Economics for an Imperfect World

Economics for an Imperfect World

Essays in Honor of
Joseph E. Stiglitz

Edited by
Richard Arnott
Bruce Greenwald
Ravi Kanbur
Barry Nalebuff

The MIT Press
Cambridge, Massachusetts
London, England

This book was set in Palatino on 3B2 by Asco Typesetters, Hong Kong, and was printed and bound in the United States of America.

Library of Congress Cataloging-in-Publication Data

Economics for an imperfect world : essays in honor of Joseph E. Stiglitz / edited by Richard Arnott ... [et al.].
    p.   cm.
 Includes bibliographical references and index.
 ISBN 0-262-01205-7 (hc. : alk. paper)
 1. Information theory in economics. 2. Rick management. 3. Uncertainty. 4. Multiple criteria decision making. I. Stiglitz, Joseph E. II. Arnott, Richard.
HB133.E3 2003
330'.01'154—dc21   2003046470

Contents

Introduction

1

Joseph E. Stiglitz and Economics for an Imperfect World

Richard Arnott, Bruce Greenwald, Ravi Kanbur, and Barry Nalebuff

Joseph Stiglitz was awarded the Nobel Prize in Economics in October 2001 for his contributions to the study of imperfect information. Eight months before this happy news, a group of his teachers, students and coauthors had come together to pay tribute to him by writing essays in his honor, marking his sixtieth birthday in 2003. This volume is the result of those contributions.

The collection of authors in this volume reflects the impact that Stiglitz has had on the profession of economics. They include four Nobel Prize winners, the president of an Ivy League University, the head of an Oxford College, the present chief economist of the World Bank, and other recognized leaders in economics from the leading universities around the world. The areas covered in this volume also reflect the "Stiglitzian" influences on much of economics today. The impact of his work is most strongly seen in the area of imperfect information, for which he won the Nobel Prize. But his influence extends to many other areas, including macroeconomics, public economics and development economics, counting in the latter the problems of transition from centrally planned to market economies. Throughout, his focus has been on the world as it actually is, with all of its imperfections—whether of information, competition, or government—rather than the world often depicted in the basic economics textbooks. Hence the title of this volume—Stiglitz's economics is truly an *Economics for an Imperfect World*.

On a more personal level, the authors who contributed to this volume along with the editors, have all felt the effect of Joe Stiglitz on their lives, in his role as student, teacher, mentor and coauthor. His remarkable impact on the economics profession is rivaled only by his personal impact on economists the world over.

Joe Stiglitz was born in Gary, Indiana, in 1943. The grim realities of that declining steel town, with its stark inequalities and sharp racial discrimination, raised questions early on about these outcomes and the processes that led to them. He did his undergraduate studies at Amherst College, where he was a student body leader. He took part in the great civil rights march in Washington, D.C. in 1963 and heard Dr. Martin Luther King, Jr., give his "I Have a Dream" speech, another lasting influence on his thinking. He completed his Ph.D. at MIT, and two of his teachers, Nobel Prize winners Paul Samuelson and Robert Solow, have contributed papers to this volume.

Stiglitz became a tenured full professor at Yale at the age of 27. Between 1969 and 1971 he was at the Institute for Development Studies in Nairobi, Kenya. The stay in a developing country led not only to his abiding interest in the problems of development, but also led him to ask questions of received economic doctrine, questions that eventually led to research that won him the Nobel Prize. After Yale, he taught at Stanford, Oxford, Princeton, and then Stanford again. This quarter-century of research established him as one of the giants of economics, his contributions ranging across every part of the discipline and winning him the coveted Clark Medal of the American Economic Association. His coauthors from that prolific period are well represented in this volume. At every university where he taught, he imbued generations of graduate students with his infectious enthusiasm for ideas and his belief in the capacity of economic analysis to lead to a better world, provided it brought to center stage the imperfections of the real world. These students are proud to have studied under him and many of them, now leading economists in their own right worldwide, have contributed chapters to this volume.

In 1993 Stiglitz left academia for the world of policy to join President Clinton's Council of Economic Advisers, of which he eventually became chairman, thereby holding a cabinet level position in the Clinton administration. In 1997 he left the White House to become senior vice president and chief economist of the World Bank, a move that saw a strengthening of the close involvement with development that started his career, which he maintained throughout the years. In both of these policy positions, Stiglitz argued against the strictures of orthodox economic policy, especially where it emanated from a market fundamentalism that he believed was not warranted in a world of imperfect information, imperfect competition, and imperfect markets. In both of these positions, he came into conflict with the U.S. Treasury's espousal of orthodox economic policies that he believed were not serving the interests of the population at large, in particular the poor. After the East Asia crisis, Stiglitz spoke out against what he saw as policies that were economically wrong-headed and detrimental to growth and poverty reduction in poor countries. The World Bank came under pressure from the U.S. Treasury to silence him, but rather than be silenced he resigned and returned to academia in 2000, first to Stanford and now at Columbia University.

At first sight it is rather odd that there should be a need to develop a new economics for an imperfect world. Surely, all of economics should be about the world as it is. Even the use of the term "imperfections" stands in contradistinction to the usually assumed "perfections" of the world analyzed in our basic textbooks—perfect information, perfect competition, and so on. This was certainly true thirty-five years ago, when Stiglitz began his economics education. It is sadly still the case for many basic textbooks, although increasingly there are exceptions, and advanced textbooks do treat of the imperfections of the real world. As Stiglitz has argued, however, in the policy world it still appears that those who analyze and advise draw their basic instincts from the perfect information, perfect competition world of Economics 101, rather than the living, breathing world that we inhabit.

A key feature of that real world is asymmetric information. In most situations, the two sides of the market have vastly different information about the good or service being transacted. In particular, sellers typically know more about what they are selling than buyers do. This can lead to adverse selection where low-quality products drive out good-quality products unless other actions are taken. What sorts of actions? Agents may choose to signal information that they have and that other parties do not. For those with high-quality products, it may be worthwhile doing this rather than be shut out from the market as bad quality drives out good. Or one side of the market may offer a menu of transaction terms, relying on the choices by the other side to screen transactors of one type from another. Offering such a menu may be better than continuing with imperfect information, but for it to play its role as a screening device, the menu has to have a structure that will separate out different types into preferring different parts of the menu. The theory then predicts that the types of transactions that one sees will be different from those that would emerge in a world of perfect information. Combining signaling and screening further enriches the scope of the analysis.

Stiglitz's research often starts with a simple truth and then shows the profound consequences of that idea. Take, for example, the demonstration of the internal contradiction of perfect competition (Grossman and Stiglitz 1980). A long tradition in economics argues that one of the features, indeed virtues, of perfect competition is that prices reflect all of the information in the market. But if that is the case, then no one has any incentive to gather any information. They can get it for free by looking at prices. If no one gathers information, however, then the prices do not have any information to reflect. This paradox lays the basis for the argument that imperfect information in markets is likely to be the rule rather than the exception. Adam Smith's invisible hand can be, at best, an imperfect guide.

Many if not most features of real-world transactions can only be understood in an imperfect information framework. The work of Joe Stiglitz, his fellow Nobel Prize winners for 2001 George Akerlof and Michael Spence, and many others, including contributors to this volume, elaborates on this point. Whether it be education as a screening device (Stiglitz 1975), the insurance market (Rothschild and Stiglitz 1976), market prices as aggregators and disseminators of information (Grossman and Stiglitz 1980), unemployment as a worker discipline device (Shapiro and Stiglitz 1984), price dispersion as a way of screening through search (Salop and Stiglitz 1982), credit rationing (Stiglitz and Weiss 1981), macroeconomic fluctuations (Greenwald, Stiglitz, and Weiss 1984), or any of a host of other issues analyzed in the articles listed in his bibliography at the end of this volume, Stiglitz has led the way in showing how the imperfect information paradigm can help us understand economic phenomena much better. The enormous richness and potential of the paradigm he helped to create are reflected in the chapters in part I of this volume, which analyze problems ranging from insurance and financial regulation, through cultural equilibria and cooperation, to industrial organization. They are a fitting tribute to the continued vitality and relevance of his contributions in the area of imperfect information.

Although the Nobel Prize was awarded for Stiglitz's seminal contributions on imperfect information, his influence on economics stretches far beyond even this gigantic achievement. Emerging partly from the imperfect information paradigm, but also from a realization of other sorts of imperfections in markets, he has made equally seminal contributions to macroeconomics, public economics, and the economics of development and transition. The chapters in Part II of this volume reflect his contributions in these areas.

Nobel Prize winners Robert Solow and George Akerlof are among those who contribute chapters on macroeconomics and unemployment, on which Stiglitz made an early contribution with his teacher (Solow and Stiglitz 1968). A key aspect of his work in these areas is the recognition of the pervasiveness of imperfect competition. One of his most cited papers is Dixit and Stiglitz (1977), which developed an elegant model that has become the workhorse of the new literature on monopolistic competition, with applications in industrial organization and in trade, as amply demonstrated by two of the chapters in part II. Joe's work in public economics is characterized by the recognition of the imperfections of governments and the limited range of governmental instruments. The design of tax and expenditure policies in this real world setting is enormously important for policy, but also exciting as an area of theoretical enquiry. Atkinson and Stiglitz (1980) remains as important a part of graduate courses in public economics as when it first came out almost a quarter of a century ago. This Atkinson-Stiglitz perspective is present in the public economics chapters in Part II, including a paper coauthored by Nobel Prize winner Kenneth Arrow. Finally, chapters on development and transition problems round out this tribute. As noted earlier, development issues have influenced his thinking profoundly (Stiglitz 1974). But, equally, development thinking has been influenced greatly by him, especially at a conjuncture where the economics of Economics 101 appear to be deployed to prescribe policies for countries where they are clearly not applicable. Failures of information, markets, and governments are pervasive, and a sophisticated analysis is needed that also takes into account the needs of the poorest and most vulnerable (Stiglitz 2002). The chapters in part II illustrate this well.

Joe Stiglitz turns sixty in 2003. Many of us who knew him first as a student, then as a teacher or as a colleague, see no diminution in his energies and in his creativity. This is good news. The world will go on being imperfect, and it will be important for him to go on producing more economics for an imperfect world, and to go on encouraging others to do so as well.

References

Atkinson, A. B., and J. E. Stiglitz. 1980. *Lectures in Public Economics*. London: McGraw-Hill.

Dixit, A. K., and J. E. Stiglitz. 1977. "Monopolistic Competition and Optimal Product Diversity." *American Economic Review* 67 (3), June: 297–308.

Greenwald, B., J. E. Stiglitz, and A. Weiss. 1984. "Informational Imperfections in the Capital Markets and Macroeconomic Fluctuations." *American Economic Review* 74 (2), May: 194–199.

Grossman, S., and J. E. Stiglitz. 1980. "On the Impossibility of Informationally Efficient Markets." *American Economic Review* 70 (3), June: 123–136.

Rothschild, M., and J. E. Stiglitz. 1976. "Equilibrium in Competitive Insurance Markets: An Essay on the Economics of Imperfect Information." *Quarterly Journal of Economics* 90 (4), November: 629–649.

Salop, S., and J. E. Stiglitz. 1982. "A Theory of Sales: A Simple Model of Equilibrium Price Dispersion with Identical Agents." *American Economic Review* 72 (5), December: 1121–1130.

Shapiro, C., and J. E. Stiglitz. 1984. "Equilibrium Unemployment as a Worker Discipline Device." *American Economic Review* 74 (3), June: 433–444.

Solow, R., and J. E. Stiglitz. 1968. "Output, Employment and Wages in the Short Run." *Quarterly Journal of Economics* 82, November: 537–560.

Stiglitz, J. E. 1974. "Alternative Theories of Wage Determination and Unemployment in L.D.C.'s: The Labor Turnover Model." *Quarterly Journal of Economics* 88 (2), May: 194–227.

Stiglitz, J. E. 1975. "The Theory of Screening, Education and the Distribution of Income." *American Economic Review* 65 (3), June: 283–300.

Stiglitz, J. E. 2002. *Globalization and Its Discontents*. New York: W. W. Norton.

Stiglitz, J. E., and A. Weiss. 1981. "Credit Rationing in Markets with Imperfect Information." *American Economic Review* 71 (3), June: 393–410.

I

Imperfect Information

2   A Small Pearl for Doctor Stiglitz's Sixtieth Birthday: When Risk Averters Positively Relish "Excess Volatility"

Paul A. Samuelson

Sometimes, even within the pure realm of deductive mathematics, experimental exploration may generate a conjecture or even a valid theorem. What fruit flies, maize, and phage do for the genetical biologist—serve as convenient special testing grounds for general microbiological truths—simple cases of two-outcome ("binary") investment probabilities can sometimes provide speedy ways of testing modern finance principles. (By modern finance I mean the Bachelier to Black-Scholes-Merton theories and beyond, most of which go back only to about the mid-twentieth century.)

One day I fooled around idly with some finger exercises in portfolio theory and was given a shock of surprise by the mathematics. Which would be better for an investor faced with an all-or-nothing choice between stock A that with even-odds turns every $1.00 of ante into $2.00 or into $0.50, or stock B that turns $1.00 into $4.00 or into $0.25?

Of course the investor's degree of risk tolerance must influence which one is chosen. A risk-neutral investor will certainly go for higher mean-money B rather than A. A near-paranoid investor with scant tolerance for loss will instead pick the less-volatile A even though its mean-money return is only ten-seventeenths that of B.

My custom is to start off with a 1738 Bernoullian who acts to maximize the expected value of log (wealth outcomes). He will be precisely indifferent between A and B. (Some will say, but not I, since A and B are equal and since he is a risk averter who shuns unnecessary volatility, he'll opt for less-volatile A.) Readers will realize that those less risk averse than Bernoulli, such as 1728 Cramer, who maximize $E\{\sqrt{\text{wealth outcomes}}\}$, will opt for B. Contrariwise, a more risk-averse investor than Bernoulli who maximizes $E\{(-1/\text{Wealth})\}$, would pick "safer" A over B.

These choosings between *all*-in-stock A or *all*-in-stock B are a bit remote from conventional portfolio problems. In them, an investor can avoid all-or-none choices. Instead she usually will face absolutely safe cash that promises an interest rate worse than A's or B's best outcome but better than either of their worst outcomes. Cash's safe return could be zero, or it could be say 5 percent. For brevity, I'll set it at 0 percent. Whatever the investor's degree of smooth risk aversion, she can always beat A by mixing it with some positive cash ratio.

The same goes for her definite gain from mixing B with some positive cash. MBA quizzes ask students what fraction of the portfolio should optimally be in cash and what remaining fraction in A? Or the B-cum-optimal cash might be the quiz question. For Bernoulli, uncomplicated linear algebra says: $x^* = 0.5$ in cash and $1 - x^* = 0.5$ in A is optimal. By sheer coincidence (of my contrived example), Bernoulli calculates 0.5 cash in B, too!

To be honest, originally I stupidly expected that if one were made to choose between A-cum best cash and B-cum cash, since all A and all B were "equivalent," then the rational investor would do better to break the previous tie by avoiding more-volatile B. I'd have felt less ashamed if I had originally (fallaciously) argued: A-cum cash and B-cum cash will still be equally preferable, when for each the cool cash has optimally quenched their respective volatilities.

One's mathematics shouts out any intuitive errors. Complete optimality calculations of expected log utility of A&Cash and B&Cash show the latter to be definitely the better choice. To ensure that this oddity was not peculiar to the special Bernoulli case, I worked out the $U = \sqrt{W}$ and the $U = -W^{-1}$ cases, only to get the same "counterintuitive" result.

Capitulating to the $2 + 2 = 4$ arithmetic, I leaped to the general conjecture:

THEOREM   Whenever $E\{U(W_A)\} = E\{U(W_B)\} = U(W_{AB})$, and the probability distribution around (W_{AB}) is for B uniformly more dispersed around (W_{AB}) than it is for A, then best $W^*_{B\&C} >$ best $W^*_{A\&C}$:

$$E\{U(W_A)\} < E\{U(W^*_{A\&Cash})\} < E\{U(W^*_{B\&Cash})\} > E\{U(W_B)\}.$$

Admittedly, this was a stretch. Why believe that what holds for *binary* wealth outcomes would hold for *general* multidiscrete-outcome cases and for probability-density cases?

Experience planted that belief stretch. Consider the similar but different case where stocks α and β have the same mean-money outcomes: α converts initial \$1 into $1/2$ or 2 with even odds; β turns \$1 into 0 or 2 $1/2$ with even odds. Then for risk averters who abhor money volatility around the money mean, when

$$E\{W_\alpha\} = E\{W_\beta\} = \overline{W} = 1\tfrac{1}{4} \tag{1a}$$

and

$$\text{Min}\{W_\beta\} < \text{Min}\{W_\alpha\} < \overline{W} < \text{Max}\{W_\alpha\} < \text{Max}\{W_\beta\}$$
$$0 < \tfrac{1}{2} < 1\tfrac{1}{4} < 2 < 2\tfrac{1}{2} \tag{1b}$$

and

$$U'(W) > 0 > U''(W), \tag{1c}$$

then $E\{U(W_\beta)\} < E\{U(W_\alpha)\}$. $\tag{1d}$

Numerous papers on "stochastic dominance" justify the stretch from even-odds binary outcome where

$$\text{prob}\{\text{Max } W\} = 1 - \text{prob}\{\text{Min } W\} \tag{2a}$$

to the most general probability cases where W can have multiple discrete values.

$$\text{prob}\{W_1 = a_1\} = p_1, \ldots, \text{prob}\{W_n = a_n\} = p_n \tag{2b}$$

$$\sum_1^n p_j = 1; p_j > 0 \text{ for } j = 1, 2, \ldots, n. \tag{2c}$$

And the same result applies when W's probability density is $p(W)\,dW = P'(W)\,dW$; and applies as well for the general Stieltjes integral case where

$$\text{Prob}\{W \leq w\} = P(w); \int_0^\infty dP(w) = 1 \tag{2d}$$

$$P(w + |h|) \geq P(w); P(0-) = 0, \text{limited Liabiability}$$

$$P(0) \geq 0; \lim_{w \to \infty} P(w) = 1. \tag{2e}$$

Having learned something, I was inclined to publish a short note. But then somebody suggested to me that this result was already in Diamond-Stiglitz (1974). I looked there and realized that indeed my brainchild was already floating somewhere there, but exactly where I was not sure. And the same vague uncertainty pertained to Rothschild-Stiglitz (1971).

For a Joe Stiglitz, who exudes theorems hourly from every pore, the best of all presents may be one that leaves to him some task of putting it together correctly. Maybe he will find that my little pearl is after all only a grain of sand?

Rationalizations

I conclude with some informal brainstorming. How intuitively can we understand the pseudoparadox that risk averters who shun money volatility as such, seemingly embrace volatility when choosing between pairs of securities that are on an all-or-none basis exactly indifferent?

Here is one literary consideration. Suppose as an extreme case that A had already been safe cash itself. Then the option to add cash as a diversifier to what is already cash can accomplish nothing for it. Thus

$$A \approx A\&C \approx B \leq B\&Cash.^* \qquad QED. \tag{3}$$

Using a reliable intuitive stretch, one realizes that cash usefully improves on volatile B more than it can for an admissible less-volatile A.

A somewhat similar comfort can come from recalling a historical Waugh-Samuelson dialogue. During World War II, Frederick Waugh published "Does the Consumer Benefit from Price Instability?" in the 1944 *Quarterly Journal of Economics*. What he proved was that with no time preference and symmetric intertemporal tastes, then over two periods one will be better off buying at $(p + h, p - h)$ prices than at $(p\ p)$ prices. Moonlighting from the wartime MIT Radiation Laboratory, I submitted to *Econometrica* a paper entitled "The Consumer Does Benefit from **Feasible** Price **Stability**" (2002, emphasis added). The meticulous assistant editor lost that accepted paper, and in my zeal to defeat Adolf Hitler I let the matter drop until decades later when the Waugh effect got rediscovered.

My point was not that Waugh's "hypothesis I implies conclusions II" was incorrect. But rather that, if its innuendo persuaded Congress to pass (in the interest of price instability) a law requiring equal harvests (q q) to be replaced by carryover and storage creating unequal (q + Δ q − Δ), consumer's utility would be *reduced* and not enhanced. Why? Because the entailed unequal (p_1 p_2) auction prices must then definitely violate Waugh's hypothesized ability to purchase at prices that averaged in the mean the same as the equalized equilibrium prices.

What is afoot in the debate is that, by the weak axiom of revealed preference, the direct utility function, $U(q_1, q_2) \equiv U(q_2, q_1) = U(q_1) + U(q_2)$, is quasi-concave in its arguments whereas its *dual* utility function in the normalized price space

$$^*U(p_1, p_2) = \underset{q_1, q_2}{\text{Max}}\ U(q_1, q_2) \text{ s.t.} \tag{4a}$$

$$p_1 q_2 + p_2 q_2 = 1 \tag{4b}$$

must be quasi-convex in its arguments. Something like the flip-flop from concavity to convexity is involved in the Diamond-Stiglitz (or Rothschild-Stiglitz) innovative papers. An easy Mill-Cobb-Douglas case is illustrative. Here

$$U(q_1, q_2) = U(q_1) + U(q_2) = \log q_1 + \log q_2 \tag{5a}$$

$$U(p_1, p_2) = {}^*U(p_1) + {}^*U(p_2) = \log(1/2p_1) + \log(1/2p_2) \tag{5b}$$

$$U'(q) > 0 > U''(q) \text{ and } {}^*U'(p) < 0 <^* U''(p). \tag{5c}$$

Note the crucial reversal of signs in equation (5c).

Similar perhaps to the Waugh effect is the familiar 1817 Ricardian pitch for specialization and trade between Portugal and England. You and your neighbor are each benefitted when, so to speak, you can buy at both your own and your neighbor's scarcity prices.

Acknowledgments

I owe thanks to Janice Murray for editorial assistance; to the MIT Sloan School and the Alfred P. Sloan Foundation for partial support; and, as usual, to Bob Solow for safety-netting.

References

Diamond, Peter, and Joseph Stiglitz. 1974. "Increases in Risk and in Risk Aversion." *Journal of Economic Theory* 8:337–360.

Rothschild, Michael, and Joseph Stiglitz. 1971. "Increasing Risk II: Its Economic Consequences." *Journal of Economic Theory* 3:66–84.

Samuelson, Paul A. 1972. "The Consumer Does Benefit from Feasible Price Stability." *Quarterly Journal of Economics* 86:476–493. Reproduced as chapter 261 in *The Collected Scientific Papers of Paul A. Samuelson*, vol. 4. Cambridge, Mass.: The MIT Press, 1977.

Waugh, Frederick V. 1944. "Does the Consumer Benefit from Price Instability?" *Quarterly Journal of Economics* 58:602–614.

3

On the Role of Good Faith in Insurance Contracting

Avinash Dixit and Pierre Picard

The law of insurance contracts usually stipulates that an applicant for insurance must not deliberately conceal any relevant information about his risks from the insurer. This principle of good faith (*uberrima fides*) is implemented with different strictness under common law or statute law. In the United States and the United Kingdom, at the time of making the contract, the insured is obliged to disclose to the insurer all material information affecting the risk; see Clarke (1997, 583).[1] The insurer can cancel the contract ex post facto and refuse to pay any claims if willful misrepresentation is found. In France, courts may order a lower payout on the claim even if the misrepresentation is not intentional; if it is, the insurer gets no indemnity and may be subject to an additional fine (Farshian 2002; Lambert-Faivre 1991).

The good faith principle can mitigate adverse selection at a low cost, since it allows the insurer to verify the insured's assertions ex post facto, only if a claim is filed. Dixit (2000) examines this in an extension of the Rothschild-Stiglitz (1976) model (henceforth R-S) of a competitive insurance market. A random investigation will be carried out when a customer who has asserted himself to be low-risk files a claim. If he is found to be truthful, the insurance indemnity paid exceeds his loss; if untruthful, the claim is denied. This combination of reward and punishment enables better separation of types, and achieves a Pareto improvement over the R-S equilibrium. Lastly, the good faith principle extends the range of high-risk and low-risk proportions for which a competitive equilibrium exists.

In Dixit's model, individuals are perfectly privately informed about their risk types, so any misrepresentation is intentional. In reality, people may be unaware of their risk type and believe themselves to be low-risk in good faith. For example, some people may have a genetic or behavioral predisposition to diabetes, but live normal lives without any symptoms, until some sudden change in diet or lifestyle triggers the disease and requires costly insulin treatment. Even if it then becomes clear that the disease must have been latent for many years, the insurer cannot allege bad faith on part of the cutomer. In this chapter we extend the Dixit (2000) model further by distinguishing between unknowing and intentional misrepresentation of type.

We allow two different types of investigation involving different costs: (1) of the insured's actual risk type (low or high), and (2) of signal receipt, that is, whether the insured was aware of his risk type. The law allows the company to rescind the contract, and may also levy a fine on the insured, if the latter investigation is made and shows that the insured, when he chose the low-risk contract, knew himself to be high-risk. We characterize the optimal contract (the company's probabilistic investigation strategies and promises of payouts conditional on its investigations and their outcomes) subject to the provisions of the law and the usual profit and incentive constraint. Not all features of the contracts that are optimal in our model are observed in reality, and we discuss possible reasons.

A brief statement of our results, with an intuition for the differences between them and the original R-S model, follows. In R-S, information is revealed by the insurance applicants' self-selection. The low-risk types are better able to withstand partial coverage than are high-risk types (the single crossing property); therefore revelation always comes at the cost of partial insurance for the low-risk types. In contrast, in our model the insurance companies can carry out investigations to elicit information, and then reward good-faith disclosures and punish bad-faith misrepresentations. This allows richer contract forms: zero indemnity when bad faith is established, partial coverage when neither good nor bad faith is established (as in R-S), and a reward in the form of over-coverage when good faith is established. To elicit truth telling, the gap between the payouts in the cases of good and bad faith is important; this gap can be achieved at a lower efficiency cost by combining such rewards and punishments.

Verifying the risk type may be used as a first step in a sequential claim handling procedure. If type verification reveals high risk, then the insurer may decide to investigate the policyholder further by performing a signal investigation, to establish whether the misrepresentation of risk was intentional. Alternatively, the company may directly investigate whether the insured had received the signal. We establish the condition under which it chooses the direct or the sequential procedure. We also show that the optimal signal investigation (direct or sequential) is always random, that is, performed with probability less than one.

The law of contract usually places the burden of proving bad faith on the insurer. In the section on onus of proof we suggest that this is usually the most efficient solution, unless the policyholder can prove good faith at a much lower cost.

1   The Setting

There is a large population facing individual risks of accident. All individuals maximize the expected utility $E[U(W)]$, where W denotes wealth, the utility function U satisfies $U' > 0$ and $U'' < 0$, and $E[.]$ is the expectation operator. They face an idiosyncratic risk of accident. If no insurance is taken out, we have $W = W_N$ in the no-accident state and $W = W_A$ in the accident state; $A = W_N - W_A$ is the loss from an accident. Individuals differ according to their probability of accident π. We have $\pi = \pi_\ell$ for a low-risk individual (or ℓ-type) and $\pi = \pi_h$ for a high-risk individual (or h-type), where $0 < \pi_\ell < \pi_h < 1$. The fraction of high-risk individuals is λ, with $0 < \lambda < 1$.

Each individual receives a signal $\sigma \in \{b, g\}$ about his risk type: low-risk individuals always gets g but high-risk individuals get g with probability q and b with probability $1 - q$, with $0 < q < 1$. Then someone who has received the bad signal b is sure to be of high-risk h-type:

$\text{Prob}(h\text{-type} \mid \sigma = b) = 1.$

Using Bayes' law, the probability that someone who has received the good signal g is nevertheless of the high-risk type, which we denote by α, is

$$\alpha \equiv \text{Prob}(h\text{-type} \mid \sigma = g) = \alpha = \frac{\lambda q}{\lambda q + (1 - \lambda)} \in (0, \lambda).$$

Thus the lower is α, the more precise is the signal.

When an individual gets signal b, he knows he is of h-type and his accident probability is π_h. When an individual perceives g, his accident probability is

$$\hat{\pi} = \alpha\pi_h + (1 - \alpha)\pi_\ell = \frac{\lambda q\pi_h + (1 - \lambda)\pi_\ell}{\lambda q + (1 - \lambda)}.$$

We also find it useful to denote by β the conditional probability that someone who has received the good signal g and has incurred an accident is of the high-risk h-type. Using Bayes' theorem again, we have

$$\beta \equiv \text{Prob}(h\text{-type} \mid \sigma = g, \text{Accident}) = \frac{\pi_h \alpha}{\hat{\pi}} = \frac{\pi_h \alpha}{\pi_h \alpha + \pi_\ell(1 - \alpha)}.$$

Then it is easy to verify that

$$\pi_\ell < \hat{\pi} < \pi_h, \qquad \beta > \alpha.$$

Insurance companies are assumed to be risk neutral, they have no administrative cost, and there is free entry in the insurance market. Each company can offer one type of contract. Of course the market may have different types of contracts offered by different companies. It is sufficient to consider two types of contracts, respectively labeled C_h and C_ℓ, designed for the h-types and ℓ-types respectively. No company offering a C_h contract will object if an ℓ-type chooses it, so such contracts will not have any investigation or rescinding provisions. A company offering a contract C_ℓ intended for ℓ-types, however, would make a loss if h-types selected it, either accidentally (in good faith) or intentionally (in bad faith). The good-faith principle allows safeguards against this. The company can make an investigation upon receipt of a claim by an individual who has chosen C_ℓ. The company can find out the individual's true type at cost c_t, and it can also verify the perceived signal at cost c_s, either after a type investigation has revealed that the policyholder is a high-risk individual (the sequential procedure) or without verifying the type first (the direct procedure). If a signal investigation reveals that a C_ℓ-policyholder had received b, then he is proved to have been in bad faith. Then the company is allowed to cancel the contract; we assume that it must return the premium, but allowing it to retain the premium causes only minor algebraic changes. We also assume that the courts levy an exogenously specified fine f on the customer. If the policyholder had received g, he was in good faith even though a type investigation may show him to be h-type. What the contract specifies in this eventuality is determined by the usual optimization and equilibrium considerations; but no fines are levied.

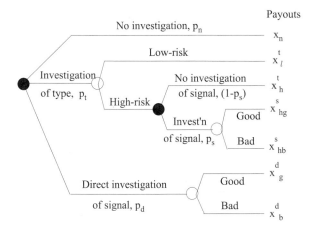

Figure 3.1
The insurer's randomized strategies

We use the following notation for the contracts:

$$C_h = (k_h, x_h), \qquad C_\ell = (k_\ell, x_n, x_\ell^t, x_h^t, x_{hb}^s, x_{hg}^s, x_b^d, x_g^d; p_n, p_t, p_s, p_d),$$

where k_h, k_ℓ are the insurance premiums paid in advance, the various p's are the probabilities of investigation if a claim is made, and the various x's are the net payouts to the policyholder[2] in the various contingencies of investigations and their outcomes. Figure 3.1 shows the contingencies, the probabilities, and the payouts. All the x's must be nonnegative; the probabilities must all be nonnegative, and satisfy $p_n + p_t + p_d = 1$, $0 \le p_s \le 1$.

We assume that the insurance companies commit to these verification strategies.[3] We disregard the sequential procedure in which signal investigation comes before type investigation, since it would be suboptimal (see proposition 4).

Thus, except for the more general nature of the C_ℓ contracts to allow for verification, our setting directly follows Rothschild and Stiglitz (1976). Our notion of equilibrium is also the same as theirs. As explained by Kreps (1990, 649), this is a subgame perfect Nash equilibrium of the following game. At the first stage, each of the large number of potential insurance companies decides whether to offer a contract, and if so, chooses the type and specification of its contract. At the second stage, each consumer chooses whether to accept a contract, and if so, what contract. Then each consumer's outcome (accident or no accident) is realized, those who have suffered accidents file claims, the insurance companies follow through with their committed investigation strategies, and depending on the outcome of the investigations that may be carried out, pay the appropriate indemnities.

Let s_b be the probability for an individual who has perceived $\sigma = b$ to take out the C_ℓ contract—this is the probability of acting in bad faith—and let s_g be the probability for an individual who has perceived g to choose the C_h contract, with $0 \le s_b$, $s_g \le 1$. The full insurance contracts with fair premium are denoted by C_h^* and C_ℓ^*, respectively for h-types and for ℓ-types, that is $C_h^* = (k_h^*, x_h^*) = (\pi_h A, A - \pi_h A)$ and $C_\ell^* = (k_\ell^*, x_\ell^*) = (\pi_\ell A, A - \pi_\ell A)$.

For the same reasons as in Rothschild-Stiglitz (1976) and Dixit (2000), there cannot be a pooling equilibrium where just one type of contract is on offer. The following definition characterizes a candidate separating equilibrium:

DEFINITION 1   A candidate equilibrium of the insurance markets consists of two contracts $C_\ell = (k_\ell, x_n, x_\ell^t, x_h^t, x_{hb}^s, x_{hg}^s, x_b^d, x_g^d; p_n, p_t, p_s, p_d)$ and $C_h = (k_h, x_h)$ offered by different insurers, and contract choice strategies s_b, s_g such that:

1. s_b maximizes the expected utility of individuals who have received signal b and s_g maximizes the expected utility of individuals who have received g, given (C_ℓ, C_h).

2. Insurers make nonnegative profit at equilibrium.

3. No company can offer a contract $C_\ell' \ne C_\ell$ or $C_h' \ne C_h$ (where C_ℓ' is labelled as available only to low-risk individuals), which, offered in addition to C_ℓ, C_h would make positive profits, assuming that individuals make optimal choice among this enlarged menu of contracts.

2   Equilibrium Contract and Verification

We now proceed to analyze when this candidate equilibrium is actually an equilibrium and obtain its properties. We begin with a characterization result:

PROPOSITION 1   In a market equilibrium, we have

1. $s_b = s_g = 0$
2. $C_h = C_h^*$
3. C_ℓ maximizes

$$(1 - \hat{\pi})U(W_N - k_\ell) + \hat{\pi}[p_n U(W_A + x_n) + p_t(1 - \beta)U(W_A + x_\ell^t)$$

$$+ \beta p_t(1 - p_s)U(W_A + x_h^t) + \beta p_t p_s U(W_A + x_{hg}^s) + p_d U(W_A + x_g^d)] \quad (1)$$

subject to

$$U(W_N - \pi_h A) \geq (1 - \pi_h)U(W_N - k_\ell) + \pi_h[p_n U(W_A + x_n) \quad (2)$$

$$+ p_t(1 - p_s)U(W_A + x_h^t) + p_t p_s U(W_A + x_{hb}^s - f)$$

$$+ p_d U(W_A + x_b^d - f)] \quad (3)$$

$$(1 - \hat{\pi})k_\ell - \hat{\pi}[p_n x_n + (1 - \beta)p_t x_\ell^t + \beta p_t(1 - p_s)x_h^t$$

$$+ \beta p_t p_s x_{hg}^s + p_d x_g^d + p_t c_t + (\beta p_t p_s + p_d)c_s] \geq 0 \quad (4)$$

$$x_n, x_\ell^t, x_h^t, x_{hb}^s, x_{hg}^s, x_b^d, x_g^d, p_t, p_d, p_n \geq 0, \qquad p_t + p_d + p_n = 1, \quad 0 \leq p_s \leq 1.$$

4. The good faith principle enlarges the set of parameter values for which this equilibrium exists. When equilibrium exists both with and without the principle, the one without the principle is the same as the Rothschild-Stiglitz equilibrium, and the one with the principle is Pareto superior.

The proof is the same as that in Rothschild and Stiglitz (1976) and Dixit (2000). Since there are two information sets, the equilibrium has the same structure as the standard R-S equilibrium: it is separating, with full insurance at fair price for b-recipients. Competition ensures that C_ℓ maximizes the expected utility of g-recipients subject to the b-recipients' self-selection constraint and to the company's no-expected-loss constraint. The reason for the possible nonexistence of the equilibrium is that a pooling contract can give everyone higher expected utility, specifically, g-recipients do better than with C_ℓ. If the good faith principle did not apply, the maximization problem solved by C_ℓ would be more constrained because the x's could not be made contingent on an investigation. Therefore nonexistence could arise for more parameter values. Pareto superiority follows from the fact that the less-constrained problem yields a higher value of the objective function (expected utility of the g-recipients). And since, in the absence of the good-faith principle, the findings of an investigation cannot be used, the company would not make a costly investigation. Therefore the equilibrium without the principle, if it exists, must be the same as in R-S.

Proposition 2 characterizes the payout to a policyholder who has received signal g and chosen contract C_ℓ.

PROPOSITION 2 $0 = x^s_{hb} = x^d_b \leq x^t_h < x_n < A - k_\ell < x^t_\ell = x^s_{hg} = x^d_g.$

The formal proofs of this and the subsequent propositions are in the appendix; the text gives the intuitive arguments. x^s_{hb} or x^d_b is paid to policyholders when bad faith has been proved: for obvious incentives reasons it is optimal to enforce the highest possible penalty in this case, that is, canceling the contract and returning the premium which correspond to $x^s_{hb} = x^d_b = 0$. Next, x^t_h is a low payment for being shown to be a high-risk type even though there is no investigation of signal receipt (bad faith), and x_n is an intermediate settlement if no investigation is carried out at all. $A - k_\ell < x^t_\ell$ shows that there is overinsurance when a risk-type investigation reveals that the policyholder is a ℓ-type. Overinsurance is a reward for truthtelling, since a ℓ-type always perceives g; however, we also have $x^t_\ell = x^s_{hg} = x^d_g$ because for insurance reasons it is optimal not to punish the h-types who have received g (whether the fact that the individual is a high risk has been established or not). In other words, when good faith is established, high-risk individuals should not be penalized by comparison with low-risk types.

Insurance contracts in reality do not usually have so many different levels of payoffs contingent on the company's investigation. Companies usually make low initial offers without any investigation. Excessive payouts, if investigations reveal good faith, are not common. Experience rating in dynamic contexts, however, may serve a similar purpose. It is also possible that the designers of insurance contracts have simply not yet realized the usefulness of rewards as an additional instrument for separation purposes.

PROPOSITION 3   Ceteris paribus, there exists $\bar{\alpha} > 0$ such that $x^t_h = 0$ when $0 < \alpha < \bar{\alpha}$.

Proposition 3 states that, when the signal is precise enough (i.e., α is small enough), no insurance indemnity should be paid to a policyholder who has chosen C_ℓ and who proves to be a h-type, after a type investigation (but no signal investigation) has been carried out.

This makes intuitive sense. If the signal is sufficiently precise, then the revelation that a C_ℓ-chooser has h-type is close to being proof of bad faith. The difference is that the law does not allow zero indemnity for being close to proof; it is merely efficient for the voluntary private contract to make this provision.

PROPOSITION 4   A sequential procedure with direct investigation of signal followed by investigation of risk type is not optimal.

The intuition is as follows. If signal investigation reveals bad faith, then the type of the policyholder is known to the company, and type investigation is unnecessary. If signal investigation reveals good faith, then the type of the policyholder is still unknown to the company (as well as to the policyholder), but optimal insurance should lead to the same payout, whether the individual is type-h or type-ℓ. In either case, investigation of type would be useless, and being costly, should not be done.

PROPOSITION 5   In the optimal verification strategy, $p_s p_t < 1$, and $p_d < 1$.

Proposition 5 means that the optimal verification strategy is random. It is not optimal always to verify the risk type and the signal in the sequential procedure or the signal in the direct procedure. Investigating the signal (either directly or sequentially) is used as an incentive device to deter b-recipients from being dishonest. Sure investigation, however, would go too far: the b-recipients self-selection constraint would be met with some slack. A small decrease in the signal verification probability p_s or p_d would decrease the insurance cost but still keep the self-selection constraint satisfied.

PROPOSITION 6   If $c_s(1 - \beta) < c_t$ and $p_t > 0$, then $p_s = 0$. If $c_s(1 - \beta) > c_t$, then $p_d = 0$.

The direct and the sequential investigation procedures are alternatives, and only the less costly of the two is chosen. Direct verification of signal costs c_s. Verification of the type costs c_t; the signal need be verified sequentially only if the type is seen to be high, and the probability of this contingent on an accident is β. Thus the total expected cost of the sequential procedure is $c_t + \beta c_s$. Proposition 6 states that insurers only use the less costly of the two procedures for signal verification.

3   The Onus of Proof

We have so far assumed that the law places the burden of proof on the insurance company when it alleges bad faith. Now we examine briefly the difference made if the burden is on the insured to prove good faith. For simplicity, we suppose that the insurance payout cannot depend on the information gathered by the insurer through investigation, except when bad faith of the policyholder is proved in which case the contract may be rescinded. In our model, this means $x_h^t = x_n = x_\ell^t = x_{hg}^s = x_g^d$. Let x_ℓ denote this common payout. Also, $x_{hb}^s = x_b^d = 0$.

First, consider the case where the burden of proving bad faith is on the insurance company. From proposition 1, the insurance policy offered to g-recipients at the market equilibrium is obtained by maximizing

$$(1 - \hat{\pi})U(W_N - k_\ell) + \hat{\pi}U(W_A + x_\ell)$$

with respect to $k_\ell, x_\ell, p_t, p_s, p_d \geq 0$ subject to the b-recipients' self-selection constraint

$$U(W_N - \pi_h A) \geq (1 - \pi_h)U(W_N - k_\ell) + \pi_h\{[1 - (p_d + p_t p_s)]U(W_A + x_\ell)$$

$$+ (p_d + p_t p_s)U(W_A - f)\}$$

and the no-expected loss constraint

$$(1 - \hat{\pi})k_\ell - \hat{\pi}[x_\ell + p_t c_t + (\beta p_t p_s + p_d)c_s] \geq 0,$$

with $p_t + p_d \leq 1$ and $p_s \leq 1$. Let us call this maximization problem P1.

Now consider the alternative legal system where the onus of the proof rests on the policyholder. Assume type investigation has revealed high risk and that the policyholder has to prove good faith in court to receive the insurance indemnity. Let D denote the costs to a g-recipient to prove good faith in court, which may cover monetary expenditures as well as time spent in legal proceedings. Now the company only investigates the type. If type h is revealed, and the policyholder is unable to prove good faith in court, he has to pay the fine f and the contract is rescinded. We assume that D is small enough and f is large enough that proving good faith in court to be the optimal strategy of g-recipients. This is the case if $x_\ell > D - f$ which is assumed here. Then the policy offered to g-recipients at the market equilibrium is obtained by maximizing

$$(1 - \hat{\pi})U(W_N - k_\ell) + \hat{\pi}[(1 - p_t\beta)U(W_A + x_\ell) + p_t\beta U(W_A + x_\ell - D)]$$

with respect to $k_\ell, x_\ell, p_t \geq 0$ subject to

$$U(W_N - \pi_h A) \geq (1 - \pi_h)U(W_N - k_\ell) + \pi_h[(1 - p_t)U(W_A + x_\ell)$$

$$+ p_t U(W_A - f)],$$

and

$$(1 - \hat{\pi})k_\ell - \hat{\pi}(x_\ell + p_t c_t) \geq 0,$$

with $p_t \leq 1$. Call this maximization problem P2.

Welfare maximization requires that the onus of the proof rests with the insurer when the expected utility of g-recipients is higher in problem P1 than in problem P2 and the onus of the proof should rest with the policyholder in the other case. Proposition 7 characterizes the threshold value of D above which the onus of the proof should rest on the company.

PROPOSITION 7   The onus of the proof should rest on the insurance company when $D > D^*$ and on the policyholder when $D < D^*$, where the threshold D^* satisfies $D^* < \inf\{c_s, (c_s - c_t)/\beta\}$. In particular, when $D = c_s$ the onus of the proof should rest on the insurer.

The intuition for proposition 7 is that the cost to policyholders of establishing good faith cannot be insured. Hence, individuals run the risk of having to prove good faith. When the cost to the insurer of proving bad faith is not larger than the cost to the policyholder of proving good faith, that is, when $\inf\{c_s, (c_s - c_t)/\beta\} \leq D$, then the onus of the proof should rest with the insurer. This is also true if D is slightly larger than $\inf\{c_s, (c_s - c_t)/\beta\}$, hence the result on the threshold D^*. This suggests that the usual legal practice of placing the burden of proving bad faith on the insurer may be the most efficient one, unless the insured's cost of proving good faith is especially low.

Appendix

Proof of Proposition 2   Let $\mathcal{L}$ be the Lagrangean and let μ_1, μ_2 and θ be Lagrange multipliers for (2), (3), and (4) respectively, with μ_1, $\mu_2 \geq 0$. The expressions for the derivatives of the Lagrangean with respect to the choice variables are:

$$\partial\mathscr{L}/\partial k_\ell = [\mu_1(1 - \pi_h) - (1 - \hat{\pi})]U'(W_N - k_\ell) + \mu_2(1 - \hat{\pi}) \tag{5}$$

$$\partial\mathscr{L}/\partial x_n = p_n\{[\hat{\pi} - \mu_1\pi_h]U'(W_A + x_n) - \mu_2\hat{\pi}\} \tag{6}$$

$$\partial\mathscr{L}/\partial x_\ell^t = p_t(1 - \beta)\{\hat{\pi}U'(W_A + x_\ell^t) - \mu_2\hat{\pi}\} \tag{7}$$

$$\partial\mathscr{L}/\partial x_h^t = p_t(1 - p_s)\{[\beta\hat{\pi} - \mu_1\pi_h]U'(W_A + x_h^t) - \mu_2\hat{\pi}\beta\} \tag{8}$$

$$\partial\mathscr{L}/\partial x_{hg}^s = p_t\beta p_s[\hat{\pi}U'(W_A + x_{hg}^s) - \mu_2\hat{\pi}] \tag{9}$$

$$\partial\mathscr{L}/\partial x_{hb}^s = -\mu_1\pi_h p_t p_s U'(W_A + x_{hb}^s - f) \tag{10}$$

$$\partial\mathscr{L}/\partial x_b^d = -\mu_1\pi_h p_d U'(W_A + x_b^d - f) \tag{11}$$

$$\partial\mathscr{L}/\partial x_g^d = p_d[\hat{\pi}U'(W_A + x_g^d) - \mu_2\hat{\pi}] \tag{12}$$

$$\partial\mathscr{L}/\partial p_t = \hat{\pi}\{(1 - \beta)U(W_A + x_\ell^t) + \beta(1 - p_s)U(W_A + x_h^t)$$
$$+ \beta p_s U(W_A + x_{hg}^s)\}$$
$$-\mu_1\pi_h\{(1 - p_s)U(W_A + x_h^t) + p_s U(W_A + x_{hb}^s - f)\}$$
$$-\mu_2\hat{\pi}\{(1 - \beta)x_\ell^t + \beta(1 - p_s)x_h^t + \beta p_s x_{hg}^s + c_t + \beta p_s c_s\}$$
$$-\theta \tag{13}$$

$$\partial\mathscr{L}/\partial p_s = \hat{\pi}\beta p_t[U(W_A + x_{hg}^s) - U(W_A + x_h^t) - \mu_2(x_{hg}^s - x_h^t)]$$
$$-\hat{\pi}\mu_2\beta p_t c_s + \mu_1\pi_h p_t[U(W_A + x_h^t) - U(W_A + x_{hb}^s - f)] \tag{14}$$

$$\partial\mathscr{L}/\partial p_d = \hat{\pi}[U(W_A + x_g^d) - \mu_2 x_g^d] - \mu_1\pi_h U(W_A + x_b^d - f)$$
$$-\mu_2\hat{\pi}c_s - \theta \tag{15}$$

$$\partial\mathscr{L}/\partial p_n = [\hat{\pi} - \mu_1\pi_h]U(W_A + x_n) - \mu_2\hat{\pi}x_n - \theta \tag{16}$$

Note that if an investigation probability is zero, then the net payments corresponding to the outcome of such an investigation are irrelevant and can be set equal to the value determined formally from the first-order conditions which sets the derivatives of the Lagrangean with respect to that net payment equal to zero.

First we prove that $\mu_1 > 0$. Assume the opposite, namely $\mu_1 = 0$. Then (5)–(12) give $x_h^t = x_n = A - k_\ell = x_\ell^t = x_{hg}^s = x_g^d$. Using (13), (15), and (16) then yield $\partial\mathscr{L}/\partial p_t < \partial\mathscr{L}/\partial p_n$ and $\partial\mathscr{L}/\partial p_d < \partial\mathscr{L}/\partial p_n$, which give $p_t = p_d = 0$ and $p_n = 1$. (3) then implies $x_n = (1 - \hat{\pi})A$ and $k_\ell = \hat{\pi}A$, which contradicts (2) since $\hat{\pi} < \pi_h$. Hence $\mu_1 > 0$.

Next, $\partial\mathscr{L}/\partial x_{hb}^s < 0$ and $\partial\mathscr{L}/\partial x_b^d < 0$ give $x_{hb}^s = x_b^d = 0$.

To prove $x_n > 0$, assume the contrary, that is, $x_n = 0$. Using (6) then gives

$$(\hat{\pi} - \mu_1 \pi_h) U'(W_A) - \mu_2 \hat{\pi} \leq 0.$$

Since $\beta < 1$, this implies

$$\left(\hat{\pi} - \frac{\mu_1 \pi_h}{\beta} \right) U'(W_A) - \mu_2 \hat{\pi} < 0.$$

Hence $\partial \mathscr{L} / \partial x_h^t < 0$ if $p_t > 0$ and $0 < 1 - p_s < 1$; this gives $x_h^t = 0$. In such a situation, (2) would not be binding which gives $\mu_1 = 0$, hence a contradiction. We deduce that $x_n > 0$ and $0 < \mu_1 < \hat{\pi} / \pi_h$.

Setting the derivatives of the Lagrangean with respect to $k_\ell, x_n, x_\ell^t, x_h^t, x_{hg}^s$ and x_g^d equal to zero then gives

$$U'(W_A + x_h^t) = \frac{\mu_2 \hat{\pi} \beta}{\hat{\pi} \beta - \mu_1 \pi_h} > \frac{\mu_2 \hat{\pi}}{\hat{\pi} - \mu_1 \pi_h} = U'(W_A + x_n)$$

$$> \frac{\mu_2 (1 - \hat{\pi})}{(1 - \hat{\pi}) - \mu_1 (1 - \pi_h)} = U'(W_N - k_\ell)$$

$$> \mu_2 = U'(W_A + x_\ell^t) = U'(W_A + x_{hg}^s) = U'(W_A + x_g^d)$$

when $x_h^t > 0$, which gives

$$W_A + x_h^t < W_A + x_n < W_N - k_\ell < W_A + x_\ell^t = W_A + x_{hg}^s = W_A + x_g^d.$$

Proof of Proposition 3   Let $\mu_1(\alpha)$ be the value of μ_1 written as a function of α, everything else being held unchanged in the model. We know from the proof of proposition 2 that $\mu_1(\alpha) > 0$ for all α in $(0, 1)$. Let us show that there exist $\mu_1^* > 0$ and $\alpha^* > 0$ such that $\mu_1(\alpha) > \mu_1^*$ when $\alpha < \alpha^*$. Suppose that is not the case. Then we can find a sequence α^n, $n = 1, 2, \dots$ such that α^n and $\mu_1^n = \mu_1(\alpha^n)$ simultaneously go to zero when n go to infinity. Let C_ℓ^n be the corresponding sequence of equilibrium C_ℓ contracts. Note that $\hat{\pi}$ goes to π_ℓ when α goes to zero. When n goes to infinity, C_ℓ^n converges toward the full insurance contract C_ℓ^* with $p_t = p_s = 0$, which contradicts the self-selection constraint (2). Hence, when $\alpha < \bar{\alpha} = \inf\{\alpha^*, \mu_1^*\}$, we have $\alpha < \mu_1(\alpha)$ which gives $\hat{\pi} \beta = \alpha \pi_h < \mu_1 \pi_h$. In such a case, we have $\partial \mathscr{L} / \partial x_h^t < 0$, which gives $x_h^t = 0$.

Proof of Proposition 4   Assume that the risk type is investigated with probability δ when direct verification of signal has revealed that the policyholder has perceived g. Then in the expected utility of g-recipients, $p_d U(W_A + x_g^d)$ is replaced by

$$p_d(1 - \delta)U(W_A + x_g^d) + \delta\alpha p_d U(W_A + x_{gh}^d) + \delta(1 - \alpha)p_d U(W_A + x_{g\ell}^d),$$

where x_{gh}^d and $x_{g\ell}^d$ respectively denote the net payout when investigation reveals high risk and low risk. Nothing is changed in the b-recipients' self-selection constraint. In the firm's no-expected loss constraint, $p_d x_g^d$ is replaced by

$$p_d(1 - \delta)x_g^d + \delta\alpha p_d x_{gh}^d + \delta(1 - \alpha)p_d x_{g\ell}^d$$

and $p_d c_s$ is replaced by $p_d(c_s + \delta c_t)$. Using

$$\partial \mathcal{L}/\partial x_g^d = \partial \mathcal{L}/\partial x_{gh}^d = \partial \mathcal{L}/\partial x_{g\ell}^d = 0$$

gives

$$x_g^d = x_{gh}^d = x_{g\ell}^d.$$

We deduce

$$\partial \mathcal{L}/\partial \delta = -\mu_2 p_d c_t < 0$$

establishing that we have a corner solution with $\delta = 0$.

Proof of Proposition 5 If $p_s p_t = 1$ or $p_d = 1$ then the expected utility of a b-recipient from claiming to have perceived g would be

$$(1 - \pi_h)U(W_N - k_\ell) + \pi_h U(W_A - f),$$

which is less than from buying no insurance and, a fortiori, less than from buying the C_h^* contract. So the incentive constraint is slack which contradicts $\mu_1 > 0$.

Proof of Proposition 6 We can simplify (13)–(16) by observing that these formulae involve many expressions of the form

$$KU(W_A + x) - Hx,$$

where the x is defined by

$$KU'(W_A + x) = H.$$

Hence, in the derivatives of the Lagrangean with respect to investigation probabilities, we may use

$$KU(W_A + x) - Hx = H\Phi(x),$$

where

$$\Phi(x) = \frac{U(W_A + x)}{U'(W_A + x)} - x.$$

Without loss of generality, we normalize utility so that $U(W_A - f) = 0$. Then $\Phi(0) > 0$ and

$$\Phi'(x) = -\frac{U(W_A + x)U''(W_A + x)}{[U'(W_A + x)]^2} > 0.$$

Also define $\theta' = \theta/\mu_2\hat{\pi}$ and $x_g = x_\ell^t = x_{hg}^s = x_g^d$. Then

$$\partial\mathscr{L}/\partial p_t = \mu_2\hat{\pi}\{[1 - \beta(1 - p_s)]\Phi(x_g) + \beta(1 - p_s)\Phi(x_h^t)$$

$$-c_t - \beta p_s c_s - \theta'\} \tag{17}$$

$$\partial\mathscr{L}/\partial p_s = \mu_2\hat{\pi}\beta p_t[\Phi(x_g) - \Phi(x_h^t) - c_s] \tag{18}$$

$$\partial\mathscr{L}/\partial p_d = \mu_2\hat{\pi}[\Phi(x_g) - c_s - \theta'] \tag{19}$$

$$\partial\mathscr{L}/\partial p_n = \mu_2\hat{\pi}[\Phi(x_n) - \theta'] \tag{20}$$

Now note that

$$\partial\mathscr{L}/\partial p_t \le 0 \ (= 0 \text{ if } p_t > 0)$$

$$\partial\mathscr{L}/\partial p_s \le 0 \text{ if } p_s = 0 \ (= 0 \text{ if } 0 < p_s < 1, \ \ge 0 \text{ if } p_s = 1)$$

$$\partial\mathscr{L}/\partial p_d \le 0 \ (= 0 \text{ if } p_d > 0).$$

Assume first $c_s(1 - \beta) < c_t$ and $p_t > 0$. Suppose in addition that $p_s > 0$. We have

$$\partial\mathscr{L}/\partial p_t = [1 - \beta(1 - p_s)]\Phi(x_g) + \beta(1 - p_s)\Phi(x_h^t) - c_t - \beta p_s c_s - \theta' = 0$$

and

$$\partial\mathscr{L}/\partial p_s = \Phi(x_g) - \Phi(x_h^t) - c_s \ge 0,$$

which implies

$$\Phi(x_g) \ge c_t + \beta c_s + \theta'.$$

Using $c_s(1 - \beta) < c_t$ then gives

$$\Phi(x_g) > c_s + \theta',$$

which in turn gives $\partial\mathscr{L}/\partial p_d > 0$. This contradicts the optimality condition on p_d. Hence $p_s = 0$ when $c_s(1 - \beta) < c_t$ and $p_t > 0$.

Similar steps prove that when $c_s(1 - \beta) > c_t$, $p_d = 0$.

Proof of Proposition 7 The optimal expected utility of g-recipients in problem P2 is decreasing with D and it is less than the expected utility reached in problem P1 if $D > D^*$. Concavity of U implies

$$(1 - p_t\beta)U(W_A + x_\ell) + p_t\beta U(W_A + x_\ell - D) < U(W_A + x_\ell - p_t\beta D).$$

Hence, the optimal expected utility of g-recipients in problem P2 is lower than the level that would be reached by maximizing

$$(1 - \hat{\pi})U(W_N - k_\ell) + \hat{\pi}U(W_A + x_\ell - p_t\beta D)$$

subject to the same constraints as in problem P2. This modified problem will be called problem P3.

Suppose first that $c_t < (1 - \beta)c_s$, which implies $p_d = 0$ in problem P1. Observing that $p_s = 1$ is optimal in this problem, it can then be rewritten as maximizing

$$(1 - \hat{\pi})U(W_N - k_\ell) + \hat{\pi}U(W_A + x_\ell),$$

with respect to $k_\ell, x_\ell, p_t \geq 0$ subject to

$$U(W_N - \pi_h A) \geq (1 - \pi_h)U(W_N - k_\ell)$$
$$+ \pi_h[(1 - p_t)U(W_A + x_\ell) + p_t U(W_A - f)]$$
$$(1 - \hat{\pi})k_\ell - \hat{\pi}[x_\ell + p_t(c_t + \beta c_s)] \geq 0$$

and $p_t \leq 1$.

Let $x'_\ell = x_\ell + p_t\beta c_s$. With this notation, problem P1 can then be rewritten as the maximization of

$$(1 - \hat{\pi})U(W_N - k_\ell) + \hat{\pi}U(W_A + x'_\ell - p_t\beta c_s),$$

with respect to k_ℓ, x'_ℓ and p_t subject to

$$U(W_N - \pi_h A) \geq (1 - \pi_h)U(W_N - k_\ell)$$
$$+ \pi_h[(1 - p_t)U(W_A + x'_\ell - p_t\beta c_s) + p_t U(W_A - f)]$$
$$(1 - \hat{\pi})k_\ell - \hat{\pi}(x'_\ell + p_t c_t) \geq 0$$

and $p_t \leq 1$.

Comparing problems P1 and P3 shows that $D > c_s$ is a sufficient condition for the optimal expected utility of g-recipients in P1 to be higher than that in P3, and therefore a fortiori higher than that in problem P2.

Similar steps show that if $c_t > (1 - \beta)c_s$, a sufficient condition for the optimal expected utility of g-recipients in problem P1 to be higher than the level reached in problem P2 is $D > (c_s - c_t)/\beta$.

Hence, we have

$D^* < c_s$ if $c_t < (1 - \beta)c_s$

$D^* < (c_s - c_t)/\beta$ if $c_t > (1 - \beta)c_s$,

which may be rewritten as

$D^* < \inf\{c_s, (c_s - c_t)/\beta\}$.

Acknowledgments

We are very grateful to Karla Hoff for suggesting many improvements to the first draft. We also thank Barry Nalebuff for perceptive comments. Dixit thanks the U.S. National Science Foundation, and Picard thanks the Fédération Française des Sociétés d'Assurance (FFSA) for research support.

Notes

1. The courts sometimes extend the notion of "material fact" to opinions such as the prognosis of a specialist; see Clarke (1997, 596–597).

2. So $k_h + x_h$, $k_\ell + x_n$ etc. are the gross indemnity amounts.

3. This is problematic. In equilibrium no one acts in bad faith, so the company is tempted ex post to save the cost of the investigation. Picard (2002) relaxes the assumption of commitment and finds that semiseparating equilibria can arise where customers randomize.

References

Clarke, Malcolm A. 1997. *The Law of Insurance Contracts*. London: LLP Limited.

Dixit, Avinash. 2000. "Adverse selection and insurance with Uberima Fides," in *Incentives, Organization, and Public Economics: Essays in Honor of Sir James Mirrlees*, ed. Peter J. Hammond and Gareth D. Myles. Oxford: Oxford University Press.

Farshian, Alain. 2002. "Assurance-vie, secret medical et déclaration inexacte." *Le Monde Argent*, 24–25 March.

Kreps, David. 1990. *A Course in Microeconomic Theory*. Princeton, NJ: Princeton University Press.

Lambert-Faivre, Yvonne. 1991. *Droit des assurances*. Paris: Dalloz.

Picard, Pierre. 2002. "Costly risk verification without commitment in competitive insurance markets." Mimeo., Universite Paris X, manuscript.

Rothschild, Michael, and Joseph E. Stiglitz. 1976. "Equilibrium in competitive insurance markets: An essay on the economics of imperfect information." *Quartely Journal of Economics* 90 : 630–649.

4 Markets under Stress: The Case of Extreme Event Insurance

Dwight Jaffee and Thomas Russell

The investigation of why markets fail and the analysis of the appropriate public policy response to such failures have been major themes in the work of Stiglitz. In this chapter we continue with these themes, examining why insurance markets for extreme (i.e., low probability/high loss) events often experience difficulties in the period following the occurrence of the event. The focus is on natural disaster insurance, such as earthquakes and hurricanes, as well as on terrorist insurance. The analysis of the failure of such markets builds on several strands of the research by Stiglitz, including his work on insurance markets, credit rationing, and principal-agent problems within firms; see, for example, Rothschild and Stiglitz (1976), Stiglitz and Weiss (1981), and Greenwald and Stiglitz (1990).

Referring to the terrorist events of September 11, 2001, most insurance firms reacted by raising prices, canceling policies, placing limits on coverage, or even withdrawing from the terrorist insurance line altogether. This behavior is documented in General Accounting Office (GAO) (2002). According to the GAO, insurance companies withdrew from the terrorism market because they did not wish to deal with the increased uncertainty due to the probability and cost of future attacks. This issue of "ambiguity aversion" is addressed later in the chapter.

Since terrorism insurance is a requirement in many industries, for example, office building construction and airline transportation, the collapse of the terrorism insurance market has precipitated a demand for alternative risk sharing arrangements. Foremost among these are proposals for the federal government to provide some form of insurance of last resort. (A federal terrorism insurance bill was signed by President Bush on November 26, 2002, as this chapter was in the final editorial stages. The bill is briefly discussed in the final section.)

Drawing on our previous research on the operation of catastrophe insurance markets, Jaffee and Russell (1997), this chapter seeks to answer two basic questions about such markets:

1. Why do extreme insurance markets tend to collapse following a major event?

2. What is the best public policy response to this market failure?

1   Extreme Insurance Market Failure: The Puzzle

The standard explanations for insurance market failures are the problems caused by moral hazard and adverse selection. These problems are not completely absent in the case of extreme events, but they are unlikely to be a major contributor to an explanation for the puzzle of market collapse. In the case of terrorism insurance, for example, it is clear that enhanced airport security can lower the probability of attack, and terrorism insurance could blunt the incentive to take such measures. On the other hand, airport security measures are federally mandated, in part for externality reasons set out in Kunreuther and Heal (2002), so moral hazard cannot play a large role in this case.

There is more at stake here than simply the fact that premiums rise after an extreme event. We can readily grant that the likelihood of future terrorist attacks was higher after September 11, 2001, than before, but this simply calls for higher premiums. Alternatively, we may assume that the degree of uncertainty surrounding terrorism went up, either increasing the variance of claims or increasing parameter uncertainty, but again this could be handled by an appropriate adjustment in the price.

What is hard to understand, for example, is the reaction of the insurers of Chicago's airports. Prior to the event, Chicago carried $750 million of terrorist insurance for an annual premium of $125,000. Post September 11, their insurers would only offer $150 million of coverage for the new premium of $6.9 million. Even if the increase in premium is understandable, why was the quantity so severely rationed?[1]

In view of the observed rationing of catastrophe and terrorist insurance, it is natural to ask whether extreme event insurance is different from ordinary casualty lines, such as auto insurance. It is clear that governments do behave as if some lines of insurance present special difficulties for private markets. For example, the U.S. government already provides insurance against (among other risks) catastrophic nuclear accidents, political risks in overseas trade, riots, floods, bank runs, and marine and aviation war risks; see General Accounting Office (2001) and Moss (2002). Moreover, in those countries exposed to terrorist attacks earlier, including Northern Ireland, Great Britain, and Israel, terrorism insurance is uniformly provided by the government. Similarly, the states of California and Florida have actively intervened in the markets for earthquake and hurricane insurance respectively.

Although the fact of government provision in these lines of insurance is not in dispute, the exact reason for state provision is far from clear. On terrorism insurance, for example, GAO (2001) states:

It seems clear, given insurers' increased recognition of their exposures in the aftermath of the unprecedented events on Sept. 11, 2001, that coverage for terrorist acts is not now amenable to normal insurance underwriting, risk management, and actuarial techniques. As a result insurers and re-insurers are concerned about their ability to set an appropriate price for insurance coverage for terrorist acts. Given this uncertainty if this kind of insurance were to be offered at all, it is likely that either the price insurers set would be prohibitively high or so low as to invite insolvency.

Pricing terrorism risk is certainly not a simple task, but neither is pricing commercial satellite risk, and this is done at Lloyd's on a nod and a handshake. Given that probabilities of loss are uncertain, each insurer would need to guard against the problem of the winner's curse. As in the case of Lloyd's syndicates, however, each insurer could underwrite only a fraction of the total loss, and in this way the problem of being at the optimistic end of the loss probability prediction spectrum would be mitigated.[2]

2   Risk Bearing and Insurance: Is Extreme Event Insurance Different?

The primitives of insurance theory are now revisited to try to understand why insurance firms may operate differently across lines. As noted by Samuelson (1963), the essence of insurance is the subdividing, not the pooling of risk. It is normally the case, however, that insurers, whether they are organized as mutuals or as joint stock companies, in fact do pool risks. This sets up a tension between pooling and subdividing, a tension made clear by Ross (1999):

After all, when an insurance company or a "swaps shop" opens its doors, it attracts n independent risks, it does not cut up some larger existing risk. The presumption is that the race between a financial market which cuts up risks and a business that adds them is won by the market....

Elsewhere, Jaffee and Russell (2002), we provide a simple model of the insurance firm which is designed to capture the essence of the pooling/subdividing issue; see also Gollier (2002). The key result of that analysis is that investors would always be willing to participate in an insurance syndicate portfolio as long as either the premium loading (the premium in excess of the expected loss) is sufficiently large and/or the number of investors is sufficiently large (meaning that each investor takes on a sufficiently small share of the portfolio). This conclusion is true, moreover, even when the expected loss or variance of each policy is large and/or when the individual risks are highly (even perfectly) correlated. Of course, when the risks are larger or more highly correlated, then the premium loading or the number of investors will itself have to be larger to induce investors to purchase a share of the portfolio.

The Special Case of Extreme Event Insurance

Extreme event insurance is just a specific type of casualty risk in terms of the above findings. In particular, the result that investors can always be induced to hold such an insurance portfolio if the premium loading or the number of shareholders is made sufficiently large, applies to extreme event insurance as much as any other casualty risk. In this context, terrorist insurance, or any type of extreme event insurance, is not of another kind.

On the other hand, the parameter values that reasonably apply to extreme event insurance might be significantly different from those that apply to more standard casualty lines, such as auto insurance. In particular, for extreme risks: (1) the size of the risks are larger; (2) the correlation coefficients between individual risks may be higher, and (3) the performance guarantee costs may be higher (as a result of 1 and 2).

The implication is that the premium loading and the number of investors necessary to induce investors to hold an extreme event insurance portfolio is likely to be larger than for more traditional casualty risks, but this is a question of degree, not of kind.

Thus, if capital markets are perfect and all investors hold highly diversified market portfolios, then an equity position in an insurance firm should be an efficient structure for holding even large and highly correlated extreme risks. Three sets of capital market imperfections exist, however, that could frustrate this result: (1) asymmetric information within the syndicate, (2) bankruptcy/agency costs, and (3) a variety of institutional impediments to accumulating capital reserves against future possible losses. These imperfections are now considered in turn.

Asymmetric Information

In forming an insurance syndicate, there is always the possibility that some members will have more information about the risks at issue than others. This problem is distinct from the insured/insurer adverse selection problem referred to earlier. But this source of asymmetric information can also lead to market failure. It is unclear, however, why asymmetric information should be a more important problem for an insurance firm selling extreme risks to capital market investors than a firm selling, say, auto insurance risks. Although extreme risks may be large and there may be substantial uncertainty surrounding the estimates of these risks, none of this uncertainty should cause substantial asymmetry between the insurance firm and its capital market investors treated as a group.

Bankruptcy/Agency Costs

If the losses created by an extreme event threaten an insurance firm with bankruptcy, then there is a potential for deadweight bankruptcy costs and related agency costs. In particular, it is clear that the probability that an insurance firm would be made bankrupt by a particularly bad extreme loss during one year is substantially higher than the probability that the same firm would be made bankrupt by a particularly bad run of, say, auto insurance losses during a year. It could thus be quite sensible for the insurance firm's managers to refuse to take on extreme risks for fear that a "big one" will cause the loss of their jobs due to the bankruptcy of their firm.

On the other hand, it would appear that agency costs created by prospective bankruptcy could be avoided by appropriate financial structures for the insurance firm. Specialist insurance firms, for example, could be created to hold only terrorist risks, thus avoiding the possibility that a major terrorist loss could disrupt an otherwise profitable insurance firm. As another example, traditional insurance firms could securitize their terrorist risks, selling them directly to capital market investors. In fact, markets for securitizing natural disaster risks, such as earthquakes and hurricanes, have already been developed. Thus, while bankruptcy/agency costs might be a short-run problem for traditional insurance firms in providing extreme event insurance, in principle the problem should be solved by quite straightforward institution or security design. These arrangements face a number of practical difficulties, however, and its remains to be seen whether or not these difficulties can be overcome.

Impediments to Raising Capital

Extreme event losses tend to be large, often exceeding the annual premiums collected for the coverage by a factor of 10 and possibly by as much as 100. In particular, if the event occurs early in the life of a syndicate, the premiums accumulated to that date will fall far short of the loss, leaving the syndicate responsible for the shortfall.[3] Even with the risk spreading associated with reinsurance, any one risk bearing entity, and certainly the industry as a whole, must have access to substantial capital if it is to pay these losses. And surely the insurance rating agencies, such as A. M. Best, will consider adequate capital an essential factor to assign a high quality rating. This compares with routine lines such as auto insurance or dental insurance, where one year's premiums will almost always cover one year's losses, thus requiring the insurance firm to place little of its own capital at risk.

In a previous paper on natural catastrophe insurance, Jaffee and Russell (1997), we discussed why it may be difficult or costly for insurance entities to raise capital against possible future losses. In particular, that paper describes three fundamental problems with retaining earnings or raising capital in anticipation of possible future losses:

1. U.S. accounting rules preclude "ear-marking" retained profits or other capital funds as "reserves" against future losses, if the actual events have not yet occurred. Insurance firms, of course, are always

free to retain their earnings, but the accounting rules preclude pre-committing these funds to pay only catastrophe losses.

2. U.S. tax rules require full taxation of profits that are retained as reserves against future losses. This makes retained earnings an expensive way to accumulate funds against possible future losses.

3. A firm that accumulates liquidity to cover future large losses could become a takeover target due to its large cash assets. Since the liquidity cannot be precommitted to catastrophe losses, a third party could take over the firm, allow the policies to mature, and then use the liquidity for another purpose.

3 Post-Event Behavior

The previous section examined the conditions necessary for the formation of an extreme event insurance syndicate. In fact, following the September 11 event, a previously well-functioning market for terrorist insurance became highly ineffective. Similar breakdowns in insurance markets occur regularly following similar catastrophic events such as hurricanes and earthquakes. This section presupposes that the extreme event has occurred. Going forward, we consider why the simple occurrence of a low probability, high consequence, event should cause the failure of a previously well functioning insurance market.

The occurrence of an event, of course, may contain information requiring the reassessment of the means, variances, and covariances of the underlying risks. But after an appropriate adjustment in premiums, it would appear insurance syndicates should again be viable. Clearly, however, this is not what happens. Typically, following an extreme event, insurance markets are seriously disrupted. Two sets of explanations are offered for this type of market failure, one associated with post-event capital market imperfections, the other with behavioral responses to bad draws.

Post-Event Capital Market Imperfections

After a major event wipes out most of the industry's capital, firms might be expected to use the financial markets to replenish their capital base. With minor exceptions, however, insurance firms have not issued new equity to replenish their capital following an extreme event. This is puzzling, since the period following an event is in many ways the perfect time for a syndicate to raise new capital. Rates normally harden following an event, and this will be reflected in higher stock prices, reducing the cost of equity. The markets have responded in exactly this way since September 11, yet insurance firms have not used the financial markets to replenish their capital in any significant way.

Jaffee and Russell (1997) discuss two main difficulties that insurance firms may have in accessing capital markets after the event:

1. Potential investors in the new securities will be concerned that their funds will be used to pay off past losses, not to support new profitable initiatives. This is a more extreme version of the classic Myers (1977) debt overhang argument, with insurance policy claimants playing the role of Myers's bond holders.

2. The potential for asymmetric information may lead potential investors to evaluate future risks at a higher level than does the issuing firm, causing the new investors to require a lower price for the new securities than the firm is willing to accept.

On the other hand, a number of insurance derivatives have been created in recent years, including option and futures contracts and catastrophe bonds.[4] These securities are motivated by the notion that catastrophe events represent, by and large, zero beta risks, so that capital market investors should be willing to take on these risks at a price that reflects only the expected loss, with little or no risk premium above that amount. These instruments have also been analyzed in Jaffee and Russell (1997). They point out that these securities have also failed to provide an effective mechanism for transferring catastrophe risks from insurance firms to the capital markets for three basic reasons:

1. Just as with new security issues, the potential for asymmetric information may lead potential investors to evaluate future risks at a higher level than does the issuing firm.

2. With the future and option instruments, the need to provide adequate performance guarantees has restricted the amount of risk transfer to relatively small amounts.

3. Investors may believe that catastrophic events will depress the economy and stock market generally, creating a positive, possibly

even very large, expected beta value, and thus raising the cost of the catastrophe insurance securities.

The absence of new issues of capital to restore the capital lost by the extreme events could also reflect the hope for federal government assistance. For whatever reason, it is clear that new capital does not immediately flow into catastrophe lines following an event, so that private insurers either limit coverage or withdraw from the line completely. The chapter now turns to behavioral explanations for this phenomenon, including a new explanation based on a behavioral interpretation of attitudes to risk.

Explanations for Post-Event Behavior: Ambiguity Aversion

The occurrence of an extreme event will frequently trigger an increase in uncertainty surrounding future events. How does this increase in uncertainty affect markets? Froot and Posner (2001), using an expected utility framework, have investigated this issue in the context of the observed high rate of return on catastrophe bonds. Perhaps rather surprisingly, they show that parameter uncertainty has a very small effect on cat bond spreads, and indeed in the case of independence between event probabilities and parameter uncertainty, the latter has no effect on these spreads.

Bantwal and Kunreuther (2000) also investigated the issue of catastrophe bond pricing. They assume investors are ambiguity averse in the Gilboa and Schmeidler (1989) sense; that is, faced with a set of probability density functions, G, investors act to maximize expected value $= \int u(x) \min f(x) \, dx$ for $f(x)$ in G. Bantwal and Kunreuther showed that ambiguity aversion would require that cat bonds offer a premium over the risk free rate, though not as large as that observed. Hogarth (2002) has also recognized the relevance of ambiguity aversion for analyzing attitudes toward catastrophic risks, particularly terrorist insurance.

As an example of such ambiguity aversion, suppose that there are fixed binary probabilities before the event, the probability of the event not occurring being P. Suppose that after the event the probability parameter P itself becomes uncertain, the new probability being $P - e$ with probability $1/2$ and $P + e$ with probability $1/2$. An ambiguity averse investor now sees two possible density functions over payoffs, $G = \{[P - e, 1 - (P - e)], [P + e, 1 - (P + e)]\}$, where the first entry in each square bracket is the probability of the event not occurring. This has no effect on pricing in the Froot and Posner framework, but in the ambiguity averse framework the payoff on a cat bond now becomes $(H)(P-e) + (0)(1-(P+e)) = H(P-e)$, where H is the contractual payoff if the event does not occur and 0 is the payoff if it does; for a similar analysis, see Dow and Werlang (1992). In this case, even given that the cat bond has no nondiversifiable risk, its reduced expected payoff will require it to be priced to yield a premium vis a vis the zero beta excess return. This premium might better be called an ambiguity premium than a risk premium. By itself this will cause required yields to rise following an event, but it is not clear that by itself this will cause the market to fail. For this we need further effects.

Explanations for Post-Event Behavior: Fairness

Fairness as discussed by Kahneman, Knetsch, and Thaler (1986) provides a further effect to consider. In this view, when events require a sharp increase in price, markets may fail because the seller is reluctant to incur the bad will caused by an apparently unfair price increase. That fairness may play a significant role in the explanation of the regulation of insurance markets has been discussed elsewhere, see Jaffee and Russell (1998).

It is less obvious that fairness plays a significant role with extreme event insurance. First, Kahneman, Knetsch, and Thaler note that unfairness is generally associated with price increases for which there is no obvious cost justification. The losses created by extreme events—earthquakes, hurricanes, or terrorist attacks—however, are all widely reported, which blunts any accusations of opportunism from raising premiums. Second, the primary concern of buyers of extreme event insurance appears to be availability, not price. For example, we noted above the example of Chicago's O'Hare, in which premiums rose fifty-fold, hardly an indication that fairness is a key issue. We now explore another explanation which may be called irrational abhorrence.

Irrational Abhorrence

The models of decision making that underlie the analysis of insurance presented so far have all been relentlessly cognitive. Recently, however, some researchers have recognized that decisions under uncertainty involve additional psychological considerations. In a recent survey Loewenstein et al. (2001) have called this new approach "risk as feelings." A withdrawal of supply is predicted in the "risk as feelings" literature, where noncognitive factors lead to inaction rather than wrong action in the face of some risks.[5] These noncognitive factors have been extensively studied by Slovic and his collaborators. Peters and Slovic (1996), for example, reduced the psychological dimensions of risk to two primary factors, *dread* defined by Loewenstein et al. as "the extent of perceived lack of control, feelings of dread, and *perceived catastrophic potential* (italics added) and *risk of the unknown* defined as the extent to which the hazard is judged to be unobservable, unknown, new, or delayed in producing harmful impacts.

That dread could lead to inaction and, in the context of terrorist insurance, to a withdrawal of supply, is consistent with the findings of Damasio and his colleagues, see Bechara et al. (1997). As reported in this study, subjects were told that they could earn hypothetical money by turning over cards from one of four decks. Two of the decks contained high payouts ($100) and two contained low payouts ($50). The high paying decks, however, also contained a "catastrophe," a card marked with a very high loss.

On average, healthy subjects sampled from all four decks until they drew the cat card, at which point they thereafter avoided the catastrophe deck. The observation that individuals shun investment opportunities that have just experienced a major loss does provide a unifying framework for the analysis of a number of extreme event phenomena. Two issues are focused on here.

Good and Bad Multiple Equilibria

Since the essence of insurance is risk sharing, it is essential that anyone contemplating joining an insurance syndicate believes that there are enough other potential members of the syndicate to make his or her share of the risk small. For example, this appears to have been the case pre-September 11. Following the event, however, even if a nonemotional investor believes that the syndicate could be profitable if sufficiently subdivided, the syndicate will not be viable if (1) the event causes a sufficient number of investors to become unavailable, or (2) it causes sufficient investors to have the belief that a sufficient number of investors will be unavailable.

In the latter case the belief that the syndicate was not viable becomes a self-fulfilling prophecy.

Heterogeneous Response

It appears unlikely that all investors will pass on a positive profit project just because it once generated a bad draw. It is known that some individuals are less prone to "irrational abhorrence" than others; see Peters and Slovic (2000). The basis of this variation across individuals lies outside the scope of economics, but there does appear to be an interesting difference between the response of individuals and the response within corporations. For example, following the cancellation of the 2002 Soccer World Cup insurance by the large French insurer AXA, Warren Buffett, an executive who exercises strong individual control over his insurance companies, quickly offered to fill the gap; see *Business Week* (2002) for an intriguing discussion of Buffett's willingness to take on such risks.

It would appear that the tendency to stay away from projects that have suffered a loss is more pronounced in corporations with all their well-known agency problems than it is in entities run by single individuals. This may seem somewhat paradoxical, however, because we would expect that systematic quantification would be more prevalent in entities run by professional managers.

4   Public Policy and the Market for Extreme Event Insurance

How should public policy be conducted when insurance firms and / or capital markets "dread" the prospects of carrying catastrophe insurance risks? This section discusses a range of alternative policy solutions.[6] Assume here that premium setting by insurance firms is not constrained by issues of fairness or by regulations.

Public Entities to Bear the Risk

One obvious solution is to create a public or quasi-public entity to hold the catastrophic insurance risks; for further analysis, see Cummins and Doherty (2002). The California Earthquake Authority (CEA), created as a quasi-public entity to hold California earthquake risks after the Northridge quake of 1994, is one example. Participating primary insurers transferred all their earthquake risks to the CEA, thus insulating their firms from all earthquake claims. The CEA, however, also had no claim on government resources, leaving only its initial capitalization, its premium income, and its retained profits to meet claims. The result is that in the event of a huge quake, policyholders will not receive full payment for their losses. This possibility was explicitly recognized in the legislation creating the CEA, although there is the question of what a government would actually do in the event.

The Pool Re agency for terrorist insurance in Great Britain, created after the 1993 IRA attack in Central London, expands the quasi-public role of the CEA by having the British Treasury provide a reinsurance policy to backstop all its losses; see Tillinghast-Towers Perrin (2001). The result is that the British government guarantees full payment on any terrorist losses. A major drawback to Pool Re, however, is that the primary decisions of insurance underwriting and pricing are taken out of the hands of the private market.[7] It is thus useful to consider catastrophe bonds as an instrument that could retain the participation of the private firms in the underwriting process, while allowing the government to limit the losses faced by these firms were an extreme event to occur.

Catastrophe Bonds as Insurer of Last Resort

A limited number of catastrophe bonds have been issued by insurance firms to hedge their hurricane and earthquake risks, but the high risk premium required so far by capital market investors has limited their usefulness. To overcome this pricing problem, the government could purchase specific tiers of catastrophe bonds, representing the riskiest layers of the catastrophe risks. The catastrophe bonds would substitute for the role held by the British Treasury as insurer of last resort under the British Pool Re plan. The advantage of the catastrophe bonds is that the primary insurance firms could underwrite and hold the policies directly, using the catastrophe bonds to hedge the tiers of extreme event risk that might otherwise threaten their solvency. Catastrophe bonds sold by insurance firms to the government would represent the securitization of insurance risks, and government ownership of the bonds can be seen as parallel to the implicit and explicit guarantees that the U.S. Treasury currently provides to Fannie Mae and Freddie Mac to back their mortgage market securitization.

Lender of Last Resort versus Insurer of Last Resort

Guaranteed catastrophe bonds still imply a potential government presence as the insurer of last resort, so it is worth considering whether even that role can be minimized. One notion would be to transfer the *insurer* of last resort function to that of *lender* of last resort. The concept of the lender of last resort could be applied to catastrophe insurance if a government agency, possibly the Federal Reserve itself, stood ready to make loans to insurance firms that were in need of liquidity. These loans might appear similar to catastrophe bonds, but (1) would be issued only after the losses occurred, and (2) would be collateralized by assets of the insurance firm. The loans would be repaid from the insurance firms' ongoing profits. A difficulty, of course, is that the government would face potential default risk on these loans. Furthermore, it is an open question whether access to such a lender of last resort, without an insurer of last resort, would provide sufficient incentive for major insurance firms to continue to commit their capital and other resources to extreme event lines of insurance.

Current Developments for Government Terrorist Insurance

In the year following the 9/11 event, real estate markets continued to operate tolerably well in the absence of any government program, although there was considerable pressure from both the real estate and insurance industries to provide government protection against the higher layers of terrorist risks. Finally, on November 26, 2002, President Bush signed a federal terrorism bill into law. Passage of this bill finds this paper in its final editing stages, so our comments here are brief and preliminary.[8] The bill shares the risks of terrorism between the private markets and the insurance industry. At the lowest level of actual losses, the insurance industry will bear the losses directly, as if there were a deductible limit. At higher levels of losses, there is coinsurance between the industry and the government, with the government share reaching 90 percent of the total. Losses above $100 billion are prorated, although it is possible that the government might then step in with post-event support. Some components of the government insurance require post-event repayments by the insurance industry (in the form of mutual insurance), whereas other components are provided without charge by the government. Another intriguing component of the bill is that all casualty insurance carriers are *required* to offer terrorism insurance to their clients, although there are no restrictions on the price at which this coverage must be offered. The presumption is that market competition will force firms to offer coverage at sensible prices. At this writing, no data are yet available on the type of coverage that is actually being offered.

5 Conclusion

The attempt here has been to understand why the occurrence of an extreme event causes supply problems in the market for extreme event insurance. Although more standard explanations such as ex post moral hazard and adverse selection in syndicate formation surely contribute to an explanation of the market failure, the timing of this failure as a response to the occurrence of a loss suggests that the "there is nothing to fear but fear itself" syndrome may play an important role. Consistent with the "risk as feelings" literature, government action may be required even when disruptions are temporary, caused by "irrational abhorrence."

In this case, the goal of government policy should be not to replace the market, but rather to calm the market until it restores itself. The alternatives for government policy range from direct government insurance (such as in Northern Ireland and Israel), to insurer of last resort (such as with the British Policy Re or possibly with guaranteed catastrophe bonds), and finally just to be lender of last resort. Generally speaking, the less government intervention the better, but the key is to make sure that capital continues to flow into these lines.

Memories fade after an extreme event, and with the help of government guarantees, it is to be expected that markets will soon return to normal operation. At that time, government support can be withdrawn.

Acknowledgments

We would like to thank seminar participants at the National Bureau of Economic Research and the Weimer School of Advanced Studies in Real Estate, and Barry Nalebuff for helpful comments on an earlier version of this chapter. Any errors are the responsibility of the authors.

Notes

1. The primary carriers of insurance might answer that the quantity of insurance was rationed because reinsurance was not available. That merely pushes the question one step back. See City of Chicago (2001) for O'Hare insurance costs.

2. We are grateful to Barry Nalebuff for calling our attention to the role of the winner's curse in this context.

3. This problem could be avoided by creating decade-long insurance contracts, with premiums still paid at the initial date of the contract. Policyholders, however, would then face a serious counterparty/performance risk. The fact that we do not see such long-term contracts suggests the performance risk issue is serious.

4. Catastrophe bonds are a class of securities issued by insurance or reinsurance firms. The issuer places the proceeds from the bond sale in Treasury securities. If the cat event does not occur, the Treasury securities are sold to repay the principal to the bondholders. If the cat event does occur, then the insurance firm receives the proceeds from the Treasury bond sale, and the firm is also relieved of its obligation to repay the principal and any further interest on the bonds.

5. Refusal to trade can be motivated by other non-Laplacian models. If the individual exhibits behavior represented by a Choquet integral, for example, then refusal to trade can be a consequence of "model uncertainty." See Routledge and Zin (2001).

6. For other concurrent discussions, see Cummins and Doherty (2002) and Kunreuther (2002).

7. Otherwise, the private markets would have incentive to cherry pick, keeping the best terrorist risks in their own portfolio and passing the others to the public pool.

8. For a more complete discussion of the bill, see Thomas Russell (2003).

References

Bantwal, V., and Howard Kunreuther. 2000. "A Cat Bond Premium Puzzle?" *The Journal of Psychology and Financial Markets*, vol. 1, 76–91.

Bechara, A., H. Damasio, D. Tranel, and A. R. Damasio. 1997. "Deciding Advantageously before Knowing the Advantageous Strategy." *Science*, 1293–1295.

Business Week. 2002. "Buffett Jumps in Where Others Fear to Tread." July 15, 120–122.

City of Chicago. 2001. Press release. "Chicago CFO Warns Congress of Huge Insurance Rate Hikes." October 25. Available online at ⟨http://www.ci.chi.il.us/Mayor/2001Press/news_press_insuranceratehikes.html⟩.

Cummins, J. David, and Neil A. Doherty. 2002. "Federal Terrorism Reinsurance: An Analysis of Issues and Program Design Alternatives." Paper presented at the NBER Insurance Conference, February 1.

Dow, James, and Sergio Werlang. 1992. "Uncertainty Aversion, Risk Aversion, and the Optimal Choice of Portfolio." *Econometrica*, vol. 60, 197–204.

Froot, Kenneth, and Steven Posner. 2001. "The Pricing of Event Risks with Parameter Uncertainty." NBER working paper no. 8106.

General Accounting Office. 2002. "Terrorism Insurance: Rising Uninsured Exposure to Attacks Heightens Potential Economic Vulnerabilities." Statement of Richard J. Hilliman, U.S. Government Accounting Office, February 27.

General Accounting Office. 2001. "Terrorism Insurance: Alternative Programs for Protecting Insurance Consumers." U.S. Government General Accounting Office.

Gilboa, Itzhak, and David Schmeidler. 1989. "Maxmin Expected Utility with Non-Unique Prior." *Journal of Mathematical Economics*, vol. 18, 141–153.

Gollier, Christian. 2002. "Insurability." University of Toulouse working paper, January 18.

Greenwald, Bruce, and Joseph Stiglitz. 1990. "Asymmetric Information and the New Theory of the Firm: Financial Constraints and Risk Behavior." *American Economic Review*, vol. 80, 160–165.

Hogarth, Robin M. "Insurance and Safety After September 11: Has the World Become a 'Riskier' Place?" from the Social Science Research Council Web page. After September 11, Perspectives from the Social Sciences, Recovery. Available online at ⟨http://www.ssrc.org/sept11/essays/hogarth.htm⟩.

Jaffee, Dwight, and Thomas Russell. 1997. "Catastrophe Insurance, Capital Markets, and Uninsurable Risks." *Journal of Risk and Insurance*, vol. 64, no. 2, 205–230.

Jaffee, Dwight, and Thomas Russell. 1998. "The Causes and Consequences of Rate Regulation in the Auto Insurance Industry," in *The Economics of Property-Casualty Insurance*, ed. David Bradford. Cambridge, MA: National Bureau of Economic Research (also NBER working paper no. 5245).

Jaffee, Dwight, and Thomas Russell. 2002. "Extreme Events and the Market for Terrorist Insurance." Fisher Center for Real Estate and Urban Economics, working paper 02–282.

Kahneman, D., J. L. Knetsch, and R. Thaler. 1986. "Fairness as a Constraint on Profit Seeking: Entitlements in the Market." *American Economic Review*, vol. 76, 894–920.

Kunreuther, Howard. 2002. "The Role of Insurance in Managing Extreme Events: Implications for Terrorism Coverage." *Business Economics*, April.

Kunreuther, Howard and G. Heal. "Interdependent Security: The Case of Identical Agents." Wharton Risk Management and Decision Processes Center working paper 02-06-HK (2002).

Kunreuther, Howard, Jacqueline Meszaros, Robin Hogarth, and Mark Spranca. 1995. "Ambiguity and Underwriter Decision Processes." *Journal of Economic Behavior and Organization*, vol. 26, 337–352.

Loewenstein, G. F, E. U. Weber, C. K. Hsee, and N. Welch. 2001. "Risk as Feelings." *Psychological Bulletin*, vol. 127, 267–286.

Moss, David A. 2002. *When All Else Fails: Government as the Ultimate Risk Manager*. Cambridge: Harvard University Press.

Myers, S. C. 1977. "Determinants of Corporate Borrowing." *Journal of Financial Economics* 5:147–176.

Peters, E., and Slovic, P. 1996. "The Role of Affect and Worldviews as Orienting Dispositions in the Perception and acceptance of Nuclear Power." *Journal of Applied Social Psychology*, vol. 26, 1427–1453.

Peters, E., and Slovic, P. 2000. "The Springs of Action: Affective and Analytical Information Processing in Choice." *Personality and Social Psychology Bulletin*, vol. 26, no. 12, 1465–1475.

Ross, Stephen. 1999. "Adding Risks: Samuelson's Fallacy of Large Numbers Revisited." *Journal of Financial and Quantitative Analysis*, vol. 34. No3, September.

Rothschild, Michael, and Joseph Stiglitz. 1976. "Equilibrium in Competitive Insurance Markets: An Essay on the Economics of Imperfect Information." *Quarterly Journal of Economics*, vol. 90, 630–649.

Routledge, Bryan, and Stanley Zin. 2001. "Model Uncertainty and Liquidity." NBER working paper, November.

Russell, Thomas. 2003. "The Costs and Benefits of the Terrorism Risk Insurance Act: A First Look." Paper presented at NBER Insurance Conference, January.

Samuelson, Paul. 1963. "Risk and Uncertainty: A Fallacy of Large Numbers." *Scientia* 98.

Stiglitz, Joseph, and Andrew Weiss. 1981. "Credit Rationing in Markets with Imperfect Information." *American Economic Review*, vol. 71, 393–410.

Tillinghast-Towers Perrin. 2001. "Update." available at ⟨http://www.towers.com/towers/services_products/Tillinghast/update_pool_re.pdf⟩.

5 Per-Mile Premiums for Auto Insurance

Aaron S. Edlin

... the manner in which [auto insurance] premiums are computed and paid fails miserably to bring home to the automobile user the costs he imposes in a manner that will appropriately influence his decisions.

—William Vickrey, 1968

Americans drive 2,360,000,000,000 miles each year, and the cost of auto accidents is commensurately large:[1] roughly $100 billion in accident insurance,[2] and, according to the Urban Institute (1991), an additional $320 billion in uninsured accident costs per year, far more than the cost of gasoline. (Figures are given in 1995 dollars throughout).

Every time drivers take to the road, and with each mile they drive, they expose themselves and others to the risk of accident. Surprisingly, though, most auto insurance premiums have largely lump-sum characteristics and are only weakly linked to mileage. Mileage classifications are coarse, and low-mileage discounts are extremely modest and based on self-reported estimates of future mileage that have no implicit or explicit commitment.[3] (Two noteworthy exceptions are premiums on some commercial policies[4] and a few recent pilot programs.)[5] Few drivers therefore pay or perceive a significant insurance cost from driving an extra mile, despite the substantial accident costs involved.

An ideal tort and insurance system would charge each driver the full social cost of her particular risk exposure on the marginal mile of driving. Otherwise, people will drive too much and cause too many accidents (from the vantage of economic efficiency). The extent of this potential problem is apparently severe if we consider that insurance costs almost as much as gasoline ($590 compared with $670 per year per private passenger vehicle in 1995) and that insurance costs may dramatically understate total accident costs.

In principle, insurance companies could levy a substantial charge for driving an extra mile, as new car leases do; however, this would require them to incur the cost of verifying mileage (through periodic odometer checks or by installing a monitoring and broadcasting device in vehicles). A central point of this chapter is that externalities make their incentives to do so considerably less than the social incentives. If insurance company C is able to reduce the driving of its insureds, although it will save on accident payouts, substantial "external" savings will be realized by other insurance carriers and their insureds who will get into fewer accidents with C's insureds. These externalities follow from Vickrey's observation that if two drivers get into an accident, even the safer driver is typically a "but for" cause of the accident in the sense that had the driver opted for the metro, the accident would not have occurred.[6] (see also Shavell 1987). Externalities help explain why we are only just now seeing pilot per-mile premiums programs.

Accident externalities suggest a valuable role for policy, and this chapter investigates the potential benefits of two proposals that would increase the marginal charge for driving, and consequently reduce driving and accidents. The first proposal is per-mile premiums, advocated by Litman (1997), Butler (1990), and the National Organization for Women. Under a per-mile premium system, the basic unit of exposure would shift from the car-year to the car-mile, either by requirement or by subtler policy tools, so that the total premiums of driver i would be $m_i p_i$, where m_i is the miles i travels and p_i is her per-mile rate. An individual's per-mile rate, p_i, would vary among drivers to reflect the per-mile risk of a given driver and could depend upon territory, driver age, safety records or other relevant characteristics used today for per-year rates. (In fact, the technology now used experimentally by Progressive in Texas also allows prices to vary by time of the day and by location.)[7]

The second proposal is to couple per-mile premiums with a Pigouvian tax to account for the "Vickrey" accident externality. Both these proposals differ fundamentally from the uniform per-gallon gas tax proposals of Vickrey (1968),[8] Sugarman (1993), and Tobias (1993), because under gas tax proposals, unlike per-mile premiums, the additional cost of driving would be independent of driver age, driver safety records, or in some cases of territory (all highly important indicia of risk), yet would depend upon fuel efficiency (a relatively poor risk measure).

This chapter begins by developing a simple model that relates miles driven to accidents, formalizing Vickrey's insights about the externalities of driving—this contribution is mainly pedagogical. The second contribution is to provide the first estimates of the potential benefits of per-mile premiums that take into account Vickrey's externalities as well as the resulting fact that as driving falls, so too will accident rates and per-mile premiums.[9] Third, the benefits of a per-mile premium policy are estimated coupled with a Pigouvian tax. (It's natural to consider taxing per-mile premiums to account for accident externalities once one incorporates externalities.) Finally, congestion cost reductions are included.

Nationally, the average insured cost of accidents is roughly 4 cents per mile driven, but we estimate that the marginal cost—the cost if an extra mile is driven—is much higher, roughly 7.5 cents, because of accident externalities. In high traffic-density states like New Jersey, Hawaii, or Rhode Island, we estimate that the marginal cost is roughly 15 cents. For comparison, gasoline costs roughly 6 cents per mile, so an efficient Pigouvian charge for accidents at the margin would dramatically increase the marginal cost of driving and would presumably reduce driving substantially.

Even without a Pigouvian charge to account for accident externalities, a system of per-mile premiums that shifted a fixed insurance charge to the margin would be roughly equivalent to a 70 percent hike in the gasoline price and could be expected to reduce driving nationally by 9.5 percent, and insured accident costs by $17 billion per year. After subtracting the lost driving benefits of $4.4 billion, the net accident reductions would be $12.7 billion or $75 per insured vehicle per year. The net savings would be $15.3 billion per year if per-mile premiums were taxed to account for the external effect of one person's driving on raising others' insurance premiums.

These estimates are probably a lower bound on what savings would actually be under a per-mile system, because they use state level data and assume that drivers and territories are homogeneous within a state. In a per-mile system, just as in the current per-year system, heterogeneity in accident risk would be reflected in per-mile rates that vary by territory, driver age, and driver accident record. Since the most dangerous drivers in the most dangerous territories would face the steepest rise in marginal driving cost and therefore reduce driving the most, actual benefits could be considerably larger than our estimates.

The main reason insurance companies have not switched to per-mile premiums is probably that monitoring actual mileage with yearly odometer checks appears too costly, given their potential gains, as suggested by Rea (1992) and Williamson et al. (1967, 247).[10] Our analysis suggests, however, that the gains a given insurance company could realize by switching to per-mile premiums are considerably less than the social gains. A single company and its customers might stand to gain only $31 per vehicle per year from the switch, far less than the potential social gains of $58 per insured vehicle that we estimate when we include the Vickrey externality (i.e., the reduction in others' insurance costs.) Moreover, the $31 in private gains would be temporary from an insurer's vantage and would all go to consumers once other firms match its new policies.[11] This discrepancy implies that the social gains from per-mile premiums might justify the monitoring costs (and the fixed costs of transition), even if no single insurance company could profit from the change itself.

Other external benefits could make the discrepancy between the private gains from per-mile premiums and the social gains even larger. A great deal of accident costs are uninsured or underinsured (more than half, according to the Urban Institute) and the driving reductions caused by per-mile premiums should reduce these costs just as they reduce insured accident costs.[12] Policy intervention looks more attractive still when nonaccident benefits such as congestion are taken into account. Congestion reductions raise our estimates of the benefits from per-mile premiums by $5.7 billion. This brings our estimates of total national benefits from per-mile premiums to $18.2 billion ($24.7 billion with a Pigouvian tax), or $107.5 per insured vehicle ($146.2 with a Pigouvian tax). Benefits would be higher still, if pollution costs, road maintenance costs, and other externality costs are higher than we assume here.[13]

The fact that accident and congestion externalities could make up more than two-thirds of the benefits from per-mile premiums suggests that even if monitoring costs are so large that it is rational for insurance companies to maintain the current premium structure, it is likely that per-mile premiums could still enhance efficiency in many states. Likewise, it suggests that as mileage monitoring technology becomes cheaper (e.g., global positioning system technology), insurance companies may be slower at adopting these technologies than is socially efficient.

Section 1 presents a simple model of accidents that formalizes Vickrey's insights about accident externalities and incorporates congestion. Section 2 describes the data. Section 3 simulates driving and accident reductions under per-mile premiums. Section 4 concludes and explores the policy implications of this research.

1   A Simple Model of Accidents and Congestion

A model relating driving to accidents is developed here and used to simulate the consequences of various pricing scenarios. For simplicity, an entirely symmetric model is constructed in which drivers, territory, and roads are undifferentiated and identical. The central insights continue to hold in a world where some drivers, roads, and territories are more dangerous than others, with some provisos. The relationship between aggregate accidents and aggregate miles will only hold exactly if the demand elasticity is the same across types of driving and drivers. Otherwise, accidents will be either more or less responsive to driving according to whether extra miles are driven by more or less dangerous drivers under more, or less dangerous conditions.

Attention is limited to one and two vehicle accidents, ignoring the fact that many accidents only occur because of the coincidence of three or more cars.[14] Accidents involving two or more cars are treated as if they all involve only two cars because multivehicle accidents are not separated in the accident data. Refined data would increase estimates of the benefits from the driving reductions associated with per-mile premiums because the size of accident externalities increase with the number of cars involved in collisions.

Let

m_i = miles traveled by driver i per year

M = aggregate vehicle miles traveled per year by all drivers

l = total lane miles

D = traffic density, or traffic volume $= M/l$

f_i = probability that i is driving at any given time

δ_1 = damages from one-vehicle accident

δ_2 = damages to each car in a two-vehicle accident

Holding speed constant, the fraction of the time that i is driving, f_i, will be proportional to the miles driven, m_i; hence $f_i = pm_i$, for some p. For convenience, imagine that the l lane miles are divided into L "locations" of equal length. An accident occurs between drivers i and j if they are in the same location and neither brakes or takes other successful evasive action. The chance that i is driving and j is in the same location is $f_i(f_j/L)$. Let q be the probability of accident conditional upon being in the same location. The expected rate of damages to i from two-car accidents with $j \neq i$ will then be

$$a_{2i,j} = \delta_2 f_i \frac{f_j}{L} q.$$

Summing over $j \neq i$ and substituting pm_j for f_j and pm_i for f_i yields expected damages to i from two-car accidents:

$$a_{2i} = \delta_2 p^2 m_i \frac{q\Sigma_{j \neq i} m_j}{L}.$$

Letting $c_2 \equiv \delta_2 p^2 l/L$, we have

$$a_{2i} = c_2 m_i \frac{(M - m_i)}{l},$$

or, assuming m_i is small relative to M,

$$a_{2i} \approx c_2 m_i \frac{M}{l} = c_2 m_i D.$$

Ignoring multiple-car accidents, the total expected accident damages suffered by driver i are then

$$a_i = c_1 m_i + c_2 m_i D.$$

The first term in the equation reflects the fact that a driver may be involved in an accident even if driving alone (e.g., falling asleep at night and driving into a tree), with c_1 representing the expected accident costs from driving a mile alone. The second term reflects the fact that the chance of getting into an accident with other vehicles in that mile increases as the traffic density D increases.

The linearity of this model in m_i ignores the possibility that practice and experience could bring down the per-mile risk, as well as the offsetting possibility that driving experience (which is generally a safe experience) could lead to complacency and conceit. Empirical estimates of the elasticity of an individual's accidents with respect to that individual's mileage, as surveyed in Edlin (1999), range from 0.35 to 0.92, but as Edlin (1999) discusses, this work has been limited by the scarcity of reliable microlevel data pairing mileage and accidents, and it probably yields downward biased estimates because of noisy mileage data and also because of the difficulty of controlling for the factors that cause any given driver to drive very little (which are likely related to accident propensity).[15]

Summing over each driver i yields the total accident costs:

$$A = c_1 M + c_2 MD = c_1 M + c_2 M^2 / l. \tag{1}$$

Observe that the cost of two-car accidents $c_2 M^2 / l$ increases with the square of total miles driven. This nonlinearity is the source of the externality effect.

The marginal total accident cost from driving an extra mile is

$$\frac{dA}{dM} = c_1 + 2c_2 D. \tag{2}$$

In contrast, the marginal cost of accidents to driver i is only

$$\frac{da_i}{dm_i} = c_1 + c_2 D. \tag{3}$$

The difference between these two costs, $c_2 D$, is the externality effect. It represents the fact that when driver i gets in an accident with another driver, driver i is typically the "but for" cause of both drivers' damages in the sense that, "but for" driver i having been driving, the accident would not have happened. (Strangely enough, it is entirely possible that both drivers are the "but for" cause of *all* damages). This model could overstate the externality effect because of accident substitution: if driver A and B collide, it is possible that driver A would have hit driver C if driver B weren't there. On the other hand, it understates the externality effect to the extent that some collisions require more than two vehicles.

A different view of the accident externality of driving is found by observing that the average cost of accidents per mile driven is:

$$\frac{A}{M} = c_1 + c_2 D. \tag{4}$$

A given driver who drives the typical mile expects to experience the average damages A/M. Yet, this driver also increases D, which means that this driver also causes the accident rate for others to rise at a rate of $(d(A/M))/(dM) = c_2(dD)/(dM) = c_2/l$. Multiplying this figure by the M vehicle miles of driving affected again yields an externality c_2D.

The basic "micro" intuition behind the accident externality is simple. If a person decides to go out driving instead of staying at home or using public transportation, she may end up in an accident, and some of the cost of the accident will not be borne by either her or her insurance company; some of the accident cost is borne by the other party to the accident or that party's insurance company. Although the average mile is not subsidized, the marginal mile is![16] The "macro" intuition is that the more people drive on the same roads, the more dangerous driving becomes. (A little introspection will probably convince most readers that crowded roadways are more dangerous than open ones; in heavy traffic, most drivers feel compelled to a constant vigilance to avoid the numerous moving hazards.)[17] A given driver or insurance company pays the average cost of accidents. The driver does not pay for the fact that driving raises the average cost of others through a crowding effect.

1.1 Gains from Per-Mile Premiums

The current insurance system, which is characterized (somewhat unfairly as note 3 concedes) as involving lump-sum premiums, is now compared with two alternative systems: (1) competitive per-mile premiums and (2) Pigouvian per-mile premiums. As derived above, the break-even condition for insurance companies charging per-mile premiums is

$$p = \frac{A}{M} = c_1 + c_2M/l. \tag{5}$$

This equation can be viewed as the supply curve for insurance as a function of the number of vehicle miles travelled requiring insurance. In a more sophisticated model, and in practice, rates would vary by risk class i, and break-even competitive prices would be $p_i = A_i/M_i = c_{1i} + c_{2i}M/l$.

Let the utility of each of the n drivers be quasi-linear in the consumption of nondriving goods y and quadratic in miles m:

$$V(y,m) = y + am - \frac{n}{b}m^2. \tag{6}$$

Then, the aggregate demand for vehicle miles traveled will be linear:

$$M = M_0 - bp\frac{n}{2}. \tag{7}$$

The equilibrium miles, M^*, and per-mile price, p^*, are found by solving (5) and (7). If drivers continued to drive as much under per-mile premiums as they do under per-year, that is, if $b = 0$ so that demand were completely inelastic, then competitive insurance companies would break-even by charging

$$p = c_1 + c_2 M_0/l.$$

For $b > 0$, however, as driving falls in reaction to this charge, the accident rate per-mile will also fall (because there will be fewer cars on the road with whom to collide). As the per-mile accident rate falls, premiums will fall in a competitive insurance industry, as we move down the average cost curve given by (5).

Figure 5.1 depicts the situation. Let c_0 be the nonaccident costs of driving (gas, maintenance, etc.) and assume that drivers pay these costs in addition to per-mile insurance premiums p. If drivers pay per-year premiums so that $p = 0$, then they demand M_0 miles of driving. The social gain from charging per-mile accident premiums p^* in this model equals the reduction in accident costs less the lost benefits from foregone driving, the shaded region in figure 5.1. This surplus S is given by

$$S = \frac{1}{2}\left(\frac{dA}{dM}\bigg|_{M_0} + \frac{dA}{dM}\bigg|_{M^*}\right)(M_0 - M^*) - \frac{1}{2}p^*(M_0 - M^*). \tag{8}$$

The first term is the reduction in accident costs that results from a fall in driving from M_0 to M^*. The second is the driving benefits lost from this reduction net of the nonaccident cost savings $c_0(M_0 - M^*)$.

The marginal accident cost dA/dM is given by (2). Note that because the marginal accident cost dA/dM lies above the average cost A/M, the competitive per-mile premium $p^* = A/M$ is less than the socially optimal accident charge p^{**} which would lead to M^{**} miles being driven, as depicted in figure 5.1. Competition does not yield socially optimal accident charges because of the accident externality.

For optimal charges, the government would need to impose a Pigouvian tax of $[(dA/dM|_{M^{**}})/(A/M^{**}) - 1] \times 100$ percent on insurance premiums A/M^{**} to yield Pigouvian per-mile premiums. Pigouvian per-mile premiums could be implemented with a uniform

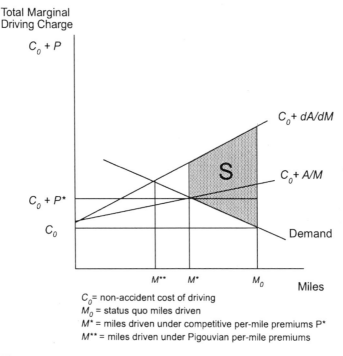

Figure 5.1
The social gains from per-mile premiums

percentage tax on competitive per-mile premiums in either a fault-based tort system or a no-fault tort system, as long as every driver stands an equal chance of being at fault. If drivers differ in fault propensity, then it will be easier to impose Pigouvian taxes in a no-fault system: In a fault-based system, by contrast, the percentage tax rate would need to vary among people, and curiously it would need to be higher for faultless drivers because they will frequently be nonnegligent despite being as much a "but for" cause of accidents as faulty drivers.

The benefit calculation assumes that the number of drivers would remain unchanged in a switch to per-mile premiums. In fact, the number of drivers would probably increase under a per-mile system because the total price of a small amount of driving (say 2,000 miles per year) would fall. Although the extra drivers, who drive relatively little, will limit driving reductions and hence accident reductions somewhat, they would probably increase the accident savings net of lost driving benefits. The reason is that these extra drivers gain substantial driving benefits, as evidenced by their willingness to pay insurance premiums. In the case of Pigouvian per-mile premiums, the entry of these extra drivers necessarily increases the benefits from accident cost reductions net of lost driving benefits.

2 Data

As a proxy for auto accident costs, A in the model above, state-level data are used on total private passenger auto insurance premiums from the National Association of Auto Insurance Commissioners (1998, table 7). Premiums paid for comprehensive coverage are subtracted, so that we are left only with accident coverage. If the insurance industry is competitive, these figures represent the true economic measure of insured accident costs, which includes the administrative cost of the insurance industry and an ordinary return on the capital of that industry. These premium data are for private passenger vehicles, so we adjust these figures to account for commercial premiums by multiplying by 1.14, the national ratio of total premiums to noncommercial premiums.[18]

Insured accident costs do not come close to comprising all accident costs. The pain and suffering of at fault drivers is not insured, for example, and auto insurance frequently does not cover their lost wages. (In no-fault states, pain and suffering is also not compensated below certain thresholds). These omitted damages are substantial and their inclusion would raise our estimates of the cost of driving and the benefit of driving reduction significantly. Pain and suffering is often taken to be three times the economic losses from bodily injury. In addition, out of pocket costs are also not fully compensated according to Dewees, Duff, and Trebilcock (1996).

Other data come from a variety of sources. Data on the miles of lanes by state come from table HM-60, 1996 Highway Statistics, FHWA. Annual vehicle miles by state come from table VM-2, 1996 Highway Statistics, FHWA. Data on the distribution of fuel efficiency among vehicles in the current U.S. fleet, and the distribution of miles by fuel efficiency of car come from the 1994 Residential Transportation Energy Consumption Survey. Gasoline prices by state come from the Petroleum Marketing Monthly, EIA, table 31 ("all grades, sales to end users through retail outlets excluding taxes") and table EN-1 (federal and state motor gasoline taxes).

3 Policy Simulations

3.1 Methodology

This section estimates and compares the potential benefits of charging per-mile premiums with and without a Pigouvian tax. Competitive per-mile premiums are determined for each of the fifty states s by calibrating equations (7) and (5) with state data and gas elasticity studies and then solving them for M_s^* and p_s^*; equilibrium per-mile premiums are just sufficient to allow insurance companies to break even, exactly covering accident costs. The Pigouvian per-mile premiums simulations assume a tax on premiums to account for the externalities of accidents. Both sets of simulations assume that an individual pays premiums in proportion to the miles she drives.

The consequences of each policy option are estimated under two models of accident determination—linear and quadratic. The linear model assumes that accident costs in state s are proportional to miles driven, namely, that $A_s = c_{1s}M_s$. The coefficient c_{1s} is estimated by dividing total accident insurance premiums A_s by total miles driven M_s. The linear model takes no account of the externalities from driving, nor the related fact that as people reduce their driving, accident rates per mile should fall because there are fewer drivers on the road with whom to have an accident.

The quadratic model includes a term that is quadratic in miles as in equation (1) to account for the externality effect. The one and two-car accident coefficients are determined for the quadratic model as described in the appendix.

A linear model is estimated for two reasons. First, the efficiency savings under a linear model are the straightforward gains from more efficient contracting that a single company (with a small market share) and its customers could together expect to receive if they alone switched to per-mile pricing. (Once other firms followed suit all these gains would go to customers.) Comparing the linear model with the quadratic model, therefore, allows us to see how much of the accident savings are external to a given driver and insurance company. The second reason to be interested in the linear model results is the possibility of substantial learning-by-doing in driving. If driving more lowers an individual's accident rate so that the typical individual has an accident elasticity with respect to miles of $1/2$,[19] then after accounting for the externality effect, the aggregate elasticity of accidents with respect to miles should be approximately 1 as assumed in the linear model.

Estimates of the results of these policies naturally depend upon the price responsiveness of driving. Estimates of the price responsiveness of driving are plentiful and generally come from observed changes in the price of gasoline. Edlin (2002) provides a methodology for converting gasoline demand elasticities into elasticities with respect to per-mile charges using the fuel efficiency composition of the existing U.S. vehicle fleet.

The benchmark case here assumes that the aggregate elasticity of gasoline demand with respect to the price of gasoline is 0.15. This figure is 25 percent lower than the short-run elasticity of 0.2 that the two comprehensive surveys by Dahl and Sterner (1991 a,b) conclude is the most plausible estimate, and also substantially lower than the miles elasticity estimated by Gallini (1983). From the perspective of social policy, we should be interested in long run elasticities, which appear to be considerably larger than short run. Edlin (2002) discusses short and long run elasticity estimates more extensively. Edlin (2002) also provides details on calibrating the model of . section 1 in each state, and on simulating the consequences of per-mile premiums.

3.2 Equilibrium Per-Mile Premiums and Driving Reductions

Table 5.1 presents estimates of equilibrium per-mile premiums and driving reductions, assuming a competitive insurance industry that sets per-mile premiums equal to the average insurance cost of accidents per mile driven in selected states. For all states, see Edlin (2002). Equilibrium per-mile premiums are quite high, exceeding the cost of gasoline in many states. Even with the modest gasoline price elasticity of 0.15 assumed here, the resulting driving reduction is substantial. The national reduction in vehicle miles traveled, $M_0 - M^*$, is approximately 10 percent in both models, and exceeds 15 percent in high-traffic states.

Reductions in driving would naturally be much larger in states that currently have high insurance costs and would thus face high per-mile premiums. Since New Jersey currently has much higher insurance costs per vehicle mile traveled (VMT) than Wyoming, for example, we estimate that equilibrium per-mile premiums would be 6.5 cents per-mile in New Jersey compared with 1.8 cents in Wyo-

Table 5.1
Per-mile premiums: Equilibrium charges and driving reductions

Selected states	$A = c_1M + c_2M^2/l$ Quadratic model		$A = c_1M$ Linear model	
	Marginal charge (cents/mile)	VMT reductions (percentage)	Marginal charge (cents/mile)	VMT reductions (percentage)
Delaware	4.4	10.9	4.9	12.1
Hawaii	6.8	15.4	7.9	18.0
Massachusetts	5.8	14.2	6.7	16.4
New Jersey	6.5	16.4	7.7	19.4
New York	5.6	13.7	6.4	15.6
Ohio	3.3	8.4	3.6	9.1
Oklahoma	2.5	6.5	2.6	6.8
Wyoming	1.8	4.4	1.8	4.6
All U.S.		9.2		10.0

Note: In 1995 dollars.

ming, and that these changes would reduce New Jersey's VMT by 16.4 percent and Wyoming's by 4.4 percent.

The driving reduction is somewhat less in the quadratic model than it is in the linear ones, because in the quadratic model, as driving is reduced, the risk of accidents also falls and with it per-mile premiums. In Massachusetts, the per-mile charge falls from 6.7 cents per mile to 5.8 cents per mile as driving is reduced. Since equilibrium per-mile premiums are lower in the quadratic model, the total driving reduction is lower than in the linear model.

Per-mile premiums estimates here have not been adjusted for uninsured drivers because data on the percentage of uninsured drivers is poor. Actual premiums would likely be higher as a result, but it wouldn't change estimates of aggregate driving reductions significantly because even though the per-mile premium would be higher for insured miles, it would be zero for uninsured miles.[20]

3.3   Accident Cost Reductions Net of Lost Driving Benefits

Estimates show that the driving reductions under per-mile premiums would in turn reduce insurance (and accident) costs by $17 billion in total across the United States according to the quadratic model. Even after subtracting lost driving benefits (the second term

Table 5.2
Yearly accident savings from per-mile premiums (net of lost driving benefits)

Selected states	$A = c_1M + c_2M^2/l$ Quadratic model		$A = c_1M$ Linear model	
	Total (millions of $)	Per insured vehicle ($)	Total (millions of $)	Per insured vehicle ($)
Delaware	54	106	22	43
Hawaii	132	188	57	81
Massachusetts	622	155	263	66
New Jersey	1040	198	453	86
New York	1339	139	574	60
Ohio	410	52	165	21
Oklahoma	80	34	35	15
Wyoming	6	16	3	8
All U.S.	12686	$75	5310	$31

Note: In 1995 dollars.

in equation (8)), the benefits remain substantial in both models. Nationally, these net accident savings range from $5.3 billion to $12.7 billion per year, as table 5.2 reports.

The difference between the $5.3 billion estimate under the linear model and the $12.7 billion under the quadratic model is dramatic: accounting for accident externalities raises the estimate of benefits by 150 percent. Such a large difference makes sense. If a price change for driver A causes her to drive less, much of her reduction in accident losses is offset by her lost driving benefits. In contrast, every driver with whom she might have had an accident, gains outright from the reduced probability of having an accident with A who is driving less. Taking this externality effect into account, nationally, the net gain is $75 per insured vehicle under the quadratic model, as reported in table 5.3. Since insurance companies and their customers don't take the externality benefits into account, however, their view of the gain from per-mile premiums is probably closer to the $31 of the linear model. In high traffic density states, the gain per insured vehicle is quite high—approximately $150 in Massachusetts and New York and nearly $200 in Hawaii and New Jersey in the quadratic model.

A Pigouvian accident tax has the potential to raise benefits still further. In the quadratic model, which takes account of the accident externalities, the marginal cost of accidents exceeds the average cost.

Table 5.3
U.S. benefits from other premium schedules

	Quadratic model	Linear model
Per-mile premiums		
Net accident savings		
U.S. total (billions of dollars)	12.7	5.3
Per insured vehicle (dollars)	75.0	31.4
Reduced delay costs (external)		
U.S. total (billions of dollars)	5.5	6.0
Per insured vehicle (dollars)	32.5	35.6
Total benefits		
U.S. total (billions of dollars)	18.2	11.3
Per insured vehicle (dollars)	107.5	67.0
Pigouvian tax and per-mile premiums		
Net accident savings		
U.S. total (billions of dollars)	15.3	5.3
Per insured vehicle (dollars)	90.6	31.4
Reduced delay costs (external)		
U.S. total (billions of dollars)	9.4	6.0
Per insured vehicle (dollars)	55.6	35.6
Total benefits		
U.S. total (billions of dollars)	24.7	11.3
Per insured vehicle (dollars)	146.2	67.0

Note: In 1995 dollars.

In consequence, the Pigouvian tax is substantial: an appropriate Pigouvian tax would be about 90 percent on insurance premiums in high traffic density states such as New Jersey and about 40 percent in low density states like North Dakota. On average across the United States, the Pigouvian tax would be 83 percent under the quadratic model. The Pigouvian tax makes national driving reductions 15.7 percent instead of 9.2 percent. National net accident savings grow to $15.3 billion from $12.7 billion per year as seen in table 5.3.

As the introduction points out, benefit estimates here are biased downward because we use aggregate data at the state level, thereby not taking into account the substantial heterogeneity by territory and by driver in accident costs. Per-mile premium policies would most likely be implemented so that per-mile rates varied among drivers or vehicles based upon the same territory, driving record, and other factors that are currently used to vary per-year rates. If high-risk drivers (whether because of age, territory, or other factors) pay the highest per-mile rates, then driving reductions will be concentrated among these drivers, where they are most effective at reducing accidents.

All of these benefit estimates depend critically on driving elasticities. Driving reductions and net accident savings are higher (respectively lower) if the aggregate gas demand elasticity is higher (respectively lower) than 0.15. Nationally, net accident benefits go from $9 billion for an elasticity of 0.1 to $16 billion for an elasticity of 0.2 in the quadratic model.

Our simulations ignore the fact that more drivers will choose to become insured once they have the option of economizing on insurance premiums by only driving a few miles. Today, some of these low-mileage drivers are driving uninsured while others are not driving at all. To the extent that per-mile premiums attract new drivers, the reduction in vehicle miles traveled will not be as large as our simulations predict. Surprisingly, though, this observation does not mean that the social benefits are lower than predicted. In fact, they are probably higher. The per-year insurance system is inefficient to the extent that low-mileage drivers who would be willing to pay the true accident cost of their driving choose not to drive, because they must currently pay the accident cost of those driving many more miles. Giving them an opportunity to drive and pay by the mile creates surplus if their driving benefits exceed the social cost. (Their benefits would always exceed the social cost under Pigouvian per-mile premiums since they are choosing to pay the social cost.)

3.4 Delay Costs from Congestion

Congestion will fall if driving is reduced, and this constitutes one ancillary benefit of per-mile premiums and of the Pigouvian accident tax. In a fundamental respect, congestion is the counterpart to accidents. In the simplest model of congestion, congestion occurs when driver i and j would be in the same location at the same time except that one or both brakes to avoid an accident. Such a formulation undoubtedly understates the marginal cost of congestion substantially, because as two vehicles slow down they generally force others to slow down as well. A cascade of such effects becomes a traffic jam. Indeed, measured traffic flow rates as a function of the number of cars traveling suggest that during periods of congestion the marginal congestion cost of driving is often many times, up to and exceeding ten times, the average congestion experienced—at least during highly congested periods.[21]

Congestion cost savings that are external to the driving decision should also be added to the benefits from per-mile premiums. Assuming that the mile foregone is a representative mile and not a mile drawn from a particularly congested or uncongested time, the person foregoing the mile will escape the average cost of delay. This savings should not be counted, though, among our benefits from driving reductions because it is internalized. Viewed differently, each person derives no net benefit from her marginal mile of driving, because she chooses to drive more miles until driving benefits net of congestion cost just equal operating costs. Yet, as there is less traffic on the road, other drivers will experience reduced delays and this external effect should be added to our calculations. The external effect, as with accidents, equals the difference between the marginal and average cost of delay. To be conservative in our simulations, we ignore the traffic jam cascade discussed above and assume that the marginal cost of congestion is twice the average cost, so that the portion of the marginal cost that is external to the driving decision equals the average cost.

A detailed study by Schrank, Turner, and Lomax (1995) estimates that the total cost of congestion in the form of delay and increased fuel consumption in the United States exceeded $49 billion in 1992 and $31 billion in 1987 in 1995 dollars.[22] This study valued time at $8.50/hr. in 1987 and $10.50/hr. in 1992, which would appear a considerable undercounting to those who would far prefer to be at work than stuck in a traffic jam. If we project this figure to $60 billion in 1995, this amounts to an average delay cost of 2.5 cents for every mile driven. Under the assumption above the average delay cost equals the external marginal cost from congestion.

Table 5.3 gives estimates of the national portion of congestion reduction that is external and should be added to net accident benefits. In all models, estimated externalized gains from congestion reductions are large, ranging from $5.5 billion to $9.4 billion per year as seen in table 5.3.

These calculations are based upon the average cost of delay. Congestion delays are concentrated during certain peak time periods and at certain locations. It turns out that this fact simply means that the congestion reductions from per-mile pricing are concentrated during these time periods and these locations. Our calculations are robust provided that the elasticities of demand for congested miles and noncongested miles are comparable, and that the externalized marginal cost is a constant multiple of average cost.[23] The concentration of congestion costs simply suggests that we would be even better off if driving were priced particularly high during congested periods and somewhat lower otherwise.

3.5 Total Benefits

Table 5.3 gives total estimated annual national benefits from competitive per-mile premiums and Pigouvian per-mile premiums. The total benefits are expressed both in aggregate and per insured vehicle. These annual benefits are quite high and suggest that charging by the mile on a national basis would be socially beneficial if verifying miles could be achieved for less than $107.50 per car each year. In some high traffic density states, per-mile premiums could be socially beneficial even if the cost of verifying miles approached $200 per vehicle. External benefits made up $13 billion of estimated benefits from per-mile premiums since net accident savings were only $5 billion under the linear model, as reported in table 5.3. The gains with a Pigouvian tax were $146 per insured vehicle nationally.

The total benefits are quite large even for the linear model where accidents are proportional to mileage. Under the linear model, the total benefits of per-mile premiums are $67 per insured vehicle. As mentioned early, this model would be roughly accurate if individual elasticities of accidents with respect to miles were 0.5, because then the externality effect would make the social elasticity roughly one, as in a linear model.

The methodology used here might overstate accident externalities because the theoretical model does not account for accident substitution (the possibility that an accident would have occurred even if one involved vehicle were not there), or understate externalities because many accidents require the coincidence of more than two cars at the same place at the same time. A potential upward bias results because c_1 and c_2 are held constant, which does does not account for the fact that as driving becomes more dangerous, drivers and states take precautionary measures. States react to higher accident rates with higher expenditures on safety by widening roads and lengthening freeway on-ramps. Drivers also make financial expenditures, buying air bags or anti-lock brakes, and nonfinancial expenditures, by paying more attention and slowing down to avoid accidents when driving in heavy traffic. All these precautionary measures mitigate the impact of extra traffic density on accidents. At the margin, if precautions are chosen optimally so that the marginal cost of precautions equals their marginal benefit, then the envelope theorem guarantees that we would still be properly capturing the sum of accident and prevention costs (i.e., we can treat prevention as being fixed). On balance, the estimation methodology appears reasonable even if rough. The regression results of Edlin and Karaca (2002) suggest that the calibration methodology in this chapter understates externalities.

A final caution is that these estimates neglect environmental gains that would result if the current price of gasoline does not adequately account for emissions, noise pollution, and road maintenance. Likewise, they would overstate gains if current gasoline taxes exceed those nonaccident noncongestion costs. Our estimates also did not account for underinsured and uninsured accident costs. Including these latter figures into estimates of eliminated accident externalities would raise the estimated benefits by several billion dollars more.

4 Conclusions and Policy Implications

In both models, the aggregate benefits of per-mile premiums are quite large. They are concentrated in states with high traffic density where accident costs and the externality effect appear particularly large. Aggregate benefits reach $11 billion nationally, or over $67 per insured vehicle even under the linear model, and are substantially larger ($18 billion) under the quadratic model. In high traffic density states like New Jersey, the benefits from reduced accident costs, net of lost driving benefits could be as high as $198 per insured vehicle, as indicated in table 5.2.

Why then are most premiums so weakly linked to actual mileage and closer to per-year than per-mile premiums? Standard contracting analysis predicts that an insurance company and its customers would not strike a deal with a lump-sum premium if an individual's accidents increase with his driving, and if vehicle miles are freely observable. By reducing or eliminating the lump-sum portion and charging the marginal claim cost for each mile of driving, the contract can be made more profitable for the insurance company and also more attractive to its customers: as individuals reduce their driving, the insurance carrier saves more in claims than customers lose driving benefits. Hence the "mystery."

The primary reason we don't see per-mile premiums is probably monitoring costs, the reason suggested by Rea (1992) and by some insurance executives. Traditionally the only reliable means of verifying mileage was thought to be bringing a vehicle to an odometer-checking station. In addition to the monitoring costs involved, a firm charging per-mile premiums would also suffer abnormally high claims from those who committed odometer fraud. The significance of monitoring costs/fraud costs as an explanation is supported by the fact that commercial policies (where the stakes are larger) are sometimes per-mile, and now that cheap technologies exist that allow mileage verification at a distance, at least two firms are now experimenting with per-mile premiums (see the introduction). Adverse selection provides another explanation that tends to close the per-mile premiums market.[24]

If monitoring costs are what limit the use of per-mile premiums policies, then to encourage their use would appear unwise because lack of use may be a good signal that the policies' benefits do not justify their costs. This chapter highlights another reason, though, why such policies are not common, a reason that suggests policy intervention could be valuable. In particular, the social gains from accident reduction as drivers reduce driving could substantially exceed the private gains (realized by drivers and insurance carriers), at least in high-traffic density states. In New Jersey, for example, estimates show that the private gains as captured by the linear model are $86 per insured vehicle as compared with social gains of $198 once external gains are included (see table 5.2). Hence, most of the benefits from switching to per-mile premiums or some other premiums schedule that reduces driving are *external*. The accident externality is surely one big reason that insurance companies have not made such a switch. If monitoring costs and other transaction costs lie in the gap between $86 and $198, then per-mile premiums would be efficient in New Jersey, but they might not materialize in a free market. Congestion reductions make the external benefits from per-mile premiums even larger, increasing the chance of market failure.

Mandating per-mile premiums as the Texas legislature recently considered and rejected might be unwise, though, even if per-mile premiums are efficient on average, because monitoring costs remain substantial and could vary across individuals. (Heterogeneity across individuals favors policy options that would allow more individual flexibility.) Even if mandates are not justified, if driving does cause substantial external accident costs as the theory and the empirical work here suggest, then some policy action could be justified.

The simplest policy option in states such as Massachusetts, which already have regular checks of automobiles for safety or emissions, would be to record odometer readings at these checks and transfer this information together with vehicle identification numbers to insurance companies. This would remove the need for special stations for odometer checking, or for installing special monitoring devices in vehicles. Private monitoring costs would also be reduced if the government increased sanctions for odometer fraud. Legislation such as the new Texas law that legalizes or otherwise facilitates switching the insurance risk exposure unit from the vehicle-year to the vehicle-mile can only help.

A second policy option would be to impose a tax on premiums sufficient to account for the accident externality of an additional driver. If insurance companies continued to have a weak mileage-premiums link, then people would at least still face efficient incentives at the margin of whether to become drivers. Moreover, insurance companies then would have increased incentives to create a strong mileage-premiums link, and drivers would face second-best incentives at the margin of deciding how many miles to drive. By making insurers pay the total social accident costs imposed by each of their drivers, a tax would give insurers the incentive to take all cost-effective measures to reduce this total cost. An externality tax would align the private incentives to incur monitoring costs and to charge per-mile premiums with the social incentives, so that insurance companies would switch premium structures to per-mile or to a schedule that better reflects accident cost whenever monitoring costs and transition costs become low enough to justify the switch. Such a tax would also make per-mile premiums higher to reflect both per-mile claim costs and the tax. The consequent driving, accident, and delay reductions would likewise be larger. An alternative to a tax that would be more difficult to administer, but perhaps easier to legislate, would be a subsidy to insurance companies that reduce their customers' driving equal to the resulting external accident cost reductions.

Another possible policy option would be to require insurance companies to offer a choice of per-mile or per-year premiums (at reasonable rates) as proposed by the National Organization for Women. A fourth option would be to facilitate the formation of an insurance clearinghouse that allowed individual per-mile premiums to be paid or billed at the pump when gasoline is purchased—again, an attempt to lower monitoring costs.

Wisdom demands, however, that enthusiasm for costly policy changes be tempered until more research is done in this area. Estimates used here are only a first cut and suffer from all the potential biases suggested and no doubt some we neglected to mention. Future research should include covariates and panel data. Simulation estimates here of the benefits from per-mile premiums and of the Pigouvian tax depend upon the size of the externality effect, the assumed linear accident/mileage profile for individuals,[25] the responsiveness of driving to price, and use of insured accident costs. Each of these areas warrants considerably more examination. For example, if the estimates of the Urban Institute (1991) are correct, and total accident costs are 4.2 times higher than the insured costs considered here, then the true benefits of premium restructuring could be much larger than estimated. Finally, we note that it would also be quite informative to break down externalities by vehicle type.

Appendix
Estimation of the Quadratic Model for Each State

To estimate a quadratic accident model for each state, we modify the model of section 1, assuming that each state's idiosyncratic errors ε_s enter multiplicatively as follows:

$$\frac{A_s}{M_s} = (c_1 + c_2 D_s)(1 + \varepsilon_s). \tag{9}$$

$$= c_{1s} + c_{2s} D_s, \tag{10}$$

where, $c_{1s} = c_1(1 + \varepsilon_s), c_{2s} = c_2(1 + \varepsilon_s)$ and where s indexes states.

We utilize national data on the percentage of accidents involving multiple cars. Assume that national accident costs are given by

$$A = c_1 M + c_2 MD,$$

where the costs of one- and two-car accidents are, respectively,

$$A_1 = c_1 M$$

and

$$A_2 = c_2 M D.$$

Let $\bar{a}$ be the average damage per insured vehicle from an accident, so that two-vehicle accidents have total damages of $2\bar{a}$ and one-vehicle accidents have damages $\bar{a}$. Let r denote the proportion of accidents that involve two vehicles. (Nationally, 71 percent of crashes were multiple-vehicle crashes in 1996, and we assume that multicar accidents involve only two cars, since we don't have data on the number of cars in multicar accidents and since this assumption makes our benefit estimate conservative.)[26]

If N is the total number of accidents in a state we have

$$A = N(1 - r)\bar{a} + 2Nr\bar{a},$$

so that

$$N\bar{a} = \frac{A}{1 + r}.$$

This implies that the total cost of one-car accidents is

$$A_1 = \frac{(1 - r)}{1 + r} A,$$

and similarly for two-car accidents

$$A_2 = \frac{2r}{1 + r} A.$$

The one and two-car accident coefficients can then be determined from the formulas:

$$\hat{c}_1 = \frac{A_1}{M} = \frac{(1 - r)A}{1 + r} \frac{1}{M}$$

and

$$\hat{c}_2 = \frac{A_2}{M^2} l = \frac{2r}{1 + r} A \frac{l}{M^2}.$$

Using the observed national data on accident costs (A), miles traveled (M), and lane miles (l), we estimate that the one-vehicle coefficient $\hat{c}_1$ is roughly .007 dollars per-mile, while $\hat{c}_2$ is 1.1×10^{-7} dollars per-mile squared per lane mile. This means that roughly 18 percent of costs are attributed to one-car accidents.

We find the state-specific coefficients for one and two vehicle accidents as follows:

$$\hat{c}_{1s} = \hat{c}_1(1 + \hat{\varepsilon}_s)$$

$$\hat{c}_{2s} = \hat{c}_2(1 + \hat{\varepsilon}_s)$$

$$\hat{\varepsilon}_s = \frac{A_s}{\hat{c}_1 M_s + \hat{c}_2 M_s D_s} - 1.$$

Acknowledgments

I am grateful for a faculty fellowship from the Alfred P. Sloan Foundation, support from the World Bank, a grant from the UC Berkeley Committee on Research, Visiting Olin Fellowships at Columbia Law School and Georgetown University Law Center, and for the comments and assistance of George Akerlof, Richard Arnott, Severin Borenstein, Patrick Butler, Amy Finkelstein, Steve Goldman, Louis Kaplow, Todd Litman, Eric Nordman, Mark Rainey, Zmarik Shalizi, Joseph Stiglitz, Steve Sugarman, Jeroen Swinkels, Michael Whinston, Janet Yellen, Lan Zhao, several helpful people in the insurance industry, and seminar participants at Cornell, Georgetown, New York University, the University of Toronto, the University of Pennsylvania, the University of Maryland, The National Bureau of Economic Research, and The American Law and Economics Association Annual Meetings. The opinions in this chapter are not necessarily those of any organization with whom I have been affiliated.

Notes

1. U.S. Department of Commerce (1997, table 1030). Figure for 1994.

2. After subtracting comprehensive insurance coverage, which covers fire, theft, vandalism and other incidents unrelated to the amount of driving, the remaining premiums for private passenger vehicles totaled $84 billion in 1995 in 1995 dollars. See National Association of Insurance Commissioners (1997). In additon, commercial premiums are approximately 15 percent of premiums for private passenger vehicles. Insurance Information Institute (1998, 22).

3. For example, State Farm distinguishes drivers based upon whether they report an estimated annual mileage of under or over 7,500 miles. Drivers who estimate annual

mileages of under 7,500 miles receive 15 percent discounts (5 percent in Massachusetts). The 15 percent discount is modest given that those who drive less than 7,500 miles per year drive an average of 3,600 miles compared to 13,000 miles for those who drive over 7,500 per year, according to author's calculations from the 1994 Residential Transportation Energy Consumption Survey of the Department of Energy, Energy Information Administration. The implied elasticity of accident costs with respect to miles is 0.05, an order of magnitude below what the evidence suggests is the private or social elasticity of accident costs. The link between driving and premiums may be attenuated in part because there is significant noise in self-reported estimates of future mileage, estimates whose accuracy does not affect insurance pay-outs.

Insurance companies also classify based upon the distance of a commute to work. These categories, however, are also coarse. State Farm, for example, classifies cars based upon whether they are used for commuting less than 20 miles per week, in between 20 and 100 miles per week, or over 100 miles per week.

Finally, miles driven are indirectly factored into premiums through experience rating, so that premiums rise with accidents. To the extent that insurance companies offer customers banking services (a loan upon accident), miles are priced in the form of higher future premiums. People certainly take experience rating into account when deciding whether to report an accident, but it seems doubtful that they do so when deciding how much to drive. Our estimates assume that they do not.

4. For private and public livery, taxicabs, and buses, because "rates are high and because there is no risk when the car is not in operation, a system of rating has been devised on an earnings basis per $100 of gross receipts or on a mileage basis" (Bickelhaupt 1983, 613). For details on per-mile commercial insurance, see "Commercial Automobile Supplementary Rating Procedures," Insurance Services Office.

5. One experiment is in Texas and another in the U.K. See *Wall Street Journal* (1999), or Carnahan (2000) for information on the Texas pilot program run by Progressive Corporation and ⟨*http://news.bbc.co.uk/hi/englishbusiness/newsid-1831000/1831181.stm*⟩, ⟨*http://www.norwich-union.co.uk*⟩ for information on Norwich-Union's program in the U.K.

6. Likely exceptions include accidents where a driver plows into a long line of cars.

7. See *Wall Street Journal* (1999).

8. Vickrey's first suggestion was that auto insurance be bundled with tires hoping that the wear on a tire would be roughly proportional to the amount it is driven. He worried about moral hazard (using a tire until it was threadbare), but concluded that this problem would be limited if refunds were issued in proportion to the amount of tread remaining.

9. Externalities turn out to increase the benefit estimates by 140 percent, over what one would calculate in a linear model of accidents (i.e., a model without externalities) as studied by Litman (1987) and Rea (1992).

10. Monitoring costs are cited as the principal reason by actuaries I have interviewed (see also Nelson 1990).

11. In a competitive industry, insurance companies cannot profit from a coordinated change because the efficiency gains would be competed away in lower prices.

12. See, for example, Dewees, Duff, and Trebilcock (1996) for evidence of substantial undercompensation. See also the estimates of the Urban Institute (1991).

13. We assume in this article that existing gasoline taxes of 20–40 cents per gallon account for these costs. Many estimates, however, suggest that these costs may be much higher. Delucchi (1997) estimates that the pollution costs of motor vehicles in terms of extra mortality and morbidity are $26.5 to 461.9 billion per year in the United States.

14. For example, one car may stop suddenly causing the car behind to switch lanes to avoid a collision—the accident occurs only if another car is unluckily in the adjacent lane.

15. For an example of such a downward bias, consider Hu et al. (1998) who study an elderly population. Omitted bad health variables seem likely to be positively correlated with worse driving and probably with less driving as well. Mileage data in that study also come from surveys and seem highly susceptible to measurement error.

16. Another way to derive our formula for accidents, in which two-vehicle accidents are proportional to the square of miles driven, is to begin with the premise that the marginal cost of a mile of driving equals the expected cost of accidents to both parties that will occur during that mile: $dA_{2-car}/dM = 2(A_{2-car}/M)$. The unique solution to this differential equation, in which the elasticity of accidents with respect to miles is 2, is $A_{2-car} = c_2 M^2$.

17. This vigilance no doubt works to offset the dangers we perceive but seems unlikely to completely counter balance them. Note also that the cost of stress and tension that we experience in traffic are partly accident avoidance costs and should properly be included in a full measure of accident externality costs.

18. See p. 22 in the Insurance Information Institute 1998 Fact Book.

19. See, for example, the estimates in Hu et al. (1998) that were discussed in Edlin (1999).

20. Let u be the fraction of uninsured drivers and $\hat{p}$ be our estimate of true per-mile premiums. If premium $\hat{p}/(1-u)$ is charged on $(1-u)$ percent of miles, then the aggregate mile reduction is identical to our estimate given linear demand. Some revenue shortfall could be expected because priced miles fall by a larger percentage than in our estimate. This is approximately offset, however, by the fact that insured accident losses could be expected to fall by more than we estimate, because driving reductions would be concentrated in the insured population.

21. Author's calculation based upon traffic flow tables. GAO, "Traffic Congestion: Trends, Measures, and Effects," GAO/PEMD-90-1, November 1989, p. 39.

22. My summation for the fifty urban areas they studied. See table A-9, p. 13, and table A-15, p. 19, in Shrank, Turner and Lomax (1995). See also Delucchi (1997), who estimates congestion costs at $22.5 to 99.3 billion.

23. To understand why, consider a model with two types of miles: A, B. Let the initial quantities of driving these miles be a, b, and let C_a, C_b be the total cost of delay during driving of types A, B, respectively. Then, the average cost of delay is $c = (C_a + C_b)/(a+b)$, and the average cost of delay during driving of the two types is $c_a = C_a/a, c_b = C_b/b$. The externalized marginal congestion costs are likewise c_a, c_b. Observe that if a uniform per mile price p is charged for both types of miles, the congestion savings will be $p\varepsilon/g[ac_a + bc_b] = p\varepsilon/g(C_a + C_b)$, where g is the initial gas cost per

mile of driving, and ε is the elasticity of miles with respect to the price of gasoline. This is equivalent to what we would calculate if we treated the two types of miles equivalently, with c as the externalized marginal cost of miles. Then we would estimate the congestion reduction as: $p\varepsilon/g[a + b]c = p\varepsilon/g(C_a + C_b)$.

24. Adverse selection is another reason that a given insurance company may not want to switch to per-mile premiums on its own. Even if the insurance company knows the average miles driven per year by drivers in a given risk pool, it does not (currently) know the miles that given individuals drive. If it charges a per-mile premium equal to the current yearly premium for the pool divided by the average number of miles driven by drivers in the pool, it will lose money. Those who drive more miles than the average will leave the pool for a firm charging per-year rates and those who drive less miles will stay with this insurance company. The remaining drivers are adversely selected, because low mileage drivers in any given per-year risk class with a given accident experience level will tend to be worse drivers than high mileage drivers in the same risk class. (Long-run historical accident costs divided by miles driven would be a sensible measure of per-mile risk.) This adverse selection means that the insurance company will have to charge a relatively high per-mile price to break even, given the selection problem and the possibility that high-mileage drivers can choose to pay fixed annual premiums with other insurance companies. In principle, the insurance company could probably find a sufficiently high per-mile price that would increase profits. One could understand, however, the hesitancy of a marketing director to propose to his CEO that the insurance company change its pricing structure in a way that would make its prices less attractive than other insurance companies' to a large percentage (probably more than half) of its current customers.

25. Note that our estimates of the size of the accident externality effect are largely independent of the shape of the typical individual's accident profile, because these estimates are based upon cross-state comparisons of the effects of different traffic density levels on insurance premiums normalized by the amount of driving done. If an individual's elasticity of accident costs with respect to miles is closer to $1/2$ instead of 1, as assumed here, then the elasticity of total (social) accident costs with respect to that individual's driving should be roughly 1, because of the externality effect. This observation suggests that if an individual's accidents are that unresponsive to driving, then the linear model should roughly predict the social gains from switching to per-mile premiums.

26. The statistic 71 percent is found by taking the ratio of the number of multiple vehicle crashes to total crashes in table 27, U.S. Department of Transportation (1997). This figure understates the number of accidents that involve multiple vehicles because if a single vehicle crashes into a fixed object, for example, that is a single vehicle crash even if the vehicle swerved to avoid another car.

References

Bickelhaupt, David Lynn. 1983. *General Insurance.* 11th ed. Homewood, Ill.: Irwin.

Butler, Patrick. 1990. "Measure Exposure for Premium Credibility." *National Underwriter*, April 23, 418–419.

Carnahan, Ira. 2000. "Insurance by the Minute." *Forbes*, 86–88.

Cooter, Robert, and Thomas Ulen. 1988. *Law and Economics.* New York: HarperCollins.

Dahl, C., and Sterner. 1991a. "A Survey of Econometric Gasoline Elasticities." *Energy Economics* 13, no. 3, 203–210.

Dahl, C., and Sterner. 1991b. "Analyzing Gasoline Demand Elasticities: A Survey." *Energy Economics* 13, no 3, 203–210.

Delucchi, Mark A. 1997. "The Annualized Social Cost of Motor-Vehicle Use in the United States, Based on 1990–1991." Institute of Transportation Studies, UC Davis.

Dewees, Don, David Duff, and Michael Trebilcock. 1996. *Exploring the Domain of Accident Law: Taking the Facts Seriously.* New York: Oxford University Press.

Edlin, Aaron S. 1999. "Per-Mile Premiums for Auto Insurance." National Bureau of Economic Research working paper.

Edlin, Aaron S. 2002. "Per-Mile Premiums for Auto Insurance." Economics Department, University of California, Berkeley, working paper E02-318. Available online at ⟨http://repositories.cdlib.org/iber/econ/E02-318⟩.

Edlin, Aaron S., and Pinar Karaca. 2002. "The Accident Externality from Driving." Available online at ⟨http://www.bepress/aaronedlin⟩.

Gallini, Nancy T. 1983. "Demand for Gasoline in Canada." *Canadian Journal of Economics* 16, 299–324.

Hu, Patricia S., David A. Trumble, Daniel J. Foley, John W. Eberhard, and Robert B. Wallace. 1998. "Crash Risks of Older Drivers: a Panel Data Analysis." *Journal of Accident Analysis and Prevention*, vol. 30, no. 5, 569–581.

Insurance Information Institute. 1998. "The Fact Book." New York: Insurance Information Institute.

Litman, Todd. 1997. "Distance Based Vehicle Insurance as a TDM Strategy." *Transportation Quarterly*, vol. 51, no. 3, Summer 119–138.

Lundy, R. 1964. "The Effect of Traffic Volumes and Number of Lanes on Freeway Accident Rates." Cal. Div. of Highways, Traffic Bull. no. II, July.

Nelson, Dale. 1990. "Response." *Contingencies*, May/June.

National Association of Insurance Commissioners. 1998. "State Average Expenditures & Premiums for Personal Automobile Insurance."

Rea, Samuel, A. 1992. "Insurance Classifications and Social Welfare," in *Contributions to Insurance Economics*, ed. George Dionne. Boston: Kluwer.

Schrank, David, Shawn Turner, and Timothy Lomax. 1995. "Urban Roadway Congestion—1982 to 1992. vol. 2: Methodology and Urbanized Area Data." Texas Transportation Institute.

Shavell, Steven. 1987. "Economic Analysis of Accident Law." Cambridge, Mass.: Harvard University Press.

Sugarman, Stephen. 1993. "Pay at the Pump Auto Insurance: The California Vehicle Injury Plan (VIP) For Better Compensation, Fair Funding, and Greater Safety." Institute of Governmental Studies, UC Berkeley 1993.

Tobias, Andrew. 1993. *Auto Insurance Alert: Why the System Stinks, How to Fix It, and What to Do in the Meantime.* New York: Simon and Schuster.

Urban Institute. 1991. "The Costs of Highway Crashes: Final Report." June.

U.S. Department of Commerce. 1997. "Statistical Abstract of the United States."

U.S. Department of Transportation. 1997. "Traffic Safety Facts 1996," December.

Vickrey, William. 1968. "Automobile Accidents, Tort Law, Externalities, and Insurance: An Economist's Critique," *Law and Contemporary Problems* 464, 33.

Wall Street Journal. 1999. "Insurance by the Mile." December 9, A1.

Williamson, Oliver, Douglas G. Olson, and August Ralston. 1967. "Externalities, Insurance, and Disability Analysis." *Economica*, August, 235–253.

6

Capital Adequacy Regulation: In Search of a Rationale

Franklin Allen and Douglas Gale

1 The Flight from Theory

Financial crises have become a popular academic subject since the recent events in Asia, Russia, and elsewhere. Of course, financial crises are nothing new; they are part of the long and colorful history of the development of the financial system. They are also an important part of the history of central banking. Central banks were originally established for a wide variety of reasons, such as enhancing the payments system and raising money to help governments finance wars. They later took on the prevention and control of financial crises as one of their central functions. The Bank of England perfected the technique in the nineteenth century. The U.S. Federal Reserve System, founded in the early twentieth century, was a slow learner and only mastered the technique in the 1930s. (A more detailed discussion of the history of central banking is contained in chapter 2 of Allen and Gale 2000a).

For the most part, the development of central banking and financial regulation has been an essentially empirical process, a matter of trial and error driven by the exigencies of history rather than formal theory. An episode that illustrates the character of this process is the Great Depression in the United States. The financial collapse in the United States was widespread and deeply disruptive. It led to substantial changes, many of which shape our current regulatory framework. The SEC was established to regulate financial markets. Investment and commercial banking were segregated by the Glass-Steagall Act (subsequently repealed and replaced by the Gramm-Leach-Bliley Act of 1999). The Federal Reserve Board revised its operating procedures in the light of its failure to prevent a financial collapse. The FDIC and FSLIC were set up to provide deposit insurance to banks and savings and loan institutions.

Looking back, there is no sign of formal theory guiding these changes. Everyone appears to have agreed the experience of the Great Depression was terrible; so terrible that it must never be allowed to happen again. But why was this set of institutions and rules adopted? And why are many of them still with us today? The mind set of the 1930s continues to influence thinking about policy. According to this mindset, the financial system is extremely fragile and the purpose of prudential regulation is to prevent financial crisis at all costs. In addition, policy making continues to be an empirical exercise, with little attention to theoretical reasoning.

The Basel Accords, which impose capital adequacy requirements on the banking systems of the signatory countries around the world, are a case in point. Practitioners have become experts at the details of a highly complex system for which there is no widely agreed rationale based in economic theory. What is the optimal capital structure? What market failure necessitates the imposition of capital adequacy requirements? Why can't the market be left to determine the appropriate level of capital? Good answers to these questions cannot be found in the theoretical literature.

It is not our intention to pass judgment on the practical value of any of the innovations mentioned above, but simply to point out that this empirical procedure is unusual. Indeed, the area of financial regulation is somewhat unique in the extent to which the empirical developments have so far outstripped theory. In most areas of economics, when regulation becomes an issue, economists have tried to identify some specific market failure that justifies intervention. Sometimes they have gone further to derive the optimal form of regulation. But there is no theory of optimal prudential regulation.

In the literature on capital adequacy, it is often argued that capital adequacy requirements are necessary to control the moral hazard problems generated by the existence of deposit insurance. Deposit insurance was introduced in the 1930s to prevent bank runs or, more generally, financial instability. Deposit insurance, however, encourages risk shifting behavior on the part of banks (see, e.g., Merton 1977), which can be controlled by requiring the shareholders to post a "bond" in the form of adequate levels of capital in the bank. Thus, capital adequacy requirements are indirectly justified by the desire to prevent financial crises. A large literature investigates the effect of capital adequacy requirements on risk taking. Although the effect of capital adequacy requirements is usually to decrease risk taking, the reverse is also possible (see, e.g., Kim and Santomero 1988; Furlong and Keeley 1989; Gennotte and Pyle 1991; Rochet 1992; Besanko and Kanatas 1996).

The incentive to take risks may also be offset by the loss of charter value when a firm goes bankrupt (see, e.g., Bhattacharya 1982). This effect will be smaller the more competitive the structure of the banking market. Keeley (1990) has provided evidence that the sharp increase in U.S. bank failures in the early 1980s was due to increased competition in the banking sector and the associated fall in charter values.

Hellman, Murdock, and Stiglitz (1998, 2000) develop a model that allows for the effect of both a higher charter value and capital adequacy requirements on risk-taking incentives. Controls on deposit interest rates are necessary, in addition to capital adequacy requirements, to achieve a Pareto-efficient allocation of resources. These interest-rate controls increase charter value and provide an extra instrument for controlling risk taking. A Pareto improvement is possible even without the use of deposit insurance.

A review of the literature shows that the justification for capital adequacy requirements is found in the existence of deposit insurance. It could be argued that an important question is being begged here: one bad policy (deposit insurance) does not justify another (capital adequacy requirements). Even if it is assumed that deposit insurance prevents financial crises, it is not clear why we should want to reduce the incidence of financial crises, still less eliminate them altogether. We have argued elsewhere that, under standard conditions, the incidence of financial crises may be socially optimal in a laisser faire system (Allen and Gale 1998, 2000b). And if not, for example, if financial crises involve deadweight losses, it should be recognized that regulation also involves administrative costs and distorts economic decisions. Any analysis of optimal policy must weigh the costs and benefits of regulation. This can only be done in a model that explicitly models the possibility of crises.

Hellman, Murdoch, and Stiglitz (1998) is an exception in the literature on capital adequacy requirements. Rather than simply taking the existence of deposit insurance as given, the authors also examine what happens in the absence of deposit insurance. In the rest of the literature, the rationale for deposit insurance and in particular its role in preventing financial crises is discussed but not explicitly modeled. In the absence of explicit modeling of the costs of financial crises, it is difficult to make a case for the optimality of intervention. As a corollary, it is difficult to make a case for capital adequacy requirements as a means of offsetting the risk taking generated by deposit insurance.

This chapter argues that, in the absence of a welfare-relevant pecuniary externality, banks will choose the socially optimal capital structure themselves, without government coercion. The model is simple and is intended to pose a challenge to advocates of capital adequacy requirements to do a better job of rationalizing the system that currently dominates the policy debates on prudential regulation.

In a series of related papers (Allen and Gale, 1998, 2000a–e, 2001), we have described a model that integrates intermediation and capital markets in a way that proves useful for the analysis of asset-price volatility, liquidity provision, financial crises, and related issues. The model can be briefly described as follows.

There are two types of assets in the economy, short-term assets that yield an immediate but low return and long-term assets that yield a higher but delayed return. Risk averse individuals want to invest to provide for future consumption. They are uncertain, however, about their preferences about the timing of consumption. If they invest in the long-term asset, they earn a high return, but it may not be available when they want to consume it. If they invest in the short-term asset, they have the certainty that it will be available when they want it, but they have to forego the higher return of the long-term asset. In short, there is a trade-off between liquidity and rate of return.

Banks are modeled as institutions that provide an optimal combination of liquidity and return. Here, we are simply following Diamond and Dybvig (1983) and a host of other writers, see for example, Chari and Jagannathan (1988), Jacklin and Bhattacharya (1988), Postlewaite and Vives (1987), and Wallace (1988, 1990). Banks take deposits from consumers and invest them in a portfolio of long- and short-term assets. In exchange, the bank gives the individual a deposit contract, that is, an option to withdraw from the bank. The amount withdrawn depends on the date at which the option is exercised, but for a given date, liquidity is guaranteed. By pooling independent risks, the bank is able to provide a better combination of liquidity and return than an individual could achieve alone. The aggregate demand for liquidity is less volatile than individual risks, so the bank can guarantee the same degree of liquidity while investing a smaller fraction of the portfolio in short-term assets, thus giving the depositor the benefit of the higher returns from the long-term assets.

Bank behavior can be represented as the solution of an optimal contracting problem. Banks compete for customers by offering combinations of a portfolio and a deposit contract. Free entry into the banking sector guarantees that banks will earn zero profit in equilibrium and will offer the combination of portfolio and contract that maximizes the depositor's expected utility. Otherwise another bank could enter, offer a more attractive contract, and take away the first bank's customers.

Risk can take the form of shocks to asset returns or the demand for liquidity. This chapter focuses on asset-return shocks. These shocks provide a role for financial markets. Specifically, we introduce markets for securities that allow banks to insure against aggregate shocks. We also introduce markets on which banks can buy and sell the long-term assets to obtain or provide liquidity.

The introduction of these two types of markets has important implications for the welfare properties of the model. First, the existence of markets on which assets can be liquidated ensures that bankruptcy involves no inefficiency ex post. Firesale prices transfer value to the buyer but do not constitute a deadweight loss. Secondly, ex ante risk sharing is optimal if there is a complete set of Arrow securities for insuring against aggregate shocks.

For a long time, policymakers have taken it as axiomatic that crises are best avoided. By contrast, in the present framework, with complete markets, a laisser-faire financial system achieves the constrained-efficient allocation of risk and resources. When banks are restricted to using noncontingent deposit contracts, default introduces a degree of contingency that may be desirable from the point of view of optimal risk sharing. Far from being best avoided, financial crises can actually be *necessary* to achieve constrained efficiency. By contrast, avoiding default is costly. It requires either holding a very safe and liquid portfolio and earning lower returns, or reducing the liquidity promised to the depositors. In any case, the bank optimally weighs the costs and benefits and chooses the efficient level of default in equilibrium.

The important point is that avoidance of crises should not be taken as axiomatic. If regulation is required to minimize or obviate the costs of financial crises, it needs to be justified by a microeconomic welfare analysis based on standard assumptions. Furthermore, the form of the intervention should be derived from microeconomic principles. After all, financial institutions and financial markets exist to facilitate the efficient allocation of risks and resources. A policy that aims to prevent financial crises has an impact on the normal functioning of the financial system. Any government intervention may impose deadweight costs by distorting the normal functioning of the financial system. One of the advantages of a microeconomic analysis of financial crises is that it clarifies the costs associated with these distortions.

The model described so far has no role for capital. Banks are like mutual companies, operated for the benefit of their depositors, with no investment provided and no return received by the entrepreneurs who set them up. Capital can be added to the model by assuming the existence of a class of risk neutral investors who are willing to invest in the bank in return for an equity share. These investors are assumed to have a fixed opportunity cost of capital, determined by the best investment returns available to them outside the banking sector. We assume this return is at least as great as the return on the long-term asset. These investors can also speculate on the short- and long-term assets, for example, holding the short-term asset to buy up the long-term asset at a firesale price in the event of a default. This kind of speculation provides liquidity. It is superfluous in the case of complete Arrow securities, but plays an essential role in equilibrium with incomplete markets.

The rest of the chapter is organized as follows. Section 2 describes the model in two settings. First, we consider the classical world of Modigliani-Miller in which markets are complete and capital structure is irrelevant. This sets a benchmark in which laisser faire is optimal and there is no justification for bank capital, let alone capital adequacy requirements. Second, we consider what happens when markets are incomplete and show that capital structure affects the risk sharing provided by the bank. The bank chooses the socially optimal capital structure in a laisser-faire equilibrium, however so once again there is no rationale for government imposition of capital adequacy requirements. The focus in section 2 is on risk sharing under symmetric information. Section 3 considers asymmetric information and makes a similar argument: unless there is a welfare-relevant pecuniary externality, the bank can internalize the agency problem and the private optimum is also the social optimum. There is no need for government intervention. Section 4 points out the value of continuous monitoring of capital structure as a means of avoiding risk-shifting behavior. Section 5 contains a brief conclusion.

2   A Simple Model of Risk Sharing

A variation of the model found in Allen and Gale (2000b) is used here. The main difference between the model presented there and the one here is that bank capital can be provided by risk-neutral investors.

Dates
There are three dates $t = 0, 1, 2$ and a single good at each date. The good is used for consumption or investment.

Assets
There are two assets, a short-term asset (the *short asset*) and a long-term asset (the *long asset*).

• The short asset is represented by a storage technology: one unit of the good invested at date t yields one unit at date $t + 1$, for $t = 0, 1$.

• The long asset takes two periods to mature and is more productive than the short asset: one unit invested at date 0 produces a random return $\tilde{R}$ at date 2. The long asset is more productive than the short asset: $E[\tilde{R}] > 1$.

Consumers
There is a continuum of ex ante identical consumers, whose measure is normalized to unity. Each consumer has an endowment consisting of one unit of the good at date 0 and nothing at subsequent dates. Ex post, there are two types of consumers, *early consumers*, who consume at date 1, and *late consumers*, who consume at date 2. The probability of being an early consumer is denoted by $0 < \lambda < 1$ and consumption at date $t = 1, 2$ is denoted by c_t. The consumer's ex ante utility is

$$\lambda U(c_1) + (1 - \lambda)U(c_2).$$

We adopt the usual "law of large numbers" convention and assume that the fraction of early consumers is identically equal to the probability λ. The period utility function $U : \mathbf{R}_+ \to \mathbf{R}$ is twice continuously differentiable and satisfies the usual neoclassical properties, $U'(c) > 0, U''(c) < 0$, and $\lim_{c \searrow 0} U'(c) = \infty$.

Investors

There is a continuum of risk neutral investors who have a large endowment at date 0 and maximize expected consumption at date 2. They can invest directly in the short and long asset and they can also hold equity in financial institutions. Investors have access to the short and long assets, as do banks, but in some cases we assume they also have access to investment opportunities that are not available to the banks. The maximum expected return available to investors (measured in terms of consumption at date 2) is denoted by $\rho \geq E[\tilde{R}]$.

Uncertainty

There are two aggregate states of nature H and L. The return to the long asset $\tilde{R}$ is a function of the state of nature:

$$\tilde{R} = \begin{cases} R_H & \text{w.pr. } 1 - \varepsilon \\ R_L & \text{w.pr. } \varepsilon \end{cases}$$

where $0 < R_L < R_H$.

Information

All uncertainty is resolved at date 1. The true state H or L is revealed and each consumer learns his ex post type, that is, whether he is an early consumer or a late consumer. Note that knowledge of the true return $\tilde{R}$ is available one period before the return itself is available.

Banking

A bank is a cooperative enterprise that provides insurance to consumers. At date 0, consumers deposit their initial endowments in a bank, which offers them a deposit contract promising d_t units of consumption if they withdraw at date $t = 1, 2$. The bank holds a portfolio (x, y) consisting of x units of the long asset and y units of the short asset. The bank can also obtain e units of capital from risk-neutral investors, in exchange for a claim on the bank's profits.

2.1   Equilibrium with Arrow Securities

Suppose that there are default-free Arrow securities for the two states H and L at date 0 and a capital market at date 1. One unit of an Arrow security corresponding to state $s = H, L$ pays one unit of the good at date 1 if state s occurs and nothing otherwise. The capital market at date 1 allows goods at date 2 to be exchanged for goods at date 1. Let q_s denote the price of one unit of the Arrow security for state s measured in terms of the good at date 0. Let p_s denote the price of one unit of the good at date 2, measured in terms of the good at date 1. Then $q_s p_s$ is the price, in terms of the good at date 0, of one unit of the good at date 2 in state s. Clearly, there are complete markets for hedging aggregate uncertainty.

In this version of the model, we assume that investors and banks have access to the same assets, that is, the short asset and the long asset. In fact, with complete markets, it does not make sense to distinguish the set of assets available to banks and markets. If investors had access to a third type of asset not available to banks, the returns to this asset would be reflected in the prices of Arrow securities. Trading Arrow securities would be equivalent to investing in the assets available to investors. In that sense, there is no loss of generality in assuming that $\rho = \bar{R}$.

Suppose that a risk-neutral investor had the opportunity to purchase a security that pays z_s units of the good at date 2 in state $s = H, L$. The investor would be indifferent between this security and one that paid the expected value $\bar{z} = (1 - \varepsilon)z_H + \varepsilon z_L$ in each state at date 2. In equilibrium, the price of these securities must be the same. Otherwise, there would be an opportunity for arbitrage. Thus,

$$q_H p_H z_H + q_L p_L z_L = (q_H p_H + q_L p_L)\bar{z}.$$

The no-arbitrage condition holds for any payoffs (z_H, z_L), which will only be true if

$$(q_H p_H, q_L p_L) = \alpha(1 - \varepsilon, \varepsilon)$$

for some constant $\alpha > 0$. Since one unit of the good at date 0 produces (R_H, R_L) at date 2, if anyone holds the long asset at date 0 it must be the case that

$$1 = q_H p_H R_H + q_L p_L R_L$$

$$= (q_H p_H + q_L p_L)\bar{R}$$

$$= \alpha\bar{R},$$

so $\alpha = \bar{R}^{-1}$. Thus, the prices of contingent commodities at date 2 are completely determined and, moreover, allow any agent with access to the market to convert an arbitrary security into one paying its expected value in each state.

A similar argument about securities paying off at date 1 proves that

$$(q_H, q_L) = \beta(1 - \varepsilon, \varepsilon),$$

and if anyone holds the short asset at date 0 it can be shown that $\beta = 1$.

We assume that banks and investors can participate directly in these markets, but that consumers cannot.

Suppose that a planner, with access to these markets, was given the task of allocating investments and consumption to maximize the expected utility of the depositors. It does not matter what assets the planner invests in at date 0 because the existence of complete markets and the absence of arbitrage opportunities means that the planner's wealth is independent of investment decisions. Given one unit of the good per depositor at date 0, the planner's task is to allocate consumption so as to maximize expected utility subject to a budget constraint. If c_s^t denotes the consumption of the typical depositor in state s at date t, then the planner's problem can be written as follows:

max $E[\lambda U(c_s^1) + (1 - \lambda)U(c_s^2)]$

s.t. $\sum_s (q_s \lambda c_s^1 + q_s p_s (1 - \lambda) c_s^2) \leq 1.$

The budget constraint can be explained as follows. In state s, each early consumer receives c_s^1 and each late consumer receives c_s^2. There are λ early consumers, so the total demand for the good at date 1 is λc_s^1 and the cost, measured in terms of the good at date 0, is $q_s \lambda c_s^1$. Similarly, there are $1 - \lambda$ late consumers so the total demand for the good at date 2 is $(1 - \lambda)c_s^2$ and the cost, measured in terms of the good at date 0, is $q_s p_s (1 - \lambda)c_s^2$. Summing these terms over dates and states gives the total cost of consumption in terms of the good at date

0, which is the left-hand side of the budget constraint. The right-hand side is the initial endowment of goods at date 0.

The no-arbitrage restrictions on the prices of contingent commodities allow us to exchange a random consumption bundle for its expected value. For example, the value of (c_H^1, c_L^1) is the same as $(\bar{c}^1, \bar{c}^1)$, where $\bar{c}^1 = (1 - \varepsilon)c_H^1 + \varepsilon c_L^1$. Since depositors are risk averse, it is always optimal to substitute $(\bar{c}^1, \bar{c}^1)$ for (c_H^1, c_L^1). A similar argument holds for consumption at date 2. Thus, the planner's problem reduces to

$$\max \quad \lambda U(c^1) + (1 - \lambda)U(c^2)$$

$$\text{s.t.} \quad \lambda c^1 + \bar{R}^{-1}(1 - \lambda)c^2 \leq 1.$$

The first-order conditions for an optimum are

$$U'(c^1) = \bar{R}U(c^2),$$

which implies that $c^1 < c^2$. Thus, the optimal consumption allocation is nonstochastic and gives more consumption to the late consumers than to the early consumers.

Now consider what a bank could achieve on behalf of its depositors. The first-best consumption allocation (c^1, c^2) can be implemented by a deposit contract (d_1, d_2), where d_1 is the payoff promised to early consumers and d_2 is the payoff promised to late consumers. Note that this deposit contract is incentive compatible. If the bank cannot distinguish early consumers from late consumers and $d_1 > d_2$, the late consumers have an incentive to withdraw d_1 at date 1, store it until date 2 and then consume it. So the deposit contract is incentive compatible if and only if $d_1 \leq d_2$, which is the case here. Since the solution to the planner's problem is the first best, the bank cannot do any better. Thus, $(d_1, d_2) = (c^1, c^2)$ is the solution to the bank's decision problem.

PROPOSITION 1 If there exist complete markets for insuring aggregate risks, the bank can achieve first-best (Pareto-efficient) risk sharing without the introduction of bank capital.

In this model, the only function of capital is to improve cross-sectional risk sharing between investors (shareholders) and depositors in the bank. This can be achieved just as well using Arrow securities, so bank capital is redundant.

To see this, consider what would happen if bank capital were introduced. Suppose that risk neutral investors subscribe e units of capital at date 0 to buy shares in the bank. The profits are all paid at date 2. Let π_s denote the profits in state $s = H, L$. The bank's budget constraint can be written as follows:

$$\sum_s (q_s \lambda c_s^1 + q_s p_s \{(1 - \lambda)c_s^2 + \pi_s\}) \le 1 + e.$$

Assume that the investors have access to the same assets as the banks, that is, the short and long assets. Then the opportunity cost of capital ρ is exactly $\bar{R}$. The supply of capital is perfectly elastic as long as investors receive the opportunity cost of capital. In equilibrium, this means that

$$e = \sum_s q_s p_s \pi_s.$$

Substituting this into the bank's budget constraint, we get the same budget constraint as before:

$$\sum_s (q_s \lambda c_s^1 + q_s p_s (1 - \lambda)c_s^2) \le 1.$$

Thus, capital makes no difference to the feasible set of consumption allocations available to depositors. This proves the following Modigliani-Miller-type result:

PROPOSITION 2   Capital structure is irrelevant because Arrow securities can be used to undo any changes in the debt to equity ratio. Any capital ratio (including zero) is optimal for the bank.

The assumption of a complete set of Arrow securities is quite restrictive. In practice, such securities do not exist. The use of dynamic trading strategies or derivatives, however, may achieve an equivalent allocation of risk. In that case, proposition 2 can be interpreted as saying that capital adequacy requirements impose no economic costs on the banking system.

Finally, we note that what is optimal for a bank is not necessarily socially optimal. In this model, however, the banks operate like a representative agent. (The risk-neutral investors serve to fix the prices of contingent commodities, but do not play any other role in equilibrium). In equilibrium, what is optimal for the bank (and its depositors) is optimal for society as a whole. There is no scope for welfare-improving intervention by the banking authorities and, in particular, no role for capital adequacy regulation. We state this corollary of proposition 2 as a proposition.

PROPOSITION 3   Whatever level of capital is chosen, the laisser-faire equilibrium is Pareto-efficient. The imposition of capital adequacy requirements cannot improve economic welfare.

Equilibrium without Arrow Securities

To provide an opportunity for welfare-improving intervention, some kind of friction or market failure must be introduced. Here we assume that markets for liquidity services are incomplete. Specifically, there are no markets for Arrow securities (or their equivalent).

In this case, there is a role for capital in promoting improved risk sharing. If banks use noncontingent liabilities to finance investment in risky assets, there is a risk of bankruptcy in bad states where asset returns are low. Even if bankruptcy involves no deadweight costs ex post, depositors end up bearing risk and the allocation of this risk may be suboptimal in the absence of Arrow securities. By using capital to finance investment, the bank increases the total value of its portfolio in each state. The depositors (debt holders) receive all the value in bad states, where the bank is bankrupt, and the shareholders receive the excess returns (total value minus debt) in good states. From the point of view of depositors, there has been a shift in returns from the good states to the bad states, equalizing consumption across states and improving risk sharing.

How far can this process go? It depends on the cost of capital, that is, the difference between the return on external investments and the bank's portfolio. So far, we have assumed that the risk-neutral investors have access to the same set of investments as the banks, that is, the long asset and the short asset. In that case, there is no cost to the bank of acquiring more capital and the first best can be achieved.

Suppose the bank acquires e units of capital at date 0 and chooses a portfolio (x, y), where x is the investment in the long asset and y is the investment in the short asset and the budget constraint

$$x + y = 1 + e$$

is satisfied. The investment in the short asset is chosen to satisfy the bank's budget constraint at date 1:

$$\lambda d_1 = y,$$

where (d_1, d_2) is the first-best deposit contract achievable with complete markets. The investment in the long asset is chosen to satisfy the bank's budget constraint at date 2 in the low state:

$$(1 - \lambda)d_2 = R_L x.$$

In the high state, there will be a surplus that goes to the shareholders as profit:

$$(1 - \lambda)d_2 + \pi_H = R_H x.$$

Clearly, we can choose e, x, and y to satisfy these constraints for the given contract of (d_1, d_2). We need to check that the shareholders are receiving their opportunity cost of capital. Recall that the bank's complete-markets budget constraint assures us that

$$\lambda d_1 + \bar{R}^{-1}(1 - \lambda)d_2 = 1.$$

This implies that

$$(1 - \varepsilon)\pi_H = \bar{R}e$$

as required.

As long as the returns on assets held by the bank are equal to the best returns available to the investors elsewhere in the economy, there is no (net) cost to the bank of acquiring capital. The bank invests capital in the long asset. The returns on the investment in the long asset are just enough to cover the investors' opportunity cost of capital. The bank's portfolio is now larger, however, and this enables the bank to pay the depositors the same amount (d_1, d_2) in both states without risk of default. This is just what an efficient allocation of risk requires: there is no risk of default and the depositors' consumption is equalized in all states. In this case, capital provides the same services as complete markets.

Note that the preceding discussion focused on the *smallest* amount of capital that allows the bank to achieve the first best. A higher level of capital would do just as well and would allow shareholders to receive positive profits in the low state as well as in the high state, but the depositors' welfare would be unchanged.

The introduction of capital allows optimal risk sharing with incomplete markets, as long as the net cost of capital is zero. As every CEO knows, however, capital is expensive. A more realistic assumption is that capital is costly, that is, the return on bank assets is not as high as the opportunity cost of capital. The rest of this section considers the case $\rho > \bar{R}$. We discuss the motivation for this assumption in section 2.3.

When capital is costly, risk sharing may be incomplete. Banks, which are forced to use noncontingent deposit contracts as liabilities, find it costly to avoid default. They either have to raise a large amount of capital, or hold a large amount of the short asset, or distort the deposit contract. They may find it optimal to default. The possibility of default allows greater flexibility and superior risk sharing. In some cases, banks that seek to maximize depositors' expected utility will find it optimal to default.

The model is easily adapted to allow for the possibility of default, which can occur if the level of capital is less than the first best. If there is no default in equilibrium at date 1, the representative bank offers a deposit contract (d_1, d_2), early consumers at date 1 receive the promised payment d_1 and the late consumers are the residual claimants at date 2. The bank must pay the late consumers d_2 if possible, and the liquidated value of the portfolio otherwise. Without loss of generality we can put $c_L \leq c_H = d_2$. In one case, there is no default at date 2 and the late consumers receive d_2 in both states. In the other case there is default in state L (only), and consumers receive d_2 in state H and the liquidated value of the portfolio in state L. In the first case, the bank's decision problem (DP) can be written as

max $\lambda U(d_1) + (1 - \lambda)U(d_2)$

s.t. $x + y \leq 1 + e$

$\lambda d_1 + (1 - \lambda)p_H d_2 + p_H \pi_H \leq y + p_H R_H x$

$\lambda d_1 + (1 - \lambda)p_L d_2 + p_L \pi_L \leq y + p_L R_L x$

$d_1 \leq d_2$

$(1 - \varepsilon)\pi_H + \varepsilon\pi_L \geq \rho e,$

where π_s is profits in state s. Note that profits are assumed to be paid at date 2. The first constraint is the budget constraint at date 0: the investment in assets is bounded by the depositors' endowment and the capital provided by investors. The second and third constraints are the date-1 budget constraints corresponding to states H and L, respectively: the left-hand side is the present value of depositors' consumption and profits and the right-hand side is the value of the bank's portfolio. The fourth constraint is the incentive constraint: late consumers have no incentive to imitate early consumers. The final constraint ensures that investors earn the rate ρ on the capital invested in the bank.

In this case, the demand for consumption at date 1 is the same in both states, as is the supply. Excess supply implies that $p_s = 1$, for $s = H, L$, which is inconsistent with equilibrium (the short asset is dominated). Thus, demand must equal supply and there is a single price $p_H = p_L = p$ that clears the asset market at date 2. Investors will only hold the short asset if $p\rho = 1$, but in that case $p\bar{R} < 1$, so no one will be willing to hold the long asset. This cannot be an equilibrium. So there is no provision of liquidity by the investors. Since capital is costly, we want to minimize the amount, holding constant the consumption of the depositors. Thus, $\pi_L = 0$. Further, since there is no liquidity provision by investors, we can assume without loss of generality that the bank holds enough of the short asset to pay the consumers at date 1 and enough of the long asset to provide consumption for the late consumers at date 2. The bank's DP reduces to

max $\lambda U(d_1) + (1 - \lambda)U(d_2)$

s.t. $x + y \leq 1 + e$

$\lambda d_1 \leq y$

$(1 - \lambda)d_2 \leq R_L x$

$d_1 \leq d_2$

$(1 - \varepsilon)(R_H - R_L)x \geq \rho e.$

This leads to first-best risk sharing, but the depositors' expected utility is reduced relative to the equilibrium with Arrow securities because of the cost of capital. To see this, consider the first-order conditions for this problem (as usual ignoring the incentive constraint, which turns out not to be a binding constraint at the optimum):

$$U'(d_1) = \mu_2$$

$$U'(d_2) = \mu_3$$

$$\mu_1 = \mu_2$$

$$\mu_1 = \mu_3 R_L + \mu_4(1 - \varepsilon)(R_H - R_L)$$

$$\mu_1 = \rho\mu_4$$

or

$$U'(d_1) = U'(d_2)R_L + \frac{U'(d_1)}{\rho}(1 - \varepsilon)(R_H - R_L),$$

which implies

$$\rho = \rho\frac{U'(d_2)}{U'(d_1)}R_L + (1 - \varepsilon)(R_H - R_L). \tag{1}$$

To check our earlier analysis of the first-best, suppose that $\rho = \bar{R}$. Then the first-order condition reduces to $\rho U'(d_2) = U(d_1)$ and we have the first-best allocation once again.

If the opportunity cost of funds to investors is greater than the return on bank assets, $\rho > \bar{R}$, increasing capital imposes a real cost on the bank depositors. They will have to give up part of the return on their investments to compensate the shareholders for the lower average return of bank assets. This trade-off between cost of capital and improved risk sharing will limit the extent to which it is optimal to share risk between shareholders and depositors.

Assume $\rho > \bar{R}$ in (1) gives $\rho U'(d_2) > U'(d_1)$. Risk sharing is no longer complete. As ρ increases, d_1 and d_2 draw closer together until at last the incentive constraint is binding. A further increase in ρ will make default in state L an optimal response.

Default occurs in state L at date 2 when the value of bank assets is sufficient to allow the bank to make the payment promised to early consumers at date 1 but not the payment promised to late consumers at date 2. Although the late consumers receive less than d_2, they will not run on the bank if they are still receiving more than d_1. The representative bank will sell the long asset in exchange for liquidity in the bad state, so investors must be willing to hold the short asset. The demand for liquidity in the good state is lower than the demand in the bad state, so the prices of future consumption at date 1 are $p_H = 1$ and $p_L = p$. To induce investors to hold the short asset, we must have

$$\rho = (1 - \varepsilon) + \varepsilon \frac{1}{p}.$$

The decision problem of the representative bank can be written as follows:

max $\lambda U(d_1) + (1 - \lambda)\{(1 - \varepsilon)U(d_2) + \varepsilon U(c_L)\}$

s.t. $x + y \leq 1 + e$

$\lambda d_1 + (1 - \lambda)d_2 + \pi_H \leq y + R_H x$

$\lambda d_1 + (1 - \lambda)pc_L \leq y + pR_L x$

$d_1 \leq c_L$

$(1 - \varepsilon)\pi_H \geq \rho e.$

If ρ gets even higher, it may be optimal to consider default at date 1 in state L.

Default at date 1 is different from default at date 2. At date 2, default simply means that the depositors receive less than was promised, but they still receive the total value of the remaining bank assets. The default event has no other equilibrium implications. Default at date 1 requires the bank to cease operating and liquidate all its assets in an attempt to meet its obligations. This has two important implications. First, the late consumers must withdraw at date 1; if they delay, there will be no assets left for them at date 2. Second, the sale of long assets will depress the asset price (raise the short-term interest rate), which in turn affects the liquidity of other banks. (Note that the asset price is affected only if a nonnegligible number of banks defaults simultaneously). Thus, default at date 1 constitutes a crisis in a way that the comparatively benign default at date 2 does not.

In each of the cases studied, it can be shown that capital is reduced when the cost of capital $\rho - \bar{R}$ is increased. When the difference between ρ and $\bar{R}$ is sufficiently large, the optimal level of capital is zero.

PROPOSITION 4   If the cost of capital is high, the optimal level of capital may be positive, but it will not guarantee complete (first-best) risk sharing. For a sufficiently high cost of capital, the optimal (for the bank) level of capital is zero.

It is worth stopping to ask why first-best risk sharing cannot be achieved between risk-neutral equity holders and risk-averse debt holders. Technically, the reason is limited liability. If the shareholder's liability is limited to their investment, so is the depositors' insurance in the worst states. Because the cost of capital is positive, the liability constraint may be binding and risk sharing will be less than complete. If the equity holders and debt holders could write a complete contingent contract, they would replicate the effect of complete Arrow securities, but this would require payments from the equity holders to the debt holders in the worst states. As we have seen, complete Arrow securities effectively imply the (net) cost of capital is zero.

This suggests an interesting way that risk sharing could be improved: multiple liability has been discussed by Macey and O'Hara (2000). Double or higher multiple liability was common in the United States until the introduction of deposit insurance in the 1930s. Absent collection and liquidity costs, multiple liability provides a way of increasing effective capital without increasing capital costs. With double liability, for example, the debt holders receive the same insurance indemnity in bad states with half the capital cost. In the limit, no capital is required, only liability.

PROPOSITION 5 If shareholder liability is a multiple m of their investment, first-best risk sharing is achieved in the limit as m diverges to infinity.

This is like the situation at Lloyd's of London, where names invest their capital in various ways to get the highest rate of return and simultaneously use it as collateral to underwrite insurance contracts. There are two drawbacks to this solution, illiquidity and collection costs.

If the shareholders' liability is limited to the capital invested in the bank's portfolio, the receiver can easily dispose of those assets, assuming no fraud on the part of the bank's management. If the shareholders' liability extends to assets they own, it may be very costly for the receiver to pursue the shareholders and enforce their liability. Again, Lloyd's of London provides a useful illustration. These costs limit the effectiveness of multiple liability as a source of inexpensive insurance.

Illiquidity is another problem. If the best returns achieved by shareholders outside the bank are generated by illiquid investments, the shareholders may have difficulty meeting their liability to the bank when the bank defaults. Another way of putting the same point is that part of the cost of capital is the need to maintain a certain portion of the bank's portfolio in liquid investments.

What can government intervention accomplish? Because markets are incomplete, the equilibrium allocation may not be Pareto-efficient. The bank chooses its portfolio and deposit contract, however, to maximize the welfare of the depositors, taking as given the prices in the market. So there is a market failure only if banks are facing the "wrong" prices. There are two possible ways in which prudential regulation can improve economic welfare. First, it could execute intertemporal trades that banks, investors, and depositors cannot achieve, effectively replacing missing markets. Second, it could alter the allocation of resources in a way that changes prices and causes economic decision makers to change their own intertemporal decisions. The first kind of intervention is not as interesting as the second. If regulatory authorities can replace missing markets, there is an obvious welfare gain; but it is not obvious what technological advantage the authorities have over the market when it comes to executing intertemporal trades. For example, if there are missing markets because transaction costs are high, the regulatory authorities will be subject to the same transaction costs. It is unrealistic to assume that they have a technological advantage in this activity. In any case, even if regulators have a superior technology available, we cannot argue that there is a market failure if the market allocation is efficient relative to the available technology. The market must be judged relative to the technology available to it.

The second possibility is more interesting. We say that an equilibrium is *constrained efficient* if it is impossible to make every agent better off (or some better off and no one worse off), by changing the allocation of goods and services at the first date, while relying on the existing (incomplete) markets at the second and subsequent dates. Constrained inefficiency does imply that markets have failed to produce the most efficient allocation possible relative to that technology. The pecuniary externality created by intervention does not require a superior transaction technology, just a manipulation of agents' incentives by changing prices. This is the idea that lies behind a famous result of Geanakoplos and Polemarchakis (1986), who show that in a model of perfectly competitive general equilibrium with incomplete markets, the equilibrium allocation is generically constrained inefficient. A welfare-improving intervention does not require the regulator to make intertemporal trades that are impossible for the market. The regulator only needs to affect the allocation of resources at a single point in time and leave it to the market to respond intertemporally to the changed incentives.

In the present model, there is no welfare-relevant pecuniary externality. Asset prices at the second date are uniquely determined by the opportunity cost of capital and the investors' first-order conditions for an optimal portfolio. An increase in the required capital adequacy ratio or reserve ratio may change the bank's portfolio, but it will not change asset prices. Since the bank is already maximizing the expected utility of the depositors taking prices as given, there is no feasible welfare improvement.

PROPOSITION 6   Equilibrium is constrained efficient. There is no scope for using capital adequacy requirements to improve economic welfare.

To see why this result holds, consider the welfare impact of imposing a capital requirement $\bar{e}$ above the equilibrium level. Each case considered earlier requires a different argument.

If there is no default at date 2, the banks do not use the asset market at date 1. At the market-clearing price, the investors do not want to hold the short asset, so there will be no trade at date 1 in the new equilibrium. Forcing the banks to hold more capital by imposing a constraint $e \geq \bar{e}$ reduces expected utility.

If there is default in the bad state at date 2, the investors provide liquidity by holding speculative balances of the short asset. It is optimal for the investors to hold the short asset only if $p_H = 1$, $p_L = p$ and

$$\rho = (1 - \varepsilon) + \varepsilon \frac{1}{p}.$$

This condition uniquely determines the price p. Thus, forcing the banks to hold more capital by imposing a constraint $e \geq \bar{e}$ does not change the prices at which banks can sell the long asset. At these prices, the banks can sell as much as they wish, just as they could in the original equilibrium. Thus, the maximum expected utility they can achieve is the solution to the DP given above with the added constraint $e \geq \bar{e}$. Obviously, adding a constraint to the problem will not increase expected utility. A similar argument applies if there is default at date 1.

The conditions under which proposition 6 holds are nongeneric. Still, it makes the point that without a welfare-relevant pecuniary externality, intervention cannot be justified. If there were a welfare-relevant payoff externality, the Geanakoplos-Polemarchakis theorem suggests that there will typically be some intervention that can make everyone better off, but it does not identify the nature of the intervention and in general it is very hard to say what the intervention will look like. Even in simple examples, the general equilibrium effects of a regulatory intervention can contradict our intuition about the policy's likely impact (cf. Allen and Gale 2000b). Without a theory of optimal policy, intervention is a shot in the dark.

2.3   The Cost of Capital

Before leaving the issue of risk sharing, we need to say something in defense of the assumption that the opportunity cost of capital ρ is greater than the return on the long asset. One rationalization, pointed out above, is that investors have access to assets that are not available to the banks. There are various other ways in which this assumption could be rationalized. Here, a simple story will suffice.

Suppose that there is a third asset, which pays a return $\rho/(1 - \varepsilon)$ in the high state and nothing in the low state. Risk neutral investors will choose to invest all of their wealth in this asset because it offers the highest expected return $\rho > \bar{R}$. Thus, ρ is the opportunity cost of capital. Now suppose some investors are persuaded to become shareholders and provide capital for the bank. The bank gains nothing from investing this capital in the risky asset. The risky asset provides no returns in the low state and the entire marginal return in the high state has to be paid to the shareholders to cover their opportunity cost of capital. An investment in the risky asset cannot improve risk sharing. To improve risk sharing (change the feasible set of consumption allocations), the bank will have to invest some of the capital in the original two assets. Thus, without loss of generality we can restrict the bank's investments to the short and long asset. Then we are back to the model analyzed here.

There are other stories one could tell. We could assume that the opportunity cost of capital is set by an asset that is more illiquid than the long asset, for example, one that only yields a return after date 2. Like the risky asset that yields nothing in state L, this asset will not help the bank improve risk sharing for the depositors, and we can assume without loss of generality that the bank does not hold it. This again yields a wedge between the opportunity cost of capital and the return on bank assets.

Risk aversion would provide another justification for an opportunity cost of capital higher than $\bar{R}$. If investors are risk averse they have to be compensated for taking on the risk that depositors shed. In this case, it may not be possible to represent the opportunity cost by an exogenous parameter ρ, but there will be an economic cost of increasing capital and the optimal capital ratio may be incompatible with first-best risk sharing.

2.4 Costly Crises

The costs of financial crises have not been emphasized, but they are obviously an important part of any rationalization of prudential regulation. In the present model, the intertemporal allocation of consumption is distorted when a bank ceases to operate because the depositors lose their access to financial markets and hence to the highest equilibrium returns. This is a cost of crises, but it appears a rather small one compared with the real effects of major financial upheavals. As Bernanke and Gertler (1989) have argued, financial crises have (negative) wealth effects that increase the cost of intermediation, reduce investment in real capital, and so reduce activity throughout the economy. This and other transmission mechanisms from the financial to the real sector are known as *financial accelerators*. Their absence is perhaps the most glaring limitation of our model.

There is a large amount of empirical evidence about the destructive effects of financial crises on the real economy and these appear to be the motivation for much of the concern with financial stability and prudential regulation. Introducing nontrivial costs of financial crises is clearly the best way to provide a foundation for prudential regulation. As with everything else, however, there will be costs and benefits of financial crises, and it is not obvious until we have analyzed these issues carefully that eliminating crises is optimal or that there are not better ways of reducing the deadweight costs of crises. What is needed (and what we do not have) are models of financial crises in which it is possible to derive the optimal prudential regulation policy, whether it be in the form of regulation of capital adequacy or some other.

3 Asymmetric Information and Capital Structure

The risk-sharing example makes the point that, under certain circumstances, capital adequacy requirements are, at best, unnecessary and, at worst, harmful. Banks, left to themselves, will choose the optimal capital structure. If regulation forces them to increase capital ratios, the result will be a reduction of economic welfare. This example ignores a number of other ways in which capital structure may influence bank behavior and economic welfare, particularly those associated with asymmetric information (moral hazard, adverse selection).

In the presence of moral hazard, debt finance may be associated with risk shifting. Banks are financed by debt-like liabilities (deposits) and this can produce an incentive to take excessive risk. Capital, like collateral, counteracts this tendency, because it increases the shareholders' sensitivity to downside risk. One rationale that is given for capital adequacy regulation is to reduce the incentive for banks to take risks.

In the absence of capital adequacy regulation, however, reputation may ensure that banks do not take excessive risks in a situation of moral hazard. Bhattacharya (1982) points to the work of Klein and Leffler (1981) on reputation and quality and suggests its applicability in this context. Depositors will infer the incentives of banks to take risk and realize that the value of a reputation for prudence makes it incentive-compatible for the bank to adopt a low-risk strategy. Hellman, Murdock, and Stiglitz (1998) also mention this incentive.

The assumption that adequate capital is necessary to prevent excessive risk taking does not by itself provide an argument for capital adequacy requirements. The bank can internalize this agency cost and adopt the optimal capital structure without any assistance from the regulator. In the absence of a pecuniary externality, there is no reason to think that the privately optimal capital structure is not socially optimal.

The same argument can be made in connection with other determinants of optimal capital structure. If there are deadweight losses from bankruptcy, for example, because illiquid markets imply that an orderly liquidation is difficult to achieve, or because there is loss of charter value or assets cannot be managed as efficiently by other banks, these costs should be internalized in the bank's choice of the optimal capital structure. Only if there is a pecuniary externality and markets are incomplete will there be an argument for regulation.

It is not clear that any of these considerations are actually the ones that motivate the regulators who set capital adequacy requirements. But whatever the motivation, the onus appears to be on the regulator to identify the pecuniary externality so that one can assess the importance of the market failure and the effectiveness of capital adequacy requirements as a solution. Financial fragility, the idea that one bank failure may trigger others and bring down the whole financial system, would be an example of a pecuniary externality on a very large scale. Perhaps this is what motivates the system of capital adequacy requirements. If so, we need better models of financial fragility before we can provide a theoretical basis for the current system.

4 Monitoring and Survival Strategies in a Volatile Environment

Another function of capital is to make continuous monitoring unnecessary. Imagine a world in which the following assumptions are satisfied:

• Monitoring is continuous
• Portfolio is marked to market
• Portfolio value changes continuously
• Markets are perfectly liquid

In this world, banks would never make losses without the forbearance of the regulator. When the net worth of the bank reaches zero, the assets and liabilities will be liquidated and the bank closed without loss to depositors. There is no need for capital to act as a buffer for creditors (depositors), since the creditors are always paid in full. Similarly, there is no incentive for risk shifting. The problem of moral hazard is resolved by continuous monitoring. These are strong assumptions. If monitoring is not continuous, if asset returns are not continuous, or if asset markets are illiquid, there may be deadweight losses associated with bankruptcy. Yet, that is not necessarily a market failure that can be rectified by setting high capital adequacy requirements. The bank will internalize these costs and choose the optimal capital structure to maximize shareholder value. Again, in the absence of a pecuniary externality, the private optimum will be the social optimum.

5   Concluding Remarks

The chapter began by noting the lack of theory in the practice of financial regulation. We have argued here that theoretical analysis should be an important component of policy analysis. In the area of banking regulation, little theory has typically been used. Instead, historical experience has been the guide. Capital adequacy regulations are one of the most important aspects of banking regulation. We have suggested that the theoretical rationale for their existence is not as straightforward as might be expected at first sight. Much work remains to be done in this area.

References

Allen, F., and D. Gale. 1998. "Optimal Financial Crises." *Journal of Finance* 53: 1245–1284.

Allen, F., and D. Gale. 2000a. *Comparing Financial Systems*. Cambridge, MA: MIT Press.

Allen, F., and D. Gale. 2000b. "Banking and Markets." Working paper 00-44B, Wharton Financial Institutions Center, University of Pennsylvania.

Allen, F., and D. Gale. 2000c. "Financial Contagion." *Journal of Political Economy* 108: 1–33.

Allen, F., and D. Gale. 2000d. "Optimal Currency Crises." *Carnegie-Rochester Series on Public Policy* 53: 177–230.

Allen, F., and D. Gale. 2000e. "Bubbles and Crises." *The Economic Journal* 110: 236–256.

Allen, F., and D. Gale. 2001. "Financial Fragility." Working paper 01-37, Wharton Financial Institutions Center, University of Pennsylvania.

Bernanke, B., and M. Gertler. 1989. "Agency Costs, Net Worth, and Business Fluctuations." *American Economic Review* 79 (1989): 14–31.

Besanko, D., and G. Kanatas. 1996. "The Regulation of Bank Capital: Do Capital Standards Promote Bank Safety?" *Journal of Financial Intermediation* 5: 160–183.

Bhattacharya, S. 1982. "Aspects of Monetary and Banking Theory and Moral Hazard." *Journal of Finance* 37: 371–384.

Chari, V., and R. Jagannathan. 1988. "Banking Panics, Information, and Rational Expectations Equilibrium." *Journal of Finance* 43: 749–760.

Diamond, D., and P. Dybvig. 1983. "Bank Runs, Deposit Insurance, and Liquidity." *Journal of Political Economy* 91: 401–419.

Furlong, F., and M. Keeley. 1989. "Capital Regulation and Bank Risk-Taking: A Note." *Journal of Banking and Finance* 13: 883–891.

Gennotte, G., and D. Pyle. 1991. "Capital Controls and Bank Risk." *Journal of Banking and Finance* 15: 805–824.

Geanakoplos, J., and H. Polemarchakis. 1986. "Existence, Regularity, and Constrained Suboptimality of Competitive Allocations When the Asset Market Is Incomplete," in eds. *Essays in honor of Kenneth J. Arrow: Volume 3, Uncertainty, information, and communication,* ed. W. Heller, R. Starr, and D. Starrett, 65–95. Cambridge, New York, and Sydney: Cambridge University Press.

Hellmann, T., K. Murdock, and J. Stiglitz. 1998. "Liberalization, Moral Hazard in Banking, and Prudential Regulation: Are Capital Requirements Enough?" Working paper 1466R, Graduate School of Business, Stanford University.

Hellmann, T., K. Murdock, and J. Stiglitz. 2000. "Liberalization, Moral Hazard in Banking, and Prudential Regulation: Are Capital Requirements Enough?" *American Economic Review* 90: 147–165.

Hellwig, M. 1994. "Liquidity Provision, Banking, and the Allocation of Interest Rate Risk." *European Economic Review* 38: 1363–1389.

Jacklin, C., and S. Bhattacharya. 1988. "Distinguishing Panics and Information-based Bank runs: Welfare and Policy Implications." *Journal of Political Economy* 96: 568–592.

Keeley, M. 1990. "Deposit Insurance, Risk, and Market Power in Banking." *American Economic Review* 80: 1183–1200.

Kim, D., and A. Santomero. 1988. "Risk in Banking and Capital Regulation." *Journal of Finance* 43: 1219–1233.

Klein, B., and K. Leffler. 1981. "The Role of Market Forces in Assuring Contractual Performance." *Journal of Political Economy* 89: 615–641.

Macey, J., and M. O'Hara. (2000). "Solving the Corporate Governance Problems of Banks: A Proposal." Cornell University, unpublished.

Merton, R. 1977. "An Analytic Derivation of the Cost of Deposit Insurance and Loan Guarantees: An Application of Modern Option Pricing Theory." *Journal of Banking and Finance* 1: 3–11.

Postlewaite, A., and X. Vives. 1987. "Bank Runs as an Equilibrium Phenomenon." *Journal of Political Economy* 95: 485–491.

Rochet, J-C. 1992. "Capital Requirements and the Behaviour of Commercial Banks." *European Economic Review* 36: 1137–1178.

Rochet, J-C., and J. Tirole. 1996. "Interbank Lending and Systemic Risk." *Journal of Money, Credit, and Banking* 28: 733–762.

Wallace, N. 1988. "Another Attempt to Explain an Illiquid Banking System: The Diamond and Dybvig Model with Sequential Service Taken Seriously." *Federal Reserve Bank of Minneapolis Quarterly Review* 12 (Fall): 3–16.

Wallace, Neil. 1990. "A Banking Model in Which Partial Suspension Is Best." *Federal Reserve Bank of Minneapolis Quarterly Review* 14 (Fall): 11–23.

7   Learning Revisited

Margaret Bray

I became interested in learning when I was a graduate student at Oxford, supervised by Joe Stiglitz and Jim Mirrlees. I was puzzled by economists' use of the term equilibrium, particularly by rational expectations equilibrium. Coming from a background in mathematics, I thought of equilibrium as steady state of a dynamic system, which if it existed, would emerge from an explicit model of the dynamics. I rapidly discovered that the formal mathematical definitions of equilibrium in economic theory hinged on beliefs and made no explicit reference to dynamics. Beliefs about the future play a crucial role in models of savings and investment, and more generally in any model of forward looking decision making. Beliefs about current but unobservable variables are important in game theory, and central to the economics of asymmetric information. Economic models give us a mapping from agents' beliefs to their decisions, to outcomes. Equilibrium is defined as a fixed point of that mapping, in which agents' beliefs about outcomes are correct. Defining equilibrium in this way works mathematically, but raises the question how agents come to have these beliefs. I wanted to know whether a learning story could provide an answer. This raised some issues, which are best understood in the context of a simple model.

1 Learning and Equilibrium

Consider a model of a market in which the price p_t of a good at date t is determined by the expectation p_t^e of the price at t which is formed on the basis of data known at date $t - 1$

$$p_t = x + ap_t^e + u_t. \tag{1}$$

Bray and Savin (1986) derive a version of this model from a generalization of the cobweb model, where demand at t depends on price p_t,
but supply is determined earlier as a function of expected price p_t^e.
Assume that $E_{t-1}u_t = 0$ where $E_{t-1}u_t$ is the expectation of u_t at date
$t-1$. In the rational expectations equilibrium of this model agents
believe that $p_t^e = (1-a)^{-1}x$ implying that $p_t = (1-a)^{-1}x + u_t$ so
$E_{t-1}p_t = p_t^e = (1-a)^{-1}x$; agents' beliefs are correct. The terminology
rational expectations equilibrium introduced by Muth (1961) suggests the concept is an extension of the standard rationality postulate, that agents make choices in an internally consistent fashion.
One story about agents' beliefs is that they understand the world in
which they live, know the numerical values of the parameters x and
a, figure out the rational expectations equilibrium, and behave accordingly. I do not find this story plausible and think it requires
much more than rationality. The term "rational expectations" is too
firmly established to change, but "model consistent expectations" is
closer to capturing the essence of the idea. A plausible account of
how rational expectations equilibrium can come about requires a
plausible story of learning.

Consider the following argument. Assume that the economy is in
rational expectations equilibrium, so $p_t = (1-a)^{-1}x + u_t$. Further,
make assumptions that ensure that $1/t \sum_{i=1}^{t} u_i \to 0$. (Sufficient conditions for this are that that $\{u_t\}$ is a sequence of independent and
identically distributed random variables with zero mean and finite
variance). Then $\bar{p}_t = 1/t \sum_{i=1}^{t} p_i = (1-a)^{-1}x + 1/t \sum_{i=1}^{t} u_i$ tends to
$(1-a)^{-1}x$ almost surely as t tends to infinity. An econometrician
making repeated observations of the rational expectations equilibrium would in the limit learn how to form rational expectations. This
looks like a learning story, but it is fundamentally flawed. It starts
from the assumption that the economy is in rational expectations
equilibrium, so it cannot be an explanation of how the economy gets
to a rational expectations equilibrium. It is not even an argument
that the economy will stay in a rational expectations equilibrium
once it gets there, because in finite samples $\bar{p}_t$ will differ from
$(1-a)^{-1}x$. But it does suggest two approaches to learning, differing
in the frequency with which estimates are updated.

First, suppose that agents update estimates rarely. Agents start
with a price expectation $p_t^e = p_0^*$. Then the price will be $p_t = x +
ap_0^* + u_t$. If agents observe many iterations of the model without
changing their expectations, they learn that the average price

is $p_1^* = x + ap_0^*$ which differs from p_0^* unless $p_0^* = (1-a)^{-1}x$. Agents learn that they are wrong, but they do not learn the rational expectations equilibrium value of p_t^e unless they started with rational expectations. Suppose this process is repeated many times, giving a succession of expectations, $p_0^*, p_1^* \ldots p_n^*$ where $p_j^* = x + ap_{j-1}^*$. If $|a| < 1$, p_n^* converges to the rational expectation equilibrium value $(1-a)^{-1}x$. This story of periodic updating gives convergence for a range of values of a, but I do not find it convincing. Why should agents forbear from changing their expectations while data accumulates?

The alternative approach supposes that agents' expected price is the average of past prices so $p_t^e = \bar{p}_{t-1}$. This is the least squares estimate of the mean of a stationary distribution. Bray (1983) offers a matrix version of this model. Bray (1982) and Bray and Savin (1986) worked with more complicated least squares models, but the general idea is the same. If $p_{t+1}^e = \bar{p}_t$ then $p_t = x + a\bar{p}_{t-1} + u_t$ implying that

$$\bar{p}_t = \frac{1}{t}p_t + \frac{t-1}{t}\bar{p}_{t-1}$$

$$= \frac{1}{t}(x + a\bar{p}_{t-1} + u_t) + \frac{t-1}{t}\bar{p}_{t-1} \tag{2}$$

so

$$\bar{p}_t - \frac{x}{1-a} = \left(1 - \frac{1-a}{t}\right)\left(\bar{p}_{t-1} - \frac{x}{1-a}\right) + \frac{1}{t}u_t. \tag{3}$$

This is a suggestive equation. If $a < 1$ then $0 < (1 - (1-a)/t) < 1$ for all sufficiently large t, so $|E_{t-1}(\bar{p}_t - x/(1-a))| < |\bar{p}_{t-1} - x/(1-a)|$. Further the term $1/tu_t$ is small for large t, and as $Eu_t = 0$ it seems plausible that sums of such terms are likely to be small. So $a < 1$ seems to be a good candidate for a sufficient condition for $\bar{p}_t$ to tend to its rational expectations equilibrium value of $x/(1-a)$. If $a > 1$ then $|E_{t-1}(\bar{p}_t - x/(1-a))| > |\bar{p}_{t-1} - x/(1-a)|$ for all t; convergence to rational expectations seems most unlikely. This intuition suggests $a < 1$ as a condition for convergence of this "econometric" learning model to a rational expectations equilibrium. The formal result is

PROPOSITION 1 Suppose that $p_t = x + a\bar{p}_{t-1} + u_t$ where $\bar{p}_{t-1} = 1/(t-1)\sum_{i=1}^{t-1}p_i$, and $\{u_t\}$ is a sequence of independent random variables with $Eu_t = 0$ and $\operatorname{var} u_t = \sigma^2$. If $a < 1$ p_t converges to $x/(1-a)$ with probability one.

The result is proved in the appendix by showing that

$$\bar{p}_t - \frac{x}{1-a} = \prod_{i=T+1}^{t}\left(1 - \frac{1-a}{i}\right)\left(\bar{p}_T - \frac{x}{1-a}\right) + z_{Tt},$$

where

$$z_{Tt} = \sum_{i=T+1}^{t-1} \prod_{j=i+1}^{t}\left(1 - \frac{1-a}{j}\right)\frac{1}{i}u_i + \frac{1}{t}u_t.$$

The proof then shows that if $1 > a$ then $\prod_{i=T+1}^{t}(1 - (1-a)/i)$ tends to zero and z_{Tt} tends to zero with probability one. If $a > 1$

$$\prod_{i=T+1}^{t}\left(1 - \frac{1-a}{i}\right) > 1 + (a-1)\sum_{T+1}^{t}\frac{1}{i},$$

which tends to infinity as t tends to infinity. In addition as

$$z_{Tt} = \left(1 + \frac{a-1}{t}\right)z_{Tt-1} + \frac{1}{t}u_t,$$

var z_{Tt} tend to infinity. When $a > 1$ the proof of convergence breaks down, and intuition suggests that convergence is unlikely.

The key features of this approach to learning is the use of an econometric technique, based on a model specification that would be correct if the model were in rational expectations equilibrium. The model is misspecified outside rational expectations equilibrium when the agents are learning. Intuition suggests conditions for convergence to rational expectation equilibrium, however, despite the model mis-specification. I showed that in three different models (Bray 1982, 1983, Bray and Savin 1986) conditions analogous to $a < 1$ were indeed sufficient for for convergence to rational expectations equilibrium when agents learn using econometrically based ordinary least squares or averaging techniques. Proving these results was a frustrating business. The convergence condition seemed intuitively obvious; computer simulation confirmed the intuition, but the results were difficult to prove, and the proofs were long and inelegant.

The question of whether least squares learning converged to a rational expectations equilibrium could be asked of a wide variety of models, but I could only get results for particular models. I never found a general approach; but Marcet and Sargent (1989) and Woodford (1990) did, drawing on work in the control theory literature by Ljung (1977). Evans and Honkapohja have used these results in a wide variety of models; their book (Evans and Honkaphja 2001) is a masterly overview of what can be done. Ljung's results are not simple, either to state or prove (see chapter 6 of Evans and Honka-pohja (2001)). If there is a simple, direct and elegant way to approach these problems, it has not been found. The essential concept is what Evans (1989) calls expectational stability. Suppose that there is a family of models parameterized by $\phi \in \Phi \subset R^n$ and a mapping $T : \Phi \to \Phi$ with the property that if agents believe that model ϕ holds, model $T(\phi)$ in fact holds. A rational expectations equilibrium is a fixed point of T, a value ϕ^* for which $T(\phi^*) = \phi^*$. In the simple model described by equation 1 ϕ is the expectation p_t^e of p_t and $T(\phi) = x + a\phi$, so $\phi^* = x/(1 - a)$. The condition for expectational sta-bility is that the differential equation

$$\frac{d\phi}{d\tau} = T(\phi) - \phi \tag{4}$$

should be stable in a neighbourhood of ϕ^*. For the simple model of equation 1 the expectational stability condition is that $d\phi/d\tau = x - (1 - a)\phi$ should be stable, that is $a < 1$. The expectational stability of a rational expectations equilibrium is closely related to the con-ditions under which least squares learning converges to the rational expecations equilibrium.

To get some intuition for why this is so, suppose that the learning process at t takes an average of past data, so

$$\phi_t = \phi_{t-1} + \gamma_t(T(\phi_{t-1}) - \phi_{t-1}),$$

where $\gamma_t = 1/t$ which implies that

$$\frac{\phi_t - \phi_{t-1}}{\gamma_t} = T(\phi_{t-1}) - \phi_{t-1}. \tag{5}$$

Let $\tau(t) = \sum_{i=1}^t \gamma_i$. The left hand side of 5 is then $(\phi_t - \phi_{t-1})/(\tau(t) - \tau(t-1))$ which tends to $d\phi/d\tau$ as t becomes large. The lim-iting behavior of the differential equation $d\phi/d\tau = T(\phi) - \phi$ in a neighbourhood of ϕ^* is the same as the limiting behavior of the dif-ference equation $\phi_t = \phi_{t-1} + \gamma_t(T(\phi_{t-1}) - \phi_{t-1})$. Evans and Honka-pohja (2001) show that various auxilliary assumptions, which are satisfied for this simple model, are necessary to establish that ex-pectational stability implies convergence of the learning process to the rational expectations equilibrium. Under much weaker conditions, failure of expectational stability of a rational expectations equilibrium implies that there is probablility zero that a learning process converges to that rational expectations equilibrium.

There are two key features of models in which agents' least squares learning converges to rational expectations equilibrium. First, agents must include the rational expectations equilibrium in the class of models they consider; in Bayesian language the rational expectations equilibrium must be in the support of the prior. Agents lack knowledge needed to form rational expectations, but they have enough insight to pick the right family of models to work with. Second, agents give equal weight to all data, be it recent or long past. This condition can be weakened somewhat. As $p_{t+1}^e = \bar{p}_t$ equation 2 can be written as

$$p_{t+1}^e = p_t^e + \gamma_t(p_t - p_t^e),$$

where $\gamma_t = 1/t$. The term γ_t is known as the gain. The gain determines the size of the response to new data. In this case the gain is decreasing. As data accumulates proportionately, less weight is given to a new piece of data. The proof of proposition 1 uses the fact that if t is sufficiently large $1 - (1-a)\gamma_t > 0$, whilst $\sum_{t=1}^{\infty} \gamma_t = \infty$ and $\sum_{t=1}^{T} \gamma_t^2 < \infty$. The proof would still work with alternative gain sequences which had these properties. If the gain is a constant so $\gamma_t = \gamma$ for all t

$$p_{t+1}^e = p_t^e + \gamma(p_t - p_t^e) = \gamma p_t + (1 - \gamma)p_t^e. \tag{6}$$

The convergence proof then breaks down, as $\lim_{T \to \infty} \sum_{t=1}^{T} \gamma_t = \infty$. Equation 6 implies that

$$p_{t+1}^e = \gamma \left(\sum_{j=0}^{\infty} (1 - \gamma)^j p_{t-j} \right).$$

Using different language, constant gain expectations are adaptive expectations where price expectations are a weighted average of past prices, with geometrically declining weights. Section 3 pursues this example, and shows that expectations are not rational, even in the limit. This is unfortunate, because consant gain or adaptive learning schemes are attractive in situations where there are nonstationary random variables. They can even generate rational expectations, as the following example shows.

2   Adaptive Expectations Can Be Rational

Up to now I have worked with a model in which the rational expectations equilibrium value of the expected price is constant. In this case someone observing the economy in rational expectations equilibrium could appropriately use the arithmetic mean as estimator in the rational expectations equilibrium price. I now replace the constant x by a term x_t which follows a random walk, and show that, in the limit of the rational expectations equilibrium, agents use an adaptive or constant gain learning rule to forecast the price.

PROPOSITION 2   Suppose that

$$p_t = x_t + ap_t^e + u_t$$

and

$$x_t = x_{t-1} + e_t,$$

where $\{e_t\}$ and $\{u_t\}$ are independent sequences of normal random variables with zero mean, and variances σ_e^2 and σ_u^2. Then in rational expectations equilibrium

$$p_t^e = p_{t-1}^e + \gamma_t(p_t - p_{t-1}^e),$$

where

$$\gamma_t = \frac{\sigma_{t-1}^2 + \sigma_e^2}{(1-a)(\sigma_{t-1}^2 + \sigma_e^2 + \sigma_u^2)}$$

$$\sigma_t^2 = \frac{(\sigma_{t-1}^2 + \sigma_e^2)\sigma_u^2}{\sigma_{t-1}^2 + \sigma_e^2 + \sigma_u^2}$$

and

$$\lim_{t \to \infty} \gamma_t = \frac{\sigma^{*2}}{(1-a)\sigma_u^2},$$

where σ^{*2} is the solution to

$$\sigma^{*2} = \frac{(\sigma^{*2} + \sigma_e^2)\sigma_u^2}{\sigma^{*2} + \sigma_e^2 + \sigma_u^2}.$$

The proof is in the appendix.

3 Constant Gain Learning

Constant gain learning rules are particularly attractive when the variable being forecast has a changing distribution, making it attractive to give more weight to recent data. In the example of section 1, where $p_t = x + a p_t^e + u_t$ and $p_t^e = \bar{p}_{t-1}$, the model converges to rational expectations equilibrium. Agents may be tempted to use a constant gain learning rule of the form

$$p_t^e = p_{t-1}^e + \gamma(p_{t-1} - p_{t-1}^e).$$

This implies that

$$p_t = x + a p_t^e + u_t$$

$$= x + a(p_{t-1}^e + \gamma(p_{t-1} - p_{t-1}^e)) + u_t$$

so

$$p_{t+1}^e = p_t^e + \gamma(p_t - p_t^e)$$

$$= \gamma(x + a p_t^e + u_t) + (1 - \gamma)p_t^e$$

implying that

$$p_{t+1}^e - \frac{x}{1-a} = (1 - \gamma(1-a))\left(p_t^e - \frac{x}{1-a}\right) + \gamma u_t. \tag{7}$$

Iterating this equation implies that

$$p_{t+1}^e - \frac{x}{1-a} = \gamma \sum_{j=0}^{t}(1 - \gamma(1-a))^j u_{t-j} + (1 - \gamma(1-a))^t\left(p_0^e - \frac{x}{1-a}\right).$$

Assuming that $\{u_t\}$ is a sequence of independent and identically distributed random variables with $E u_t = 0$ and $\operatorname{var} u_t = \sigma^2$ for all t and taking expectations gives

$$E p_{t+1}^e - \frac{x}{1-a} = (1 - \gamma(1-a))^t\left(E p_0^e - \frac{x}{1-a}\right)$$

so if $-1 < (1 - \gamma(1-a)) < 1$ $E p_t^e$ tends to $x/(1-a)$. Also

$$E\left(p_{t+1}^e - \frac{x}{1-a}\right)^2$$

$$= \gamma^2 \sum_{j=0}^{t}(1 - \gamma(1-a))^{2j}\sigma^2 + (1 - \gamma(1-a))^{2t}E\left(p_0^e - \frac{x}{1-a}\right)^2$$

implying that if $-1 < (1 - \gamma(1 - a)) < 1$ var p_t^e tends to $\gamma^2\sigma^2/$
$(1 - (1 - \gamma(1 - a))^2)$. Thus in the limit p_t^e has a covariance stationary distribution with mean $x/(1 - a)$ if $0 < \gamma(1 - a) < 2$. Assuming
that the gain γ is positive, this condition cannot be satisfied unless
$1 > a$, in which case it is satisfied if $\gamma < 2/(1 - a)$.

As

$$p_{t+1} - \frac{x}{1 - a} = a\left(p_{t+1}^e - \frac{x}{1 - a}\right) + u_{t+1},$$

equation 7 implies that

$$p_{t+1} - \frac{x}{1 - a} = (1 - \gamma(1 - a))\left(p_t - \frac{x}{1 - a}\right) - (1 - \gamma)u_t + u_{t+1}.$$

Thus the price follows an ARMA(1,2) process. With this learning
process the expected price does not converge to the rational expectations value $x/(1 - a)$. In the limit $Ep_t^e = Ep_t = x/(1 - a)$, the
unconditional expectation of both the price and the price expectation are at their rational expectations value. Expectations, however, do not converge to rational expectations. Using a constant
gain or adaptive learning rule rather than a learning rule with a decreasing gain $\gamma_t = 1/t$ prevents convergence to rational expectations
equilibrium.

These examples suggest that the relationship between rational and
adaptive expectations is delicate. There are circumstances in which
rational expectations are adaptive. In the example here this occurs
when intercept x_t follows a random walk rather than being constant. More generally, as Evans and Honkapohja point out, forming
adaptive expectations, that is using a constant gain, or equivalently
giving more weight to more recent data, is appropriate when
parameters change through time. But if parameters are in fact constant, giving equal weights to past and present data, so using a
decreasing gain, makes convergence possible, in this case convergence to the rational expectations equilibrium. In models such as this
one, where expectations affect outcomes, there is the further compli-
cation that using constant gain learning methods, in a situation where
decreasing gain learning would converge to rational expectations,
induces persistent dynamics, which might themselves encourage
agents to use constant gain learning processes.

4 Learning and Bounded Rationality

The idea that agents forecast using the most basic of textbook econometrics, averages or ordinary least squares did not have any deep theoretical or empirical justification; it simply appealed to the fact that econometrics is in reality used to generate forecasts. Moreover, the statement that "agents behave like econometricians" has no content without some assumptions on the specification of the models agents are working with. Even nonparametric statistics involves assumptions about which variables are relevant. The key feature of the econometric learning models I worked with is that agents use specifications that would be correct in rational expectations equilibrium. This is essential for convergence to the rational expectations equilibrium. If agents rule out the rational expectations equilibrium, they will never learn it. If the econometrics is interpreted in Bayesian fashion, the rational expecations equilibrium must be in the support of the initial prior. Because agents' expectations affect the data-generation process, learning changes the dynamics of the model, so a specification that would be correct in rational expecatations equilibrium is incorrect when agents are learning. Standard results on convergence of estimators do not apply. Nevertheless, it is possible to obtain convergence results.

If we take full rationality as meaning that agents work with correctly specified models, the econometric learning literature embraces a form of bounded rationality. I expected, but never encountered, difficulties with seminar audiences and referees over this approach to learning. Perhaps the appeal is that the learning processes I studied did not move very far from rational expectations in the sense that they included the rational expectations equlibrium in the model specification and converged to rational expectations for appropriate parameter values. David Kreps and I worked with an approach to learning that embedded agents' inference problems in a more elaborate rational expectations equlibrium (Bray and Kreps 1987). This approach avoided bounded rationality altogether, but it begged the question of how agents learned what they needed to know to work in the more elaborate equilibrium.

A major limitation of the econometric learning literature is its mechanical view of how econometric learning proceeds. Agents simply run ordinary least squares. In reality, econmetricians test their models and experiment with model specification. With rapid convergence to rational expectations equilibrium, the transient mis-specification induced by the the learning process may well escape notice. So the speed of convergence is important, but seems very difficult to get analytical results on. Gene Savin and I (Bray and Savin 1986) used computer simulation to look at convergence rates and specification, and we found unsurpisingly that they depended upon the distance of the intial prior from the rational expectations value and the weight given to the intial prior.

Rational expectations equilibrium, and the closely related concept of Nash equilibrium in a game, have remained and I expect will remain the most widely used means of handling beliefs and expectations in mathematically formulated economic models. Without the mathematical formulation it would be impossible to implement the concepts. But as the examples in this chapter demonstrate, whether or not a rule for forming expectations corresponds to rational expectations, all the time or in the limit, depends crucially on context. Rational expectations are right in context. The great difficulty for real-world decision making is that, unlike actors in models, we do not know what the context is. Hence, I think the increasing interest in psychologically based and behavioral economics (Rabin 1998, Shleifer 2000).

Appendix

Proof of Proposition 1

Iterating equation 3 gives

$$\bar{p}_t - \frac{x}{1-a} = \prod_{i=T+1}^{t} \left(1 - \frac{1-a}{i}\right)\left(\bar{p}_T - \frac{x}{1-a}\right) + z_{Tt}, \tag{A1}$$

where

$$z_{Tt} = \sum_{i=T+1}^{t-1} \prod_{j=i+1}^{t} \left(1 - \frac{1-a}{j}\right)\frac{1}{i}u_i + \frac{1}{t}u_t. \tag{A2}$$

If T is sufficiently large $(1 - (1-a)/i) > 0$ for all $i > T$ so $\ln(1 - (1-a)/i)$ is real valued. As $\ln(1+y)$ is a concave function with value 0 and slope 1 at $y = 0$ $\ln(1+y) \leq y$, so letting $y = (1-a)/i$ gives

$$\ln\left(\prod_{i=T+1}^{t}\left(1-\frac{1-a}{i}\right)\right) = \sum_{i=T+1}^{t}\ln\left(1-\frac{1-a}{i}\right) \leq -\sum_{i=T+1}^{t}\frac{1-a}{i}.$$

If $1 > a$ the right-hand side of this inequality tends to minus infinity as t tends to infinity, which implies that

$$\lim_{t\to\infty}\prod_{i=T+1}^{t}\left(1-\frac{1-a}{i}\right) = 0.$$

Thus the first term on the right-hand side of A1 tends to zero almost surely. To prove that the second term tends to zero define a sequence w_{Tt} by $w_{TT} = 0$ and

$$w_{Tt} = z_{Tt} - \sum_{i=T+1}^{t}\frac{1}{i}u_i. \tag{A4}$$

Equations A2 and A4 imply that

$$w_{Tt} = \left(1-\frac{1-a}{t}\right)w_{Tt-1} - \frac{1}{t}(1-a)\sum_{i=T+1}^{t-1}\frac{u_i}{i}.$$

Thus using the triangle inequality if $1 > a$ and T is large enough that $1 - (1-a)/t > 0$ for all $t > T$

$$|w_{Tt}| \leq \left(1-\frac{1-a}{t}\right)|w_{Tt-1}| + \frac{1}{t}(1-a)\left|\sum_{i=T+1}^{t-1}\frac{u_i}{i}\right|.$$

A simple induction argument implies that, as $w_{TT} = 0$, given any $\varepsilon > 0$, if

$$\left|\sum_{i=T+1}^{r}\frac{u_i}{i}\right| < \frac{\varepsilon}{2} \quad \text{for all } r > T,$$

then $|w_{Tt}| < \varepsilon/2$ for all $t > T$, and so from equation A4 $|z_{Tt}| < \varepsilon$ for all $T > t$. The next step uses Kolmogorov's inequality which states that if $y_1, y_2 \ldots y_n$ are independent random variables with $Ey_i = 0$ and $Ey_i^2 < \infty$, then for all $\eta > 0$

$$P(|y_1 + y_2 \ldots + y_r| > \eta \text{ for some } r) \leq \eta^{-2}\sum_{r=1}^{n}\text{var}(y_r).$$

Thus as $\{u_t\}$ is a sequence of independent random variables with $Eu_t = 0$ and $\text{var}\, u_t = \sigma^2$ if T is sufficiently large since

$$P\left(\left|\sum_{i=T+1}^{r}\frac{u_i}{i}\right| > \frac{\varepsilon}{2} \text{ for some } r > T\right) \leq \frac{4}{\varepsilon^2}\sum_{i=T+1}^{\infty}\frac{\sigma^2}{i^2}.$$

The right-hand side of this inequality tends to zero as T tends to infinity. Thus given any $\delta > 0$ by choosing T sufficiently large

$$P\left(\left|\sum_{i=T+1}^{r}\frac{u_i}{i}\right| < \frac{\varepsilon}{2} \text{ for all } r > T\right) > 1 - \delta$$

and so

$$p(|z_{Tt}| < \varepsilon \text{ for all } t > T) > 1 - \delta.$$

Taken together with A1, A2, and A3, this proves the result.

Proof of Proposition 2

Let $\mu_{t-1} = E_{t-1}x_{t-1}$ and $\sigma^2_{t-1} = \text{var}_{t-1}\,x_{t-1}$. As

$$p_t = x_t + ap_t^e + u_t \tag{A5}$$

$$p_t^e = E_{t-1}p_t = \frac{1}{1-a}E_{t-1}x_t = \frac{\mu_{t-1}}{1-a} \tag{A6}$$

and using the formula for a conditional normal distribution

$$E_t x_t = \mu_t = E_{t-1}x_t + \theta_t(p_t - E_{t-1}p_t)$$

$$= \mu_{t-1} + \theta_t(p_t - E_{t-1}p_t), \tag{A7}$$

where

$$\theta_t = \frac{\text{cov}_{t-1}(x_t, p_t)}{\text{var}_{t-1}\,p_t}$$

and

$$\sigma^2_t = \text{var}_{t-1}\,x_t - \frac{[\text{cov}_{t-1}(x_t, p_t)]^2}{\text{var}_{t-1}(p_t)}.$$

As

$$x_t = x_{t-1} + e_t,$$

$\text{var}_{t-1}\,x_t = \sigma^2_{t-1} + \sigma^2_e$. As $p_t^e = E_{t-1}p_t$ is known at $t-1$ equation A5 implies that $\text{cov}_{t-1}(x_t, p_t) = \text{var}_{t-1}\,x_t = \sigma^2_{t-1} + \sigma^2_e$ and $\text{var}_{t-1}(p_t) = \text{var}_{t-1}(x_t + u_t) = \sigma^2_{t-1} + \sigma^2_e + \sigma^2_u$. Hence

$$\theta_t = \frac{\sigma_{t-1}^2 + \sigma_e^2}{\sigma_{t-1}^2 + \sigma_e^2 + \sigma_u^2}$$

and

$$\sigma_t^2 = \sigma_{t-1}^2 + \sigma_e^2 - \frac{(\sigma_{t-1}^2 + \sigma_e^2)^2}{\sigma_{t-1}^2 + \sigma_e^2 + \sigma_u^2} = \frac{(\sigma_{t-1}^2 + \sigma_e^2)\sigma_u^2}{\sigma_{t-1}^2 + \sigma_e^2 + \sigma_u^2} \tag{A8}$$

Thus from A6 and A7

$$p_{t+1}^e = E_t p_{t+1} = \frac{\mu_t}{1-a} = \frac{\mu_{t-1}}{1-a} + \frac{\theta_t}{1-a}(p_t - E_{t-1}p_t)$$

$$= p_t^e + \gamma_t(p_t - p_t^e),$$

where $\gamma_t = \theta_t/(1-a)$.

The limit for γ_t is obtained by showing that σ_t^2 tends to σ^{*2} where σ^{*2} satisfies

$$\sigma^{*2} = \frac{(\sigma^{*2} + \sigma_e^2)\sigma_u^2}{\sigma^{*2} + \sigma_e^2 + \sigma_u^2}. \tag{A9}$$

From A8 and A9

$$|\sigma_t^2 - \sigma^{*2}| = \left| \frac{(\sigma_{t-1}^2 + \sigma_e^2)\sigma_u^2}{\sigma_{t-1}^2 + \sigma_e^2 + \sigma_u^2} - \frac{(\sigma^{*2} + \sigma_e^2)\sigma_u^2}{\sigma^{*2} + \sigma_e^2 + \sigma_u^2} \right|$$

$$= \left(\frac{\sigma_u^2}{\sigma_{t-1}^2 + \sigma_e^2 + \sigma_u^2} \right) \left(\frac{\sigma_u^2}{\sigma^{*2} + \sigma_e^2 + \sigma_u^2} \right) |\sigma_{t-1}^2 - \sigma^{*2}|$$

$$< \alpha |\sigma_{t-1}^2 - \sigma^{*2}|,$$

where

$$\alpha = \frac{\sigma_u^2}{\sigma^{*2} + \sigma_e^2 + \sigma_u^2}.$$

Thus as $0 < \alpha < 1$, σ_t^2 tends to σ^{*2},

$$\lim_{t \to \infty} \theta_t = \frac{\sigma_{t-1}^2 + \sigma_e^2}{\sigma_{t-1}^2 + \sigma_e^2 + \sigma_u^2} = \frac{\sigma^{*2} + \sigma_e^2}{\sigma^{*2} + \sigma_e^2 + \sigma_u^2} = \frac{\sigma^{*2}}{\sigma_u^2}$$

and

$$\lim_{t \to \infty} \gamma_t = \frac{\sigma^{*2}}{(1-a)\sigma_u^2}.$$

References

Bray, M. 1982. "Learning, Estimation and the Stability of Rational Expectations." *Journal of Economic Theory* 26:318–339.

Bray, M. 1983. "Convergence to Rational Expectations Equilibrium," in *Individual Forecasting and Aggregate Outcomes*, ed. R. Frydman and E. S. Phelps. Cambridge: Cambridge University Press.

Bray, M., and D. M. Kreps. 1987. "Rational Learning and Rational Expectations," in *Arrow and the Ascent of Modern Economic Theory*, ed. G. R. Feiwel, 597–628. New York: New York University Press.

Bray, M., and N. Savin. 1986. "Rational Expectations Equilibria, Learning and Model Specification." *Econometrica* 54:1129–1160.

Evans, G. W. 1989. "The Fragility of Sunspots and Bubbles," *Journal of Monetary Economics* 23:297–317.

Evans, G. W., and S. Honkapohja. 2001. *Learning and Expectations in Macroeconomics.* Princeton University Press.

Ljung, L. 1977. "Analysis of Recursive Stochastic Algorithms." *IEEE Transactions on Automatic Control* 22:551–575.

Marcet, A., and T. J. Sargent. 1989. "Convergence of Least Squares Learning in Environments with Hidden State Variables and Private Information." *Journal of Political Economy* 97:1306–1322.

Muth, J. F. 1961. "Rational Expectations and the Theory of Price Movements." *Econometrica* 29:315–335.

Rabin, M. 1998. "Psychology and Economics." *Journal of Economic Literature* 36:11–46.

Shleifer, A. 2000. *Inefficient Markets: An Introduction to Behavioral Finance.* New York: Oxford University Press.

Woodford, M. 1990. "Learning to Believe in Sunspots." *Econometrica* 58:277–307.

8 Regulating Nonlinear Environmental Systems under Knightian Uncertainty

William Brock and
Anastasios Xepapadeas

Stiglitz has recently been active in questioning standard approaches to policy making such as the "Washington Consensus" and thinking about alternatives to it (Stiglitz 1998a,b). It is fair to say that his critiques have stimulated valuable controversy and debate. Prestigious economists have weighed in on both sides of the debate. The reader will find much discussion of this issue in a brief search on the Internet. His paper (Stiglitz 1998a) examines financial instabilities and the role played by incomplete and imperfect capital markets during financial liberalizations. Economists argue vigorously about the relative roles played by market imperfections and government imperfections in causing financial instabilities. His Prebisch Lecture (Stiglitz 1998b) goes further and not only challenges much of conventional development policy but also proposes rather major modifications. One analytical and potentially econometrically tractable way of thinking about such disputes is to use concepts of scientific model uncertainty.

An intelligent policymaker might operate in the face of scientific model uncertainty by using concepts from econometrics like Bayesian model averaging coupled with recent advances in decision theory such as modeling "Knightian uncertainty." This approach was taken by Brock and Durlauf (2001) in an attempt to constructively critique policy applications of empirical growth analysis and to suggest a modified approach that is still empirically disciplined. The idea is to first objectively represent the amount of scientific uncertainty in what we can learn from empirical exercises when there are levels of uncertainty present, such as theory uncertainty and model uncertainty, above and beyond the usual sampling uncertainty in parameter estimates for a given model. This "true" amount of uncertainty is typically larger than representations of uncertainty in conventional econometric studies. Second, given levels of uncertainty that must be faced by the policymaker, the policymaker should indulge in "robust" policy making that appropriately makes some attempt to hedge against worst cases as well as maximize the usual estimated net benefit.

This chapter illustrates how the conceptualization of Knightian uncertainty can be applied to the classic problem of regulating human impacted ecosystems and how it can lead to a type of precautionary principle. Stiglitz has written extensively in the environmental area. For example, we believe that a version of his pair of classical papers on growth and exhaustible resources (Stiglitz 1974a,b) could be extended to include stochastic shocks and model uncertainty about the impact of human activities upon the regenerative power of the ecosystem as well as uncertainty about the elasticity of substitution between ecosystem inputs and human produced inputs into the economic process. In such an extension of Stiglitz's work, one could develop a policy analysis framework under Knightian uncertainty that could lead to potentially useful conceptions of macrogrowth precautionary principles as well as useful insights into the interaction among uncertainties in different parts of the system.

An example of what this approach might look like is Pizer (1996), except that we would add uncertainty about the elasticity of substitution between inputs and, especially, nonlinear regeneration dynamics for the ecosystem that allow multiple stable states for appropriate parameter values. In this way Pizer's Bayesian analysis would allow data to speak to these uncertainties as well as the uncertainties that he models. We believe this kind of analysis would help explain which uncertainties matter the most and how scientific resources should be allocated across attempts to reduce uncertainties. This chapter makes a very modest start on this challenging project by considering optimal management of a human impacted ecosystem under deterministic nonlinear ecosystem dynamics under Knightian uncertainty.

Thus, this chapter considers an environmental system where many agents (e.g., countries) contribute to the accumulation of a pollutant with global characteristics (e.g., greenhouse gasses). We analyze cooperative and noncooperative solutions under uncertainty associated with the process of pollution accumulation. The presence of nonlinear feedbacks in the natural system could result in multiple steady state equilibria. The novelty in our approach lies in that we: (1) seek to explore situations with a potential heterogeneity in risk aversion between a regulator, acting as a Stackelberg leader that seeks to implement a cooperative solution, and individual agents that behave in a noncooperative way; and (2) analyze the implications of this heterogeneity for regulation when nonlinear dynamics could steer the dynamic system toward alternative basins of attraction.

Heterogeneity in risk aversion is a possibility that appears once we start considering as a possible way to model uncertainty the ideas of the "least favorable prior" decision theory (Gilboa and Schmeidler 1989), which results in the use of maximin expected utility theory. Sims (2001), for example, hints at this heterogeneity by indicating that the same maximin criterion should not be imposed on private agents and optimizing policymakers.

Here, heterogeneity in risk aversion is introduced in the following way. In the cooperative solution, the regulator faces Knightian uncertainty, which is of the e-contamination type (Epstein and Wang 1994). Here is a simplified form of e-contamination that will serve as a preview. The regulator computes expected utility for each of k models, attaches probability p_k to each model k (typically by using available evidence and something like a Bayesian procedure), and chooses a regulatory instrument to maximize a weighted sum of the form

$$(1 - e) \sum_k p_k E_k U_k(a) + e \min_k E_k U_k(a),$$

where $E_k U_k(a)$ is the expected utility of action a under model k, p_k is the (posterior) probability of model k, and e is a weight between zero and one. The regulator attaches weight e to the "worst case" and weight $1 - e$ to the conventional expected utility and chooses a regulatory action, a, to maximize this weighted sum. Another way of thinking about it is that the regulator believes "nature" is "mean" with probability "e" and "benign" with probability "$1 - e$". When "e" is positive, we say that the regulator is "first-order risk averse." At the risk of repeating, heterogeneity in risk aversion here is of the following form. In the cooperative solution, the regulator is first-order risk averse. In the noncooperative solution the agents are "second-order risk averse" and are expected utility maximizers.[1]

This heterogeneity could be defended along different lines. A regulator could face a dynamical system with at least two different time

scales with unobservables at a slow time scale that can cause bifur-
cations. These unobservable slow-moving dynamics may or may not
be influenced by responses of the regulatees to controls chosen by
the regulator. In any event, these unobservable dynamics can cause
flips to undesirable steady states,[2] which hurt the regulator's objective. It would be interesting but complex to formalize this interaction
between time scales, unobservable slow moving bifurcational dynamics, multiple stable states in the fast moving dynamics, and the
regulator's information set being coarser than the regulatees' information set, which influences the dynamics that the regulator is
attempting to control. Here, we abstract away this complexity by
positing that the regulator, a Stackelberg leader, views a problem as
facing a regulatory objective that is e-contaminated Knightian.

Another line of approach could be to consider the case where the
regulator's employment contract and its incentive schedule are "as
if" the regulator gets punished more severely if something unusual
happens in response to an instrument choice than if something opposite in sign that is positive happens. To protect against this possibility, the regulator could operate under the "least favorable prior",
implying uncertainty aversion.

Using an open loop, most rapid approach path (MRAP) concept[3]
as the equilibrium concept for the noncooperative solution, we show
that the deviation between the cooperative optimal steady state
(OSS) and the noncooperative OSS can be broken down into two
components: one which is due to the public bad externality of the
global pollutant, while the other is due to the heterogeneity in risk
aversion between regulator and agents. The second effect can be
identified as a precautionary effect. Thus the regulatory instrument
should account both for the public bad externality and the uncertainty aversion effect, which implies that under heterogeneity in the
type of risk aversion regulation is more stringent.

Finally, we examine regulation when the regulator faces random
shocks to the initial values of the regulated system that can move the
system to an undesired basin of attraction. We derive the optimal regulation in a framework where the parameters of the e-contamination
in Knightian uncertainty are *endogenized*. Thus, at a second level
our contribution to the literature here is having the e-contamination
parameter and the implied worst case outcome *derived* from the
underlying structure of the problem rather than imposed in a some-

what ad hoc matter which has been the most common way of handling Knightian uncertainty of the e-contamination type.

1 The Cooperative Solution

There are $i = 1, \ldots, n$ players (e.g., countries) that emit pollutant a_i per unit time with global effects. Gross benefits from a_i are pa_i where p is some fixed price (small countries, small players). The environmental cost of the accumulated pollutant for player i is $c_i(x), c_i' > 0$, $c_i'' > 0$. The pollutant accumulates according to

$$\dot{x} = \sum_{i=1}^{n} a_i - bx + f(x), x(0) = x_0, \quad x \in X \subset \mathscr{R}_+, \tag{1}$$

where $f(x)$ is a nonnegative, increasing, convexo-concave and bounded, twice differentiable function, with $f(0) = 0, f'(0) = f'(\infty) = 0$ reflecting the nonlinearity associated with feedbacks of the natural system.

The cooperative problem assuming symmetric players is

$$\max \int_0^\infty e^{-\rho t}[pa - nc(x)]\, dt \sum_{i=1}^{n} a_i = a, \text{ s.t.(1) and } 0 \le a \le a^{\max}. \tag{2}$$

Equation (1) can be written as $a = \dot{x} + bx - f(x)$. Substituting into (2), the problem can be rewritten in the MRAP formulation as

$$\max_a \int_0^\infty e^{-\rho t}[p(bx - f(x)) - nc(x) + \rho px]\, dt, \text{ s.t. } 0 \le x \le x^{\max}. \tag{3}$$

The cooperative OSS is determined by

$$\max_a W(x, b) = \max_a [p(bx - f(x)) - nc(x) + \rho px]. \tag{4}$$

with first-order necessary conditions (FONC)

$$p(b + \rho - f'(x)) = nc'(x). \tag{5}$$

We assume that $\max[W(x, b)]/\rho$ (which is just the value implied by (3)) is an adequate approximation to the true value $V(b|x_0)$ defined by (2) for initial condition x_0 in a closed interval containing $x^* = \operatorname{argmax}\{W(x, b)\}$. This assumption is maintained for all parameter values in the discussion that follows until otherwise noted.

This approximation will tend to be better the more negative is $g(x) = -bx + f(x)$ between x_0 and $x^* = \text{argmax}\{W(x, b)\}$ and the larger is $a^{\max}$ in (2). Of course this approximation can be poor if there is an x_{trap} such that $g(x_{trap}) < 0$, $x_0 > x_{trap}$, $x^* < x_{trap}$ and W falls off rapidly enough for $x \geq x_{trap}$. Suppose a unique global maximum solution $x^c = x^*$ to (4) exists. Then the approach to the cooperative optimal steady state is according to

$$a = 0 \qquad\qquad\qquad \text{if } x > x^c$$

$$a = bx^c - f(x^c) \qquad \text{if } x = x^c \tag{6}$$

$$a = a^{\max} \qquad\qquad\quad \text{if } x < x^c$$

Given the nonlinearity in transition equation (1), the first-order condition (5) might have more than one solution. Brock and Starrett (1999) determine conditions under which there is an odd number of solutions for (5). Therefore,

$$\text{if } -[pf''(x^c) + nc''(x^c)] \quad \begin{array}{l} < 0 \\ \text{then} \\ > 0 \end{array} \quad \begin{array}{l} x^c \text{ local maximum} \\ \\ x^c \text{ local minimum} \end{array} \tag{7}$$

This is shown in figure 8.1. The OSSs are defined by the intersection of the R curve and the C curve. Local maxima are (x_{r1}^c, x_{r3}^c) and local minimum is x_{r2}^c.

If we assume an adjustment mechanism in the neighborhood of the OSS of the form $\dot{x} = \phi[p(b + \rho - f'(x)) - nc'(x)]$, $\phi > 0$ it is clear that since the slope at any equilibrium point x^c is given by (7), local maxima are locally stable equilibria, while local minima are locally unstable. Given the properties of f, the curve $R(x) = p(b + \rho - f'(x))$ satisfies $R(0) = R(\infty) = p(b + \rho)$, while the curve $C(x, n) = nc'(x)$ satisfies $C(0, n) = 0$, $C' > 0$. Hence, there is $\bar{n}$ such that $n > \bar{n}$ implies that there is only one intersection of C with R, C intersects R from below, and (7) is strictly negative at this unique intersection. In this case only one globally stable OSS exists. Therefore, cooperation of many players acts as a stabilizer and could eliminate multiple equilibria. This is shown in figure 8.1 where the C_m curve drawn for $n_m > \bar{n}$ intersects R only once at F to define a unique OSS.

Suppose that the planner managing the cooperative solution faces Knightian uncertainty about the parameters of the natural system. Assume that the uncertainty for b—that is, uncertainty about the self-cleaning process in a shallow lake where phosphorus accu-

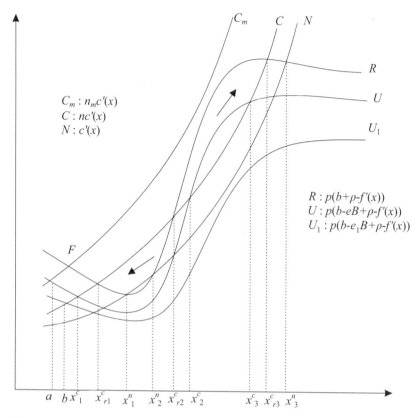

Figure 8.1
Cooperative and noncooperative equilibrium

mulates, or about the CO_2 absorption capability of oceans—is of the
e-contamination type $P(e) = (1 - e)b + em$, $m \in M(B)$, where b represents a point mass of unity at b and M represents the entire set of
probability measures with support $[b - B, b + B]$. This relates to a
major theme in Stiglitz's recent work mentioned in the introduction.
He argues, for example, that conventional policymakers may not be
using the right models. Think of "b" as the "consensus model," and
think of him as arguing for models represented by measures with
most mass concentrated on $b - B$, and some of his critics as arguing
for models represented by measures concentrated towards $b + B$.
How might a Knightian policymaker act when faced by the debate
among experts unleashed by him (e.g., Stiglitz's book 2002). One
way she might act is given by equation (8).

Following Epstein and Wang (1994, 288, eq. (2.3.1), (2.3.2)) we assume the planner wishes to choose total emissions a to maximize $W(x, b)$. Then the e-contamination MRAP problem under Knightian uncertainty is to maximize

$$\int W dP(e) = (1 - e)W(b, x) + e \lfloor \inf \int W(x, b) \, dm \rfloor. \tag{8}$$

It can be shown by using the envelope theorem in (4) that $W(x, b)$ is increasing in b. Since M contains all probability measures over b values with support $[b - B, b + B]$, then (8) can be written as

$$\max_x \int W dP(e) = \max_x [(1 - e)W(x, b) + eW(x, b - B)]. \tag{9}$$

The equivalent to FONC (5) under Knightian uncertainty is

$$p(b - eB + \rho - f'(x)) = nc'(x). \tag{10}$$

By comparing (5) to (10) the following result can be stated.

PROPOSITION 1 Under uncertainty aversion the regulator is first-order risk averse for all the local maxima $x^c(e)$ of the welfare maximization problem (8), and it holds that $(dx^c(e))/de < 0$. Under risk aversion the regulator is second-order risk averse and $(dx^c(e))/de = 0$. For proof and precise definition of second-order risk averse see the appendix.[4]

In terms of figure 8.1 the solution for the first-order risk averse regulator is given by the intersections of the U curve with the C curve. Local maxima are (x_1^c, x_3^c) and local minimum is x_2^c. On the other hand, the solution for a second-order risk averse regulator is given by the intersections of the R curve and the C curve. The deviations $x_{1r}^c - x_1^c$ and $x_{3r}^c - x_3^c$ can be characterized as the reductions in the socially optimal steady state for the accumulation of the pollutant due to precautionary effect.

It can also be noted in the same figure that if e or B are sufficiently large such that $p(b - eB + \rho - f'(x))$ shifts further down like curve U_1, then there is only one globally stable OSS for the uncertainty averse regulator at b. In this case uncertainty aversion eliminates multiple equilibria and directs the system toward the smallest concentration of the pollutant. This effect is not, however, present when the regulator is second-order risk averse.

2 The Noncooperative Solution

In the noncooperative case, each player (country) i maximizes its own payoff given the best response $\bar{a}_j$ of the rest of the $j \neq i$ players. Thus each player solves the open loop problem

$$\max_{a_i} \int_0^\infty e^{-\rho t}[pa_i - c(x)]\,dt$$

$$\text{s.t. } \dot{x} = a_i + \sum_{j \neq i}^n \bar{a}_j - bx + f(x), \quad 0 \leq a_i \leq a^{\max} \tag{11}$$

Because players are symmetric, a_i is the same for all i. Using the MRAP formulation the noncooperative OSS is determined under symmetry by

$$\max_x W^i(x,b) = \max_x \left[p\left(bx - \sum_{j \neq i}^n \bar{a}_j - f(x)\right) - c(x) - \rho p x \right] \quad \forall i \tag{11$'$}$$

with FONC

$$p(b + \rho - f'(x)) = c'(x). \tag{12}$$

If a solution x^n to (12) exists, then the approach to the non-cooperative locally stable OSS follows a MRAP. Furthermore, as in the cooperative case, local maxima are locally stable and local minima are locally unstable.

By comparing (5) to (12) the public bad type of externality characterizing the global pollutant can be easily identified through the $nc'(c)$ term. Then the well-known result that the pollutant accumulation at the noncooperative solution exceeds the pollutant accumulation at the cooperative solution immediately follows. As shown in figure 8.1, where the two solutions are compared, the C curve shifts down to the N curve for the noncooperative case, and the solution is determined by the intersection of the N curve with the R curve.

Suppose $\tilde{b} = b + e\omega$ where ω is a mean zero random variable with support on $[b - B, b + B]$ for B such that $b - B > 0$. Also suppose that the approximation $V(b', x_0) = \max[W(x, b')]/\rho$ is good for all $b' = b + e\omega$ for all initial conditions x_0 in a compact interval centered at x^*. Under this assumption we saw in proposition 1 that this mean preserving spread in b has no effect on the social optimal x^*. The same argument shows that it has no effect on individual players' choice of optimal x. Then, each player solves the problem $\max_x EW^i(x, b + e\omega)$ with FONC $p(b + \rho - f'(x)) = c'(x)$.

The deviation between the cooperative and the noncooperative solutions, as shown in figure 1 for the two locally stable OSSs, is $x_3^n - x_3^c, x_1^n - x_1^c$. This deviation can be broken into two parts, attributed to two different sources:

1. The public bad externality $PB = (x_1^n - x_{r1}^c)$ or $(x_3^n - x_{r3}^c)$ due to the shift of the C curve to the N curve.

2. The uncertainty aversion effect $U = (x_{r3}^c - x_3^c)$ or $(x_{r1}^c - x_1^c)$ due to the shift of the R curve to the U curve. This effect can be identified as a precautionary effect stemming from the fact that the regulator is uncertainty averse with respect to the values of the natural system.

Regulation that seeks to attain the socially optimal outcome should correct for both the public bad externality and the heterogeneity in risk aversion effect.

3   Regulation[5]

The regulator seeks to implement the cooperative OSS, x^c, using a linear tax τ on emissions. Then, the noncooperative OSS under regulation is determined as

$$\max_x W^i(x, b, \tau) = \max_x \left[(p - \tau)\left((b + \rho)x - \sum_{j \neq i}^n \bar{a}_j - f(x) \right) - c(x) \right] \quad (13)$$

The FONC imply that the optimal τ should be chosen so that

$$(p - \tau)(b + \rho - f'(x)) - c'(x) = 0 \text{ implies } x = x_i^c, \quad i = 1, 3 \quad (13)'$$

The tax impact is determined in the following proposition.

PROPOSITION 2   Let x_i^n be an unregulated noncooperative steady state $(\tau = 0)$. Then $(dx_i^n/d\tau) < 0$ if x_i^n is locally stable (local maximum), and $(dx_i^n/d\tau) > 0$ if x_i^n is locally unstable (local minimum). (For proof see the appendix.)

Assume first that the regulator's objective is the sum of individual objectives and that the regulator wants to implement x_{r1}^c, which is the global social optimum (figure 8.1). If we set τ such that $p - \tau = p/n$, it is easy to see that x_{r1}^c is Nash equilibrium. This is so because the relevant part of each Nash player's objective function is proportional to $W(x,b)$ under this value of τ, or $W^i(x,b,\tau) = (1/n)W(x,b)$. The R curve shifts downward until it intersects the N curve at the point corresponding to x_{r1}^c. Assume second that the regulator has Knightian objective $W(x,b,eB)$ given by (9). Then the regulator wishes to implement a lower value of x, i.e. x_1^c in figure 8.1 than that implementable in Nash equilibrium with $p - \tau = p/n$. While it is beyond our scope here to give a thorough treatment it appears that, in many cases, a value of τ can be found such that the regulator's target x^* can be implemented via Nash equilibrium. For the Knightian objective it can be shown after combining (10) and (13') that the implementing τ^* should satisfy $(p - \tau^*)/p = c'(x_1^c)/[nc'(x_1^c) + epB]$.

Now drop the assumption that $V(b|x_0)$ can be well approximated by $\max[W(x,b')]/\rho$ so that the initial condition matters. It is beyond our scope here to do a full analysis, but one can show that if the regulator's objective is the sum of the individual players' objectives, then each Nash player solving problem (13) subject to $0 \le a_i \le a^{\max}$ ends up implementing the social objective in "open loop" dynamic Nash equilibrium if $p - \tau = p/n$. This is so because the x-dependent part of (13) is proportional to the social optimization problem. Hence, since the same limits $0 \le a_i \le a^{\max}$ are on each of the n Nash players as on each of the n agents in the social problem, the same optimal path, $x(.)$ will be chosen by (13) as open-loop dynamic Nash equilibrium as will be chosen by the collective of n socially optimally coordinated agents.

It appears to be possible to create examples where there are two types of agents so that one instrument τ potentially cannot hit two targets which are needed to implement social optimum. Suppose costs are given by $c_i(x) = (1/2)B_i x^2$, $i = 1, 2, B_1 > B_2$. Put $p_1 = p_2 = p$ and let $n = n_1 + n_2$. Call 1's, "greens" and call 2's, "browns." Greens and browns value income from loadings at p per unit, but greens are hurt more than browns by the ecosystem damages caused by x. Social welfare is the discounted sum of $p(n_1 a_1 + n_2 a_2) - c_1(x) - c_2(x)$. Greens have desired $x_1 < x_2$, which is the brown's desired x. To find an illustrative example, go to the extreme and make B_2 almost zero so that x_2 is huge. Thus, socially optimal x_1 is chosen close to the value of a problem with $n = n_1, B = B_1$, so we would try to implement that value with Nash equilibrium by choosing $\tau = p(1 - 1/n_1)$. But 2's facing this τ would get a net of p/n_1 for each unit of loading and would choose a huge x. Hence their Nash "best reply" would over-brown the lake at this τ. But if you lowered τ to induce the browns toward a lower x, the greens would over-green the lake. This speculation suggests that another instrument is needed to implement social optimum.

Also note about regulation that if there is an x_{trap} such that $-bx_{trap} + f(x_{trap}) < 0$ while the target of regulation is $x^* < x_{trap}$, then the target cannot be achieved for any initial state $x_0 > x_{trap}$. This is the result of irreversibility once the state of the system exceeds x_{trap}, which is induced by the nonlinearity of the natural system.

3.1   Regulation under Large Rare Shocks

In trying to develop a general theory of regulation with multiple basins of attraction, we consider now the possibility that large rare random shocks could move initial conditions from one basin of attraction to the other. It is clear that optimal regulation should take into account such an event.

Let q denote the probability that a large shock moves the initial value $x(0) = x^0$ of our system to the high pollutant accumulation basin of attraction. To expose the effects of large rare shocks in a clearer way, assume that $B = 0$ in (9) so there is no uncertainty about the natural parameter b of the system. Then the optimal regulation problem for the regulator is to determine an optimal tax τ^* such that

$$\tau^* = \arg\max[(1 - q)W(x_1^n(\tau)) + qW(x_3^n(\tau))]. \tag{14}$$

$x_i^n(\tau)$, $i = 1, 3$ is a solution of (13)$'$, W is defined by (4).

PROPOSITION 3   For an optimal tax that solves (14), $d\tau^*/dq > 0$. (For proof, see the appendix.)

Thus the regulator will react to an increase in the probability that a random shock might move the system to a "bad" basin of attraction by increasing the optimal tax.

Problem (14) can be interpreted in a way that is very close to the e-contamination formulation of Knightian uncertainty (9) with $q = e$. In the Knightian formulation (9), the second term has been transformed to reflect the worst case scenario which is the worst possible value that nature can choose for b. In (14) the worst possible choice of nature would be to shock the initial condition in such a way that the system moves to the high pollutant accumulation basin of attraction and converges eventually to the high pollutant accumulation steady state x_3^n. Thus (14) can be regarded as an e-contamination formulation of Knightian uncertainty about the basin of attraction of the system, with the e-contamination parameter being the probability that nature would choose the worst possible case. This parameter can even be endogenized if we consider that the probability of the system ending in the high pollutant accumulation basin of attraction can be affected by the choice of the optimal tax τ.

Let the timing be such that the regulator chooses τ and nature adds a random shock. Assume that before the shock the system is in the basin of attraction of the low pollutant accumulation steady state, x_1^c (figure 8.2). The system will jump to the basin of attraction of the high pollutant accumulation steady state if the shock is such that the initial value passes to the right of point J, which separates the two locally stable basins of attraction.

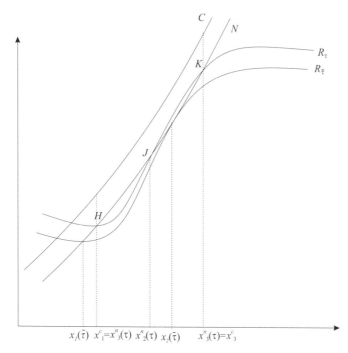

Figure 8.2
Regulation

The tax affects the position of this basin-separation point, however, since increasing the tax reduces the high pollutant accumulation basin of attraction JK. The regulator could choose a tax: (1) so that the probability of a shock moving the system to a high pollutant accumulation basin of attraction is zero, or (2) by optimally taking into account the effect of the tax on the basin separation point.

To make the probability of the system being shocked to a high pollutant accumulation basin of attraction zero, the high pollutant accumulation steady state should be eliminated. This means choosing the tax so that curve R_τ in figure 8.2 shifts downward to the point where the intersections at J and K are eliminated. Proposition 4 defines this tax.

PROPOSITION 4 Let $\bar{\tau}$ be a tax rate such that $(p - \bar{\tau})(b + \rho - f'(x(\bar{\tau}))) - c'(x(\bar{\tau})) = 0$ has two solutions:

$$x_1(\bar{\tau}) : pf''(x_1(\bar{\tau})) + c''(x_1(\bar{\tau})) > 0$$

$$x_2(\bar{\tau}) : pf''(x_2(\bar{\tau})) + c''(x_2(\bar{\tau})) = 0$$

Then for any $\tau > \bar{\tau}$ the high pollutant accumulation basin of attraction is eliminated and the regulated system has only one steady state with low pollution accumulation (figure 8.2). (For proof see the appendix.)

The tax rate $\bar{\tau}$ can be obtained iteratively by gradual increases until the point of tangency between the N curve and the $R_{\bar{\tau}}$ is reached. To determine the optimal tax rate by taking into account the effect of the tax on the basin separation point let $F_S(z) = \Pr[S > z]$ be the cumulative distribution function of a random shock S. If $x^0 + S < x_2^n(\tau)$ where $x_2^n(\tau)$ is the locally unstable steady state of the regulated system, corresponding to point J in figure 8.2, then the system converges to the locally stable low pollutant accumulation steady state $x_1^n(\tau)$ corresponding to point H in figure 8.2. If $x^0 + S > x_2^n(\tau)$, then the system converges to the locally stable high pollutant accumulation steady state $x_3^n(\tau)$ corresponding to point K in figure 8.2. Then the optimal taxation problem is defined as

$$\max_\tau [F_S(x_2^n(\tau))W(x_1^n(\tau)) + (1 - F_S(x_2^n(\tau)))W(x_3^n(\tau))] \tag{15}$$

with FONC

$$F'_S(x_2^n(\tau))\frac{dx_2^n(\tau)}{d\tau}[W(x_1^n(\tau)) - W(x_3^n(\tau))] + F_S(x_2^n(\tau))\frac{\partial W(x_1^n(\tau))}{\partial x_1^n}\frac{dx_1^n(\tau)}{d\tau}$$

$$+ (1 - F_S(x_2^n(\tau)))\frac{\partial W(x_3^n(\tau))}{\partial x_3^n}\frac{dx_3^n(\tau)}{d\tau} = 0. \qquad (16)$$

Comparing (15) to (14) and (9), it is clear that the e-contamination parameter is now determined by $1 - F_S(x_2^n(\tau))$, and it has been endogenized since the probability that nature will choose the high accumulation basin of attraction depends on the optimal tax choice. It can be seen in (16) that in the FONC the first term reflects the marginal effect of a tax change on the probability that the shock will take the system to the high pollutant accumulation basin of attraction which is $F'_S(x_2^n(\tau))(dx_2^n(\tau))/d\tau$, weighted by the difference in welfare between the low and the high pollutant accumulation which is $W(x_1^n(\tau), b) - W(x_3^n(\tau), b - B)$.

4 Concluding Remarks

This chapter introduces a new framework of analysis of environmental regulation issues, using a nonlinear representation of the natural system, where there is heterogeneity in risk aversion between regulator and regulatees, the regulator facing Knightian uncertainty of the e-contamination type (i.e., being uncertainty averse), while the regulatees are risk averse.

We are able to identify a precautionary effect, induced by risk aversion heterogeneity, contributing to the deviation between cooperative and noncooperative solutions, in addition to the public bad externality effect. We examined regulation in this context and we identified potential difficulties in regulation when agents are heterogeneous. We also consider regulation under large rare shocks that could move the system to an undesirable basin of attraction. In this framework we obtain an endogenization of the e-contamination parameter of Knightian uncertainty, which is an advance relative to the ad hoc way in which this parameter has been chosen up to now.

This chapter made an initial foray into a general theory of regulation of dynamical systems with multiple basins of attraction and a hierarchy of time scales. For example, it showed how a 2-hierarchy of time scales, that is, rapid MRAP adjustment of state variable x with random shocks occurring to the initial state on a slower time scale, generate a regulation problem that is mathematically similar to some recent formulations of Knightian uncertainty. Examples of such regulation problems include: (1) regulation of nutrient loadings into watersheds of potentially eutrophic lakes (Carpenter, Brock, and Hanson 1999) where the lake ecosystem dynamics may possess alternative stable states (oligotrophic is low nutrient and is good, eutrophic is high nutrient and is bad), (2) regulation of global climate change (Keller, Bolker, and Bradford 2001) where there may be thresholds and alternative stable states in oceanic dynamics, and (3) general regulation of human-dominated ecosystems where the ecosystem dynamics may possess at least two alternative stable states, one of which is good, the other bad (Gunderson and Holling 2002).

Many of these cases have the property that human management will appear to be doing a fairly good job for a while—namely, the system appears to be resilient to the normal range of shocks. Then a rare but large shock occurs and the system appears to collapse into a bad state which is difficult and costly to reverse. Gunderson and Holling (2002) review many cases of ecosystem management that appear to fit this pattern. A main cause of the unpleasant surprise when a large shock occurs appears to be a slow moving state variable that is either ignored or is unobserved and whose dynamics are coupled to the faster moving dynamics of observed state variables which management is attempting to target. Increases in this slow moving variable degrade the ability of the ecosystem to absorb large shocks. A formal modeling of this slow variable effect in the context of management of nutrient inflows into the catch basin of a lake is carried out by Ludwig, Carpenter, and Brock (2002) (hereafter LCB).

In many of these cases where a slow loss of resilience is occurring, it will be hard to detect this gradual increase in vulnerability to collapse induced by large shocks. This is so because the faster moving state variable x (which is phosphorous sequestered in algae in the lake water in LCB) has the curvature in $g(x, M) = -b(M)x + f(x, M)$ slowly increasing in a slow moving state variable M (which is sedimented phosphorous in the lake bottom in LCB). For values of M where the zero-loading equation $dx/dt = g(x, M)$ has only $x = 0$ as a stable state, standard sensitivity analysis would tend to reveal robust performance to a fairly wide range of estimated parameter values different from data generated by the system.

Notes

1. Let $\tilde{\varepsilon}$ be a random variable such that $E(\tilde{\varepsilon}) = 0$ and consider the lottery $x + t\tilde{\varepsilon}$. Its risk premium π is defined by $\delta_{x-\pi(t)} \sim x + t\tilde{\varepsilon}$. The agent's attitude towards risk at x is of order 1, (first-order risk aversion) if for every $\tilde{\varepsilon} \neq \delta_0$, $E[\tilde{\varepsilon}] = 0$, $\partial\pi/\partial t|_{t=0^+} \neq 0$. It is of order 2, (second-order risk aversion) if for every such $\tilde{\varepsilon}$, $\partial\pi/\partial t|_{t=0^+} = 0$ but $\partial^2\pi/\partial t^2|_{t=0^+} \neq 0$ (see Segal and Spivak 1990).

2. See for example Carpenter, Brock, and Hanson (1999).

3. We doubt that the use of an alternative equilibrium concept such as the closed loop (feedback-subgame perfect) changes the substantive conclusions or the methodological advances developed here.

4. The appendix can be provided by the authors on request.

5. We thank Barry Nalebuff for questioning our previous discussion which prompted us to develop the results in this section.

References

Brock, W., and S. Durlauf. 2001. "Growth Empirics and Reality." *The World Bank Economic Review* 15(2): 229–272.

Brock, W., and D. Starrett. 1999. "Nonconvexities in Ecological Management Problems." *SSRI working paper* no. 2026.

Carpenter, S., W. Brock, and P. Hanson. 1999. "Ecological and Social Dynamics in Simple Models of Ecosystem Management." *Conservation Ecology*. Available online at ⟨http://www.consecol.org/journal/vol3/⟩.

Epstein, L., and T. Wang. 1994. "Intertemporal Asset Pricing under Knightian Uncertainty." *Econometrica* 63: 283–322.

Gilboa, I., and D. Schmeidler. 1989. "Maxmin Expected Utility with Non-Unique Prior." *Journal of Mathematical Economics* 18: 141–153.

Gunderson, L. and Holling, C. eds. 2002. *Panarchy: Understanding Transformations in Human and Natural Systems*. Washington, D.C.: Island Press.

Keller, K., Bolker, B., and D. Breadford. "Uncertainty Climate Thresholds and Optimal Economic Growth." Available online at ⟨www.princeton.edu~klkeller⟩.

Ludwig, D., Carpenter, S., and W. Brock. 2002. "Optimal Phosphorus Loading for a Potential Eutrophic Lake." SSRI working paper, 2002–9, University of Wisconsin.

Pizer, W. 1996. *Modelling Long-Term Policy under Uncertainty*, Ph.D. Thesis, Department of Economics, Harvard University.

Segal, U., and A. Spivak. 1990. "First Order Versus Second-Order Risk Aversion." *Journal of Economic Theory*, 51: 111–125.

Sims, C. 2001. "Pitfalls to Minimax Approach to Model Uncertainty." Website, Princeton University Department of Economics.

Stiglitz, J. 1974a. "Growth with Exhaustible Natural Resources: Efficient and Optimal Growth." *Review of Economic Studies* 41: 123–137.

Stiglitz, J. 1974b. "Growth with Exhaustible Natural Resources: The Competitive Economy." *Review of Economic Studies* 41: 139–152.

Stiglitz, J. 1998a. "Knowledge for Development: Economic Science, Economic Policy, and Economic Advice." World Bank Conference on Development Economics, Washington, D.C., April 20–21.

Stiglitz, J. 1998b. "Towards a New Paradigm for Development: Strategies, Policies, and Processes." 1998 Prebisch Lecture at UNCTAD, Geneva, October 19.

Stiglitz, J. 2002. *Globalization and Its Discontents*. New York: W. W. Norton. New York.

9 Conflicting Preferences and Voluntary Restrictions on Choices

Jacob Glazer and Andrew Weiss

I do not understand what I do. For what I want to do I do not do, but what I hate I do.

—Paul, Romans 7:15

Perhaps the most basic assumption in modern economic theory is that each individual can be represented by a set of internally consistent (noncontradictory) preferences and endowments. By internally consistent preferences we mean that people today place positive values on future outcomes if and only if they will value those outcomes at the time they are realized.

This is not an innocuous assumption. One implication of this assumption is that people would never voluntarily choose to restrict or penalize future choices. However, people do restrict their choices. Consider the purchase of Antabuse, a drug that induces vomiting if the individual consumes alcohol. Clearly, if the consumer has consistent preferences, buying Antabuse is a strictly dominated strategy. If the consumer later drinks alcohol he is worse off having bought antabuse, since he will vomit and will have spent money on the drug. If the consumer does not drink alcohol later, the purchase of Antabuse has reduced his wealth by the cost of the drug. Ainslie (1992), Elster (1984, 1985), Schelling (1984, 1992), Sen (1977), Shefrin and Thaler (1988), and Thaler (1987) present examples in which people appear to choose dominated strategies.

Research in neurophysiology supports the view that the brain contains semiautonomous decision makers, each of which dominates the individual's decision-making process under different circumstances.[1] An individual could genuinely regret actions that he has taken and may want to stop himself from taking similar actions in the future.

By precluding certain choices in the near future, the present "self" allies itself with preferences that will be dominant in the distant future. Thus, an individual may avoid bars or smoke-filled rooms, because he knows that in those situations a set of preferences will become dominant that will lead him to drink or smoke, and he will later regret those choices. Voluntarily imposing restrictions on future choices does not require a high level of reasoning ability. George Ainslie (1974) has shown that even pigeons try to prevent themselves from making some choices.[2]

Economic analysis has been based on notions of a unified and internally consistent self for two reasons.[3] First, it was not clear that rigorous analytic results could be obtained without making these assumptions.[4] Second, it was not known if realistic psychological assumptions would affect the results in interesting ways.

This chapter addresses those two issues by showing how an applied economic problem can be formulated and solved in a model that allows for conflicting preferences. The results differ from those we would have derived by assuming that all individuals had consistent preferences.

The particular examples studied here are testing for drug use and smoking in the workplace. Smoking and drug use are activities in which conflicting preferences are widely acknowledged. People often claim that they would like to be discouraged or even prevented from smoking or using drugs in the future. Also smokers and drug users often judge their past use as a mistake.

In the model used here, testing for drug use or smoking serves some of the same functions as rehabilitation programs in which lapses are punished. Just as those rehabilitation programs are valuable, so is testing for drug use. In standard models, testing only serves to reallocate jobs between drug users and nonusers. In our model testing has the additional benefit of helping some individuals stop themselves from using drugs. However, if the workers who would most benefit from penalizing drug use are less desirable employees, the sorting effects of these tests could lead to too little testing.

The objective here is not to provide a new psychological theory, rather it is to show how a real economic problem can be analyzed while allowing agents to have conflicting preferences. Consequently, preference shocks have been introduced in an especially simple way, and those preference shocks have been embedded in a fairly standard model of asymmetric information. The assumption *of* conflicting preferences appears to also prove fruitful for analyzing a wide range of other aspects of behavior, including savings, food consumption, and time allocation.

1 Testing in the Workplace

1.1 The Model

In our model, firms decide whether (and how frequently) to test workers for behavior that is harmful to both the worker and the firm. For example, firms could be testing for smoking or drug abuse (or high cholesterol).[5] Firms may want to test for these health-related aspects of behavior to reduce their medical costs or because that behavior is correlated with other aspects of job performance such as absenteeism. The main result is that there can be subsidies for testing and taxes on labor that make everyone strictly better off and that are budget balancing.

There are many identical risk-neutral firms, each hiring at most one worker. There are more firms than workers. Workers are also risk neutral.

In period 0, each firm offers a single contract, consisting of a probability t of testing its worker for smoking (taking drugs, eating fatty food) and a wage Y to be paid to the worker if he is not detected smoking. If the worker is detected smoking, his wage is normalized to zero.[6] Firms can commit to {t, Y}. Workers apply to every firm offering the contract(s) they most prefer. Each firm hires at most one worker from its applicants and employs him in period 1. In period 1 the worker may smoke. At the end of period 1 the worker is tested with probability t and paid Y if not detected. The test is accurate: there are no false positives. Firms have a cost of testing c(t), which is strictly increasing and discontinuous at $t = 0$, corresponding to a fixed cost for having a testing program.[7]

In period 1 workers may get utility from smoking. This utility is a random variable, u, realized only after the worker has chosen his contract. Workers know their distribution of u before choosing a contract. $F_i(u)$ denotes the distribution of u for worker i. $F_i(u)$ is continuously differentiable.

Workers who smoke in period 1 regret it in future periods. This regret has a present value of R in period 1. A worker who has accepted a contract $\{t, Y\}$ smokes in period 1 if and only if $(1 - t)Y + u - R \geq Y$, or $u > R + tY$; that is, if her pleasure from smoking in period 1 is greater than her (expected) future disutility from having smoked.

Let u^* denote the value of u such that the two sides of the last inequality are equal. Then the probability of worker i smoking is

$$p(t, Y, i) = 1 - F_i(u^*) = 1 - F_i(R + tY) \tag{1}$$

In period 0 each worker applies to the firm(s) offering the contract that maximizes his expected utility. Applications are costless.

There are three types of workers, all workers of the same type are identical. Workers know their type, but firms do not. That is, each worker looks the same to every firm. Firms know the characteristics of each type of worker.

We refer to the first type of workers as B or bad. The utility they get from smoking enters into their overall utility function when they apply to firms in period 0. Consequently, in period 0 they have no desire to restrain themselves from smoking if they later have a high realization of u. Testing unambiguously lowers their overall utility. One may think of these as committed addicts. They have the unified preferences customary in standard models. If such a worker smokes, his utility level in period 0 is $u + (1 - t)Y$, if he does not smoke it is Y. (For simplicity, assume no discounting between periods 0 and 1.) A type B worker will work for a firm offering the contract $\{t, Y\}$ that maximizes his period 0 utility function:

$$U^B(t, Y) = [1 - p(t, Y, B)t]Y + p(t, Y, B)[E(u|u > u^*)],$$

$$\text{where } E(u|u > u^*) = \frac{1}{p(t, Y, B)} \int_{u^*}^{\infty} f(u) \, du \tag{2}$$

The second type of workers is type A or ambivalent. Type A workers have the same distribution of period 1 preferences as type B. In period 0, however, they do not value the (expected) pleasure they will obtain from smoking in period 1. This assumption about type A's preferences is what makes our model different from traditional models.

Type A workers will work for a firm offering the contract that maximizes their period 0 utility function

$$U^A(t, Y) = [1 - p(t, Y, A)t]Y - p(t, Y, A)R. \tag{3}$$

The omission of u and inclusion of R in the maximization problem of type A workers are the crucial differences between types A and B. For type A workers, more testing may increase or decrease their period 0 utility.

There are also workers who never smoke who are labeled here as type G or good. Their distribution of preference shocks is such that $u - R$ is always negative. Their period 0 utility function is

$$U^G(t, Y) = Y. \tag{4}$$

Workers choose the contract that maximizes their utility in period 0. If workers are indifferent between two different contracts, we assume they choose the one that generates the greatest profits to the firms. If a contract is being offered by more firms than the number of workers who want that contract, we assume that there is an ordering among firms that is common to all workers and that determines which firms hire workers. This assumption yields positive profit equilibria. All the other results go through if we assume that when several firms offer the same contract, workers choose randomly among those firms.

Most of our analysis will be carried out graphically in (t, Y) space. It is helpful, therefore, to look first at the period 0 indifference curves of the workers in this space. In figure 9.1 the horizontal line I^G rep-

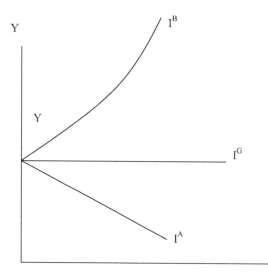

Figure 9.1
The indifference curves for each type of workers

resents a typical indifference curve of type G workers. All contracts that lie on this indifference curve give a type G worker the same expected utility. Since a type G worker never smokes, his utility is affected only by income Y and not by the probability of being tested. His indifference curves are horizontal lines, a higher line represents greater utility.

The period 0 indifference curves of the B types are increasing in (t, Y) space.[8] I^B in figure 9.1 is a type B indifference curve. To keep type B workers indifferent among contracts with different probabilities of being tested, they have to be paid more at the contract with the higher probability of testing.

A representative indifference curve for type A can be increasing, decreasing, or nonmonotonic.[9] We assume that the indifference curves of type A workers are downward sloping in (t, Y) space, that is, holding Y fixed the type A workers (at the time they apply for work) prefer working for firms that test workers. Type A workers like to be tested, because testing decreases their probability of smoking in period 1. In period 0 they value that deterrence.

We now discuss the firm's problem. Q_s denotes the firm's net profit if the worker smokes, Q_n denotes its profits if the worker does not smoke, $Q_n > Q_s$. We assume that Q_s and Q_n are independent of the worker's type. If a firm offers contract $\{t, Y\}$ and hires a worker of type i, its expected profit will be:

$$\pi^i(t, Y) = (1 - p(t, Y, i))Q_n + p(t, Y, i)Q_s - c(t) - Y(1 - p(t, Y, i)t) \quad (5)$$

Figure 9.2 displays the isoprofit curves in (t, Y) space for a firm hiring different types of workers. For all types of workers testing is costly, and because the cost of testing is discontinuous at $t = 0$ the isoprofit curves are discontinuous there.

If a firm hires a type G worker, its expected profit is strictly decreasing with t, because for those workers testing has no productivity-enhancing effects to outweigh its costs.[10] The π^G curve represents a locus of equal profit contracts for a firm hiring type G workers.

Testing reduces the probability that types A and B will smoke. If this productivity-enhancing effect outweighs the cost of testing, the isoprofit line will increase with the probability of testing t. In that case, the expected profit from hiring a type A or B worker would be greater, the greater is the probability of the worker being tested. The isoprofit curves for a firm hiring either A or B workers need not be monotonic. There can be ranges of values of t for which the expected

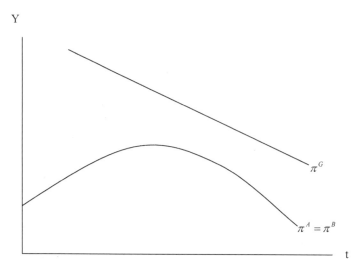

Figure 9.2
The iso-profit curves for a firm attracting each type of worker

profits of the firm are increasing with t, and other values of t for which expected profits are decreasing with t. The curve π^B in figure 9.2 describes a possible isoprofit curve for a firm hiring a type B worker. To focus on issues of conflicting preferences, we assume that $F_B(u) = F_A(u)$, for all u, such that the isoprofit curves for a firm hiring a type A worker are the same as for a firm hiring a type B worker. Thus, the only difference between a type A and a type B worker is the weight they give in period 0 to their pleasure from smoking in period 1.

There is a constant vertical difference between any two isoprofit curves or any two indifference curves of a given type of worker. We use π^i to denote an isoprofit curve of a firm that hires a type i worker; π^{ij} denotes an isoprofit curve of a firm that hires randomly from the pool of workers of types i and j; and π^{ABG} denotes the isoprofit curve of a firm hiring randomly from the pool of all workers.

1.2 Equilibrium

An equilibrium is a profile of contracts and applications by workers so that no firm can increase its profits by offering a different contract, and no worker can increase his utility by applying to a different firm.

PROPOSITION: There are parameter values that support each of the following equilibria:

• Complete pooling: all workers choose the same contract with no testing (in figure 9.3a the point ABG represents this contract).

• Types G and A choose the same contract; type B chooses a contract with a lower probability of testing (see points AG and B in figure 9.3b).

• Types G and B choose the same contract; A chooses a contract entailing a higher probability of testing.

• Complete separation: each type chooses a different contract. The contract chosen by type A will have the highest probability of testing, and the contract chosen by type B the lowest.

In all the equilibria above all firms break even. There are also separating equilibria in which the contract chosen by the type G workers generates positive profits and the contracts chosen by types A and B break even. (An analysis of that case is available from the authors upon request.)

Before providing proofs of these results, we shall discuss the properties of these equilibria.

If either the type A or type B workers are the only type choosing a particular contract, then the contract they choose would be the same as what they would get in the perfect information case. If the type B workers choose the same contract as some other type, they are choosing a zero testing contract. Types A and B cannot be pooled separately from type G. Type B workers take the contract with the lowest probability of being tested.

Types A and G can be pooled at an interior contract. This result is at odds with the standard result in screening models—that pooling equilibria must lie on a boundary (as in figure 9.3a). The reason our model generates interior pooling equilibria is that the profitability of the various types is not monotonic in the slopes of their indifference curves. Consequently although the firm is making positive profits from type G workers at the pooling equilibrium illustrated in figure 9.3b, a deviating contract that attracts type G but not type A would also attract type B and would generate losses. The lack of monotonicity also generates the positive profit equilibria.[11]

Figures 9.3a and 9.3b illustrate (qualitative) sufficient conditions for these equilibria to exist. Y^{ABG} is the wage that breaks even when

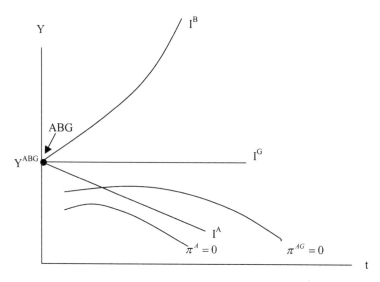

Figure 9.3a
Equilibrium contract when all workers choose the same contract

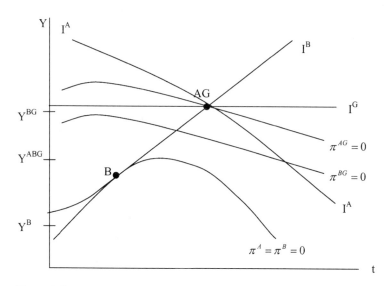

Figure 9.3b
Equilibrium pair of contracts when types A & G choose the same contract, and type B chooses a different contract

workers are not tested and types A, B, and G are hired. Y^{BG} and Y^B are defined similarly. Figure 9.3a is a complete pooling equilibrium. All firms are offering the same contract; there is no testing and firms have zero expected profits. For complete pooling equilibria to exist, it is sufficient, first, that everywhere, except at $t = 0$, the $\pi^{AG} = 0$ isoprofit curve lies below the I^G line that passes through the point ABG, and, second, that the I^A indifference curve that passes through the point ABG lies above the π^A isoprofit curve. It is not difficult to show that parameter values exist guaranteeing that these conditions hold, for example, high setup costs of testing.

We now prove that these conditions are sufficient to guarantee the existence of a complete pooling equilibrium. If a firm offers a contract that lies above the I^B indifference curve, it attracts all three types of workers and hence loses money. This follows from our first condition, which ensures that this deviating contract is above the $\pi^{AG} = 0$ isoprofit curve, and hence is also above $\pi^{ABG} = 0$ isoprofit curve. If the firm offers a contract below the I^B indifferent curve but above the I^G one, it will attract only the G and A types of workers and will again lose money since, again by our first condition, this contract is above the $\pi^{AG} = 0$ isoprofit curve. If the firm offers a contract above I^A but below I^G, it will attract only type A workers, but it will lose money, since our second condition ensures that this contract is above the $\pi^A = 0$ curve. Any other contract will not attract workers.

Figure 9.3b illustrates an equilibrium where type A and type G workers take the same contract, while type B workers take a different contract. The B contract is the point on $\pi^B = 0$ that generates the highest utility for type B, and the AG contract lies on the intersection of the type B indifference curve through their contract and the $\pi^{AG} = 0$ isoprofit curve. Type B workers are indifferent between the contract they take and the contract that the other workers take, whereas type A and G workers strictly prefer the contract they take to the one that type B workers take. Type B workers may be choosing a contract at $t = 0$ or a contract at which their indifference curve is tangent to $\pi^{BG} = 0$. The latter case is illustrated in figure 9.3b. If the type B indifference curve through point B in figure 9.3b were to intersect the vertical axis below Y^B, then the relevant type B indifference curve for this equiilibrium would be the one passing through Y^B.

The proof of this result proceeds along the same lines as the proof that contract ABG in figure 9.3a can be an equilibrium. In a similar fashion we can show that pooling types B and G and separating type A can characterize an equilibrium, as can completely separating every type. It can also be shown that equilibria exists where the firms make positive profit. (An analysis of these equilibria is available from the authors upon request.)

1.3 Welfare Analysis

THEOREM: If in equilibrium the probability of testing a type A worker is less than what it would have been if firms could costlessly identify type A workers, then subsidies exist for testing and budget balancing taxes on wages that make everyone better off on their period 0 preferences.

(Proof: See the appendix.)

The following Pareto-improving government interventions are possible:

1. If the original contract was characterized by complete pooling, then after government intervention two contracts are offered: One with zero testing, that is taken by types B and G, and one with positive testing, taken only by type A workers.

2. If the original contract was characterized by pooling G and A, then after government intervention three contracts are offered. Type B workers take the contract with the lowest probability of testing, type A workers take the contract with the highest probability of testing, and type G take an intermediate contract.

In both cases (1) and (2) there is too little testing of type A workers. We are able to make every type better off because there is an efficiency gain from inducing the type A to take the contract that they would if their type was known. By redistributing enough of that efficiency gain to type A, we can offset their loss from not being pooled with type G and make each type better off in period 0.

To implement these policies, the government must take into account the presence of individuals with inconsistent preferences. If policymakers incorrectly believed that all people had consistent preferences; that is, there were only types B and G in the population, the policies that would be advocated would be very different from those implied by our theorem. In particular, there are plausible circumstances in which the government would subsidize testing only if it was aware that some workers had conflicting preferences.

2 Conclusion

A model has been analyzed here in which some people want to be protected from their own impulses to smoke or take drugs. They can do this by working for a firm that tests workers for that behavior and penalizes workers who fail the test. Because of informational asymmetries, the market equilibrium may by characterized by too little testing. In that case subsidies for testing that are financed by wage taxes can make everyone better off. The desire to protect oneself from urges to smoke or take drugs is due to the intertemporal consequences of that behavior.

Savings is another area in which people are highly vulnerable to preference shocks. A consumption binge that lasts a very short time can reverse a lifetime of savings. There is anecdotal evidence that welfare recipients suffer greatly toward the end of their payment period. The well-being of recipients might be improved considerably by paying them weekly, even if transaction costs were to lower their total payments. The frequency of payments is not an issue that we usually think of as having large effects on welfare, but it may.

Appendix

Proof of the Theorem

Suppose that the initial equilibrium is characterized by complete pooling at $(0, Y^{ABG})$, the point ABG in figure 9.4.

Suppose further that the contract type A workers would receive under perfect information would entail some testing $\hat{t} > 0$. That contract $(\hat{t}, \hat{Y})$ will break even.

The following balanced budget combination of taxes and subsidies induces a new (unique) equilibrium in which the expected utility of all workers is increased. The government gives a subsidy S to firms that test their workers with probability $\hat{t}$ and pay a (postsubsidy) wage no greater than $\hat{Y} + S$; all other firms pay a tax of T. The values of T, S and $\hat{t}$ are derived below.

Let Y^{BG} represent the wage such that $\pi^{BG}(0, Y^{BG}) = 0$; that is, BG denotes the point $(0, Y^{BG})$ in figure 9.4. Let α and β represent the fractions of type A and B workers in the population:

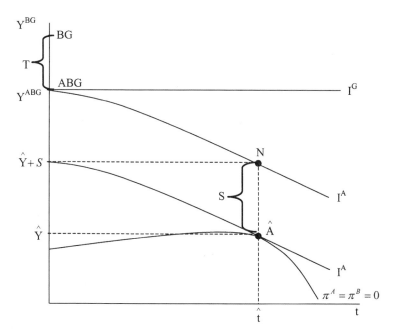

Figure 9.4
A Pareto-improving tax-subsidy scheme. T—Tax; S—Subsidy.

$$Y^{BG} = \frac{1}{1-\alpha}\{\beta[p(0, Y^{BG}, B)Q_s + (1 - p(0, Y^{BG}, B)Q_n]$$

$$+ (1 - \alpha - \beta)Q_n\}. \tag{A1}$$

Choose T such that

$$T = Y^{BG} - Y^{ABG}. \tag{A2}$$

If firms could costlessly identify each worker's type, then type A workers would receive the contract $(\hat{t}, \hat{Y})$, the contract generating the highest utility level for type A along the zero profit locus for those workers. We assume that $\hat{t} > 0$, thus $(\hat{t}, \hat{Y})$ corresponds to point $\hat{A}$ in figure 9.4.

Define a subsidy S such that if a type A worker choosing contract $(\hat{t}, \hat{Y})$ were to get subsidy S, he would be as well off as at the pooling contract $(0, Y^{ABG})$; thus

$$U^A(\hat{t}, \hat{Y} + S) = U^A(0, Y^{ABG}) \tag{A3}$$

Contract $(\hat{t}, \hat{Y} + S)$ corresponds to point N in figure 9.4.

Consider the following tax-subsidy pair. Each firm that tests its new hire with probability $\hat{t}$ and pays a wage less than or equal to $\hat{Y} + S$ receives a subsidy S that satisfies (A3). Firms that hire workers at any other contract pay a tax T as defined by (A2). In the new equilibrium, two contracts are offered: $(0, Y^{ABG})$ and $(\hat{t}, \hat{Y} + S)$. All type A workers choose firms that offer the contract $(\hat{t}, \hat{Y} + S)$; all other workers choose firms that offer contract $(0, Y^{ABG})$. Firms that hire workers at contract $(0, Y^{ABG})$ make before tax profits of $Y^{BG} - Y^{ABG}$ and after tax profits of zero. Firms that offer contract $(\hat{t}, \hat{Y} + S)$ also make zero profits after receiving the subsidy S. It is easy to verify that this is an equilibrium. The arguments are the same as those used previously for equilibria when government intervention did not take place.

We now show that this equilibrium is unique. Given that the tax T is paid by firms offering any contract other than $(\hat{t}, \hat{Y} + S - \Delta)$, where $\Delta \geq 0$, all the isoprofit and indifference curves are shifted downward by the distance T, except at $(\hat{t}, \hat{Y} + S - \Delta)$. Therefore, if the only equilibrium that existed previously was the completed pooling one $(0, Y^{ABG})$, then after the government intervention the only possible equilibrium that does not involve $\hat{t}$, and some wage less than or equal to $\hat{Y} + S$ being offered by any firm, is characterized by complete pooling at contract $(0, Y^{ABG} - T)$. This contract, however, cannot be an equilibrium. If all firms offered this contract, a firm could deviate and offer the contract $(\hat{t}, \hat{Y} + S - \varepsilon)$, where ε is a small positive number. From (A3) and the definition of $(\hat{t}, \hat{Y})$, a value of ε exists such that the deviating firm will attract a type A worker and make a positive profit on that worker. If the deviating firm were also able to attract type G workers or B and G workers, it would do even better.

Now, we show that there cannot be a complete pooling equilibrium at some contract $(\hat{t}, \hat{Y} + S - \Delta)$, for $\Delta \geq 0$. If all firms were to offer that contract, one firm could deviate and offer a contract $(0, Y^*)$ lying ε below the indifference curve of A through $(\hat{t}, \hat{Y} + S - \Delta)$. This contract would attract types B and G but not type A, and would lie below Y^{ABG}, and hence it would make positive profits. This contract could either be offered by a new firm or by one of the existing firms. The same argument explains why an equilibrium cannot involve a contract $(\hat{t}, \hat{Y} + S - \Delta)$ that pools just types A and G. A new firm can always enter with a contract that attracts types B and G and makes positive profits. We know already that there cannot be an equilibrium with pooling only types A and B. Therefore, the equilibrium we have constructed is unique.

Under the new equilibrium, all workers get the same expected utility as they got before the government intervention. We will show, however, that even though all workers get the same utility, the government collects more in taxes than it pays in subsidies. Thus, the government can redistribute this surplus and make everyone better off.

Normalize the population of workers to one. In equilibrium, the government collects $(1 - \alpha)T$ as taxes and pays αS as subsidies. We shall prove that $\alpha S < (1 - \alpha)T$.

Let Y^A be the wage such that $\pi^A(0, Y^A) = 0$. Then

$$Y^A = p(0, Y^A, A)Q_s + (1 - p(0, Y^A, A))Q_n. \tag{A4}$$

Notice that $U^A(0, Y^A) < U^A(\hat{t}, \hat{Y})$. Using (A1) and (A4) it is easy to show that

$$\alpha Y^A + (1 - \alpha)Y^{BG} = Y^{ABG} \tag{A5}$$

$$U^A(0, Y^{ABG}) = U^A(\hat{t}, \hat{Y} + S) \text{ (by the definition of S).} \tag{A6}$$

$$= S + U^A(\hat{t}, \hat{Y}) \text{ (form 3)).} \tag{A7}$$

Therefore,

$$U^A(0, Y^{ABG}) > S + U^A(0, Y^A) \text{ (by the definition of } (\hat{t}, \hat{Y})) \tag{A8}$$

$$S < U^A(0, Y^{ABG}) - U^A(0, Y^A) = Y^{ABG} - Y^A \tag{A9}$$

$$\alpha S < \alpha(Y^{ABG} - Y^A) \tag{A10}$$

$$\alpha S < (1 - \alpha)(Y^{GB} - Y^{ABG}) \text{ (from A5)} \tag{A11}$$

$$\alpha S < (1 - \alpha)T \text{ (from A2)} \tag{A12}$$

Now consider the other case where there is too little testing: types G and A are pooled at an interior contract that entails less testing than is optimal for type A, while type B workers are taking the zero profit contract. The proof is the same as above. The partial pooling contract GA, shown in figure 9.3b, can be treated the same as contract ABG in the proof above. Since before transfers the type G would be receiving the same wage and be tested with the same probability as before, the type B would not choose that contract. Any deviation to lower testing of G would attract type B workers, and type A workers would again get a subsidy at the contract that supports an equilibrium in which they are getting the optimal amount of testing.

Acknowledgments

We are grateful for NIDA for financial support. Some of this research was conducted while Weiss was a visiting Professor at Tel Aviv University. We benefited from valuable conversations with Eric Maskin, Robert Frank, Douglas Gale, David Kreps, Itzhak Gilboa, Gleen Loury, Motty Perry, Ariel Rubinstein and participants in seminars at Harvard University, Cornell University, Tel Aviv University and Boston University. The relevance of Romans, chapter 7, to our research was suggested by Glenn Loury.

Notes

1. See Gazzaniga (1985).

2. Ainslie constructed the following experiment. If pigeons pecked at a red key, they got two seconds of food; if they did not, with a three-second delay, they got four seconds of food. They almost always pecked at the key. He then gave them a means of deactivating the red key. One-fourth of the pigeons consistently deactivated the red key. This result was robust to changes in experimental design.

3. It is tempting to call these pre-Freudian notions, but it is more accurate to call them enlightenment notions, since they would be alien to the way people viewed themselves both before and after the enlightenment era.

4. Shefrin and Thaler have presented stimulating discussions of how conflicting preferences can explain a wide range of economic behavior.

5. We shall ignore the legal and ethical issues surrounding such testing programs.

6. Our results do not depend on the assumption that each firm can only offer a single contract. If we keep the assumption that firms have the option of not hiring any workers, we can allow firms to offer menus of contracts without affecting our results. Workers who chose contracts that generated losses for the firm would not be hired. On the other hand, several of our results depend on firms not being able both to offer a menu of contracts and commit to hiring t randomly from their applicants, regardless of their choice of a contract. The implications of allowing firms to offer menus were suggested to us by Eric Maskin.

7. If the cost of testing were continuous complete, pooling equilibria won't exist, but there can be a partial pooling equilibrium in which subsidizing testing increases welfare.

8. This can be proven by using (2) to show that $dY/dt|_{U^B = \bar{U}} > 0$.

9. This can be proven by using (3) to show that $dY/dt|_{U^A = \bar{U}}$ can be either positive or negative.

10. Since $\pi^G(t, Y) = Q_n - Y - c(t)$, we get that $dY/dt|_{\pi^G(t,Y)=0} = -c'(t) < 0$.

11. This positive profit equilibrium can be broken if firms can offer a menu of contracts and commit to hiring applicants who choose contracts that generate losses. By offering contracts in the neighborhood of each of the existing contracts and making this commitment, a firm would attract all workers and make positive expected profits on the worker it hired. It seems unreasonable, however, to expect that a firm will hire a worker who it knows will be unprofitable. It is not clear how a firm could commit itself to hire and retain those unprofitable workers.

References

Ainslie, George. 1974. "Impulse Control in Pigeons." *Journal of the Experimental Analysis of Behavior*, vol. 21: 485–489.

Ainslie, George. 1992. *Pico-Economics*. Cambridge: Cambridge University Press.

Elster, Jon. 1984. *Ulysses and the Sirens*, rev. ed., Cambridge: Cambridge University Press.

Elster, Jon. 1985. "*Introduction.*" *The Multiple Self*, ed. Jon Elster. Cambridge: Cambridge University Press.

Gazzaniga, Michael. 1985. *The Social Brain*. New York: Basic Books.

Schelling, Thomas. 1984. *Choice and Consequence*. Cambridge: Harvard University Press.

Schelling, Thomas. 1992. "Self-Command, A New Discipline," in *Perspectives on Intertemporal Choice*, ed. George Loewenstein and Jon Elster. New York: Russell Sage Foundation Press.

Sen, Amartya. 1977. "Rational Fools: A Critique of the Behavioral Foundations of Economic Theory." *Philosophy and Public Affairs* 6.

Shefrin, H. M., and R. H. Thaler. 1988. "The Behavioral Life-Cycle Hypothesis." *Economic Inquiry*, October 26: 609–643.

Thaler, R. 1987. "Anomalies: Saving, Fungibility and Mental Accounts." *Journal of Economic Perspectives* 1 (Winter), 197–201.

10 Punctuality: A Cultural Trait as Equilibrium

Kaushik Basu and Jörgen W. Weibull

A people's culture, norms and habits are important determinants not just of the quality of social life but of economic progress and growth. Certain aspects of habits, preferences, and behaviors are associated with whole groups of people and thought of as the nuts and bolts of culture. When a lay person hypothesizes that a certain nation or social class has done badly because the people are given to sloth, or when the anthropologist collects evidence to demonstrate that the Yanomami Indians of South America are so poor because they have little respect for property rights, or, for that matter, when the Yano-mami Indians think of anthropologists as a not quite human group, they are all subscribing to some view of shared cultural traits and how these traits can have consequences for the quality of life and well-being of the group in question.[1]

It is a short step from this to think of culture as something that is preordained, indelibly etched onto a people's psyche, and thus beyond the ambit of their choice. When in 1950 the British chargé d'affaires in Korea, Alec Adams, pronounced how they (the colonial masters stationed in Korea) entertained "the lowest opinion of Korean mores, ability and industry," and, more importantly, how he found it "hard to believe that they will ever be able to successfully govern themselves," he was subscribing to this view of innateness of culture (Clifford 1994, 29). This erroneous prediction, so close to the Korean economic take-off, could not have contributed much to Adams' reputation as an economic forecaster. In his treatment of culture as something beyond the reach of a people's choice, however, he was not alone.

In this chapter we take the view that while the importance of culture is undeniable, the innateness of culture is not; and that societies can constructively think in terms of breaking out of cultural traps.

This is a large topic, however, so we want to work here with a single example to demonstrate how a human trait that is widely believed to be cultural and, in all likelihood, is so to a large extent, is at the same time a matter of choice. While each individual may have no interest in opting out of his or her cultural trait, society as a whole may have such an interest, and each individual may in fact prefer to change if he or she had the assurance that so would others. In other words, the same set of people with the same innate preferences, endowments, and abilities can settle into different cultural practices.

The example chosen here is punctuality and, by association, the related concepts such as tardiness, laziness, and diligence. As the next section describes, social psychologists often think of punctuality as a cultural trait—something that is shared by the individuals in a certain group, for instance, a community, social class, or region. This may be true, but, at the same time, punctuality may have little to do with innate characteristics or preferences of the group. It may be simply an equilibrium response of individuals to what they expect others to do (and what they expect others to expect from them). The same society, in other words, can get caught in a punctual equilibrium or a tardy equilibrium. This is not to deny that punctuality may be habit-forming, and the habit could be subject to evolutionary erosion or bolstering. The aim here is to focus on one core element of such a large agenda, namely the fact that punctuality can be both a shared social trait and an equilibrium response on the part of every individual.

The idea of multiple equilibria is a familiar one in economics. One of the earliest formal modeling of it in the context of a social phenomenon was that by Stiglitz (1975), who has in subsequent work continued to stress its importance in understanding certain social realities, especially economic underdevelopment and high unemployment (see Stiglitz 2000; Hoff and Stiglitz 2000; Basu, Genicot, and Stiglitz 2002), and there is a now a substantial literature on the subject. There is also a recent literature about coordination over time (e.g., Hvide 2001; Ostrovsky and Schwarz 2001). In the equally substantial literature in sociology and social psychology on punctuality, however, there is very little recognition of this. This chapter aims to bring these two literatures together. We show that punctuality is a phenomenon where the possibility of multiple equilibria arises naturally and therefore this ought to be recognized also in social-psychological analyses of punctuality. Following a method that Stiglitz has used so effectively, we use this simple example to illustrate a bigger point—in our case about certain pervasive social phenomena that in popular discourse are treated as cultural and innate.

The disposition of the rest of the chapter is as follows. Section 1 discusses the literature on punctuality, section 2 gives a simple example, section 3 a simple model, and section 4 concludes by briefly probing into some deeper aspects of unpunctuality. (A background calculation for the analysis in section 4 is provided in an appendix.)

1 Punctuality

Punctuality, or the ability of different individuals to exchange some words and then coordinate on time, is one of the crucial ingredients of modern life and progress. Social scientists—largely outside of economics—who did research on this, appreciated this fact well. Zerubavel (1982, 2) writes: "Standard time is thus among the most essential coordinates of intersubjective reality, one of the major parameters of the social world. Indeed social life would probably not have been possible at all were it not for our ability to relate to time in a standard fashion." And, following Durkheim, Clayman (1989, 660) observes, "As a general principle, organized social life requires that human activities be coordinated in time." Given this realization, it is natural that punctuality has been a subject of intensive research in social psychology and sociology (see, e.g., Lockwood 1930; Mcleary 1934; Dudycha 1937, 1938; Levine, West, and Reis 1980; Marin 1987; Kanekar and Vaz 1993).

This large social science literature researching the causes of punctuality appears to have treated punctuality as a matter of preference or a person's innate behavior trait. Thus, underlying Dudycha's (1938) empirical inquiry into punctuality is the presumption that people's punctuality is prompted by their "attitudes towards punctuality," that punctuality reflects a person's "early training" in school and at home. Based on a study of fifteen men and twenty-two women in Cleveland State University, Richard and Slane (1990, 397) concluded that a person's "punctuality style is a persistent personality characteristic" and a trait that correlates well with a person's innate anxiety level, with punctual people exhibiting less anxiety in general.

These social psychologists and sociologists soon recognized that punctuality is not entirely an idiosyncratic individual trait, however, but a characteristic that often exhibits systematic variation across groups. Several studies have located systematic differences across the genders (e.g., Lockwood 1930; Dudycha 1937). But these differences appear milder than those across nations or geographical regions. Kanekar and Vaz (1993) motivate their study of undergraduate students in Bombay University by observing that (377–378) "Indians are notorious for their unpunctuality."[2] In their celebrated study of punctuality patterns in Brazil and the United States, Levine, West, and Reis (1980) found systematic variations across these two societies. Taking extra care not to use politically incorrect language, they observe that (542) "Brazilians and people from the United States do differ in their time-related behavior in the direction predicted by stereotype."

This raises the question: why these differences across nationalities? People have tried to explain these systematic differences through deep cultural moorings or religion, such as the "fatalistic nature of the Latin personality" or the Hindu belief in determinism. When they have looked for more proximate causes, they have found explanations in disruptive factors in the environment, which make it difficult for people to have control over time, or clocks and watches which do not function well. By studying a number of watches in Brazil and the United States, Levine, West, and Reis (1980, 542) find strong evidence in support of their hypothesis that one reason Brazilians are less punctual is that "public clocks and personal watches [are] less accurate in Brazil than in the United States."[3] Even in the early study of Dudycha (1938), he found that among the 307 college students surveyed, 20 attributed their lack of punctuality to "incorrectly set clocks or watches."

Such explanations leave open some important questions about the direction of causality, but that is not our concern here. Before describing our model, it is worth recounting, however briefly, one of the first proper empirical studies of punctuality. Lockwood's (1930) research is interesting, despite its occasional eccentricities, because it is based on a serious attempt to make sense of data on tardiness available from school records. During 1928–1929 in Rushville High School, Rushville, Indiana, data were collected from students who arrived late to school and had to report at the principals office. They were made to fill out a form asking for the extent of delay in minutes and the cause of the delay. Lockwood classified the causes into eight categories: "work," the inevitable "clock wrong," "started late," "automobile trouble," "accidental or unusual cause," "sickness," the somewhat baffling category of "no reason," and then "overslept." He explained that he had difficulty classifying some of the declared causes of delay, such as, "tore my trousers," "held up by a long freight train," and (here we must express a certain admiration for the imagination of the student concerned) "stopped to look at a queer animal in a store window." The problem of classifying these were solved by putting them in the category of "accidental or unusual cause." In some ways Lockwood was more careful about the causality of tardiness than subsequent writers. Thus he notes (539), "While everyone realizes the great difficulty of synchronizing clocks, the excuse 'clock wrong' can in no way justify tardiness." He found that boys were more often late than girls, but girls, when late, were later than boys. He noted that lack of punctuality could become a habit and concluded that tardiness is more "a parent problem" than "a pupil problem."

We recognize that all the above explanations may have some truth. None of them touches on a less obvious explanation, however, which has little to do with innate characteristics or preferences or habit, but has much to do with equilibrium behavior. What we want to show is that even if none of the above factors were there, and in fact even if all human beings were identical, we could get differences in punctuality behavior across cultures. Moreover, these differences could be small within each nation or community but vary across nations or communities, exactly as observed. This is because whether we choose to be punctual or not may depend on whether others with whom we interact are punctual or not. It will be argued here that it is in the nature of the problem of coordinating over time that the extra effort needed to be punctual becomes worthwhile if the others with whom one has to interact are expected to be punctual. To illustrate the argument, a simple example and a simple model are presented in the next two sections.

Though our analysis is abstract, we try to capture a kind of social reality that sociologists have written about, such as how ghetto culture breeds ghetto culture, making it virtually impossible for an individual to escape it. Hence, our argument could be thought of as a formalization of Wilson's (2002, 22) observation, "Skills, habits, and styles are often shaped by the frequency with which they are found in the community." (See also Swidler 1986.)

The basic idea that leads to our explanation of why punctuality is a shared trait within cultures is not the obvious one that punctuality has externalities, namely, that one person's greater punctuality makes life easier for others who have to interact with him. It is the somewhat more complex idea of how one person's greater punctuality increases the worth of the other person's effort to be more punctual that is germane to our analysis. Again, as a technical concept this is well known in economics and arises in the guise of strategic complementarity or supermodularity in game theory and industrial organization theory. What is interesting is the observation that the problem of time coordination gives rise to supermodularity so naturally. No special or contrived assumptions are needed to get this result. It seems to be there in the nature of things. This is what we will try to demonstrate in the next two sections.

2   Example

Imagine two individuals who have made an appointment. Each individual has two choices: to be on time or to be late. Let B be the gain or benefit to each person of the meeting starting on time, and let C be the cost to each person of being on time. Being late has the advantage that you can finish what you were doing. If you are reading a novel and not fussy about being punctual, you can finish the novel and then get up for your meeting even though that may mean some delay. A punctual person, on the other hand, has to put down the novel and leave early. Clearly, an unpunctual person always has the option of being punctual. Hence, it appears reasonable to assume that being punctual incurs a cost, here captured by C. Assume $B > C$, that is, both individuals are better off if they are both on time than if they are both late. If both are on time, then they each thus obtain the "net benefit" or "net return" $B - C > 0$, while if both are late, then they each by definition obtain 0 "net benefit" (the reference value). If one individual is on time and the other is late, then the meeting starts late, and the punctual individual accordingly obtains the net benefit $-C$. The latecomer in this case incurs zero net benefit.

If the two individuals make their choices independently, this interaction can be represented as a symmetric simultaneous-move game with the following payoff bimatrix (the first entry in each box being the payoff, here net benefit, to the row player, and the second entry is the payoff to the column player):

	on time	late
on time	$B - C, B - C$	$-C, 0$
late	$0, -C$	$0, 0$

This is a coordination game with two pure Nash equilibria, *(on time, on time)* and *(late, late)*, respectively. The strategy pair *(on time, on time)* is a strict equilibrium: if an individual expects the other to be on time (with a sufficiently high probability), then being late is strictly worse (since by assumption $B - C > 0$). This strategy pair is also Pareto-dominant: it gives each individual the highest possible payoff, $B - C$, in the game. Hence, this is the outcome that both individuals would prefer to happen, and it is also the outcome that a benevolent social planner would prescribe. *(Late, late)* is also a strict equilibrium: if an individual expects the other to be late (with a sufficiently high probability), then the *unique* best choice is to be late too (since by assumption C is positive). This equilibrium, however, gives a lower payoff to both individuals than *(on time, on time)*.

On top of these two pure Nash equilibria, there is also a Nash equilibrium in mixed strategies, in which both individuals randomize between being on time or being late. This equilibrium probability is the same for both players and is such that it makes the other individual indifferent between being on time and being late.[4] The mixed equilibrium, however, is unstable in the sense that if one individual expects the other to be on time with a probability that is slightly above (below) the equilibrium probability, then it is in that individual's self interest to be on time with probability one (zero). Hence, any perturbation of behaviors in a recurrently interacting population will take the population to one of the strict equilibria.

What prediction does game theory give in this class of games? All three Nash equilibria are perfect in the sense of Selten (1975), and, viewed as singleton-sets, each of them is srategically stable in the sense of Kohlberg and Mertens (1986). Hence, even the mixed equilibrium survives these demanding refinements of the Nash equilibrium concept. Evolutionary game theory, however, rejects the mixed equilibrium: the equilibrium strategy to randomize between being on time and being late is not evolutionarily stable (Maynard Smith and Price 1973; Maynard Smith 1982). A population playing this strategy can be "invaded" by a small group of "mutants" who are always punctual: these earn the same payoff on average when meeting the "incumbents" who randomize, but they fare better when meeting each other.[5] By contrast, each of the two pure strategies is evolutionarily stable.

Which of the two pure-strategy equilibria is more likely in the long run if individuals in a given population (culture or society) are randomly matched in pairs to play the above punctuality game? Kandori, Mailath, and Rob (1993) and Young (1993) provided models with precise predictions for such recurrently played games. The basic driving force in their models is that individuals most of the time chose the action which is best in the light of the recent past play of the game. For instance, if in the recent past virtually all individuals were late, then such an individual will choose to be late for the next meeting. A second driving force, however, is that now and then, with a small fixed probability, individuals make mistakes or experiments and instead play the other action. In both models, the combined long-run effect of these two forces is that the risk dominant equilibrium will be played virtually all the time.[6] The concept of risk dominance is due to Harsanyi and Selten (1988), and singles out the equilibrium with the lowest strategic risk, in the sense of being most robust to uncertainty about the other player's action.[7] In the above punctuality game, the socially inefficient equilibrium (late, late) is risk-dominant if and only if

$$\frac{C}{B} > \frac{1}{2}. \tag{1}$$

Likewise, (on time, on time) is risk-dominant under the reversed inequality. In other words, the long-run outcome is (late, late) if the cost C of leaving early is more than half the benefit of starting the meeting early.

The next section briefly considers a simple model that generalizes the present example in two relevant dimensions.[8]

3   A Simple Model

Many situations where punctuality matters involve more than two individuals, and usually an element of randomness is attached to arrival times. Suppose that there are n persons who decide at time $t = 0$ to have a meeting at time $t = 1$. Just as in the preceding example, the meeting cannot start until all n persons arrive. We are therefore considering an instance of what are called minimum effort games (Bryant 1983; Carlsson and Ganslandt 1998). Each person can plan to be punctual or tardy, for example, by choosing an early or late departure time. A punctual person, one who leaves early, arrives at the agreed-upon time $t = 1$ with probability one. Tardiness or unpunctuality is naturally associated with some degree of randomness in behavior, an aspect neglected in the preceding example (see also the section on unpunctual behavior). Hence, a tardy person, who leaves late, has a probability $p < 1$ of arriving on time and a probability $1 - p$ of being late, that is, of arriving at, say, time $t = 2$.

Let B be the benefit or gain to each person of the meeting starting on time, that is, at $t = 1$ (as opposed to time $t = 2$). And let $C < B$ be the cost to each person of being punctual (leaving early). If k of the n persons choose to be punctual, the expected gross benefit (gross in the sense of not taking account of the cost C of being punctual) to each person is thus B multiplied by the probability of everybody being on time. Assuming statistical independence in the delays of tardy persons, the expected gross benefit is thus simply $B(k) = p^{n-k}B$. Let $\Delta B(k)$ denote the increase in the expected gross benefit when, starting with k persons being punctual, one of the tardy persons chooses to instead be punctual:

$$\Delta B(k) = B(k + 1) - B(k) = p^{n-k-1}(1 - p)B. \tag{2}$$

Suppose all individuals decide independently whether to be punctual or tardy (whether to leave early or late), and that each of them strives to maximize his or her expected net benefit, that is the expected gross benefit of an early meeting minus the cost of punctuality, if this is the individual's choice. If individual i believes that k other persons will choose to be punctual (leave early), then also i will choose to be punctual if and only if the resulting increase in the expected gross benefit is no less than the cost of punctuality, that is if and only if $\Delta B(k) \geq C$. Note that the expected return $\Delta B(k)$ to punctuality here increases in the number k of others who are punctual. This simple model illustrates that punctuality has a natural strategic complementarity (or supermodularity) property: if one more individual is punctual, then the marginal return to punctuality increases.

It is now easy to see that there may be multiple Nash equilibria in this punctuality game. For instance, everybody choosing to be punctual (leave early) is an equilibrium if and only if $C \leq \Delta B(n - 1) =$

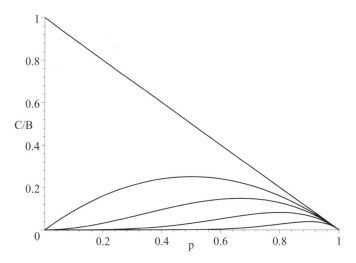

Figure 10.1
The parameter region where full punctuality and full tardiness coexist in equilibria,
for $n = 2, 3, 5, 10$ (lower curves for higher n)

$(1 - p)B$. Likewise, everybody choosing to be tardy (leave late) is an
equilibrium if and only if $\Delta B(0) = p^{n-1}(1 - p)B \leq C$. Hence, both
these polar equilibria coexist if and only if

$$p^{n-1}(1 - p) \leq \frac{C}{B} \leq 1 - p. \tag{3}$$

Figure 10.1 displays the timely arrival probability p of a tardy person
on the horizontal axis and the cost-benefit ratio C/B on the vertical
axis. The four curves plot the equation $C/B = p^{n-1}(1 - p)$ for $n =
2, 3, 5, 10$, respectively, where lower curves correspond to larger n.
Hence, for all parameter combinations $(p, C/B)$ below the straight
line $C/B = 1 - p$, all punctual is an equilibrium, and for all parameter
combinations $(p, C/B)$ above the relevant curve (depending on n), all
tardy is an equilibrium. Multiple equilibria do exist for a large set of
parameter combinations $(p, C/B)$, and this set is larger the more
people, n, are involved in the meeting, as shown in figure 10.1.

The simple idea behind this model may hold some clues to tardiness, inefficiencies of several kinds, and to the poor quality of work
and other such phenomena observed in developing countries. It
shows how, despite having no innate difference of significance, two
groups can get locked into very different behaviors: one where they

are all tardy and one where they are all punctual. A social scientist who neglects this strategic aspect may be tempted to believe that if two societies exhibit sharply different behaviors, then they must have innate differences, such as different preferences or different religious outlooks on life or different genes. What we have just seen is that none of this is necessary. Some of the cultural differences that we observe across societies could simply be manifestations of different equilibria in otherwise identical societies.

In reality, certain behaviors tend to become habits. A person may then suffer some dissonance cost if he or she has to behave otherwise. It is arguable that punctuality behavior falls into this category. Hence, even though one's decision to be punctual or not may be founded in trying to achieve some objectives, if one is punctual or unpunctual for a long time, one may develop a direct preference for such behavior. Though it would be interesting to model the possibility of growing attachment to certain kinds of behavior and dissonance cost associated with trying to break out of it, we do not embark on such a study here.

There are many other and more direct ways, however, in which the model can be generalized to accommodate a wider range of situations. For example, suppose that instead of the meeting only going ahead with a quorum of all n people, the meeting goes ahead at the early date, $t = 1$, irrespectively of how many have arrived, though with a diminished benefit to all present.[9] Those who arrive late simply miss the meeting and obtain utility zero. More specifically, suppose that if m individuals are on time, the meeting takes place with these individuals, each of whom receives the gross benefit $A(m)$, a nondecreasing function of the number m of individuals who are present at time $t = 1$. The model above corresponds to the special case when $A(m) = 0$ for all $m < n$ and $A(n) = B$.

Suppose that k individuals choose to be punctual (leave early) and hence arrive on time with certainty. Each of the remaining $n - k$ tardy individuals arrive on time with probability p. The expected gross benefit to each punctual person is then

$$P(k) = E[A(k + X)] - C, \tag{4}$$

where (again assuming statistical independence), the random number X of tardy individuals who happen to arrive on time has a binomial distribution with parameters $n - k$ (the number of trials) and p

(each trial's success probability), $X \sim Bin(n - k, p)$. Likewise, the expected benefit to each tardy person is

$$T(k) = pE[A(k + 1 + X')], \tag{5}$$

where $X' \sim Bin(n - k - 1, p)$. The same argument as above leads to a sufficient condition for the existence of multiple equilibria, with condition (3) as a special case. In other words, as long as the payoff to punctuality depends positively on the number of other individuals who are punctual, the multiple equilibrium structure emerges naturally.

Another natural modification of this simple model is to let people choose departure time more freely. This is the topic of the following subsection.

3.1   Fine-tuned Departure Times

In many real-life situations individuals do not have a binary choice between being punctual (leave early) or tardy (leave late). Instead, a whole range of intermediate degrees of punctuality are available choice alternatives. The departure time for a meeting can often be chosen on a more or less continuous scale. Suppose that each individual i can choose his or her departure time t_i anywhere in the time interval $[0, 1]$. Suppose also that the probability p_i that individual i will arrive in time (that is, by time $t = 1$) is a decreasing function of i's departure time. This is the case, for example, if the travel time to the venue of the meeting is a random variable with a fixed distribution. Then $p_i = F_i(1 - t_i)$, where F_i is the cumulative distribution function of travel time for the individual (here assumed independent of departure time, but which may depend on i's location, mode of transportation etc.). Let $C_i(t)$ be i's cost or disutility of departing at time t, which we assume is decreasing in t. Suppose, for example, that the cost is lost income: If i's wage rate is w_i per time unit until he or she departs for the meeting, then $C_i(t) = C_0 - w_i t_i$. Let $B_i > 0$ denote the gross benefit to individual i of a meeting at the agreed-upon time $t = 1$. Assuming statistically independent travel times, the expected net benefit (or utility) to individual i is then

$$u_i = B_i \prod_{j=1}^{n} F_j(1 - t_j) - C_0 + w_i t_i. \tag{6}$$

Suppose all individuals simultaneously choose their departure times. What are then the equilibrium outcomes? We focus on the special case of two persons with identically and exponentially distributed travel times. To keep the example consistent with the basic model, however, we truncate the travel-time distribution so that even the latest departure, at $t = 1$, results in arrival by $t = 2$ for sure. The cumulative probability distribution function for travel time x is hence $F(x) = (1 - e^{-\lambda x})/(1 - e^{-\lambda})$.

In this case, a necessary first-order condition for an interior Nash equilibrium (that is, one where $0 < t_i < 1$ for $i = 1, 2$) is that the departure time of each individual i satisfies

$$t_i = 1 + \frac{1}{\lambda} \ln\left(\frac{w_i}{\lambda B_i}\right) + \frac{2}{\lambda} \ln(1 - e^{-\lambda}) - \frac{1}{\lambda} \ln(1 - e^{\lambda t_j - \lambda}) \qquad (7)$$

This equation specifies i's optimal departure time as a function of i's wage rate, gross benefit of a punctual meeting, and i's expectation of j's departure time (see the appendix for a derivation). We note that i's departure time is increasing in i's wage rate, decreasing in his or her gross benefit from a punctual meeting, and increasing in i's expectation of j's departure time. Note, in particular, that the higher wage an individual has or, more general, the higher an individual's opportunity cost of interrupting his or her usual activity, the later he or she departs and the more likely it is that he or she will be late.

Equation (7) thus specifies the best-reply curve for each individual, and the intersections between these two curves constitute the interior Nash equilibria (see figure 10.2) where the solid curve is 1's best departure time as a function of the expected departure time of individual 2, and the dashed curve is 2's best departure time as a function of the expected departure time of individual 1. When generating this figure, we assigned individual 1 a higher wage/benefit ratio: $w_1/B_1 > w_2/B_2$. Consequently, in both equilibria, individual 2 chooses an earlier departure time than individual 1 and is therefore more likely than individual 1 to be on time.

Besides these two interior equilibria, there is one equilibrium on the boundary, namely when both individuals leave as late as possible, $t_1 = t_2 = 1$, in which case the meeting will be late with probability one. That this is indeed a Nash equilibrium can be seen directly from equation (6): if one individual is expected to leave at time 1, then the probability is zero for an meeting at that time, and hence it

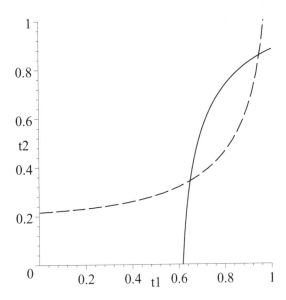

Figure 10.2
Interior equilibria in the special case $n = 2$, truncated exponential travel times with $w_1/B_1 = 1$ and $w_2/B_2 = 0.3$

is best for the other individual to leave as late as possible, that is, at time one.

Note finally that one of the interior equilibria, the one associated with later departure times, is dynamically unstable: a small shift in j's departure time gives an incentive for i to shift his or her departure time in the same direction. Hence, just as in the introductory example there are two stable extreme equilibria and one unstable equilibrium between these.

4   What Is Unpunctual Behavior?

One question that we have been on the verge of raising but did not is: what constitutes unpunctual behavior? The reason why we could get away without confronting this question directly is because it was obvious in each of the examples considered above as to which behavior was associated with punctuality and which with the absence of it. Once we go beyond specific examples to confront the general question of what is the essence of the lack of punctuality, however, we run into a host of conceptual problems.

A person who is late and unpredictably so is clearly unpunctual. This is a case of sufficiency, however, but not necessity in describing a person as unpunctual. Problems arise when we go beyond this clear case. Consider, for instance, a person who invariably shows up half an hour after the time he is supposed to show up. Is this person unpunctual? It all depends on what we mean by the time he is supposed to show up, that is, what we take to be the base time to which he adds 30 minutes.

First, consider the case where he comes 30 minutes after whatever time he is *told* to come (and maybe he expects other people to come 30 minutes after the time he tells them to come) and this is common knowledge. In this case we may indeed think of him as punctual. We will simply have to remember to tell him to come 30 minutes before the time we wish him to come; and when he invites someone for dinner, that person has to remember to go 30 minutes after the time he is asked to go. When in France you are invited for dinner, something like this is true. Both sides know that if the announced time for the dinner is 7:00 p.m., then the intended time is 7.30.

Even here there may be a problem if meetings are called and dinner guests are invited by way of a public announcement of the time of the meeting or dinner, and we live in a society where some people follow the above time convention, while others take the announcement literally. It may then not be possible to fine-tune the message reaching each person, and so the person who is in the habit of arriving 30 minutes late will indeed be late (unless the host targets the information for him and ends up having the other guests arrive early) and will be considered unpunctual. If information could be fined-tuned appropriately for each person, however, we would have to simply think of this person as someone who uses language differently.

Now consider the case when the latecomer, call him individual i, is a person who comes 30 minutes after what he believes is the time he is expected to come. In this case he is unequivocally unpunctual, and his behavior becomes hard to predict when he has to interact with another rational individual. Consider first the case where he has to use a certain facility, for instance, a laboratory or a tennis court, which can be booked according to a fixed (say, hourly) schedule. If this person treats the time when the facility is booked for his use as the time he is expected to show up, then, by virtue of his habit of delay, there will be 30-minutes of loss during which the facility stands idle waiting for him.

The problem gets messier if there is another person involved, who, for instance, calls a meeting with i. If the other person, say j, who calls the meeting, knows i's type, she may ask him to come 30 minutes before the time j wants him to show up. But if i knows that j knows his type, he may show up one hour after the time she asks him to come. If she knows that he knows that she knows his type, however, she may give him a time that is one hour before the desired time, and so on in an infinite regress. Indeed, if i's type is common knowledge, it is not clear whether it is at all possible for i to communicate with j about time. Time coordination, in other words, may become impossible with such a person. We would, nevertheless, not hesitate to call him unpunctual.

In closing, while this chapter considered problems involving timing decisions alone, it is possible that timing decisions interact with other kinds of decisions, causing a wider domain of reinforcement. Instead of one person's tardiness reinforcing other people's tardiness, it may reinforce other kinds of inefficiencies in other people. Consider, for example, the problem of watch synchronization and tardiness. Some social scientists believe, that the former causes the latter. Economists, on the other hand, are usually dismissive of this and think of tardiness as the cause of why people are content using clocks and watches that do not function properly. The kind of analysis we undertook here suggests that the causality may run in both directions. We can conceive of an equilibrium in which it is not worthwhile for watch producers to incur the extra cost needed to produce better watches, because there is so much lack of punctuality around that it is not worthwhile for individuals to spend much more on better watches that would help them to be more punctual.

In the introduction we wrote about how, as Stiglitz and others have suggested, economic underdevelopment may be a kind of suboptimal equilibrium in an economy with multiple equilibria. What we are suggesting—and this clearly needs more research—is that other kinds of social phenomena, such as tardiness or the lack of work culture, which are widely observed in less economically developed countries, may not be purely matters of coincidence or immutable habit but a necessary concomitant of that equilibrium.

Appendix

A necessary first-order condition for an interior Nash equilibrium in the model in the section on fine-tuning is that the departure time of each individual i (for $i = 1, 2$ and $j \neq i$) satisfies

$$\frac{\partial u_i}{\partial t_i} = -B_i F(1 - t_j) f(1 - t_i) + w_i = 0.$$

Equivalently,

$$\frac{1 - e^{-\lambda(1-t_j)}}{1 - e^{-\lambda}} \frac{\lambda e^{-\lambda(1-t_i)}}{1 - e^{-\lambda}} = \frac{w_i}{B_i},$$

or

$$e^{\lambda t_i - \lambda} = \frac{w_i}{\lambda B_i} \frac{(1 - e^{-\lambda})^2}{1 - e^{\lambda t_j - \lambda}}.$$

Taking the logarithm of both sides, one obtains

$$\lambda t_i - \lambda = \ln\left(\frac{w_i}{\lambda B_i}\right) + 2\ln(1 - e^{-\lambda}) - \ln(1 - e^{\lambda t_j - \lambda}),$$

which gives equation (7).

Acknowledgments

This chapter was begun in early 1997, with the essential ideas already laid out then. Yet, through a series of what is best described as temporal lapses and procrastination, the paper remained at the level of notes till very recently. During this long process we have accumulated many debts to colleagues and friends, but suffice it to mention here Abhijit Banerjee, Glenn Ellison, Karla Hoff, Geraint Jones, Eva Meyersson Milgrom, Barry Nalebuff, Lena Palseva, and Mark Voorneveld, who all gave helpful comments.

Notes

1. While these are meant to be illustrative examples and not statements of fact, that the Yanomami view anthropologists as a rather special class is, however, probably true. "Anthropologists," writes Tierney (2000, 14), "have left an indelible imprint upon the Yanomami. In fact, the word *anthro* entered the Indians' vocabulary.... The Yanomami consider an *anthro* to be a powerful nonhuman with deeply disturbed tendencies and wild eccentricities."

2. In contrast, one of us (Basu) was told by the late Sir Arthur Lewis how he found Indians to be punctual. It is worth noting that his sample of experience must have been predominantly Indians in England and the Americas. Our chapter will show how the same people may behave differently when they find themselves in a different setting.

3. While we do not know of any similar studies in India, our observation that time is often asked of strangers in India with the question, "Sir, what is the time by your watch?" makes us believe that time does have an element of watch dependency in India, similar to Brazil.

One may wonder why broken watches should be treated as a cause of unpunctuality, for they could, equally, make people show up early. We abstain from including this aspect in our analysis, though chronological uncertainty, and the awareness of others' chronological uncertainty, may well affect punctuality in the way found by Levine, West, and Reis.

4. In this equilibrium, each player is on time with probability $p = C/B$.

5. A (pure or mixed) strategy in a symmetric and finite two-player game is an evolutionarily stable strategy (ESS), if there is an "invasion barrier" against all other (pure or mixed) strategies, in the sense that if the population share playing such a "mutant" strategy is below this barrier, then its payoff is on average lower than that to the "incumbent" strategy, see Maynard Smith and Price (1973), Maynard Smith (1982), and Weibull (1995).

6. As the probability of mistakes or experiments goes to zero, the long-run probability for the risk dominant equilibrium tends to one.

7. Consider any symmetric 2 × 2 coordination game (such as our punctuality game). One of the two pure-strategy equilibria is said to *risk-dominate* the other if the strategy used in the first equilibrium is optimal for a wider range of probabilities—attached to the other player's equilibrium action—than the strategy in the other equilibrium. This condition is equivalent to the condition that the unique mixed-strategy equilibrium in such a game assigns less than probability 1/2 to the first strategy.

8. An interesting extension which we will not elaborate on, however, would be to allow for the possibility that a latecomer is embarrassed to have others wait. In the simple model given above, this would correspond to a negative payoff, rather than zero payoff, assigned to the strategy late when played against on time.

9. We are grateful to Geraint Jones for suggesting this generalization.

References

Basu, K., G. Genicot, and J. Stiglitz. 2002. "Minimum Wage Laws and Unemployment Benefits when Labor Supply is a Household Decision," in *Markets and Governments*, ed. K. Basu, P. Nayak, and R. Ray. New Delhi: Oxford University Press.

Bryant, J. 1983. "A Simple Rational-Expectations Keynes-Type Model." *Quarterly Journal of Economics* 98: 525–528.

Carlsson, H., and M. Ganslandt. 1998. "Noisy Equilibrium Selection in Coordination Games." *Economics Letters* 60: 23–34.

Clayman, S. 1989. "The Production of Punctuality: Social Interaction, Temporal Organization and Social Structure." *American Journal of Sociology* 59: 659–691.

Clifford, M. 1994. *Troubled Tiger*. London: M. E. Sharpe.

Dudycha, G. 1937. "Sex Differences in Punctuality." *Journal of Social Psychology* 8: 355–363.

Dudycha, G. 1938. "A Qualitative Study of Punctuality." *Journal of Social Psychology* 9: 207–217.

Harsanyi, J., and R. Selten. 1988. *A General Theory of Selection in Games*. Cambridge, Mass.: MIT Press.

Hoff, K., and J. Stiglitz. 2000. "Modern Economic Theory and Development," in Meier, Gerald and Stiglitz, Joseph eds. *Frontiers of Development Economics*. Oxford and New York: Oxford University Press.

Hvide, H. 2001. "Some Comment on Free-Riding in Leontief Partnerships." *Economic Inquiry* 39: 467–473.

Kandori, M., G. Mailath, and R. Rob. 1993. "Learning, Mutation, and Long-Run Equilibria in Games." *Econometrica* 61: 29–56.

Kanekar, S., and L. Vaz. 1993. "Effects of Gender and Status upon Punctuality Norms." *Journal of Social Psychology* 133: 377–384.

Kohlberg, E., and J.-F. Mertens. 1986. "On the Strategic Stability of Equilibria." *Econometrica* 54: 1003–1037.

Levine, R., L. West, and H. Reis. 1980. "Perceptions of Time and Punctuality in the United States and Brazil." *Journal of Personal and Social Psychology* 38: 541–550.

Lockwood, L. A. 1930. "Causes of Tardiness." *School Review* 38: 538–543.

Mcleary, R. 1934. "The Control of Tardiness in One High School." 42: 440–446.

Marin, G. 1987. "Attributions for Tardiness among Chilean and United States Students." *Journal of Social Psychology* 127: 69–75.

Maynard Smith, J., and G. Price. 1973. "The Logic of Animal Conflict." *Nature* 246: 15–18.

Maynard Smith, J. 1982. *Evolution and the Theory of Games*. Cambridge: Cambridge University Press.

Ostrovsky, M., and M. Schwarz. 2001. "Waiting Time ands and Coordination." Mimeo., Harvard University.

Richard, D., and S. Slane. 1990. "Punctuality as a Personal Characteristic: Issues of Measurement." *Journal of Psychology* 124: 397–402.

Selten, R. 1975. "Reexamination of the Perfectness Concept for Equilibrium Points in Extensive Games." *International Journal of Game Theory* 4: 25–55.

Stiglitz, J. 1975. "The Theory of Screening, Education and the Distribution of Income." *American Economic Review* 65: 283–300.

Stiglitz, J. 2000. "Democratic Development as the Fruits of Labor," in *Joseph Stiglitz and the World Bank: The Rebel Within*, ed. Ha-Joon Chang. London: Anthem Press.

Swidler, A. 1986. "Culture in Action: Symbols and Strategies." *American Sociological Review* 51: 273–286.

Tierney, P. 2000. *Darkness in El Dorado: How Scientists and Journalists Devastated the Amazon.* New York: Norton.

Weibull, J. 1995. *Evolutionary Game Theory.* Cambridge, Mass.: MIT Press.

Wilson, W. J. 2002. "Social Theory and the Concept 'Underclass.'" Mimeo., Harvard University.

Young, P. 1993. "The Evolution of Conventions." *Econometrica* 61: 57–84.

Zerubavel, E. 1982. "The Standardization of Time: A Sociohistorical Perspective." *American Journal of Sociology* 88: 1–23.

11

A Few Righteous Men: Imperfect Information, Quit-for-Tat, and Critical Mass in the Dynamics of Cooperation

Serge Moresi and Steven Salop

In the *Wealth of Nations*, Adam Smith ([1776] 1910) wrote that it was self-interest guided by the invisible hand of the market that leads the economy to a beneficial outcome, not the benevolence or humanity of the butcher, the brewer, or the baker. The development of models of imperfect information and strategic interaction by Joseph Stiglitz, John Nash, and others has demonstrated the limitations of the invisible hand (Nash 1950; Stiglitz 1975).

The failure of self-interest to generate a cooperative equilibrium is illustrated in the one-shot Prisoners' Dilemma game, where defection is the dominant strategy. Escape from the Prisoners' Dilemma is possible with enforceable agreements, fear of governmental, religious or social sanctions, altruism and other ethical motivations (Smith ([1790] 1976); Ullman-Margarlit 1977; Frank 1988; and Sen 2000). In a repeated play context, cooperation can be sustained by adopting "conditional cooperation" strategies, such as Tit-for-Tat (Shubik 1959; Axelrod 1984; and Taylor 1987). In fact, when individuals interact repeatedly and have perfect information about the past behavior of their partners, any outcome from zero cooperation to universal co-operation can be sustained as an equilibrium (Friedman 1971).

Good information, however, is essential for successful coopera-tion. When pairs of individuals interact repeatedly, each obtains a (private) reputation within the relationship. Similarly, if individuals interact in sequential business relationships with different partners over time, then conditional cooperation strategies require informa-tion about a partner's previous interactions with others. Your incen-tives to cooperate today are reduced if future partners will not know whether you defected in a previous relationship (Ellison 1994). In a large open society, however, this type of public reputation informa-tion may be unavailable.

The incentives to cooperate in the absence of public reputation information are explored here, using an infinite-horizon model of sequential relationships in which individuals initially are paired randomly. In the equilibrium with identical profit-maximizing individuals, each cooperates in the initial interaction with a new partner with some probability. If both individuals cooperate at first, they choose to form a long-term cooperative relationship until one member dies. If one party defects, then the victim quits the relationship and both are paired with others in the next period.

We assume that an individual's defection is not public information, but is known only to the victim and the defector. A person does not know whether his new partner is a new entrant into the community, someone who previously defected, or someone who previously cooperated but then quit a relationship after a partner's defection or death.[1]

We refer to the strategy of quitting the relationship after your partner defects as Quit-for-Tat (QFT).[2] This QFT strategy is reminiscent of the Shapiro and Stiglitz (1984) unemployment model, where apparently shirking workers are terminated by the firm and thrown into the pool of involuntarily unemployed.

A full cooperation equilibrium never exists in this imperfect information model. The incentives to defect and then switch to a new uninformed partner are too strong in the absence of public reputation information. Three possible steady-state equilibria exist. One equilibrium involves zero cooperation in which each person defects every period. Under certain conditions, however, there also are two partial cooperation QFT equilibria, one with a low incidence of cooperation and one with a high incidence. In these QFT equilibria, a fraction of individuals cooperate initially with new partners (or each individual follows a mixed strategy in the initial interaction with a new partner) and then follow a QFT strategy thereafter.

Given this structure, suppose that there were a mass of ethical or religious people in society who never defect in the initial interaction, but do quit a relationship if their partner defects. In principle, these "righteous" people might increase or decrease the incentives of others to defect.[3] On the one hand, the righteous might be the proverbial "suckers-born-every-minute." Defectors could exploit their current cooperating partners and then exit the relationship and find new cooperating suckers to exploit tomorrow. On the other hand, they might induce better behavior by others who find it in their self-interest to cooperate in the hope of achieving a long-term relationship with a righteous individual (Salop 1978).

We show that, under some conditions, the adoption of religious/ethical norms by a sufficient critical mass of families (individuals and their progeny) will lead to a *cooperation* bandwagon and dramatically increase the equilibrium amount of cooperation in society. This is because the QFT equilibrium with a high incidence of cooperation is stable, while the low-incidence equilibrium is unstable. Moreover, if people are patient enough so that the discount rate tends to zero, then the required critical mass of the righteous also tends to zero.

These results are reminiscent of the Kreps et al. (1982) finitely repeated game, where the presence of a small fraction of "committed cooperators" significantly increases the amount of cooperation by profit-maximizing individuals. In their paper, however, profit-maximizing individuals start with cooperation and eventually switch to defection as the end of the game approaches. Here, they start with partial cooperation and eventually enter into a long-term relationship of full cooperation.

Thus, despite the lack of public reputation information in our model, a publicly anonymous moral minority can generate a moral rebirth for society at large. For example, in Genesis, God informs Abraham that He is going to destroy Sodom and Gomorrah because of its evil behavior. Abraham asks whether God would save the city if there were as few as fifty righteous inhabitants. When God assents, Abraham then asks about (or negotiates) the outcome if there were only forty-five (or forty or fewer) righteous inhabitants. God ultimately concludes that the city would be saved if there were at least ten moral inhabitants (Genesis 18:16–19:38). One interpretation of this story consistent with our model is that ten moral inhabitants might be enough to create a moral rebirth, thereby spurring the other inhabitants to behave better.[4]

The chapter is organized as follows. Sections 2 and 3 set up the basic model without any righteous individuals and solve for the steady-state equilibria. Section 4 discusses the main properties of these partial cooperation equilibria. In particular, the equilibrium with low incidence of cooperation is unstable while the equilibrium with high incidence of cooperation is stable. (The equilibrium with zero cooperation is stable as well.) The impact of adding a mass of righteous individuals into the model is then examined.

2   Basic Model

At the beginning of the first period, a large number of ex ante identical individuals are randomly paired. Each pair then plays a (symmetric) Prisoners' Dilemma game: players simultaneously decide whether to cooperate or defect. For now, assume that there are no commitments. Each obtains a payoff C if both cooperate or D if both defect. If one player cooperates and the other defects, the cooperator's payoff is S (sucker) and the defector's is T (temptation). We assume $T > C > D > S$, so that the game is a Prisoners' Dilemma.

At the end of each period, after observing their payoffs, the players independently and simultaneously decide whether to stay matched and play together again next period, or to exit the relationship and obtain a new partner from the pool of unmatched individuals. The players exit and are repaired with a different partner unless both decide to continue with the relationship. If both decide to remain in the match, they play the same game again in the next period. They again choose simultaneously whether to cooperate or defect. That is, we assume that individuals in a relationship cannot make binding commitments.

A new generation of (identical) individuals is born and arrives in the market at the beginning of each period. The new generation enters the pool of unmatched individuals and joins the pairing process. This assumption ensures that there will always be a large number of unmatched individuals. At the same time, a fraction of the population may die and exit from their relationships or the unmatched pool. Individuals evaluate future payoffs using a common discount factor δ.[5] For most of the analysis, we assume $0 < \delta < 1$.

We assume information is imperfect. Decisions in previous relationships are private information.[6] Thus, a defector can exit his or her current relationship and start fresh by reentering the unmatched pool incognito. This also means that individuals cannot condition decisions on their partner's history in previous relationships. We assume, however, that previous decisions within the relationship are known to both matched players. Thus, within a relationship, decisions to cooperate or defect next period and exit can be made conditional on the partner's behavior in the current period.

Attention is focused on steady-state equilibria in which the fraction α of cooperators among unmatched individuals and the fraction

β of cooperators among the individuals in long-term relationships are constant over time. (Note that this definition does not require that the fraction of unmatched individuals in the entire population be constant over time.)

3   Steady-State Equilibria

An equilibrium with no cooperation always exists. There is never an equilibrium with universal cooperation, and there may be partial cooperation (i.e., less than universal cooperation) equilibria.

THEOREM 1   There is an equilibrium with zero cooperation (i.e., $\alpha = \beta = 0$).

The proof of theorem 1 is straightforward. Consider the following strategy: "In each period, defect and then change partner." If all follow that strategy, nobody has an incentive to change strategy.

THEOREM 2   Universal cooperation (i.e., $\alpha = \beta = 1$) is *not* an equilibrium.

The proof of theorem 2 is also straightforward. If all the unmatched people cooperate ($\alpha = 1$), then each individual has an incentive to defect and change partners in every period.[7]

Under certain conditions, there are "partial cooperation" equilibria in which only a fraction of the unmatched individuals cooperate (i.e., $0 < \alpha < 1$) and all matched individuals in long-term relationships cooperate (i.e., $\beta = 1$). These partial cooperation equilibria can be supported by the following two-phase (symmetric) QFT strategies. Phase I describes how unmatched people behave when they first meet a partner. Phase II describes how players decide whether to quit or stay, and how they play after that decision.

Phase I (Partial Cooperation)   Cooperate with probability α in the current period. At the end of the period, play according to phase II.

Phase II (Quit-for-Tat)   (1) If the outcome of the current period was not mutual cooperation, then quit the relationship and in the next period change partner and play according to phase I. (2) If the outcome of the current period was mutual cooperation, then offer to stay together with your partner. If your partner also decides to stay, cooperate with certainty in the next period and play according to phase II again at the end of that period. If your partner quits or dies, return to the unmatched pool, find a new partner and play according to phase I.

We are left with finding values of α such that this two-phase strategy is an equilibrium strategy. A necessary condition is that no individual has an incentive to deviate when play is in phase I (given that the partner is using the above strategy). That is, the individual must be indifferent between cooperating and defecting. As shown in Moresi and Salop (2002), this condition leads to a quadratic equation in α,

$$A\alpha^2 - B\alpha + F = 0, \tag{1}$$

where $A = \delta(T - D)$, $F = (1 - \delta)(D - S)$ and $B = A + F + C - T$. By the quadratic formula, equation (1) has two solutions:

$$\alpha_1 = [B - (B^2 - 4AF)^{1/2}]/(2A), \tag{2}$$

and

$$\alpha_2 = [B + (B^2 - 4AF)^{1/2}]/(2A), \tag{3}$$

that are real and lie between 0 and 1 *if and only if*

$$B^2 > 4AF, \quad B > 0, \quad \text{and} \quad 2A > B + (B^2 - 4AF)^{1/2}. \tag{4}$$

These conditions are necessary for a steady-state equilibrium with partial cooperation to exist.[8]

For sufficiency, we also need to show that no individual has an incentive to deviate when play is in phase II. In particular, the individual must prefer to cooperate rather than defect. It is better to co-operate *if and only if*

$$C/(1 - \delta) \geq T + \delta V, \tag{5}$$

where $V = [\alpha_i T + (1 - \alpha_i)D]/(1 - \delta)$ is an individual's equilibrium expected utility evaluated at the beginning of phase I.[9]

This leads to the following theorem.

THEOREM 3   Two partial cooperation *QFT* equilibria exist if and only if the conditions in equations (4) and (5) are satisfied. The fractions of cooperators among unmatched individuals in the two equilibria, α_1 and α_2, then are given by equations (2) and (3), respectively.

This theorem is proved in Moresi and Salop (2002).[10] To illustrate, suppose that $T = 5$, $C = 3$, $D = 1$ and $S = 0$. Then, equations (4) and

(5) are not satisfied if $\delta = 0.8$, but they are both satisfied if $\delta = 0.9$. More generally, the theorem 3 conditions are satisfied for all Prisoners' Dilemmas if the discount factor δ is sufficiently close to 1.

For later use, we note that equations (2) and (3) imply a limit result. As δ tends to 1 (i.e., when people are "very patient"), the fraction of the unmatched individuals who cooperate in the low-cooperation equilibrium (α_1) tends to 0, while the fraction in the high-cooperation equilibrium (α_2) tends to $(C - D)/(T - D)$.[11]

4   Stability and Committed Cooperators

We assume hereafter that the conditions in theorem 3 are satisfied, so that there are three possible equilibria. Figure 11.1 below illustrates the two partial cooperation equilibria.

Figure 11.1 shows the expected payoff of an unmatched individual who decides to cooperate (or defect). The expected payoff is the line labeled V_C (or V_D) and is a function of the fraction α of unmatched individuals who cooperate. The two points where V_C and V_D intersect correspond to the two partial cooperation equilibria. The origin is the zero cooperation equilibrium.

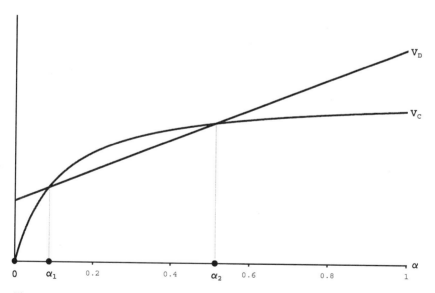

Figure 11.1
Steady-state equilibria

Figure 11.1 shows that the partial cooperation equilibrium with a low incidence of cooperation (α_1) is unstable. If α is slightly smaller (greater) than α_1, then V_C is smaller (greater) than V_D. Thus, starting at $\alpha = \alpha_1$, if α falls (increases) by a small amount, then individuals prefer to defect (cooperate) which will further reduce (increase) the fraction α of cooperating unmatched individuals. If the market is initially to the left of α_1, the market will move toward the zero co-operation equilibrium. If instead the market is initially to the right of α_1, then it will move toward the high cooperation equilibrium (α_2).[12]

Consider a market initially at a steady-state zero cooperation equilibrium, so that the entire population is in the unmatched pool. Now assume that an exogenous fraction γ of the population instantaneously and permanently become "righteous" (committed cooperators) and give birth to righteous progeny. These righteous people cooperate in every period and change partners only if their current partners defect. The remaining population fraction $1 - \gamma$ are "profit-maximizing" individuals. We assume that righteous have the same constant birth and mortality rates (b and m) as the profit-maximizing. Finally, we assume that an individual's type is private information. We then can show that a critical mass of committed cooperators can tip society to the high cooperation equilibrium.

THEOREM 4   If the mass of righteous individuals γ exceeds the critical mass γ^*, then the only steady-state equilibrium is the high cooperation equilibrium α_2, where

$$\gamma^* = \alpha_1 \frac{b + (1 - m)m + (1 - m)^2 \alpha_1}{b + (1 - m)m + (1 - m)^2 \alpha_1^2}. \tag{6}$$

The proof of theorem 4 is provided in Moresi and Salop (2002). Intuitively, suppose that the profit-maximizing individuals do not change their behavior, despite the presence of righteous individuals, but continue to defect and change partners in every period. In this hypothetical scenario, all the profit-maximizing individuals stay in the unmatched pool until they die, while some of righteous people eventually exit the unmatched pool and enter long-term relationships with other righteous people. It follows that the fraction of righteous people in the unmatched pool, which in this scenario is also the fraction α of cooperating people in the unmatched pool, decreases over time and converges to a steady state level which is below the initial fraction γ of righteous people. In theorem 4, the critical mass condition $\gamma > \gamma^*$ ensures that the fraction α of cooperating people in the unmatched pool is always greater than α_1 (even if all the profit-maximizing individuals always defect). It then follows that the only steady-state equilibrium is the α_2 equilibrium.

Corollary of Theorem 4   As the discount factor δ tends to 1, the critical mass γ^* of righteous individuals tends to 0. In the limit, the only steady-state equilibrium is the high-cooperation equilibrium regardless of how small the fraction of righteous individuals.

This last result supports the view that a few righteous people may well be enough to move society from no cooperation to a high incidence of cooperation. (The proof follows directly from equation (6) and the fact that α_1 tends to 0 as δ tends to 1.)

Notes

1. When individuals can obtain imperfect information about their partners, the results may depend on whether that information is public or private (see Mailath and Morris 2002). For simplicity, we assume that individuals cannot obtain any information on new partners.

2. See Hayashi and Yamagishi (1998) for experiments with QFT.

3. We assume that the behavior of these righteous individuals is exogenous and the other individuals are profit-maximizing. In contrast, evolutionary models assume that people select strategies by a trial-and-error learning process in which they gradually discover that some strategies are better. See Weibull (1995) for the role of evolutionary game theory in the field of behavioral ethics.

4. Another interpretation is that God was willing to spare thousands of immoral inhabitants to save ten moral people. This alternative interpretation fails because God had the option of saving solely the few moral inhabitants, just as he saved Lot and his daughters. (Lot's wife did not fully cooperate with God's orders and perished.)

5. The discount factor δ reflects both the rate of time preference and the mortality rate.

6. Nor does an individual know whether his partner is a new entrant or not. In addition, we assume that players cannot use correlated strategies.

7. Contagious punishments à la Ellison (1994) are not practical because the number of players is infinite.

8. We ignore the nongeneric case where $B^2 = 4AF$.

9. Intuitively, if the individual cooperates, then he remains in a long-term relationship and obtains the expected present value $C/(1 - \delta)$. If instead he decides to defect, then his payoff is equal to T in the current period (since his partner is cooperating) plus δV in future periods (since his partner will quit). The equilibrium expected utility V can be evaluated by assuming that an individual defects all the time (since he is indifferent

in phase I), in which case he remains in the unmatched pool forever and obtains an expected payoff equal to $\alpha_i T + (1 - \alpha_i)D$ in each period.

10. We also show that the two partial cooperation equilibria, α_1 and α_2, can be supported by strategies where individuals do not quit after a defection, but instead stay together and behave as if they just met. This amounts to a "probabilistic" punishment strategy.

11. Moresi and Salop (2002) provide additional comparative statics results and derive the steady-state size of the unmatched pool with constant birth and mortality rates.

12. Moresi and Salop (2002) formally analyze equilibrium stability by introducing some inertia into the model. That is, we consider the alternative assumption that people do not constantly reoptimize their behavior but, for example, choose a lifetime strategy once, when they first arrive in the market. This alternative assumption does not change the steady-state equilibria.

References

Axelrod, R. 1984. *The Evolution of Cooperation*. New York: Basic Books.

Ellison, G. 1994. "Cooperation in the Prisoner's Dilemma with Anonymous Random Matching." *The Review of Economic Studies* 61: 567–588.

Frank, R. 1988. *Passions Within Reason: The Strategic Role of the Emotions*. New York: W. W. Norton.

Friedman, J. 1971. "A Non-Cooperative Equilibrium for Supergames." *Review of Economic Studies* 38: 1–12.

Hayashi, N., and T. Yamagishi. 1998. "Selective Play: Choosing Partners in an Uncertain World." *Personality and Social Psychology Review* 2: 276–289.

Kreps, D., P. Milgrom, J. Roberts, and R. Wilson. 1982. "Rational Cooperation in the Finitely Repeated Prisoners' Dilemma." *Journal of Economic Theory* 27: 245–252.

Mailath, G., and S. Morris. 2002. "Repeated Games with Almost-Public Monitoring." *Journal of Economic Theory* 102: 189–228.

Nash, J. 1950. "Equilibrium Points in N-Person Games." *Proceedings of the National Academy of Sciences* 36: 48–49.

Moresi, S., and S. C. Salop. 2002. "Imperfect Information, Quit-for-Tat and Probabilistic Punishments in Repeated Prisoners' Dilemma Games." Mimeo.

Salop, S. C. 1978. "Parables of Information Transmission in Markets," in *The Effect of Information on Consumer and Market Behavior*, ed. A. Mitchell. American Marketing Association.

Sen, A. 2000. *What Difference Can Ethics Make?* Presented at the international meeting on "Ethics and Development" of the Inter-American Development Bank. Available online at ⟨http://www.iadb.org/etica/ingles/lis-doc1-i.cfm⟩.

Shapiro, C., and J. E. Stiglitz. 1984. "Equilibrium Unemployment as a Worker Discipline Device." *American Economic Review* 74: 433–444.

Shubik, M. 1959. *Strategy and Market Structure: Competition, Oligopoly, and the Theory of Games*. New York: Wiley.

Smith, A. [1776] 1910. *An Inquiry into the Nature and Causes of the Wealth of Nations*. London: Dent & Sons.

Smith, A. [1790] 1976. *The Theory of Moral Sentiments*. Oxford: Clarendon Press.

Stiglitz, J. E. 1975. "Information and Economic Analysis," in *Current Economic Problems*, ed. Michael Parkin and A. R. Nobay. Cambridge: Cambridge University Press.

Taylor, M. 1987. *The Possibility of Cooperation*. Cambridge: Cambridge University Press.

Ullmann-Margalit, E. 1977. *The Emergence of Norms*. Oxford: Clarendon Press.

Weibull, J. 1995. *Evolutionary Game Theory*. Cambridge, MA: MIT Press.

12

Market Structure, Organizational Structure, and R&D Diversity

Joseph Farrell, Richard J. Gilbert, and Michael L. Katz

An extensive literature examines the relationship between market structure and research and development (R&D) activities, primarily comparing privately and socially optimal investment levels, along a single dimension. In practice, however, there are many different research paths that a firm might pursue. Hence, progress also hinges on the research directions chosen by firms and the extent to which firms diversify their approaches to R&D by pursuing multiple directions simultaneously.

Many people suspect that a diversity of approaches goes along with a diversity of approachers, and antitrust authorities have expressed concern over the effects of mergers, for instance, on research diversity.[1] But it is not immediately clear why this should be a concern. After all, a single organization can have incentives to pursue diverse approaches. Put simply, why can't a single organization do everything a group of firms can do, plus take advantage of coordination where beneficial? This question is answered here by exploring how market structure and organizational structure affect the social portfolio of R&D approaches.

Stiglitz is no stranger to these issues. Two lines of his research are directly on point. One is his work on R&D competition when each firm can pursue multiple paths simultaneously. Sah and Stiglitz (1987) established conditions under which the total number of paths pursued in a market is independent of the number of firms. While provocative, this result applies to a limited set of market structures. Several additional settings are examined here. We call the influence of market structure on diversity the role of external factors.

Sah and Stiglitz (1985, 1986, 1988) also provided a second line of directly relevant work, this time on organizational design. Sah and Stiglitz explored how the architecture of an economic organization—

who collects information, with whom it is communicated, and how decisions are made—affects the quality of decision making. Below, we build on their model of hierarchical architectures to examine how firms' choices of internal organization affect R&D diversity. We call this the role of internal factors.

The remainder of this chapter is organized as follows. Section 1 lays out several assumptions maintained throughout the analysis. Section 2 establishes a benchmark by examining a firm that is the sole potential innovator and is a unitary, profit-maximizing decision maker. Section 3 examines external factors by considering the interaction of several unitary, profit-maximizing decision makers. Specifically, it examines whether highly concentrated industries will predictably give rise to different R&D portfolios than less concentrated industries. Section 4 turns to internal issues and examines how organizational choices interact with market structure to affect the equilibrium R&D portfolio.

1 Our Choice of Research Path

Many factors influence firms' R&D strategies, and to identify diversification incentives we begin by eliminating or holding constant potentially confounding influences. First, with product innovation, the value of R&D diversity as a response to uncertainty may become confounded with the value of product variety.[2] To avoid this problem, we restrict attention to process innovations and assume throughout that each firm has a product of fixed characteristics.

Second, we restrict attention to situations in which R&D activities along different paths are substitutes for one another. We do this because complementarities could introduce economies of scope that can separately influence the choice of R&D portfolios. We define a project as a level of effort along a particular R&D path. We assume that each project, j, gives rise to a stand-alone cost level, c^j, and that a firm's unit cost is equal to the lowest realized cost level over the set of projects the firm has undertaken: firm i's unit production costs are $c_i = \min\{c^1, c^2, \ldots, c^k\}$ when firm i undertakes projects 1 through k.

Third, we also want projects to be substitutes rather than complements in terms of the interaction of effort levels across projects. Throughout most of the analysis we assume that there are no technological spillovers within or across firms: the distribution of results from project j undertaken by firm i is independent of the efforts devoted to other projects by firm i or its rivals.[3]

Fourth, we want to distinguish the incentive to diversify R&D paths from incentives for firms to choose different types of R&D projects. The economics literature suggests that incumbent firms with market power have stronger incentives than new competitors to invest in incremental innovations.[4] Furthermore, a large business strategy literature suggests that incumbent firms tend to look to innovate in areas they already know.[5] While theses biases are themselves of considerable interest, we focus on diversification narrowly defined to identify clearly various forces at work. Thus, we assume that, conditional on the level of effort, each of the different substitute projects has the same cost distribution as any other.

2   Unitary Monopoly

We begin by comparing the diversification incentives of a profit-maximizing monopolist with those of a total-surplus-maximizing decision maker. Consider a set of portfolios of R&D projects where each portfolio entails the same level of aggregate R&D expenditures. Each portfolio gives rise to a distribution function for the firm's cost level. A profit-maximizing decision maker chooses the portfolio that maximizes the expected value of $\pi(c)$, the monopoly profits earned with unit production cost level c. A welfare-maximizing decision maker chooses the portfolio that maximizes the expected value of $W(c)$, the sum of profits and consumer surplus when the firm chooses the monopoly price corresponding to marginal cost c. Note that both profits and welfare are decreasing functions of c. Moreover, profits are convex in c; a profit maximizer has incentives to take risks with R&D. Does the firm do so to an efficient degree?

As is well known, a monopolist facing a downward-sloping demand function undertakes too little cost-reducing R&D because a fall in marginal costs leads to an equilibrium increase in consumer surplus. A similarly general result does not exist for the monopolist's attitude toward risk. Define $x(p)$ as the quantity demanded at price p, $r(c)$ as the monopoly price given costs c, and $x^*(c) \equiv x(r(c))$. By the envelope theorem, $\pi'(c) = -x^*(c)$. The change in total surplus is $W'(c) = (r - c)dx^*/dc - x^*(c)$. Using the Lerner condition, $W'(c) = -x^*(c)(1 + \varphi(c))$, where $\varphi(c) \equiv dr/dc \geq 0$ is the pass-through rate.

Suppose that $\varphi(c)$ is constant over c, as is the case with linear, constant elasticity, or rectangular (i.e., all consumers have the same reservation price) demand. Integrating the expression for the derivatives of profits and welfare demonstrates that $W(c) = \alpha + (1 + \varphi)\pi(c)$, where α is a constant. Therefore, when $\varphi(c)$ is constant, profit-maximizing and welfare-maximizing decision makers have identical preference orderings over risky portfolios that require equal R&D expenditures.

When the pass-through rate varies with c, a profit-maximizing monopolist may have different attitudes toward risk in c than a welfare maximizer. One measure of preferences toward risk is the Arrow-Pratt coefficient of absolute risk aversion, $-u''(x)/u'(x)$, where $u(x)$ is a payoff function. Twice differentiating the expressions for welfare and profits yields

$$W''(c) = -\frac{dx}{dr}\varphi(c)(1 + \varphi(c)) - x^*(c)\varphi'(c)$$

and

$$\pi''(c) = -\frac{dx}{dr}\frac{dr}{dc} = \left[-\frac{r}{x}\frac{dx}{dr}\right]\frac{dr}{dc}\frac{x}{r} = \eta\varphi(c)\frac{x}{r} > 0,$$

where $\eta \equiv -(r/x)(dx/dr)$ is the elasticity of demand. Combining the previous calculations,

$$-\frac{W''(c)}{W'(c)} = -\frac{\pi''(c)}{\pi'(c)} - \frac{\varphi'(c)}{1 + \varphi(c)}. \tag{1}$$

Consider a choice between one R&D portfolio that yields a non-degenerate distribution of cost levels and another requiring the same R&D expenditures that yields a particular cost level with certainty. When the pass-through rate everywhere increases with c, the coefficient of absolute risk aversion is everywhere higher for the profit-maximizing monopolist and thus, whenever the welfare maximizer weakly prefers the risky R&D portfolio, so does the profit maximizer.[6] Similarly, if the pass-through rate decreases with c, then whenever the profit maximizer weakly prefers the risky R&D portfolio, so does the welfare maximizer.

As is well known, the Arrow-Pratt measure is of limited usefulness for analyzing choices between two risky portfolios. Ross (1981) has proposed a stronger measure for dealing with such situations. Modifying his definition to fit the present setting, $W(c)$ is said to be "strongly more risk loving" than $\pi(c)$ if and only if $\inf_c(W''(c)/\pi''(c)) \geq \sup_c(W'(c)/\pi'(c))$. If one decision maker is strongly more risk loving than the other, then when the second one would choose the riskier of two portfolios, so would the first (Ross 1981, application 1). Application of this measure generally requires consideration of specific demand functions. One can make the following observations, however, which limit the possible nature of any divergence between private and social attitudes toward risk in c. Using our earlier expressions for the derivatives of profits and welfare, $(W''(c))/(\pi''(c)) = 1 + \varphi(c) - (r/\eta)(\varphi'(c)/\varphi(c))$ and $(W'(c))/(\pi'(c)) = 1 + \varphi(c)$. Hence, if $\varphi'(c) > 0$, the welfare maximizer cannot be strongly more risk loving than the profit maximizer. Similarly, if $\varphi'(c) < 0$, the profit maximizer cannot be strongly more risk loving than the welfare maximizer.

The previous analysis compares private and social attitudes toward risk in cost realizations. But to understand any divergence between the privately chosen degree of diversification and the social optimum, one must also understand the generally complex relationship between riskiness and diversification. A profit-maximizing monopolist will—from a social perspective—tend to underinvest in cost-reducing R&D. To distinguish this effort bias from any diversification bias, we assume that the firm has a fixed total R&D expenditure of E and we examine the effects of spreading expenditure over additional projects. In choosing the degree of diversification, at least two factors come into play in addition to the firm's attitudes toward risk: (1) different projects are substitutes, and (2) changing the level of effort devoted to an R&D project changes its distribution of returns.

Consider the first additional factor. Because the outputs of successful R&D projects are perfect substitutes, there is no incremental private or social value to adding a project whose distribution of resulting cost reductions mirrors that of a project already in the firm's portfolio.[7] Thus, all else equal, there is value in pursuing negatively correlated projects even if the decision maker is risk loving.

Now focus on the second factor by supposing the outcomes of different projects are independent and identically distributed, conditional on effort levels, with common distribution function $G(c|e)$, where e is the amount of effort devoted to that project. We normalize the price of effort at 1 and assume that there is an additional fixed cost of F per project. If the optimal allocation of effort across k active projects is uniform, then $E = k(e + F)$ and the lowest realized cost has density $kg(c|E/k - F)(1 - G(c|E/k - F))^{k-1}$, where g is the density associated with G.

A central question is whether differences in attitudes toward risk lead a profit-maximizing monopolist to choose a different value of k than would a total-surplus maximizer. Building on yet another line of Stiglitz's work (Diamond and Stiglitz 1974; Rothschild and Stiglitz 1970, 1971), one portfolio of projects is said to be riskier than the other if the distribution of costs associated with the first portfolio is equal to the distribution of the second plus a mean preserving spread. Unfortunately, characterizing the effects of k on a portfolio's distribution of cost realizations can be difficult because the distribution of returns from each project in a portfolio generally varies as total effort is distributed more thinly across projects.

One case in which the private and social portfolio decisions can readily be compared is an R&D technology such as in Sah and Stiglitz (1987), in which any project has only two possible outcomes, success and failure. Suppose that failure leaves a firm's cost unchanged, while success lowers the firm's marginal cost to c^*. Let $\rho(e)$ denote a project's probability of success given that effort level e is devoted to that project. We assume throughout that $\rho(0) = 0$, $\rho'(e) > 0$, and $\rho''(e) < 0$. For a fixed level of total R&D expenditure, both the social and private programming problems are to allocate the expenditure across projects to maximize the probability that at least one project succeeds. This common program can be expressed as

$$\min \prod_{i=1}^{k}(1 - \rho(e_i))$$

$$\text{subject to } kF + \sum_{i=1}^{k} e_i \leq E,$$

where k is the total number of projects receiving positive effort. It immediately follows that: (1) attitudes toward risk have no effect on the optimal choice of project diversity, and (2) any privately optimal allocation of R&D effort is also socially optimal.

For the analysis that follows, it is useful to characterize the optimal allocation of effort more fully. Forming the Lagrangian and differentiating yields first-order conditions

$$\rho'(e_i) \prod_{j \neq i}(1 - \rho(e_j)) = \mu \qquad i = 1, 2, \ldots, k, \tag{2}$$

where μ is the multiplier for the budget constraint. For any two projects i and j receiving positive effort, one must have $\rho'(e_i)(1 - \rho(e_j)) = \rho'(e_j)(1 - \rho(e_i))$. When $(\rho'(e))/(1 - \rho(e))$ is strictly decreasing in e, all active projects must receive the same level of effort.[8] We assume that this condition is satisfied.

Now suppose that E is endogenous. The argument above implies that all active projects will receive a common level of effort, e. The firm chooses e and k to maximize expected profits. Let π be the expected incremental profit from a successful project. The optimal level of effort satisfies equation (2) with $\mu = 1/\pi$ and, ignoring integer constraints, the marginal R&D project must just break even in equilibrium,

$$\pi\rho(e)(1 - \rho(e))^{k-1} = F + e.$$

These two equations imply

$$\frac{\partial\rho(e)/\partial e}{\rho(e)} = \frac{1}{F + e}. \tag{3}$$

Making sufficient assumptions about the curvature of $\rho(e)$, there is a unique optimal per-project effort level, e^*.[9] Notice that e^* depends on neither k nor π. Finally, define $\rho \equiv \rho(e^*)$.

3   External Concerns

This section examines the interaction of multiple unitary decision makers. The R&D decisions of different firms interact in several ways. One is through product-market competition: successful R&D by one firm affects the returns to R&D that are enjoyed by product-market rivals. Other effects can arise when intellectual property rights, such as patents, enable an initial innovator to preempt later ones following a similar R&D path or when firms conducting R&D compete for scarce inputs, such as trained research personnel.

Our interest is in how market structure—acting through its influence on the nature of these interactions—shapes the market-wide portfolio of R&D projects.[10] As Sah and Stiglitz (1987) observed, many models of R&D investment forcibly underestimate the R&D diversification that may arise in concentrated market structures by flatly assuming that each firm undertakes only a single R&D project. Sah and Stiglitz emphasized that such an assumption is unrealistic and provided a set of circumstances in which a highly concentrated industry undertakes the same total number of R&D projects as a more atomistic one. Below, we generalize their result and show how it depends on assumptions made about the interactions identified above. We find that equilibrium R&D diversity generally depends on market structure, but in complex ways not well captured by the conventional one-project-per-firm assumption.

Innovation Competition with Nonexclusive Intellectual Property Rights

Following Sah and Stiglitz (1987), assume that each of N producers of a homogeneous product can pursue one or more cost-reducing R&D projects. For simplicity, assume that all firms have the same constant marginal costs $c_i = c^0$, $i = 1, \ldots, N$ before any discovery is made. The outcomes of the projects are stochastically independent, whether pursued by the same firm or by different ones. Firms draw from an infinite pool of projects, so that the chance of any two firms undertaking the same project is nil. The results of all undertaken projects become common knowledge before price or output decisions are made. As in our earlier example, an unsuccessful project leaves a firm's cost unchanged, while a successful project lowers the firm's marginal cost to $c^* < c^0$. The marginal cost reduction from an additional successful project is zero.

The intellectual property rights regime is such that successful R&D by one firm neither allows other firms to take advantage of the results of that R&D nor precludes other firms from making use of their own successful R&D. We have in mind an environment in which R&D projects are protected by trade secrets. Secrecy prevents a firm from appropriating a rival's successful R&D, but it does not prevent any firm from exploiting the results of its own R&D.[11]

Nash-Bertrand Competition

Sah and Stiglitz (1987) showed that the total, market-wide number of R&D projects pursued in equilibrium is independent of the number of firms in the industry when firms are Nash-Bertrand product-market competitors. With Bertrand competition and constant marginal costs, all producers earn zero profits if more than one firm succeeds at R&D or if all of them fail. Firm i earns positive product-market profits, π, if and only if its R&D alone succeeds.

If firm j engages in k_j R&D projects, $j = 1, 2, \ldots, N$, then firm i's net expected profit is

$$\pi q(k_i) \prod_{j \neq i} (1 - \rho)^{k_j} - k_i m,$$

where $q(k_i) = 1 - (1 - \rho)^{k_i}$ is the probability that at least one of firm i's projects succeeds, $\prod_{j \neq i} (1 - \rho)^{k_j}$ is the probability that all projects by other firms fail, and $m = F + e^*$ is the cost of an optimally scaled R&D project. With Bertrand competition and constant marginal costs, the equilibrium total number of R&D projects, $K^* = \sum_{j=1}^{N} k_j$, satisfies

$$\pi \rho (1 - \rho)^{K^*} \leq m \leq \pi \rho (1 - \rho)^{K^* - 1}.$$

The Sah and Stiglitz result that the extent of R&D diversity is independent of market structure under these conditions is evident from these inequalities: K^* is independent of the number of firms in the industry.[12]

Consider the productive and allocative efficiency properties of the equilibrium. An important property of Bertrand competition is that if at least one project is successful, all equilibrium production is by a firm with the lower cost level, c^*. Thus, production efficiency is independent of how the projects are spread across firms. This property does not hold for other forms of product-market competition and, as will be shown below, this has important implications for the effect of R&D competition on industry costs and welfare. Turning to allocative efficiency, the equilibrium price is lower if two or more firms have successful R&D projects than if only one firm does. Hence, as long as demand is not perfectly inelastic, allocative efficiency depends on the distribution of projects across firms.[13]

Before discussing the Sah and Stiglitz invariance result further, we observe that, with independently and identically distributed R&D projects, K is a useful measure of R&D diversity. When the returns to different R&D projects are correlated to various degrees, the extent of diversity also depends on the extent of correlation among the projects firms choose to pursue. For the reasons discussed in the section on unitary monopoly above, a firm has incentives to pursue a portfolio of R&D projects whose returns are negatively correlated. It is easy to see that, under Nash-Bertrand competition with undifferentiated products, there also is an incentive for a firm to choose projects with returns negatively correlated with those of rival firms because there is no value in being successful if another firm has been successful as well.

A Perfect Cartel

The reason why the total number of R&D projects in the industry does not depend on the total number of firms under homogeneous Bertrand competition is that the incremental private benefit of a successful R&D project: (a) is zero if there is at least one other successful project, whether pursued by the same firm or by another, and (b) is independent of the number of firms and the set of unsuccessful projects if it is the unique successful project. Thus, a firm contemplating an incremental project calculates the profitability of the project based on the total number of projects in the industry, not on their allocation among firms.

As we will illustrate with the models of this subsection and the next, the Sah and Stiglitz invariance result is not robust to the nature of product-market competition. Before considering these formal models, it is useful to understand intuitively where the result breaks down. As long as any two successful projects are perfect substitutes, one success for a firm makes additional successes worthless regardless of the nature of product-market competition. The extent to which success by one firm affects the value of success for its rivals, however, does vary with the nature of competition. In particular, under many forms of competition, there is a positive prize associated with being one of several firms to have successfully innovated. Thus, property (a) of the Sah-Stiglitz model is not generally satisfied.[14] Turning to property (b), this too does not generally hold because other firms will affect the successful innovator's product-market output and price, and in many models a change in the number of rivals (with the same costs as one another) will change the value of being a unique successful innovator.

Consider the polar opposite case from Bertrand competition: firms collude perfectly on price. We continue to assume that firms compete in research and development. Specifically, assume that demand is inelastic at quantity D^0 up to the reservation value v and firms share industry revenues vD^0 equally. Firm i's expected profit is

$$\frac{D^0}{N}[(v - c^0) + (c^0 - c^*)(1 - (1 - p)^{k_i})] - k_i m$$

when it undertakes k_i R&D projects. Each firm's optimal number of R&D projects satisfies

$$\frac{D^0}{N}(c^0 - c^*)\rho(1 - \rho)^{k^*} \leq m \leq \frac{D^0}{N}(c^0 - c^*)\rho(1 - \rho)^{k^*-1}.$$

The inequalities imply that k^* is a nondecreasing function of D^0/N, which clearly falls as N rises. The total industry number of R&D projects is not, in general, invariant to the structure of the industry.[15] With our assumed R&D technology, a second success by a given producer is worthless to that firm. The value of its first success, however, is now independent of whether other firms have succeeded or not. Moreover, the value of success depends on the producer's share of total output, and each firm's optimal investment in R&D, k^*, is decreasing in the number of firms. Hence, neither property (a) nor (b) of the Sah and Stiglitz model now holds.

Although the total number of R&D projects can increase with N, expected welfare in this example is a nonincreasing function of the number of firms in the industry. Expected industry profits (which are equal to expected total surplus in this model) fall as N rises because there is less diffusion of a successful innovation. A firm with lower production costs sells only D^0/N units of output, and thus expected production costs are higher when a given number of R&D projects are spread across more firms. Moreover, each firm's expected marginal cost of output rises with the number of firms because each firm undertakes fewer R&D projects. Thus, while more firms may contribute to greater R&D diversity as measured by the total number of projects, expected total surplus falls and expected production costs rise.

Because the firms do not compete in price with one another in this assumed cartel, licensing would be jointly profitable. We implicitly assumed above that informational asymmetries and the intellectual property rights regime make such licensing infeasible. Under different informational and property right assumptions, however, the invariance result would reappear. Specifically, the number of R&D projects would be independent of the number of firms if (1) a monopoly licensor could fully extract the value of its innovation from its licensees, and (2) two or more successful innovators would compete in the licensing market in Nash-Bertrand fashion, driving the equilibrium license fee to zero. When conditions (1) and (2) are satisfied, properties (a) and (b) of the Sah-Stiglitz model hold. Condition (1) is necessary because a firm fully internalizes the benefits of innovation for its own sales, which are a function of N, while the total benefits of industry-wide licensing are independent of N.

Nash-Cournot Oligopoly

Suppose the N firms are Nash-Cournot competitors in the product market. Unlike a perfect cartel, a firm's payoff from innovation depends on the number of other firms that innovate successfully. Unlike Bertrand competition, the firm's payoff from innovation can be positive even if it shares the market with other successful innovators.

Assume that N firms sell a homogeneous product with linear inverse demand with intercept A and slope $-b$. Define the average marginal cost of all firms other than firm i: $\tilde{c}_{-i} \equiv 1/(N-1) \sum_{j \neq i} \tilde{c}_j$, where $\tilde{c}_j$ is a random variable that takes the value c^* with probability $q(k_j) = 1 - (1-p)^{k_j}$ and c^0 with probability $1 - q(k_j)$. Standard analysis (see, e.g., Vives 1999 and Yi 1999) shows that firm i's profit as a function of industry cost realizations is[16]

$$\pi_i(c_i, \tilde{c}_{-i}) = \frac{1}{b} \left[\frac{A - c_i + (N-1)(\tilde{c}_{-i} - c_i)}{N+1} \right]^2.$$

In a Cournot oligopoly, firm i's profit depends on the average of all other active firms' costs and does not depend upon how those costs are distributed among its rivals. Let $\bar{c}_{-i}$ be the expected value of $\tilde{c}_{-i}$. Firm i's expected profit is

$$E\pi_i(c_i, \tilde{c}_{-i}) = \frac{1}{b} \left[\frac{A - c_i + (N-1)(\bar{c}_{-i} - c_i)}{N+1} \right]^2 + \frac{(N-1)^2}{b(N+1)^2} \text{var}(\tilde{c}_{-i})$$

$$= \pi_i(c_i, \bar{c}_{-i}) + \frac{(N-1)^2}{b(N+1)^2} \text{var}(\tilde{c}_{-i}).$$

If firm i undertakes k_i R&D projects, its expected profit net of R&D expenditures is

$$(1-p)^{k_i} E\pi_i(c^0, \tilde{c}_{-i}) + (1 - (1-p)^{k_i}) E\pi_i(c^*, \tilde{c}_{-i}) - k_i m$$

and the expected benefit to firm i from an additional R&D project is

$$p(1-p)^{k_i} [\pi_i(c^*, \tilde{c}_{-i}) - \pi_i(c^0, \tilde{c}_{-i})] - m.$$

In a symmetric equilibrium, each of N firms invests in k R&D projects. Then $\bar{c}_j = c^* + (1-p)^k(c^0 - c^*)$ for all $j = 1, \ldots, N$. Figure

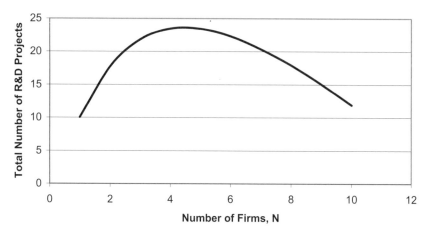

Figure 12.1
Total number of R&D projects versus number of firms for Nash-Cournot case

12.1 shows the total number of R&D projects in a symmetric N-firm oligopoly when $A = 80$, $b = 1$, $\rho = .1$, $c^0 = 10$, $c^* = 6$, and $m = 5$. This example ignores integer constraints and assumes projects are divisible. As figure 12.1 shows, total investment in R&D has an inverted-U shape. That is, the equilibrium total number of R&D projects reaches a maximum at intermediate levels of market concentration.

Intuitively, two offsetting forces are at play as the number of firms rises. First, as the number of firms rises, each firm's sales fall and, thus, so do the benefits of successful, unit-cost-reducing R&D. This effect leads each firm to do less R&D as the number of firms rises. (Dasgupta and Stiglitz 1980 demonstrate this result in a model with free entry.) Second, unlike the Nash-Bertrand case, each firm can benefit from successful R&D even if other firms succeed as well. This effect can raise the total industry incentives to conduct multiple projects. Up to some number of firms (four in this example), the total industry investment in R&D increases, but it falls for larger numbers of firms.

In the present model, even if an increase in the number of firms leads to a larger total number of R&D projects, it leads (weakly) to fewer projects per firm. Moreover, unlike the Nash-Bertrand case, a Nash-Cournot competitor whose R&D succeeds does not serve the entire market. As a result, both firm and industry expected unit costs increase with the number of firms, even if the total number of R&D projects and, therefore, the probability of successful R&D also increase with the number of firms. Recall that the perfect cartel equilibrium exhibits a similar pattern. The total number of R&D projects can increase with the number of firms, but expected unit costs at the firm and industry levels weakly increase with more firms.

In contrast to the case of a perfect cartel facing inelastic demand, the beneficial impact on prices of an increase in the number of Cournot competitors can outweigh the negative impact on industry costs. For the parameter values in the example reported in figure 12.1, expected welfare increases with N up to six firms, and decreases for larger numbers of competitors.

Innovation Competition with Exclusive Success or Scarce R&D Inputs

When innovation is protected through intellectual property laws that grant the right to exclude others (*e.g.*, patent), if one firm succeeds along a particular path, then other firms may be unable to make use of the results of their R&D if they have followed the same research path.[17] Thus, when there are finitely many potential paths, or some firms can choose their R&D paths after observing the choices of their rivals, the possibility of preemption arises. We will show how preemption can give rise to an incentive to diversify as a "spoiler" strategy.

Consider a model in which each firm allocates effort along two paths, A and B, each of which is a patent race. While innovations on the two paths are perfect substitutes for reducing production costs, a patent for an innovation on one path does not block use of an innovation on the other one. On each path, each firm's probability of success is an increasing function of its own efforts and a decreasing function of its rival's. Thus, firm 1 has success probability $a(e_1^A, e_2^A)$ along path A, where e_i^A is firm i's effort along path A. Firm 2 has a symmetric success probability, $a(e_2^A, e_1^A)$. We use analogous notation for path B. Unlike in the nonexclusive case, at most one firm can succeed on any given path.

Private payoffs are as follows: if one firm succeeds along at least one path and its rival succeeds along neither, then gross payoffs are $(\pi^M, 0)$, where π^M denotes monopoly profits in the product market. If each firm succeeds along a different path, then gross payoffs are (π^D, π^D), where π^D denotes the per-firm duopoly payoffs and $2\pi^D < \pi^M$. Firm 1's expected payoff is

$$a(e_1^A, e_2^A)[1 - b(e_2^B, e_1^B)]\pi^M + a(e_1^A, e_2^A)b(e_2^B, e_1^B)\pi^D$$

$$+ b(e_1^B, e_2^B)[1 - a(e_2^A, e_1^A)]\pi^M + b(e_1^b, e_2^B)a(e_2^A, e_1^A)\pi^D - e_1^A - e_1^B.{}^{18}$$

A similar expression holds for firm 2. Hence, the marginal return to e_1^A is (using subscripts on $a(\cdot,\cdot)$ and $b(\cdot,\cdot)$ to denote partial derivatives):

$$a_1(e_1^A, e_2^A)[(1 - b(e_2^B, e_1^B))\pi^M + b(e_2^B, e_1^B)\pi^D]$$
$$- a_2(e_2^A, e_1^A)b(e_1^B, e_2^B)[\pi^M - \pi^D] - 1.$$

The term -1 is the direct cost of firm 1's marginal effort along path A. The first term (beginning with a_1) is the expected private value of increasing firm 1's own success along path A, while the term with a_2 (recall that $a_2 < 0$) captures the private value of reducing firm 2's probability of succeeding along path A, which is valuable to firm 1 in the event that firm 1 succeeds along B. The term with a_2 is a raising-rival's-cost effect: firm 1 tries to succeed along path A in part to stop firm 2 from doing so. This component of firm 1's private benefit is proportional to firm 1's probability of success along path B. Note that

$$\frac{\partial^2 \pi_1(e_1^A, e_1^B)}{\partial e_1^A \partial e_1^B} = -[a_1(e_1^A, e_2^A)b_2(e_2^B, e_1^B) + b_1(e_1^B, e_2^B)a_2(e_2^A, e_1^A)]$$

$$\times [\pi^M - \pi^D] > 0.$$

Thus, there is a private complementarity between success on A and success on B. Intuitively, if a firm knows it is going to succeed along one path, it has strong private incentives to succeed along the other to protect the profits it can earn from being the unique successful innovator.

In contrast to the private incentives, there is a social substitutability between success along path A and success along path B. If the firm succeeds along path A, there is no social value to the firm's succeeding along path B as well because there is no incremental cost reduction. The private complementarity can create a private incentive to diversify along both paths even if the technology of R&D is characterized by increasing returns to effort along any one path so that specialization would be efficient. Moreover, with nonexclusive success, increasing returns to R&D would give rise to private incentives to specialize efficiently.

Similarly to preemptive patenting, a firm can have incentives to diversify its projects to raise rivals' R&D costs. If some inputs for R&D have upward sloping supply curves, then a firm may expand its R&D along a particular path to make R&D more expensive for its competitors, thereby decreasing their probabilities of success along that path.

4   Internal Considerations

So far, we have assumed that firms behave as unitary decision makers acting to maximize profits subject to market competition. This is, at best, an approximation; a well-run firm solves a complex multilayer principal-agent problem and can thus be viewed as maximizing profits subject to many constraints, only some of which come from product-market competition. This section briefly examines the effects of various private responses to the need to aggregate and exchange information within an organization to make decisions.

To focus on the influence of organizational design on the choice of R&D portfolios, we first consider a setting in which the equilibrium number of R&D projects is independent of the number of firms, holding organizational structure constant across firms, then we examine how changing the organizational structure affects the equilibrium number of R&D projects.

Similar to the first model of the section on external concerns, consider a market in which firms are Nash-Bertrand competitors in the product market and choose among stochastically independent projects, each of which has only two possible outcomes: success and failure. In contrast to the earlier model, assume that there are two classes of R&D projects: good and bad. A good project has a probability of success, $p(e) > 0$ for all $e > 0$ and $p(0) = 0$, while a bad project has a zero probability of success for any level of effort.

Suppose the manager choosing whether to undertake an R&D project believes that a fraction $\omega \in (0, 1)$ of the projects proposed by the organization's staff are good. Let π be the prize from having the sole successful project. As earlier, the prize is 0 if two or more firms have successful projects. The expected incremental value of a marginal project is equal to

$$\max_{e} \omega p(e) H \pi - e - F,$$

where H is the probability that all other projects (of that firm or any other) fail. Inserting ω into the derivation in the section on unitary monopoly, the optimal level of effort per project, e^*, is given by equation (3) and is independent of ω and π.

In a symmetric equilibrium with K projects, $H = (1 - \omega\rho)^{K-1}$, where as before $\rho \equiv \rho(e^*)$. When $\omega\rho\pi > F + e^*$, it is profitable for at least one firm to engage in R&D and, ignoring integer constraints, the equilibrium number of projects satisfies

$$\omega\rho(1 - \omega\rho)^{K-1}\pi = F + e^* = m, \tag{4}$$

As expected, the equilibrium number of projects is independent of N.

In what follows, it is useful to understand the relationship between the equilibrium number of R&D projects, K^*, and the probability that a project is good, ω. We can examine this relationship by taking the natural logarithm of the condition for the equilibrium number of projects and totally differentiating with respect to ω:

$$\left[\frac{1}{\omega} - \frac{(K^* - 1)\rho}{1 - \omega\rho}\right] d\omega + \ln(1 - \omega\rho)\, dK^* = 0.$$

Hence,

$$\frac{dK^*}{d\omega} = -\frac{1 - \omega\rho k^*}{\omega(1 - \omega\rho)\ln(1 - \omega\rho)}. \tag{5}$$

The denominator is negative, and the sign of $dK^*/d\omega$ is equal to the sign of $1 - \omega\rho K^*$.

By equation (4), $K^* = 1 - [(\ln \omega\rho\pi - \ln m)/(\ln(1 - \omega\rho))]$, and thus

$$1 - \omega\rho K^* = 1 - \omega\rho + \omega\rho\left[\frac{\ln \omega\rho\pi - \ln m}{\ln(1 - \omega\rho)}\right]. \tag{6}$$

Because $0 < \omega\rho < 1$, the first two terms on the right-hand side of equation (6) sum to a positive number and the denominator of the third term is negative. By equation (4), $m < \omega\rho\pi$ and thus the third term is negative.

If π is sufficiently large, the sum of the three terms is negative. Hence, given any positive value of $\omega\rho$, if π is sufficiently large, then a change in organizational design that increases ω will result in fewer equilibrium R&D projects industry wide. An increase in the effectiveness of project selection will reduce equilibrium R&D diversity. Conversely, for any admissible value of $\omega\rho$, if π is sufficiently close to $m/(\omega\rho)$ from earlier, the sum of the three terms is positive. Hence, for a given value of ω, if π is sufficiently close to $m/(\omega\rho)$ from earlier, an increase in the effectiveness of project selection will result in greater equilibrium R&D diversity.

While the equilibrium number of projects undertaken may rise or fall with ω, the equilibrium probability that at least one project will succeed always rises. The reason is as follows. From equation (4), $(1 - \omega\rho)^{K^*-1}$ is equal to $m/(\omega\pi\rho)$, which falls as ω rises. The probability that all projects fail is $(1 - \omega\rho)^{K^*} = (1 - \omega\rho)(1 - \omega\rho)^{K^*-1}$. Because both factors on the right-hand side of this equality fall as ω rises, the probability that all projects fail must fall as ω rises.

Thus far we have taken ω to be exogenous. Various aspects of organizational design, however, affect an enterprise's ability to pursue a favorable selection of R&D projects. One element is the extent to which internal reward structures align employee incentives with those of shareholders. Suppose, for example, that the R&D staff in an organization have very low-powered incentives. Then the technical staff may propose bad projects because these projects generate utility to the staff as interesting research problems even though they hold no commercial promise. Conversely, in an organization that has compensation and promotion schemes that align the incentives of R&D staff with those of stockholders, higher-level managers can correctly assume that a higher percentage of projects advanced by the technical staff are good projects.

A second factor is how the organization aggregates diverse information and views held by different members of the organization. The design of organizations to accomplish this task was the subject of an important line of research reported in Sah and Stiglitz (1985, 1986, 1988). Here, we analyze a model building on this line of research. Firms choose from the same, infinitely large pool of potential projects. When a firm chooses a project, the firm can expend resources to evaluate the project before committing effort to it. Unlike in Sah and Stiglitz, projects are substitutes for one another and, thus, there are declining incremental social and private values of undertaking additional projects.

An organization chooses how many evaluations of a proposed R&D project to conduct. Each evaluation incurs a cost, s, to obtain a binary signal of whether the project is good or bad. We say that an evaluator approves a project when the signal indicates that the project is good. The probability that a single evaluator will approve a project is γ if the project is in fact good and β if the project is in fact bad. We assume that evaluations are informative (i.e., $\gamma > \beta$) and that the evaluations are independent of one another conditional on the true type of the project.

As defined by Sah and Stiglitz, under an L-level hierarchy, a project is evaluated sequentially and a negative evaluation at any point leads to the project's being rejected without any further evaluation. Thus, a project is accepted if and only if all L levels of the hierarchy give it a positive evaluation. When ω_0 is the prior probability that a project is good, if the project has been approved by an L-level hierarchy, then the posterior probability that the project is good is

$$\omega(L) = \left[\frac{\omega_0 \gamma^L}{\omega_0 \gamma^L + (1 - \omega_0)\beta^L}\right].$$

Note that $\omega(L)$ goes to 1 as L goes to infinity, and $\omega(L)$ goes to ω_0 as L goes to 0.

On average, a proposed project will be evaluated

$$\zeta(L) \equiv \omega_0 \left[\frac{1 - \gamma^L}{1 - \gamma}\right] + (1 - \omega_0)\left[\frac{1 - \beta^L}{1 - \beta}\right]$$

times. The fraction of proposed projects that a L-level hierarchy will deem good and therefore eligible for investment is $\omega_0 \gamma^L + (1 - \omega_0)\beta^L$. Consequently, the evaluation cost per approved project in an L-level hierarchy is $(s\varsigma(L))/(\omega_0 \gamma^L + (1 - \omega_0)\beta^L)$, which is an increasing function of L. The expected evaluation cost per undertaken project increases with the number of levels in the hierarchy because each project has to be reviewed at each level, and the organization has to sort through a larger number of projects to select one in which to invest.

Evaluation costs are in addition to per-project R&D costs, $F + e^*(L)$, where $e^*(L)$ satisfies

$$\frac{\partial p(e^*)/\partial e}{p(e^*)} = \frac{1}{F + e^*(L) + \dfrac{s\varsigma(L)}{\omega_0 \gamma^L + (1 - \omega_0)\beta^L}}.\ [19]$$

By the concavity of $p(\cdot)$, $e^*(L)$ is increasing in L. Hence, the sum of the effort and evaluation costs per undertaken project, $m(L) \equiv F + e^*(L) + (s\varsigma(L)/(\omega_0 \gamma^L + (1 - \omega_0)\beta^L))$, is increasing in L. An additional level increases the probability that R&D projects approved for investment will succeed, but the cost per undertaken project also rises.[20]

Suppose there are N hierarchies, each of which has L levels. Define $\rho^*(L) \equiv \rho(e^*(L))$. Generalizing our earlier discussion of the Bertrand case, if the firms undertake a total of K projects, no firm can increase its expected profits by screening one more or one fewer project if

$$\omega(L)\rho^*(L)(1 - \omega(L)\rho^*(L))^{K-1}\pi \geq m(L) \geq \omega(L)\rho^*(L)(1 - \omega(L)\rho^*(L))^K\pi.$$

Thus, ignoring integer constraints,

$$\omega(L)\rho^*(L)(1 - \omega(L)\rho^*(L))^{K^*-1}\pi = m(L).$$

As before, the equilibrium number of R&D projects under Bertrand competition is independent of the number of firms in the industry holding L fixed. The number of projects does, however, depend on the size of the hierarchies, which may itself depend on the number of firms.

Our analysis above identifies several effects on R&D from increasing the number of layers in each hierarchy. The net result depends on technological parameters. Figure 12.2 reports the results of simulations with $\omega_0 = 0.2$, $\gamma = 0.6$, $\beta = 0.4$, and $\pi = 300$ under the assumption that the scale of R&D projects is technologically fixed such that $F + e^*(L) = 5$ and $\rho^*(L) = 0.1$ for all L. The figure illustrates the equilibrium outcome for various levels of the cost per evaluation, s. Given these parameters, for small values of L, π is sufficiently close to $m/(\omega(L)\rho^*(L))$ from earlier that $dK^*/d\omega$ is positive. For larger values of L, however, $dK^*/d\omega$ is negative. When there are no per-

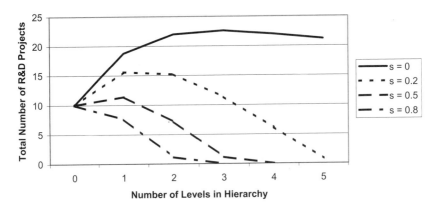

Figure 12.2
Dependence of total number of R&D projects on the number of hierarchy levels

project evaluation costs ($s = 0$), an increase in L increases the probability of success for each project undertaken and, from our earlier result, increases the total probability that R&D is successful for the market as a whole. Furthermore, for small hierarchies, the numerator in equation (5) is positive and the total number of R&D projects in the market increases with the number of layers in each hierarchy. The results change dramatically, however, when project evaluations are costly. For example, when $s = 0.8$, the total number of R&D projects and the total probability of successful R&D fall with the number of layers in each hierarchy, and firms do not do any R&D at all if the number of levels in the hierarchies exceeds 2.

Although we have treated the number of hierarchical levels as given, in practice each firm chooses the number of levels in its organization. We next briefly explore some of the forces at work. We show that, under the assumption that the scale of R&D projects is technologically fixed at e^* with success probability p, a larger reward for successful innovation leads firms to invest in (weakly) more layers of hierarchy.

Suppose there is a fixed cost of S per level of hierarchy within an organization in addition to the per-evaluation cost, s. A firm's choice of k and L can be broken into two steps. For any given probability of success, $1 - \alpha$, the firm chooses k and L to

$$\min km(L) + LS$$

subject to $[1 - p\omega(L)]^k \leq \alpha.$ \hfill (7)

The firm then chooses α to maximize $(1 - \alpha)\pi - \Phi(\alpha)$, where $\Phi(\alpha)$ is the optimized value of the objective function in the subproblem above and π is the prize associated with having at least one successful project.[21] By standard revealed preference arguments, $\Phi(\cdot)$ is a nonincreasing function and the firm's choice of α is nonincreasing in π.

We next examine the comparative statics of L varying α exogenously.[22] It will be convenient to define $\theta(L) \equiv \ln[1 - p\omega(L)]$ and write inequality (7) as $k\theta(L) \leq \ln \alpha$.

The Kuhn-Tucker conditions for the choice of k and L include

$$k[m(L) + \vartheta\theta(L)] = 0 \hfill (8)$$

and

$$L[S + km'(L) + k\vartheta\theta'(L)] = 0, \hfill (9)$$

where ϑ is the multiplier for the constraint. If $k > 0$, then equation (8) implies that $\vartheta = (-m(L))/(\theta(L))$. Substituting this expression into equation (9) yields the necessary condition

$$L\left[S + km(L)\left(\frac{m'(L)}{m(L)} - \frac{\theta'(L)}{\theta(L)}\right)\right] = 0. \tag{10}$$

By equation (10), if $S > 0$, then $L > 0$ only if

$$\frac{m'(L)}{m(L)} < \frac{\theta'(L)}{\theta(L)}. \tag{11}$$

Now consider two values of the failure probability, $0 < \alpha_1 < \alpha_2$. Define $k_1' \equiv (\ln \alpha_1)/\theta(L_2)$ and $k_2' \equiv (\ln \alpha_2)/\theta(L_1)$. By construction, (k_1', L_2) satisfies the constraint in the firm's program when the failure probability is α_1, and (k_2', L_1) satisfies the constraint when the failure probability is α_2. The optimality of (k_1, L_1) and (k_2, L_2) implies

$$k_1' m(L_2) + L_2 S \geq k_1 m(L_1) + L_1 S$$

and

$$k_2' m(L_1) + L_1 S \geq k_2 m(L_2) + L_2 S.$$

Adding these two inequalities and rearranging terms yields

$$(k_1' - k_2)m(L_2) \geq (k_1 - k_2')m(L_1). \tag{12}$$

Using the definitions of the k_i' and the fact that the constraint in the firm's program is satisfied with equality by each (k_i, L_i) pair, it follows that inequality (12) is satisfied if and only if

$$[\ln \alpha_1 - \ln \alpha_2]\left[\frac{m(L_2)}{\theta(L_2)} - \frac{m(L_1)}{\theta(L_1)}\right] \geq 0. \tag{13}$$

By hypothesis, $0 < \alpha_1 < \alpha_2$. Thus, the first term in square brackets is negative. Hence, the second term in square brackets must be nonpositive. By inequality (11), $(m(L))/(\theta(L))$ is increasing in L (recall that $m(\cdot)$ is a positive, increasing function, while $\theta(\cdot)$ is a negative, decreasing function).[23] Therefore, inequality (13) can be satisfied only if $L_1 \geq L_2$.

Now return to our earlier model of a perfect cartel of N firms with no licensing. In that model, π is a decreasing function of N and the analysis above establishes that the equilibrium value of L is nonincreasing in N. Intuitively, as N rises, each firm conducts less R&D and has fewer projects over which to spread the fixed costs of hierarchy. Hence, with fewer firms, firms will invest in more layers of hierarchy and engage in more accurate project evaluations.

The analysis also suggests that in a model of Bertrand competition with differentiated products and asymmetric market shares, the firms with larger shares—and thus larger potential gains from successful cost-reducing innovation—will invest in larger hierarchies. The possibility that smaller firms will choose smaller hierarchies raises a number of interesting issues about the types of research conducted by small and large firms within an industry.

5   Closing Remarks

Drawing inspiration from some of Stiglitz's pathbreaking work, we have explored how both external and internal factors might affect firms' R&D portfolios. Much work remains to be done. We hope that this chapter—written by a modified hierarchy that at times threatened to become a Sah and Stiglitz polyarchy[24]—will be instrumental in stimulating that work by developing some promising paths along which others may proceed.

Acknowledgments

Farrell thanks SIEPR for research support through a Cain Fellowship.

Notes

1. See Robinson (1999) and Rubinfeld and Hoven (2001) on the proposed merger of Lockheed-Northrop and Grumman.

2. A large literature exists on deterministic product selection, which establishes that a monopolist may choose greater or less variety than is socially optimal and than would a multifirm market. Stiglitz is a prominent contributor to this literature. See Dixit and Stiglitz (1977). See also Katz (1980).

3. Notice that this assumption does not imply that the resulting cost levels of different projects are uncorrelated conditional on the effort levels.

4. See Gilbert and Newbery (1982) and Katz and Shapiro (1987).

5. Christensen (1997) argues that market leaders in the computer disk drive industry repeatedly failed to embrace the next technological revolution because they focused

too much on meeting customer demands for incremental improvements to existing technologies. Henderson (1993) invokes organizational factors and economic incentives to explain why new entrants in semiconductor photolithography equipment often leapfrogged existing market leaders.

6. This result is a variant of the following result, which applies to two decision makers with monotonically increasing, concave objective functions who are choosing between a lottery and a sure thing. (In our setting, two decision makers with monotonically decreasing, convex objective functions choose between a lottery and a sure thing.) If one decision maker everywhere has a higher coefficient of absolute risk aversion than the other, then if the decision maker with a higher coefficient of absolute risk aversion weakly prefers the lottery, so does the decision maker with the lower coefficient. See, for example, Kreps (1990, 86).

7. More precisely, there is no incremental value to a project for which there is no state of the world that occurs with positive probability in which that project has a strictly lower cost realization than any other project in the firm's portfolio.

8. If $(p'(e))/(1 - p(e))$ is strictly increasing in e, the firm undertakes only one R&D project.

9. A sufficient condition is for the elasticity of $p(e)$ with respect to e to be non-increasing in e because then $(ep'(e))/(p(e))$ must cross $e/(F + e)$ once from earlier.

10. By "structure" we mean the underlying tastes and technology. In much of what follows, we treat the number of firms as an exogenously given element of market structure. This should be viewed as a short hand for the endogenous determination of the number of firms as a result of tastes, technology, and possibly government policies, such as antitrust.

11. This secrecy also makes licensing difficult. For a discussion of the difficulties of selling information, see Arrow (1962, 614–616). For a discussion of licensing in the presence of the potential theft of information shown to the prospective buyer, see Anton and Yao (1994).

12. When industry demand is perfectly inelastic, one can extend this result to projects that have more than two possible outcomes. The reason is that a project's value depends only on how much better it is than the next-most-successful project, regardless of who owns it.

13. This point is made by Sah and Stiglitz (1987, 103, 104).

14. Sah and Stiglitz (1987, 107) themselves make this point.

15. The equilibrium industrywide total number of projects is $K \equiv Nk^*$. Ignoring integer constraints, the sign of dK/dN is equal to the sign of $\ln((q(k^*))/(1 - q(k^*)))$ where $q(k) \equiv 1 - (1 - p)^k$. The sign is positive if k^* is sufficiently large and negative if k^* and p are sufficiently small.

16. We assume that all firms are active producers, which is the case for $c^0 - c^*$ sufficiently small.

17. We assume that a successful innovator has no obligation to share the fruits of its R&D with product-market rivals and that rival firms cannot use independent invention as a defense to an infringement claim.

18. For simplicity, in this subsection we assume $F = 0$.

19. This result is another application of the derivation in the section on unitary mono-poly and implicitly assumes sufficient curvature of $p(e)$ to ensure that a unique solu-tion exists.

20. Moreover, if—unlike the present model—there is a limited number of good proj-ects, then a firm's mistakenly rejecting a good project, which becomes more likely as L increases, will be costly.

21. The value of π depends both on the nature of product-market competition and the intensity of R&D competition that the firm faces. Here, our reduced form allows for arbitrary forms of product competition and assumes that the firm makes its R&D decisions holding its rivals' R&D strategies fixed.

22. We ignore integer constraints, and the analysis provides a heuristic examination of the forces at work.

23. Again, this is a heuristic argument because equation (8) need hold only at the respective optima.

24. Projects within this chapter were sequentially evaluated and were rejected if they received two negative evaluations. In a polyarchy, a project is accepted as soon as it receives a favorable evaluation.

References

Anton, James J., and Dennis A. Yao. 1994. "Expropriation and Inventions: Appropri-able Rights in the Absence of Property Rights." *American Economic Review* 84(1): 190–209.

Arrow, Kenneth J. 1962. "Economic Welfare and the Allocation of Resources for In-vention," in *The Rate and Direction of Inventive Activity: Economic and Social Factors*, ed. Richard R. Nelson. Princeton: Princeton University Press.

Christensen, Clayton M. 1997. *The Innovator's Dilemma*. Boston: Harvard Business School Press.

Dasgupta, Partha, and Joseph Stiglitz. 1980. "Industrial Structure and the Nature of Innovative Activity." *Economic Journal* 90: 266–293.

Diamond, Peter A., and Joseph E. Stiglitz. 1974. "Increases in Risk and in Risk Aver-sion." *Journal of Economic Theory* 8(3): 337–360.

Dixit, Avinash, and Joseph E. Stiglitz. 1977. "Monopolistic Competition and Optimal Product Diversity." *American Economic Review* 67: 297–308.

Henderson, Rebecca. 1993. "Underinvestment and Incompetence as Responses to Radical Innovation: Evidence from the Photolithographic Alignment Equipment In-dustry." *The RAND Journal of Economics* 24(2): 248–270.

Gilbert, Richard J., and David Newbery. 1982. "Preemptive Patenting and the Persis-tence of Monopoly." *American Economic Review* 72(2): 514–526.

Hoven, John, and Daniel L. Rubinfeld. 2001. "Innovation and Antitrust Enforcement," in *Dynamic Competition and Public Policy: Technology, Innovation, and Antitrust Issues*, ed. J. Ellig. New York: Cambridge University Press.

Katz, Michael L. 1980. "Multiplant Monopoly in a Spatial Market." *Bell Journal of Economics* 11(2): 519–535.

Katz, Michael L., and Carl Shapiro. 1987. "R&D Rivalry with Licensing and Imitation." *American Economic Review* 77(3): 402–420.

Kreps, David M. 1990. *A Course in Microeconomic Theory.* Princeton: Princeton University Press.

Reinganum, Jennifer. 1989. "The Timing of Innovation: Research, Development, and Diffusion," in *The Handbook of Industrial Organization*, ed. R. Schmalensee and R. D. Willig. Amsterdam: North-Holland.

Robinson, Constance K. 1999. "Leap-frog and Other Forms of Innovation." Address before the American Bar Association, Chicago, IL, June 10.

Ross, Stephen A. 1981. "Some Stronger Measures of Risk Aversion in the Small and the Large with Applications." *Econometrica* 49(3): 621–638.

Rothschild, Michael, and Joseph E. Stiglitz. 1970. "Increasing Risk: I. A Definition," *Journal of Economic Theory* 2(3): 225–243.

Rothschild, Michael, and Joseph E. Stiglitz. 1971. "Increasing Risk II: Its Economic Consequences." *Journal of Economic Theory* 3(1): 66–84.

Sah, Raaj Kumar, and Joseph E. Stiglitz. 1985. "Human Fallibility and Economic Organization," *American Economic Review* 75(2) Papers and Proceedings of the Ninety-Seventh Annual Meeting of the American Economics Association (May), 292–297.

Sah, Raaj Kumar, and Joseph E. Stiglitz. 1986. "The Architecture of Economic Systems: Hierarchies and Polyarchies." *American Economic Review* 76(4): 716–727.

Sah, Raaj Kumar, and Joseph E. Stiglitz. 1987. "The Invariance of Market Innovation to the Number of Firms." *The Rand Journal of Economics* 18(1): 98–108.

Sah, Raaj Kumar, and Joseph E. Stiglitz. 1988. "Committees, Hierarchies and Polyarchies." *The Economic Journal* 98(391): 451–470.

Vives, Xavier. 1999. *Oligopoly Pricing.* Cambridge, MA: MIT Press.

Yi, Sang-Seung. 1999. "Market Structure and Incentive to Innovate: The Case of Cournot-Oligopoly." *Economics Letters*, 65: 379–388.

13   Patent Oppositions

Jonathan Levin and Richard
Levin

In just over two decades, a succession of legislative and executive
actions has served to strengthen substantially the rights of patent
holders.[1] At the same time, the number of patents issued in the
United States has nearly tripled from 66,290 in 1980 to 184,172 in
2001. Although the surge in patenting has been widely distributed
across technologies and industries, decisions by the Patent and
Trademark Office and the courts have expanded patent rights into
three important areas of technology where previously the patentability of innovations had been presumed dubious: genetics, software,
and business methods.[2] As in other areas of innovation, patents in
these fields must meet standards of usefulness, novelty and nonobviousness. A serious concern, however, in newly emerging areas
of technology is that patent examiners may lack the expertise to assess
the novelty or nonobviousness of inventions, leading to a large
number of patents likely to be invalidated on closer scrutiny by the
courts.

Although similar examples could be drawn from the early years of
biotechnology and software patenting, economists in particular will
appreciate that many recently granted patents on business methods
fail to meet a common-sense test for novelty and nonobviousness.
Presumably this occurs because the relevant prior art is unfamiliar
to patent examiners trained in science and engineering. Consider
U.S. Patent No. 5,822,736, which claims as an invention the act of
classifying products in terms of their price sensitivities and charging
higher markups for those with low price sensitivity, rather than
a constant markup for all products. The prior art most relevant
to judging the novelty of this application is neither documented
in earlier patents nor found in the scientific and technical literature normally consulted by patent examiners. Instead, it is found in

textbooks on imperfect competition, public utility pricing, or optimal taxation.

The almost certain unenforceability of this particular business method patent may render it of limited economic value, but other debatable patents have already been employed to exclude potential entrants or extract royalties. A much publicized example is Jay Walker's patent (U.S. Patent No. 5,794,207) covering the price-matching system used by Priceline. After several years of legal wrangling, Microsoft Expedia agreed to pay royalties for allegedly infringing on this patent. Many economists, however, would object that Walker's patent covers only a slight variation on procurement mechanisms that have been used for hundreds if not thousands of years. Interestingly, in terms of prior art, Walker's patent application cites several previous patents but not a single book or academic article on auctions, procurement, or market exchange mechanisms.

If challenged in court, a patent on the inverse elasticity rule would likely be invalidated for failing to meet the test of novelty or non-obviousness. The Walker patent, a closer call, also might not survive such scrutiny. But current U.S. law permits third party challenges only under very limited circumstances. An administrative procedure, reexamination, is used primarily by patentees to amend their claims after becoming aware of uncited prior art, but it is also available to third parties who seek to invalidate a patentee's claims by identifying prior art, in the form of an earlier patent or publication, that discloses the precise subject matter of the claimed invention.[3]

Broader objections to a patent's validity can be adjudicated only in response to a patent holder's attempts to enforce rights against an alleged infringer. In response to an infringement suit, the alleged infringer may file a counterclaim of invalidity. In response to a "desist or pay" letter, the alleged infringer may seek a declaratory judgment to invalidate the patent. Generally speaking, such proceedings are very expensive and time consuming. A recent survey estimated the median cost of a litigated patent infringement suit at $1.5 million in cases involving stakes of $1 million to $25 million; when the stakes exceed $25 million, the median cost of a suit was estimated to be $3 million (American Intellectual Property Law Association 2001). A typical infringement suit might take two to five years from initial filing to final resolution.

What are the costs of uncertainty surrounding patent validity in areas of emerging technology? First, uncertainty may induce a considerable volume of costly litigation. Second, in the absence of litigation, the holders of dubious patents may be unjustly enriched and the entry of competitive products and services that would enhance consumer welfare may be deterred. Third, uncertainty about what is patentable in an emerging technology may discourage investment in innovation and product development until the courts clarify the law, or inventors may choose to incur the cost of product development only to abandon the market years later when their technology is deemed to infringe. In sum, a timelier and more efficient method of establishing ground rules for patent validity could benefit innovators, followers, and consumers alike.

One recently suggested remedy is to expand the rights of third parties to challenge the validity of a patent in a low-cost administrative procedure before sinking costly investments in the development of a potentially infringing product, process, or service (see Merges 1999; Levin 2002). Instead of the current reexamination procedure, which allows post-grant challenges only on very narrow grounds, the United States might adopt an opposition procedure more akin to that practiced in Europe, where patents may be challenged on grounds of failing to meet any of the relevant standards: novelty, nonobviousness, utility, written description, or enablement. The European system requires only minimal expenditure by the parties. When interviewed, senior representatives of the European Patent Office estimated expenditures by each party at less than $100,000. The time required for adjudication, however, is extremely long, nearly three years, owing to very generous deadlines for filing of claims, counterclaims, and rebuttals.[4]

The idea of a streamlined, efficient U.S. administrative procedure for challenges to patent validity is clearly gaining momentum in the response to mounting concern about the quality of patents in new technology areas. In its recently released *21st Century Strategic Plan*, the Patent Office stated as one of its intended actions: "Make patents more reliable by proposing amendments to patent laws to improve a [sic] post-grant review of patents" (U.S. Patent and Trademark Office 2002).

This chapter makes a modest attempt to evaluate the potential costs and benefits of introducing such a post-grant opposition process. The next two sections develop a simple model of patent enforcement and patent oppositions. We model patent oppositions as essentially a cheaper and earlier way to obtain a ruling on patent validity. One further difference between patent opposition and litigation captured by the model is that patent oppositions can be generated by potential infringers, while litigation must be initiated or triggered by the patent holder. The analysis divides naturally into two cases: one where the potentially infringing use of the patent is rivalrous (i.e., competes directly with the patentee's product) and one where the uses are nonrivalrous (i.e., independent or complementary). The key difference between these cases is that in the former, the patent holder wants to deter entry, while in the latter the patent holder simply wants to negotiate for a large licensing fee.

Several effects of introducing an opposition process are identified. First, if the parties foresee costly litigation in the absence of an opposition, they have a clear incentive to use the cheaper opposition process to resolve their dispute. This lowers legal costs and potentially prevents wasteful expenditure on product development. At the same time, giving the parties a lower cost method of resolving disputes can lead to oppositions in cases when the entering firm might either have refrained from development or been able to negotiate a license without litigation. These new oppositions have a welfare cost in that the firms incur deadweight costs from preparing their opposition suits. Nevertheless, these oppositions generate potential benefits. They can prevent unwarranted patents from resulting in monopoly profits. More broadly, if decisions under the opposition process are more informed than those made directly by the patent examiners, the rewards to patent holders end up more closely aligned with the true novelty and nonobviousness of their invention. From a dynamic welfare standpoint, this has the favorable effect of providing more accurate rewards for innovation.

The model suggests that, in some cases, introducing an opposition process will have an unambiguous welfare benefit, while in other cases there will be a trade-off between static welfare costs and static and dynamic welfare benefits. Section 3 uses available information on the cost of litigation and plausible parameters for market size and the cost of development to provide a rough quantitative sense of the welfare effects. Our general conclusion is that the costs of introducing an opposition system are likely to be small in relation to the potential benefits.

Section 4 concludes with a discussion of some aspects of the opposition process not captured in our simple modeling approach. The model provides a reasonable assessment of how an opposition system affects the gains and losses realized by a single inventor, a single potential infringer, and their respective customers. It ignores, how-ever, substantial positive externalities from greater certainty and more timely information about the likely validity of patents that would flow to other parties contemplating innovation and entry in a new technology area. In this respect, our analytic and quantitative findings probably understate the full social benefit of introducing a low-cost, timely system for challenging patent validity.

1   A Model of Patent Enforcement

We start by developing a simple benchmark model from which we can investigate the effect of an opposition process. There are two firms. Firm A has a newly patented innovation, while firm B would like to develop a product that appears to infringe on A's patent. The dilemma is that the legitimacy of A's patent is uncertain. In the event of litigation, B may be able to argue convincingly that part or all of it should be voided.

The interaction between the firms unfolds as follows. Initially Firm B must decide whether to develop its technology into a viable prod-uct. Let k denote the costs of development. If B does not develop, A will be the monopoly user of its technology. If B does develop, it can enter negotiations to license A's technology. If negotiations are suc-cessful, B pays a licensing fee (the precise amount will be determined by bargaining) and both parties use the technology. If B does not obtain a license, it may still introduce its product. In this event, A can either allow B to market its product unhindered or file suit to enforce its intellectual property rights. If it files suit, the parties enter litigation.

We adopt a simple formulation for thinking about litigation in which each party incurs a cost L to prepare its case. At trial, the court assesses the validity of A's patent and whether B's patent infringes upon it. We focus on the determination of validity, since this is the aspect of patent disputes for which an opposition process has rele-vance. Let p_A and p_B denote the subjective probabilities that firms A and B assign to the court upholding the patent, and let p denote the true objective probability of validity. We assume that the firms' sub-jective probabilities (but not the true objective probability) are com-monly known though not necessarily equal.[5]

If the court invalidates the relevant parts of firm A's patent, B is free to market its product. In contrast, if the patent is upheld, A has the option of excluding B from the market. Firm B may try

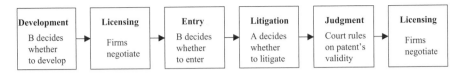

Figure 13.1
Timing in the benchmark model

again to negotiate a license but if it fails A proceeds to market alone.

The firms' profits depend on whether B's product reaches the market and whether they incur litigation costs. Let $\pi_{A|B}$ and π_A denote the gross profits that A will realize if B's product does or does not reach the market. Let π_B denote the gross profits that B's product will generate. In making decisions, the firms must factor in these eventual profits as well as development costs, litigation costs, and licensing fees in the event of a licensing agreement.

We model licensing negotiations, both pre-litigation and post-litigation, using the Nash bargaining solution. This means that if there are perceived gains to licensing, each party captures its perceived payoff in the absence of a license and the additional surplus generated by the agreement is divided equally.

The timing of the benchmark model is displayed in figure 13.1. After development, the firms can negotiate a license. If this fails, B must make a decision about whether to enter and A can respond by litigating. If there is litigation, the court rules on the patent's validity at which point the parties have another opportunity to negotiate a license.

In thinking about this benchmark situation and the effects of an opposition process, we have found it useful to distinguish two prototypical situations. In the first, which we refer to as the case of nonrivalrous innovation, the firms have a joint interest in bringing firm B's product to market. This is the situation, for instance, when firm A's patent covers a research tool or perhaps a component of a product that B can produce at lower cost than A. In the second case, rivalrous innovation, firm B's product will compete directly with A's and the introduction of B's product will decrease joint profits through intensified competition. Think, for instance, of A as a drug company and B as a rival with a closely related therapeutic.

We analyze these situations separately for a simple reason. When innovations are nonrivalrous, litigation and opposition hearings will not bar entry. They serve only to affect the terms of licensing agreements. In contrast, with rivalrous innovation, litigation is an instrument for firm A to defend its monopoly status. We assume that antitrust law precludes A from paying B not to enter or from designing a licensing agreement that manipulates future competition.[6] Thus if A's patent rights are upheld, it denies its rival access to the market. Changing the method for resolving disputes from litigation to an opposition may substantively affect what products eventually reach market.

1.1 Nonrivalrous Innovation

We start by considering nonrivalrous innovation. To focus attention on this case, we make the following parametric assumption, which is sufficient to ensure that introducing firm B's product generates a joint gain for the two firms.

ASSUMPTION NR $\pi_{A|B} + \pi_B - 2k \geq \pi_A$.

In fact, this assumption is slightly stronger than is needed to ensure nonrivalry. A weaker condition would be that $\pi_{A|B} + \pi_B - k \geq \pi_A$. The stronger condition has the benefit of guaranteeing that firm B will have a sufficient incentive to develop prior to negotiating a license rather than needing to seek a license prior to development. Since the effect of an opposition proceeding turns out to be essentially the same in this latter case, we omit it for the sake of clarity.[7]

To analyze the model, we work backward. First, we describe what happens if the parties wind up in litigation. We then consider whether litigation will occur or whether B will negotiate a license or simply enter with impunity. Finally, we consider B's incentives to develop its product.

Outcomes of Litigation

Suppose that firm B introduces its product without a license and firm A pursues litigation. Two outcomes can result. If the court voids the relevant sections of A's patent, B can enter without paying for a license. If the court upholds A's patent, B must seek a license. Because the products are nonrivalrous, there is a gain $\pi_{A|B} + \pi_B - \pi_A > 0$ to be realized from an agreement. Development costs do not appear in the calculation of the gain from introducing B's product because they have already been sunk. Nash bargaining means that this gain is split equally through a licensing fee F_V:

$$F_V = \frac{1}{2}(\pi_A - \pi_{A|B}) + \frac{1}{2}\pi_B.$$

Here, we use the subscript V to refer to bargaining under the presumption that A's patent is valid.

Factoring in these two possible outcomes of litigation, we can calculate the (subjective) expected payoffs to the two firms upon entering litigation. These are $\pi_{A|B} - L + p_A F_V$ for Firm A and $\pi_B - k - L - p_B F_V$ for firm B.

Determinants of Litigation

We now back up and ask what will happen if firm B develops its technology.

The first question is whether A has a credible threat to litigate if B attempts to market its product without a license. Since A's subjective gains from litigation are $p_A F_V - L$, it will want to pursue litigation only if

$$p_A F_V - L \geq 0. \tag{A}$$

If this inequality fails, Firm A has a weak patent—the benefit of enforcing it is smaller than the litigation costs. If A's patent is weak, firm B can simply ignore it and enter without fear or reprisal. Indeed, even if an opposition system is in place, B would never want to use it since A's patent is already of no meaningful consequence. This makes the weak patent case relatively uninteresting from our perspective. For this reason, we assume from here on that A's patent is not weak.

Given that firm A has a credible threat to litigate, we now ask whether litigation will actually occur. The parties will end up in court if and only if the following two conditions are met:

$$\pi_B - p_B F_V - L \geq 0 \tag{B}$$

and

$$(p_A - p_B)F_V - 2L \geq 0. \tag{L}$$

The first condition says that firm B would rather endure litigation than withdraw its product. The second condition says that the two firms have a joint incentive to resolve the patent's validity in court rather than reach a licensing agreement with validity unresolved. Note that this can only occur if the parties disagree about the probable outcome in court (i.e., if $p_A > p_B$). Moreover, it is more likely to occur if litigation costs are small relative to the value generated by B's product.

If either condition (B) or condition (L) fails, litigation will not occur. Rather, the parties will negotiate a license without resolving the patent's validity. The specific license fee is determined by Nash bargaining with the parties splitting the surplus above their threat points should negotiations fail. If (B) fails, firm B does not have a credible threat to litigate so Nash bargaining results in a licensing fee F_V. In essence, the parties treat the patent as if it were valid. In contrast, if firm B has a credible threat to litigate but there is no joint gain to licensing after litigating (i.e., (L) fails), the alternative to licensing is litigation. In this case, B will pay a somewhat lower fee F_U:

$$F_U = \frac{1}{2}(p_A + p_B)F_V.$$

Here, the subscript U refers to bargaining under uncertainty about the validity of the patent. Intuitively, the licensing fee is lower when there is uncertainty about the patent's validity.

Development

The last piece of the model is to show that firm B has an incentive to develop its product regardless of whether it anticipates licensing or litigation. The worst outcome for B is that (B) fails and it is forced to pay a licensing cost F_V. Even in this case, however,

$$\pi_B - k - F_V = \frac{1}{2}(\pi_{A|B} + \pi_B - \pi_A) - k \geq 0.$$

So B still has an incentive to develop its product, a conclusion that follows directly from assumption NR.

We can now summarize the benchmark outcomes when innovation is nonrivalrous.

PROPOSITION 1 Suppose innovation is nonrivalrous and that firm A's patent is not weak. The possible outcomes are:

• *Litigation.* If both (B) and (L) hold, firm B develops its product and there is litigation to determine patent validity. If the patent is upheld, firm B pays F_V for a license.

Table 13.1
Profits with nonrivalrous innovation

	A's profit	B's profit
Litigation	$\pi_{A|B} + pF_V - L$	$\pi_B - k - pF_V - L$
Licensing	$\pi_{A|B} + \{F_U, F_V\}$	$\pi_B - k - \{F_U, F_V\}$

- *Licensing without Litigation.* If either (B) or (L) fails, firm B develops and negotiates a license. The fee is either F_U if (B) holds or F_V if not.

Table 13.1 summarizes the objective payoffs to the two firms in each scenario.

1.2   Rivalrous Innovation

Next we consider the case of rivalrous innovation. To do this, we assume that introducing firm B's product reduces joint profits. The following assumption is sufficient to imply this.

ASSUMPTION R $\pi_{A|B} + \pi_B/p_A + 2L/p_A < \pi_A$.

As in the previous section, this is slightly stronger than is needed. A weaker condition that would guarantee rivalry is that $\pi_{A|B} + \pi_B - k < \pi_A$. The stronger condition implies that if firm B chooses to enter, then not only will firm A have an incentive to litigate (ruling out the weak patent case), it will not want to license just to avoid costly litigation. We rule out this latter situation in an effort to keep the model as simple as possible. Nevertheless, it can be worked out and in such a circumstance the effect of an opposition process corresponds closely to the nonrivalrous environment described above.[8]

To analyze the possible outcomes, we again work backward. We first consider what would happen in the event of litigation, then ask whether litigation will occur if B develops, and finally consider the incentive to develop.

Outcomes of Litigation

If firm B introduces its product and there is litigation, there are two possible outcomes. If the court voids the patent, B can market its product without paying any licensing fee. If the court upholds A's patent, the rivalry of the products means that A will deny B a license.

Thus the firms' (subjective) profit expectations entering litigation are $p_A \pi_A + (1 - p_A)\pi_{A|B} - L$ for firm A and $(1 - p_B)\pi_B - k - L$ for firm B.

Determinants of Litigation

Now consider what will happen should B develop its product. If B attempts to introduce its product, assumption R implies that A will certainly want to initiate litigation because:

$$p_A(\pi_A - \pi_{A|B}) - L \geq 0. \tag{A}$$

That is, assumption R rules out the weak patent case where firm A is not willing to defend its intellectual property rights.

At the same time, firm B is willing to introduce its product and face litigation if and only if

$$(1 - p_B)\pi_B - L \geq 0. \tag{B}$$

If this inequality fails, the litigation cost outweighs B's expected benefit from a product introduction. If it holds, B will introduce its product and the parties will end up in court. To see this, we note that under assumption R, the sum of the perceived gains from litigation necessarily outweigh the litigation costs so long as (B) is satisfied. In particular, combining (B) and assumption R shows that

$$p_A(\pi_A - \pi_{A|B}) - p_B \pi_B - 2L \geq 0, \tag{L}$$

so there is a joint gain to litigation versus a licensing agreement.

Development

Finally we consider firm B's incentive to develop. If B would not introduce a product it developed, it should certainly not develop. On the other hand, B's subjective expected profits from litigation are greater than zero if

$$(1 - p_B)\pi_B - L - k \geq 0. \tag{E}$$

Importantly, whenever (E) holds, so will (B). That is, if B is willing to develop in expectation of litigation, it certainly wants to litigate having sunk the development costs. Intuitively, B is more likely to develop and endure litigation if litigation costs are relatively low, if A's patent does not seem certain to be upheld, or if the potential profits from entry are large.

It is now easy to summarize the equilibrium outcomes.

Table 13.2
Profits with rivalrous innovation

	A's profit	B's profit
Litigation	$p\pi_A + (1-p)\pi_{A|B} - L$	$(1-p)\pi_B - k - L$
No entry	π_A	0

PROPOSITION 2   Suppose that B's product is rivalrous. The possible outcomes are

· *Litigation*. If (E) holds, firm B will develop its product and there will be litigation. Firm B will enter if and only if firm A's patent is voided.

· *Deterrence*. If (E) fails, firm B is deterred from developing by the threat of ligation.

Table 13.2 summarizes the firm's expected payoffs in these two cases.

2   An Opposition Process

This section introduces an opposition process that allows for the validity of A's patent to be assessed immediately following the granting of the patent. Then, starting with the benchmark outcomes derived in the previous section, the effect of allowing for opposition hearings is examined.

With an opposition process, the timing proceeds as follows. After the grant of the patent, firm B is given the opportunity to challenge firm A's patent. Prior to initiating a challenge, B can approach A and attempt to license its technology. If B does not obtain a license, it must decide whether to challenge. If B declines to challenge, everything unfolds exactly as in the earlier case; that is, B retains the option of developing and either licensing or facing litigation. On the other hand, if B initiates a challenge, the parties enter a formal opposition hearing.

We model the opposition proceeding essentially as a less expensive way of verifying patent validity than litigation. In an opposition proceeding, each firm incurs a cost $C \leq L$ to prepare its case. There are several reasons to believe that the costs of an opposition would be lower than litigation should the United States adopt an opposition process. First, an opposition hearing would be a relatively streamlined administrative procedure rather than a judicial process with all the associated cost of extensive discovery. Second, as noted above, the cost of an opposition in Europe are estimated by European Patent Office officials to be less than 10 percent of the cost of litigation. Although the crossover to the United States is imperfect, it suggests that an opposition procedure could be made relatively inexpensive if that were a desired goal.

Once the parties present their cases in an opposition hearing, an administrator rules on the patent's validity. We assume that the firms assign the same subjective probabilities (p_A and p_B) to A's patent being upheld in the opposition process as in litigation, and also that the objective probability p is the same. Similarly if A's patent is upheld in the opposition, firm B must obtain a license to market its product. (In particular, firm A need not endure another round of costly litigation to enforce its property rights against B.) Conversely if the relevant parts of A's patent are voided, B can develop and market its product without fear of reprisal.

2.1 Nonrivalrous Innovation

We now derive the equilibrium outcomes with an opposition process and contrast these to the benchmark outcomes without an opposition.

The first question is whether firm B has any incentive to use the opposition process. If not, the change will have no effect. Assume as before that firm A's patent is not weak (in which case the patent can simply be ignored). Firm B has an incentive to use the opposition process if and only if

$$\pi_B - k - p_B F_V - C \geq \Pi_B. \tag{BC}$$

Here Π_B denotes firm B's subjective expected payoff should it decline to challenge. That is, Π_B is the payoff derived for B in the previous section.

If firm B has a credible threat to use the opposition process, an opposition proceeding will still only occur if the parties do not have a joint gain from negotiating a settlement. The sum of their subjective expected payoffs from an opposition hearing exceeds their joint payoff from licensing if and only if

$$(p_A - p_B)F_V - 2C \geq 0. \tag{C}$$

Note that this condition is precisely the same as characterizes whether there is a joint gain from litigation, only the litigation cost L is replaced by the opposition cost C.

If both (BC) and (C) hold, the result is an opposition proceeding. If the patent is upheld, B will be forced to pay a fee F_V for a license. On the other hand, if (BC) holds but (C) does not, there will be licensing under uncertainty at a fee F_U.

It is easy to see that the effect of introducing the opposition process depends on the relevant no-opposition benchmark. If the result without an opposition process was litigation, then because the incentives to enter an opposition process are at least as strong as the incentives to enter litigation (since $C \leq L$), the new outcome will be an opposition hearing. Importantly, because an opposition is less expensive than litigation, both firms benefit from the introduction of the opposition process.

In contrast, suppose the result without an opposition process would be licensing at a fee of either F_V or F_U. In this case, simple calculations show that both (BC) and (C) may or may not hold. The new outcome depends on the exact parameters. One possibility with the opposition system in place is that there is no change. Another possibility is that firm B goes from not having a credible threat to fight the patent's validity in litigation to having a credible threat to launch an opposition. In this event, the licensing fee drops from F_V to F_U. The last possibility is that an opposition proceeding occurs.

What is certain in all these cases is that firm B's expected payoff with the opposition proceeding is at least as high as without it. This should be intuitive. Introducing the opposition process gives firm B an option—it can always decline to challenge and still get its old payoff. On the other hand, A's expected payoff may increase or decrease. The case where litigation costs decrease benefits A; the case where licensing fees decrease hurts A. The case where an opposition proceeding replaces licensing certainly hurts A if the earlier licensing fee would have been F_V, but could potentially benefit A if the licensing fee would have been F_U.

The next result summarizes oppositions in the nonrivalrous case.

PROPOSITION 3 Suppose products are nonrivalrous and that A's patent is not weak. The introduction of a opposition process will have the following effects, depending on the outcome in the benchmark case of no oppositions.

• *Litigation.* If the benchmark outcome was litigation, the outcome with an opposition process will be an opposition. Legal costs are reduced and both firms benefit.

• *Licensing.* If the benchmark outcome was licensing, the outcome with an opposition process may be the same, or licensing prior to development, or an opposition. Legal costs may be higher, but license fees will tend to go down for invalid patents and up for valid patents. The social welfare effects are ambiguous, because the dead weight loss from the opposition process is offset by the increased incentive to file valid patents.

In the simple static model here, the direct welfare effects are limited to the cost of conflict resolution and the change in licensing fees. An important point, however, is that the impact on A depends on whether its patent is valid. In particular, the opposition process tends to help A if its patent is valid and hurt it if its patent is invalid. Because the opposition process tends to more closely align the rewards to innovation with truly novel inventions, it appears clear that in a richer dynamic model, where A was to make decisions about R&D expenditures and patent filing, the opposition process would have an additional positive incentive effect. We argue in the section on welfare effects that this effect might be fairly large in practice relative to the costs of oppositions.

2.2 Rivalrous Innovation

We now turn to the case of rivalrous innovation and again consider the effects of introducing the opposition process.

The first question again is whether firm B has an incentive to make use of the opposition procedure. Firm B is willing to initiate an opposition if and only if

$$(1 - p_B)(\pi_B - k) - C \geq \Pi_B. \tag{BC}$$

Again Π_B denotes firm B's subjective expected payoff in the absence of oppositions.

Unlike in the nonrivalrous case, (BC) is not just a necessary condition for an opposition proceeding to occur but also a sufficient condition. If (BC) holds, then assumption R implies that the joint benefit from the opposition proceeding exceeds the costs. In particular, combining (BC) and assumption R shows that

$$p_A(\pi_A - \pi_{A|B}) - p_B(\pi_B - k) - 2C \geq 0,$$

so there is no gain from licensing rather than facing the opposition process. Thus if (BC) holds, the new outcome is an opposition, while if it fails the outcome is unchanged from the no-opposition benchmark.

To see how the opposition process affects previous outcomes, imagine that the result without an opposition process was litigation. In this case, B was willing to face litigation for an opportunity to market its product so it will certainly be willing to ante up the opposition costs. By using the opposition route rather than the litigation route, B can also avoid sinking the development cost k in the event that A's patent is upheld rather than voided. It follows that previous litigation over the validity of A's patent will be replaced by opposition hearings.

In contrast, suppose the result without an opposition process was that firm B chose not to enter. Now the introduction of oppositions may encourage B to initiate a challenge. Firm B can enter if the challenge succeeds. From a welfare standpoint, this potential change has a cost: both firms will have to spend C on the challenge. It also has the benefit of increased competition. Though B's entry will decrease industry profits, the increase in consumer surplus typically will exceed this loss. Thus the net welfare gain depends on whether the potential increase in market surplus is greater than 2C.

As in the nonrivalrous case, firm B always gains from the introduction of the opposition process. Since it need not use the opposition option, it can certainly do no worse. Firm A's situation is more complex. If it previously would have had to litigate, it benefits from the cheaper opposition process. If it previously was able to deter entry without litigation, it loses from having to pay the opposition costs and loses substantially if its patent, which would not have been litigated, is held invalid and its monopoly profits disappear.

PROPOSITION 4   Suppose products are rivalrous. Depending on the benchmark outcome, an opposition system has the following effects:

• *Litigation*. If the outcome without oppositions was litigation, the new outcome is an opposition hearing. This reduces dispute costs and saves on wasted development costs in the event of a valid patent.
• *Deterrence*. If the outcome without oppositions was deterred entry, the new outcome may be an opposition. If it is, dispute costs increase but firm B is able to enter if the patent is invalid.

As in the nonrivalrous case, there is a potential dynamic welfare effect in addition to the static effects. The static welfare effects are limited to the cost of conflict resolution, the possible reduction in monopoly power and the potential savings on wasted development. Dynamically, the opposition process also serves to reward valid patents and punish invalid patents. The better alignment of rewards with true innovation should tend to provide better incentives for R&D and patent filing decisions.

3 Welfare Effects of a Opposition Process

Figure 13.2 summarizes the welfare effects of introducing an opposition system. The first column distinguishes cases in which firms A and B are nonrivalrous and rivalrous. The second column classifies the possible behaviors under a regime comparable to the current status quo. As the figure illustrates, there are four possible outcomes: litigation and licensing without litigation in the nonrivalrous case, and litigation and deterrence without litigation in the rivalrous case.

The figure's third column indicates how behavior changes when firm A's patent is subject to challenge in an opposition proceeding. Seven possible outcomes are possible, as described in the previous section. Columns four and five indicate the static welfare and dynamic incentive effects of each outcome.

One striking implication of our model, which is apparent from inspection of figure 13.2, is that once a challenge procedure is available, full-scale litigation never occurs. This conclusion depends on several of the model's assumptions about full information that are unlikely to represent with accuracy every empirical situation. For example, some patents are (allegedly) infringed and thus may become the subject of lawsuits, without the knowledge of the (alleged) infringer, who may be ignorant that his product, process, or service is potentially covered by the patent. Or, suppose that both firms A and B initially agree that the probability of a patent's validity is very low. This is the weak patent case that we noted, but did not analyze, in which B's entry is accommodated by A. In such a circumstance, B would not file a challenge, but if, subsequent to B's entry, A revised its estimate of validity significantly upward, it might sue for infringement. Finally, an opposition system would rule only on the validity of A's patent or specific claims within the patent. It would not pass judgment on whether a particular aspect of B's product

Type of innovation	Behavior w/o oppositions	Behavior w/ oppositions	Static welfare effect	Dynamic welfare effect
Nonrivalrous	Litigation - license if valid - free entry if invalid	Opposition (1) - license if valid - free entry if invalid	Gain = 2(L–C)	Positive
	Licensing w/o litigation	No Change (2)	None	None
		License at F_U not F_V (3)	None	Ambiguous
		Opposition (4) - license if valid - free entry if invalid	Loss = 2C	Positive due to sorting of valid/invalid patents.
Rivalrous	Litigation - monopoly if valid - free entry if invalid	Opposition (5) - monopoly if valid - free entry if invalid	Gain = 2(L–C) + k if valid	Positive
	Deterrence w/o litigation	No Change (6)	None	None
		Opposition (7) - monopoly if valid - free entry if invalid	Loss = 2C; Gain from eliminating monopoly if invalid.	Positive due to sorting of valid/invalid patents.

Figure 13.2
The welfare effects of patent oppositions

infringed on A's patent. For all these reasons, we clearly would not expect an opposition system to supplant litigation entirely.

To get a sense of the likely magnitude of the welfare effects displayed in figure 13.2, we constructed a simple simulation model, which we calibrated with empirically plausible parameter estimates. The theoretical model contains nine parameters (π_A, $\pi_{A|B}$, π_B, p_A, p_B, p, L, C and k). We add three more in order to make welfare calculations. The first of these additional parameters is the consumer surplus generated by the entry of firm B. The other two represent an attempt to capture the dynamic incentive effects implicit in an otherwise static model. Thus, we assume that firm A's profits not only enter directly into a social welfare function that sums consumer and producer surpluses, but that extra weight is given to A's profits when it has a valid patent and some weight is subtracted when it licenses or exclusively exploits an invalid patent.

With so many parameters to vary, a comprehensive presentation of simulation results would be tedious. Therefore we limit ourselves to describing just two plausible cases: one nonrivalrous and the other rivalrous. In both cases we assume that the present value of firm A's monopoly profit from its patent is $100 million and that firm B must spend $20 million to develop its innovation. We also assume that patent litigation costs each party $2.5 million, which, given the size of the market, is consistent with the estimates reported by the American Intellectual Property Law Association. We assume, given the U.S. propensity to spend on lawyers, that the cost of an opposition proceeding would be 20 percent of the cost of litigation, or $500,000 for each party. This is a conservative assumption in light of the report of the European Patent Office that oppositions cost less than $100,000. Finally, in both nonrivalrous and rivalrous examples, we assume that the objective probability of the validity of firm A's patent is 0.55, corresponding to the empirical frequency of validity calculated by Allison and Lemley (1998) on all litigated patent cases from 1989 through 1996.

In the nonrivalrous case, we assume that firm B's entry would yield it a gross profit of $60 million and generate an equivalent amount of consumer surplus. We also assume no decline in firm A's gross profit given B's entry. This leaves us free to examine what happens as we vary first the subjective probabilities of validity and then the dynamic welfare parameters. For simplicity, we assume that the subjective probabilities of A and B are symmetric around the objective probability of 0.55.

Under these circumstances, if the firms have similar expectations about the validity of the patent, there will be no litigation prior to the introduction of a challenge system and no use of the opposition procedure thereafter. This situation is represented as case (2) in figure 13.2. The introduction of an opposition system has no effect on either static or dynamic welfare.

If the expectations of the firms diverge by more than 0.032 but less than 0.166 (i.e., as firm A's subjective probability of validity increases from 0.566 to 0.633), there would be no litigation prior to the introduction of a challenge system, but firm B would initiate an opposition proceeding. This situation is represented as case (4) in figure 13.2. There is a net static welfare loss equal to the total cost of an opposition proceeding, or $1 million. Still, the opposition process has advantages because it sorts out valid from invalid patents. If, when the patent is valid, we give an additional positive weight of only 14 percent to firm A's profit as a proxy for the incentive effect, then the welfare benefits of an opposition system outweigh the cost of a proceeding. If we subtract an equal percentage from A's profit when its patent is ruled invalid, we need add only an 8 percent weight to offset the cost of the opposition proceeding. If we give substantial weight to these incentive effects, such as counting as a component of social welfare 150 percent of A's profit in the case of a valid patent and only 50 percent if the patent is invalid, then introducing an opposition system increases social welfare by $6.4 million.

The final possibility arises when the divergence in subjective probabilities exceeds 0.166 (i.e., firm A's subjective probability exceeds 0.633). In this instance, there is an unambiguous social benefit of the difference between the total cost of litigation and the total cost of opposition, as represented in case (1) in figure 13.2. Given our assumptions, this produces a gain of $4 million. Since our model implies that half the gain is realized by firm A, there is a small (favorable) dynamic incentive effect. In this case, however, the gain comes not from sorting valid from invalid patents, but because firm A captures a portion of the social saving.

To explore the rivalrous case, we vary only two parameters and assume that the present value of post-entry gross profits of firms A and B are now $45 million. Again, if the subjective probabilities of validity are close together, litigation will not occur, because firm B's entry can be deterred without it. In this instance, if the difference in subjective probabilities does not exceed 0.1 (i.e., firm A's subjective probability does not exceed 0.6), there will be no litigation, but B will challenge A if oppositions are permitted. As shown in case (7) in figure 13.2, there is a static welfare loss equal to the total cost of the challenge ($1 million) if the patent is valid. If the patent is not valid, there is a substantial net gain of $29 million, representing the incremental producer plus consumer surplus ($50 million) created by B's entry minus the development cost ($20 million) minus the cost of the challenge ($1 million).

Finally, if firms A and B have subjective probabilities that differ by more than 0.1, litigation will occur when oppositions are not permitted. If oppositions are allowed, a challenge will be lodged and, as in case (5) in figure 13.2, there will be an unambiguous gain in static welfare, amounting to $4 million if the patent is invalid and $24 million if the patent is valid, because B will not sink the cost of development if it loses a challenge.

Thus, it appears that the cost of introducing an opposition procedure is quite small relative to the potential static welfare gains and dynamic incentive effects. A static welfare loss arises only when a challenge is lodged under circumstances that would not have given rise to litigation, such as when the parties do not differ greatly in their subjective expectations of the patent's validity. In such instances the loss is never greater than the cost of both parties participating in the administrative proceeding, which, if European experience is any guide, is likely to be modest. By contrast, both the potential static and dynamic welfare gains that arise under other circumstances will be considerably larger. The low cost opposition procedure will often supplant higher cost litigation; larger profits to the innovator will provide a favorable dynamic incentive, and wasteful development expenses may sometimes be avoided. All of these effects are likely to be larger in magnitude than the cost of an opposition proceeding.

4   Discussion

The analysis of our two firm model of a patentee and potential entrant makes clear that in this simple framework an opportunity to contest the validity of an issued patent is likely to yield net social benefits. In the model, however, benefits and costs are evaluated strictly by the standard welfare metrics in the product markets occupied by firms A and B, assuming that there are no additional firms that might potentially infringe on A's patent. As a result, the model fails to capture several additional effects and likely benefits of introducing an opposition system.

First, opposition proceedings should speed the education of patent examiners in emerging technologies. Third parties will tend to have far greater knowledge of the prior art in fields that are new to the Patent and Trademark Office. Allowing the testimony of outside experts to inform the opposition proceedings should have substantial spillovers in pointing patent examiners to relevant bodies of prior art, thus making them more likely to recognize nonnovel or obvious inventions when they first encounter them.

Second, in an emerging area of technology, a speedy clarification of what is patentable and what is not confers substantial external benefit on those who wish to employ the new technologies. Because precedent matters in litigation and would presumably matter in opposition proceedings, a decision in one case, to the extent it articulates principles and gives reasons, has implications for many others. Clarifying the standard of patentability in an area could have significant effects on firms developing related technologies, even if these technologies are unlikely to infringe on the patent being examined. Early decisions making clear the standard of patentability would encourage prospective inventors to invest in technology that is appropriable and shun costly investments in technology that might later prove to be unprotected.

More narrowly, clarifying the validity of a patent has an obvious effect on future users of the technology.[9] In fact, it is not difficult to broaden our two firm model to allow for future infringers on A's patent. One important change then is that A's future profits are likely to depend on whether or not a definitive decision is handed down about the validity of its patent. In principle, this future patent value effect might make A either more or less inclined to grant an early infringer a license. To the extent that A becomes more inclined to grant a license, this can lead to one new outcome not captured in the model—the firms may negotiate a license even if B's product is rivalrous. In this case, the introduction of oppositions can result in a hearing when without the opposition process the result would have been licensing, with consequent positive and negative welfare effects.

In closing, little guidance has been offered about the specific design of a system permitting post-grant review of patent validity. To be effective, such a system should have a broader mandate than the current reexamination process, which is not an adversary proceeding and which allows third party intervention on only very limited grounds. Presumably, a more thoroughgoing U.S. system would allow challenges to validity on any of the familiar grounds now available to litigants in a court proceeding. The testimony of experts and the opportunity for cross-examination would seem desirable as a means of probing questions of novelty and nonobviousness. Still, it would be important to avoid extensive prehearing discovery, unlimited prehearing motions, and protracted hearings. The costs of using a challenge system should be kept substantially below that of full-scale infringement litigation or its benefits will become negligible. In designing an opposition system, we would do well to examine the diverse experience with administrative proceedings in various federal agencies and imitate the best practices.

Acknowledgments

We are indebted to the members and staff of the Intellectual Property committee of the National Academy of Science's board on Science, Technology and Economic Policy for stimulating our thinking on this topic. We also thank Barry Nalebuff and Brian Wright for helpful comments. Among Joe Stiglitz's prodigious contributions, his work on innovation and market structure occupies only a small corner of the terrain. His interest in the subject, however, was sufficient to inspire one of us to write a dissertation under his direction. In this field, as in so many others, he has captured important insights about public policy using very simple economic models. We offer this contribution in the hope that we have followed in his footsteps.

Notes

1. Notable among these actions are the Bayh-Dole Patent and Trademark Amendments Act of 1980, the creation of the Court of Appeals for the Federal Circuit in 1982, the Hatch-Waxman Drug Price Competition and Patent Restoration Act of 1984, the Process Patent Amendments Act of 1988, and the Trade-Related Aspects of Intellectual Property Rights (TRIPS) Agreement of 1994.

2. Three landmark cases about, respectively, genetics, software, and business methods, are Diamond v. Chakrabarty, 447 U.S. 303 (1980); Diamond v. Diehr, 450 U.S. 175 (1981); and State Street Bank & Trust Co. v. Signature Financial Group, Inc. 149 F.3d 1368 (Fed Cir 1998).

3. Prior art invalidating the inverse elasticity patent could probably be found. On the other hand, patents such as Walker's that are close but not identical to past published ideas typically cannot be overturned on reexamination.

4. See Graham, Hall, Harhoff, and Mowery (2002) for this and other detail on the European Patent Office's opposition procedure.

5. The assumption that p_A, p_B are commonly known, but not necessarily equal, means that firms will not update beliefs when they negotiate as in standard asymmetric information models. Rather, they "agree to disagree" about patent validity. This is a simple way to capture the fact that parties may sometimes end up in court rather than settle. Note that the uncertainty about patent validity is the only uncertainty in the model. For instance, there is no uncertainty or learning about whether B's development will succeed or about the size of the product market. Accounting for these realistic forms of uncertainty would change the quantitative, but not the qualitative, conclusions of our model.

6. See Meurer (1989) for a model in which the patent holder may use the terms of a licensing agreement to restrict future competition.

7. Note that our definition of nonrivalry does allow firm A's profits to decrease if B enters. A more traditional notion of nonrivalry might require that $\pi_{A|B} \geq \pi_A$. Our more encompassing definition focuses on joint profitability, which is natural once one realizes that firm A will be capture some of firm B's profits through licensing fees.

8. There is also another reason why the firms might want to avoid litigation, which is that if there are other potential entrants, firm A may incur a larger cost from having its patent invalidated than from just allowing B's entry. We discuss the case of multiple entrants in section 4.

9. See Choi (1998) for a model where there is a single patent holder and several potential infringers. Choi points out that a free-rider problem may arise in this environment, whereby a potential infringer on a patent may hesitate to introduce its product in hopes that another infringer on the same patent will enter first and the ensuing litigation will clarify the patent's validity. This kind of free-rider problem could also arise with an opposition process, though it would be mitigated to the extent that the cost of oppositions can be kept low.

References

Allison, John, and Mark Lemley. 1998. "Empirical Evidence on the Validity of Litigated Patents." *American Intellectual Property Law Association Quarterly Journal* 26: 185–277.

American Intellectual Property Law Association. 2001. *Economic Survey.*

Choi, Jay Pil. 1998. "Patent Litigation as an Information Transmission Mechanism." *American Economic Review* 88 (December): 1249–1263.

Graham, Stuart, Bronwyn Hall, Dietmar Harhoff, and David Mowery. 2002. "Post-Issue Patent 'Quality Control': A Comparative Study of U.S. Patent Re-Examinations and European Patent Oppositions." Mimeo.

Levin, Richard. 2002. Testimony before the FTC-DOJ Joint Hearings on Competition and Intellectual Property Law, Washington, D.C., February 6.

Merges, Richard. 1999. "As Many as Six Impossible Patents before Breakfast: Property Rights for Business Methods and Patent System Reform." *Berkeley Technology Law Journal* 14 (spring): 577–616.

Meurer, Michael. 1989. "The Settlement of Patent Litigation." *Rand Journal of Economics* 20 (spring): 77–91.

U.S. Patent and Trademark Office. 2002. *The 21st Century Strategic Plan*. June 3.

14   The Economics of Vertical Restraints

Patrick Rey

Producers and distributors often use more sophisticated contracts than the simple linear prices that are at the heart of microeconomics textbooks. Instead, their relationships are often governed by contractual provisions, broadly named vertical restraints, that not only set more general terms for payments (nonlinear prices—two-part tariffs, discounts—royalties, fees, etc.), but may also limit producers' or distributors' decisions (resale price maintenance—RPM—tie-ins) or intrabrand competition (exclusive dealing, franchising, exclusive territories).

Vertical restraints have been the object of lively debates among competition policymakers, who have adopted rather contrasted attitudes: exclusive territories, for instance, are still more tolerated in North America than in Europe. In many countries, the attitude has moreover changed drastically over time. In the United States, for instance, the Supreme Court first declared resale price maintenance (RPM) illegal in *Dr Miles* (1911). In 1937, however, the *Miller-Tydins* Act allowed price floors and in 1952, the *McGuire* Act further allowed producers to impose resale prices to all dealers as soon as one of them accepted RPM; in 1975, the per se illegality of RPM was reaffirmed, but its enforcement has still fluctuated.

The academic debate on the motivations for vertical restraints and their impact on economic welfare is also quite lively. Those who strongly believe in free markets state that business practices can emerge and develop only when efficient; businesses "know their business" better than economists or regulators do, and competition agencies should thus let firms design their arrangements as they wish. Others advise against any arrangement that may restrict one party's freedom of trade, which is the case of practically any vertical restraint.

This chapter offers an economic perspective on this debate. Section 1 discusses the efficiency benefits derived from enhanced vertical coordination, while sections 1 and 2 review the potential anticompetitive concerns that have been identified and which have been the object of much work in the last decade. A brief conclusion follows.

1   Vertical Coordination

This theme has been the first to be formally analyzed in the literature. The emphasis is placed on coordination problems between upstream and downstream firms, within a given vertical structure; it is thus possible to ignore the interaction with other vertical structures and most of the models that have been used consider the case of a unique producer, dealing with either one or several retailers.[1]

A vertical structure faces a number of decision variables: wholesale and retail prices, franchise fees, quantity purchased by the distributors, quantity eventually sold to customers, selling efforts, distributors' locations, and so forth. Some of these variables are controlled by the producer, while others are monitored by the distributors. While some decisions only affect the sharing of the pie, others affect the total surplus of the vertical structure; their decentralization thus generates externalities (one party's decisions affecting the other parties' profits), which can cause inefficiencies if not correctly taken into account. It is thus natural for the partners to look for means of coordination between these decisions, and vertical restraints can be used for that purpose.

To illustrate this, I will discuss two frequently quoted externalities for retail prices and services.

Double Marginalization

Double marginalization was the first coordination problem formally analyzed (Spengler 1950); the intuition is simple: if producers and distributors each add markups over their costs, the resulting double markup leads to excessive prices. The externality stems from the fact that each partner, when setting a price (the wholesale price for the producer or the retail price for the distributor), does not take into account the effect of this price on the other partner's profit. For instance, the distributor does not take into account that an increase in price, which decreases the final demand, also reduces the producer's

Producer

cost c

$\downarrow w$

Distributor

cost γ

$\downarrow p$

Consumers

$q = D(p)$

Figure 14.1
Double marginalization

profit. This externality is likely to lead to a final price above the level that would maximize the aggregate profits of both the producer and the distributor.

Consider, for example, a producer and a distributor that are monopolists with constant marginal costs, c for the producer and γ for the distributor. Let w and p denote, respectively, the producer's wholesale price and the distributor's retail price, and $q = D(p)$ denote consumer demand (see figure 14.1).

The aggregate profits of the two firms only depend upon the retail price, p. The price that maximizes these joint profits is the monopoly price, characterized by

$$p^m(c) = \arg\max_{p}\{(p - c - \gamma)D(p)\}. \tag{1}$$

In such a situation, however, each firm has an incentive to set its price above its own perceived cost. To make some profit, the producer must charge a wholesale price above cost ($w > c$); but then, the retailer chooses price p so as to maximize the retail profit:

$$p^m(w) = \arg\max_{p}\{(p - w - \gamma)D(p)\}. \tag{2}$$

which leads to a higher price than the (joint profit maximizing) monopoly price ($w > c$ implies $p^m(w) > p^m(c)$).[2] The manufacturer's and distributor's aggregate profits are thus lower than what they could get by setting the retail price at the monopoly level; consumers, too, would be better off facing an integrated monopoly.

The two partners can solve this double marginalization problem in various ways. The most obvious solution consists in dictating the retail price with RPM ($p \leq p^m$); the wholesale price can then be used to share the pie. A price ceiling ($p \leq p^m$)—equivalently, a minimal quota $q \geq q^m = D(p^m)$—would suffice here. Alternative solutions include nonlinear tariffs $T(q)$, where q denotes the quantity sold to the distributor and T the total payment to the manufacturer; for example, a two-part tariff of the form

$$T(q) = A + cq, \tag{3}$$

that includes a wholesale unit price w equal to the manufacturer's cost ($w = c$) and a franchise fee A. The distributor's profit margin then coincides with joint profits:

$$(P(q) - \gamma)q - T(q) = (P(q) - \gamma - c)q - A, \tag{4}$$

where $P(.)$ is the inverse demand function, and this leads the distributor to adopt the correct retail price; the franchise fee A can then be used to share the profits as desired.

Yet another solution consists in introducing a strong intrabrand competition among distributors. In that case, assuming perfect price competition à la Bertrand, distributors set $p = w + \gamma$. The manufacturer can thus get the entire monopoly profit through an appropriate wholesale price, $w = p^m - \gamma$.

This simple analysis yields several insights. First, vertical restraints allow the manufacturer and the distributor to maximize joint profits. Furthermore, different vertical restraints (RPM, quantity quotas, nonlinear tariffs) appear as substitutes for a better efficiency. Last, vertical restraints employed to solve double marginalization problems not only increase joint profits but also benefit consumers and thus hence enhance total welfare.[3]

Retail Services

Distributors provide a range of services that affect the demand for the goods they are offering: door delivery, presale advice, salespersons or cashiers to reduce waiting times, bigger showrooms, aftersale services, parking facilities, and so forth.

These efforts generate both vertical externalities between the manufacturer and its distributors and horizontal externalities between distributors. An important issue concerns the appropriability of these efforts: providing presale advice can for example give rise to free-rider problems, whereas increasing the number of cashiers is unlikely to benefit rival distributors. The existence of vertical or horizontal externalities usually prevents a distributor from getting the full benefits of the services it provides, resulting in fine in insufficient levels of service.

To analyze this issue, introduce in the previous framework an additional variable, e, representing retail effort. Thus, the distributor now chooses both the retail price p and an effort level e, which increases consumer demand $D(p, e)$ and the retail cost $\gamma(e)$ (see figure 14.2).

From the vertical structure as a whole, only p and e matter: these variables are thus now the two targets that affect joint profits. Their optimal values are:

$$(p^m, e^m) = \arg\max_{p,e}\{(p - c - \gamma(e))D(p, e)\}. \tag{5}$$

We can equivalently reason with the quantity q and the effort e, using $p = P(q, e)$, where P denotes the inverse demand function; under standard concavity assumptions, the optimal 3-uple (p, e, q) is then characterized by

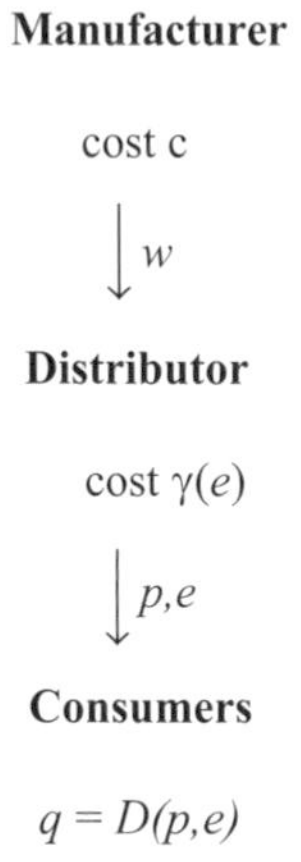

Manufacturer

   cost c

   $\downarrow w$

Distributor

   cost $\gamma(e)$

   $\downarrow p, e$

Consumers

   $q = D(p,e)$

Figure 14.2
Retail services

$$\partial_q P(q^m, e^m)q^m + (p^m - c - \gamma(e^m)) = 0,$$

$$\partial_e P(q^m, e^m) - \gamma(e^m) = 0, \tag{6}$$

$$P(q^m, e^m) = p^m.$$

These optimal values a priori differ from the socially desirable ones, characterized by

$$P(q^S, e^S) = c + \gamma(e^S),$$

$$\partial_e S(q^S, e^S) = \gamma'(e^S)q^S, \tag{7}$$

$$P(q^S, e^S) = p^S.$$

where $S(q, e) = \int_0^q P(x, e)\, dx$ represents total consumer surplus. Note that firms and consumers are likely to disagree over the level of services. Firms are interested in the additional number of consumers they can attract and thus focus on marginal consumers, thereby neglecting inframarginal consumers. Hence, if marginal consumers are willing to pay more for services (i.e., inframarginal consumers would prefer to have less services and lower prices), it may be in the joint interest of the manufacturer and the distributor to offer more services (at a higher price), at the expense of the majority of consumers and total welfare (see Spence 1975). This divergence of objectives between firms and consumers is more likely to matter when the vertical structure enjoys a substantial market power. When consumers have attractive alternatives, an increase in retail price and service is unlikely to hurt consumers—those who could be hurt would turn to their favorite alternative.

When facing a wholesale price w, the distributor chooses $(p^d(w), e^d(w))$, characterized by

$$(q^m(w), e^m(w)) = \arg\max_{p, e}\{(p - w - \gamma(e))D(p, e)\}. \tag{8}$$

The manufacturer then chooses w so as to maximize its own profits, given the distributor's reaction:

$$\tilde{w} = \arg\max_w\{(p^r(w) - w - \gamma(e^r(w)))D(p^r(w), e^r(w))\}. \tag{9}$$

This leads the manufacturer to adopt a wholesale price w higher than its unit cost, and thus the distributor chooses in turn an excessively high price (double marginalization) and too little effort, compared with what would maximize joint profits. The basic reason is that, when choosing its level of effort, the distributor does not take into account the positive impact of this effort on the manufacturer's profits, $(w - c)D(p, e)$.[4]

To solve this multiple coordination problem, the manufacturer can seek to control the distributor's decisions, for example, by setting a price ceiling and requiring a minimal level of service. A two-part tariff would be as effective: charging $T(q) = A + cq$ leads the distributor to choose both the level of effort and the price that maximize joint profits, since retail profits then coincide, up to a constant, with aggregate profits. The franchise fee, A, can then be adjusted so as to achieve the desired sharing of the profits.

In contrast, intrabrand competition does not necessarily facilitate coordination on retail services. Intrabrand competition pushes distributors to reflect consumers' relative preferences over prices and services, and consumer preferences usually differ from firms' preferences. While intrabrand competition leads retailers to adapt to consumer preferences, however, the producer may react in a way that more than counterbalances this effect. As a result, from a welfare viewpoint, the situation that prevails under linear wholesale prices and intrabrand competition may be either better or worse than under joint-profit maximization (see Caillaud-Rey 1987; Scherer 1983; Comanor 1985).

Therefore, alternative vertical restraints allow the manufacturer and the distributor(s) to achieve joint-profit maximization. In contrast with the case of pure double marginalization, however, the restraints used to solve coordination problems are not necessarily socially desirable, particularly when the vertical structure enjoys a substantial market power, since the divergence between the marginal and inframarginal consumers' willingness to pay for services may then be important.[5] Vertical restraints are more likely to be socially desirable when retail services are subject to free riding since intrabrand competition is then likely to generate an insufficient level of effort, both from the firms' and the consumers' viewpoints (see, e.g., Mathewson-Winter 1984).

Policy Implications

Producers and retailers make many different decisions that affect their joint profits. Accounting for the associated coordination problems yields the following observations: First, in most cases, a simple wholesale price fails to ensure good coordination between the manufacturer and its distributor(s); various vertical restraints can then be combined to enhance this coordination. Second, while these restraints benefit the firms, they may also benefit consumers and thus increase total welfare, although not necessarily so. When interbrand competition is weak and a vertical structure thus enjoys substantial market power, the theoretical analysis alone remains ambiguous on the welfare impact of vertical restraints, and a case-by-case study is in order. In contrast, for those goods that are subject to strong interbrand competition, vertical restraints that allow a manufacturer and its distributors to achieve a better coordination not only increase their profits but are also likely to increase consumer surplus and total welfare.

2   Interbrand Competition

The possible anticompetitive uses of vertical restraints are now reviewed. Note that most restraints tend to reduce downstream competition; as a result, downstream firms may be tempted to use vertical restraints to circumvent a ban on explicit cartels through sham agreements with a virtual upstream party. Although this is clearly a trivial misuse of vertical restraints, which is likely to be banned in most countries, occasional examples still occur from time to time.[6] First, the impact on interbrand competition between existing manufacturers is considered before turning to foreclosure issues.

Altering Interbrand Competition

Because they directly affect the nature of downstream intrabrand competition between distributors and, indirectly, the behavior of the upstream manufacturer, vertical restraints alter the strategic interaction between rival structures. In short, altering intrabrand competition modifies interbrand competition as well. Several aspects have been explored along this line of reasoning: competition-dampening, tacit collusion and interlocking relationships. Various approaches build on the insight that vertical restraints can be used to commit oneself to behave in a certain way vis-à-vis rivals.

Competition Dampening
Several papers have shown, for example, that vertical restraints such as exclusive territories, which reduce intrabrand competition within

a given distribution network, also reduce interbrand competition between rival manufacturers by reducing their incentives to undercut each other.[7] Suppose, for example, that competing manufacturers distribute their products through distinct retail networks. If they maintain strong intrabrand competition within their retailers, then for each product the retail price will closely reflect the evolution of its wholesale price; as a result, the situation resembles one of direct, face-to-face competition between manufacturers. If, instead, manufacturers reduce intrabrand competition, for example, by assigning exclusive territories to their distributors, these distributors have more freedom for setting their prices; typically, the retail price for one product then responds (at least partially) to increases in rival manufacturers' wholesale prices, which encourages the rival manufacturers to raise their prices. Thus, reducing intrabrand competition leads to an indirect mode of competition between manufacturers, which perceive less elastic demands upstream and are more incline to maintain high prices. Assigning exclusive territories to retailers is an effective way for a manufacturer to commit itself to a "friendlier" behavior vis-à-vis its rivals, which in turn encourages them to charge higher prices.

Suppose, for example, that two manufacturers produce imperfect substitutes and distribute them through distinct retail networks (see figure 14.3).

Assume first that, within each retail network, retailers fiercely compete à la Bertrand. Retail prices then simply reflect perceived costs: $p_i = w_i + \gamma$, and the manufacturers thus directly dictate the retail prices of their products. The resulting price equilibrium is characterized by:

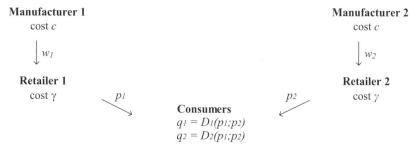

Figure 14.3
Competition dampening

$$\frac{p_i - c - \gamma}{p_i} = \frac{1}{\varepsilon_i(p_1, p_2)} \tag{10}$$

where $\varepsilon_i(p_1, p_2)$ denotes the direct price elasticity of the demand for product i.

If, instead, manufacturers assign exclusive territories to their distributors, each distributor only faces competition from distributors of the rival product; if territories are representative of the overall population, then, given the wholesale prices (w_1, w_2), downstream competition leads to a retail price equilibrium $p_i^r(w_1, w_2)$ characterized by

$$\frac{p_i^r(w_1, w_2) - w_i - \gamma}{p_i^r(w_1, w_2)} = \frac{1}{\varepsilon_i(p_i^r(w_1, w_2), p_i^r(w_1, w_2))}. \tag{11}$$

These reaction functions alter the perception of the demand by the manufacturers, which becomes:

$$\tilde{D}_i(w_1, w_2) = D_i(p_1^r(w_1, w_2), p_2^r(w_1, w_2)). \tag{12}$$

In particular, the elasticity of the demand for product i, as perceived by manufacturer i, becomes:

$$\tilde{\varepsilon}_i(w_1, w_2) = \lambda_i(w_1, w_2)\varepsilon_i(p_1^r(w_1, w_2), p_2^r(w_1, w_2))$$
$$- u_i(w_1, w_2)\eta_i(p_1^r(w_1, w_2), p_2^r(w_1, w_2)), \tag{13}$$

where $\lambda_i(w_1, w_2)$ denotes the elasticity of product i's equilibrium retail price with respect to its wholesale price, w_i, $\mu_i(w_1, w_2)$ denotes product j's equilibrium retail price elasticity with respect to the wholesale price w_i, and $\eta_i(q_1, q_2)$ denotes the cross price elasticity of the demand for product i. If the products are (possibly imperfect) substitutes ($\eta_i > 0$), distributors that find that their costs have increased are likely to absorb some of the cost increase ($\lambda_i < 1$); if, in addition, retail prices are strategic complements, rival retailers will also increase their prices ($\mu_i > 0$), which tends further to reduce the producer's perceived loss in sales.[8] Both of these effects attenuate the elasticity of the demand perceived by the manufacturers and thus induce higher (wholesale and retail) prices in equilibrium. Exclusive territories thus reduce both intrabrand and interbrand competition.[9] This insight has been empirically validated by Slade's (1998) analysis of the impact of the U.K. Beer Orders, which forced brewers to sell-off their integrated pubs and led to a situation of exclusive vertical structures such as studied here.[10]

This analysis, however, raises several issues. One issue concerns the extent to which internal arrangements are observed by rivals,[11] and another relates to the set of admissible contracts: in the absence of any restriction, firms could easily achieve full collusion (see Katz 1991). Still, the intuition is clear: internal vertical arrangements can be used to limit competition between rival vertical structures, particularly in markets where interbrand competition is initially imperfect.

Note that all vertical restraints do not generate such competition-dampening effects. As shown above, the key idea is that vertical restraints allow manufacturers to commit themselves to behave in a certain way vis-à-vis their rivals. This commitment can only be achieved by delegating some decision power to distributors, for example, as in granting exclusive territories. In contrast, vertical restraints that increase the direct control of manufacturers over their distributors, such as RPM, cannot serve such a purpose. In the above example, RPM would lead to the same situation as with fierce intrabrand competition. Moreover, if intrabrand competition is imperfect—for example, because retailers are differentiated by their location—then RPM would lead to stronger interbrand competition.

Interlocking Relationships

The chapter has focused so far on situations where manufacturers distribute their products through distinct retail channels. For most consumer goods, however, retailers carry competing products and the picture is thus somewhat different. While there is both upstream and downstream competition, each manufacturer deals with several retailers and each retailer also deals with several manufacturers. In this context of interlocking relationships, Rey-Vergé shows that vertical restraints can have an even more drastic impact on competition: RPM can eliminate both upstream and downstream competition. To see the argument, consider a situation similar to the previous one, except that (1) the two retailers (now labeled A and B) are differentiated, so that each manufacturer prefers to deal with both retailers (there are thus four relevant products for the consumers, who can choose between brands and between stores); and (2) manufacturers use two-part tariffs to avoid double marginalization problems (see figure 14.4).

Manufacturer i's profit is given by

$$(w_{iA} - c)D_{iA}(p_{1A}, p_{2A}, p_{1B}, p_{2B}) + F_{iA}$$

$$+ (w_{iB} - c)D_{iB}(p_{1A}, p_{2A}, p_{1B}, p_{2B}) + F_{iB}) \tag{14}$$

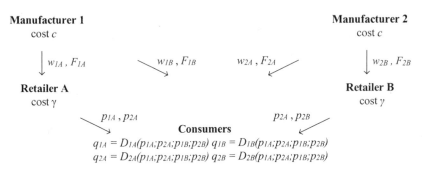

Figure 14.4
Interlocking relationships

Franchise fees must be acceptable by the two retailers A and B and must therefore satisfy:

$$(p_{1A} - w_{1A} - \gamma)D_{1A}(p_{1A}, p_{2A}, p_{1B}, p_{2B})$$

$$- F_{1A} + (p_{2A} - w_{2A} - \gamma)D_{2A}(p_{1A}, p_{2A}, p_{1B}, p_{2B}) - F_{2A} \geq 0,$$

$$(p_{1B} - w_{1B} - \gamma)D_{1B}(p_{1A}, p_{2A}, p_{1B}, p_{2B})$$

$$- F_{1B} + (p_{2B} - w_{2B} - \gamma)D_{2B}(p_{1A}, p_{2A}, p_{1B}, p_{2B}) - F_{2B} \geq 0. \qquad (15)$$

Hence, given the rival's wholesale tariffs, the maximal profit that producer i can get is given by (for $i \neq j = 1, 2$)

$$(p_{iA} - c - \gamma)D_{iA}(p_{1A}, p_{2A}, p_{1B}, p_{2B}) + (p_{jA} - w_{jA} - \gamma)D_{jA}(p_{1A}, p_{2A}, p_{1B}, p_{2B})$$

$$- F_{jA} + (p_{iB} - c - \gamma)D_{iB}(p_{1A}, p_{2A}, p_{1B}, p_{2B})$$

$$+ (p_{jB} - w_{jB} - \gamma)D_{jB}(p_{1A}, p_{2A}, p_{1B}, p_{2B}) - F_{jB}. \qquad (16)$$

In the absence of any vertical restraint, competition leads to a somewhat competitive outcome, all the more so that manufacturers and/or retailers are close substitutes. This is not entirely clear here, since retailers act as common agents for both manufacturers—and Bernheim-Whinston (1985, 1986) emphasize that common agency help maintaining monopoly prices and quantities. But here, competition also exists downstream among the agents. To prevent this competition from driving prices down, manufacturers must charge wholesale prices above marginal costs; but then, as seen from (1.16), each manufacturer has an incentive to free-ride on the rival's upstream margin, which leads to prices below the monopoly level.

Now, if manufacturers use RPM, they no longer need to rely on wholesale prices to maintain high retail prices. They can thus (1) set retail prices to the monopoly level; (2) charge wholesale prices that simply reflect production costs ($w_i = c$); and (3) use franchise fees to recover the resulting profits. Indeed, if one manufacturer does this, it is its rival's interest to do it too. For example, if manufacturer 2's adopts this policy, than manufacturer 1's profit boils down to:

$$(p_{1A} - c - \gamma)D_{1A}(p_{1A}, p_{2A}^M, p_{1B}, p_{2B}^M)$$

$$+ (p_{2A}^M - c_{2A} - \gamma)D_{2A}(p_{1A}, p_{2A}^M, p_{1B}, p_{2B}^M) - F_{2A}$$

$$+ (p_{1B} - c - \gamma)D_{1B}(p_{1A}, p_{2A}^M, p_{1B}, p_{2B}^M)$$

$$+ (p_{2B}^M - c_{2B} - \gamma)D_{2B}(p_{1A}, p_{2A}^M, p_{1B}, p_{2B}^M) - F_{2B}, \tag{17}$$

and thus coincide, up to a constant, with the integrated monopoly profits; manufacturer 1 thus has an incentive to maintain high retail prices for its own products. In addition, since profits can be shared through franchise fees as well as through wholesale prices, manufacturer 1 is willing to "sell at cost" and recover profits through the franchise fees. Therefore, *RPM* allows firms to sustain monopoly prices, in spite of the fact that, in principle, there is competition both upstream and downstream.[12]

Collusion

Courts often argue that vertical restraints can help manufacturers to sustain a cartel.[13] Only recently, however, has this argument been captured formally. Jullien-Rey (2002) stresses that, by ensuring more uniform prices, RPM makes price cuts easier to detect and so facilitates tacit collusion. In the absence of RPM, retail prices are partially driven by wholesale prices but also respond to local shocks in retail costs or demand conditions. Therefore, short of monitoring the entire distribution of retail prices, it may be difficult to detect changes in wholesale prices. Instead, through RPM, manufacturers can maintain uniform prices, and any deviation from a collusive agreement can be detected at once. The paper shows that, while RPM entails some inefficient price rigidity, manufacturers may still prefer to use it because it indeed facilitates collusion. In fact, manufacturers adopt RPM precisely when it allows them to maintain sufficiently higher collusive prices so as to offset the loss of profits generated by price rigidity.

Foreclosure

In some circumstances, vertical restraints can foreclose market access and prevent entry by potential efficient competitors. One possible strategy is to sign up available distributors into exclusive dealing arrangements, thereby forcing potential new suppliers to set up their own distribution systems; such exclusive arrangements raise the entry cost of potential rivals if there are large economies of scope or scale in distribution or if retail entry is difficult and costly; for example, if there is a limited supply of retailers, at least of comparable quality or a scarcity of comparable retail locations.

These strategies are part of more general raising rivals' costs strategies that have had already been informally explored by Krattenmaker-Salop (1986). This anticompetitive role of exclusive provisions, however, has long been contested by the so-called Chicago critique, which pointed out that distributors would not agree to forego opportunities to deal with more efficient suppliers and/or to reduce supply competition. A first answer to that critique, formalized by Aghion and Bolton (1987), is that incumbent manufacturers can use part of the additional profits to "bribe" the distributors into the exclusive agreements.

More precisely, consider a market with two incumbent firms, a manufacturer M and a distributor D, and one potential alternate supplier M', whose unit cost can be lower than the incumbent's one (see figure 14.5). Assuming the possibility of downstream entry, an exclusive arrangement between M and D would effectively prevent M' from entering the market; however, D will not accept such an arrangement without compensation, since D would prefer to turn to M' whenever it is more efficient. Moreover, M will not be able to bribe the distributor into the exclusive agreement when M' has in-

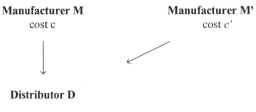

Figure 14.5
Vertical foreclosure

deed lower costs than M, since the pair $M' - D$ is then more profitable than the pair $M - D$. But Aghion and Bolton show that the two incumbents (M and D) may still prefer to partially prevent the entry of M' if, by so doing, they can extract some rents from the entrant. This can indeed be achieved through a provision for liquidation damages, whereby D must pay a certain amount to M if it turns to M'. M' would then have to compensate D for at least the same amount, so that the liquidation damages are eventually supported by the entrant. If the entrant costs are perfectly known to the incumbents, they can adjust the amount of the liquidation damages so as to extract almost all the surplus of the entrant, and entry will thus occur whenever the entrant is more efficient. In contrast, if the entrant's cost and profitability is uncertain, then the amount of liquidation damages will be optimally set at an average level, resulting in inefficient entry deterrence if the entrant's cost advantage is not large enough. Entry will thus occur less often but, whenever it occurs, the joint profits of the two incumbent firms will increase through the liquidation damages eventually paid by the entrant. (This increase in the joint profits of the two incumbent firms can ex ante be shared between them through an adjustment of the wholesale price.)

Building on this insight, Rasmusen, Ramseyer, and Wiley (1991) have further shown that exclusive dealing can completely deter entry of efficient entrants when: (1) there is poor coordination among distributors and (2) entry requires a minimal scale to be viable. The idea is that incumbent suppliers can then "bribe" some distributors into exclusive arrangements (ruling out viable entry), by sharing with them the extra rents that they can gain when dealing with the remaining distributors.[14]

Comanor and Rey (2000) point out that the entry of a new competitor at one stage (upstream or downstream) not only introduces or reinforces competition at that stage but also triggers of reinforces competition in the industry as a whole, and that it may thus result in a decrease in the joint profits of the incumbent firms. Whenever this is the case, incumbents have an incentive to prevent entry to protect their initial rents. More precisely, consider a market with an inelastic demand characterized by a reservation price r, and two incumbents, a manufacturer M with unit cost of production c and distributor D with unit retail cost γ. Finally, suppose that there exists an alternate potential supplier M' with a lower unit cost c', and that the incumbent manufacturer (but not the alternate supplier) can set up its own retail network D' that has a higher retail cost γ' than the incumbent distributor.[15] In the absence of M', M prefers to deal with D rather than setting its own and less efficient distribution system. Moreover, the two incumbents, then with a monopoly position, can charge the monopoly price $(p^m = r)$ and share the corresponding profits (normalizing market size to 1):

$$\pi_P + \pi_D = r - c - \gamma \tag{18}$$

In that situation, the entry of M' generates upstream competition between the two suppliers, but it also triggers competition between two vertical structures: an efficient one $(M' - D)$ with total unit cost $c' + \gamma$, and a less efficient one $(M - D'$, where D' denotes M's distribution system) with total unit cost $c + \gamma' > c' + \gamma$. As long as this second structure is an effective competitor $(c + \gamma' < r)$, upstream competition leads to a wholesale price equal to c, the largest of the unit costs of production, and competition between vertical structures leads to a retail price equal to $c + \gamma'$, the largest of the two total unit costs; the joint profits of the incumbents are thus lower than in the absence of the alternate supplier:

$$\pi_P + \pi_D = \gamma' - \gamma < r - c - \gamma \tag{19}$$

Hence, the two incumbents M and D would prefer to enter in an exclusive arrangement, thereby ruling out the entry of the alternate supplier. Even if initially M has all the bargaining power vis-à-vis D, in which case D would a priori be eager to promote new upstream entry and competition, M can convince D to enter into this arrangement by offering a compensating reduction in the wholesale price.[16]

Foreclosure may also arise even in the absence of upstream competition. Consider, for example, an industry where an essential input (sometimes referred to as a bottleneck or essential facility) is controlled by a monopolist M, and used by potentially competitive downstream firms D_1, D_2, and so forth. The traditional concern then is that the upstream monopolist may deny or limit access to its input to eliminate or restrict competition in the downstream market. This traditional "market power leverage" concern, however, has been contested by the Chicago school, which correctly pointed out that there is a single profit to be gained, and the monopolist can directly achieve this profit in the input market. Since then, however, Hart and Tirole (1990) have stressed that the upstream monopolist can find it difficult to exert its market power without some form of exclusion. The incentive for foreclosure then is not to extend, but to restore market power in the monopoly segment.

The basic idea is straightforward and has already been understood in the specific contexts of patent licensing and of franchising. A patentholder is the owner of a technology that can be used as an input in productive processes. The patentholder is unlikely to make much money if it cannot commit not to flood the market with licenses, since, if everyone holds a license, intense downstream competition destroys the profit created by the upstream monopoly position. Therefore, a patentholder would like to promise that the number of licenses will remain limited. There is a commitment problem, however; once the patentholder has granted n licenses, it is tempted to sell additional licenses, which depreciates the value of the existing n licenses. Such expropriation is ex post profitable for the licensor, but reduces its ex ante profit since licensees, anticipating this opportunism, will not pay a full price for their licenses. A similar point can be made for franchising. Franchisees are unlikely to pay much to franchisors if they do not have the guarantee that competitors will not set up shop at their doorsteps.

The licensing and franchising examples involve binary decisions (grant or not a license or franchising agreement), but the commitment problem is general and extends to situations in which downstream firms purchase variable amounts of an essential input. And the loss of monopoly power associated with the commitment problem is likely to be more severe, the more competitive the downstream segment, for example, the larger the number of downstream firms and the more substitutable are the downstream units.[17]

In essence, a bottleneck owner faces a commitment problem similar to that of a durable-good monopolist; such a monopolist may not achieve the monopoly profit because it may be tempted to "create its own competition." By selling more of the durable good at some date, it depreciates the value of units sold at earlier dates; the prospect of further sales in turn makes early buyers wary of expropriation and makes them reluctant to purchase. Similarly, once it has contracted with a downstream firm for access to its essential facility, the bottleneck owner has an incentive to provide access to other firms as well, even though those firms will compete with the first one and reduce its profits. This opportunistic behavior reduces ex ante the bottleneck owner's profit (in the example just given, the first firm is willing to pay and buy less). The analogy with Coase's durable good analysis also extends to the means of restoring monopoly power: vertical integration, exclusive dealing, retail price floor, reputation of the monopolist not to expropriate, and so forth.[18] For example, M could tie its hands by offering an exclusive contract to an independent downstream firm (or, more generally, a contract that specifies the number of other suppliers or franchisees within a given area). The other has M integrating vertically and refusing to supply to independent downstream firms. The integrated monopolist then internalizes the negative externality imposed on its downstream subsidiary when it sells to independent downstream firms. In the example above, both strategies enable M to obtain the monopoly profit.[19]

3   Conclusion

Vertical restraints have been the subject of intense debates, both in courts and in academia. In the last decades, competition authorities have been inclined to adopt a more tolerant attitude. For the United States, this is partially explained by the success of the so-called Chicago critique, which correctly identified several weaknesses in the original concerns. This critique has had the beneficial effect of forcing industrial economists to reconsider the arguments and to put them on firmer grounds. This chapter has summarized recent developments showing that vertical restraints can indeed be used to serve anticompetitive purposes.

This is not meant to suggest that vertical restraints are necessarily or most likely to be anticompetitive. Indeed, vertical restraints can generate efficiency gains, some of which (enhancing intrabrand vertical coordination) have been presented here at the beginning. Still, recent literature clearly advocates for a rule of reason, trading off costs and benefits on a case-by-case basis, rather than a per-se legality status. Furthermore, the literature has identified the motivations and factors that may help guide the implementation of such a rule of reason.

Acknowledgments

This chapter builds on several works, most of them joint ones. I wish to address special thanks to Jean Tirole and Joseph Stiglitz for giving me the opportunity to explore with them this topic, and Bernard Caillaud, Bill Comanor, Bruno Jullien, and Thibaud Vergé whom I have had the pleasure to work with. I also thank Nancy Gallini, Frédéric Jenny, Kai-Uwe Kühn, Steve Salop, Marius Schwartz, Leonard Waverman, and Ralph Winter for stimulating discussions and comments.

Notes

1. To fix ideas, I will use the terms *producer* and *retailer* to designate the upstream and downstream firms; however, the analysis applies to any similar vertical structure.

2. The monopoly price increases with the cost; see Tirole (1988) for a simple revealed preference argument.

3. These conclusions rely on the assumption of perfect information. Rey-Tirole (1986) shows that if (1) local shocks affect retail cost or demand and (2) distributors are risk-averse but have *ex post* better information on local conditions, then joint profit maximization can no longer be achieved, because the arrangements that best use the distributors' information also put more risk on their side; in addition, compared with firms' choices, consumers have a stronger preference for intrabrand competition.

4. This is not totally correct: it is true that given the retail price, the distributor tends to choose an insufficient level of effort, and that given the effort level, the distributor tends to choose too high a price; however, because of cross effects, it may be the case that the retail price that is eventually chosen is actually lower than the monopoly price.

5. Winter (1993) offers a detailed analysis of firms' and consumers' objectives when retailers' efforts aim at reducing consumers' shopping time. See also Marvel-McCafferty (1984) and Klein-Murphy (1988).

6. When the Swiss cartel office started to increase its pressures for lowering the prices for German books, the official bookstore cartel decided to drop its cartel status, turning to a single intermediary to handle all trade between German publishers and Swiss bookstores, with RPM as part of the vertical arrangement with the importer.

7. See, for example, Rey-Stiglitz (1985, 1995). A similar idea has been formulated by Vickers (1985) and further explored by Bonanno-Vickers (1988) to show that manufacturers may prefer, for strategic purposes, to delegate the marketing of their products to independent distributors. Related ideas have been developed in the marketing literature (see, for example, McGuire-Staelin 1983), and other papers have enriched the delegation model (see, for example, Gal-Or 1991).

8. See Rey-Stiglitz (1995) for a formal analysis of these conditions.

9. Equilibrium prices depend upon the exact content of the vertical arrangements and in particular on whether franchise fees are allowed or not. Prices are likely to be higher when franchise fees are ruled out, due to double marginalization problems.

10. Barron and Umbeck (1984) reach a similar conclusion in their analysis of the U.S. reform of gas distribution.

11. For example, distributors may not observe rival manufacturers' wholesale tariffs. Similar effects, however, may arise as long as distributors have some knowledge of these tariffs, even if these tariffs are subject to private renegotiation. See Caillaud-Rey (1994) for an overview of the literature on strategic delegation.

12. There are many equilibria. Rey-Vergé shows, however, that the equilibrium just described is the only one when accounting for the need to give retailers incentives to provide efforts and services. In addition, this equilibrium, which yields monopoly prices and quantities, clearly maximizes firms' aggregate profits.

13. For example, in *Business Electronics*, the U.S. Supreme Court repeated its previous statement justifying the per se illegality of RPM: "Our opinion in *GTE Sylvania* noted a significant distinction between vertical nonprice and vertical price restraints. That is, there was support for the proposition that vertical price restraints reduce interbrand price competition because they 'facilitate cartelizing'." See 485 U.S. 717 (1988) at 725.

14. See the discussion in Segal-Whinston (2000).

15. The assumption that only the incumbent manufacturer can enter downstream is central to the analysis; it reflects the fact that long-time established firms are in better position to master the production-distribution interface. In particular, incumbent manufacturers have a better knowledge of actual or potential actors that may help set up a new distribution system. The analysis also applies when incumbents' reputation, say, give them a comparative advantage in setting up new products or new distribution channels (e.g., consumers may be willing to buy a new products in their usual store or their usual brand in a new store, but more reluctant to buy a new brand in a new store).

16. A large literature exists on the entry deterrence effect of tying arrangements. See Whinston (1990), Nalebuff (1999, 2000), and Carlton-Waldman (2000).

17. This insight has been validated by experimental studies conducted by Martin, Normann, and Snyder (2002).

18. See Rey-Tirole (1997) for a more comprehensive list of strategies.

19. More generally, a vertically integrated M may not refuse to supply, but limit instead the sales of its input to independent downstream firms. This may be the case when independent downstream firms create value, for example, by offering differentiated products. In that case, vertical integration is more efficient than alternative profit-preserving means such as exclusive dealing; resorting to exclusive dealing would completely foreclose efficient downstream firms and reduce consumer choices.

References

Aghion, P. and P. Bolton. 1987. "Contracts as Barriers to Entry." *American Economic Review* 77:388–401.

Barron and J. R. Umbeck. 1984. "The Effects of Different Contractual Arrangements: The Case of Retail Gasoline." *Journal of Law and Economics*, 27:313–328.

Bernheim, B. D., and M. Whinston. 1985. "Common Marketing Agency as a Device for Facilitating Collusion." *Rand Journal of Economics* 16:269–281.

Bernheim, B. D., and M. Whinston. 1986. "Common Agency," *Econometrica* 54:923–942.

Bonanno, G., and J. Vickers. 1988. "Vertical Separation." *Journal of Industrial Economics* 36:257–265.

Caillaud, B., and P. Rey. 1987. "A Note on Vertical Restraints with the Provision of Distribution Services." INSEE and M.I.T discussion paper.

Caillaud, B., and P. Rey. 1994. "Strategic Ignorance in Producer-Distributor Relationships." Mimeo.

Carlton, D., and M. Waldman. 2000. "The Strategic Use of Tying to Preserve and Create Market Power in Evolving Industries." Working paper NBER DP no. 6831, 1998.

Comanor, W. S. 1985. "Vertical Price Fixing and Market Restrictions and the New Antitrust Policy." *Harvard Law Review* 98:983–1002.

Comanor, W. S., and P. Rey. 2000. "Vertical Restraints and the Market Power of Large Distributors." *Review of Industrial Organization* 17(2):135–153.

Gal-Or, E. 1991. "Duopolistic Vertical Restraints." *European Economic Review* 35:1237–1253.

Hart, O., and J. Tirole. 1990. "Vertical Integration and Market Foreclosure." *Brookings Papers on Economic Activity, Microeconomics* 205–285.

Jullien, B., and P. Rey. 2002. "Resale Price Maintenance and Collusion." Mimeo.

Katz, M. L. 1991. "Game-Playing Agents: Unobservable contracts as Precommitments." *Rand Journal of Economics* 22–3:307–328.

Klein, B., and K. M. Murphy. 1988. "Vertical Restraints as Contract Enforcement Mechanisms." *Journal of Law and Economics* 31:265–297.

Krattenmaker, T. G., and S. C. Salop. 1986. "Anticompetitive Exclusion: Raising Rivals' Costs to Achieve Power Over Price." *The Yale Law Journal* 96(2):209–293.

Martin, S., H.-T. Normann, and C. Snyder. 2002. "Vertical Foreclosure in Experimental Markets." *RAND Journal of Economics*, 32:3, 2002, 466–496.

Marvel, H., and S. McCafferty. 1984. "Resale Price Maintenance and Quality Certification." *Rand Journal of Economics* 15:340–359.

Mathewson, G. F., and R. A. Winter. 1984. "An Economic Theory of Vertical Restraints." *Rand Journal of Economics* 15:27–38.

McGuire, T. W., and R. Staelin. 1983. "An Industry Equilibrium Analysis of Downstream Vertical Integration." *Marketing Science* 2:161–191.

Nalebuff, B. 1999. "Bundling." Mimeo.

Nalebuff, B. 2000. "Competing against Bundles." Mimeo.

Rasmusen, E. B., M. Ramseyer, and J. S. Wiley. 1991. "Naked Exclusion." *American Economic Review* 81(5):1137–1145.

Rey, P., and J. E. Stiglitz. 1988. "Vertical Restraints and Producers Competition." *European Economic Review* 32:561–568.

Rey, P., and J. E. Stiglitz. 1995. "The Role of Exclusive Territories in Producers' Competition." *Rand Journal of Economics* 26:431–451.

Rey, P., and J. Tirole. 1986. "The Logic of Vertical Restraints." *American Economic Review* 76:921–939.

Rey, P., and J. Tirole. 1997. "A Primer on Foreclosure." IDEI, Toulouse. Forthcoming in *Handbook of Industrial Organization*, ed. M. Armstrong and R. H. Porter.

Scherer, F. M. 1983. "The Economics of Vertical Restraints." *Antitrust Law Journal* 52:687–707.

Segal, I., and M. Whinston. 2000. "Naked Exclusion: Comment." *American Economic Review* 90(1):296–309.

Slade, M. 1998. "Beer and the Tie: Did Divestiture of Brewer-Owned Public Houses Lead to Higher Beer Prices?" *The Economic Journal* 108:565–602.

Spence, A. M. 1975. "Monopoly, Quality and Regulation." *Bell Journal of Economics* 6:417–429.

Spengler, J. J. 1950. "Vertical Integration and Antitrust Policy." *Journal of Political Economy* 58:347–352.

Tirole, J. 1988. *The Theory of Industrial Organization*. Cambridge, MA: MIT Press.

Vickers, J. 1985. "Delegation and the Theory of the Firm." *The Economic Journal* 95:138–147.

Whinston, M. 1990. "Tying, Foreclosure, and Exclusion." *American Economic Review* 80:837–860.

Winter, R. 1993. "Vertical Control and Price Versus Nonprice Competition." *The Quarterly Journal of Economics* 153:61–76.

II

Macroeconomics, Public Economics, and Development

15   Stumbling Toward a Macroeconomics of the Medium Run

Robert M. Solow

A lot of important events happened in 1968. Lyndon Johnson decided not to run for reelection. The Vietnam War went on and on. There were riots in the streets of Chicago at the Democratic national convention. Student disorders were at their most disorderly in many universities. And Detroit won the World Series, beating the St. Louis Cardinals.

One of the least memorable events of 1968 was the publication in the *Quarterly Journal of Economics* of an article by Joseph Stiglitz and me, called "Output, Employment, and Wages in the Short Run." He was all of 25 years old at the time, and it shocks me to realize that I was then a couple of years younger than my youngest child is now. The article fell with a dull thud; it attracted no attention to speak of. The *Quarterly Journal* published one response, which was based on a total misunderstanding of the paper.

We thought that our paper had some serious things to say. It was certainly a very early attempt to model the notion that aggregate output is sometimes limited by aggregate demand (in the sense that many firms would be willing and able to produce more at current prices and wages, but are deterred by the difficulty of finding buyers) and sometimes limited by aggregate supply (in the sense that at any higher output marginal cost would exceed marginal revenue). We adopted explicitly the short-side principle that aggregate output at any time is the smaller of aggregate supply and aggregate demand. (We went one step further and supposed that momentary output adjusts toward the smaller of supply and demand.)

We had anticipated the Barro-Grossman book and the French fixed-price models of Bénassy, Drèze (sic), and Younès, culminating in Edmond Malinvaud's *Theory of Unemployment Reconsidered* (1977).

I used Malinvaud's book for several years in teaching macro-economics to graduate students. I dropped it only when it became all too clear that the students did not find it nearly as interesting as I did, and neither did most grown-up economists. Macroeconomics was then being carried on by other means.

It is true that we did not explore the specifically general-equilibrium aspects of these fixed-price-with-quantity-adjustment models, or the subtleties of defining effective demand, for example, when employers' demand for labor is limited by their inability to sell goods, while workers' demand for goods is limited by their inability to sell labor. On the other hand, one of the major complaints about the French fixed-price models was exactly the fixity of nominal prices and wages. But our paper took care of that by incorporating ultra-short-run adjustment equations (price and wage Phillips curves) by which nominal prices responded to supply-demand tensions and changes in wages, while nominal wages responded to unemployment and changes in prices.

To see just how ahead-of-its-time that was, here is Alan Blinder in the 1998 *American Economic Review*: "This sharp dichotomy between rapid price adjustments and sluggish wage adjustment has no basis in empirical reality. Instead, both prices *and* wages appear to be extremely sticky.... [B]oth wages and prices are viewed as largely predetermined in the short run, and dynamic adjustment equations (Phillips curves) describe their evolution over time."

Perhaps the Solow-Stiglitz paper left everyone cold because it was explicitly motivated by the wish to understand the precise relation between the neoclassical theory of distribution (factor prices related to factor supplies and technology via marginal products) and the theory espoused by Nicholas Kaldor and Joan Robinson (factor prices—or shares—related to differential saving rates for wages and profits). We showed that it all turned on whether the function of factor prices was to clear factor markets or to clear goods markets, and thus ultimately on whether aggregate output was in any particular instance limited on the side of aggregate supply or aggregate demand. Eventually all this came to appear merely quaint and not a part of serious macroeconomics. One of my goals here is to free the model from this distraction altogether.

I also want to focus on a different limitation of the 1968 article. It was—again explicitly—short-run in the Keynesian sense that the stock of capital goods was treated as constant, although investment was recognized as an important component of aggregate demand. Thus, it was characteristic of most of the applied macroeconomics of the time.

The short-run theory of output as a whole was a theory of aggregate demand with constant capital stock; the long-run theory—neoclassical growth theory—was essentially a theory of aggregate supply with capital accumulating over time. Our 1968 paper at least had the merit of bringing supply-limited equilibria—and disequilibria—into the short-run picture in a consistent way.

Here, I would like to take a stab at incorporating the process of capital accumulation as well, as a primitive step toward connecting aggregative modeling of the short run and the long run. Evsey Domar and Roy Harrod knew that the stock of capital, built up by investment decisions and persisting long afterward, was the main link between the short run and the long.

When I say primitive, I mean it. I think this is a difficult problem, not so much technically as substantively. The hard part is to know what behavior assumptions make sense. Growth theory imagines tranquil enough conditions so that it is reasonable to assume complete information and model-consistent expectations or even perfect foresight. In short-run macroeconomics we are habituated to certain ad hoc assumptions; or else we are unhappy with them, and pretend to "microfoundations" that are at bottom just about equally ad hoc.

It is in the in-between phases that there are no widely accepted conventions and no obvious compromises. I should state upfront that I will not adopt the currently popular device of treating the Ramsey model as a descriptive model, assuming that the observed economy is tracing out the desired path of a unitary long-horizon intertemporal optimizer. I realize that for some economists this is the hallmark of a consistent macroeconomics for every run. For me, it is a judgment call and a bad one.

Any medium-run macromodel has to distinguish explicitly between actual and potential aggregate output. In the (very) short run, potential output can be taken as fixed and ignored. For the long run, the convention is that actual and potential output coincide. I will deal with them in the following simple way. Let Y and Z stand for current and potential output respectively. Growth theory is about the evolution of potential output; the aggregate production function sets $Z = F(K, L)$, where K is the stock of capital and L is "maximal" employment, defined any way you like. At any moment, uL of the maximally available workers are unemployed; when that is the case, a fraction $q = q(u)$ of the capital stock is also left idle.

Keep in mind that the measurement of L already makes allowance for frictional and similar unemployment. There should obviously also be a theory of q and its relation to u, but I will treat it as a given. Then current output $Y = F[(1 - q)K, (1 - u)L]$. I am ignoring techno- logical progress as a distraction. It would be possible to think of L as "labor measured in efficiency units" in the usual way.

The aggregate utilization rate Y/Z is an important quantity in the short-to-medium run. It can be calculated by division. Cobb-Douglas strikes again: if $F(K, L) = AK^aL^{1-a}$, then $Y/Z = (1 - q)^a(1 - u)^{1-a}$ in- dependent of K and L. This is a form of Okun's law. Various easy approximations are available, for instance $Y/Z \approx \exp\{-aq - (1 - a)u\}$. This comes from the same property that makes Cobb-Douglas so convenient for modeling factor-augmenting technological change.

The 1968 paper, given its motivation, approached aggregate demand by way of an IS curve with the marginal propensity to save from wage income smaller than that applying to profits. Investment spending was left exogenous. The obvious implication was that ag- gregate demand would appear as an increasing function of the real wage. That sort of connection is no longer interesting; therefore, here I will omit the notion of differential saving propensities altogether and lump all income together tn the consumption function.

Instead, in pursuit of a different goal, I will incorporate a permanent- income-like quantity, by letting potential output Z serve as a surro- gate for permanent income. In the purest form, I could set $C = cZ$, with a constant marginal and average propensity to consume per- manent income. Instead, however, I let c itself be a function of Y/Z: the formulation $C = c(Y/Z)Z$ has some flexibility. If $c(.)$ is constant, we have a pure permanent-income consumption function, as noted. If $c(Y/Z) = cY/Z$, we have a pure current-income consumption function. In any case, $1 - c(1)$ is the appropriate saving rate for growth theory when, by assumption, $Y = Z$. Probably $c(.)$ is approxi- mately constant when $Y \approx Z$; but I am not sure what to expect about the marginal propensity to consume when Y is substantially higher or lower than Z.

One reasonable requirement, however, is that the marginal propensity to consume from current income be smaller than the marginal propensity to consume from permanent income. When $C = c(Y/Z)Z$, this implies that $c'(x)/c(x) < 1/(1 + x)$ (where x is temporarily written for Y/Z)); and this in turn implies that $c(Y/Z) <$ $c(0)(1 + Y/Z)$. Neither of these appears informative, and they are only necessary conditions anyway.

Finding a simple and suitable investment function is much harder. In a sense, I create this problem for myself by trying to avoid direct intertemporal reasoning and the accompanying need to represent expectations explicitly. That would just get in the way of the main goal, which is to write down a plausible short-run investment function that will easily take on the appropriate neoclassical form, if the economy works its way into a growth process with $Y = Z$. In the 1968 paper, we took I as exogenous; the question is how to escape from that limitation, while keeping to the spirit of the 1968 paper.

The textbook IS curve—I will ignore depreciation throughout, merely for notational simplicity—makes do with something like $I = i(r, Y/Z)Y$, where r is the interest rate or some related measure of the cost of capital. That would be a reasonable starting point for my purposes too, except that $i(r, 1)$ bears no explicit relationship to any conventional growth-theoretic concept. One could imagine, in a rather pre-Keynesian way, that the interest rate equilibrates saving and investment when $Y = Z$, which would mean that r solves $1 - c(1) = i(r, 1)$. Even that would still leave the problem of relating $i(\cdot, \cdot)$ to the production function.

If the textbook IS curve is at one end of a bridge, the textbook neoclassical growth model is at the other. A (neoclassical) growth path, not necessarily a steady state, is by definition a solution of $dK/dt = sF(K, L)$, given $L(t)$ and an initial condition for K. Alternatively, set $k = K/L(t)$ and $F(K/L, 1) = f(k)$. Then a growth path satisfies $dk/dt = sf(k) - nk$ if, as usual, $L(t) = L_0 e^{nt}$. Aggregate saving is $sF(K,L)$, where s is $1 - c(1)$.

Since capital is just congealed output, competitive equilibrium requires $r = F_K(K,L)$ and, by constant returns to scale, $K = g(r)L$, where g is the inverse function of $F_K(K/L,1) = f'(k)$. For such a path to be followed, r must always move to equate saving and investment: that is, $sF(K,L) = I = dK/dt = g(r)dL/dt + Lg'(r)dr/dt$. A simpler way to write this equation is $sf(k) = g(r)n + g'(r)dr/dt$. The rate of interest has to keep tracking the marginal product of capital along the growth path. The two terms on the right-hand side of the last equation take care of the widening and deepening of capital, respectively.

This is precisely where the neoclassical and Keynesian faces of the neoclassical synthesis make contact, and I do not know quite how to fit them together. Suppose r has the wrong value. Then Y will come unglued from Z; any theory has to decide how it believes Y is then determined. The more or less Keynesian answer is that Y adjusts to make saving equal to investment; the ISLM apparatus takes over. If r is too high, Y must fall to reduce the excess of saving over investment; if r is too low, Y must rise to reduce the excess of investment over saving. A standard stability argument enters here. (There is also the price level to think about, and I will come to that.) The neoclassical answer is that r does not have the wrong value; r is market-determined to equate saving and investment or, alternatively, the supply of and demand for capital.

Cobb-Douglas is again a simplification, but it can not help with the basic conceptual difficulty. If and when the economy approaches a growth path, it should be with $k = (r/a)^{-1}/(1-a)$. It is then routine to calculate the required path of r, and also the required investment, from the equations given just above. The question is how the economy gets there from here. It is easy to see how seductive it must be just to avoid all this messiness by adopting the Ramsey model for both the short and long run. Only common sense—or one version of it—stands in the way.

Now I go back to the short run and the construction of an IS curve, when $I = i(r, Y/Z)Y$. There has been no government in this model; but if there is some source of autonomous expenditure, we can call it A. The IS curve is then:

$$Y = c(Y/Z)Z + i(r, Y/Z)Y + A;$$

it is to be remembered that Y stands for aggregate demand in this context, and the IS curve is meant to specify a sustainable level of aggregate demand. This is a routine IS curve because $Z = F(K,L)$ is predetermined. It is convenient to divide both sides by Z; then if we write x for Y/Z:

$$x = c(x) + i(r, x)x + b,$$

where b stands for the ratio of (real) autonomous spending to potential output. In this form, the IS curve determines the demand-side utilization rate for the economy, as a function of r and the amount of autonomous spending relative to potential.

What about r? First of all, it should clearly stand for the real rate of interest. The routine textbook introduces an LM curve (involving the nominal interest rate, of course). But most of us would agree with Alan Blinder's observation that "the LM curve no longer plays any role in serious policy analysis, having been supplanted by the assumption that the central bank controls the short-term nominal interest rate." (David Romer's article "Keynesian Macroeconomics without the LM Curve," contains a full argument. See Romer 2000.) So I shall just replace r by R-p' in the IS curve and treat R (or even r) as the central bank's policy instrument. (I use the notation p' to mean $p^{-1}dp/dt$, the rate of inflation.) Serious policy analysis would have to get to the long-term real interest rate via some notion about term structure; but that would take me too far afield. I turn back to the 1968 paper, instead, and carry on from there.

Figure 15.1 is patterned after a 1968 diagram, but is different and more complex for two reasons. The first is that the treatment of aggregate demand has been extended to include investment, as already explained. The second is that in 1968 we treated labor as the only variable factor of production in the short run. Now I am allowing the input of capital services to vary in the short run, even with the stock predetermined, as the facts require. This complicates the short-run aggregate supply curve in the following way.

Potential output is $Z = F(K, L)$. Current output is $Y = F[(1 - q(u))K, (1 - u)L]$. Let w be the nominal wage and $v = w/p$ be the real wage. Presented with w and p, the representative firm will wish to produce with the ratio of utilized inputs satisfying $f(j) - jf'(j) + kf'(j)q'(u) = v$. Here $j = (1 - q)k/(1 - u)$ is the ratio of utilized capital to actual employment. If u and $q(u)$ were identically zero, $j = k$ and this would be a standard marginal-productivity equation. It differs slightly because of the need to insert j for k, and because the employment of an extra unit of labor increases output by more than the marginal product of labor, by virtue of the accompanying utilization of a little more capital according to $q'(u)$. The LHS can be inverted to give a decreasing inverse $j = \phi(v)$. The first key point is that this equation determines u and $q(u)$ as a function of v and the K and L given by history.

Aggregate supply, then, is $Y^s = F[(1 - q)K, (1 - u)L]$ when u and $q(u)$ are such as to make $j = \phi(v)$. In figure 15.1 the vertically measured quantities are normalized relative to the full-utilization output

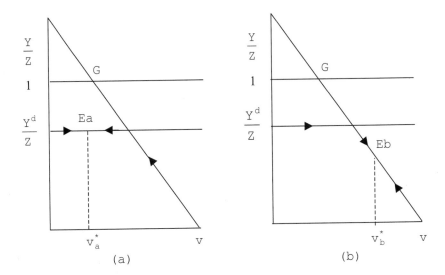

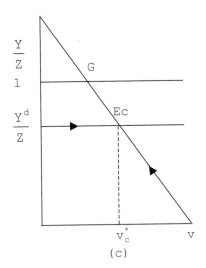

Figure 15.1

Z, so the appropriate aggregate supply curve is Y^s/Z as a function of v. It was noted earlier that with Cobb-Douglas technology this version of Okun's Law is independent of K and L.

We can now interpret figure 15.1, drawn for the current values of K,L and $R - p'$ and the level of autonomous spending relative to potential. The horizontal line at height 1 is the locus where $Y^d = Z$. The lower horizontal is a normalized IS curve; it shows current Y^d/Z. (It is possible for Y^d to exceed Z; u would then have to be negative, meaning that some frictional unemployment has been eroded. I will ignore that possibility.) The downward-sloping curve at the right is the supply curve just derived. Along a neoclassical growth path, the economy is always at point G. The interesting stuff is elsewhere in the diagram.

For wage and price dynamics I follow the original Solow-Stiglitz formulation with only notational changes. We postulated Phillips-like equations for both p and the nominal wage w. Thus, (remembering that p' and w' are proportional rates of change) $p' = G(Y^d/Y^s) + mw'$ and $w' = H(1 - u) + np'$. Since we know how to get from u to Y^d/Y^s, it is no great abuse to think directly of $w' = H(Y^d/Y^s) + np'$. Since $v = w/p$, $v' = w' - p'$ and one eventually finds that $v' = (1 - mn)^{-1}[(1 - m)H(Y^d/Y^s) - (1 - n)G(Y^d/Y^s)]$. This is enough to let us think qualitatively about figure 15.1, which is all I want to do.

The fact that this version of the model—unlike the 1968 version—makes aggregate demand independent of the real wage is a simplification. We know that Y^d/Y^s increases from left to right in the diagram. Now both G(.) and H(.) are increasing functions of Y^d/Y^s; wage and price inflation are both faster when excess demand is higher. Suppose anyway that there is one and only one value of Y^d/Y^s at which $(1 - m)H(Y^d/Y^s) - (1 - n)G(Y^d/Y^s) = 0$, and therefore one value of v for which $v' = 0$. A vertical line is drawn in figure 15.1 at that value of v denoted v^*. (If there were more than one such line, the model can still do business, but in a much more complicated way. In 1968 we allowed for many more possibilities.) I shall also assume that $v' > 0$ to the left of that line and $v' < 0$ to the right. That amounts to the assumption that the rate of price inflation is more sensitive than the rate of wage inflation to the demand-supply balance in the economy as a whole. This is obviously a good-behavior condition: in its absence the real wage would tend to run away in one direction or the other.

Now I turn to the dynamics of output. In 1968 we did not require that $Y = \min(Y^d, Y^s)$. Instead we postulated that current employment would adjust toward the level corresponding to the smaller of demand and supply. That still seems like a sensible procedure, and it could be used here unchanged. In pursuit of simplicity, however, I will instead adopt the assumption that current output is always equal to the smaller of supply and demand. The two possible configurations are shown in figures 15.1a and 15.1b, along with arrows indicating direction of motion.

In figure 15.1a, the temporary equilibrium is at E_a, where output is limited on the demand side and the real wage has stabilized at v_a^*. Figure 15.1b illustrates a supply-limited equilibrium at E_b with real wage v_b^*. In both cases, it should be remembered, the vertical axis measures aggregate output relative to potential, so output is growing at the trend rate.

More is going on than meets the eye. The aggregate demand calculations were made, and the diagrams drawn, as of a given real rate of interest. But the rate of price inflation is perpetually changing along the $(v, Y/Z)$-trajectory, because both the supply-demand balance and the rate of wage inflation are changing. Without an offsetting monetary policy, the aggregate demand curve would shift from moment to moment. So the story told by the diagrams requires the central bank to be maneuvering the nominal interest rate R so as to maintain $R - p' = r$ constant. (And the term-structure issue is being ignored altogether.) Romer (2000) argues that many central banks in fact follow a real-interest-rate oriented policy.

Figure 15.1b illustrates another point. At E_b output and employment are supply limited; there is classical unemployment. A small increase in the nominal and real interest rate to lower the aggregate demand curve will not alter that directly. But tighter monetary policy will have two indirect effects operating through the contraction of aggregate demand. It will lower Y^d/Y^s and thus lead to lower price and wage inflation. On the assumptions I have been making, however, p' will fall more than w', the real wage will tend to rise and keep rising until the old demand-supply balance is restored. But then the unemployment rate will be higher than initially, and wage and price inflation will go back to where they were initially. None of this is to be taken quite literally, because the underlying assumptions are deliberately simplistic, but the basic mechanism seems sensible to me.

Another possible assessment exists of a situation like Figure 15.1b. As it stands, or especially after a further contraction of demand, E_b involves output well below potential. Alternatively, v_b^* is too far to the right. The modern solution might be simply to redefine potential output. Remember, that potential output is defined as $F(K, L)$, where L is the maximally available supply of labor after the deduction of frictional and other "necessary" unemployment. If this necessary or "natural" rate of unemployment were higher, L would be smaller and thus potential output would be less. The ratio of current output to potential would be higher, and the redrawn figure 15.1 would look more promising. One might achieve a configuration like figure 15.1c. As a notorious skeptic about natural-rate theory, I will not pursue this avenue any further; it can easily drift into blithely defining away a real problem. But neither do I have anything useful to say about other endogenous mechanisms to drive the economy to a position like that in figure 15.1c in a reasonable length of time.

In any case, E_c is only a halfway house. As stated earlier, a neoclassical growth path is represented by a point like G_c, where the economy is realizing its (independently defined) potential and growing at a rate equal to the sum of population growth and labor-augmenting technical progress. Even apart from the informational asymmetries and other deficiencies dear to the mature Stiglitz's heart, I am not willing to bet that the natural processes of a market economy will steer it to G_c automatically.

G_c is defined as the intersection of the normalized supply curve with the horizontal at $Y^d / Z = 1$. Within this model, the central bank can try to find a path for the nominal interest rate that will eventually achieve and maintain a real interest rate for which $Y^d / Z = 1$.

Even if that were accomplished, there remains the possibility already discussed that the v for which $Y^d = Z$ is not the v for which $v' = 0$. For someone who is not willing to define this problem away via the "natural" rate of unemployment, the model is one policy instrument short. (It occurs to me now that natural-rate theory was also born in 1968, surely a blind coincidence.)

I have left two other items hanging. One is the absence of a government, and therewith of fiscal policy and a serious monetary or financial mechanism. Having those things might make it easier to imagine getting to G_c, but would not appear to offer a solution to the v^* problem. The second is the hare that I started earlier and then abandoned: how to model the transition from a short-run behavioristic investment function to a full neoclassical equilibrium. That will surely require some forward-looking behavior, just not so much as to strain credulity.

References

Blinder, Alan. (1997). "Is There a Core of Practical Macroeconomics That We Should All Believe?" *American Economic Review* (Papers and Proceedings) 87:240–243.

Malinvaud, Edmond. 1977. *The Theory of Unemployment Reconsidered*. Oxford: Blackwell.

Romer, David. 2000. "Keynesian Macroeconomics without the LM Curve." *Journal of Economic Perspectives* 14:149–170.

Solow, Robert, and Joseph Stiglitz. 1968. "Output, Employment and Wages in the Short Run." *Quarterly Journal of* Economics 82:537–560.

16

Waiting for Work

George A. Akerlof, Andrew
K. Rose, and Janet L. Yellen

The relation between wages and unemployment has been a prime focus of Stiglitz's research throughout his career (see, for example, Shapiro, and Stiglitz 1984, and Greenwald and Stiglitz 1988 and 1993). His contributions have been central to the development of efficiency wage theory and the new Keynesian macroeconomics.

This chapter presents a different perspective on the relation between wages and unemployment, and thus it is a fitting contribution to celebrate our longstanding collaboration with Stiglitz. His interest in unemployment is just one facet of his broader concern with poverty and its cure, both at home and abroad. We admire the passion, intellect and purposefulness with which he has pursued this important research and policy agenda as well as his constant good humor, grace, and ever-present smile.

This chapter develops a model of "wait unemployment" designed to accord with three well-documented empirical regularities: high-skilled workers suffer more moderate cyclical fluctuations in employment and unemployment than low-skilled workers;[1] low-skilled workers gain substantially improved access to "good jobs" during expansions;[2] and job-changers experience larger procyclical real wage movements than workers who remain in the same job.[3] We do not attempt to model the shocks that cause cyclical fluctuations in job opportunities, treating both the flow of new jobs and the wages associated with them as exogenous. The focus, instead, is on the process governing skill patterns of wages, employment, and unemployment during a cyclical recovery.

Although this model takes the supply of jobs in the aggregate as "exogenous," it is assumed that more skilled workers, should they choose, can bump less skilled workers for available job vacancies since firms prefer to hire the most able workers available. Consistent with the evidence about job downgrading and upgrading, such bumping occurs during recessions in this model; but the extent of cyclical downgrading is endogenously limited by the willingness of workers who are laid off in a downturn rationally to wait to accept jobs until business conditions improve.

The unemployment experienced by skilled workers in this model during recessions thus reflects their decision to "wait for work": these workers find it rational to hold out for the "good jobs," which will appear later in an expansion, rather than locking-in the lower wages paid by the less good jobs that are available to them during the initial stages of a recovery.

The model is motivated in part by the observation that labor is not the only factor of production that experiences periods of idleness. Office buildings sometimes stand unoccupied for extended periods of time and oil reserves sit idly underground. In the case of oil (and other exhaustible natural resources), a well-developed theory (Hotelling 1931) explains why the owners wait to extract their resource. In the equilibrium of the Hotelling model, the owners of oil reserves are compensated for waiting by an increase in the price of oil at the rate of interest.

In contrast to oil, the use of office buildings in one period does not preclude their use in other periods. In this respect, workers more closely resemble office buildings than oil, yet office-space gluts are fairly common. In Houston during the 1990s, for example, vacancy rates were extraordinarily high in many completed office buildings. The Hotelling model can be adapted to explain the existence of vacant office buildings, provided that a significant fixed cost must be borne when office space is occupied or vacated. If such costs are sufficiently large, there is a lock-in effect: a building owner who rents office space today to one tenant forgoes the possibility of renting the same space in later periods to other tenants. If long-term rental rates increase more rapidly than the rate of interest, it pays the owner of an unoccupied building to leave the space vacant and wait until conditions improve to rent out space.[4] This is true even if there are tenants willing to pay to occupy the space now.

In contrast, if the rental rates on long-term leases increase at less than the rate of interest, the building owner maximizes the present value of his income by renting all available space now, since the reward to waiting for higher rents in the future does not make up for the loss in rentals today. Analogous to the market for oil, in equilibrium, long-term rental rates will rise at precisely the rate of interest with the stock of excess office space being gradually eliminated over time.

The theory of wait unemployment developed here is exactly analogous to Hotelling's model as it would be applied to vacant office space. The cyclical unemployment of workers seeking long-term (primary-sector) jobs is analogous to the vacancies in office buildings whose owners seek long-term tenants. The labor supply function in this model is perfectly elastic. Thus, the model can rationalize the finding that large variations in employment are accompanied by small procyclic variations in wages concentrated among those workers who change jobs.

The model thus accounts for large aggregate fluctuations in employment without empirically implausible elasticities of substitution between leisure in different time periods. It offers an alternative rationale for a high elasticity of labor supply with respect to transitory wage movements: if the wage were rising more rapidly than the rate of time preference, a rational worker seeking a new, long-term job would optimally wait for work rather than commit to the best job currently available. This behavior occurs even if workers place no value at all on leisure. Analogously, the supply elasticity of office space with respect to transitory changes in long-term rental rates is infinite in the Hotelling office-space model, even though owners place no value on vacancies per se.

The incidence of wait unemployment (both its distribution across skill groups and its aggregate amount), as well as the paths of wages over time by skill, are endogenously determined in the model in much the same way that the path of extraction of oil over time and the length of time that must elapse before the oil is fully depleted and a backstop technology comes into use is endogenously determined in the Hotelling model.

Section 1 presents the model. Section 2 analyzes how the amount of wait unemployment and the path of wages vary across individuals as the economy emerges from an exogenously caused recession and describes simulations of the model for reasonable parameter values. Section 3 concludes.

1   Description of the Model

This model of the labor market focuses on the determination of wages and employment in the "spot" market where newly created jobs are filled. The number of new jobs created at each date and the wage distribution of these new positions are exogenously determined. Workers vary in skill and employers fill new jobs with the best workers available at the offered wage. Workers maximize the present value of lifetime income. Wait unemployment occurs when an individual who could obtain work today decides to hold out for better opportunities in the future. The model is used to characterize the equilibrium paths of wages and wait unemployment by skill type as the economy emerges from a recession and individual workers are reabsorbed into employment.

Specifically, we study how the labor market responds to a "shock" at time 0 that destroys a fraction of existing jobs, leaving θ people unemployed. Individuals differ in skill, indexed by x. It is assumed, for simplicity, that x is uniformly distributed between 0 and 1 among the θ people unemployed due to the shock. In addition to the workers whose unemployment results from the shock, it is assumed that an ongoing process of job destruction (cum creation), quits, and new entry into the labor force produces a flow of new entrants into the unemployment pool.[5] During a short period of time, dt, new workers arrive into the unemployment pool at the rate α dt. The skill of these new entrants into the unemployment pool is also uniformly distributed between 0 and 1. Workers who are unemployed receive a benefit that is a proportion b of their steady-state wage, w_s, the wage that workers of that skill type earn in a long-run equilibrium with full employment.

Assume that in deciding whether or not to accept the best currently available job offer in the spot market, unemployed individuals maximize the present discounted value of lifetime income with future income discounted at rate δ. The authors abstract from uncertainty and assume perfect foresight about future job opportunities.

These assumptions about labor demand are intended to mirror key findings of internal labor market and efficiency wage theorists about the personnel practices of "primary sector" firms offering "good" long-term jobs.[6] In particular, we assume that firms hire workers into "jobs" filling each vacancy with the best worker willing to accept a job offer at the time the vacancy appears. (This model assumes that firms can observe the skill (x) of applicants and therefore rank them.) Jobs are characterized by the wages they pay with a job of type w paying its incumbent a wage of w. With respect to job creation, it is assumed that new jobs arrive at the rate λdt and the distribution of wages of the λdt jobs created between time t and t + dt is uniform between 0 and $\overline{w}$. Accordingly, there is a uniform distribution (of density $\lambda dt/\overline{w}$) of new jobs paying a wage w between 0 and $\overline{w}$.

Two further assumptions are made about jobs—both extreme for the sake of analytic simplicity: first, that the wage associated with a given job remains fixed over time; and second, that workers are completely immobile, so that they are indefinitely locked-in to any job they accept.

The assumption of a fixed wage is intended to capture the empirical finding that primary-sector jobs shield workers from spot market fluctuations in the labor market so that the wages earned by job stayers are relatively insensitive to cyclical fluctuations, whereas those received by newly hired workers vary significantly and procyclically, conditioning on worker quality. This assumption mirrors the findings of Rayack (1991), Weinberg (2001) and Baker, Gibbs, and Holmstrom (1994b).

Baker, Gibbs, and Holmstrom find strong cohort effects among workers at a large employer whose employment policies they have studied in detail. Their data provide striking evidence that the starting wages of different new-hire cohorts fluctuate over time and that starting wages exert a continued influence on the wage paths of the cohort throughout their careers. Our own empirical research (Akerlof, Rose, and Yellen 1990) similarly finds a long-lasting impact of the intitial conditions prevailing when a worker starts a job on that worker's wage path over time. Such discrimination among cohorts may partly explain why, contrary to our extreme assumption, quits in the U.S. economy are procyclic (see Akerlof, Rose, and Yellen 1988). In booms, mobile workers leave bad jobs that they acquired in recessions; the less mobile workers, whose behavior we model, remain stuck in these bad jobs.

The extreme assumption of complete lock-in is motivated by the empirical finding of long average job tenures (see, for example, Akerlof and Main 1981), and an important role in primary-sector jobs for investments in firm-specific human capital and rising rewards to tenure that make mobility costly. (We could amend the model to allow for "short-term" (secondary-sector) job opportunities for unemployed workers with high discount rates, low job-switching costs or liquidity constraints. In this model, these workers would experience unemployment only when their respective spot wage falls below the value of their leisure and unemployment benefits.

The presence of such workers in this model would add to the un-employment of long-term job seekers.[7]

Evidence about the sensitivity of incumbent wages to spot market developments and the extent of lock-in are not uniformly supportive of our assumptions. In particular, Beaudry and DiNardo (1991) find strong evidence of "upward flexibility" in wages, suggesting that firms negotiate implicit wage contracts with workers that shield incumbents from losses when spot market wages decline but match spot market wages whenever the spot market wage exceeds the ini-tial contract wage. Contrary to our model, Beaudry and DiNardo's finding suggests that job mobility is costless even among workers in long-term jobs. Similarly, the mobility and hiring patterns observed by Baker, Gibbs, and Holmstrom suggest that general, rather than firm-specific human capital, is more important in explaining wage and career trajectories.

2 Solution of the Model

A solution to this model consists of a description of the equilibrium paths both for the wage rate of each skill type and the unemploy-ment rate of each skill type at each date during the transition to the steady state as the stock of initially unemployed workers, along with the flow of new entrants, is matched with the flow of new jobs. We denote these $w(x, t)$ and $u(x, t)$. We first describe the steady state of this model, in which there is no unemployment, and then the approach to the steady state.

The Steady State

In the steady state, unemployment disappears and the flow of new entrants into the labor market is matched with the flow of new jobs. New entrants and new jobs flow into the labor market at the rates αdt and λdt, respectively. We assume that $\alpha < \lambda$. Under this assump-tion, the flow of new jobs is more than sufficient to provide employ-ment to all new entrants into the labor force. At each time, new entrants queue by skill and slot themselves in order of quality into the flow of new jobs becoming available. In a steady state, the wage received by skill type x, denoted $w_s(x)$, is determined by the equi-librium condition that the number of new jobs paying at least $w_s(x)$

should just match the number of incoming workers at least as skilled as x, leading to the following equation:

$$\left[\int_{w_s(x)}^{\overline{w}} \frac{\lambda}{\overline{w}}\, dw \right] dt = \alpha(1 - x)\, dt. \tag{1}$$

The left-hand side of (1) is the number of new jobs paying a wage at least as great as $w_s(x)$. The right-hand side of (1) is the number of workers at least as skilled as x who are entering the unemployment pool. Solution of (1) yields a specific formula for the steady-state wage $w_s(x)$:

$$w_s(x) = \overline{w}\left[1 - \frac{\alpha}{\lambda}(1 - x) \right]. \tag{2}$$

In the steady state with $\alpha < \lambda$, some newly created jobs are never filled. If, contrary to our assumption, $\alpha > \lambda$, workers of skill type less than $1 - \lambda/\alpha$ are permanently unemployed.

Wages and Unemployment Along the Path to the Steady State

Along an equilibrium path to the steady state, all jobs accepted by workers of the same skill type must yield the same intertemporal utility. This follows from the fact that individuals who maximize intertemporal utility will never accept a job at any date t' if they can get higher utility by accepting a job at another date, t''. As a result, an initially unemployed worker of type x receives utility U(x) dependent only on his skill type and not on the date of job acceptance. Since firms give preference to more qualified job candidates, workers of higher skill index x will receive jobs with a higher utility.

   To solve for the path of wages received by a given skill type x along the path to the steady state, it is necessary to determine T_x, which is the first date at which workers of type x receive the steady-state wage and also the last date at which they have any unemployment. The methodology is similar to that used in a natural resource problem.

   In a natural resources problem, the price path of a resource is computed conditional on the date of first use of the backstop technology. Then the date of first use of the backstop technology is determined by the condition that the demand for the resource up to that date exactly exhausts the supply of the resource. T_x is analogous to the date of use of the backstop technology. As in the natural resource problem, the equilibrium wage path is computed conditional on T_x. Then T_x is determined by the condition that the demand for labor of type x along the equilibrium wage path between 0 and T_x must match the supply of labor of type x over the same period.

The Wage Path Conditional on T_x

The wage paid to skill type x at the date T_x is the steady state wage, $w_s(x)$, given by (2). Knowing that $w(x, T_x) = w_s(x)$, it is possible to find the wages for type x workers at all preceding dates conditional on T_x, since the present discounted value of the income stream of a worker accepting a job at $t < T_x$ and at T_x must be the same. A job accepted at T_x yields intertemporal utility $U(x)$, which is the sum of two components: the present discounted value of the income, $bw_s(x)$, received from unemployment insurance between 0 and T_x, plus the present discounted value of the steady state wage, which is received beyond T_x. This utility is

$$U(x) = bw_s(x)\frac{1 - e^{-\delta T_x}}{\delta} + \frac{w_s(x)}{\delta}e^{-\delta T_x}. \tag{3}$$

The reservation wage of type x labor at time t, $w(x, t)$, is then just that wage that yields the same total utility $U(x)$ for an initially unemployed worker who instead accepts a job at date $t < T_x$. The utility from accepting a job paying $w(x, t)$ at t is

$$U(x) = bw_s(x)\frac{1 - e^{-\delta t}}{\delta} + \frac{w(x, t)e^{-\delta t}}{\delta}. \tag{4}$$

Equating (4) and (3) yields $w(x, t)$:

$$w(x, t) = w_s(x)e^{-\delta(T_x - t)} + bw_s(x)(1 - e^{-\delta(T_x - t)}). \tag{5}$$

Computation of T_x

To solve for T_x, we equate the number of jobs created between 0 and T_x that yield utility at least as great as $U(x)$ with the number of initially unemployed workers and new entrants to the labor force between 0 and T_x with skills at least as great as x.

In this example it is possible to show that if type x labor has no unemployment at T_x, then no higher grade of labor will be unemployed. Consequently, the number of new jobs taken by labor with skill at least as great as x is the sum of two parts: the first component is the stock of workers with skill at least as great as x who were initially unemployed (at T_x they are all employed); the second component is the flow between 0 and T_x of workers who entered the labor force with skill at least as great as x. (All of these workers will also be employed at T_x in jobs that are at least as good as those taken by labor of type x.) There are $(1 - x)\theta$ workers who are initially unemployed, with skill at least as great as x who become reemployed by date T_x; and there are $\alpha(1 - x)T_x$ workers who enter the labor pool with skill at least as high as x. Consequently, $(1 - x)\theta + (1 - x)\alpha T_x$ jobs are taken between 0 and T_x which are at least as good as the jobs taken by workers of skill level x.

How many jobs preferable to those taken by group x are created between 0 and T_x? At time t the rate of such "superior" job creation is

$$\int_{w(x,t)}^{\overline{w}} \frac{\lambda}{\overline{w}} = dw, \tag{6}$$

where $w(x, t)$ is the reservation wage of labor of type x. Any job paying a higher wage than the reservation wage of type x labor is superior to that paying $w(x, t)$. Between 0 and T_x, the total number of such jobs created is

$$\int_0^{T_x} \left[\int_{w(x,t)}^{\overline{w}} \frac{\lambda}{\overline{w}} dw \right] dt. \tag{7}$$

To solve for T_x, we equate the number of jobs created between 0 and T_x offering utility at least as great as $U(x)$, given by (7), with the number of initially unemployed workers and new entrants to the labor force between 0 and T_x with skills at least as great as x. This results in the equation

$$\int_0^{T_x} \left[\int_{w(x,t)}^{\overline{w}} \frac{\lambda}{\overline{w}} dw \right] dt = \theta(1 - x) + \alpha(1 - x)T_x. \tag{8}$$

Substitution of the formula for the wage, given by (5), into (8) yields an implicit equation for T_x:

$$T_x - \frac{1 - e^{-\delta T_x}}{\delta} = \frac{\dfrac{\theta}{\lambda}(1 - x)}{(1 - b)\left(1 - \dfrac{\alpha}{\lambda}(1 - x)\right)}. \tag{9}$$

The Unemployment Path by Skill

The unemployment rate of type x labor at time t, $u(x,t)$, defined as the fraction of the initially unemployed workers of this skill type who are still out of a job at time t, can now be easily obtained. At time T_x there is no unemployment of type x workers or workers with greater skill. Therefore, for any $t < T_x$, the number of unemployed workers at least as skilled as x plus the number of workers who will enter the labor force between t and T_x with skill at least as great as x must equal the number of new jobs that will be created between t and T_x with wages at least as great as $w(x,t)$:

$$\int_x^1 \theta u(\phi, t) d\phi + (1 - x)\alpha(T_x - t) = \int_t^{T_x} \left[\int_{w(x,t)}^{\overline{w}} \frac{\lambda}{\overline{w}} dw \right] dt. \tag{10}$$

The first term on the left-hand side of (10) is the total number of unemployed workers with skill at least as great as x; the second term is the number of new entrants to the labor market with skill at least as great as x between t and T_x. The right-hand side of (10) is the total number of jobs yielding at least as much utility as $U(x)$ which are created between t and T_x. The unemployment rate of workers of type x at time t, $u(x,t)$, is obtained by total differentiation of (10) with respect to x. Use of (2) and (5) to substitute for $w(x,t)$ and use of (9) to compute dT_x/dx yields the following simple formula for the unemployment rate:

$$u(x, t) = \frac{1}{1 - \frac{\alpha}{\lambda}(1 - x)} \frac{1 - e^{-\delta(T_x - t)}}{1 - e^{-\delta T_x}} - \frac{\alpha(1 - b)(T_x - t)}{\theta}$$

$$+ \alpha(1 - b)\frac{1 - e^{-\delta(T_x - t)}}{\theta \delta}. \tag{11}$$

Differentiating (11) with respect to x and making use of the fact that T_x is higher for lower x, it is easy to verify that, at each date, unemployment rates are inversely related to skill; less skilled workers experience higher unemployment throughout the transition to the full-employment steady state. The more skilled workers experience a more rapid decline in unemployment than the less skilled, who linger longer in the unemployment pool as the economy emerges from recession. This theory thus rationalizes the fact that the degree of procyclicality in unemployment and employment is inversely correlated with skill. Higher skilled workers have lower unemployment rates, but unemployment is not confined solely to the lowest skilled workers in recession.

Although more skilled workers can always bump less skilled workers for jobs, and thus there is no "involuntary" unemployment, there are (endogenous) limits to the bumping that occurs. The rate at which skilled workers currently take jobs determines the current wage gradient with respect to skill. Too great a current skill/wage gradient makes it rational for workers to wait rather than to take the jobs that are currently available to them. Unemployment results so that the current skill/wage gradient is not too steep.

This model generates a path for aggregate wages that is slightly procyclic due to the fact that not all newly created jobs are taken and, as recovery occurs, the wage cut off of those that are taken rises. Quality-adjusted wages vary procyclically as the average skill of new hires into given quality jobs falls in booms. With the more realistic assumption (see, for example, Okun 1973 or Vroman 1977) that the average quality of new jobs rises in booms, both quality-adjusted and aggregate wages would be significantly procyclic.[8]

As should be intuitive, an increase in α or decrease in λ serves to lengthen the amount of time it takes for the unemployment of any group to be absorbed. The unemployment rate of each group at each date is also greater the higher the unemployment benefit, b. These benefits raise an individual's reservation wage path by providing positive income in periods in which waiting occurs.

As a consequence, individuals become more patient, in the sense that their wages need to rise at a slower rate to make waiting worthwhile. In the absence of unemployment benefits, wages must rise at the rate α to compensate a worker for waiting. With unemployment benefits, the required rate of increase is approximately $\alpha(1 - b)$. Interestingly, although not shown in equation (11), the taxation of the marginal unemployment benefits of workers of greater skill will increase the unemployment of lower skill workers because it will induce the higher skill workers to take up the jobs that would otherwise be available to lower skilled workers.

Simulations

Figures 16.1 and 16.2 illustrate the key properties of this model for reasonably chosen parameter values. The parameters which need to be selected are θ, the percent of the labor force initially unemployed,

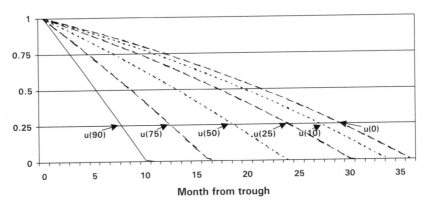

Figure 16.1
Fraction of initial unemployment remaining by skill percentile by month from trough with benchmark parameters

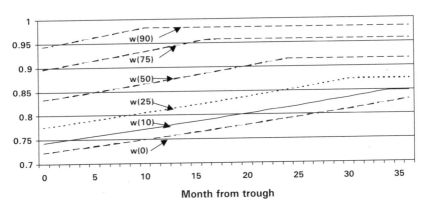

Figure 16.2
Wages as a fraction of maximum wage by skill percentile by month from trough with benchmark parameters

α, the rate of flow into the labor pool as a fraction of the labor force, λ, the rate at which new jobs are created, b, the fraction of income replaced by unemployment insurance, and δ, the rate of discount. We chose $\theta = 5$ percent; in other words, we examine a recession that starts with 5 percent excess unemployment. The model does not represent the unemployment of persons who are in the secondary labor market or on temporary layoff waiting to be recalled. Nor does it reflect the unemployment of those at the margin between being in and out of the labor force. For this reason we chose α, the flow into the unemployment pool, to be quite low relative to total turnover. Total turnover in manufacturing is approximately 60 percent per year. We chose α to be 5 percent per year. Further, we chose b = 0.5, and $\delta = 0.1$.

The major reason for choosing such a high rate of discount is to mitigate the extreme assumption in the model that jobs last forever. Workers' leaving their jobs with a constant probability is similar to an addition to the rate of discount in this model. The final parameter chosen was λ, the rate of job creation; λ was chosen so that the length of the recovery would be thirty-six months, the typical length of recoveries in the United States. That is we chose, T_0, the length of time for the lowest index labor to lose all its unemployment, to be three years. λ was then chosen so that with the values of α, b, and δ already selected, T_0 would be three years (according to formula (9) for T_0). Figures 16.1 and 16.2 show simulated paths of unemployment and wages with these benchmark parameters.

Note how modest the fluctuations in real wages are over this cycle. This model generates a semielasticity of real wages with respect to changes in the aggregate unemployment rate approximately equal to $-\delta(1 - b)T_0/\theta$, or -0.03 with our benchmark parameters. This theoretical prediction of our model accords closely with actual estimates of the impact of a one-percentage point change in the aggregate unemployment rate on the real wages of new job holders. For example, using data from 1979–1986 from the National Longitudinal Survey of Youth, we estimate a significant unemployment semielasticity with respect to real wages of -0.028 for "job changers" and -0.039 for school-leavers entering full-time employment for the first time (see Akerlof, Rose, and Yellen 1990 for a detailed description of these empirical results). Similarly, Bils (1985) estimates an unemployment semielasticity of real wages between $-0.035 - 0.04$ for job changers.

3   Concluding Remarks

This chapter has presented a theory of the skill-incidence of unemployment and wages for an economy emerging from a recession. It rationalizes the consistent finding that less-skilled workers experience more pronounced procyclical fluctuations in employment and unemployment than those with greater skill. The model provides an equilibrium theory of upward mobility in a high-pressure economy as observed by Okun (1973) and others: in booms, less advantaged workers have better odds of escaping from dead-end jobs and acquiring primary-sector jobs with steeper returns to tenure (see, most recently, Hines, Hoynes, and Krueger 2002). In recessions, declining job opportunities induce some workers to wait for work rather than lock in to the less desirable jobs that are available. The number of workers unemployed at each skill level is endogenously determined so that the reward to waiting due to the procyclic movement in real wages exactly compensates for income lost due to current unemployment. Simulations of the model suggest that for reasonable parameter values, the model's theoretical predictions are consistent with existing empirical estimates of the degree of real wage cyclicality.

Acknowledgments

This chapter is adapted from our earlier unpublished paper with the same title, NBER working paper no. 3385, May 1990.

Notes

1. See, for example, Hoynes (2000) and Hines, Hoynes, and Krueger (2002).

2. The phenomenon by which low-skilled workers move toward "better" jobs in a high pressure economy has been explored by Reder (1955), Okun (1973), Vroman (1977), Bils (1985), Hines, Hoynes, and Krueger (2002), and Rayack (1991).

3. See Akerlof, Rose, and Yellen (1990), Barlevy (2001), Beaudry and DiNardo (1991), Bils (1985), and Solon, Barsky, and Parker (1994).

4. This abstracts from the existence of variable costs incurred from renting space and assumes that tenancies last forever.

5. This assumption is consistent with Davis, Haltiwanger, and Schuh's (1996) finding of large gross flows in the labor market. In such an environment, it seems highly implausible that skilled workers would be unable to bump less-skilled workers for jobs if they want them.

6. See, for example, Piore (1968) and Katz and Summers (1989).

7. The presence of such workers at the beginning of a recession typically leads to greater depression of quality-adjusted wages, thus increasing the incentive to wait for workers with high switching costs or low rates of time preference.

8. See Abraham and Haltiwanger (1995) for a survey of the evidence.

References

Abraham, Katharine G., and John C. Haltiwanger. 1995. "Real Wages and the Business Cycle." *Journal of Economic Literature* 33:1215–1264.

Akerlof, George A., and Brian G. M. Main. 1981. "An Experience-Weighted Measure of Employment and Unemployment Durations." *American Economic Review* 71:1003–1011.

Akerlof, George A., Andrew K. Rose, and Janet L. Yellen. 1988. "Job Switching and Job Satisfaction in the U.S. Labor Market." *Brookings Papers on Economic Activity*: 495–592.

Akerlof, George A., Andrew K. Rose, and Janet L. Yellen. 1990. "Waiting for Work." National Bureau of Economic Research working paper no. 3385.

Baker, George, Michael Gibbs, and Bengt Holmstrom. 1994a. "The Internal Economics of the Firm: Evidence from Personnel Data." *Quarterly Journal of Economics* 109:881–919.

Baker, George, Michael Gibbs, and Bengt Holmstrom. 1994b. "The Wage Policy of a Firm." *Quarterly Journal of Economics* 109:921–955.

Barlevy, Gadi. 2001. "Why Are the Wages of Job Changers So Procyclical?" *Journal of Labor Economics* 19:837–878.

Beaudry, Paul, and John DiNardo. 1991. "The Effects of Implicit Contracts on the Movement of Wages Over the Business Cycle: Evidence from Micro Data." *Journal of Political Economy* 99:665–688.

Bils, Mark J. 1985. "Real Wages Over the Business Cycle: Evidence from Panel Data." *Journal of Political Economy* 93:666–689.

Davis, Steven J., John C. Haltiwanger, and Scott Schuh. 1996. *Job Creation and Destruction*. Cambridge and London: MIT Press.

Greenwald, Bruce C., and Joseph E. Stiglitz. 1988. "Examining Alternative Macroeconomic Theories." *Brookings Papers on Economic Activity*: 207–260.

Greenwald, Bruce C., and Joseph E. Stiglitz. 1993. "New and Old Keynesians." *Journal of Economic Perspectives*. 7:12–44.

Hines, James R., Hilary W. Hoynes, and Alan B. Krueger. 2002. "Another Look at Whether a Rising Tide Lifts All Boats," in *The Roaring Nineties: Can Full Employment Be Sustained?*, ed. Alan B. Krueger and Robert M. Solow. New York: Russell Sage Foundation.

Hotelling, Harold. 1931. "The Economics of Exhaustible Resources." *Journal of Political Economy* 39:137–175.

Hoynes, Hilary W. 2000. "The Employment and Earnings of Less Skilled Workers Over the Business Cycle," in *Finding Jobs: Work and Welfare Reform*, ed. Rebecca Blank and David Card. New York: Russell Sage Foundation.

Katz, Lawrence F., and Lawrence H. Summers. 1989. "Industry Rents: Evidence and Implications. Microeconomics." *Brookings Papers on Economic Activity*: 209–275.

Okun, Arthur M. 1973. "Upward Mobility in a High Pressure Economy." *Brookings Papers on Economic Activity*: 207–252.

Piore, Michael J. 1968. "The Impact of the Labor Market upon the Design and Selection of Productivity Techniques within the Manufacturing Plant." *Quarterly Journal of Economics* 82:602–620.

Rayack, Wendy L. 1991. "Fixed and Flexible Wages: Evidence from Panel Data." *Industrial and Labor Relations Review* 44:288–298.

Reder, Melvin W. 1955. "The Theory of Occupational Wage Differentials." *American Economic Review* 45:833–852.

Shapiro, Carl, and Joseph E. Stiglitz. 1984. "Equilibrium Unemployment as a Worker Discipline Device." *American Economic Review* 74:433–444.

Solon, Gary, Robert Barsky, and Jonathan A. Parker. 1994. "Measuring the Cyclicality of Wages: How Important Is Composition Bias?" *Quarterly Journal of Economics* 109:1–25.

Vroman, Wayne. 1977. "Worker Upgrading and the Business Cycle." *Brookings Papers on Economic Activity* 1977:229–250.

Weinberg, A. Bruce. 2001. "Long-Term Wage Fluctuations with Industry-Specific Human Capital." *Journal of Labor Economics* 19:231–264.

17

Welfare Economics in Imperfect Economies

Kenneth Arrow, Partha
Dasgupta, and Karl-Göran
Mäler

In several recent publications, it has been shown that there is a wealth-like measure that can serve as an index of intergenerational welfare. The index enables one to check whether welfare will be sustained along an economic forecast and to conduct social cost-benefit analysis of policy reforms, for example, investment projects. Except under special circumstances, however, the index in question is not wealth itself, but an adaptation of wealth. These results do not require that the economy be convex, nor do they depend on the assumption that the government optimizes on behalf of its citizens.[1]

An economy's wealth is the worth of its capital assets. As is widely recognized today, the list of assets should include not only manufactured capital but also knowledge and skills (human capital) and natural capital. Formally, an economy's wealth is a linear combination of its capital stocks, the weights awarded to the stocks being the latter's accounting prices.

The term accounting prices was used originally in the literature on economic planning (Tinbergen 1954). The underlying presumption was that governments are intent on maximizing social welfare. Public investment criteria were subsequently developed for economies enjoying good governance (Little and Mirrlees 1968 and 1974; Arrow and Kurz 1970). In turn, the now-extensive literature exploring various concepts of sustainable development has been directed at societies where governments choose policies to maximize intergenerational welfare.[2]

Sustainability is different from optimality. To ask whether collective well-being is sustained along an economic forecast is to ask, roughly speaking, whether the economy's production possibility set is growing. The concept of sustainability is useful for judging the performance of economies where the government, whether by design or incompetence, does not choose policies that maximize intergenerational welfare. One can argue, therefore, that the term "sustainable development" acquires bite only when it is put to work in imperfect economies. Recently the theory of intertemporal welfare indices has been extended to imperfect economies, that is, economies suffering from weak, or even bad, governance.[3] The theory's reach now extends to actual economies. The theory has also been put to use in a valuable paper by Hamilton and Clemens (1999) for judging whether in the recent past countries have invested sufficiently to expand their productive bases.[4] Among the resources making up natural capital, only commercial forests, oil and minerals, and the atmosphere as a sink for carbon dioxide were included in the Hamilton-Clemens work. Not included were water resources, forests as agents of carbon sequestration, fisheries, air and water pollutants, soil, and biodiversity. Nor were discoveries of oil and mineral reserves taken into account. Moreover, there is a certain awkwardness in several of the steps Hamilton and Clemens took when estimating changes in the worth of an economy's capital assets. Our aim of this chapter is to clarify a number of issues that arise in putting the theory of welfare indices to practical use, with the hope that the findings documented here will prove useful in future empirical work.

The authors are interested in three related questions: (1) How should accounting prices of capital assets be estimated? (2) What index should one use to evaluate policy change in an imperfect economy? (3) Given an economic forecast, what index should one use to check whether intergenerational welfare will be sustained?

Section 1 rehearses the basic theory, proving that the same set of accounting prices should be used both for policy evaluation and for assessing whether or not intergenerational welfare along a given economic path will be sustained. We also show that a comprehensive measure of wealth, computed in terms of the accounting prices, can be used as an index for questions (2) and (3) above. These results do not require that the economy be convex nor do they depend on the assumption that the government optimizes on behalf of its citizens. Section 2 uses the Ramsey-Solow model of national saving in a convex economy to illustrate the theory. The remainder of the chapter is concerned with rules for estimating the accounting prices of several specific environmental natural resources, which are transacted in a few well known economic institutions.

To make these findings easily accessible for empirical work, we report findings as a catalogue of results. Rules for estimating accounting prices of exhaustible natural resources under both free and restricted entry are derived in section 3. Section 4 shows how expenditure toward the discovery of new deposits ought to be incorporated in national accounts. Section 5 develops methods for including forest depletion; and section 6 shows how the production of human capital could be taken into account. Section 7 studies the production of global public goods.

If an economy were to face exogenous movements in certain variables, its dynamics would not be autonomous in time. Nonautonomy in time introduces additional problems for constructing the required welfare index in that the wealth measure requires to be augmented. Exogenous growth in productivity, for example, is a potential reason for nonautonomous dynamics. In section 8 we show that by suitably redefining variables it is often possible to transform a nonautonomous economic system into one that is autonomous. But such helpful transformations are not available in many other cases. In a companion paper (Arrow, Dasgupta, and Mäler 2003a) we show how, nevertheless, the required welfare index can be constructed. Additional extensions to our basic model are discussed in the final section here.

Throughout, we assume that population remains constant. In a companion paper (Arrow, Dasgupta, and Mäler 2003b) we extend the theory to cover cases where population varies over time. For simplicity, we only consider a deterministic world.

1 The Basic Model

1.1 Preliminaries

We assume that the economy is closed. Time is continuous and is denoted variously by τ and t $(\tau, t \geq 0)$. The horizon is taken to be infinite. For simplicity of exposition, we aggregate consumption into a single consumption good, C, and let **R** denote a vector of resource flows (e.g., rates of extraction of natural resources, expenditure on education and health). Labor is supplied inelastically and is normalized to be unity. Intergenerational welfare (henceforth, social welfare) at t (≥ 0) is taken to be of the Ramsey-Koopmans form,

$$W(t) = \int_t^\infty U(C(\tau)) \exp(-\delta(\tau - t)) \, d\tau, \qquad (\delta > 0), \tag{1}$$

where the utility function, $U(C)$, is strictly concave and monotonically increasing.

The state of the economy is represented by the vector $\mathbf{K}$, where $\mathbf{K}$ is a comprehensive list of capital assets. Let $\{C(\tau), \mathbf{R}(\tau), \mathbf{K}(\tau)\}_t^\infty$ be an economic program from t to ∞. Given technological possibilities, resource availabilities, and the dynamics of the ecological-economic system, the decisions made by individual agents and consecutive governments from t onward will determine $C(\tau)$, $\mathbf{R}(\tau)$, and $\mathbf{K}(\tau)$ – for $\tau \geq t$ – as functions of $\mathbf{K}(t)$, τ, and t. Thus let $f(\mathbf{K}(t), \tau, t)$, $g(\mathbf{K}(t), \tau, t)$, and $h(\mathbf{K}(t), \tau, t)$, respectively, be consumption, the vector of resource flows, and the vector of capital assets at date $\tau(\geq t)$ if $\mathbf{K}(t)$ is the vector of capital assets at t. Now write

$$(\xi(\tau))_t^\infty \equiv \{C(\tau), \mathbf{R}(\tau), \mathbf{K}(\tau)\}_t^\infty, \qquad \text{for } t \geq 0. \tag{2}$$

Let $\{t, \mathbf{K}(t)\}$ denote the set of possible t and $\mathbf{K}(t)$ pairs, and $\{(\xi(\tau))_t^\infty\}$ the set of economic programs from t to infinity.

DEFINITION 1   A "resource allocation mechanism", α, is a (many-one) mapping

$$\alpha: \{t, \mathbf{K}(t)\} \rightarrow \{(\xi(\tau))_t^\infty\}. \tag{3}$$

DEFINITION 2 α is "time-autonomous" (henceforth "autonomous") if for all $\tau \geq t$, $\xi(\tau)$ is a function solely of $\mathbf{K}(t)$ and $(\tau - t)$.

Notice that if α is time-autonomous, then economic variables at date $\tau(\geq t)$ is a function of $\mathbf{K}(t)$ and $(\tau - t)$ only. α would be non-autonomous if knowledge or the terms of trade (for a trading economy) were to change exogenously over time. In certain cases exogenous changes in population size would mean that α is not autonomous. By suitably redefining state variables, however, non-autonomous resource allocation mechanisms can sometimes be mapped into autonomous mechanisms.

DEFINITION 3 α is "time consistent" if

$$h(\mathbf{K}(\tau'), \tau'', \tau') = h(\mathbf{K}(t), \tau'', t), \qquad \text{for all } \tau'', \tau', \text{ and t.} \tag{4}$$

Time consistency implies a weak form of rationality. An autonomous resource allocation mechanism, however, has little to do with rationality; it has to do with the influence of external factors (e.g., whether trade prices are changing autonomously). In what follows, we assume that α is time consistent.

DEFINITION 3   The "value function" reflects social welfare (equation (1)) as a function of initial capital stocks and the resource allocation mechanism. We write this as

$$W(t) = V(\mathbf{K}(t), \alpha, t). \tag{5}$$

Let K_i be the ith capital stock. We assume that V is differentiable in $\mathbf{K}$.[5]

DEFINITION 4   The "accounting price," $p_i(t)$, of the ith capital stock is defined as

$$p_i(t) = \partial V(\mathbf{K}(t), \alpha, t)/\partial K_i(t) \equiv \partial V(t)/\partial K_i(t). \tag{6}$$

Note that accounting prices are defined in terms of hypothetical perturbations to an economic forecast. Specifically, the accounting price of a capital asset is the present discounted value of the perturbations to U that would arise from a marginal increase in the quantity of the asset. Given the resource allocation mechanism, accounting prices at t are functions of $\mathbf{K}(t)$, and possibly of t as well. The prices depend also on the extent to which various capital assets are substitutable for one another. It should be noted that accounting prices of private "goods" can be negative if property rights are dysfunctional, such as those that lead to the tragedy of the commons. Note too that if α is autonomous, accounting prices are not explicit functions of time, given the vector of capital stocks.

1.2 Marginal Rates of Substitution vs. Market Observables

Using (1) and (6), one can prove that, if α is time consistent, $p_i(t)$ satisfies the dynamical equation,

$$dp_i(t)/dt = \delta p_i(t) - U'(C(t))\partial C(t)/\partial K_i(t) - \sum_j [p_j(t)\partial(dK_j(t)/dt)/\partial K_i]. \tag{7}$$

(7) reduces to Pontryagin equations for costate variables in the case where α is an optimum resource allocation mechanism. We show below that, to study the evolution of accounting prices under simple resource allocation mechanisms, it is often easier to work directly with (6).

From (6) it also follows that accounting price ratios $(p_i(t)/p_j(t)$, $p_i(t')/p_i(t)$, and consumption discount rates (see what follows) are defined as marginal social rates of substitution between goods. In an economy where the government maximizes social welfare, marginal rates of substitution among goods and services equal their corresponding marginal rates of transformation. As the latter are observable in market economies (e.g., border prices for traded goods in an open economy), accounting prices are frequently defined in terms of marginal rates of transformation among goods and services. Marginal rates of substitution in imperfect economies, however, do not necessarily equal the corresponding marginal rates of transformation. A distinction therefore needs to be made between the ingredients of social welfare and market observables. Using market observables to infer social welfare can be misleading in imperfect economies. That we may have to be explicit about welfare parameters (e.g., δ and the elasticity of U) to estimate marginal rates of substitution in imperfect economies is not an argument for pretending that the economies in question are not imperfect after all. In principle it could be hugely misleading to use the theory of optimum control to justify an exclusive interest in market observables.

1.3   Sustainable Development

IUCN (1980) and World Commission (1987) introduced the concept of sustainable development. The latter publication defined sustainable development to be "development that meets the needs of the present without compromising the ability of future generations to meet their own needs" (World Commission 1987:43). Several formulations are consistent with this phrase.[6] But the underlying idea is straightforward enough: we seek a measure that would enable us to judge whether an economy's production possibility set is growing. Our analysis is based on an interpretation of sustainability that is based on the maintainence of social welfare rather than on the maintainenance of the economy's productive base. We then show that the requirement that economic development be sustainable implies, and is implied by, the requirement that the economy's productive base be maintained (theorems 1 and 2). The two equivalence results give intellectual support for the definition of sustainability we adopt here.

DEFINITION 5   The economic program $\{C(t), R(t), K(t)\}_0^\infty$ corresponds to a sustainable development path at t if $dV(t)/dt \geq 0$.

Notice that the previous criterion does not attempt to identify a unique economic program. In principle any number of technologically and ecologically feasible economic programs could satisfy the criterion. On the other hand, if substitution possibilities among capital assets are severely limited and technological advances are unlikely to occur, it could be that there is no sustainable economic program open to an economy. Furthermore, even if the government were bent on optimizing social welfare, the chosen program would not correspond to a sustainable path if the utility discount rate, δ, were too high. It could also be that along an optimum path social welfare declines for a period and then increases thereafter, in which case the optimum program does not correspond to a sustainable path locally but does so in the long run.

Optimality and sustainability are different notions. The concept of sustainability helps us to better understand the character of economic programs and is particularly useful for judging the performance of imperfect economies.

We may now state

THEOREM 1 $dV(t)/dt = \partial V(t)/\partial t + \sum_i [p_i(t)dK_i(t)/dt].$ (8)

Moreover, if α is autonomous, then $\partial V(t)/\partial t = 0$, and (8) reduces to

$$dV(t)/dt = \sum_i [p_i(t)dK_i(t)/dt].$$ (9)

Call the right-hand side (RHS) of (9) "genuine" investment at t. Equation (9) states that at each date the rate of change in social welfare equals genuine investment.

Theorem 1 is a local measure of sustainability. Integrating (9) yields a nonlocal measure:

THEOREM 2   For all $T \geq 0$,

$$V(T) - V(0) = \sum_i [p_i(T)K_i(T) - p_i(0)K_i(0)]$$

$$- \int_0^T \left[\sum_i \{dp_i(\tau)/d\tau\} K_i(\tau) \right] d\tau.$$ (10)

Equation (10) shows that in assessing whether or not social welfare has increased between two dates, the capital gains on the assets that have accrued over the interval should be deducted from the difference in wealth between the dates.

Both theorems 1 and 2 are equivalence results. They do not say whether α gives rise to an economic program along which social welfare is sustained. For example, it can be that an economy is incapable of achieving a sustainable development path, owing to scarcity of resources, limited substitution possibilities among capital assets, or whatever. Or it can be that the economy is in principle capable of achieving a sustainable development path, but that because of bad government policies social welfare is unsustainable along the path that has been forecast. Or it can be that α is optimal, but that because the chosen utility discount rate is large, social welfare is not sustained along the optimum economic program. Or it can be that along an optimum path social welfare declines for a period and then increases thereafter.

1.4   Project Evaluation

Imagine that even though the government does not optimize, it can bring about small changes to the economy by altering the existing resource allocation mechanism in minor ways. The perturbation in question could be small adjustments to the prevailing structure of taxes for a short while, or it could be minor alterations to the existing set of property rights for a brief period, or it could be a small public investment project. Call any such perturbation a policy reform.[7]

Consider an investment project as an example. It can be viewed as a perturbation to the resource allocation mechanism α for a brief period (the lifetime of the project), after which the mechanism reverts back to its earlier form. We consider projects that are small relative to the size of the economy. How should they be evaluated?

For simplicity of exposition, we suppose there is a single manufactured capital good (K) and a single extractive natural resource (S). The aggregate rate of extraction is denoted by R. Let the project's lifetime be the period [0, T]. Denote the project's output and inputs at t by the vector $(\Delta Y(t), \Delta L(t), \Delta K(t), \Delta R(t))$.[8]

The project's acceptance would perturb consumption under α. Let the perturbation at t (≥ 0) be C(t). It would affect U(t) by the amount $U'C(t)$. Since the perturbation includes all "general equilibrium effects," however, it would be tiresome if the project evaluator were required to estimate C(t) for every project that came up for consideration. Accounting prices are useful because they enable the evaluator to estimate C(t) indirectly. Now, it is most unlikely that consumption and investment have the same accounting price in an imperfect economy. So we divide $\Delta Y(t)$ into two parts: changes in consumption and in investment in manufactured capital. Denote them as $\Delta C(t)$ and $\Delta(dK/dt)$, respectively.

U is the unit of account.[9] Let $w(t)$ denote the accounting wage rate. Next, let $\hat{q}(t)$ be the accounting price of the extractive resource input of the project and $\lambda(t)$ the social cost of borrowing capital (i.e., $\lambda(t) = \delta - [dp(t)/dt]/p(t)$).[10]

From the definition of accounting prices, it follows that

$$\int_0^\infty [U'C(\tau)] \exp[-\delta\tau] \, d\tau$$

$$= \int_0^T [U'\Delta C(\tau) + p(\tau)\Delta(dK(\tau)/d\tau) - w(\tau)\Delta L(\tau)$$

$$- \lambda(\tau)p(\tau)\Delta K(\tau) - (\tau)\Delta R(\tau)] \exp[-\delta\tau] \, d\tau. \tag{11}$$

But the RHS of (11) is the present discounted value of social profits from the project (in utility numeraire). Moreover, $\int_0^\infty [U'C(\tau)] \cdot \exp[-\delta\tau] \, d\tau = \Delta V(0)$, the latter being the change in social welfare if the project were accepted. We may therefore write (11) as

$$\Delta V(0) = \int_0^T [U'\Delta C(\tau) + p(\tau)\Delta(dK(\tau)/d\tau) - w(\tau)\Delta L(\tau)$$

$$- \lambda(\tau)p(\tau)\Delta K(\tau) - (\tau)\Delta R(\tau)] \exp[-\delta\tau] \, d\tau. \tag{12}$$

Equation (12) leads to the well-known criterion for project evaluation:

THEOREM 3 A project should be accepted if and only if the present discounted value of its social profits is positive.

1.5 Evaluating Projects and Assessing Sustainability

To make the connection between theorems 1 and 3, we study how genuine investment is related to changes in future consumption brought about by it. Imagine that the capital base at t is not $K(t)$ but $K(t) + \Delta K(t)$, where as before, Δ is an operator signifying a small difference. In the obvious notation,

$$V(\alpha, \mathbf{K}(t) + \Delta \mathbf{K}(t)) - V(\alpha, \mathbf{K}(t)) \approx \int_t^\infty U' \Delta C(\tau) \exp[-\delta(\tau - t)] \, d\tau. \quad (13)$$

Now suppose that at t there is a small change in α, but only for a brief moment, Δt, after which the resource allocation mechanism reverts back to α. We write the increment in the capital base at $t + \Delta t$ consequent upon the brief increase in genuine investment as $\Delta \mathbf{K}(t)$. So $\Delta \mathbf{K}(t)$ is the consequence of an increase in genuine investment at t and $\mathbf{K}(t + \Delta t) + \Delta \mathbf{K}(t)$ is the resulting capital base at $t + \Delta t$. Let Δt tend to zero. From equation (13) we obtain:

THEOREM 4   Genuine investment measures the present discounted value of the changes to consumption services brought about by it.[11]

1.6   Numeraire

So far we have taken utility to be the unit of account. In applied welfare economics, however, it has been found useful to express benefits and costs in terms of current consumption. It will pay to review the way the theory being developed here can be recast in consumption numeraire. For simplicity of exposition, assume that there is a single commodity, that is, an all-purpose durable good that can be consumed or reinvested for its own accumulation. Assume too that utility is isoelastic and that the elasticity of marginal utility is η. Define (t) to be the accounting price of the asset at t in terms of consumption at t; that is,

$$\bar{p}(t) = p(t)/U'(C(t)). \quad (14)$$

It follows from (14) that

$$[dp(t)/dt]/p(t) = [dp(t)/dt]/p(t) + \eta[dC(t)/dt]/C(t). \quad (15)$$

Let $\rho(t)$ be the social rate of discount in consumption numeraire. $\rho(t)$ is sometimes referred to as the consumption rate of interest (Little and Mirrlees 1974). From (1),

$$\rho(t) = \delta + \eta[dC(t)/dt]/C(t).[12] \quad (16)$$

Using (16) in (15), we obtain the relationship between the asset's prices in the two units of account:

$$[d\bar{p}(t)/dt]/\bar{p}(t) = [dp/dt]/p(t) + \rho(t) - \delta.[13] \quad (17)$$

2 Illustration

It will prove useful to illustrate the theory by means of a simple example, based on Ramsey (1928) and Solow (1956). Imagine that there is an all-purpose durable good, whose stock at t is $K(t)$ (≥ 0). The good can be consumed or reinvested for its own accumulation. There are no other assets. Population size is constant and labour is supplied inelastically. Write output (GNP) as Y. Technology is linear. So $Y = \mu K$, where $\mu > 0$. μ is the output-wealth ratio. GNP at t is $Y(t) = \mu K(t)$.

Imagine that a constant proportion of GNP is saved at each moment. There is no presumption that the saving rate is optimum; rather, it is a behavioral characteristic of consumers, reflecting their response to an imperfect credit market. Other than this imperfection, the economy is assumed to function well. At each moment expectations are fulfilled and all markets other than the credit market clear. This defines the resource allocation mechanism, α. Clearly, α is autonomous in time. We now characterise α explicitly.

Let the saving ratio be s $(0 < s < 1)$. Write aggregate consumption as $C(t)$. Therefore,

$$C(t) = (1 - s)Y(t) = (1 - s)\mu K(t). \tag{18}$$

Capital is assumed to depreciate at a constant rate $\gamma(> 0)$. Genuine investment is therefore

$$dK(t)/dt = (s\mu - \gamma)K(t). \tag{19}$$

$K(0)$ is the initial capital stock. The economy grows if $s\mu > \gamma$, and shrinks if $s\mu < \gamma$. To obtain a feel for orders of magnitude, suppose $\gamma = 0.05$ and $\mu = 0.25$. The economy grows if $s > 0.2$, and shrinks if $s < 0.2$.

Integrating (19), we obtain

$$K(\tau) = K(t)\exp[(s\mu - \gamma)(\tau - t)], \qquad \text{for all } \tau \text{ and } t, \tau \geq t \geq 0, \tag{20}$$

from which it follows that

$$C(\tau) = (1 - s)\mu K(\tau) = (1 - s)\mu K(t)\exp[(s\mu - \gamma)(\tau - t)],$$
$$\text{for all } \tau \text{ and } t, \tau \geq t \geq 0. \tag{21}$$

If the capital stock was chosen as numeraire, wealth would be $K(t)$, and NNP would be $(\mu - \gamma)K(t)$. Each of wealth, GNP, NNP, consumption and genuine investment expands at the exponential rate $(s\mu - \gamma)$ if $s\mu > \gamma$; they all contract at the exponential rate $(\gamma - s\mu)$ if $s\mu < \gamma$. We have introduced capital depreciation into the example so as to provide a whiff (albeit an artificial whiff) of a key idea, that even if consumption is less than GNP, wealth declines when genuine investment is negative. Wealth declines when consumption exceeds NNP.

Current utility is $U(C(t))$. Consider the isoelastic form

$$U(C) = -C^{-(\eta-1)}, \qquad \text{where } \eta > 1. \tag{22}$$

δ is the social rate of discount if utility is numeraire. Let $\rho(t)$ be the social rate of discount if consumption is the unit of account. It follows that

$$\rho(t) = \delta + \eta[dC(t)/dt]/C(t) = \delta + \eta(s\mu - \gamma). \tag{23}$$

The sign of $\rho(t)$ depends upon the resource allocation mechanism α. In particular, $\rho(t)$ can be negative. To see why, suppose the unit of time is a year, $\delta = 0.03$, $\gamma = 0.04$, $s = 0.10$, $\eta = 2$, and $\mu = 0.20$. Then $\eta[dC(t)/dt]/C(t) = -0.04$ per year, and (23) says that $\rho(t) = -0.01$ per year.[14]

Social welfare at t is

$$V(t) = \int_t^\infty U(C(\tau)) \exp[-\delta(\tau - t)] \, d\tau. \tag{24}$$

Using (21) and (22) in (24), we have

$$V(t) = -[(1 - s)\mu K(t)]^{-(\eta-1)} \int_t^\infty \exp\{-[(\eta - 1)(s\mu - \gamma) + \delta](\tau - t)\} \, d\tau,$$

or, assuming that $[(\eta - 1)(s\mu - \gamma) + \delta] > 0$,

$$V(t) = -[(1 - s)\mu K(t)]^{-(\eta-1)}/[(\eta - 1)(s\mu - \gamma) + \delta]. \tag{25}$$

V is differentiable in K everywhere. Moreover, $\partial V(t)/\partial t = 0$. Equations (20) and (25) confirm theorem 1.[15]

We turn now to accounting prices.

Utility Numeraire

Begin by taking utility to be numeraire. Let $p(t)$ be the accounting price of capital. Now

$$p(t) \equiv \partial V(t)/\partial K(t) = \int_t^\infty U'(C(\tau))[\partial C(\tau)/\partial K(t)]\exp[-\delta(\tau - t)]\,d\tau. \quad (26)$$

Using (25) in (26), we have

$$p(t) = (\eta - 1)[(1 - s)\mu]^{-(\eta-1)}K(t)^{-\eta}/[(\eta - 1)(s\mu - \gamma) + \delta]. \quad (27)$$

Using equations (20), (21), (25), and (27) it is simple to check that $p(t) \neq U'(C(t))$, except when $s = (\mu + (\eta - 1)\gamma - \delta)/\mu\eta$. Let s^* be the optimum saving rate. From equation (25), we have

$$s^* = (\mu + (\eta - 1)\gamma - \delta)/\mu\eta. \quad (28)$$

Note that $p(t) < U'(C(t))$ if $s > s^*$, which means there is excessive saving. Conversely, $p(t) > U'(C(t))$ if $s < s^*$, which means there is excessive consumption.

Consumption Numeraire

Write $\bar{p}(t) = p(t)/U'(C(t))$.   (29)

Using (26) in (29) yields

$$\bar{p}(t) = \int_t^\infty [U'(C(\tau))/U'(C(t))][\partial C(\tau)/\partial K(t)]\exp[-\delta(\tau - t)]\,d\tau. \quad (30)$$

Now use (21), (22) and (30) to obtain

$$\bar{p}(t) = \int_t^\infty (1 - s)\mu\exp(-\rho(\tau - t))\exp(s\mu - \gamma)\,d\tau, \quad (31)$$

where $\rho = \delta + \eta(s\mu - \gamma)$.
    (31) simplifies to

$$\bar{p}(t) = (1 - s)\mu/[\rho - (s\mu - \gamma)]. \quad (32)$$

Observe that $\bar{p}(t) > 1$ (resp. < 1) if $s < s^*$ (resp. $> s^*$).[16]
    To obtain a sense of orders of magnitude, suppose $\eta = 2$, $\mu = 0.20$, $\gamma = 0.05$, and $\delta = 0$. From (28) we have $s^* = 0.625$. Now imagine that $s = 0.40$ (by Ramsey's criterion, this is undersaving!). Using (23) we have $\rho = 0.06$ per unit of time. So (32) reduces to $(t) = 4$. In other words, a saving rate that is approximately 30 percent short of the optimum corresponds to a high figure for the accounting price of investment: investment should be valued four times consumption.

Although intergenerational equity is nearly always discussed in terms of the rate at which future well-being is discounted (see, e.g., Portney and Bryant 1998), equity would be more appropriately discussed in terms of the curvature of U. Let the unit of time be a year. Suppose $\gamma = 0$, $\delta = 0.02$, and $\mu = 0.32$. Consider two alternative values of η: 25 and 50. It is simple to confirm that $s^* = 0.038$ if $\eta = 25$ and $s^* = 0.019$ if $\eta = 50$. Intergenerational equity in both consumption and welfare (the latter is a concave function of the former) can be increased indefinitely by making η larger and larger: C(t) becomes flatter as η is increased. In the limit, as η goes to infinity, s^* tends to γ (equation (28)), which reflects the Rawlsian maximum-minimum consumption as applied to the intergenerational context.[17]

Having illustrated the theory by means of an example, we now proceed to obtain rules for estimating accounting prices by focusing on specific categories of capital assets and several well known institutional imperfections.[18]

3   Exhaustible Resources: The Closed Economy

Accounting prices of exhaustible resources when depletion rates are optimal have been much studied (e.g., Dasgupta and Heal 1979; see what follows). What is the structure of their accounting prices when resources are instead common pools?

Two property-rights regimes suggest themselves: open access and restricted entry. They in turn need to be compared to an optimum regime. It is simplest if we avoid a complete capital model, so we resort to a partial equilibrium world: income effects are assumed to be negligible. Let R(t) be the quantity extracted at t. Income is the numeraire. Let U(R) be the area under the demand curve below R. So $U'(R)$ is taken to be the market demand function. U is taken to be an increasing and strictly concave function of R for positive values of R. To have a notation that is consistent with the one in the foregoing example, we take the social rate of interest to be an exogenously given constant, ρ.

Social welfare at t is,

$$V(t) = \int_t^\infty U(R(\tau)) \exp[-\rho(\tau - t)] \, d\tau. \tag{33}$$

Let S(t) be the stock. Then,

$$dS(t)/dt = -R(t). \tag{34}$$

3.1 The Optimum Regime

Consider first an optimizing economy. Assume that extraction is costless (constant unit extraction cost can be introduced easily). Let $p^*(t)$ denote the accounting price of the resource underground (equivalently, the Hotelling rent, or the optimum depletion charge per unit extracted). We know that

$$dp^*(t)/dt = \rho p^*(t). \tag{35}$$

This is the Hotelling rule. Moreover, optimum extraction, $R^*(t)$, must satisfy the condition

$$U'(R(t)) = p^*(t). \tag{36}$$

Assume that $U'(R)$ is isoelastic:

$$U(R) = -R^{-(\eta-1)}, \qquad \text{where } \eta > 1. \tag{37}$$

Then

$$R^*(t) = (\rho/\eta)S(0)\exp(-\rho t/\eta). \tag{38}$$

We next consider the two imperfect regimes.

3.2 Restricted Entry

For vividness, assume that there are N identical farmers ($i, j = 1, 2, \ldots, N$), drawing from an aquifer. Extraction is costless. We model the situation in the following way:[19]

At t, farmer i owns a pool of size $S_i(t)$. Each pool is separated from every other pool by a porous barrier. Water percolates from the larger pool to the smaller one. Let λ_{ij} (> 0), be the rate at which water diffuses from pool i to pool j. We assume that $\lambda_{ij} = \lambda_{ji}$. Denote by $R_i(t)$ the rate at which i draws from his pool. There are then N depletion equations:

$$dS_i(t)/dt = \sum_{N\backslash i}[\lambda_{ji}\{S_j(t) - S_i(t)\}] - R_i(t), \tag{39}$$

where "$\sum_{N\backslash i}$" denotes summation over all j other than i.

The payoff function for farmer i at time t is

$$\int_t^\infty U(R_i(\tau))\exp[-\rho(\tau - t)]\,d\tau. \tag{40}$$

Farmers play noncooperatively. For tractablity, we study an open loop solution: Farmers are assumed to be naive (when computing optimum extraction rates, each takes the others' extraction rates as given).[20]

Let $p_i(t)$ be the (spot) personal accounting price of a unit of i's own resource pool. The present value Hamiltonian for i's optimization problem would then be

$$H(t) = U(R_i(t)) \exp(-\rho t)$$

$$+ \left[\sum_{N \backslash i} (\lambda_{ji}\{S_j(t) - S_i(t)\}) - R_i(t) \right] p_i(t) \exp(-\rho t). \tag{41}$$

It follows from (41) that $p_i(t)$ obeys the equation

$$dp_i(t)/dt = \left[\rho + \sum_{N \backslash i} (\lambda_{ji}) \right] p_i(t). \tag{42}$$

For notational simplicity, assume that $\lambda_{ij} = \lambda$ for all i, j. Then (42) reduces to

$$dp_i(t)/dt = [\rho + (N - 1)\lambda]p_i(t). \tag{43}$$

Write $[\rho + (N - 1)\lambda] = \beta$. We conclude that the rush to extract because of insecure property rights amounts to each extractor using an implicit discount rate, β, which is in excess of the social discount rate ρ.[21] Assume now that the elasticity of demand is a constant, $\eta\ (> 1)$. The optimum rate of extraction is therefore

$$R(\tau) = (\beta/\eta)S(t) \exp[-\beta(\tau - t)/\eta], \qquad \text{for all } \tau \geq t. \tag{44}$$

To have a meaningful problem, we take it that $\beta/\eta > \beta - \rho$ (see what follows).

Let $p(t)$ be the resource's (social) accounting price. We know that $p(t) = \partial V(t)/\partial S(t)$. Using (38), it follows that

$$p(t) = \int_t^\infty U'(R(\tau))[\partial R(\tau)/\partial S(t)] \exp[-\rho(\tau - t)]\, d\tau. \tag{45}$$

Write $\bar{p}(t) = p(t)/U'(R(t))$. Then (43) and (45) imply

$$\bar{p}(t) = (\beta/\eta) \int_t^\infty \exp[-(\rho - \beta(\eta - 1)\eta)](\tau - t)]\, d\tau, \tag{46}$$

or $$\bar{p}(t) = \beta/[\beta - \eta(\beta - \rho)] > 1. \tag{47}$$

(Notice that $\bar{p}(t) = 1$ if $\beta = \rho$.)

As a numerical illustration, consider the case where $\rho = 0.06$, $\beta = 0.10$, and $\eta = 2$. In this case, $\bar{p}(t) = 5$, which reflects a considerable imperfection in the resource allocation mechanism in question: the resource's accounting price is five times its market price.

3.3 Open Access

We next study an open-access pool. To have a meaningful problem, we now assume that extraction is costly. For simplicity, let the unit extraction cost be a constant k (> 0). Under open access, Hotelling rents are dissipated completely. Therefore, the equilibrium extraction rate, $R(t)$, is the solution of the equation

$$U'(R(t)) = k. \tag{48}$$

Equation (48) confirms that, for any given level of reserves, there is excessive extraction. Let $\bar{R}$ be the solution of (48). We then have

$$dS(t)/dt = -\bar{R}. \tag{49}$$

Reserves remain positive for a period $T = S/\bar{R}$. Let us normalize utility by setting $U(0) = 0$. It follows that

$$V(t) = \int_t^{(t+S(t)/\bar{R})} [U(\bar{R}) - k\bar{R}] \exp(-\rho(\tau - t))\, d\tau. \tag{50}$$

Let $p(t)$ be the accounting price of the unextracted resource. Then,

$$p(t) = \partial V(t)/\partial S(t) = [(U(\bar{R}) - k)/\bar{R}] \exp(-\rho S(t)/\bar{R}) > 0. \tag{51}$$

Write $\bar{p}(t) = p(t)/U'(\bar{R})$, which is the ratio of the resource's shadow price to its unit extraction cost. Then, from (48) and (51),

$$\bar{p}(t) = [(U(\bar{R}) - k\bar{R})/k\bar{R}] \exp(-\rho S(t)/\bar{R}) > 0. \tag{52}$$

(52) resembles a formula proposed by El Serafy (1989) for estimating depletion charges.[22] The charge is positive because an extra unit of water in the aquifer would extend the period of extraction. Notice that (t) is bounded above by the ratio of the Marshallian consumer surplus to total extraction cost; furthermore, it increases as the aquifer is depleted and attains its upper bound at the date at which the pool is exhausted. If reserves are large, $\bar{p}(t)$ is small, and free access involves no great loss—a familiar result.

What are plausible orders of magnitude? Consider the linear demand function. Assume therefore that

$$U(R) = aR - bR^2, \quad \text{where } a > k \text{ and } b > 0. \tag{53}$$

From (48) and (53),

$$\bar{p}(t) = (a - k)/2b. \tag{54}$$

Substituting (53) and (54) in (52),

$$\bar{p}(t) = [(a - k)/2k]\exp[-2b\rho S(t)/(a - k)]. \tag{55}$$

Equation (55) says that

$$\bar{p}(t) \geq 1 \text{ iff } \rho S \leq [(a - k)/2b]\ln[(a - k)/2k]. \tag{56}$$

(55) expresses the magnitude of $\bar{R}$ in terms of the parameters of the model. Suppose, for example, that $\rho = 0.02$ per year, $S/\bar{R} = 100$ years (i.e., at the current rate of extraction, the aquifer will be exhausted in 100 years), $(a - k)/2k = 20$ (e.g., $k = \$0.50$ and $(a - k) = \$20$). Then

$$\bar{p} = 20\exp(-2) \approx 7. \tag{57}$$

We should conclude that the value to be attributed to water at the margin is high (about seven times extraction cost). As the date of exhaustion gets nearer, the accounting price rises to its upper bound, twenty.

4 Exploration and Discoveries

How should one account for expenditure on explorations of new deposits of exhaustible resources? We imagine that the rate at which new reserves are discovered, N, is an increasing function of (1) current expenditure on explorations, E, and (2) the accumulated expenditure on explorations, M, but is a declining function of (3) accumulated extraction, Z(t). Denote the discovery function by $N(E(t), M(t), Z(t))$, where

$$dM(t)/dt = E(t), \tag{58}$$

and $\quad dZ(t)/dt = R(t). \tag{59}$

We revert to the model containing one manufactured capital good, K, and an exhaustible natural resource, S. In the familiar notation, $Y = F(K, R)$ is taken to be the aggregate production function. The remaining equations of motion are

$$dK(t)/dt = F(K(t), R(t)) - C(t) - E(t). \tag{60}$$

$$dS(t)/dt = N(E(t), M(t), Z(t)) - R(t). \tag{61}$$

The model has four capital assets K, S, M, and Z. Their accounting prices are denoted by p_K, p_S, p_M, and p_Z, respectively. Social welfare is given by (1). From theorem 1, we have

$$dV(t)/dt = p_K(t)[F(K(t), R(t)) - C(t) - E(t)]$$
$$+ p_S(t)[N(E(t), M(t), Z(t)) - R(t)]$$
$$+ p_M(t)E(t) + p_Z(t)R(t). \tag{62}$$

There are two cases to consider:

1. Assume that $\partial N/\partial M = 0$ (implying that $p_M = 0$) and $\partial N/\partial Z < 0$ (implying that $p_Z(t) < 0$). Even in this case genuine investment is not the sum of investment in manufactured capital and changes in proven reserves $(N(t) - R(t))$. This is because new reserves are valued differently from existing reserves. Note too that exploration costs should not be regarded as investment.

Consider now the special case where the mining industry optimizes.[23] Then $p_K(t) = p_S(t)\partial N/\partial E$. If, in addition, $p_S(t)N(t)$ can be approximated by $p_K(t)E(t)$, one could exclude discoveries of new reserves from genuine investment, but regard instead exploration costs as part of that investment.

2. Suppose $\partial N/\partial M > 0$. If the industry optimizes, we have

$$p_K(t) = p_M(t) + p_S(t)\partial N/\partial E, \tag{63}$$

and so $p_K(t) > p_M(t)$. It follows that genuine investment should now include not only new discoveries and investment in manufactured capital (as in case 1) but also exploration costs, using an accounting price that is less than that of manufactured capital.

5 Forests and Trees

As stocks, forests offer a multitude of services. Here we focus on forests as a source of timber. Hamilton and Clemens (1999) regard the accounting value of forest depletion to be the stumpage value (price minus logging costs) of the quantity of commercial timber and fuelwood harvested in excess of natural regeneration rates. This is an awkward move, since the authors do not say what is intended to happen to the land being deforested. For example, if the deforested land is converted into an urban sprawl, the new investment in the sprawl would be recorded in conventional accounting statistics.[24] But if it is intended to be transformed into farmland, matters would be different: the social worth of the land as a farm should be included as an addition to the economy's stock of capital assets. In what follows, we consider the simple case where the area is predicted to remain a forest.

Let the price of timber, in consumption numeraire, be unity and let ρ (assumed constant) be the social rate of discount. Holding all other assets constant, if B(t) is aggregate forest land at, we may express social welfare as V(B(t)). The accounting price of forest land is then $\partial V(t)/\partial B(t)$, which we write as s(t).

Consider a unit of land capable of supporting a single tree and its possible successors. If the land is virgin, if a seed is planted at $t = 0$, if F(T) is the timber yield of a tree aged T, and if T is the rotation cycle, then the present discounted value of the land as a tree bearer is

$$s(0) = F(T)\exp(-\rho T)/[1 - \exp(-\rho T)]. \tag{64}$$

Suppose, instead, that at $t = 0$ the piece of land in question houses a tree aged τ. What is the value of the land?

If the cycle is expected to be maintained, we have

$$\bar{s}(0) = F(T)\exp[-\rho(T - \tau)]/\{1 - \exp[-\rho(T - \tau)]\}. \tag{65}$$

If instead the tree is logged now, but the cycle is expected to be maintained, the value of the land, after the tree has been felled, is given by (64). Depreciation of the forest, as a capital asset, is the difference between (65) and (64).

6 Human Capital

To develop an accounting framework for knowledge acquisition and skill formation, consider a modified version of the basic model of section two. In particular, the underlying resource allocation mechanism is assumed to be autonomous. Labor hours are assumed to be supplied inelastically and population is constant, we may as well then normalize by regarding the labor hours supplied to be unity.

Production of the consumption good involves physical capital, $K_1(t)$, and human capital, $H_1(t)$. Here, $H_1(t)$ is to be interpreted to be the human capital embodied in those who work in the sector producing the consumption good. Thus, if $Y(t)$ is output of the consumption good,

$$Y(t) = F(K_1(t), H_1(t)), \tag{66}$$

where F is an increasing function of its arguments.

Assume that human capital is produced with the help of physical capital, $K_2(t)$, and human capital, $H_2(t)$, and that, owing to mortality, it depreciates at a constant rate, γ. Output of human capital is given by the technology

$$G(K_2(t), H_2(t)), \tag{67}$$

where G is an increasing function of its arguments and strictly concave, representing that the input of students is given.

By assumption, all individuals at a given moment of time have the same amount of human capital. Therefore, $H_1(t)/[H_1(t) + H_2(t)]$ is the proportion of people employed in the sector producing the consumption good. Let the total quantity of human capital be H. It follows that

$$H_1(t) + H_2(t) = H(t). \tag{68}$$

Write

$$K_1(t) + K_2(t) = K(t). \tag{69}$$

For simplicity of exposition, we assume that physical capital does not depreciate. Accumulation of physical capital can be expressed as

$$dK(t)/dt = F(K_1(t), H_1(t)) - C(t), \tag{70}$$

and the accumulation of human capital as

$$dH(t)/dt = G(K_2(t), H_2(t)) - \gamma H(t). \tag{71}$$

Since the resource allocation mechanism, α, is assumed to be autonomous, we have

$$V(t) = V(\alpha, K_1(t), K_2(t), H_1(t), H_2(t)). \tag{72}$$

Let $p_1(t)$ and $p_2(t)$ be the accounting prices of physical capital and $q_1(t)$ and $q_2(t)$ the accounting prices of human capital, in the two sectors, respectively (i.e., $p_1(t) = \partial V(t)/\partial K_1(t)$, $q_2(t) = \partial V(t)/\partial H_2(t)$, and so forth). Therefore, wealth can be expressed as

$$Z(t) = p_1(t)K_1(t) + p_2(t)K_2(t) + q_1(t)H_1(t) + q_2(t)H_2(t),$$

and genuine investment by

$$I(t) = p_1(t)\, dK_1(t)/dt + p_2(t)\, dK_2(t)/dt + q_1(t)\, dH_1(t)/dt$$
$$+ q_2(t)\, dH_2(t)/dt. \tag{73}$$

If α were an optimum resource allocation mechanism, we would have $p_1(t) = p_2(t) = p(t)$, say, and $q_1(t) = q_2(t) = q(t)$, say. These prices would be related by the optimality conditions

$$U'(C(t)) = p(t); \qquad p(t)\partial F/\partial K_1 = q(t)\partial G/\partial K_2;$$

and $\quad p(t)\partial F/\partial H_1 = q(t)\partial G/\partial H_2.$

Estimating $q_1(t)$ and $q_2(t)$ poses difficult problems in practice. It has been customary to identify human capital with education and to estimate its accounting price in terms of the market return on education (i.e., salaries over and above raw labor). But this supposes, as we have assumed in the above model, that education offers no direct utility. If education does offer direct utility (and it is widely acknowledged to do so), the market return on education is an underestimate of what we should ideally be after. Furthermore, human capital includes health, which is both a durable consumption good and capital good.

An alternative is to use estimates of expenditures on health and education for the purpose in hand. Such a procedure may be be a reasonable approximation for poor societies, but it is in all probability far off the mark for rich societies.

7   Global Public Goods

Countries interact with one another not only through trade in international markets but also via transnational externalities. Hamilton and Clemens (1999) include carbon dioxide in the atmosphere in their list of assets and regard the accounting price (a negative number) of a country's emission to be the amount it would be required to pay the rest of the world if carbon emissions were the outcome of a fully cooperative agreement. Their procedure is, consequently, valid only if each country is engaged in maximizing global welfare, an unusual scenario. In what follows, we develop the required analysis.

Let G(t) be the stock of a global common at t. We imagine that G is measured in terms of a quality index which, to fix ideas, we shall regard as carbon dioxide concentration in the atmosphere. Being a global common, G is an argument in the value function V of every country. For simplicity of notation, we assume that there is a single private capital good. Let $K_j(t)$ be the stock of the private asset owned by citizens of country j and let α_j be j's (autonomous) resource allocation mechanism and α the vector of resource allocation mechanisms. If V_j is j's value function, we have

$$V_j(t) = V_j(\alpha, K_j(t), G(t)). \tag{74}$$

Let $p_j(t) = \partial V_j(t)/\partial K_j(t)$ and $g_j(t) = \partial V_j(t)/\partial G(t)$. It may be that G is an economic "good" for some countries, while it is an economic "bad" for others. For the former, $g_j > 0$; for the latter, $g_j < 0$. Let $E_k(t)$ be the emission rate from country k and let γ be the rate at which carbon in the atmosphere is sequestered. It follows that

$$dG(t)/dt = \sum_k (E_k(t)) - \gamma G(t). \tag{75}$$

Genuine investment in j is

$$I(t) = dV_j(t)/dt = p_j(t)\, dK_j(t)/dt + g_j(t)\, dG(t)/dt,$$

which, on using (75), can be expressed as

$$I(t) = p_j(t)\, dK_j(t)/dt + g_j(t)\left[\sum_k (E_k(t)) - \gamma G(t)\right]. \tag{76}$$

Note that the expression on the RHS of (76) is the same whether or not α is based on international cooperation. On the other hand, $dK_j(t)/dt$ and $dG(t)/dt$ do depend on how the international resource allocation mechanisms are arrived at (e.g., whether they are cooperative or noncooperative); and they affect the accounting prices, $p_j(t)$ and $g_j(t)$.[25]

8   Exogenous Productivity Growth

To assume exogenous growth in total factor productivity (the residual) over the indefinite future is imprudent. It is hard to believe that serendipity, not backed by R&D effort and investment, can be a continual source of productivity growth. Moreover, many environmental resources go unrecorded in growth accounting. If the use of natural capital in an economy has been increasing, estimates of the residual could be presumed to be biased upward. On the other hand, if a poor country were able to make free use of the R&D successes of rich countries, it would enjoy a positive residual.

The residual can have short bursts in imperfect economies. Imagine that a government reduces economic inefficiencies by improving the enforcement of property rights or reducing centralized regulations (import quotas, price controls, and so forth). We would expect the factors of production to find better uses. As factors realign in a more productive fashion, total factor productivity would increase.

In the opposite vein, the residual could become negative for a period. Increased government corruption could be a cause; the cause could also be civil strife, which destroys capital assets and damages a country's institutions. When institutions deteriorate, assets are used even more inefficiently than before and the residual declines. This would appear to have happened in sub-Saharan Africa during the past forty years (Collins and Bosworth 1996).

We now study sustainability in the context of two models of exogenous productivity growth.

8.1 Labor Augmenting Technical Progress

Consider an adaptation of the model explored in section 2. Physical capital and a constant labor force together produce a nondeteriorating all purpose commodity. The economy enjoys labor augmenting technological progress at a constant rate n. If K is capital and A is knowledge, we have in the usual notation,

$$Y(t) = F(K(t), A(t)), \tag{77}$$

$$dK(t)/dt = F(K(t), A(t)) - C(t), \tag{78}$$

$$\text{and} \quad dA(t)/dt = nA(t). \tag{79}$$

There are two capital goods, K and A. Let $p_K(t)$ and $p_A(t)$, respectively, be their accounting prices in utility numeraire. The sustainability criterion is then $p_K(t)\,dK(t)/dt + p_A(t)\,dA(t)/dt \geq 0$, or, equivalently,

$$dK(t)/dt + q(t)\,dA(t)/dt \geq 0, \quad \text{where } q(t) \equiv p_A(t)/p_K(t). \tag{80}$$

It is instructive to study the case where the resource allocation mechanism is optimal. The equations of motion for p_K and p_A are

$$dp_K(t)/dt = \delta p_K(t) - p_K(t)\partial F/\partial K, \tag{81}$$

and $\quad dp_A(t)/dt = \delta p_A(t) - p_K(t)\partial F/\partial A - np_A(t). \tag{82}$

Using (80)–(82) yields

$$dq(t)/dt = (\partial F/\partial K - n)q(t) - \partial F/\partial A. \tag{83}$$

Suppose F displays constant returns to scale. Define $k = K/A$ and $c = C/A$. Write $f(k) \equiv F(k, 1)$. From (78) and (79), we have

$$dk(t)/dt = f(k(t)) - nk(t) - c(t),$$

or $\quad dk(t)/dt = (\partial F/\partial K)k(t) + \partial F/\partial A - nk(t) - c(t). \tag{84}$

Adding (83) and (84) yields

$$d(q(t) + k(t))/dt = (\partial F/\partial K - n)(q(t) + k(t)) - c(t). \tag{85}$$

It is simple to confirm that $q + k$ is the present value of future consumption (discounted at the rate $\partial F/\partial K$) divided by A (the current state of knowledge). It follows that the sustainability criterion at t (condition (80)), divided by A(t), is

$$dk(t)/dt + n(k(t) + q(t)) \geq 0. \tag{86}$$

8.2 Resource Augmenting Technical Progress

Consider an alternative world, where output, Y, is a function of manufactured capital (K) and the flow of an exhaustible natural resource (R). Let A(t)R(t) be the effective supply of the resource in production at t and S(t) the resource stock at t. Then we may write

$$Y(t) = F(K(t), A(t)R(t)), \tag{87}$$

$$dK(t)/dt = F(K(t), A(t)R(t)) - C(t), \tag{88}$$

$$dA(t)/dt = n, \tag{89}$$

$$dS(t)/dt = -R(t). \tag{90}$$

There are three state variables. But we can reduce the model to one with two state variables. Thus, write $Q(t) \equiv A(t)R(t)$ and $X(t) = A(t)S(t)$. Then (88) and (89) become

$$dK(t)/dt = F(K(t), Q(t)) - C(t), \tag{91}$$

and $dX(t)/dt = nX(t) - Q(t).$ (92)

This is equivalent to a renewable resource problem, and the steady state is the Green Golden Rule, with

$$nX = Q. \tag{93}$$

Let $p_K(t)$ and $p_X(t)$ be the accounting prices of $K(t)$ and $X(t)$, respectively. Then the sustainability condition is

$$p_K(t)\, dK(t)/dt + p_X(t)\, dX(t)/dt \geq 0. \tag{94}$$

It is instructive to study the case where the resource allocation mechanism is optimal. Suppose also that F displays constant returns to scale. Following the approach of the previous example, let $q(t) = p_X(t)/p_K(t)$. Then it is easy to confirm that

$$(dq(t)/dt)/q(t) = \partial F/\partial K - n. \tag{95}$$

Moreover, the optimal use of the productivity adjusted natural resource, $Q(t)$, is determined by the condition,

$$\partial F/\partial Q = q(t). \tag{96}$$

Along the optimal program, the sustainability condition (94) is

$$F(K(t), Q(t)) - C(t) + q(t)[nX(t) - Q(t)] \geq 0, \tag{97}$$

or $(\partial F/\partial K)K(t) + (\partial F/\partial Q)Q(t) - C(t) + q(t)[nX(t) - Q(t)] \geq 0,$ (98)

or $(\partial F/\partial K)K(t) - C(t) + nq(t)X(t) \geq 0.$ (99)

Inequality (99) says that consumption must not exceed the sum of capital income and the sustainable yield.

9   Further Extensions

A number of important features of actual economies were missing in the economic models developed so far. We comment on a few of them and show how they can be included in the theory.

Intragenerational Distribution

The distribution of well-being within a generation has been ignored so far. Theoretically it is not difficult to include this. If there are N people in each generation and person j consumes C_j, her welfare would be $U(C_j)$.[26] A simple way to express intragenerational welfare would be to "concavify" U. Let G be a strictly concave, increasing function of real numbers. We may then express intragenerational welfare as $\sum_j[G(U(C_j))]$. Some people would be well off, others badly off. The formulation ensures that at the margin, the well-being of someone who is badly off is awarded greater weight than that of someone well off.

The social worth of consumption services (C) depends on who gets what. To accommodate this idea, we have to enlarge the set of commodities so as to distinguish, at the margin, a good consumed or supplied by one person from that same good consumed or supplied by another. Thus, a piece of clothing worn by a poor person should be regarded as a different commodity from that same type of clothing worn by someone who is rich. With this reinterpretation of goods and services, the results we have obtained continue to hold.

Defensive Expenditure

The model developed in section two can be specialized to include defensive expenditure against pollution. Denote by Q(t) the stock of defensive capital and X(t) investment in its accumulation. Let P(t) be the stock of pollutants and Y(t) aggregate output. We may then write

$$dP(t)/dt = G(Y(t), Q(t)) - \pi P(t), \quad \text{where } G(Y(t), Q(t)) \geq 0, \partial G/\partial Y > 0$$

$$\text{and } \partial G/\partial Q < 0. \tag{100}$$

Moreover, if defensive capital depreciates at the rate ξ, then

$$dQ(t)/dt = X(t) - \xi Q(t), \quad \text{where } \xi > 0. \tag{101}$$

In the usual notation, the accumulation equation is expressed as

$$dK(t)/dt = F(K(t)) - C(t) - X(t). \tag{102}$$

Denote by p(t) the accounting price of K, m(t) that of defensive capital, and r(t) (< 0) the accounting price of the pollutant. Wealth can then be expressed as

$$p(t)K(t) + m(t)Q(t) + r(t)P(t),$$

and genuine investment at t as

$$I(t) = p(t)\,dK(t)/dt + m(t)\,dQ(t)/dt + r(t)\,dP(t)/dt. \tag{103}$$

Equation (103) says that defensive expenditure against pollution ought to be included in the estimation of genuine investment $(m(t) \, dQ(t)/dt)$, but, so should changes in the quality of the environment be included $(r(t) \, dP(t)/dt)$. To include the former, but not the latter, would be a mistake.

Acknowledgments

Research support was provided by the William and Flora Hewlett Foundation. An early version of this chapter was presented at a workshop on Putting Theory to Work: The Measurement of Genuine Wealth, held at the Stanford Institute for Economic Policy Research during April 25–26, 2002. The chapter was completed during an intellectually most stimulating visit by the first two authors to the Beijer International Institute of Ecological Economics, Stockholm. We are most grateful to Geir Asheim for correcting an error in a previous draft. A more technical and complete presentation of the material in this chapter is presented in Arrow, Dasgupta, and Mäler (2003a).

Notes

1. Dasgupta and Mäler (2000), Dasgupta (2001a,b), and section 1 here.

2. For references to the technical literature on sustainable development, see Pezzey and Toman (2002).

3. Dasgupta and Mäler (2000) and Dasgupta (2001a,b).

4. Serageldin (1995) and Pearce, Hamilton, and Atkinson (1996) were early explorations of the practicalities of estimating a nation's comprehensive wealth.

5. Differentiability everywhere is a strong assumption. For practical purposes, however, it would suffice to assume that V is differentiable in K_i almost everywhere. The latter would appear to be a reasonable assumption even when production possibilities (including ecological processes) are realistically nonconvex. See Arrow, Dasgupta, and Mäler (2003a).

6. Pezzey (1992) contains an early, but thorough, account.

7. Over the years economic evaluation of policy reform in imperfect economies has been discussed by a number of economists (e.g., Meade 1955; Dasgupta, Marglin, and Sen 1972; Mäler 1974; Blitzer, Dasgupta, and Stiglitz 1981; Starrett 1988; Ahmad and Stern 1990; Dreze and Stern 1990), but they did not develop a formal account for intertemporal economies.

8. If the project has been designed efficiently, we would have

$$\Delta Y(t) = (\partial F/\partial K)\Delta K(t) + (\partial F/\partial L)\Delta L(t) + (\partial F/\partial R)\Delta R(t),$$

where F is an aggregate production function $(Y = F(K, L, R))$. The analysis that follows in the text does not require the project to have been designed efficiently. As we are imagining that aggregate labor supply is fixed, $\Delta L(t)$ used in the project would be the same amount of labor displaced from elsewhere.

9. Dasgupta, Marglin, and Sen (1972) and Little and Mirrlees (1974), respectively, developed their accounts of social cost-benefit analysis with consumption and government income as numeraire. Which numeraire one chooses is, ultimately, not a matter of principle, but one of practical convenience.

10. The following is how (t) could in principle be estimated: Suppose other things being the same, $\Delta R(t)$ is the change in resource use. Let this change cause displacements $C(t)$, $(dK(t)/dt)$, $(dS(t)/dt)$ in consumption, net capital accumulation, and net growth in the natural-resource base, respectively. Denote by $q(t)$ the accounting price of the resource in situ. We then have

$$\hat{q}(t)\Delta R(t) = U'C(t) + p(t)(dK(t)/dt) + q(t)(dS(t)/dt).$$

Note that if manufactured capital were to depreciate at a constant rate, say γ, the social cost of borrowing capital would be $\lambda(t) = \delta + \gamma - [dp(t)/dt]/p(t)$.

At a full-optimum, $p(t)\partial F/\partial R(t) = q(t) = \hat{q}(t)$, and $U' = p(t)$.

11. Theorem 4 is, of course, familiar for economies where the government maximizes social welfare (see Arrow and Kurz 1970).

12. To prove (16) notice that, by definition, $\rho(t)$ satisfies the equation

$$U'(C(t))\exp(-\delta t) = U'(C(0))\exp\left(-\int_0^t [\rho(\tau)]\,d\tau\right).$$

If we differentiate both sides of the above equation with respect to t, (16) follows.

13. Notice that in imperfect economies δ and η may be directly observable. See section on marginal rates of substitution.

14. These are not fanciful figures. Per capita consumption in a number of countries in sub-Saharan Africa declined over the past three decades at as high a rate as 1 percent per year, implying that for small values of δ, the consumption rate of interest would have been negative.

15. As the economy has a single asset, theorem 3 is trivially true.

16. A special case of formula (32) appears in Dasgupta, Marglin, and Sen (1972). Unlike our present work, however, the earlier publication did not provide a rigorous welfare economic theory for imperfect economies.

17. Solow (1974) and Hartwick (1977) are the key articles on this limiting case.

18. In Arrow, Dasgupta, and Mäler (2003a), we develop an example to show that the theory can be applied to nonconvex economies.

19. McKelvey (1980) has studied a special case of the model of diffusion developed in what follows.

20. For an analysis of closed loop solutions for a class of games in which firms are engaged in polluting a lake, see Xepapadeas, de Zeeuw, and Mäler (2001).

21. In the limit, as λ tends to infinity, β tends to infinity, implying that depletion is instantaneous.

22. See also Hartwick and Hageman (1993) for a fine discussion that links El Serafy's formula to Hicks' formulation of the concept of national income (Hicks 1942).

23. That the industry optimizes does not mean that the economy is following an optimum program.

24. It should be noted though that the value of urban land would be more than just the new investment: there is a contribution to the value (which could be of either sign) arising from changes in population density—both in the newly developed property and in places of origin of those who migrate to the property.

25. Social cost-benefit analysis, as sketched in the section on project evaluation, would enable a country to estimate whether it ought to alter its emissions.

26. Person-specific factors (e.g., age, health status, gender) can be included in the welfare function. This is routinely done in applied economics.

References

Ahmad, E., and N. Stern. 1990. *The Theory and Practice of Tax Reform for Developing Countries*. Cambridge: Cambridge University Press.

Arrow, K. J., P. Dasgupta, and K.-G. Mäler. 2003a. "Evaluating Projects and Assessing Sustainable Development in Imperfect Economies." *Environmental and Resource Economics*. Forthcoming.

Arrow, K. J., P. Dasgupta, and K.-G. Mäler. 2003b. "The genuine savings criterion and the value of population." *Economic Theory* 21:217–225.

Arrow, K. J., and M. Kurz. 1970. *Public Investment, the Rate of Return and Optimal Fiscal Policy*. Baltimore: Johns Hopkins University Press.

Blitzer, C., P. Dasgupta, and J. E. Stiglitz. 1981. "Project Appraisal and Foreign Exchange Constraints." *Economic Journal* 91:58–74.

Brock, W., and D. Starrett. 2000. "Non-Convexities in Ecological Management Problems." Discussion Paper no. 130, Beijer International Institute of Ecological Economics, Stockholm.

Collins, S., and B. Bosworth. 1996. "Economic Growth in East Asia: Accumulation Versus Assimilation." *Brookings Papers on Economic Activity* 2:135–191.

Dasgupta, P. 2001a. "Valuing Objects and Evaluating Policies in Imperfect Economies." *Economic Journal* 111 (Conference Issue), 1–29.

Dasgupta, P. 2001b. *Human Well-Being and the Natural Environment*. Oxford: Oxford University Press.

Dasgupta, P., and G. Heal. 1979. *Economic Theory and Exhaustible Resources*. Cambridge: Cambridge University Press.

Dasgupta, P., and K.-G. Mäler. 2000. "Net National Product, Wealth, and Social Well-Being." *Environment and Development Economics* 5:69–93.

Dasgupta, P., S. Marglin, and A. Sen. 1972. *Guidelines for Project Evaluation*. New York: United Nations.

Dreze, J., and N. Stern. 1990. "Policy Reform, Shadow Prices, and Market Prices." *Journal of Public Economics* 42:1–45.

El Serafy, S. 1989. "The Proper Calculation of Income from Depletable Natural Resources." in Y. Ahmad, S. El Sarafy, and E. Lutz, eds.. *Environmental Accounting for Sustainable Development*. Washington, DC: World Bank.

Hamilton, K., and M. Clemens. 1999. "Genuine Savings Rates in Developing Countries." *World Bank Economic Review* 13:333–356.

Harsanyi, J. C. 1955. "Cardinal Welfare, Individualistic Ethics and Interpersonal Comparisons of Utility." *Journal of Political Economy* 63:309–321.

Hartwick, J. 1977. "Intergenerational Equity and the Investing of Rents from Exhaustible Resources." *American Economic Review* 66:972–974.

Hartwick, J., and A. Hageman. 1993. "Economic Depreciation of Mineral Stocks and the Contribution of El Sarafy," in E. Lutz, ed.. *Toward Improved Accounting for the Environment*. Washington, DC: World Bank.

Hicks, J. R. 1942. "Maintaining Capital Intact: A Further Suggestion." *Economica* 9:174–179.

IUCN. 1980. *The World Conservation Strategy: Living Resource Conservation for Sustainable Development*. Geneva: International Union for the Conservation of Nature and Natural Resources.

Little, I. M. D., and J. A. Mirrlees. 1968. *Manual of Industrial Project Analysis in Developing Countries: Social Cost Benefit Analysis*. Paris: OECD.

Little, I. M. D., and J. A. Mirrlees. 1974. *Project Appraisal and Planning for Developing Countries* London: Heinemann.

Lutz, E., ed. 1993. *Toward Improved Accounting for the Environment*. Washington, DC: World Bank.

McKelvey, R. 1980. "Common Property and the Conservation of Natural Resources," in S. A. Levin, T. G. Hallam, and L. J. Gross, eds. *Applied Mathematical Ecology, 18: Biomathematics*. Berlin: Springer Verlag.

Mäler, K.-G. 1974. *Environmental Economics: A Theoretical Enquiry*. Baltimore, MD: Johns Hopkins University Press.

Meade, J. E. 1955. *Trade and Welfare*. Oxford: Oxford University Press.

Nordhaus, W. D., and Z. Yang. 1996. "A Regional Dynamic General-Equilibrium Model of Alternative Climate-Change Strategies." *American Economic Review* 86:741–765.

Pearce, D., K. Hamilton, and G. Atkinson. 1996. "Measuring Sustainable Development: Progress on Indicators." *Environment and Development Economics* 1:85–101.

Pezzey, J. C. V. 1992. "Sustainable Development Concepts: An Economic Analysis." World Bank environment paper no. 2, World Bank, Washington, DC.

Pezzey, J. C. V., and M. A. Toman. 2002. "Progress and Problems in the Economics of Sustainability," in *The International Yearbook of Environmental and Resource Economics 2002/2003*, ed. T. Tietenberg and H. Folmer. Cheltenham, UK: Edward Elgar.

Portney, P. R., and J. P. Weyant, eds. 1999. *Discounting and Intergenerational Equity*. Washington, DC: Resources for the Future.

Ramsey, F. P. 1928. "A Mathematical Theory of Saving." *Economic Journal* 38:543–549.

Serageldin, I. 1995. "Are We Saving Enough for the Future?" in *Monitoring Environmental Progress*, Report on Work in Progress, Environmentally Sustainable Development, World Bank, Washington, DC.

Solow, R. M. 1956. "A Contribution to the Theory of Economic Growth." *Quarterly Journal of Economics* 70:65–94.

Solow, R. M. 1974. "Intergenerational Equity and Exhaustible Resources." *Review of Economic Studies* 41 (Symposium Issue): 29–45.

Starrett, D. 1988. *Foundations of Public Economics*. New York: Cambridge University Press.

Tinbergen, J. 1954. *Centralization and Decentralization in Economic Policy*. Amsterdam: North Holland.

World Commission. 1987. *Our Common Future*. New York: Oxford University Press.

Xepapadeas, A., A. de Zeeuw, and K.-G. Mäler. 2001. "Feedback Equilibria for a Class of Non-Linear Differential Games in Resource Economics." Discussion paper series no. 152, Beijer International Institute of Ecological Economics, Stockholm.

18   Optimality or Sustainability?

Geoffrey Heal

1   What Is Sustainability?

Sustainability is currently one of the most widely discussed issues in the environmental field, particularly among policymakers. Two concerns lie at the heart of these discussions: a concern for the interests of those who will live in the distant future, and a concern for the constraints imposed on human activity by the ecological and biogeochemical foundations of our societies. These capture what is common to many definitions of sustainability, the best known of which is probably the Brundtland report's comment that "Sustainable development is development that meets the needs of the present without compromising the ability of future generations to meet their own needs." Other definitions are more precise, requiring for example, that utility levels be nondecreasing over time,[1] or that resource stocks be nondecreasing, or that capital stocks in total (including natural capital) be nondecreasing.[2] All of these formulations are attempting to ensure adequate welfare for future generations either directly by bounding this below or indirectly by bounding below the stocks instrumental in providing future welfare.

Do we need new concepts and models to talk intelligently about these issues, or are they already captured by existing economics? The arguement here that there are few if any substantially novel intellectual issues raised by the discussions of sustainability. It is possible to model the concerns of sustainability within the existing corpus of economics, and indeed many key ingredients of the debate about sustainability have appeared in the economics literature before under different key words. Specifically, the literature on optimal growth with exhaustible and renewable resources covered many of the ingredients of sustainability back in the 1970s, and one of the contribuitors to that literature was Joe Stiglitz. His paper in the *Review of Economic Studies Symposium* (Stiglitz 1974) posed and answered some of the questions central to many contemporary discussions of sustainability. In that paper he modeled the impact that the presence of exhaustible resources would have on an economy's long-run growth. He focused on the issue of substitutability between natural resources and capital, still seen as one of the central issues here. Proposition 4 of his paper almost uses the word sustainability, "a necessary and sufficient condition for sustaining a constant level of consumption per capita is that the ratio of the rate of technical change, γ, to the rate of population growth must be greater than or equal to the share of natural resources." On a later page he goes on to say: "The fact that there is a limited amount of natural resources and natural resources are necessary for production does not necessarily imply that the economy must eventually stagnate and then decline. Two offsetting forces have been identified: technical change and capital accumulation. Even with no technical change, capital accumulation can offset the effects of the declining inputs of natural resources, so long as capital is 'more important' than natural resources."[3] All of these discussions sound quite contemporary, even though they are now thirty years old.

Certainly a concern for the long run raises old questions, dating back to Sidgwick (1890) and Ramsey (1928). Even if we have not answered these questions fully, we have discussed them at length. Likewise we may not yet have modeled well the constraints imposed by our society's biogeochemical infrastructure, but doing so probably raises no totally new theoretical issues. Focusing on these issues raises questions about how we specify the technological constraints under which society operates, whether these involve nonlinearities, nonconvexities, irreversibilities, and so forth. Both of the issues defining sustainability—long-run welfare and constraints on growth—are also at the heart of another area of economics: optimal growth theory. Ramsey's classic work initiated this field and placed the issue of balancing the welfares of present and future squarely on the agenda. Indeed, Ramsey's comment that "discounting future utilities is ethically indefensible and arises purely from a weakness of the imagination" states a position that most environmentalists would agree with, were they aware of it.

Explored here are what we know about the trade-offs between present and future and about the specification of the resource constraints under which the economy operates, relating the ideas

emerging from sustainability to those from optimal growth. Specifically, questions asked include "Are sustainable paths optimal?" and
"Are optimal paths sustainable?" Different approaches are explored
to the present-future trade-off, those due to Ramsey, von Weizäcker
(1967), Koopmans (1960), Rawls (1972), and others. This is done in
the context of various specifications of constraints on the economy,
constraints posed by exhaustible resources, renewable resources,
resources that are a source of utility to consumers, resources used in
production, and so forth. Beginning with the simplest case, Hotelling's 1931 model, the chapter moves through different specifications
of preferences and constraints. A clear picture emerges indicating
that optimal paths are sustainable, provided that preferences and
constraints reflect fully what we know about human society's dependence on environmental systems.[4] This proviso is crucial: if
earlier generations of optimal growth models did not produce sustainable paths, it was largely because they did not reflect this dependence. Different long-run welfare functions give different degrees
of sustainability, but we shall see that no reasonable definition of
optimal choice would lead to the destruction of society's natural
resource base. So it appears safe to assert that optimal paths are
usually sustainable, using the terms "optimal" and "sustainable" in
ways that command general assent. Sustainable paths, however, may
not be optimal.[5]

What are the implications of this conclusion? Sustainability, it
appears, is not a separate goal from optimality; rather, optimality is
a refined form of sustainability. Instead of proselytizing about sustainability as a social goal, environmental economists should work to
refine the concept of optimality generally used and ensure that it
incorporates an understanding of human dependence on environmental systems.

2   The Hotelling Model

Consider first the simplest and most classical formulation of the
problem of the optimal management of a natural resource. This is
Hotelling's formulation, which assumes the resource to be exhaustible. $u(c_t)$ is a utility function that is assumed throughout to be
increasing, strictly concave and twice continuously differentiable, so
that the first derivative is positive and the second negative. u' and
u'' denote the first and second derivatives of u, respectively. c is
consumption and s_t the stock of a resource remaining at time t. The

problem can be stated formally as max $\int_0^\infty u(c_t)e^{-\delta t}\,dt$ s.t. $s_t \geq 0$ and $\dot{s}_t = -c_t$ where of course $s_t = s_0 - \int_0^t c_f\,df$. A dot over a variable is always used to denote its time derivative.

The first-order conditions for a solution require that $\dot{\lambda}_t - \delta\lambda_t = 0$, that is, $\lambda_t = \lambda_0 e^{\delta t}$. What are the implications of this for consumption paths? To start with, consider a simple case. Let $u(c_t) = \log c_t$. Then $c_t = c_0 e^{-\delta t}$ so consumption falls exponentially at the discount rate. Nothing is conserved or sustained forever, and the present and future are treated very unequally. The ratio c_t/c_0 of initial consumption c_0 to consumption at date t, c_t, decreases exponentially with time: $c_t/c_0 = e^{-\delta t}$. The inequality between generations increases exponentially over time. In the general case, we have $u''(c_t)\dot{c}_t = \delta u'(c_t)$ so that $\dot{c}/c = -(\delta/\eta)$ where $\eta = -c_t u''(c_t)/u'(c_t) > 0$ and is the elasticity of marginal utility of consumption: it is also a measure of risk aversion and of the curvature of the function $u(c)$.

The next section shows that a relatively small change to this formulation, acknowledging an explicit value for the resource stock, alters everything. It makes the problem qualitatively different. We still work with an exhaustible resource, so that the set of feasible paths is unaltered, but the valuation of the remaining stock alters optimal use patterns radically and introduces real substance into the discussion of sustainability. Making the resource renewable, which is the theme of section 4, takes this process even further. Another strategy for making the model richer is to allow for the accumulation of capital, which can to some degree substitute for the resource. This is the approach that was taken initially by Dasgupta and Heal (1974, 1979), who showed that positive consumption levels may be sustained forever, even with an exhaustible resource, provided that there is considerable scope for substitution of produced capital for the resource.

3   Valuing a Depletable Stock

It is important to recognize explicitly the mechanisms through which environmental assets contribute to economic well-being. First we change the pure depletion problem by adding the remaining stock of the resource as an argument of the utility function, so that we now recognize explicitly that the stock of the resource may be a source of value. Examples of environmental resources for which this would be appropriate include biodiversity, which as measured by the range of species or some measure of their variation is a depletable asset; once it is reduced through extinction, it can never be restored to its original value, and clearly the stock of biodiversity is a source of many services. Another example is a forest, which yields a flow of wood for consumption as well as recreational facilities and carbon sequestration services by removing CO_2 from the atmosphere. Forest are usually renewable rather than depletable, but a tropical hardwood forest may to a first approximation be thought of as depletable. Other examples are a landscape, which can be farmed to yield a flow of output or enjoyed as a stock, or the atmosphere, which can be used to yield a flow of services as a sink for pollution or enjoyed as a stock of clean air.[6]

The basic problem is now max $\int_0^\infty u(c_t, s_t)e^{-\delta t}dt$ s.t. $s_t \geq 0$ and $\dot{s}_t = -c_t$ where the only alteration from the previous section is in the inclusion of the stock as an argument of the utility function, leading to qualitatively different conclusions. Now, in contrast to the previous case, it may be optimal to preserve some of the resource stock indefinitely. How much to preserve is sensitive to the precise specification of the objective, and several alternatives are investigated here.

3.1 Utilitarian Optimal Paths

The first-order conditions require that the derivative of utility with respect to consumption must be greater than or equal to the shadow price of the resource: $u_c(c_t, s_t) \leq \lambda_t, = \lambda_t$ if $c_t > 0$ where $u_c \equiv (\partial u(c,s))/(\partial c)$ and so forth. The condition describing the movement of the shadow price over time is $\dot{\lambda}_t - \delta \lambda_t = -u_s(c_t, s_t)$.

For simplicity, consider the case when the utility function is additively separable: $u(c_t, s_t) = u_1(c_t) + u_2(s_t)$ where the u functions are increasing, strictly concave and twice continuously differentiable. Then, letting a prime denote the derivative of a function of one variable with respect to its argument, the conditions for optimality become

$$u_1'(c_t) \leq \lambda_t, = \lambda_t \text{ if } c_t > 0, \ \dot{\lambda}_t - \delta \lambda_t = -u_2'(s_t). \tag{1}$$

In the previous case, the shadow price of the resource grew indefinitely. Now, in contrast, there may be a solution at which c_t, s_t and λ_t are constant. Note that if consumption is constant, it must be zero: this is the only feasible constant consumption. And note that if the

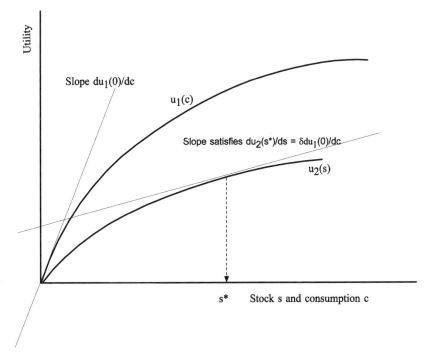

Figure 18.1
The stationary solution corresponding to equation 2 for a utilitarian optimal path
when the stock is valued

shadow price is constant, then $\delta\lambda_t = u_2'(s_t)$. So at a stationary solution
of the first-order conditions (1),

$$\delta \le \frac{u_2'(s^*)}{u_1'(0)}, \qquad \text{with equality if } c_t > 0, \tag{2}$$

where s^* is the constant value of the remaining resource stock. This
equation has a simple interpretation: it requires that the slope of an
indifference curve in the $s - c$ plane, the ratio of the marginal utilities
of the stock and flow, equal (or exceed) the discount rate. The stationary configuration for this model is shown in figure 18.1. The
constant level of the stock is one at which the derivative of utility
with respect to the stock (the slope of the curve u_2) equals the slope
of u_1, the utility-of-consumption function, at the origin, times the
discount rate δ.

Figure 18.2 shows the dynamics of an optimal policy, which involve depleting the resource stock by consuming it until it is run

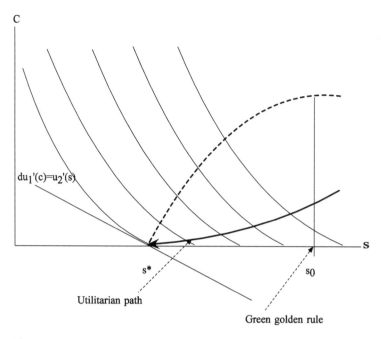

C

$du_1'(c)=u_2'(s)$

s*

s0

Utilitarian path

Green golden rule

S

Figure 18.2
The dynamics of a utilitarian optimal policy when the stock is valued

down to s^*, and then stopping consumption and preserving the stock forever. There is an important difference between the solution to the present problem, and that to the classic Hotelling problem. In the present framework, a positive stock may be preserved forever on an optimal path. Exactly how much depends on the discount rate and on the utility functions, but this is a qualitative difference between the two problems. So the concept of sustainability appears to have some relevance in the context of this solution.

When will it be optimal in this context to preserve a positive stock level forever? This depends on the behavior of the utility function as the consumption level goes to zero. If the marginal utility of consumption goes to infinity as consumption goes to zero, as is often assumed, then equation (2) has no solution and there is no stationary state. This is the case with a Cobb-Douglas function, or with a separable utility function in which $u_1(c)$ has a constant elasticity of marginal utility. In any of these cases, the indifference curves in the $c - s$ plane do not cross the horizontal axis, but asymptote toward it. These are cases in which the flow from the resources is in some sense essential. There is no substitute for it and the flow cannot be allowed to fall to zero. It is natural that in these cases no stock will be preserved. Note that whether there is a substitute for the stock—that is, the behavior of $u_2'(0)$—is not important in determining whether a positive stock remains. We can summarize this as follows:

PROPOSITION 1 Consider an optimal solution to the problem posed in section 3 when the utility function is additively separable, $u(c,s) = u_1(c) + u_2(s)$. A sufficient condition for this to involve the preservation of a positive stock forever is that the marginal utility of consumption at zero is finite, $u_1'(0) < \infty$, and that there exists a finite stock level s^*, the optimal stationary stock, such that $u_1'(0)\delta = u_2'(s^*)$. In this case, if the initial stock $s_0 > s^*$, then total consumption over time will equal $s_0 - s^*$: if $s_0 \leq s^*$, then consumption will always be zero and the entire stock will be conserved on an optimal path. If, on the other hand, the marginal utility of consumption at $c = 0$ is infinite, then it will not be optimal to conserve any positive stock level indefinitely.

3.2 The Green Golden Rule

A second difference arising from the inclusion of the stock as a source of utility comes when we ask the question, "which configuration of the economy gives the maximum sustainable utility level?" This is a question motivated by the "golden rule of economic growth," introduced in the 1960s by Phelps (1961), and by the interest here in sustainability. In the Hotelling formulation, there is no interesting answer to this question; the only utility level maintainable forever is that associated with zero consumption. In the present model, however, the question is quite interesting, as there are many utility levels that can be maintained forever. Clearly, in the very long run, no positive consumption level can be maintained and utility must be derived from the stock only. So the answer to the question, "which configuration of the economy gives the maximum sustainable utility level?" must be "the utility level associated with the initial stock (the biggest stock ever) and zero consumption." Formally, in finding the maximum utility that can be sustained indefinitely, we are maximizing $u(0,s)$ where $s \leq s_0$, and the solution is clearly to preserve the entire stock and never consume anything. This is the solution that has been called the green golden rule (Beltratti,

Chichilnisky, and Heal 1995): it is the path that of all feasible paths gives the highest value of the long-run level of utility.[7] It can be formalized as the solution to $\max_{feasible\ paths} \lim_{t \to \infty} u(c_t, s_t)$. Formally,

PROPOSITION 2   The maximum sustainable utility level is attained by conserving the entire initial stock.

3.3   The Rawlsian Optimum

An alternative approach to sustainability is using the Rawlsian definition of justice between generations. In the case of the current model, the green golden rule happens to be the optimal path in the Rawlsian sense, the one that maximizes the welfare of the generation that is least well off. On any path that involves positive consumption, the utility level is eventually nonincreasing over time. So the least-well-off generation is the "last" generation. In fact, there is no "last" generation, so more accurately the lowest welfare level is the limiting welfare level. But this is maximized by the green golden rule, which maximizes the sustainable, and so the limiting, welfare level over all feasible paths.

3.4   Overtaking

In an attempt to avoid the problems of zero discount rates, and yet give equal weight to present and future, von Weizäcker (1967) introduced the overtaking criterion:

DEFINITION 3   A path c^1 is said to weakly overtake a path c^2 if there exists a time T^* such that for all $T > T^*$, we have $\int_0^T u(c_t^1)\,dt \geq \int_0^T u(c_t^2)\,dt$. The path c^1 is said to strictly overtake c^2 if the inequality is strict.

This is an ingenious approach: it replaces infinite integrals by finite ones, and says that one path is better than another if from some date on cumulative utility on that path is greater. This is a relationship that can be checked even if both cumulative utility totals go to infinity as $T \to \infty$, so this approach does to some degree extend the applicability of an approach based on a zero discount rate. The overtaking criterion ranks paths with different limiting utility values according to those limiting values (Heal 1998). Consequently, the overtaking optimal path is the green golden rule, the path along which nothing is consumed and the entire initial stock is maintained intact. This is also the Rawlsian optimum. This is a remarkable coincidence of views. Note that with these three criteria complete conservation of the initial stock is optimal, whatever the size of the initial stock. Nothing in these arguments depends on the size of the initial stock. In some ways this is surprising; intuitively, one might believe that whether to conserve or not should depend on the size of the initial stock. This is true of the discounted utilitarian solution.

4   Renewable Resources

Now we add further to the structure of the model, this time in the specification of the constraints and the dynamics of the resource. We assume the resource to be renewable, that is, to have self-regenerating properties. The resource has a dynamic, a life of its own. We model the interaction between this dynamic and the time path of its use by humans. Animals, fish, and forests fall into this category. In fact, any ecosystem is of this type, and many of our most important natural resources are best seen as entire ecosystems rather than as individual species or subsystems. For example, soil is a renewable resource with a dynamic of its own, which interacts with the patterns of use by humans. Even for individual species, such as whales or owls, one should ideally think of the validity and the dynamics of the entire ecosystem of which they are a part. We shall see that the renewable nature of the resource makes a dramatic difference to the nature of optimal solutions. Now the future may be better treated than the present along an optimal path. If the initial resource stock is low, the optimal policy requires that consumption, stock, and utility all rise monotonically over time. Since the resource is renewable, both stocks and flows can be built up over time, provided that consumption is less than the rate of regeneration.

In this reformulation, the maximand remains exactly as before: primarily the discounted integral of utilities from consumption and from the existence of a stock, $\int_0^\infty u(c,s)e^{-\delta t}\,dt$, although as before some alternatives will be reviewed. The constraints, however, are changed. We assume that the dynamics of the renewable resource are described by $\dot{s}_t = r(s_t) - c_t$. Here r is the natural growth rate of the resource, assumed to depend only on its current stock. This describes its growth without human intervention. More complex models are possible in which several such systems interact: a well-known example is the predator-prey system. In general, r is a concave function that attains a maximum at a finite value of s. This formulation has a long and classical history, which is reviewed in Dasgupta and Heal (1979). Probably the weakest part of this specification is the ecological dynamic. As noted previously, most ecosystems are considerably more complex than suggested by the adjustment equation. In most cases they consist of many linked elements, each with its own interacting dynamics. Under some conditions, it is possible that the simple representation used here can be thought of as an aggregate representation of the ecological system as a whole, with the variable s_t not the stock of an individual type but an aggregate measure such as biomass. This is a topic for further research. It is also true, fortunately, that the general qualitative conclusions reached do not depend very sensitively on the precise specification of the ecological system.

The overall problem can now be specified as max $\int_0^\infty u(c,s)e^{-\delta t}\,dt$ s.t. $\dot{s}_t = r(s_t) - c_t$, s_0 given. First order conditions are $u_c(c_t, s_t) = \lambda_t$ and $d/dt(\lambda_t e^{-\delta t}) = -[u_s(c_t, s_t)e^{-\delta t} + \lambda_t e^{-\delta t} r'(s_t)]$. A solution to the problem is characterized by

$$\left.\begin{array}{l} u_1'(c_t) = \lambda_t \\[2mm] \dot{s}_t = r(s_t) - c_t \\[2mm] \dot{\lambda}_t - \delta\lambda = -u_2'(s_t) - \lambda_t r'(s_t) \end{array}\right\} \qquad (3)$$

In studying these equations, we first analyze their stationary solution and then examine the dynamics of this system away from the stationary solution.

4.1 Stationary Solutions

At a stationary solution, s is constant so that $r(s_t) = c_t$: in addition the shadow price is constant so that $\delta u_1'(c_t) = u_2'(s_t) + u_1'(c_t)r'(s_t)$. Hence:

PROPOSITION 4 A stationary solution to (3) satisfies

$$r(s_t) = c_t, \frac{u_2'(s_t)}{u_1'(c_t)} = \delta - r'(s_t) \qquad (4)$$

The first equation in (4) tells us that a stationary solution must lie on the curve on which consumption of the resource equals its

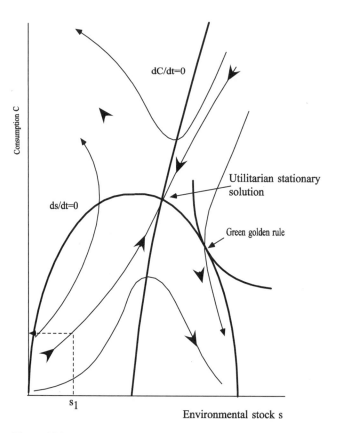

Figure 18.3
The dynamics of utilitarian optimal paths for a renewable resource

renewal rate; this is obviously a prerequisite for a stationary stock. The second gives us a relationship between the slope of an indifference curve in the $c - s$ plane and the slope of the renewal function at a stationary solution. The indifference curve cuts the renewal function from above. Such a configuration is shown as the utilitarian stationary solution in figure 18.3. This reduces to the earlier result that the slope of an indifference curve should equal the discount rate if $r'(s) = 0 \forall s$, if the resource is nonrenewable.

The dynamics of this system outside of a stationary solution are shown in figure 18.3. This shows that the utilitarian stationary solution (4) is a saddlepoint locally if it involves a stationary stock in excess of that giving the maximum sustainable yield. This is certainly the case for δ small enough. Hence, the dynamics of paths satisfying the necessary conditions for optimality are as shown in figure 18.3, and we can establish:

PROPOSITION 5   For small enough discount rates, optimal paths for the problem in section 4 tend to the stationary solution (4). They do so along a path satisfying the first-order conditions (3), and follow one of the two branches of the stable path in figure 18.3 leading to the stationary solution. Given any initial value of the stock s_0, there is a corresponding value of c_0 that will place the system on one of the stable branches leading to the stationary solution. The position of the stationary solution depends on the discount rate and moves to higher values of the stationary stock as this decreases. As $\delta \rightarrow 0$, the stationary solution tends to a point satisfying $u_2'/u_1' = r'$, which means in geometric terms that an indifference curve of $u(c,s)$ is tangent to the curve $c = r(s)$ given by the graph of the renewal function.

The renewable nature of the resource has clearly made a dramatic difference to the nature of optimal solutions. Now the future may actually be better treated than the present: if the initial resource stock is low, the optimal policy requires that consumption, stock, and utility all rise monotonically over time. Since the resource is renewable, both stocks and flows can be built up over time, provided that consumption is less than the rate of regeneration, that is, the system is inside the curve given by the graph of the renewal function $r(s)$.

4.2   The Green Golden Rule

The renewable framework can be used to ask a question that was asked before: what is the maximum sustainable utility level? There is a simple answer. First, note that a sustainable utility level must be associated with a sustainable configuration of the economy, that is, with sustainable values of consumption and of the stock. But these are precisely the values that satisfy the equation $c_t = r(s_t)$, for these are the values that are feasible and at which the stock and the consumption levels are constant. Hence, in figure 18.3, we are looking for values that lie on the curve $c_t = r(s_t)$. Of these values, we need the one that lies on the highest indifference curve of the utility function $u(c,s)$. This point of tangency, shown in the figure, is where the slope of an indifference curve equals that of the renewal function, so that the marginal rate of substitution between stock and flow equals the marginal rate of transformation along the curve $r(s)$. Hence, the maximum sustainable utility level (the green golden rule) satisfies

$$\frac{u_2'(s_t)}{u_1'(c_t)} = -r'(s_t)$$

Recall from (4) that as the discount rate goes to zero, the stationary solution to the utilitarian case tends to such a point.

Note also that any path that approaches the tangency of an indifference curve with the reproduction function is optimal according to the criterion of achieving the maximum sustainable utility. In other words, this criterion of optimality only determines the limiting behavior of the economy; it does not determine how the limit is approached. This clearly is a weakness. Of the many paths that approach the green golden rule, some will accumulate far more utility than others. One would like to know which of these is the best, or indeed whether there is such a best. We return to this later.

4.3 The Rawlsian Solution

In the nonrenewable context, we noted the coincidence of the Rawlsian optimum with the green golden rule. In the present case things do not always fit together so neatly. Consider the initial stock level s_1 in figure 18.3: the utilitarian optimum from this is to follow the path that leads to the saddle point. In this case consumption, stock, and utility are all increasing. So the generation that is least well off is the first generation, not the last, as it was in the nonrenewable case. What is the Rawlsian solution in the present model with initial stock s_1? It is easy to verify that this involves setting $c = r(s_1)$ forever. This gives a constant utility level, and it gives the highest utility level for the first generation compatible with subsequent levels being no lower. This remains true for any initial stock no greater than that associated with the green golden rule. For larger initial stocks, the green golden rule is a Rawlsian optimum and in this case we still have the coincidence noted in the previous section. Formally,

PROPOSITION 6 For an initial resource stock s_1 less than or equal to that associated with the green golden rule, the Rawlsian optimum involves setting $c = r(s_1)$ forever. For s_1 greater than the green golden rule stock, the green golden rule is a Rawlsian optimum.

4.4   Overtaking

What does the overtaking criterion imply in the case of renewable resources?

First, note that by quite standard arguments, an optimal path must satisfy the utilitarian first-order conditions for optimality with the discount rate equal to zero. These conditions have as their saddle-point stable stationary solution the green golden rule.

Second, note that all paths satisfying the above first-order conditions have well-defined limiting utility values.

Finally, note that the green golden rule is the highest possible limiting utility value, so that the path satisfying the above conditions and approaching the green golden rule overtakes any other path satisfying the same first-order conditions. Overall, then, it is clear that an overtaking optimal path follows the utilitarian first-order conditions with a zero discount rate to the green golden rule.

5   Conclusion

From a review of paths of resource use that are optimal for a variety of models, we see that many optimal paths are sustainable. They involve maintaining at least a part of the initial resource stock intact forever. In fact, it is only the simple Hotelling model that does not produce sustainable paths, but this reflects the technology of the problem rather than a conflict between optimality and sustainability. With more environmentally appropriate preferences, even this specification of the technology can give optimal paths that are sustainable and, indeed, maintain the entire initial stock intact. In the case of renewable resources, most possible optimal paths are sustainable in the sense of maintaining the resource base and growing it. Some asymptote to the maximum possible utility level, the green golden rule, and are sustainable in a very strong sense; others settle at a lower utility level, but are still sustainable. The green golden rule occupies a strategic position in the analysis in that most paths will move toward it or remain near it for long periods. The initial assertion that optimal paths are sustainable, provided that the preferences and constraints reflect fully what we know human dependence is on environmental systems, appears well documented. And some of these issues are not new; thirty years back, under the guise of optimal growth with natural resourcs, economists were investigating the issues underlying concerns about sustainability. The papers by Solow (1974), Stiglitz (1974) and Dasgupta and Heal (1974), written in the early 1970s, went a long way toward establishing the right intellectual framework. They and related papers also went on to ask and begin to answer another related and important question: will competitive markets implement optimal paths in the presence of natural resources? This is the topic of Stiglitz's second paper in the Review of Economic Studies Symposium (1974) and also of chapter 8 of Dasgupta and Heal (1979).

Acknowledgments

Prepared for presentation at the EAERE 2001 Conference, Southampton, June 2001. This chapter is a condensation of parts of the author's book *Valuing the Future: Economic Theory and Sustainability*, (Columbia University Press, 1998), with a few new insights added. Proofs of all propositions can be found in that book.

Notes

1. Pezzey (1989) and for a review see Asheim, Buchholz, and Tungodden (2001).

2. For a review see Smulders (2001).

3. Stiglitz analyzed an economy with a Cobb-Douglas production function using as inputs capital, labor and natural resources. This allowed him to derive analytical solutions for the growth paths. Partha Dasgupta and I worked (1974) with more general production functions and obtained similar characterizations.

4. As summarized, for example, in Heal (2000).

5. That sustainable paths are not optimal is sufficiently obvious that it does not require formal proof. Sustainable paths are not required by their definitions to meet first-order conditions for intertemporal efficiency.

6. This framework was introduced by Krautkraemer (1985), and developed further by him in (1986).

7. This is formalized as the maximum limiting utility value. Other formalizations, however, are in principle possible: for example, as the maximum of the lim sup of the utility values. The differences between alternatives become of significance only when positive limit sets of feasible trajectories may be limit cycles or other more complex attractors.

References

Asheim, Geir, Wolfgang Buchholz, and Bertil Tungodden. 2001. "Justifying sustainability." *Journal of Environmental Economics and Management* 41 (3), May.

Beltratti, Andrea, Graciela Chichilnisky, and Geoffrey M. Heal. 1995. "The green golden rule." *Economics Letters* 49:175–179.

Dasgupta, Partha S., and Geoffrey M. Heal. 1974. "The optimal depletion of exhaustible resources." *Review of Economic Studies*, Symposium: 3–28.

Dasgupta, Partha S., and Geoffrey M. Heal. 1979. *Economic Theory and Exhaustible Resources*. Cambridge, UK: Cambridge University Press.

Heal, Geoffrey M. 1973. *The Theory of Economic Planning*. Amsterdam: North-Holland Publishing Company.

Heal, Geoffrey M. 1985. "Depletion and discounting: a classical issue in resource economics," in R. McElvey, ed., *Environmental and Natural Resource Mathematics* 32:33–43, Proceedings of Symposia in Applied Mathematics, American Mathematical Society, Providence, RI.

Heal, Geoffrey M. 1998. *Valuing the Future: Economic Theory and Sustainability*. New York: Columbia University Press.

Heal, Geoffrey M. 2000. *Nature and the Marketplace*. Washington, DC: Island Press.

Hotelling, Harold. 1931. "The economics of exhaustible resources." *Journal of Political Economy* 39:137–175.

Koopmans, Tjalling. 1960. "Stationary ordinal utility and impatience." *Econometrica* 28:287–309.

Krautkraemer, Jeffrey A. 1985. "Optimal growth, resource amenities and the preservation of natural environments." *Review of Economic Studies* 52:153–170.

Krautkraemer, Jeffrey A. 1986. "Optimal depletion with resource amenities and a backstop technology." *Resources and Energy* 8:133–149.

Pezzey John. "Economic analysis of sustainable growth and development." Environmental Department working paper no. 15, World Bank, Washington D.C., 1989.

Phelps, Edmund S. 1961. "The golden rule of accumulation: a fable for growthmen." *American Economic Review* 51 (4):638–643.

Rawls, John. 1972. *A Theory of Justice*. Oxford, UK: Clarendon Press.

Ramsey, Frank. 1928. "A mathematical theory of saving." *Economic Journal* 38:543–559.

Sidgwick, H. 1890. *The Methods of Ethics*. London: Macmillan.

Smulders, Sjak. 2001. "Economic growth and environmental quality." Intended as chapter 21 of *Principles of Environmental Economics*, Henk Folmer and Landis Gabel, eds. Cheltenham, UK: Edward Elgar.

Solow, Robert M. 1956. "A contribution to the theory of economic growth." *Quarterly Journal of Economics* 70 (1):65–94.

Solow Robert M. 1974. "Intergenerational equity and exhaustible resources." *Review of Economic Studies*, Symposium: 29–45.

Stiglitz, Joseph E. 1974. "Growth with exhaustible natural resources: efficient and optimal paths." *Review of Economic Studies*, Symposium: 123–138.

Stiglitz, Joseph E. 1974. "Growth with exhaustible natural resources: the competitive economy." *Review of Economic Studies*, Symposium: 139–152.

von Weizäcker, Carl Christian. 1967. "Lemmas for a theory of approximately optimal growth." *Review of Economic Studies* 34 (1):143–151.

19   Labor Market Flexibility and the Welfare State

A. B. Atkinson

This chapter is concerned with a set of policy issues that are both an intellectual puzzle and of key importance for contemporary policy making. Such a subject appears highly appropriate for a volume honoring Joe Stiglitz, who combines the distinction of being one of our generation's most creative thinkers with having served as chair of President Clinton's Council of Economic Advisers and as chief economist of the World Bank. The issues can be simply stated. Are labor market reforms and scaling back the welfare state complementary or substitute economic policies? Do countries need to do both, or can they choose? If there is a choice, how should the balance be struck?

Comparisons with the United States have led many people to conclude that Continental Europe needs less rigid labor market institutions and less social spending. In their review of the reasons for the persistence of unemployment in Europe, Nickell and Layard conclude that "the key labor market institutions on which policy should be focused are unions and social security systems" (1999, 3080). Such views have influenced policymakers. When asked what structural changes were needed to support the euro, the IMF Managing Director Horst Köhler said that "the big countries in Europe must reform their social security and tax systems and make their labor markets more flexible" (reported in *IMF Survey*, June 5, 2000, 179). The OECD study by Elmeskov, Martin, and Scarpetta of key lessons for labor market reforms concluded that "comprehensiveness seems indeed to be a crucial feature of any successful strategy to reduce unemployment because reforms in different areas can reinforce each other's effects" (1998, 223). The article, "Policy Complementarities," by Coe and Snower in *IMF Staff Papers* argued that "an important group of labor market policies are complementary in the sense that the effect of each policy is greater when implemented in conjunction with the other policies than in isolation. [What is required] is deeper labor market reforms across a broader range of complementary policies" (1997, 1); (see also Orszag and Snower 1998.) These authors are careful in their definition of complementarity, which concerns the reinforcing effects of policies, but the statements have been interpreted as saying that countries cannot choose to concentrate on one arm of the strategy. They cannot, for example, succeed by making labor markets more flexible but retaining generous social protection.

It is not evident, however, that governments have to both make labor markets more flexible and cut back on social protection. Empirical studies of unemployment, such as Nickell and Layard (1999), seek to explain employment rates as linear functions of variables representing employment protection, union strength, benefit replacement rates, and so forth. This specification posits a straightforward trade-off between policy variables. On this basis, unemployment could be lowered by reducing either employment protection or benefit rates. There is room for choice, and this means that we have to ask how the policy decision should be related to the ultimate goals of efficiency and equity.

These questions are examined here in the context of a specific job search model of the labor market, set out in section 1. Since other models could well lead to other conclusions, I should note that this model has been widely employed in the macroeconomic and labor market literatures and appears to underlie much of the less formal policy discussion. In the context of this book, I should point out that the model is of an imperfect economy in the sense that, by assumption, the labor market does not clear instantaneously and there is a matching process for job filling. Such an assumption is made in part because I find it a more realistic description of how the world works than the assumption of frictionless clearing. It is made in part because it allows the introduction of a reason for the existence of transfer payments. All too often the economic analysis of the welfare state is based on models that take no account of the contingencies for which social insurance was introduced. The model is used to examine (in section 2) the complementarity or substitutability of policies and (in section 3) the balancing of the two arms of policy in the pursuit of efficiency and equity.

1 Equilibrium Unemployment

The search/matching model in its simplest form (following Mortensen and Pissarides 1999) assumes identical potential workers, $(1 - u)$ of whom are employed at a particular date at a wage w, and u of whom constitute a stock of unemployed, searching for a job. While unemployed they produce a flow of output at home, x, and receive a flat-rate transfer, b, financed by a fixed tax, t, on all workers (no taxes are levied on the employer).[1] There is a stock of job vacancies, v per head of the potential labor force, created by identical firms. The square root of the ratio of v to u, a measure of labor market tightness, is denoted by θ. The matching function is assumed to be such that the probability per unit of time of an unemployed worker getting a job offer is $m\theta$, and the probability per unit of time of a vacancy being filled is m/θ, where m is a constant: that is, a constant returns to scale matching function with an elasticity of a half. Jobs produce a constant flow of output, y, per worker (where $y > x$), so that profit over labor costs is $(y - w)$. Jobs suffer an exogenous probability, δ, per unit of time of being terminated. If the (common) discount rate is r, then the expected present value of a filled job is J where

$$J = (y - w)/(r + \delta). \tag{1}$$

The cost per unit of time to the employer of holding open a vacancy is assumed to be a constant, c. There is assumed to be free entry, so that

$$J(m/\theta) = c. \tag{2}$$

The expected present value arising from holding open a vacancy per unit of time is in equilibrium equal to c. It follows that

$$y - w = c(r + \delta)\theta/m. \tag{3}$$

This yields the job creation condition shown in figure 19.1. If wages are high, then firms will only create vacancies if the labor market is sufficiently slack that they can expect to fill the vacancy quickly. Tightness in the labor market is related to the unemployment rate by the condition that in steady state the flow of job terminations equal the flow of job matches:

$$\delta(1 - u) = m\theta u \quad \text{or} \quad (1 - u) = \theta/(\mu + \theta), \tag{4}$$

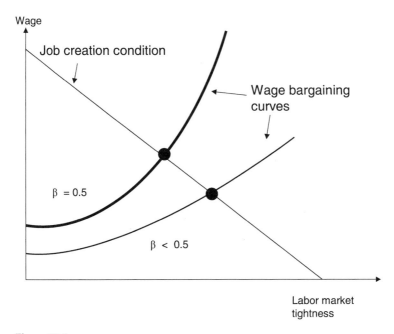

Figure 19.1
Determination of wage and degree of labor market tightness

where (δ/m) is defined to be μ. All other parameters affect the level of employment only via θ.

Workers are assumed to evaluate alternatives in terms of the expected present value of a stream of returns, discounted at constant rate r over an infinite horizon. The expected present value of job to a worker, denoted by W, and the value, U, attached to the state of being unemployed, satisfy, in steady state, the flow condition

$$rW = w - t - \delta[W - U] \tag{5}$$

$$rU = b + x + m\theta[W - U]. \tag{6}$$

We can solve for

$$(r + \delta + m\theta)(W - U) = w - t - b - x. \tag{7}$$

The wage is determined by wage bargaining such that the worker receives a fraction β of the surplus created by the match:

$$W - U = \beta[W - U + J]. \tag{8}$$

Combined with (7), and using (2) and (3), this yields the wage bargaining curve shown in figure 19.1:

$$w = \beta[y + c\theta^2] + (1 - \beta)(b + t + x). \tag{9}$$

The tighter the labor market, the larger the reservation wage (since an unemployed worker stands a better chance of getting another job), and hence the larger the bargained wage. The position of the curve depends on the strength of bargaining power: two cases are shown, one (heavy line) with equal sharing of the surplus ($\beta = 1/2$) and the other with less powerful workers ($\beta < 1/2$).

There is a unique equilibrium value for θ, which is the positive root of the quadratic:

$$f(\theta) \equiv \beta c\theta^2 + [(r + \delta)c/m]\theta - (1 - \beta)(y - b - t - x) = 0, \tag{10}$$

where it is assumed that the constant term is negative, which puts an upper limit on the policy parameters $(b + t)$. The derivative of $f(\theta)$ is positive at the equilibrium value, which means that the equilibrium level of labor market tightness is a declining function of the strength of union bargaining power, as indicated in figure 19.1, and of the cost of a job vacancy, c. A rise in c causes the job creation line to rotate clockwise, and the wage bargaining curve to shift to the left, and hence causes unemployment to rise. It may also be deduced from (10) that $c\theta$ is an increasing function of c. Since from (8) $(W - U)$ is proportional to J, and hence from (2) to $(c\theta)/m$, it follows that a rise in the costs of a vacancy increases the "premium" received by those in employment.

The policy parameters b and t are linked via the government budget constraint:

$$t(1 - u) = bu \quad \text{or} \quad t = bu/(1 - u). \tag{11}$$

This means that, using (4),

$$b + t = b/(1 - u) = b[1 + \mu/\theta] = t[1 + \theta/\mu], \tag{12}$$

or $b = t\theta/\mu$. The wage bargaining curve incorporating the government budget constraint is

$$w = \beta[y + c\theta^2] + (1 - \beta)[x + t(1 + \theta/\mu)]. \tag{9a}$$

The solution for θ is now given by the equation

$$g(\theta) \equiv \beta c\theta^2 + [(r/\delta + 1)c\mu + (1 - \beta)t/\mu]\theta - (1 - \beta)(y - t - x) = 0. \tag{13}$$

A rise in the tax rate increases the value of $g(\theta)$ and hence lowers the equilibrium value of θ. The other comparative static propositions described earlier remain valid.

The model just described is used here as exemplifying the kind of analytical framework that appears to underlie much policy discussion. Its use should not be taken as an endorsement of its properties, which are open to debate. For example, other models have reached different conclusions about the impact of hiring costs (see Bertola 1990, 1992). A reduction in the benefit level here causes the wage bargaining curve to shift down and hence increases employment, but for a different view of the economic impact of cutting unemployment insurance (see Atkinson 1999).

2   Welfare State and Labor Market Reforms: Complements or Alternatives?

The model outlined above omits much of the complexity of real world labor markets, and I do not believe that we should go down the route of calibrating it for policy analysis. Too much is left out. But what the model does allow us to do is to identify key elements in the policy debate and to trace through their implications in an explicit framework. Examined here are:

1. Policies to increase labor market flexibility, either by eliminating frictions, represented here by reducing the cost of holding open job vacancies (c), or by reducing the bargaining power of unions, represented here by reducing β.

2. Policies to reduce the generosity of social protection, represented here by reducing b.

The recent policy debate has suggested that the relation between these policies in producing employment is like that of complementary goods in producing utility. The isoquants resemble those labeled type A in figure 19.2, rather than those labeled type B, where there is substitutability. In drawing these, I have taken $(-c)$ as the positive input into employment; increasing $(-c)$ means greater flexibility. Similarly, $(-b)$ is the positive input into employment. The difference between types A and B is an important one. Where the isoquants are effectively right angles, as at the point marked, then employment cannot be increased without reducing the scale of ben-

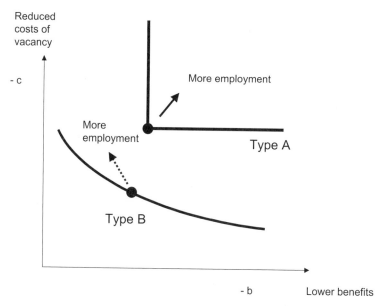

Figure 19.2
Different types of isoquant in producing employment

efits. We have to move in the direction indicated by the arrow with
a solid line. This kind of shape has been posited by some writers
when seeking to explain the apparent ineffectiveness of labor market
policies when introduced on their own. The conclusion drawn has
been that, to make progress in raising European employment, action
needs to be taken on both fronts. On the other hand, if the isoquants
look more like type B, then more employment can be produced by
simply reducing labor market frictions, or by combining this policy
with increased generosity of benefits, as indicated by the arrow with
the dotted line.

What do the isoquants look like in the present model? We can see
from (4) that, for fixed μ, the isoemployment curves are given by
constant values of θ. Leaving aside the budget constraint, we can
then see from (10) that constant θ implies a linear relation between
c and b. The employment isoquants are straight lines in $(-b, -c)$
space. A given level of employment can be attained by different
mixes of high flexibility/high social protection or low flexibility/low
social protection.

Substitutability along the isoquant does not contradict the statement that the cross-derivative of labor market tightness with the two

policy variables is positive. From the solution to the quadratic equation (10), we can show that $\partial^2\theta/\partial(-c)\partial(-b)$ is positive. We have a positive cross-derivative but linearity of the isoquants. Linearity remains true when we allow for the effect of the budget constraint: it may be seen from (13) that the isoquants in $(-b, -c)$ space remain linear. Linearity does not carry over if we consider not the cost of job creation but the level of employee bargaining power, β. Instead, the isoquants are rectangular hyperbolae. The important feature is that the asymptotes are outside the relevant space, which means that there is substitutability for the ranges of parameter values of interest. It remains that, for any benefit level b, there is a value of c that can attain the desired employment rate. The cost of achieving this reduction in c (for instance, via subsidies to job creation) may be high, but failure to move on the benefit side does not prevent the economy from attaining a specified employment target.

The use of a formal model, albeit stylized, allows us to highlight the ambiguity surrounding the use by economists of the word complementarity. This ambiguity is well known from consumer theory and was clearly set out by Sir John Hicks (whose chair at Oxford was later held by Joe Stiglitz) in *Value and Capital* (1946), where curves like those in figure 19.2 are to be found on page 43. As Hicks explains, one natural approach is to define complementarity in terms of the cross-derivative. Coe and Snower are following Edgeworth and Pareto in defining two policies as complementary in terms of cross-derivatives. As Hicks points out, however, there is no necessary link between this definition and the shape of the indifference curves. In a consumer demand context, the indifference curves are a purely ordinal notion, whereas the cross-derivative depends on the cardinalization. In a production context, it is quite possible to have substitution along an isoquant while having a positive cross-derivative.

We need to be careful, therefore, about the interpretation of the term complementary. Moreover, the consequences for policy choice are not immediate. A Cobb-Douglas production function has a positive cross-derivative, but firms are not under a technological requirement to make all adjustments by hiring both more labor and more capital (or reducing both). Such a decision is a matter for choice, and in the next section I consider how such a balance may be struck.

3   Policy Choice, Efficiency, and Equity

Governments have a choice about the mix of policies to be pursued. At the same time, a positive cross-derivative of employment with respect to labor market flexibility and benefit reductions would have consequences for policy choice. The more that the labor market becomes flexible, the greater the attraction in terms of employment increase of scaling back the welfare state. Does this then mean that measures that increase labor market flexibility imply a fall in the optimal level of transfers? To answer this question, we first need to consider the objectives of policy. We have to look at the demand side as well as the supply side.

In the discussion of the interrelation between flexibility policies and reduced social protection, both were seen as "goods" contributing to the production of employment. Employment, however, is not a final objective. This has been recognized clearly in the search model literature. When Diamond refers in the title of his article (1982) to "efficiency in search equilibrium," he has in mind not total employment but the maximization of expected net output. As shown by Hosios (1990) and Pissarides (1990, 121), there is a critical value of labor market tightness that maximizes expected net output. Reducing unemployment beyond this point is inefficient because it adds more to the cost of having unfilled vacancies than it adds to output. In the present case, expected net output, Y, is given by

$$Y \equiv (1 - u)y + ux - cv = (1 - u)y + ux - cu\theta^2. \tag{14}$$

Substituting for u from (4), and differentiating with respect to θ, we can see that Y increases with θ if

$$h(\theta) \equiv c\theta^2/2 + c\mu\theta - (y - x)/2 < 0. \tag{15}$$

It is immediately evident that this condition is satisfied for small values of θ but not for large values. There is a level of θ that generates an efficient outcome. This does not mean that governments will actually choose such a level; the explanation of their behavior is a matter for public choice theory. Comparing (10) and (15), we can see that one special case that generates net output efficiency is where $\beta = 1/2$, $r = 0$ and $b = t = 0$. This is a special case in several senses. First, it means that there is no profit income over and above that required to cover the expected costs of filling vacancies. Profit income is often neglected in discussions of labor market policy. We are concentrating here on the labor market, but developments in the capital market are also important. If increased labor market flexibility has led to reduced costs of hiring (or firing), then this may not have been competed away, but have led to higher shareholder return. (Some stock market analysts have correlated stock market performance across countries with increased labor market flexibility.) For the rest of the chapter, I set $r = 0$. There are no net profits in excess of the cost of vacancies, but it must be remembered that the level of employment is a declining function of r (see 13).

The efficiency condition depends on the relative bargaining power: whether $(1 - \beta)$ is greater or less than the elasticity of the matching function with respect to vacancies, here assumed to be a half. Where $\beta = 1/2$, introduction of unemployment benefits will not only raise unemployment but also reduce market efficiency. If efficiency is the objective, then in this situation there is no case for social protection. Concentrating just on this special case is misleading, however, since we miss the important point that the no-intervention equilibrium may well be inefficient (a point stressed by Diamond 1981). Suppose that labor market flexibility leads to a lower level of bargaining power for workers: Millard and Mortensen (1997) take a value of 0.3 for the United States, compared with 0.584 for the United Kingdom. The no-intervention equilibrium then generates a degree of labor market tightness above the efficient level; the introduction of unemployment benefits raises efficiency. This is depicted in figure 19.3. The heavy lines are the loci of labor market equilibria with different tax rates, obtained by solving equation (13). The dashed line shows $h(\theta)$, which has the same sign as the derivative of net output with respect to θ. It follows that, in the case where β is less than one-half, at point A, with zero tax, the derivative is negative, so that a rise in the tax rate would move the economy toward the efficient degree of labour market tightness. Alternatively, if we start from a situation with social protection and strong worker bargaining power, as B in figure 19.3, then reduction in worker bargaining power to point C may not only obviate the need for scaling back benefits but mean that benefits should be maintained on efficiency grounds.

Concern for the Least Advantaged

The notion that reducing unemployment may be inefficient may appear counterintuitive but reflects the criterion used for evaluation,

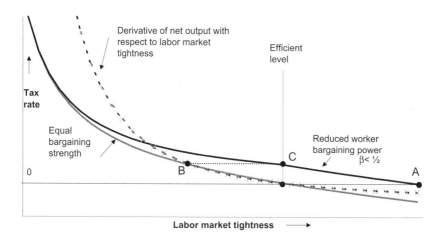

Figure 19.3
Efficiency and social protection

which is purely one of efficiency. There may be a case for reducing unemployment on distributional grounds, even if expected output is reduced (as firms find themselves unable to fill vacancies), and the chapter now turns to this argument. It should be emphasized that I am referring here to reductions in equilibrium unemployment, not to measures to reduce unemployment below its equilibrium rate, although distributional concerns may lie behind such arguments too.

To explore the distributional implications, we have to trace the recipients of income. Suppose that we cut taxes and hence unemployment benefits with the aim of reducing unemployment, moving along the menu offered by equation (13). For the employed population, we would count an increase in their number and a fall in the tax rate, but offset by a fall in the wage. For the unemployed, there would be a fall in their number, but those remaining unemployed would be worse off. There would be a rise in total profits as employment increases, and as the wage falls, but a reduction on account of the rise in the cost of filling vacancies. The assumptions of free entry and $r = 0$ means that the net effect on profits is zero.

How can these distributional differences be treated? There is room here for considerable differences of opinion. These differences may concern two distinct, but not fully independent, dimensions: (1) how we evaluate individual circumstances and (2) how we aggregate to form an overall social judgment. I concentrate on the case where individual welfare[2] is measured by current income and where we assume that the social welfare function is additive:

$$(1 - u)G(w - t) + uG(b + x), \qquad (16)$$

where $G(X)$ is an increasing, concave function. (It should be noted that the conclusions would be different if we replaced current income by the expected present value of being employed/unemployed.) The resulting assessment will depend on the judgments embodied in the form of $G(\ )$. The efficiency criterion in effect takes $G(X) = X$; that is, the social marginal valuation of income is indifferent to its distribution. At the other extreme is the situation where we are solely concerned with the circumstances of the least advantaged, a criterion associated with the name of Rawls (1971), although his theory of justice is much richer than this criterion suggests. Here, since there are always frictionally unemployed workers, a reduction in the benefit level unambiguously worsens the position of the least advantaged, regardless of any gain in employment. A rise in employment is only desirable to the extent that it allows more revenue to be raised. This underlines a special feature of the Rawlsian objective: it is focused on the least advantaged to the exclusion of concern for the number of people constituting this class.

The Rawlsian case, while special, allows us to explore the relation between labor market flexibility policies and arguments concerning the optimal scale for the welfare state. The maximization of the level of benefit, which by the government budget constraint is given by

$$b = t\theta/\mu, \qquad (17)$$

can be located from the social indifference curves in (θ, t) space, each of which is a rectangular hyperbola, as shown in figure 19.4. The menu of possibilities is given by the equilibrium relationship (13). The question in which I am interested here is the impact of increased labor market flexibility on the optimal scale, b*, of benefits. It is possible that a fall in c causes the trade-off to be less favorable to benefits; positive cross-derivative means that a reduction in benefits becomes more attractive at the margin. The slope of the possibility frontier at any t in figure 19.4 is less steep, which in itself causes the choice to shift down. But the frontier is also further out. With the improved functioning of the labor market, we can afford a higher

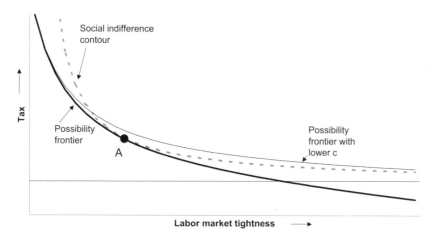

Figure 19.4
Pursuing a Rawlsian objective

level of benefits. The scale of benefits is always increased; the optimal tax rate may rise or fall.

With a Rawlsian objective, increased labor market flexibility (in the form of lower c) would lead a government to increase benefits. In terms of benefits, the possibility frontier is obtained by substituting from (17) into (13), generating the relationship between b and θ shown in figure 19.5 by the solid lines for two different values of c. (The dashed indifference curves are discussed in what follows.) The effect of a fall in c is to shift the curve outward, leading to a policy choice where labor market tightness is increased but so is the level of benefit. In the same way, an adverse shock in the labor market may be expected to lead to a policy response shared between lower benefits and higher unemployment.

Differing Distributional Weights

The Rawlsian criterion may be seen as the limiting case of a social evaluation based on the rank order of the person concerned. As Sen (1974) has proposed, a less extreme set of distributional weights are those that take the form of the rank order statistics themselves, ranging from 1 for the person at the bottom, $(1 - F)$ for the person at the F-th percentile, and zero at the top. Sen shows that such weights are equivalent to evaluating social welfare according to the mean income times $(1 - \text{Gini coefficient})$.

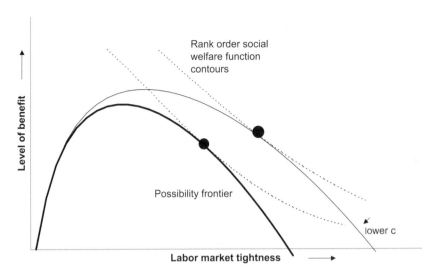

Figure 19.5
Benefit possibility frontier

With this rank order weighted objective, the value of social welfare may be calculated as (setting $x = 0$ for simplicity)

$$(1 - u)Y + ub, \tag{18}$$

where Y is value of expected net output (see equation 14). This may be seen as a weighted average of the efficiency and Rawlsian objectives, with weights given by the employment and unemployment rates. Thus, we would expect that the point chosen on the policy frontier, returning to figure 19.5, to be to the right of the peak, involving a lower level of benefit and more employment than the Rawlsian solution. The adoption of the less redistributive rank order (Gini) social welfare function may therefore lead to a less favorable view of social protection. A further important difference, however, is that the weights on Y and b in (18) are endogenous, since u is changed if we change b. A move to a more flexible labor market affects the indifference curves as well as the possibility frontier. Increased flexibility in the labor market means that there is a larger gain in net output to increasing θ: see equation (14). There is still an income effect operating, however, in the direction of causing a move to greater flexibility to lead to a rise in the optimal level of benefit.

Conclusions

The chapter began with the questions: are labor market reforms and scaling back the welfare state complementary or substitute economic policies? Do countries need to do both? If there is a choice, how should the balance be struck? I have argued that differences in view among economists about the first question are partly due to an ambiguity in their use of the word complementarity. In the job search model considered here, labor market reforms and benefit cuts are not like left and right shoes. The indifference curves, in generating employment, are not right angles. At the same time, the cross-derivative is positive: the more that the labor market becomes flexible, the greater the attraction in terms of a tighter labor market of scaling back the welfare state. But even if the slope of the possibility frontier tilts in the direction of scaling back benefits as well, the frontier is also further out. With the improved functioning of the labor market, a society can afford higher benefits, and in the case of a Rawlsian objective this would always be chosen. Or, if our concern is with efficiency, a reduction in worker bargaining power may not only obviate the need for scaling back benefits but also mean that benefits should be maintained to prevent over-shooting.

The answers just given are derived from one particular model of the labor market. (A different model is used to examine complementarities in Atkinson 2000.) This model has been widely employed in the academic literature, and it appears to underlie much policy discussion. Once we leave the world of Arrow-Debreu and enter the territory of imperfect markets, however, the conclusions drawn from theoretical models can depend sensitively on the assumptions adopted. With different assumptions about the labor market, the conclusions may change qualitatively. At the same time, the analytical issues remain. We need to be precise in the use of terms such as complementary policies. We need to be careful about the inferences drawn from complex comparative static exercises. Statements about the desirability of particular reforms can only be conditional on the objectives pursued.

Acknowledgments

This chapter is revised version of a paper presented at the L.R.R. Conference on "The Costs of Labour Market Flexibility," Moncalieri,

Turin, February 2001, and at the seminar of the Bank of Italy, March 2001. I am most grateful for comments by the participants at these seminars and by Richard Arnott and David Grubb, which have led to significant improvements.

Notes

1. As noted by Pissarides (1998), the results of comparative static analyses may be sensitive to the modeling of benefit entitlement. He considers both a fixed real benefit level, as here, and a constant replacement rate.

2. The discussion is conducted in terms of individuals, but in fact we are usually concerned about the welfare of families or households. Households may contain a mix of employed and unemployed workers.

References

Atkinson, A. B. 1999. *The Economic Consequences of Rolling-Back the Welfare State*. Cambridge, MA: MIT Press.

Atkinson, A. B. 2000. "The Welfare State and Employment." Paper prepared for the VI IESE International Conference on Job Creation, Barcelona, September.

Bertola, G. 1990. "Job Security, Employment and Wages." *European Economic Review* 34: 851–886.

Bertola, G. 1992. "Labor Turnover Costs and Average Labor Demand." *Journal of Labor Economics* 10: 389–411.

Coe, D. T., and Snower, D. J. 1997. "Policy Complementarities: The Case for Fundamental Labour Market Reform." *IMF Staff Papers* 44: 1–35.

Diamond, P. A. 1981. "Mobility Costs, Frictional Unemployment, and Efficiency." *Journal of Political Economy* 89: 798–812.

Diamond, P. A. 1982. "Wage Determination and Efficiency in Search Equilibrium." *Review of Economic Studies* 49: 217–227.

Elmeskov, J., Martin, J. P., and Scarpetta, S. 1998. "Key Lessons for Labour Market Reforms: Evidence from OECD Countries' Experiences." *Swedish Economic Policy Review* 5: 207–252.

Hicks, J. R. 1946. *Value and Capital*, 2. ed. Oxford: Oxford University Press.

Hosios, A. J. 1990. "On the Efficiency of Matching and Related Models of Search and Unemployment." *Review of Economic Studies* 57: 279–298.

Millard, S. P., and Mortensen, D. T. 1997. "The Unemployment and Welfare Effects of Labour Market Policy: A Comparison of the USA and the UK," in D. J. Snower and G. de la Dehesa, eds., *Unemployment Policy*. Cambridge: Cambridge University Press.

Mortensen, D., and Pissarides, C. 1999. "New Developments in Models of Search in the Labor Market," in *Handbook of Labor Economics*, vol. 3B, ed. O. C. Ashenfelter and D. Card. Amsterdam: North-Holland.

Nickell, S., and Layard, R. 1999. "Labour Market Institutions and Economic Performance," in *Handbook of Labor Economics*, vol. 3C, ed. O. C. Ashenfelter and D. Card. Amsterdam: North-Holland.

Orszag, M., and Snower, D. J. 1998. "Anatomy of Policy Complementarities." *Swedish Economic Policy Review* 5: 303–343.

Pissarides, C. 1990. *Equilibrium Unemployment Theory*. Oxford: Blackwell.

Pissarides, C. 1998. "The Impact of Employment Tax Cuts on Unemployment and Wages." *European Economic Review* 42: 155–183.

Rawls, J, 1971. *A Theory of Justice*. Cambridge, MA: Harvard University Press.

Sen, A. K. 1974. "Informational Bases of Alternative Welfare Approaches: Aggregation and Income Distribution." *Journal of Public Economics* 3: 387–403.

20 The Fiscal Politics of Big Governments: Do Coalitions Matter?

Luisa Lambertini and Costas Azariadis

OECD countries have experienced a remarkable increase in the size of their governments since the 1930s. Most of this increase comes from an expansion in government transfer programs.

U.S. government outlays as a percentage of GDP went from about 10 percent in 1940 to 20 percent in 2001, peaking at about 25 percent in 1983. Government transfers—defined as the sum of old-age and disability pensions, welfare, unemployment compensations, Medicare, and Medicaid—went from 1 to 11 percent of GDP over the same period, therefore accounting for the entire growth in government outlays. Government transfers, more narrowly defined by excluding Medicare and Medicaid, account for about 60 percent of the growth of government outlays.

Other industrialized economies have experienced even faster growth in government outlays and transfer programs. Total government outlays as a percentage of GDP have grown from 33 percent in 1970 to 45 percent in 2000 on average among OECD countries; about 50 percent of this growth stems from an increase in social benefits and transfers that exclude health care.

A closer look at the data reveals that most government transfer programs grew most rapidly in the period between 1970 and the mid-1980s. In the United States, for example, social security outlays doubled and income security outlays almost tripled during that period, to stabilize and then decrease after that. Other OECD economies, especially in Europe, experienced an even faster and more prolonged growth of their transfer programs.

The authors argue that a large increase in government transfers may be the result of the formation of a liberal coalition that favors such transfers. A model is developed where young unskilled workers and retirees form a dominant coalition that raises inter- and intragenerational transfers.

Several factors favor the formation of a liberal coalition. The first is widening income inequality that brings the interests of inter- and intragenerational transfer recipients together. After several decades of decline, income inequality started rising in the 1970s. Recent empirical works have attributed this widening in income inequality to a skill-biased technical change and increased trade with low-wage economies; the oil crises in 1973 and 1982 also contributed to this phenomenon.

A second factor is aging of the population. As retirees become a larger fraction of the electorate, political support for a more generous pay-as-you-go social security program builds up. In fact, all industrialized economies have experienced a steady increase in the share of the population aged 65 and above. In the United States, for example, this share has increased from 5 to 13 percent since 1929; for the OECD countries, this share has grown from 9 to 15 percent since 1950.

A third factor is that real interest rates have been low relative to the growth of real wages in mature economies. This further expanded the constituency in favor of a pay-as-you-go pension system. Intuitively, if capital is cheap and labor is expensive, individuals prefer old-age benefits to be a fraction of current labor earnings rather than the capitalization of their savings. In a dynamically inefficient economy, for example, individuals are better off with a pay-as-you-go rather than a fully funded old-age pension system. Real interest rates were low and even largely negative throughout the 1970s.

The rest of this chapter is organized as follows. Section 1 reviews the literature; section 2 presents the model and sections 3 to 5 solve for the equilibrium. Section 6 illustrates the point with a numerical exercise and section 7 concludes.

1 Toward a Theory of Large Governments

A large body literature has addressed the issue of government growth in industrialized countries.[1] We briefly review some of this literature and how our work relates to it.

An informal but popular view is that large governments and deficits characterize democracies because politicians want to purchase votes, because they have a shorter horizon than voters, or because they engage in pork-barrel spending. One issue that these views do not address is the timing of government growth. Why have governments grown so much in the 1970s and 1980s? This chapter provides an answer to this question.

The ratchet explanation states that large expansions of government are hard to reverse. The ratchet theory applies to some components of government spending better than others; for example, transfer programs have proven hard to reduce or eliminate, whereas military expenditures have fallen after each war to nearly prewar levels. We rely on the ratchet theory for the existence of a status quo in transfer programs; our goal, however, is to explain what changes the status quo and in what direction.

Wagner's law predicts that government involvement in fiscal matters increases as society develops. In other words, the income elasticity for publicly provided goods is larger than one in the short run and equal to one in the long run. The work here focuses on a complementary explanation of government size, namely on how income inequality and voting institutions affect government transfers.

Baumol (1967) suggests that productivity in the service sector has grown slower than in the rest of the economy, so that higher wages in more efficient sectors have raised the wage bill for government services. We focus instead on government transfer programs that are responsible, rather than public good provision, for nearly all government growth in the last decades.

In Meltzer and Richard (1981) the constituency in favor of welfare transfers increases when income inequality worsens. As a result, more welfare transfers take place. We extend the work of Meltzer and Richard to a setting with both intragenerational, namely welfare, and intergenerational, namely social security, transfers; we also find that widening income inequality leads to the formation of a liberal coalition that results in more intra- and intergenerational redistribution.

2 The Model

To investigate how social and economic variables influence government outlays, we use a simple dynamical general equilibrium voting model with overlapping generations of heterogeneous voters, living over two periods. Start by considering the one-sector OLG growth model by Diamond (1965). The generation born at time t will be referred to as generation t; we assume that generation t is of size

$$N_t = (1+n)^t, \qquad t = 0, 1, \ldots. \tag{1}$$

If n is positive, population grows; whereas if n is negative, population shrinks. There is a linear production technology:

$$F(K_t, L_t) = RK_t + L_t, \tag{2}$$

where K_t is the stock of capital and L_t is labor at time t; wage has been normalized to one, and $R \geq 0$ is the gross interest rate assuming that capital depreciates fully in each period. This production function is chosen for simplicity and without loss of generality: a linear production technology gives constant factor prices $(w, 1 + r) = (1, R)$. There is no public debt or fiat money; stores of value are private loans and claims on physical capital.

When young, individuals work and consume; when old, they consume only. Individuals are heterogeneous in terms of their innate economic ability or skills in production: a fraction λ of young individuals have high ability, $1 - \lambda$ have low ability. Hence, income inequality is a long-run phenomenon in our setting, unlike Stiglitz (1969).[2] Individuals with high innate ability (skilled) produce y^h in one period, whereas individuals with low innate ability (unskilled) produce y^l in one period, with $y^h > y^l > 0$.

A generation t individual maximizes the following lifetime utility function when young

$$V_t^{i,t} = u(c_t^{i,t}) + \beta u(c_{t+1}^{i,t}), \qquad \beta > 0, \qquad i = h, l, \tag{3}$$

where c is private consumption and β is the subjective discount factor. The function $u : R_+ \rightarrow R$ is strictly increasing and strictly concave in its argument. When young, the individual cares about the present discounted value of her lifetime utility. The right-hand side of (3) is maximized, subject to budget constraints

$$y_t^i(1 - \tau_t) + b_t = c_t^{i,t} + z_t^{i,t}, \qquad i = h, l, \tag{4}$$

$$c_{t+1}^{i,t} = z_t^{i,t}R + s_{t+1}, \tag{5}$$

where τ_t is a labor income tax, b_t is a welfare transfer from the government, z_t is private savings, and s_{t+1} is an old-age pension received from the government at $t+1$. Hence, a generation t-type i young individual pays net taxes $\tau_t y_t^i - b_t$ to the government. When old, a generation t individual cares only about current consumption and maximizes

$$V_{t+1}^{i,t} = u(c_{t+1}^{i,t}), \qquad i = h, l, \tag{6}$$

subject to the constraint (5). Her consumption when old therefore depends on private savings and government transfers. Over her lifetime, the generation t-type i's net tax payment to the government is $\tau_t y_t^i - b_t - s_{t+1}/R$.

We also assume that young individuals supply labor at t according to the inverse-L shaped schedule

$$L_t^i = \begin{cases} y_t^i & \text{if } \tau_t < \bar{\tau}, \qquad i = h, l \\ 0 & \text{otherwise} \end{cases} \tag{7}$$

for some $\bar{\tau} \le 1$. Since working entails some disutility, individuals supply one unit of labor only if their after-tax wage is above some minimum level.

For the purposes of this chapter, the population can be divided into three groups labeled with an the index j defined as follows: $j = 0$ for the old group; $j = 1$ for the young with high productivity; $j = 2$ for the young with low productivity. The old population consists of both high- and low-productivity individuals; since individuals work only in their youth and are taxed on their labor income, this division can be ignored.

The government in this economy engages in intragenerational (welfare benefits) and intergenerational (old-age pension) transfers, which are financed by a tax on labor income. Government policy at t is a vector of three variables

$$\pi_t = \left\{ \tau_t, b_t, \frac{s_t}{1+n} \right\} \in [0, \bar{\tau}] \times R_+^2, \qquad \bar{\tau} \le 1, \tag{8}$$

where τ is the labor income tax, b is a lump sum welfare transfer to young individuals, and s is a pension to old individuals. All fiscal variables are constrained to be positive and the labor income tax rate cannot exceed 1. The government balances the budget every period and allocates tax revenues according to the following constraint

$$\tau_t Y_t = b_t + \frac{s_t}{1+n}, \tag{9}$$

where aggregate income is $Y_t = [\lambda y_t^h + (1 - \lambda)y_t^l] > 0$ if $\tau_t \leq \bar{\tau}$, and 0 otherwise.

3   The Economic Equilibrium

The first step in solving the model is to derive the economic equilibrium, taking fiscal policy as given. The economic equilibrium consists of the savings and labor supply decisions made by young individuals. Since this is a closed economy, savings equal capital that, together with labor supply, determines production and consumption.

The labor supply decision is described in (7). The savings decision of generation t is given by

$$z_t^i(\pi_t, \pi_{t+1}) = \arg \max u(c_t^{i,t}) + \beta u(c_{t+1}^{i,t}), \qquad i = h, l, \tag{10}$$

subject to (4) and (5) and taking the fiscal policy sequence $\{\pi_t\}$ as given. The first-order condition is

$$u'(c_t^{i,t}) = \beta R u'(c_{t+1}^{i,t}). \tag{11}$$

Consumption increases over an individual's lifetime if $\beta R > 1$ and decreases if $\beta R < 1$. Let k_t denote the capital-labor ratio at t. Capital accumulation for a given fiscal policy is described by

$$L_{t+1}(\pi_{t+1})k_{t+1} = [\lambda z_t^h(\pi_t, \pi_{t+1}) + (1 - \lambda)z_t^l(\pi_t, \pi_{t+1})]L_t(\pi_t) \tag{12}$$

where $L_t(\pi_t) = \lambda L_t^h(\pi_t) + (1 - \lambda)L_t^l(\pi_t)$ is the labor supplied by generation t. Given a feasible policy sequence $\{\pi_t\}$ satisfying (9), any capital sequence $\{k_{t+1}\}$ satisfying (12) is an economic equilibrium. Notice that the economic equilibrium is uniquely defined in this economy. If $\tau_t > \bar{\tau}$, the economic equilibrium is trivial; labor supply and young individuals' income, savings, and consumption are all zero, as are capital and production. If $\tau_t \leq \bar{\tau}$, then $L_t = N_t$ and (12) reduces to

$$(1 + n)k_{t+1} = \lambda z_t^h(\pi_t, \pi_{t+1}) + (1 - \lambda)z_t^l(\pi_t, \pi_{t+1}). \tag{13}$$

4   The Political Equilibrium in Open-loop Strategies

All individuals, young and old, vote in this economy and fiscal policy is decided by majority voting. Savings are a function of current and future fiscal policy variables, as they depend on current taxes and welfare transfers and on future pensions. We consider two classes of strategies: open-loop and closed-loop strategies.

With closed-loop strategies, individuals can condition their current actions to the history of past actions; with open-loop strategies, on the other hand, such conditioning does not take place and future fiscal policy variables are taken as given. We start by studying the Nash equilibrium in open-loop strategies; the next section extends the analysis to subgame perfect equilibria in closed-loop strategies.

For simplicity, let y^h and y^l and therefore Y be time-invariant constants, and let the utility of group j at time t be $V^j(\pi_t, \pi_{t+1})$. The ideal fiscal policy for group j is the policy $\bar{\pi}_t$ solving the following optimization problem

$$\bar{\pi}_t = \arg \max \, V_t^j(\pi_t, \pi_{t+1}), \tag{14}$$

taking future fiscal policy as given, subject to (4), (5), (9), and where private savings are defined as in (10). Ideal policies (τ, b, s) in open-loop strategies are

$$\bar{\pi}_o^j = \begin{cases} (\bar{\tau}, 0, \bar{\tau}Y(1+n)) & j = 0 \\ (0,0,0) & j = 1 \\ (\bar{\tau}, \bar{\tau}Y, 0) & j = 2 \end{cases} \tag{15}$$

The ideal policy for the old is to levy the highest tax consistent with positive provision of labor and allocate all revenues to old-age pensions. Intuitively, pensions are intergenerational transfers paid by the young that benefit the old, who want them to be as large as possible. Young individuals, on the other hand, do not want old-age pensions. Young individuals with low innate ability favor redistribution and want welfare transfers; hence, their ideal policy is to levy $\bar{\tau}$ and allocate all revenues to welfare transfers. Young individuals with high innate ability dislike redistribution and want no government transfers at all, as they are the net payers in the system; hence, their ideal policy is a zero tax rate and zero transfers.

DEFINITION 1   A group is dominant if it consists of at least half the voting population.

Hence, a group is dominant if its size is at least $(2 + n)/[2(1 + n)]$.

PROPOSITION 1   If a group is dominant, the open-loop political equilibrium is the dominant group's ideal fiscal policy in open-loop strategies.

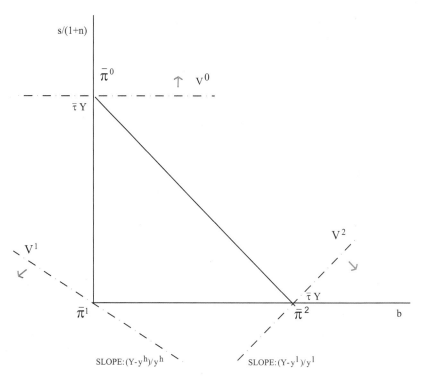

Figure 20.1
Ideal policies in open-loop strategies

The proof is simple: if a group is dominant, its ideal policy is a Condorcet winner. Figure 20.1 shows the ideal policy of the three groups in the $(b, s/(1+n))$ space. The straight line V^j is the indifference curve for group j and the arrow indicates which policy combinations would increase utility for this group.

Ideal policies cannot be a political equilibrium if no group is dominant. Intuitively, there is always a feasible fiscal policy that is strictly preferred to any of the three ideal fiscal policies by a majority of voters.

If there is no dominant group, the political equilibrium depends on the formal rules governing agenda formation and voting. Here, we model the legislative structure according to Baron and Ferejohn's (1989) closed rule. There are three steps in the legislature: recognition, proposal, and voting. At the beginning of each period, a recognition rule identifies an individual, that is, a group within the legislature; we assume that recognition is random. Once recognized, the individual makes a proposal that is voted against the status quo. If a majority of individuals vote in favor of the proposal, it is adopted; otherwise the status quo is implemented. The legislative process is repeated every period. Although rather stylized, this model reflects the endogenous nature of proposal making. The strongest assumption is that the status quo remains constant over time, which is interpreted as the existence of an apolitical fiscal policy implemented if the legislature fails to reach a majority vote.

Let the status quo be denoted by $\pi = (\tau, b, s)$. We now characterize the political equilibrium for a generic status quo when no group is dominant. At the beginning of each period, group j's probability of being recognized, p^j, is equal to its relative size in the voting population; hence, old individuals will be recognized with probability $p^0 = 1/(2+n)$, young individuals with high ability will be recognized with probability $p^1 = \lambda(1+n)/(2+n)$ and young individuals with low ability will be recognized with probability $p^2 = (1-\lambda)(1+n)/(2+n)$.

Suppose group $j = 0$, the old, is recognized. The recognized old individual proposes the policy that maximizes her utility, under the constraint that a majority of individuals prefers it to the status quo. Let π be the status quo in figure 20.2. The need for a majority prevents the old from choosing a policy too close to $\bar{\pi}_0^0$: her proposal must give another group at least as much utility as it would get in the status quo. This means that the old will either move along group 1's or group 2's indifference curve through the status quo, depending on which maximizes her utility. In figure 20.2, the old individual prefers A to B and therefore coalesces with the high ability young individual.

Formally, the old proposes the policy solving the maximization problem (14) with $j = 0$, subject to

$$\frac{s_t - s}{1 + n} \leq \frac{Y - y^h}{y^h}(b_t - b) \quad \text{and} \quad p^0 + p^1 \geq \frac{1}{2} \tag{16}$$

if she coalesces with the young with high ability, or to

$$\frac{s_t - s}{1 + n} \leq \frac{Y - y^l}{y^l}(b_t - b) \quad \text{and} \quad p^0 + p^2 \geq \frac{1}{2} \tag{17}$$

if she coalesces with the young with low ability. Equation (16) excludes all allocations above the indifference curve for group 1 through π and it requires the coalition with the young skilled to

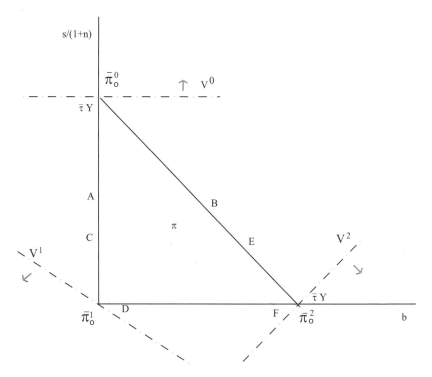

Figure 20.2
Proposals in open-loop strategies

constitute a majority. Similarly, (17) excludes all allocations above
the indifference curve for group 2 through π and requires the coalition with the young skilled to constitute a majority. The old needs
only satisfy one set of constraints. The old proposes the policy that
gives her higher utility; this is point A in figure 20.2, if she coalesces
with the young skilled, or point B if she coalesces with the young
unskilled.[3]

Consider the case where group 1, the young skilled, is recognized
to make a policy proposal. Since we are considering a constant status
quo and open-loop strategies, there is no link between the policy
chosen today and tomorrow. The young skilled proposes the policy
maximizing (14) for $j = 1$ subject to the additional constraints (17)
and $n \geq 0$ if she coalesces with the young unskilled or

$$s_t \geq s \quad \text{and} \quad p^0 + p^1 \geq \frac{1}{2} \tag{18}$$

if she coalesces with the old. If the young skilled coalesces with the old, the proposed policy is point C in figure 20.2. On the other hand, if the young skilled coalesces with the young unskilled, the proposed policy is point D in figure 20.2. With open-loop strategies, old-age pensions are simply a loss for all young individuals. Hence, for high enough values of s in the status quo so that point D lies vertically above point π^1, the young skilled coalesces with the young unskilled and proposes $\bar{\pi}^1$. For low values of s in the status quo, namely for $s/(1+n) < b\lambda(y^h - y^l)/y^l$, the decision to propose C or D depends on the parameters of the model.

Finally, consider the case where a young unskilled is recognized to make a proposal. She solves the maximization problem in (14) subject to the additional constraint (16) and $n \geq 0$ or (18). If the young unskilled coalesces with the old, the proposed policy is point E in figure 20.2; the proposed policy if she coalesces with the young skilled is point F in figure 20.2. For high enough values of s in the status quo so that point F implies positive old-age pensions, the young unskilled coalesces with the young skilled and proposes $\bar{\pi}^2$. For relatively low values of $s/(1+n)$, however, the choice between a coalition with the old or the young skilled depends on the parameters of the model.

5   The Political Equilibrium in Closed-Loop Strategies

This section studies closed-loop political equilibria. Typically, the closed-loop strategy space is much larger than the open-loop strategy space. We restrict our attention to stationary closed-loop strategies, which dictate that an agent acts in the same way in structurally equivalent subgames.[4] The subgames starting at the beginning of each period are structurally equivalent for the members of each group. For an individual born at time t, however, the subgame beginning at t and the subgame beginning at $t+1$ are not structurally equivalent, as she belongs to a group in period t but to another in period $t+1$. Therefore we consider group-specific stationary strategies.

With stationary closed-loop strategies, equilibria with constant intergenerational transfers may arise. If the real interest rate is low, young voters may prefer to pay for old-age benefits today, provided the same amount will be given to them tomorrow. On the other

hand, if the return to capital is high, private saving is a better technology for transferring resources to the future than a pay-as-you-go
pension system.

   We start by identifying each group's ideal policy in stationary
closed-loop strategies. Since individuals are not altruistic and live for
two periods, punishment lasts one period at most; we assume that a
deviation in period t is punished by reverting to open-loop strategies
in period $t + 1$. Old individuals cannot be punished in case of a deviation; hence, they play open-loop strategies in a subgame perfect
equilibrium. Young individuals, on the other hand, may be better off
by playing a closed-loop strategy. A young individual in group j,
$j = 1, 2$, at time t solves problem (14) subject to constraints (4), (5), (9)
and

$$\pi_t = \pi_{t+1} = \bar{\pi}_c^j. \tag{19}$$

Ideal subgame perfect policies are

$$\bar{\pi}_c^0 = (\bar{\tau}, 0, \bar{\tau}Y(1 + n))$$

$$\bar{\pi}_c^1 = \begin{cases} (\bar{\tau}, 0, \bar{\tau}Y(1 + n)) & \text{if } R < R^h \equiv \dfrac{Y(1 + n)}{y^h} \\ (0, 0, 0) & \text{otherwise} \end{cases} \tag{20}$$

$$\bar{\pi}_c^2 = \begin{cases} (\bar{\tau}, 0, \bar{\tau}Y(1 + n)) & \text{if } R < R^l \equiv \dfrac{Y(1 + n)}{Y(1 + n) - y^l n} \\ (\bar{\tau}, \bar{\tau}Y, 0) & \text{otherwise} \end{cases}$$

with $R^h < R^l$ if $\lambda < 1/(1 + n)$. Figure 20.3 depicts ideal stationary
closed-loop policies for the three groups. If the return to capital is
low enough, the ideal policy for the three groups coincide with the
provision of the largest feasible old-age pension and zero welfare
transfers, which is the allocation at the upper corner of the triangle.
If individuals are homogeneous so that $\lambda = 0$ or 1, then $R^h =
R^l = 1 + n$. In words, the economy must be dynamically inefficient
in the standard sense for young individuals to be in favor of a pay-
as-you-go social security program. If individuals are heterogeneous
in terms of their labor income, youth's support for a pay-as-you-go
pension system does not go hand in hand with dynamic inefficiency.
More precisely, $R^h < 1 + n$ and the economy must be more than dynamically inefficient for the young skilled to be in favor of intergenerational transfers, since they are the net payers in this fiscal

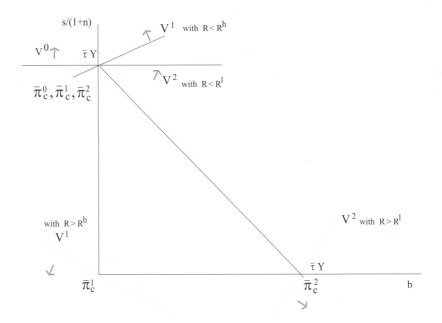

Figure 20.3
Ideal policies in closed-loop strategies

system. For the young unskilled, $R^l \lessgtr 1 + n$ if $n \gtrless 0$. With low interest rates and negative growth, they may prefer inter- to intragenerational transfers even though the economy is dynamically efficient because, together with the old, they are net recipients in the fiscal system.

The rate of return for a young person from a pay-as-you-go pension system increases with the growth rate of population, but falls with her taxable income. The intuition is simple. The higher n, the more young individuals pay into the social security system and the more old individuals receive, everything else being equal. A pay-as-you-go social security system, however, redistributes income from high- to low-labor income individuals so that the higher personal labor income, the lower the returns from the system.

Proposition 2 extends proposition 1 to closed-loop strategies. Proposition 3 summarizes the results obtained earlier.

PROPOSITION 2 If a group is dominant, the closed-loop political equilibrium is the dominant group's ideal fiscal policy in closed-loop strategies.

PROPOSITION 3   In a subgame perfect equilibrium, old individuals adopt open-loop strategies; young skilled individuals adopt closed-loop strategies and support a pay-as-you-go social security system if $R < R^h \equiv Y(1+n)/y^h$; young unskilled individuals adopt closed-loop strategies and support a pay-as-you-go social security system if $R < R^l \equiv Y(1+n)/[Y(1+n) - y^l n]$.

If no group is dominant, the political equilibrium depends on the voting rule. Let the legislative structure be the same as in the previous section. In each period, the recognized group makes a proposal that is voted by majority rule against the status quo, which is $\pi = (\tau, b, s)$, and let the probability that group j is recognized be p^j. To simplify the exposition, consumption is written as $c_t^{i,t}(\pi_t, \pi_{t+1})$ for the young and as $c_t^{i,t-1}(\pi_t)$ for the old.

First, consider the case where a member of the old group is recognized; her proposed policy is exactly the same as in open-loop strategies.

Then, consider the case where a young skilled is recognized. Young skilled individuals propose the policy $\pi_c^1 = (\tau_c^1, b_c^1, s_c^1) \in [0, \bar{\tau}] \times R_+^2$ solving the problem:

$$\pi_c^1 = \arg \max E_t V_t^{h,t} = u(c_t^{h,t}(\pi_c^1, E_t \pi_{t+1})) + \beta E_t u(c_{t+1}^{h,t}(\pi_{t+1})) \qquad (21)$$

subject to (4), (5), and the government budget constraint (9), with

$$E_t \pi_{t+1} = p^0 \pi_o^0 + p^1 \pi_c^1 + p^2 \pi_{t+1}^2$$

and

$$E_t u(c_{t+1}^{h,t}(\pi_{t+1})) = p^0 u(c_{t+1}^{h,t}(\pi_o^0)) + p^1 u(c_{t+1}^{h,t}(\pi_c^1)) + p^2 u(c_{t+1}^{h,t}(\pi_{t+1}^2)),$$

where the policy proposed by group 2 at time $t+1$, π_{t+1}^2, could be either in closed-loop or open-loop strategies. Young skilled individuals are rational and adopt closed-loop strategies if and only if they are better off doing so, namely, if

$$E_t V_t^{h,t}(\pi_c^1) \geq E_t V_t^{h,t}(\pi_o^1). \qquad (22)$$

Young unskilled individuals solve a similar problem.

The subgame perfect equilibrium when no group is dominant can be characterized as follows. If $R < \min\{R^h, R^l\}$, the policy $(\bar{\tau}, 0, \bar{\tau} Y(1+n))$ is optimal for every group; hence, it is proposed and adopted every period. If $R^h < R < R^l$, then the young skilled adopt open-loop strategies and $\pi_c^1 = \pi_o^1 = (0,0,0)$, whereas the young unskilled adopt closed-loop strategies and $\pi_c^2 = (\bar{\tau}, 0, \bar{\tau}Y(1+n))$. If $R^l < R < R^h$, then the young unskilled adopt open-loop strategies and $\pi_c^2 = \pi_o^2 = (\bar{\tau}, \bar{\tau}Y, 0)$, whereas the young skilled adopt closed-loop strategies and $\pi_c^1 = (\bar{\tau}, 0, \bar{\tau}Y(1+n))$. If $R > \max\{R^h, R^l\}$, both young groups adopt open-loop strategies, and the equilibrium is the one described in section 4.

6 Can Political Coalitions Explain the Growth in Government?

To illustrate our point, we simulate our model with parameter values matching the U.S. economy in 1967 and in 1996. Individuals maximize a CES period utility function of the following type:

$$u(c) = \frac{c^{1-1/\sigma}}{1 - \frac{1}{\sigma}}. \tag{23}$$

Individuals live for thirty years; they are young for fifteen years and old for fifteen years. Table 20.1 presents the parameter values used for the 1967 simulation; all values are on an annual basis, except for the intertemporal elasticity of substitution σ. The values of y^h and y^l capture income distribution in 1967; in that year, households in the lower 60 percent of the income distribution had an average income of \$18,000, measured in 1996 dollars, whereas households in the upper 40 percent of the income distribution had an average income of \$57,000. R is the real interest rate on government bonds with ten year maturity and n is the rate of growth of the civilian population in 1967.

The results of the simulation are reported in table 20.2. Since the real interest rate is higher than both R^l and R^h, neither young group adopts closed-loop strategies. The first column in table 20.2 indicates the recognized group; columns two to four report the proposed fiscal

Table 20.1
Parameter values for 1967

Parameter	Value	Parameter	Value	Parameter	Value
R	1.02	λ	0.4	σ	2
β	0.96	n	0.01	y^h	57,000
y^l	18,000	$\bar{\tau}$	0.2	τ	0.18
b	3,815	s	2,670		

Table 20.2
Equilibrium policies for 1967

Group recognized	Proposed policy			Utility ratio of group j
	τ_o^j	b_o^j	$s_o^j/(1+n)$	
$j = 0$	0.125	0	3,866	1.0063
$j = 1$	0.035	1,161	0	1.0621
$j = 2$	0.2	6,720	0	1.065
$E\pi_o$	0.125	2,416	1,789	
$E\pi_o$ as % GDP		3.9	3	

Table 20.3
Parameter values for 1996

Parameter	Value	Parameter	Value	Parameter	Value
R	1.038	λ	0.4	σ	2
β	0.96	n	0.009	y^h	80,000
y^l	20,000	$\bar{\tau}$	0.3	τ	0.16
b	3,815	s	2,670		

policy; columns five shows the ratio of period utility for the proposing group under the proposed policy and the status quo. The last two rows reports average fiscal policy, calculated as $E_t \pi_{t+1} = \sum_{j=0}^{2} p_j \pi_t^j$, and average fiscal policy as a percentage of output.

In this simulation, the equilibrium policies in terms of figure 20.2 are A, D, and F: when recognized, the old coalesce with the young skilled; when recognized, the young skilled coalesce with the young unskilled; when recognized, the young unskilled coalesce with the young skilled. No coalition chooses the maximum level of redistribution and taxation. Total expected transfers are 6.9 percent of GDP, which is just a bit larger than the 5 percent of the data; the average tax rate on labor income is 12.5 percent in our simulation, while it was 18 percent in the actual data.

We simulate the model for 1996 with the parameter values specified in table 20.3. The real interest rate is higher and income distribution is more unequal than in 1967. More precisely, income measured in 1996 dollars is $20,000 for the young unskilled and $80,000 for the young skilled; these are, respectively, the average income for individuals in the lower 60 percent and the top 40 percent of the actual U.S. income distribution in 1996. These figures imply

Table 20.4
Equilibrium policies in open-loop strategies for 1996

Group recognized	Proposed policy τ_o^j	b_o^j	s_o^j	Utility ratio of group j
$j = 0$	0.3	7,904	6,058	1.011
$j = 1$	0.048	2,093	0	1.056
$j = 2$	0.23	10,082	0	1.132
$E\pi_o$	0.22	7,361	2,826	
$E\pi_o$ as % GDP		9.2	3.5	

that income grew by 40 percent for the young skilled but only by 11 percent for the young unskilled between 1967 and 1996. For comparative purposes, we keep the status quo unchanged.

The outcome of the simulation is presented in table 20.4. Once again, the young groups do not adopt closed-loop strategies in equilibrium, so that all proposed policies are in open-loop strategies. Points B, D and F in figure 20.2 are the equilibrium policies: when recognized, the old coalesce with the young unskilled; when recognized, the young skilled coalesce with the young unskilled; when recognized, the young unskilled coalesce with the young skilled. There is an important change from the earlier simulation where the old coalesced with the young skilled in 1967, but coalesce with the young unskilled in 1996. Thus, increased income inequality leads to the formation of a liberal coalition between the old and the young unskilled that raises taxation and redistribution. In terms of figure 20.2, the policy proposed by the old switches from point A to point B. As a result, total expected government transfers increase from 6.9 percent for the 1967 simulation to 12.7 percent of GDP for the 1996 simulation; the actual data are 5 percent and 8.5 percent, respectively. The average tax rate on labor income is 22 percent in our simulation, against a 20 percent in the actual data.

If inequality had increased more than assumed in our 1996 simulation, the welfare state would have also increased further. More precisely, if $y^h = \$90,000$ rather than $\$80,000$ in 1996, the proposed equilibrium policies in our simulation would have been B, D, and E. In other words, a complete liberal coalition would emerge, with the young unskilled coalescing with the old when either group is recognized. Under this scenario, total government transfers reach 14 percent of GDP.

7 Conclusions

This chapter emphasizes that changes in the size of the welfare state can be explained by shifts in voting coalitions brought by changes in the economic and social structure of society. Widening income inequality, a raising share of retirees in the voting population, and low real rate of returns contribute to the formation of a coalition among the groups that favor inter- and intragenerational redistribution. We believe that these forces, among others, were at work during the rapid expansion of the welfare state in the 1970s and 1980s.

Even though our model is simple, we believe it outlines a mechanism that remains valid in a richer setting. This would include models with a more realistic production function and legislative structure.

Finally, it would be interesting to extend this model to allow for budget deficits. In an overlapping-generation model like ours, the retirees favor both more generous pay-as-you-go pension benefits and budget deficits, as both imply a transfer resources from the future to the present. The formation of a liberal coalition between the young unskilled workers and the retirees may have contributed to the budget deficits experienced by industrialized economies concurrently with the expansion of the welfare state.

Acknowledgments

Financial support by a U.C.L.A. Senate grant is gratefully acknowledged. We thank Laura Alfaro for excellent research assistance.

Notes

1. For a review of such theories, see Tullock (1990).

2. Stiglitz (1969) assumes homogenous economic ability, and he shows that wealth and income become asymptotically evenly distributed in a neoclassical growth model.

3. The formal expressions for these policies are available upon request.

4. Two structurally equivalent subgames satisfy the following conditions: (1) the structure of the subgames at the initial node are identical; (2) the sets of players to be recognized at the next recognition node are the same; and (3) the strategy sets of agents are identical.

References

Baron, David P., and John A. Ferejohn. 1989. "Bargaining in Legislatures." *American Political Science Review* 83, no. 4.

Baumol, William. 1967. "The Macroeconomics of Unbalanced Growth: The Anatomy of Urban Crisis." *American Economic Review* 57, no. 3.

Diamond, Peter A. 1965. "National Debt in a Neoclassical Growth Model." *American Economic Review* 55, no. 5.

Meltzer, Allan H., and Scott F. Richard. 1981. "A Rational Theory of the Size of Government." *Journal of Political Economy* 89, no. 5.

Stiglitz, Joseph E. 1969. "Distribution of Income and Wealth among Individuals." *Econometrica* 37, no. 3.

Tullock, Gordon. 1990. "Government Growth." Mimeo.

21

Indirect Taxation and Redistribution: The Scope of the Atkinson-Stiglitz Theorem

Robin Boadway and Pierre Pestieau

One of the oldest controversies in tax theory involves the choice between direct and indirect taxation, in particular the issue debated is when differential commodity taxes are not a component of the optimal tax system. The early literature focused on the efficiency role of commodity taxes. Under what circumstances would the Ramsey tax system applied to a given household consist of a uniform tax on commodities, or equivalently a tax on income? The famous Corlett and Hague (1953–1954) theorem settled that. If all goods are equally substitutable for leisure, differential commodity taxes should not be used. Otherwise, goods that are more complementary with leisure should bear higher commodity tax rates. As explained in Sandmo (1976), a utility function in which goods are separable from leisure, and which is homothetic in goods, satisfies this property. Although an important methodological innovation, this result is of limited interest from a policy point of view since it abstracts from the redistributive role that the tax system plays.

The question of when differential commodity taxes should be used alongside a progressive income tax as part of a redistributive tax system was addressed in a well-known paper by Atkinson and Stiglitz (1976). Their result, the Atkinson-Stiglitz separability theorem (the A-S theorem in what follows), has been seminal and has spawned a substantial literature.

Generally, the A-S theorem states that if household utility functions are separable in goods and leisure, differential commodity taxes should not be used. This result is arguably the most relevant result for policy purposes to emerge from the optimal income tax literature initiated by Mirrlees (1971). It has been subject to considerable scrutiny in the literature, and special attention has been devoted to the circumstances in which it is violated and what it implies for the structure of commodity taxes.[1] Interestingly, the analogue of the Corlett-Hague theorem applies, albeit for different reasons. As shown by Edwards, Keen, and Tuomala (1994) and Nava, Schroyen, and Marchand (1996), if weak separability is violated, higher tax rates should apply to goods that are relatively more complementary with leisure.

The purpose here is to revisit the A-S theorem. The chapter explores the robustness of the theorem to different specifications of household utility, including differences among households in needs and preferences as well as different types of labor supply. The analysis shows that the applicability of the A-S theorem depends crucially on the information available to the government. The chapter begins with a simple derivation of the A-S theorem, using a methodology that will be useful in synthesizing the various extensions. It then turns to those extensions, first focusing on the case of different preferences and needs for particular goods, then turning to the case where households can supply alternative forms of labor, including nonmarket labor.

1   The A-S Theorem

This section adopts a simplified version of the model used by Atkinson and Stiglitz (1976), retaining their essential assumptions. There are two types of households that differ only in their wage rates w_i ($i = 1, 2$), where $w_2 > w_1$, with n_i households of type i. We assume there are only two goods, denoted x and z, along with labor ℓ, and that households have identical weakly separable utility functions of the form $u(g(x, z), \ell)$.[2] The utility function is strictly concave, and both goods as well as leisure are normal. The market (pretax) income of a type-i household is $y_i \equiv w_i \ell_i$. Following Guesnerie (1995), the government is assumed to be able to observe household incomes as well as anonymous transactions in the goods market. It can therefore implement a nonlinear income tax as well as proportional commodity taxes.[3]

As is well known, only the structure of commodity taxes, and not their level, constitutes an independent policy instrument; proportional commodity taxes can be replicated by an appropriate adjustment in the income tax schedule. Therefore, we can normalize the commodity tax rate on good x to be zero and treat the tax rate on z

as the policy instrument, reflecting the differential commodity tax structure. Let t be the per unit tax on purchases of good z. If $t = 0$ in the optimum, the redistributive objectives of government can be achieved by an income tax alone. Producer prices for goods are assumed to be fixed by a linear technology (although the results also apply with a nonlinear technology) and are normalized to unity. We define the consumer price of good z to be $q \equiv 1 + t$.

To facilitate this analysis, we disaggregate household decision making into two stages.[4] In the first stage, the household chooses labor supply, earns income, pays income taxes, and ends up with disposable income. In the second stage, disposable income is allocated between the two goods. Consider the second stage first. Let c_i be disposable income, where $c_i = x_i + q z_i$. Given the separable utility function, a household of type i solves the following problem:

$$\max_{\{z_i\}} g(c_i - q z_i, z_i),$$

where c_i and q are given. From the first-order conditions, $g_z^i / g_x^i = q$,[5] we obtain the demand function $z(q, c_i)$ and the maximum value function $h(q, c_i)$. Applying the envelope theorem with respect to q and c_i, we obtain

$$h_q^i = -g_x^i z_i \quad \text{and} \quad h_c^i = g_x^i.$$

In the first stage, the household chooses labor supply, given the income tax schedule chosen by the government and the anticipated outcome of stage two. Effectively, the household is choosing earned income y_i and, via the income tax, c_i. For this stage, we follow the standard procedure of optimal income tax analysis initiated by Stiglitz (1982) of allowing the government to choose y_i and c_i implicitly by its choice of an income tax schedule. Individual utility functions are reformulated in terms of what the government can observe as follows:

$$v^i \left(h(q, c_i), \frac{y_i}{w_i} \right) \equiv u(h(q, c_i), \ell_i).$$

The government is assumed to maximize a utilitarian objective function, although any quasi-concave function in individuals' utilities would give the same results. The Lagrange expression for the optimal income and commodity tax problem of the government can then be written as

$$L = \sum_{i=1,2} n_i v^i \left(h(q, c_i), \frac{y_i}{w_i} \right) + \lambda \sum_{i=1,2} n_i (y_i + t z^i(q, c_i) - c_i)$$

$$+ \gamma \left[v^2 \left(h(q, c_2), \frac{y_2}{w_2} \right) - v^2 \left(h(q, c_1), \frac{y_1}{w_2} \right) \right].$$

The first constraint with Lagrange multiplier λ reflects the government budget constraint and assumes no net revenue requirement. The second constraint with multiplier γ is the incentive constraint and reflects the fact that this will only be binding for type-two households.

The relevant first-order conditions for purposes here are those with respect to c_1, c_2 and q:[6]

$$n_1 v_h^1 h_c^1 - \lambda n_1 \left(1 - t \frac{\partial z^1}{\partial c_1} \right) - \gamma \hat{v}_h^2 \hat{h}_c^2 = 0 \tag{1}$$

$$n_2 v_h^2 h_c^2 - \lambda n_2 \left(1 - t \frac{\partial z^2}{\partial c_2} \right) + \gamma v_h^2 h_c^2 = 0 \tag{2}$$

$$\sum_{i=1,2} n_i v_h^i h_q^i + \lambda \sum_{i=1,2} n_i \left(z_i + t \frac{\partial z^i}{\partial q} \right) + \gamma (v_h^2 h_q^2 - \hat{v}_h^2 \hat{h}_q^2) = 0, \tag{3}$$

where the "hat" refers to a type-two household that is mimicking a type-one. Multiplying (1) by z_1, (2) by z_2, and adding both equations to (3), we immediately obtain the A-S theorem:

$$t \sum_{i=1,2} n_i \frac{\partial \tilde{z}^i(q)}{\partial q} = \frac{\gamma}{\lambda} \hat{v}_h^2 \hat{h}_c^2 (z_1 - \hat{z}_2) = 0, \tag{4}$$

where we have used the envelope condition on q from the second-stage of the household's problem, $h_q^i + g_x^i z_i = 0$, which also applies to the mimicking type-two household. The function $\tilde{z}^i(q)$ represents the compensated demand for z_i, where the compensation takes the form of disposable income. The second equality follows from the fact that type-one households and the mimicking type-two households have the same disposable income c_i, but differ in their labor supplies. By separability, they will consume the same bundle of goods, so $\hat{z}_2 = z_1$. Therefore, when the income tax is being set optimally, $t = 0$, so no differential commodities taxes should be applied. This demonstrates the A-S theorem.

Using the negativity of the own substitution effect, equation (4) also implies that $t > 0$ if $z_1 > \hat{z}_2$. This occurs if z and leisure are complements: type-two mimickers take more leisure than type-one's, given that their incomes are the same (Edwards, Keen, and Tuomala 1994; Nava, Schroyen, and Marchand 1996). It is useful to give the intuition for this result. Starting at $t = 0$, an incremental increase in t will reduce the welfare of a type-i household by z_i. If the income tax schedule is adjusted so that $\Delta c_i = -z_i \Delta t$, there will be no change in utilities v^1 and v^2, and the government budget will remain balanced. But, the mimicker will be worse off, implying that the self-selection constraint becomes slack and social welfare can be improved. The same logic applies to the results obtained in the following two sections.

Next we turn to two sorts of extensions to the above analysis. In the first, taken up in the following section, we modify the manner in which goods enter the subutility function $g(x, z)$ by allowing households to have different basic needs or, equivalently, different endowments of one of the goods. The subsequent section considers a different specification for labor supply. In each case, the results depend on the relationship between the demands for z by the mimicker and the household being mimicked ($\hat{z}_2$ and z_1 in the earlier case).

2   Needs and Endowments

Suppose that, in the manner of the Stone-Geary utility function, households have some basic nondiscretionary expenditures that must be spent on one of the goods, say, z. The separable utility function can then be written $u(g(x, z - b), \ell)$, where b is nondiscretionary spending on z. One interpretation that can be given to b, following Rowe and Woolley (1999), is that of a basic *need* for good z, such as sustenance, health spending, and so forth. Alternatively, b might be interpreted as an initial endowment, as in Cremer, Pestieau, and Rochet (2001), in which case it takes a negative value.[7] The only difference between the two approaches is that initial endowments enter the overall resource constraint of the economy by adding to net output.[8] Note that b might enter into the utility function in other ways, such as multiplicatively, and a need parameter might be associated with good x as well. Since these would not affect the basic results, we analyze only the case of additive nondiscretionary expenditures in good z for simplicity.

If b were the same for all persons, it would obviously have no effect on the A-S theorem derived in the previous section. The nondiscretionary spending would simply be an element of the common utility function faced by all households, which would remain separable. Instead, we assume that b can differ across households. For expositional purposes, we assume that b can take on two values b_j, $j = 1, 2$. This implies that there can now be four household types, $\{w_i, b_j\}$, $i, j = 1, 2$. In analyzing government policy, two informational settings are considered. In one, following Cremer, Pestieau, and Rochet (2001), the government can observe neither w nor b. In the other, the government can observe b, but not w. This is the assumption adopted by Rowe and Woolley (1999) in their analysis of needs. We consider these two settings in turn, focusing on the case where b reflects needs rather than endowments.

2.1 Government Does Not Observe Needs

With both w and b unobservable, the government faces a two-dimensional screening problem. This is the case analyzed by Cremer, Pestieau, and Rochet (2001). As is well known, the analysis is complex and the results ambiguous, mainly because the directions in which the various self-selection constraints bind are ambiguous. We can simplify the analysis considerably without affecting the main results by assuming that each ability type is associated with a given need. Thus, a household with wage w_i has a need of b_i. This leaves us with at most one binding self-selection constraint that, unlike in the previous section, can bind in either direction even under a utilitarian objective function.

For example, if high-wage households also have high needs, the government may want to redistribute from the low-wage to the high-wage types. For purposes here, that does not affect the issue at hand—whether or not the A-S theorem applies—although it does affect the consequences if it does not apply. We proceed by assuming that the self-selection constraint applies downward as in the previous section.

As before, we adopt a two-stage procedure, assuming that in the first stage, labor supply and income are chosen, while in the second stage, disposable income is allocated between the two goods. The analysis of the second stage is identical to that earlier. A type-i household chooses z_i to maximize $g(c_i - qz_i, z_i - b_i)$. This yields the demand function $z(q, c_i, b_i)$, and the value function $h(q, c_i, b_i)$. The envelope theorem for q again yields $h_q^i = -g_x^i z_i$.

In the first stage, the Lagrangean expression for the government's choice of $\{c_i, y_i, q\}$ is exactly as before, and the first-order conditions on c_i and q can be used along with the envelope condition on q to obtain the analog of (4):

$$t \sum_{i=1,2} n_i \frac{\partial \tilde{z}^i(q)}{\partial q} = \frac{\gamma}{\lambda} \hat{v}_h^2 \hat{h}_c^2 (z_1 - \hat{z}_2). \tag{5}$$

Unlike in the previous section, the right-hand side is generally not zero: it will only be so if $b_1 = b_2$. It can be shown that $t > 0$ if $b_2 > b_1$ and vice versa. That is, if high-wage households also have higher needs, the tax on z should be higher (assuming that the self-selection constraint on the high-wage types is binding).

This result can be illustrated using figure 21.1, which depicts preferences and the budget constraint for a type-one person and a mimicking type-two. Define the net (after-needs) consumption of good z by $\bar{z}_i \equiv z_i - b_i$. Then, the subutility function for the two types of individuals is identical in x and $\bar{z}$, and preferences over x and $\bar{z}$ are independent of labor supply. When $t = 0$, the budget constraints for

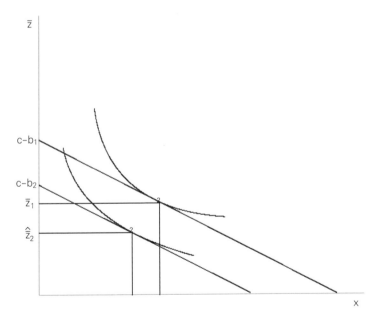

Figure 21.1
Household choices when type 2's have the highest needs

each household are given by $c_i - b_i = x_i + \bar{z}_i$. Figure 21.1 shows the choices of x_i and $\bar{z}_i$ for the two types of households when $b_2 > b_1$. As can be seen, $\bar{z}_1 - \hat{\bar{z}} < b_2 - b_1$ (recall that the "hat" refers to the mimicker), which implies that $\hat{z}_2 > z_1$. Since the mimicker purchases more of good z, the self-selection constraint can be weakened by imposing a tax on that good by the same intuition as before. The opposite result occurs if $b_1 > b_2$. Then, $z_1 > \hat{z}_2$ and it is optimal to set $t < 0$.

If the higher productivity workers have higher needs, the self-selection constraint could apply in the other direction. This is surely the case when productivity differences are very small relative to differences in needs. Then, the mimicker is of type one, and $z_2 > \hat{z}_1$. It is optimal to subsidize z in this case to relax the self-selection constraint. With four types, the pattern of self-selection constraints becomes quite complex, but as shown by Cremer, Pestieau, and Rochet (2001) the case for a nonzero tax, positive or negative, is very strong.

The upshot of this discussion is that if persons have different unobservable needs or endowments, the A-S theorem will fail to be satisfied even if the utility function is weakly separable.

2.2 Government Observes Needs

Suppose now that the government can observe household needs b_j, but it cannot observe wage rates w_i. There are now four household types, and we denote the government's policy instruments by $\{c_{ij}, y_{ij}, q\}$, $i, j = 1, 2$. Since needs are now observable, however, the population can be divided into the two identifiable need types $\{w_1, b_1; w_2, b_1\}$ and $\{w_1, b_2; w_2, b_2\}$. The second stage of the household problem is analogous to that mentioned previously, the only difference being that household demands and functions are now indexed by ij rather than simply i.

The government can now condition its policies on need, and that simplifies matters considerably. In particular, it need worry only about incentive compatibility within each need type. The Lagrangean expression for the government can be written as follows:

$$L = \sum_i \sum_j n_{ij} v^{ij}\left(h(q, c_{ij}), \frac{y_{ij}}{w_i}\right) + \lambda \sum_i \sum_j n_{ij}(y_{ij} + tz^{ij}(q, c_{ij}) - c_{ij})$$

$$+ \sum_j \gamma_j \left[v^{2j}\left(h(q, c_{2j}), \frac{y_{2j}}{w_2}\right) - v^{2j}\left(h(q, c_{1j}), \frac{y_{1j}}{w_2}\right) \right]$$

The first-order conditions with respect to disposable income and q are

$$n_{1j}v_h^{1j}h_c^{1j} - \lambda n_{1j}\left(1 - t\frac{\partial z^{1j}}{\partial c_{1j}}\right) - \gamma_j\hat{v}_h^{2j}\hat{h}_c^{2j} = 0 \qquad j = 1,2$$

$$n_{2j}v_h^{2j}h_c^{2j} - \lambda n_{2j}\left(1 - t\frac{\partial z^{2j}}{\partial c_{2j}}\right) + \gamma_j v_h^{2j}h_c^{2j} = 0 \qquad j = 1,2$$

$$\sum_i\sum_j n_{ij}v_h^{ij}h_q^{ij} + \lambda\sum_i\sum_j n_{ij}\left(z^{ij} + t\frac{\partial z^{ij}}{\partial q}\right) + \sum_j \gamma_j(v_h^{2j}h_q^{2j} - \hat{v}_h^{2j}\hat{h}_q^{2j}) = 0.$$

It should be apparent that by combining these conditions, we obtain the analog of (4) derived earlier:

$$t\sum_i\sum_j n_{ij}\frac{\partial \tilde{z}^{ij}(q)}{\partial q} = \sum_j\frac{\gamma_j}{\lambda}\hat{v}_h^{2j}\hat{h}_c^{2j}(z_{1j} - \hat{z}_{2j}) = 0.$$

The last equality comes about because within each need group j, a type-one household and a type-two mimicker have the same disposable income and the same value of b_j, so by separability, they have the same demand for good z, or $z_{1j} = \hat{z}_{2j}$. Therefore, the A-S theorem applies in this case. It also ought to be obvious that this result extends to other formulations of need, such as multiplicative. Provided the government can classify households by need, and utility functions are separable, the A-S theorem applies.

The optimal income tax system is obviously more complicated in this case, since there is a different schedule for each need type.

3   Multiple Forms of Labor

This section considers the robustness of the A-S theorem when household labor supplies are disaggregated into more than one type. For simplicity, we assume that each household can supply two types of labor, say ℓ_c and ℓ_d, whose interpretations will be discussed for various cases considered later.[9] As in the previous section, the informational restrictions that face the government will be key in determining whether the A-S theorem applies.

3.1   Two Types of Market Labor

Suppose each household supplies two types of labor to the market, receives a wage rate for each, and uses the proceeds to purchase goods. For example, the two types of labor could be two different jobs. The utility function now becomes $u(g(x, z), \ell_c, \ell_d)$. In this case, the applicability of the A-S theorem depends on whether or not incomes from the two forms of labor supply y_c and y_d are observable.

If both y_c and y_d are observable either individually or in the aggregate, the analysis of section 1 goes through with virtually no modification. The government's selection of an optimal tax policy involves selecting consumption levels and disposable incomes for the two types of households, as well as the commodity tax on z. The conditions on c_i and q are the same as before. Moreover, since the mimicker has the same disposable income as a type-one person, separability ensures that $\hat{z}_2 = z_1$, so the optimal commodity tax rate is zero $(t = 0)$.

On the other hand, suppose that, say, y_c is observable, but y_d is not. This might correspond with the case in which labor supply ℓ_d is to the underground economy, as in Boadway, Marchand, and Pestieau (1994). For this interpretation to apply, one ought to model explicitly the penalty and detection technologies associated with the underground sector. That would serve only to complicate the story, however, without affecting the main result. That result is that the A-S theorem generally no longer applies if one source of income is not observable to the government.

The intuition is straightforward, even without a formal analysis. If only y_c is observable, the government can control only that part of disposable income that comes from ℓ_c. Assuming that the wage rate of the mimicker is higher that that of a type-one household in the unobserved sector, it will generally be the case that $\hat{y}_{d2} \neq y_{d1}$. That implies that $\hat{c}_2 \neq c_1$, so that even with separable preferences, $\hat{z}_2 \neq z_1$. So, for example, if $\hat{y}_{d2} > y_{d1}$ because of the higher productivity of a type-two person, $\hat{z}_2 > z_1$, and it will be optimal to impose a tax on good z to relax the self-selection constraint.

More generally, suppose the subutility function $g(x, z)$ is homothetic. In this case, the proportions in which the two goods are consumed by the two persons will be the same. Even in this case it will be optimal to tax good z. In fact, as Boadway, Marchand, and Pestieau (1994) show, the optimal commodity tax system is a proportional one on the two goods x and z. The point is that in the absence of full observability of income, a proportional income tax is no longer a perfect substitute for a proportional commodity tax. In the optimum, there needs to be a mix of the two taxes.

3.2 Household Production

Suppose that the second form of labor supply ℓ_d represents non-market or household production with no disposable income that can be used to purchase x and z. All disposable income comes from y_c, which is observed by the government. Assume that the utility function still takes the form $u(g(x, z), \ell_c, \ell_d)$, where the argument ℓ_d incorporates the disutility of the nonmarket work as well as the product of that work. In this case, the A-S theorem still holds regardless of whether nonmarket labor is observed by the government. Indeed, if all households share the same preferences, that will not be relevant.

The analysis is a straightforward application of that used in section 1. The government controls y_c, and therefore the disposable income that is used to purchase x and z. The existence of nonmarket labor complicates things slightly because it conditions the structure of the optimal nonlinear income tax, and it might in principle affect the direction in which the incentive constraint is binding. Suppose, for example, that the self-selection constraint is binding on type-two households in the optimum. Households of type two who mimic those of type one will earn the same market income y_{c1} and obtain the same disposable income c_1. By the same analysis as above, $\hat{z}_2 = z_1$, and so $t = 0$ in the optimum. This logic still applies if the self-selection constraint binds on type-one households.

3.3 Different Preferences for Leisure

Household might differ not only by ability but according to their preferences for leisure. This adds another important and difficult dimension to redistributive policy. For one thing, governments are unlikely to be able to differentiate persons according to their preferences for leisure, that is, their laziness or diligence. For another, even if they could, it is not obvious how redistributive policies ought to differentiate among preference types. There is a school of thought that suggests that households are responsible for their own preferences, and redistributive policies ought only to compensate for ability differences (Roemer 1998; Fleurbaey and Maniquet 1999). On the other hand, as stressed by Cuff (2000), preferences for leisure might be viewed as being partly determined not just by one's attitude to work but also to the degree of difficulty individuals face in working.

Consider the simple case in which there are two ability types of households and two preference types. A convenient way to formulate the utility function when there are differences in preferences is as $u(g(x,z), \alpha \ell)$.[10] In this formulation, α can take on the values α_1 and α_2. If $\alpha_1 > \alpha_2$, preference type-one has a greater preference for leisure than preference type-two households. In the unlikely event that the government could distinguish between households with high and low preference for leisure, it could simply design two separate non-linear income tax systems for the two types, exactly analogous to the case of different needs for goods considered earlier. In this case, it is obvious that the A-S theorem applies, since within each preference type, the high-wage mimicking person would have the same disposable income as the low-wage person and by separability would consume the same bundle of goods.

If the government cannot distinguish preference types, it is again faced with a two-dimensional screening problem. Depending on the relative welfare weights attached to the two preference types, the pattern of binding self-selection constraints can vary (Boadway et al. 2002). Regardless of what the pattern might be in the optimum, however, the separability of the utility function combined with the commonality of the subutility function $g(x,z)$ implies that the A-S theorem still holds. Mimickers will have the same income and disposable income as those they are mimicking regardless of the type of either. They will consume the same bundle of goods, therefore, implying that a differential commodity tax cannot be used to separate the two types. Differences in preferences for leisure merely serve to complicate the form of the optimal nonlinear income tax.

Finally, note that differences in preference for leisure could reflect differences in need, analogous to the case of differences of need for different goods. For example, utility functions might take the form $u(g(x,z), \ell + a)$, where a reflects need and can vary from one household to another. By similar reasoning to that used earlier, the A-S theorem continues to apply in this case, regardless of whether the government can observe household needs.

3.4 Becker-Gronau Household Production

A final case to consider is the case where consumption of goods itself requires the allocation of some time, following Becker (1965), Gronau (1977), and Jacobsen Kleven (2000). One way of formulating the utility function in this case is as $u(g(x,z), \ell)$, where x and z are commodities produced by household production functions $f^x(x, \ell_x)$ and $f^z(z, \ell_z)$, where ℓ_x and ℓ_z are labor inputs into the production of the home-produced commodities.

Assuming that the household production functions are the same for both households, the A-S theorem applies directly. Mimicking households will have the same income and disposable incomes as those being mimicked, and given these assumptions they will purchase the same quantities of the two goods x and z to produce the same quantities of household goods. On the other hand, if the households had different productivities in home production, which might be a reasonable assumption, the same disposable incomes would generally give rise to different demands for x and z by mimicking type-two's and type-one's.

4   The Linear Progressive Income Tax Case

The A-S theorem represented a landmark in optimal tax theory. In the context of a standard optimal income tax setting, it showed that there is no need to supplement the income tax with differential commodity taxes when goods are weakly separable from leisure in household preferences. This result was derived under what might now be regarded as the strong assumption that all households have the same preferences. We have relaxed this assumption in two realistic ways: first, that needs for particular goods can differ across households, and second, that households may supply more than one form of labor. In each of these cases, the A-S theorem will generally be violated if the government is unable to observe the difference in needs or some types of labor supply.

These results, like the A-S theorem itself, presume that the government has full freedom to levy an optimal nonlinear income tax. It is straightforward to generalize the analysis to a more restrictive income tax regime, such as an optimal linear income tax. In this case, it is well known that differential commodity taxes should not be used if goods are separable from leisure and if the subutility function in goods is quasi-linear, that is, Engel curves for x and z are linear (Deaton 1979).

By using the same logic as before, differences in need and endowments for goods will have the same effect on the applicability of this modified A-S theorem, as in the A-S theorem under nonlinear optimal income taxation. That is, if households have different unobservable needs for one of the goods, it will generally be desirable to impose a tax or subsidy on it. On the other hand, if needs are observable, different tax schedules will apply to persons of different needs classes. Similarly, if households supply two types of labor, the modified A-S theorem applies if both types are observable, but not otherwise. The modified version still applies if there is unobserved household production or if preferences for leisure differ.

5 Conclusions

When looking at actual tax systems, one finds almost everywhere a mix of direct and indirect taxes, or more precisely of consumption and income taxes. What are the reasons for such an apparent violation of the A-S theorem? Ignorance of basic public economics and thus bad fiscal engineering? Huge compliance costs in income taxation relative to consumption taxation? Reasons developed in this chapter and elsewhere for nonapplicability of the A-S theorem? Unwillingness to implement an optimal income tax? Lack of separability of the utility function?

As usual, the answer is a bit of everything. It is clear that in developing countries, the compliance and administration costs of income taxation are so high that tax authorities have to rely on friendlier indirect taxation. The arguments developed above also have some empirical relevance. For example, it is natural to think that needs differ across individuals and are not always observable. The issue of separability is also far from being settled: most econometric studies do not lend support to such separability. It is possible that some public finance experts and policymakers miss the point of A-S theorem and believe that taxes are like eggs: you do not put them in the same basket as income taxation. Finally, there is an issue with the real-world relevance of an optimal income tax. The A-S theorem assumes that one starts with such a tax. It is far from being granted that existing income tax systems correspond to such a scheme, and without optimal income taxation there is no A-S theorem.

Acknowledgments

This chapter, like much of our work in public economics, is inspired by Joe Stiglitz. His combination of analytical virtuosity, intuition, and dedication to economic science as a vehicle for addressing pressing social concerns is an example to us all. We are grateful to Richard Arnott for comments on an earlier draft, and to our various collaborators—especially Helmuth Cremer, Michael Keen, Maurice Marchand, and Nicolas Marceau—on whose work and ideas we have drawn.

Notes

1. See Cremer, Pestieau, and Rochet (2001) and references cited therein. See also Naito (1999), who shows that if production consists of several sectors using variable proportions of different types of workers, then it pays to tax the sectors employing a relatively high proportion of skilled labor; Saez (2003), who shows that Naito's objection disappears in the long run; and Cremer and Gahvari (1995), who underline the desirable insurance effect of commodity taxation.

2. This assumption assures that the A-S theorem applies. It has been questioned on empirical grounds. See Browning and Meghir (1991).

3. Revesz (1986) has shown that if the government could levy two-part taxes consisting of commodity-specific lump-sum license fees alongside proportional commodity taxes, it might be optimal to do so even if optimal proportional commodity tax rates are zero because of separability. We assume that license fees cannot be enforced because of the possibility of resale.

4. A similar procedure has been used by Edwards, Keen, and Tuomala (1994), Nava, Schroyen, and Marchand (1996), and Cremer, Pestieau, and Rochet (2001).

5. In what follows, variables applying to households of type i are denoted by a subscript, while functions for household i are denoted by a superscript. Function subscripts refer to partial derivatives.

6. The first-order conditions on incomes y_i can be used to characterize the structure of the optimal income tax. The characterization is standard and we suppress it here. In what follows, the government is always taken to be applying the optimal income tax.

7. An interpretation of unobserved endowments that gives rise to a rationale for differential commodity taxation is the case of bequests analyzed in Boadway, Marchand, and Pestieau (2000) and Cremer, Pestieau, and Rochet (2003). In this case, the analysis is intertemporal, and the differential taxation applies to future versus present consumption. Capital income taxation then becomes the policy instrument for taxing future consumption differentially.

8. Differences in needs or endowments are also similar to heterogeneous tastes. On this, see Saez (2002).

9. This is different from the case where different households supply different types of labor. If these are not substitutable, the A-S theorem may also fail as shown by Naito (1999), noted earlier.

10. This is the formulation for the preferences for leisure used by Boadway et al. (2002), who study the design of the optimal redistributive income tax when households differ in both ability and preferences.

References

Atkinson, Anthony B., and Joseph E. Stiglitz. 1976. "The Design of Tax Structure: Direct versus Indirect Taxation." *Journal of Public Economics* 6:55–75.

Becker, Gary S. 1965. "A Theory of the Allocation of Time." *The Economic Journal* 75:493–517.

Boadway, Robin, Maurice Marchand, and Pierre Pestieau. 1994. "Towards a Theory of the Direct-Indirect Tax Mix." *Journal of Public Economics* 55:71–88.

Boadway, Robin, Maurice Marchand, and Pierre Pestieau. 2000. "Redistribution with Unobservable Bequests: A Case for Taxing Capital Income." *Scandinavian Journal of Economics* 102:253–267.

Boadway, Robin, Maurice Marchand, Pierre Pestieau, and Maria del Mar Racionero. 2002. "Optimal Redistribution with Heterogeneous Preferences for Leisure." *Journal of Public Economic Theory* 4:475–498.

Browning, Martin, and Costas Meghir. 1991. "The Effects of Male and Female Labor Supply on Commodity Demands." *Econometrica* 59:925–951.

Corlett, W. J., and D. C. Hague. 1953–1954. "Complementarity and the Excess Burden of Taxation." *Review of Economic Studies* 21:21–30.

Cremer, Helmuth, and Firouz Gahvari. 1995. "Uncertainty and Optimal Taxation: In Defense of Commodity Taxes." *Journal of Public Economics* 56:291–310.

Cremer, Helmuth, Pierre Pestieau, and Jean-Charles Rochet. 2001. "Direct Versus Indirect Taxation: The Design of the Tax Structure Revisited." *International Economic Review* 42:781–799.

Cremer, Helmuth, Pierre Pestieau, and Jean-Charles Rochet. 2003. "Capital Income Taxation When Inherited Wealth Is Not Observable." *Journal of Public Economics.* Forthcoming.

Cuff, Katherine. 2000. "Optimality of Workfare with Heterogeneous Preferences." *Canadian Journal of Economics* 33:149–174.

Deaton, Angus. 1979. "Optimally Uniform Commodity Taxes." *Economics Letters* 2:357–361.

Edwards, Jeremy, Michael Keen, and Matti Tuomala. 1994. "Income Tax, Commodity Taxes and Public Good Provision: A Brief Guide." *Finanzarchiv* 51:472–497.

Fleurbaey, Marc, and Francois Maniquet. 1999. "Compensation and Responsibility." Mimeo.

Gronau, Ruben. 1977. "Leisure, Home Production and Work—The Theory of the Allocation of Time Revisited." *Journal of Political Economy* 85:1099–1123.

Guesnerie, Roger. 1995. *A Contribution to the Pure Theory of Taxation.* Cambridge, UK: Cambridge University Press.

Jacobsen Kleven, Henrik. 2000. "Optimal Taxation and the Allocation of Time." Mimeo.

Mirrlees, James A. 1971. "An Exploration in the Theory of Optimal Income Taxation." *Review of Economic Studies* 38:175–208.

Naito, Hisahiro. 1999. "Re-examination of Uniform Commodity Taxes under a Nonlinear Income Tax System and its Implication for Productive Efficiency." *Journal of Public Economics* 71:165–188.

Nava, Mario, Fred Schroyen, and Maurice Marchand. 1996. "Optimal Fiscal and Public Expenditure Policy in a Two-Class Economy." *Journal of Public Economics* 61:119–137.

Revesz, John T. 1986. "On Some Advantages of Progressive Indirect Taxation." *Public Finance* 41:182–199.

Roemer, John E. 1998. *Equality of Opportunity.* Cambridge, U.S.: Harvard University Press.

Rowe, Nicholasm, and Frances Woolley. 1999. "The Efficiency Case for Universality." *Canadian Journal of Economics* 32:613–629.

Sandmo, Agnar. 1976. "Optimal Taxation: An Introduction to the Literature." *Journal of Public Economics* 6:37–54.

Saez, Emmanuel. 2002. "The Desirability of Commodity Taxation under Nonlinear Income Taxation and Heterogeneous Tastes." *Journal of Public Economics* 83:271–330.

Saez, Emmanuel. 2003. "Direct or Indirect Tax Instruments for Redistribution: Short-run Versus Long-run." NBER working paper. *Journal of Public Economics.* Forthcoming.

Stiglitz, Joseph E. 1982. "Self-Selection and Pareto Efficient Taxation." *Journal of Public Economics* 17:213–240.

22

Optimum Income Taxation When Earnings Are Imperfectly Correlated with Productivity

David L. Bevan

This chapter examines optimum income taxation when the informational problem is somewhat more extensive than that usually considered in this literature. It takes up a point made in Stiglitz 1987, 1021: "Views about the desirability of progressive taxation are often related to views concerning the extent to which differences in income are due to differences in effort, to differences in ability, or to differences in luck." This observation might reflect the role of luck in weakening the view that those on high incomes have a moral right to them because these incomes are earned. This chapter shows, however, that the presence of even small amounts of luck radically alters optimum progressivity even in the standard welfarist setup where considerations of rights do not arise.

Stiglitz (1982) examined the case where income was stochastic, but the government could still infer the individual's ability from his income. He found that this could imply a marginal tax rate on high incomes of 100 percent, provided income was bounded above. He observed "more generally, however, we will not be able to distinguish perfectly a low ability lucky individual from a high ability unlucky individual. This makes the design of the optimal tax structure ... far more difficult (and more interesting)" (235). This chapter sets out to address this issue.

Leaving aside a handful of very special cases, the optimum income tax problem is not analytically tractable, but requires numerical solution. This requires the structure of the problem to be specified explicitly. Stern (1976 at 123) noted four ingredients in this specification: an objective function, a preference relation or supply function for individuals, a skill structure and distribution, and a production relation. In addition, however, there is the issue of incomplete information and how this is specified. This chapter focuses on this fifth feature.

It shows that quite mild variations in the informational assumptions, given the rest of the specification, can lead to a markedly different form for the optimum tax schedule. In particular, the common finding, both in numerical exercises (Mirlees 1971; Tuomala 1990; Kanbur and Tuomala 1994; Kanbur, Keen, and Tuomala 1994; Slemrod et al. 1994) and in asymptotic analyses (Mirrlees 1971; Seade 1977) that the marginal tax rate should eventually fall with income[1] is shown not to be robust to a relaxation in the usual informational set-up. The structure of the chapter is as follows.

Section 1 outlines the informational approach adopted here, which essentially posits noise in the employer's assessment of a worker's contribution to output. In effect, the present model assumes more stringent informational problems than is usual in this literature. Section 2 briefly recapitulates the original Mirrlees model, and section 3 then augments this to take the reduction in information into account. Section 4 introduces specific functional forms to permit numerical solution of the system. With Stern's ingredients, these are chosen to replicate those used in the original numerical illustration (Mirrlees 1971, 200–207). Given the nature of these assumptions, it is natural to model the measurement error as lognormally distributed and multiplicative. Section 5 concludes.

1 Informational Assumptions

The usual informational assumption in this literature is related to the assumption on technology, that the individual's output is the deterministic product of his skill (ability) and his effort (hours worked), and that the output of individuals of different ability is homogeneous. The informational assumption is then that, whereas output is perfectly observable, ability and effort are not separately observable at all. In this stylized setting, this is of no concern to the employer, who is only interested in the worker's output and not in how it is produced. It does not matter, for example, whether a moderate output is the outcome of a high-ability individual working a little, or a low-ability individual working a lot. The government, by contrast, would like to be able to distinguish these cases and tax by ability rather than by income, but this option is precluded by the separate non-observability of effort and ability.

The first point to notice about the construction of this principal-agent problem is how much it differs from the construction of the analogous principal-agent problem involving just the employer and worker. In the simplest form of the latter, ability differences between workers are suppressed. The problem arises because the output attributable to the individual can only be observed with error, either due to intrinsic difficulties in partitioning output, or because output is the joint product of the worker's efforts and an unobservable exogenous shock. The nonobservability of effort may now become an issue for the employer, and the outcome is a wage that is imperfectly correlated with the worker's productivity.[2]

The question addressed here is what are the implications of this imperfect correlation between wages and productivity for the choice of the optimum tax schedule? To permit the analysis to focus on this core point, I assume that employers do not formulate complicated wage contracts, but simply pay workers pro rata for their imperfectly observed contribution to output.[3] For the same reason, the other features of the model closely follow those of Mirrlees's original paper.

2   Recapitulation of the Mirrlees Model

While subsequent elaborations of the 1971 paper are cast in very general terms, the difficulty of obtaining clear-cut and robust general results has meant that much weight has rested on the numerical illustrations provided in the original paper, and some limited variants of these provided by other authors, most notably Tuomala (1990). In this section, the bare bones of this special case are presented;[4] the following section adds the imperfect observability feature.

The fraction of the unit time endowment that an individual works is denoted by y. Individuals have identical preferences over consumption (x) of a composite good, and working time, $u = u(x,y)$, where u is a strictly concave, continuously differentiable function (strictly) increasing in x, (strictly) decreasing in y, defined for $x > 0$ and $1 > y \geq 0$. Individuals differ only in their skill or productivity per unit time. Skill is indexed by n with density $f(n)$, normalized so that $\int_0^\infty f(n) \, dn = 1$. Output is homogeneous. An n-person produces an amount $z(n) = ny(n)$ and aggregate output is $Z = \int_0^\infty ny(n)f(n) \, dn$. The government is able to observe the individual's earnings exactly and these in turn exactly match his contribution to output, z, where the output price is set at unity. The government chooses the income tax schedule so that an individual with income z is constrained to consume no more than $c(z) = c(ny(n)) = x(n)$ after tax. In the absence of satiation, aggregate consumption is then $X = \int_0^\infty x(n)f(n)\,dn$. The government has a net revenue requirement $\bar{R}$ so its budget constraint is $X + \bar{R} = Z$, where

$$\int_0^n [ty(t) - x(t)]f(t)\,dt = R(n) \tag{1}$$

and $\bar{R} = R(\infty)$. It also has a welfare function that is increasing in individual utilities $G = \int_0^\infty W(u^n)f(n)\,dn$ where u^n is the utility of an n-person. This can be formulated as a maximum principle problem, with $y(n)$ as the control variable and $u(n)$ and $R(n)$ as the state variables. The first-order condition for utility maximization is $u_x nc'(ny) + u_y = 0$. Hence, writing g for the derivative of u^n with respect to n:

$$g(u, y) = \frac{du^n}{dn} = u_n^n = u_x c' y = -\frac{y u_y}{n}. \tag{2}$$

We now differentiate g given n invariant, yielding

$$g_y = -[u_y + y u_{yy} - y u_{yx} u_y / u_x]/n$$

$$g_u = -y u_{yx}/n u_x.$$

The Lagrangean for the government's problem is

$$\int_0^\infty \left\{ W(u^n)f(n) + \lambda(n)\left([ny(n) - x(n)]f(n) - \frac{dR(n)}{dn} \right) \right.$$
$$\left. + \psi(n)(u_n^n - g) \right\} dn. \tag{3}$$

Integration by parts yields the Hamiltonian:

$$H = \{W(u^n) + \lambda(n)[ny(n) - x(n)]\}f(n) - \psi(n)g(n) + \lambda_n R(n) - \psi_n u^n, \tag{4}$$

with the first-order conditions:

$$H_u = (W' - \lambda/u_x)f(n) - \psi_n - \psi g_u = 0 \tag{5}$$

$$H_y = \lambda(n + u_y/u_x)f(n) - \psi g_y = 0 \tag{6}$$

$$H_R = \lambda_n = 0 \tag{7}$$

Define

$$v = \frac{1 + u_y/nu_x}{-(u_y + yu_{yy} - yu_{yx}u_y/u_x)} = \frac{\psi}{n^2 \lambda f(n)}. \tag{8}$$

Then $\psi = n^2 \lambda f(n)v$ and

$$\psi_n = \left[\frac{2}{n} + \frac{\lambda_n}{\lambda} + \frac{f'}{f} + \frac{v_n}{v}\right]\psi$$

$$= \left[\frac{2}{n} + \frac{f'}{f} + \frac{v_n}{v}\right]\psi \tag{9}$$

$$\left[\frac{2}{n} + \frac{f'}{f} + \frac{v_n}{v} - \frac{yu_{yx}}{nu_x}\right]v = \frac{(W' - \lambda/u_x)}{n^2 \lambda} \tag{10}$$

Equations 2 and 10 can be written as

$$u_n = -yu_y/n \tag{11}$$

$$v_n = -\frac{v}{n}[2 + nf'/f - yu_{yx}/u_x] + (W'/\lambda - 1/u_x)/n^2 \tag{12}$$

This pair of first-order ordinary differential equations can then be solved for the optimum schedule, once specific functional forms for u, W, and f are chosen. Mirrlees also showed[5] that there exists a number $n_0 \geq 0$ such that

$$y'' = 0 \ (n \leq n_0), \quad y'' > 0 \ (n > n_0),$$

and argued that $n_0 > 0$ for distributions of the type usually considered by economists (Mirrlees 1971, 185). In other words, it would usually be (second-best) optimal to have some of the population idle. n_0 provides a convenient method for establishing initial values for the solution.

3 Incorporating Imperfectly Observed Productivity

3.1 Representation

The simplest way of introducing this feature is to postulate a bivariate distribution of true and apparent ability. It is natural to assume that the two marginal distributions take the same form. In the original numerical illustration, true (the only) ability was assumed to be distributed in the population lognormally, $n \sim \Lambda(\mu_n, \sigma_n)$ where $\ln \mu_n$ and σ_n are the mean and standard deviation of the associated normal distribution, that is, n has median μ_n and mean $\mu_n e^{\sigma_n^2/2}$, and this assumption is maintained for the marginal true distribution. Now consider a worker i, who has true ability n_i and works y_i. His true contribution to output is therefore $q_i = n_i y_i$, but this is perceived by the employer as $z_i = m_i y_i$ where $z_i = q_i \varphi$ and φ is an error term. It follows that the same relation holds in the unobservables, so that $m_i = n_i \varphi$. We assume that the error $\varphi \sim \Lambda(\mu_\varphi, \sigma_\varphi)$, and that it may be correlated with n, with $\rho_{n\varphi}$ as the correlation coefficient in the associated bivariate normal distribution. Then it follows from the properties of the normal distribution that

$$\sigma_m^2 = \sigma_n^2 + \sigma_\varphi^2 + 2\rho_{n\varphi}\sigma_n\sigma_\varphi \tag{13}$$

$$\rho_{mn} = (\sigma_n + \rho_{n\varphi}\sigma_\varphi)/\sigma_m = \frac{\sigma_n + \rho_{n\varphi}\sigma_\varphi}{\sqrt{\sigma_n^2 + \sigma_\varphi^2 + 2\rho_{n\varphi}\sigma_n\sigma_\varphi}} \tag{14}$$

It is worth considering some special cases of this relation. Evidently, if $\rho_{n\varphi} = 1$, then so does ρ_{mn}, and the error φ is reduced to a scaling factor. The ranking of individual workers by productivity is now exactly right, but the dispersion is exaggerated in the ratio $(1 + \sigma_\varphi/\sigma_n)^2$. In all other cases, $|\rho_{n\varphi}| < 1 \Rightarrow |\rho_{mn}| < 1$. What is more, $\rho_{mn} > 0$ even when $\rho_{n\varphi} < 0$ provided $-\rho_{n\varphi} < \sigma_n/\sigma_\varphi$ and always when $\rho_{n\varphi} > 0$. Provided the variance of $\ln \varphi$ is less than that of $\ln n$, so that the measurement error is no larger than the true variation in the object measured, as appears plausible, this condition will hold. Hence a positive but imperfect correlation between true and apparent ability would appear to be robust to any plausible parameterization of the error.

We have the marginal distribution with $m \sim \Lambda(\mu_m, \sigma_m)$. Since we shall suppose that the parameters of the true skill distribution (μ_n, σ_n) and those of the error $(\sigma_\varphi, \rho_{n\varphi})$ are given, this only leaves μ_m to be determined. We make the natural assumption that the employer is accurately informed about total (average) product. We also assume that each employer has a balanced labor force, and is not specialized in some part of the ability distribution. Then if working time were uniform, $y(m) = y$, all m, this would imply the restriction that the means of the two distributions coincide, $\mu_m = \mu_n \mu_\varphi = \mu_n e^{-(\sigma_\varphi^2 + 2\rho_{n\varphi}\sigma_n\sigma_\varphi)/2}$.

We are interested in situations, however, where labor supply will not in general be uniform across worker types, and where it will respond differentially to changes in the tax regime. The relation between skill and earnings then becomes more delicate, and it is useful to separate the apparent skill index m of a worker from the wage he is paid, $z(m) = wmy(m)$, where w is common across all workers. We can then treat m as a characteristic of the worker that describes his apparent skill (and wage per unit time) relative to other workers, but does not necessarily equal his real product wage. We can choose μ_m arbitrarily, preserving the values m/μ_m. In what follows, we choose $\mu_m = e^{(\sigma_n^2 - \sigma_m^2)/2}$ since that equates average per period values of true and apparent skill.

3.2   Incorporation (1)

In place of an n-worker, we now have an (m, n) worker, where m is his apparent and n his true ability. Consider an $(m, \cdot)$ worker: he is treated as a Mirrlees m-worker, and he makes the labor supply decision $(y(m))$ and obtains the consumption $(x(m))$ of a Mirrlees m-worker. Now, however, a distribution of product is contributed by the group of workers classified as $(m, \cdot)$ workers that is $y(m)$ times the conditional distribution of n given m. Given that $m, n \sim \Lambda(\mu_n, \mu_m, \sigma_n, \sigma_m, \rho_{mn})$, and writing $h(m)$ for the expected value of this conditional distribution, we have $n|m \sim (\mu_{n|m}, \sigma_{n|m})$ where $\mu_{n|m} = \mu_n(m/\mu_m)^{\rho_{nm}\sigma_n/\sigma_m}$ and $\sigma_{n|m}^2 = \sigma_n^2(1 - \rho_{mn}^2)$. Hence, $h(m) = \mu_n(m/\mu_m)^{\rho_{nm}\sigma_n/\sigma_m} e^{\sigma_n^2(1-\rho_{mn}^2)/2}$. Incorporating the condition $\mu_m = e^{(\sigma_n^2 - \sigma_m^2)/2}$, we obtain

$$h(m) = \mu_m e^{(\sigma_m^2 - \sigma_n^2)/2} (m/\mu_m)^{\rho_{nm}\sigma_n/\sigma_m} e^{\sigma_n^2(1-\rho_{mn}^2)/2}$$

$$= \mu_m^{(1-\rho)} e^{(1-\rho^2)\sigma_m^2/2} m^\rho, \tag{15}$$

where we define $\rho = \rho_{mn}\sigma_n/\sigma_m$. Substituting from equations 13 and 14 we obtain $\rho = (\sigma_n^2 + \rho_{n\varphi}\sigma_n\sigma_\varphi)/(\sigma_n^2 + \sigma_\varphi^2 + 2\rho_{n\varphi}\sigma_n\sigma_\varphi)$. Provided there is any error at all $(\sigma_\varphi^2 \neq 0)$, then $\rho < 1$ unless $\rho_{n\varphi}$ is negative and $|\rho_{n\varphi}| \geq \sigma_\varphi/\sigma_n$.

While alternatives have been discussed for completeness, the most natural assumption would be that the measurement error is uncorrelated with ability. In that case, we get the simple relation $\rho = \sigma_n^2/(\sigma_n^2 + \sigma_\varphi^2) = \sigma_n^2/\sigma_m^2$. The associated condition, $E[m|n] = n$, all n, is seen to imply that $E[n|m] \equiv h(m) \neq m$ in general. Even for biased errors, however, within any plausible range of bias, the implication of this discussion is that $h(m) \propto m^\rho$ with $\rho < 1$ so that $h(m)/m$ is decreasing in m.

3.3 Incorporation (2)

Now consider how to recast the original model to take this effect into account. We could in principle continue to integrate over the variable n, but this would be cumbersome, since workers who share the same value of true ability are now treated differently by their employers and hence by the tax authorities. In consequence, they face different budget constraints and will generally behave differently. This difficulty does not arise if we integrate instead over the variable m. The behavior of an (m, n) worker, as already noted, is indistinguishable from that of a Mirrlees m-worker. Workers who share the same apparent ability are treated the same, face the same budget constraint, and behave the same. The characterization of social welfare is similarly unaffected if we replace n with m. The only change is that aggregate output attributable to workers with apparent skill $t \leq m$ is $Q(m) = \int_0^m h(t)y(t)f(t)\,dt$, where $h(t)$ is given by equation 15.

Making the associated changes to the government's maximization problem, we need to replace the government's budget constraint 1 by $\int_0^m [h(t)y(t) - x(t)]f(t)\,dt = R(m)$. The only changes to the Hamiltonian 4 are the switch for the variable of integration from n to m, and the replacement of the term in square brackets by $[h(m)y(m) - x(m)]$. The first-order conditions are undisturbed, with the exception of 6 which becomes

$$H_y = \lambda(h(m) + u_y/u_x)f(m) - \psi g_y = 0.$$

This alters the definition of v as follows:

$$v = \frac{h(m)/m + u_y/mu_x}{-(u_y + yu_{yy} - yu_{yx}u_y/u_x)}$$

Once this alteration is accounted for, however, the form of the two differential equations 11 and 12 remains the same.

The other way in which the changed specification alters the solution is via the definition of gross income (z). Since output and income are both defined in real terms, we must have $Q = Z$. For a predetermined value of μ_m, however, $\int_0^\infty my(m)f(m)\,dm \neq \int_0^\infty h(m)y(m)f(m)\,dm$ unless $y(m) = y$, or $\rho = 1$. We proceed by defining a wage factor w:

$$w = \frac{\int_0^\infty h(m)y(m)f(m)\,dm}{\int_0^\infty my(m)f(m)\,dm}.$$

We now have $Z = w \int_0^\infty my(m)f(m)\,dm = Q$ as required[6] and that the individual $(m, \cdot)$ worker has gross income $z(m) = wmy(m)$. The upshot is that workers are paid in proportion to their perceived productivities, and that the economy-wide average wage equals the economy-wide average product. The government is effectively choosing the consumption schedule directly in light of real output and revenue requirements. We thus have that the worker pays tax of $wmy(m) - x(m)$; writing r for the share of government revenue in total purchasing power, we have that

$$r = R/Z = 1 - X/Z$$

$$= 1 - \frac{\int_0^\infty x(m)f(m)\,dm}{w \int_0^\infty my(m)f(m)\,dm}.$$

For the purpose of comparative tax analysis, we here choose to maintain r constant.

3.4   Interpretation

It may appear that the change in the optimum problem when imperfect correlation between earnings and productivity is introduced is rather slight. This is certainly true of its structure. The question of interest here is the numerical one, however, as to how sensitive the optimum tax schedule is to plausible values of this correlation. Before turning to computation, it is worth considering the qualitative nature of the change. The central problem in optimum taxation is the trade-off between equity and efficiency. Highly able workers receive high incomes, so are desirable targets for high, redistributive taxes. The problem is that they are paid highly precisely because they are highly productive. Hence disincentive effects, leading to a reduction in their labor supply may be socially very costly.

At the other end of the spectrum, redistribution toward the low paid is desirable from the equity viewpoint, and the associated incentive effects may be relatively unimportant, because these workers are very unproductive anyway. These features help to explain two characteristics of the usual optimum calculations. First, marginal tax rates are low, and typically falling at the top of the distribution, and second, there may be a group at the bottom of the distribution for whom it is socially optimal that they do no work.

If we now introduce imperfect correlation between earnings and productivity, the nature of this trade-off is shifted, and is to some extent less stark. Highly paid workers are paid, on average, more than they are worth; the low paid are paid less than they are worth. The potential equity gains from high taxes on highly paid workers are unchanged, but the production losses from a unit reduction in their labor supply are reduced. Indeed, if the correlation were very low, the highly paid would be receiving substantial economic rents that are usually seen as appropriate targets for high taxes. The incentive effects on the low paid, however, are now more serious; while the poor are in one sense more deserving in this case, they are harder to compensate. It should be clear from this discussion that imperfect correlation of this type is likely to have complex effects, and these may not vary in any simple way with the size of the correlation coefficient. In particular, it is not clear whether a fall in the perceptibility of productivity would make the optimal tax system more or less redistributive.

4   Numerical Illustrations

4.1   Assumptions

These assumptions follow closely those chosen for the numerical illustrations in the 1971 paper. As already noted, the distribution of n was there assumed to be lognormal. Mirrlees took $\mu_n = e^{-1}$ and, for five of the six calculations reported, $\sigma_n = 0.39$; we restrict attention to these values, but now for the distribution of m. Utility is assumed to take the Cobb-Douglas form, $u = x(1 - y)^{1/\alpha}$ and the welfare function the form $G = \int_0^\infty [(u^{1-\gamma} - 1)/(1 - \gamma)]f(n)\,dn$. In the calculations, α and γ are both set at 1.[7] The net revenue requirement was set at rather arbitrary amounts in the original calculations, presumably as a consequence of the solution procedure. This was to choose trial values of λ and n_0, and iterate on n_0 until a sufficiently good fit was obtained. The ratio of aggregate consumption to aggregate production, X/Z, and hence the net revenue requirement at this solution depend on the trial value of λ originally chosen. In the present calculations, a second round of iterations are undertaken, on λ, to maintain the revenue requirement constant between experiments.

4.2   Results

Since the interest of the present exercise lies in the shape of the tax function, the results are presented graphically in figure 22.1. In panel a, the tax is purely redistributive, while in panel b it must also meet a net revenue requirement equal to 25 percent of income. Panel a graphs the marginal tax rate for four degrees of correlation between true and inferred skill.[8] The bold line plots the tax rate when the correlation is perfect, that is, this is the case considered by Mirrlees. The rate rises slightly for very low skill levels (above the level below which individuals do no work), but then falls rather slowly. It was this type of calculation that led Mirrlees to conclude (1) that asymptotic results were rather misleading, and (2) that a linear tax might not be a bad approximation to the optimal tax. The remaining three plots in the panel explore what happens as we progressively relax the link between what workers are paid and what they produce. Even when the correlation is as high as 0.95,[9] the tax schedule undergoes a substantial shift, becoming slightly u-shaped, but very close to being stationary.

As the correlation falls to 0.9, the tax schedule now shows a rather rapid rise at low skill levels, and it continues to rise steadily across the upper range. With a correlation of 0.8, this rise becomes quite marked and not dissimilar from the pattern of conventional income tax schedules adopted in practice. At low inferred skill levels, it is also now optimal for the marginal tax rate to be negative. The disincentive effects of transferring income to the low paid are now becoming serious, since these workers are on average substantially more productive than they appear to be from their wages.[10]

Panel b plots the schedules for correlations of 1.0 and 0.8 when there is a positive revenue requirement. The interesting feature here is that the displacement of the marginal schedules is rather slight for high skill levels, but shows a very marked increase at low levels. With a correlation of 0.8, the imposition of the net revenue requirement makes the optimum schedule u-shaped.

5   Conclusion

Once we allow that wages are not perfectly aligned with productivity, the shape of optimum income tax schedules may be altered

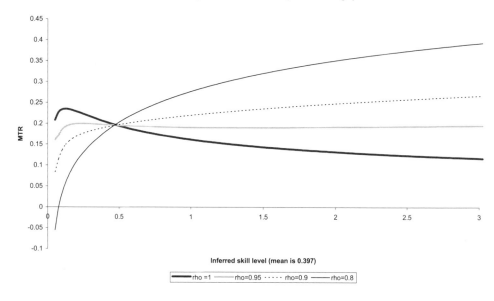

Panel a: Purely redistibutive taxation (balanced budget)

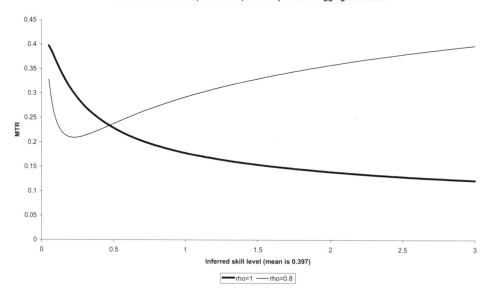

Panel b: Net revenue requirement equal to 25 percent of aggregate income

Figure 22.1
Marginal tax rate schedules (MTR) for different degrees of correlation between observed and true productivity (rho)

drastically. Even if the wage-productivity fit is good, it is likely that the marginal tax rate should rise with income, even in the lognormal case where the conventional treatment indicates a declining rate. For more realistic specifications of the skill distribution, with a thicker upper tail, this conclusion is reinforced.

Notes

1. Mirrlees (1971) demonstrated that this would not necessarily hold for distributions with a Pareto upper tail, but this point has tended to be overlooked. See, however, Diamond (1998).

2. This is true if the employer writes a second-best optimal contract, trading off the worker's risk aversion against the disincentive effect of insuring him. But it is also true of any other feasible contract, including the simplest one that pays the worker for the observed output, leaving him to bear all the risk.

3. In a companion paper, Bevan (1997), I examine the case when employers and government are tackling their principal-agent problems simultaneously, restricting attention to loglinear wage contracts and loglinear income tax schedules. In the present context, the most natural assumption is that employers cannot attribute output to individual workers, but can observe effort accurately, and have a shrewd but not perfect idea of workers' abilities. There is then no viable contact other than one that is proportional to this perceived contribution.

4. We assume differentiability of the relevant functions and restrict attention to the first-order conditions. For all the schedules computed in this chapter, it turns out that the second-order condition is strictly satisfied. See Ebert (1992).

5. Mirrlees (1971, 177) proposition 1.

6. Note that the scale of the corrections is likely to be very small for reasonable values of the correlation, that is, w is typically very close to 1.

7. These components were organised slightly differently in the original paper, with $u = \alpha \ln x + \ln(1 - y)$ and $W = -e^{-\beta u}/\beta$. For the calculations, α was set at 1 and β took the alternative values 0 and 1. These correspond to the forms in the text with α again set at 1 and γ set at 1 and 2, respectively.

8. The tax rates are plotted against the inferred skill level rather than income since it is the former that is invariant between cases. The general shape of the schedules, however, is very similar if plotted against income.

9. Since the size of these correlations is not intuitive, it is helpful to consider the implied relation between relative wages and productivity across some range of the distribution. For example, the group of workers paid twice the average wage will (on average, across the two groups) be overpaid relative to those paid the average wage by 3 percent if $\rho = 0.95$; by 6 percent if $\rho = 0.9$; and by 12 percent if $\rho = 0.8$.

10. Indeed, for lower correlations than those displayed, the marginal tax schedule becomes u-shaped, with the bottom of the u being substantially negative.

References

Bevan, D. L. 1997. "Principals and Agents when Ability Differs and Is Imperfectly Observed." Mimeo., Oxford, October.

Diamond, P. A. 1998. "Optimal Income Taxation: An Example with a U-Shaped Pattern of Optimal Marginal Tax Rates." *American Economic Review* 88:83–95.

Ebert, U. 1992. "A Re-examination of the Optimal Nonlinear Income Tax." *Journal of Public Economics* 49:47–73.

Kanbur, R., and M. Tuomala. 1994. "Inherent Inequality and the Optimal Graduation of Marginal Tax Rates." *Scandinavian Journal of Economics* 96:275–282.

Kanbur, R., M. Keen, and M. Tuomala. 1994. "Optimal Non-Linear Income Taxation for the Alleviation of Income-Poverty." *European Economie Review* 38:1613–1632.

Mirrlees, J. A. 1971. "An Exploration in the Theory of Optimum Income Taxation." *Review of Economic Studies* 38:175–208.

Mirrlees, J. A. 1976. "Optimal Tax Theory: A Synthesis." *Journal of Public Economics* 6:327–358.

Mirrlees, J. A. 1986. "The Theory of Optimal Taxation," chap. 24 in *Handbook of Mathematical Economics Vol. III*, ed. K. J. Arrow and M. D. Intriligator. Amsterdam: North-Holland, 1197–1249.

Seade, J. 1977. "On the Shape of Optimal Tax Schedules." *Journal of Public Economics* 7:203–235.

Seade, J. 1982. "On the Sign of the Optimum Marginal Income Tax." *Review of Economic Studies* 49:637–643.

Slemrod, J., S. Yitzhaki, J. Mayshar, and M. Lundholm. 1994. "The Optimal Two-Bracket Linear Income Tax." *Journal of Public Economics* 53:269–290.

Stern, N. H. 1976. "On the Specification of Models of Optimum Income Taxation." *Journal of Public Economics* 6:123–162.

Stiglitz, J. E. 1982. "Self-Selection and Pareto Efficient Taxation." *Journal of Public Economics* 17:213–240.

Stiglitz, J. E. 1987. "Pareto Efficient and Optimal Taxation and the New New Welfare Economics," in *Handbook of Public Economics*, vol. 2, ed. A. J. Auerbach and M. Feldstein. Amsterdam: North-Holland.

Tuomala, M. 1990. *Optimal Income Tax and Redistribution*. Oxford: Clarendon Press.

23   Can Government Collect Resources without Hurting Investors? Taxation of Returns from Assets

Raaj Sah and Kenji Wada

This chapter shows that it may be possible to increase the government's resources, using taxes (and subsidies) on the returns from financial assets, without hurting investors. We work with a simple yet realistic set of taxes. The return from an asset is taxed at a constant rate. Different assets can be taxed at different rates.[1] All investors face an identical set of tax rates. It is not assumed that the government can tax every asset.

This analysis is conducted with heterogeneous investors whose investment opportunity set consists of one riskless and many risky assets. Here is a simple example of the results presented later. Suppose that: (1) investors are homogeneous, (2) there are no preexisting taxes, (3) there is one riskless and one risky asset, (4) the expected return from the risky asset exceeds the positive riskless return, and (5) investors have a nonzero portfolio weight on the riskless asset. Then, a small tax on the return from the risky asset, and a small subsidy on the riskless return, increases the government's resources without hurting investors. When we say that investors are not hurt, we mean that the changes in the tax rates under consideration do not reduce the level of the expected utility for any of the investors.

Several qualitative results are presented in more general settings, with many risky assets and with heterogeneous investors. A typical result is in the form of a single condition that is intuitive and informationally parsimonious. If this condition is satisfied by even one pair of assets, then a small change in the tax rates will increase the government's resources without hurting investors. Using numerical simulations, we also describe some large changes in the tax rates that yield the same. What we mean by small changes in the tax rates is that the tax rates are perturbed only in the local neighborhood of the pre-change tax regime, whereas no such restriction applies to large changes in the tax rates. We work with a small open economy that trades freely in financial assets with the rest of the world. We show that our results hold whether the asset markets are complete or incomplete. Later in this section, we summarize the reasons why the government may be able to increase its resources. To our knowledge, the results presented here are unavailable in the literature.

One of the concerns of the literature originated by Mossin (1968), Sandmo (1977), and Stiglitz (1969, 1972) has been to study the effects of taxes on an investor's portfolio weights (hereafter referred to as weights) on different assets. The focus here is on the effects of taxes on the welfare levels of investors and is, in this sense, orthogonal to the concern just noted. In a contribution to the analysis of taxation of risky assets, Auerbach (1981, 1) notes but does not analyze or establish the possibility that the government can raise resources without hurting individuals.

Since the taxes are imposed here on the returns from financial assets, the government's revenue is random. There are three main approaches adopted in the literature toward the treatment of random government revenue. The first is to ignore the revenue (see the review by Sandmo 1985 for such examples). This approach, though appropriate for analyzing many questions, is not applicable to the issues examined here. The second approach is to satisfy the government's budget constraint in each state-of-the-world, after reimbursing the government revenue to individuals on a lump-sum basis (see, e.g., Konrad 1991). While such analyses yield some economic insights, this characterization of the government may not be the most appropriate in many contexts. Among the reasons for this are: (1) lump-sum transfers are rarely feasible in practice; (2) governments typically have the ability to save and dissave, and to lend and borrow (including from nondomestic sources), across time and the states-of-the-world; (3) governments typically do not appear to balance their budgets on a state-by-state basis; and (4) the provision of public goods is a central activity of governments.

The third approach to the treatment of the government revenue is as follows. For brevity, let m denote the random government revenue. Then, an example of this approach is to specify that the government's resources are represented by the expected value of the revenue, $E[m]$, where $E[\ ]$ is the expectation operator (see Christiansen 1993, and Koskela and Kanniainen 1984). A motivation underlying this reduced-form approach is that the government can average out its random revenues across time and the states-of-the-world through saving, dissaving, borrowing, and lending, and that these averaging activities do not entail any net cost.

A more general version of this approach is to employ a transformation function on random government revenue and calculate the expected value of this function across the states-of-the-world (see Allingham 1972 and Stiglitz 1972 for similar formulations). We use this approach and represent the government's resources as $E[g(m)]$, where $g(m)$ is the transformation function. Our conclusions do not depend on virtually any property of the transformation function $g(m)$. Also, for our analysis, it is not necessary to specify how the government's resources are employed (for example, on which public goods and services, or on which other activities), provided that an increase in the government's resources, in itself, does not decrease the welfare of any investor.[2]

Can Private Entities Collect Resources?

The government's power of taxation plays an important role in our analysis. This is because, unlike the government, a private entity (such as an investment bank) in a competitive market may not be able to collect resources by introducing private taxes or subsidies. Consider this simple illustration. Suppose that an investment bank is willing to buy or sell the riskless asset at a return higher than the riskless rate prevailing in the market. Then, investors will buy the riskless asset from this bank and sell the corresponding quantity of this asset to a competing investment bank that is trading this asset at the riskless rate prevailing in the market. In this process, the former investment bank will incur a loss, the investors will make a profit, and thus this activity will not arise. Analogous reasoning applies to the situations in which an investment bank wishes to impose a private tax on the riskless asset, or a private tax or subsidy on a risky asset, or a combination of these.

Where Do the Government's Resources Come From?

Suppose that there are no preexisting taxes on any asset, and that the government introduces a tax on the return from one of the assets. By doing so, the government creates a new post-tax joint distribution of asset returns (referred to, in the rest of this subsection, as post-tax distribution). What matters to investors is this post-tax distribution. By altering the tax rates on the returns from various assets, the government can create many different post-tax distributions. Each such post-tax distribution will in general entail a different set of random payoffs to the government and investors. Therefore, given the characteristics of investors, including their respective preferences, and given the government's transformation function, some of these post-tax distributions may be such that each investor is as well-off in the post-tax regime as he is in the pretax regime, while the quantity of the government's resources in the post-tax regime is larger than that in the pretax regime. An analogous logic applies if there are pre-existing taxes.

As noted earlier, the economy considered here is open and small. This polar abstraction is more reasonable for some countries, but obviously not for all, than another commonly used polar abstraction in which the economy is closed. Briefly discussed here are some of the implications of the abstractions that we have chosen to work with. An implication of the openness of the economy is that, in some states-of-the-world, it receives net resource inflows from the rest of the world, whereas the opposite happens in some other states-of-the-world. Another implication of openness is that the welfare of some of those in the rest of the world may be affected by a change in the home country's tax regime. Since we have not examined these welfare effects, we do not address the issue of a "free lunch." Given the openness of the economy, an implication of its smallness is that the pretax distribution of asset returns faced by the home country's investors is not affected by the change in the tax regime in the home country. A question that remains is whether some of the insights presented here have counterparts if the assumption of smallness is modified.

It should thus be apparent now that some of the critical elements of our framework (in particular, the openness and the smallness of the economy, and the specification of the government's resources) are fundamentally different from those that are typically present in the models that study the Pareto optimality (or its versions that are constrained in one manner or another) of a competitive equilibrium in closed economies (with or without complete asset markets). For this reason, our analysis and conclusions are not directly comparable to, and thus are not inconsistent with, those associated with the models just noted.

Organization of the Chapter

Section 1 begins the analysis with homogeneous investors. Section 2 presents the analysis with heterogeneous investors. In these two sections, the analysis deals with small changes in the tax rates. Section 3 summarizes some of our analysis of large changes in the tax rates. Section 4 presents some extensions of the analysis in sections 1 and 2. Section 5 concludes.

1 A Basic Model

We begin by considering homogeneous investors. Investors are risk-averse. The investment opportunities consist of one riskless and n risky assets. Depending on the context, an asset may be interpreted as an asset class rather than as an individual asset. None of the $n+1$ assets is redundant. The riskless asset is denoted by $i = 0$, and it yields a pretax return x_0. Throughout the chapter, "return" means the net return, and a distinction is made, wherever it is necessary, between the pretax and the post-tax return from an asset. We assume that $x_0 > 0$; that is, the riskless return is positive. Other values of x_0 are considered later. The risky assets are denoted by $i = 1$ to n, and their pretax random returns are represented by the column vector $\tilde{x} \equiv (\tilde{x}_1, \ldots, \tilde{x}_n)'$. Throughout the chapter, a prime denotes the transpose of a vector. The expected values of the pretax returns from the risky assets are denoted by the column vector $x \equiv (x_1, \ldots, x_n)'$, where $x \equiv E[\tilde{x}]$. The investor's initial wealth is denoted by y, and $y > 0$. The investor's weight on asset i is a_i, where

$$a_0 = 1 - \sum_{k=1}^{n} a_k. \tag{1}$$

Taxes

The column vector $t \equiv (t_0, t_1, \ldots, t_n)'$ represents the tax rates on the returns from different assets. For any asset, the sign of its post-tax return is the same as that of its pretax return; that is $t_i < 1$.

In the present context, it is not meaningful to view a positive value of t_i as a "tax" on the i-th asset, or a negative value of t_i as a "subsidy." The effect of the sign of t_i depends on whether the investor is long or short on asset i. For example, if the investor is short on the riskless asset, then a positive value of t_0 reduces the cost of this borrowing, implying a subsidy. Alternatively, if the investor is long on the riskless asset, then a negative value of t_0 raises the return from this lending, also implying a subsidy. Hence, unless explicitly needed, we use the phrase "tax" to refer to a positive, zero, or negative value of any element of t.

Utility Levels of Investors

With full tax-loss offset, the random terminal wealth of the investor, denoted by Y, is

$$Y \equiv y \left\{ 1 + \sum_{i=0}^{n} (1 - t_i) a_i \tilde{x}_i \right\}. \tag{2}$$

For brevity in summations over assets, we sometimes write x_0 as $\tilde{x}_0$, as is done in (2) above, while keeping in mind that $\tilde{x}_0$ is nonrandom.

The utility function of the investor is $u(Y)$, which is increasing and strictly concave in Y. Let $U(t)$ denote the maximized level of the investor's expected utility. That is,

$$U(t) \equiv \max_{(a_1,\ldots,a_n)} E[u(Y)]. \tag{3}$$

It is assumed throughout the essay that an investor's optimization problem, such as (3), has a unique interior solution. The first-order conditions for the optimality of (3), taking (1) and (2) into account, are

$$E[\tilde{x}_j u_Y] = (1 - t_0) x_0 E[u_Y]/(1 - t_j), \qquad \text{for } j = 1 \text{ to } n, \tag{4}$$

where $u_Y \equiv \partial u / \partial Y > 0$. Define $U_j \equiv dU/dt_j$ for $j = 0$ to n. Then,

$$U_j = -y a_j (1 - t_0) x_0 E[u_Y]/(1 - t_j), \qquad \text{for } j = 0 \text{ to } n. \tag{5}$$

Expression (5) is derived in the appendix. From (5), we obtain the following to be used later:

$$U_j/U_i = (1 - t_i) a_j/(1 - t_j) a_i, \qquad \text{for } i \text{ and } j = 0 \text{ to } n, \tag{6}$$

where it is assumed that $a_i \neq 0$.

Government's Resources

We assume that taxes are the only source of government revenue. Thus, for example, we abstract from issues related to government bonds. We also assume that the government does not directly buy or sell financial assets. This is consistent with the practice in many modern market economies, especially concerning corporate and other nongovernment securities. Among the reasons, not modeled here, is that such a participation will make the government a stakeholder in private entities, which may have adverse market consequences.

The random government revenue is HM, where H is the number of investors, and M is the revenue collected from each investor. It follows that

$$M \equiv y \sum_{i=0}^{n} t_i a_i \tilde{x}_i. \tag{7}$$

Define

$$G(t) \equiv E[g(HM)], \tag{8}$$

where the nonrandom scalar $G(t)$ denotes the government's resources. No assumption is made about the function $g(\ )$ in (8), except that $g_M(0) > 0$, where g_M denotes the derivative of g with respect to its argument. That is, if the government's revenue is zero, then a small increase in this revenue raises the government's resources. As will be seen later, even this innocuous assumption can be dropped. Further, any monotonically increasing function of $G(t)$ will leave the analysis unchanged. It is assumed that: (1) a larger amount of the government's resources, in itself, does not hurt any investor, (2) any benefit that an investor gets from the government's resources is additively separable from his utility (3), and (3) the preceding benefit has no effect on the investor's portfolio decisions.

Define $G_j \equiv dG/dt_j$ for $j = 0$ to n. From (7) and (8), we obtain

$$G_j = yHE[(a_j \tilde{x}_j + \xi_j)g_M], \quad \text{where } \xi_j \equiv \sum_{i=0}^{n} t_i \tilde{x}_i \frac{\partial a_i}{\partial t_j}, \quad \text{for } j = 0 \text{ to } n. \tag{9}$$

Small Changes in the Tax Rates

Consider a small change in the tax rates t_i and t_j that keeps the utility level of an investor unchanged. If t_j is increased by a small amount

δt_j, then the change in t_i must be

$$\delta t_i = -U_j \delta t_j / U_i. \tag{10}$$

The corresponding change in the government's resources, using (10), is $\delta G = G_i \delta t_i + G_j \delta t_j = (G_j - G_i U_j / U_i) \delta t_j$. Define a metric

$$\phi(i, j) \equiv G_j - G_i U_j / U_i. \tag{11}$$

The substitution of (6) into (11) yields

$$\phi(i, j) = G_j - G_i(1 - t_i)a_j / (1 - t_j)a_i, \qquad \text{for } i \text{ and } j = 0 \text{ to } n, \tag{12}$$

where the G_i's are given by (9). It then follows that

If $\phi(i, j)$ is positive, then the government's resources increase from a small increase in the tax on the return from asset j, and a change in the tax on the return from asset i that leaves investors unhurt. $\tag{13}$

Expression (13) yields

PROPOSITION 1. Suppose that there is an arbitrary set of preexisting taxes. Consider any pair of assets i and j, such that investors have a nonzero weight on asset i. Then, the government's resources become larger from a small increase in the tax on the return from asset j, and a change in the tax on the return from asset i that keeps investors unhurt, if the right-hand side of (12) is positive.

A noticeable feature of this proposition is as follows. To increase the government's resources without hurting investors, it is sufficient that only one of the $n(n + 1)/2$ possible pairs of assets satisfies the required condition. The same observation applies to all of the propositions presented later here, with the exception of proposition 3.

Changes in the Tax Rates in the Vicinity of the No-Tax Regime

While proposition 1 holds for any preexisting taxes, we now consider small changes in the tax rates in the vicinity of the "no-tax regime"; that is, the regime in which there are no preexisting taxes. As one would expect, the resulting conclusions are qualitatively more transparent than proposition 1.

Since all tax rates are zero, (9) implies that $\xi_i = 0$ for $i = 0$ to n. From (7), $M = 0$. Hence, $g_M(HM) = g_M(0)$ is non-random. Substitution of these into (9) yields

$$G_j = yHg_M(0)a_jx_j; \tag{14}$$

that is, G_j is proportional to a_jx_j. Combining (14) with (12), and recalling that $g_M(0) > 0$, we obtain

$$\phi(i, j) > 0 \qquad \text{if } a_j(x_j - x_i) > 0, \tag{15}$$

and the following result.

PROPOSITION 2. Suppose that there are no preexisting taxes. Consider any pair of assets i and j, such that investors have nonzero weights on both assets. Then, the government's resources become larger from a small increase in the tax on the return from asset j, and a change in the tax on the return from asset i that keeps investors unhurt, if: (1) investors have a positive (negative) weight on asset j, and (2) the expected return from asset j is larger (smaller) than that from asset i.

This proposition is highly parsimonious in its informational needs. To implement this proposition, the only information that the government needs is investors' current weights and the expected returns from various assets. The same informational parsimony holds for all of the propositions presented later that deal with tax changes around the no-tax regime.

Consider now a special case of proposition 2 in which there is only one risky asset; that is, $n = 1$. In this case, it is reasonable to assume that the expected return from the risky asset, x_1, is larger than the riskless return, x_0. This assumption ensures that investors' weight on the risky asset is positive; that is $a_1 > 0$ (see Ingersoll 1987, 68). Recall (15), and substitute into it: $i = 0$, $j = 1$, $x_1 > x_0$, and $a_1 > 0$. This yields $\phi(0, 1) > 0$.

From (13), the preceding inequality implies a small tax on the return from the risky asset (i.e., $\delta t_1 > 0$). In turn, a subsidy on the riskless return is required to keep investors unhurt. This is because, from (6) and (10), $\text{sgn}\{\delta t_0\} = -\text{sgn}\{a_0\}$, given that $a_1 > 0$. Thus, δt_0 will be negative or positive, depending on whether investors are long or short on the riskless asset. As was noted earlier, in either case, this implies a subsidy on the riskless return. These observations lead to the following conclusion.

PROPOSITION 3. Suppose that (1) there are no preexisting taxes, (2) the investment opportunities consist of one riskless and one risky asset, (3) the expected return from the risky asset exceeds the positive riskless return, and (4) investors have a nonzero weight on the riskless asset. Then, the government's resources become larger from a small tax on the return from the risky asset and a small subsidy on the riskless return that keeps investors unhurt.

Under the plausible conditions noted here, proposition 3 guarantees that the government's resources will increase, without hurting investors, if the investment opportunity set consists of a riskless and a risky asset. Some additional observations on this proposition are presented in Sah and Wada (2001).

Complete versus Incomplete Asset Markets

Recall the assertion made in the introduction that our results hold in complete as well as incomplete asset markets. To confirm this, note that there is no redundant asset in our analysis with one riskless and n risky assets. Also, we have placed no restriction on the number of the states-of-the-world. Thus, our analysis is for complete asset markets if there are only $n + 1$ states-of-the-world. Alternatively, our analysis is for incomplete asset markets if the number of the states-of-the-world is larger than $n + 1$.

2 Heterogeneous Investors

This section considers heterogeneous investors. Investors are identified by the superscript $h = 1, \ldots, H$. For brevity, the range of summation over investors is often suppressed. For investor h, the initial wealth is y^h (where $y^h > 0$), the random terminal wealth is Y^h, the utility function is $u^h(Y^h)$, the weight on asset i is a_i^h, and the maximized level of the expected utility is $U^h(t)$. Then, analogous to (1), (2), (3), and (6), we respectively have

$$a_0^h = 1 - \sum_{k=1}^{n} a_k^h, \tag{16}$$

$$Y^h \equiv y^h \left\{ 1 + \sum_{i=0}^{n} (1 - t_i) a_i^h \tilde{x}_i \right\}, \tag{17}$$

$$U^h(t) \equiv \max_{(a_1^h, \ldots, a_n^h)} : E[u^h(Y^h)], \quad \text{and} \tag{18}$$

$$U_j^h / U_i^h = (1 - t_i) a_j^h / (1 - t_j) a_i^h, \qquad \text{for } i \text{ and } j = 0 \text{ to } n. \tag{19}$$

The government's resources are $G(t) \equiv E[g(\sum_r M^r)]$, where $M^h \equiv y^h \sum_{i=0}^n t_i a_i^h \tilde{x}_i$ is the revenue collected from investor h. It follows that

$$G_j = E\left[\sum_r y^r \{ a_j^r \tilde{x}_j + \xi_j^r \} g_M \right],$$

where $\xi_j^h \equiv \sum_{i=0}^n t_i \tilde{x}_i \dfrac{\partial a_i^h}{\partial t_j}$, for $j = 0$ to n. \hfill (20)

We work with the HARA-class utility functions, defined by the equation

$$-u_Y^h(Y^h) / u_{YY}^h(Y^h) = \varepsilon_1^h + \varepsilon_2 Y^h, \tag{21}$$

where $u_{YY}^h \equiv \partial^2 u^h / \partial (Y^h)^2$, and ε_1^h and ε_2 are parameters. Note that the heterogeneity in the investors' preferences is somewhat limited here because the parameter ε_2 is the same for all investors. We later present some comments on the HARA-class and note that our results also hold for some specifications other than that in (21).

Define

$$\alpha_k^h \equiv a_k^h / (1 - a_0^h), \qquad \text{for } k = 1 \text{ to } n. \tag{22}$$

That is, α_k^h is the amount that investor h invests in the risky asset k as a fraction of his total wealth invested in all risky assets. For brevity, we refer to α_k^h as the "sub-weight" of investor h on the risky asset k. By definition, $\sum_{k=1}^n \alpha_k^h = 1$.

As is well known, (21) yields the two-fund separation property. Formally,

$$\alpha_k^h = \alpha_k, \qquad \text{for any } k = 1 \text{ to } n, \text{ and for all } h. \tag{23}$$

That is, the subweight on any risky asset k is the same for all investors (see Rubinstein 1974 at 227–228).

A property of the subweights α_k's is as follows. For even one α_k to be nonzero, as well as nontrivial (in the sense that this nonzero value of α_k has any impact on the terminal wealth), it is necessary that $a_0^h \neq 1$ for all h.[3] That is, an investor does not invest all of his wealth in the riskless asset. Accordingly, we assume that $a_0^h \neq 1$ for all h. Using this, (19), (22), and (23), we obtain

$$\phi^h(k, \ell) = G_\ell - G_k (1 - t_k) \alpha_\ell / (1 - t_\ell) \alpha_k, \qquad \text{for } k \text{ and } \ell = 1 \text{ to } n, \tag{24}$$

where the G_k's are given by (20). An important property of (24) is that the metric $\phi^h(k, \ell)$ is the same for all investors.

Next, as shown in the appendix, the evaluation of (24) in the no-tax regime yields

$$\phi^h(k, \ell) > 0 \text{ for all } h, \quad \text{if } \left[\sum_r y^r(1 - a_0^r)\right]\alpha_\ell(x_\ell - x_k) > 0. \qquad (25)$$

Note that $\sum_r y^r(1 - a_0^r)$ is the sum of all investors' initial wealth invested in all of the risky assets. We assume here that this sum is positive though, as shown later, an analogous result holds even if this sum were negative. Accordingly,

$$\phi^h(k, \ell) > 0 \quad \text{if } \alpha_\ell(x_\ell - x_k) > 0. \qquad (26)$$

We thus have the next two propositions.

PROPOSITION 4.   Suppose that there is an arbitrary set of preexisting taxes, and that heterogeneous investors have the HARA-class utility functions defined by (21). Consider any pair of risky assets k and ℓ, such that investors have a nonzero weight on asset k. Then, the government's resources become larger from a small increase in the tax on the return from asset ℓ, and a change in the tax on the return from asset k that keeps each investor unhurt, if

the right-hand side of (24) is positive.   (27)

A notable aspect of this proposition is as follows. Here, there is an arbitrary number of heterogeneous investors. Yet there is only one condition, namely (27), that needs to be satisfied (and not, say, one condition for each investor) for the government's resources to increase without hurting investors. Moreover, as noted earlier, it is sufficient that this one condition be satisfied for any one of the many possible pairs of assets. The same observation applies to the other propositions that deal with heterogeneous investors, namely, the next proposition and proposition 6 presented later.

PROPOSITION 5.   Suppose that there are no preexisting taxes, and that heterogeneous investors have the HARA-class utility functions defined by (21). Consider any pair of risky assets k and ℓ, such that investors have nonzero weights on both assets. Then, the government's resources become larger from a small increase in the tax on the return from asset ℓ, and a change in the tax on the return from asset k that keeps each investor unhurt, if (1) investors have a positive (negative) subweight on asset ℓ, and (2) the expected return from asset ℓ is larger (smaller) than that from asset k.

Isoelastic Utility Functions

Propositions 4 and 5 apply to taxes on any pair of risky assets, but not to taxes on a pair consisting of the riskless and any one of the risky assets. We now present a result that includes pairs of taxes of the latter type. Suppose that the investors' utility functions are isoelastic; that is, $u^h(Y^h) = (Y^h)^{1-\varepsilon}/(1-\varepsilon)$, where $0 < \varepsilon < \infty$ is the parameter of relative risk-aversion. This is a special case of (21) with $\varepsilon_1^h = 0$, and $\varepsilon_2 = 1/\varepsilon$. This utility function, sometimes called the CRRA utility, includes the log utility function as a special case. Accordingly, propositions 4 and 5 hold in the present case. A further implication of the isoelastic utility function is that all investors have the same weight on any given asset. That is,

$$a_i^h = a_i, \qquad \text{for any } i = 0 \text{ to } n, \text{ and for all } h. \tag{28}$$

Define $y \equiv \sum_r y^r/H$ as the average initial wealth per investor. Then, using (19) and (28), we obtain

$$\phi^h(i, j) = G_j - G_i(1 - t_i)a_j/(1 - t_j)a_i, \qquad \text{for } i \text{ and } j = 0 \text{ to } n, \tag{29}$$

where the G_j's are given by (9). Thus, the right-hand side of (29) is the same as that of (12).

Further, in the no-tax regime, we have the same expression as (15), but now it applies to all investors. That is,

$$\phi^h(i, j) > 0 \qquad \text{if } a_j(x_j - x_i) > 0. \tag{30}$$

These observations lead to

PROPOSITION 6. Suppose that heterogeneous investors have isoelastic utility functions. Then, the conclusions of propositions 1, 2, and 3 hold without any modification.

The reason underlying proposition 6 is simple. To an investor, what matters for the present analysis is his set of portfolio weights. For investors with isoelastic utility functions (with heterogeneous levels of wealth, but the same parameter of relative risk-aversion), this set is identical across investors.

3   Large Changes in the Tax Rates: A Summary

In the preceding two sections, the focus was on small changes in the tax rates. Separately, we have analyzed whether some large changes in the tax rates can increase the government's resources. Due to space constraints, only a verbal summary of this analysis is presented below; the key details are in Sah and Wada (2001).

Consider the following framework. There are many risky assets and one riskless asset. Investors have mean-variance (M-V) utilities. That is, the welfare level of investor h is $E[Y^h] - v^h Var[Y^h]/2$, where his post-tax random terminal wealth Y^h is described by (17), and v^h is his risk-aversion parameter. Note that this M-V specification is different from the one that arises if a quadratic utility function (which is a special case of the HARA-class utility functions considered earlier) is used. Investors are heterogeneous in their initial wealth levels and in their risk-aversion parameters. The government's resources are defined in an M-V fashion; in particular, $G \equiv E[\sum_h M^h] - \rho Var[\sum_h M^h]/2$, where $M^h \equiv y^h \sum_{i=0}^n t_i a_i^h \tilde{x}_i$ is the random government revenue collected from investor h. For simplicity, we deal only with positive values of ρ.

We know from mean-variance portfolio analysis (Ingersoll 1987, 88) that there is an efficient-frontier that represents the feasible and relevant portfolio choices of all investors. A commonly used graphical description of this efficient-frontier is that the standard deviation of the portfolio return is on the horizontal axis, the resulting expected return of the portfolio is on the vertical axis, and the efficient-frontier is an upward sloping straight line of which the intercept is the riskless return (the relevant riskless return here is the post-tax one). The optimal choice of any one investor is a point on the efficient-frontier, and the optimal choices of a heterogeneous group of investors will in general be represented by many different points on the efficient-frontier. Therefore, the welfare level of each of the investors can be kept unchanged, while changing the tax vector, by considering those combinations of changes in the tax rates which leave the efficient-frontier unaltered.

Next, using the standard analytics of mean-variance portfolio analysis, it can be shown that, in general, a change in the tax rate on the riskless return (recall that t_0 represents this tax rate) affects both the intercept and the slope of the efficient-frontier, whereas a change in the tax rate on the return from a risky asset (recall that $(t_1, \ldots, t_n)$

represent these tax rates) affects the slope but not the intercept of the efficient-frontier. Therefore, in our analysis, we keep t_0 unchanged, while examining combinations of changes in $(t_1, \ldots, t_n)$ such that the efficient-frontier remains unaltered. Note that this analysis does not require any information on the initial wealth levels of investors, because this information is not relevant for constructing the efficient-frontier.

In our numerical simulations, the investment opportunity set consists of one riskless and two risky assets. The tax rate t_0 is set at zero, and the only changes considered are those in t_1 and t_2. To keep the efficient-frontier unaltered, only one of these two tax rates, t_1 and t_2, can be changed independently of the other. We define the prechange regime to be the one in which there are no taxes; i.e., $t_1 = t_2 = 0$. It follows that $G = 0$ in this benchmark regime. The data on annual real returns are taken from Ibbotson (1996), for each year from 1926 to 1995. These data for the United States are treated as pretax data. The riskless return corresponds to that from the T-bills. The returns from the two risky assets correspond respectively to those from (1) the T-bonds, and (2) an equally weighted portfolio of small- and large-cap stocks. We find a number of combinations of t_1 and t_2 for which is G positive. That is, the government's resources increase as a result of nonlocal changes in the tax rates on the returns from assets. This conclusion holds for several sets of values of the parameters ρ and $(v^1, \ldots, v^H)$.

4 Some Extensions

This section summarizes some extensions of the analysis presented in sections 1 and 2. Each extension is independent of the others.

Investor's Preferences

In a part of section 2 it was assumed that investors have the HARA-class utility functions defined by (21). This class includes many of the utility functions commonly used in financial economics, such as quadratic, cubic, exponential, and isoelastic. Further, what matters for the corresponding results in that section is the two-fund separation property and not the nature of the underlying utility functions. Thus, analogs of these results will hold under all those conditions in which investors exhibit the two-fund separation property. Ingersoll

(1987, 164) summarizes several such conditions in terms of restrictions on investors' preferences and/or the distribution of the asset returns.

Riskless Return

Our analysis has been based on the assumption that the riskless return is positive. For expositional brevity, we do not consider negative values of the riskless return, though such values do not alter the economic conclusions of the essay. If the riskless return is zero, then the analysis becomes considerably simpler. Note from (5) that if $x_0 = 0$, then $U_j = 0$, for $j = 0$ to n. That is, taxes have no effect on the expected utility of an investor (which was originally established by Sandmo 1977, 1989). Thus, the government's resources can be increased, whether or not there are preexisting taxes, if at least one of the G_j's is nonzero, for $j = 0$ to n. This is because a small increase or decrease in the tax rate t_j will increase G if G_j is respectively positive or negative. The implementation of this conclusion is especially easy for changes in the tax rates in the vicinity of the no-tax regime. For instance, with homogeneous investors, it follows from (9) that, in this case, $\text{sgn}\{G_j\} = \text{sgn}\{a_j x_j\}$.

Zero Weight on an Asset

For simplicity, consider homogeneous investors. It follows from (5) that if an investor has a zero weight on asset i, then his expected utility remains unchanged due to a change in the tax rate t_i. Therefore, using the reasoning presented in the preceding paragraph, the government's resources can be increased through a small increase or decrease in t_i, depending on whether G_i is positive or negative. This conclusion, however, does not translate for use around the no-tax regime because, in this case, (9) implies that G_i is zero.

Other Assumptions

We assumed earlier that $g_M(0) > 0$; that is, a slight increase in the government revenue increases the government's resources if the current government revenue is zero. Consider the opposite assumption; namely that $g_M(0) < 0$. This reverses the sign of the inequalities (15), (26), and (30). This reversal merely requires a rewording of the corresponding propositions that deal with tax changes around the no-tax regime.

An assumption used in deriving proposition 5 was that $\sum_r y^r(1 - a_0^r) > 0$; that is, the amount invested by all investors in all of the risky assets is positive. Suppose instead that the sign of the preceding expression is negative. Then, the sign of the inequality (26) will be reversed, resulting in a simple restatement of proposition 5.

5 Concluding Remarks

Ever since the work of Harberger, we have known that the garnering of resources for public goods and services imposes direct costs on private individuals, and, in addition, can entail significant indirect costs. If the level of public resources can be increased for a given set of private costs, then it is typically the case that the private costs can be reduced for a given level of public resources. While we recognize this, it is not our aim to look for free lunches. This chapter does not even raise the issue of a free lunch, because we have looked at changes in the tax regime in a small open economy without accounting for the effects that such changes may have on the rest of the world, and how the rest of the world might respond to such changes. At the same time, it is the case that a small open economy is a more appropriate abstraction for many countries than another commonly used abstraction, namely, that of a closed economy. It is also the case that, in many contexts, policy decisions are made within a country without much attention to its implications on the rest of the world and, for one reason or another, without significant responses from the rest of the world. The possibility of being able to reduce the private costs of raising public resources appears intriguing to us, even if it may be meaningful only within specific contexts such as the one just noted.

Appendix

DERIVATION OF (5).   The use of the envelope theorem on (3), while using (2), yields

$$U_j = -ya_jE[\tilde{x}_ju_Y], \qquad \text{for } j = 0 \text{ to } n. \tag{A1}$$

Substitution of (4) into (A1) yields the desired expression.

DERIVATION OF (25).   Here, each element of t is zero. From its definition, $M^h = 0$. Thus, $\sum_r M^r = 0$, and $g_M(0)$ is nonrandom. Further, $\xi_j^h = 0$ from (20). Substitution of these and (22) and (23) into (20) yields: $G_j = g_M(0)[\sum_r y^r(1 - a_0^r)]x_j\alpha_j$. This and (24) yield $\phi^h(k, \ell) > 0$ for all h, if $g_M(0)[\sum_r y^r(1 - a_0^r)]\alpha_\ell(x_\ell - x_k) > 0$. The desired expression follows since $g_M(0) > 0$.

Acknowledgments

We present this essay to celebrate and honor Joe Stiglitz. From Raaj, it is also a token of appreciation to a friend. Joe's intense scholarly originality has deeply impacted many parts of economics. As a public servant and social thinker, he has unflinchingly created alternative visions for a better world. More than anything else, it was Joe's idealism that led him to become an economist. It is heartwarming that, unlike many whose idealism withers with the passage of time, Joe's has flourished richly. And his ever-present warmth and liveliness. God bless!

We thank Carlos da Costa, John Donaldson, Allison Garrett, Seok-Kyun Hur, Ravi Kanbur, Robert Lucas, Rajnish Mehra, and the late Sherwin Rosen for their help. We thank Richard Arnott for his extensive comments and suggestions. Wada acknowledges a special debt to Keio University for its generous financial support.

Notes

1. Gains from different asset classes are taxed at different rates in a number of countries. Price Waterhouse (1996) provides many examples.

2. Note that the government's instruments in the present analysis are quite limited. For example, the tax rates on the returns are proportional. Our conclusions will only be reinforced if the set of instruments that the government can use were larger (e.g., nonlinear tax rates on the returns from assets) than that specified here. We work with the simplifying assumption that the investors pay taxes only to their home government, and that no foreigners pay taxes to this government, but these aspects can easily be modified. We also assume that the government can prevent the domestic investors' tax noncompliance (including through arbitrage with the rest of the world); for example, by requiring that these investors are served only by domestically regulated brokers.

3. This can be seen by using (16) and (22) to rewrite (17) as $Y^h = y^h\{1 + (1 - t_0)a_0^h x_0 + (1 - a_0^h)\sum_{k=1}^n (1 - t_k)\alpha_k \tilde{x}_k\}$. Suppose $\alpha_\ell \neq 0$. Then, the value of α_ℓ has no impact on Y^h if $a_0^h = 1$.

References

Allingham, M. G. 1972. "Risk-Taking and Taxation." *Zeitschrift fur Nationalokonomie* 32:203–224.

Auerbach, Alan J. 1981. "Evaluating the Taxation of Risky Assets." Discussion paper no. 857. Cambridge, MA: Harvard Institute of Economic Research.

Christiansen, Vidar. 1993. "A Normative Analysis of Capital Income Taxes in the Presence of Aggregate Risk." *Geneva Papers on Risk and Insurance Theory* 18:55–76.

Ingersoll, Jonathan E., Jr. 1987. *Theory of Financial Decision Making*. Totowa, NJ: Rowman and Littlefield.

Konrad, Kai. 1991. "Risk Taking and Taxation in Complete Capital Markets." *Geneva Papers on Risk and Insurance Theory* 16:167–177.

Koskela, Erkki, and Vesa Kanniainen. 1984. "Changing Tax Base and Risk-Taking." *Oxford Economic Papers* 36:162–174.

Mossin, Jan. 1968. "Taxation and Risk-Taking: An Expected Utility Approach." *Economica* 35:74–82.

Price Waterhouse. 1996. *Individual Taxes—A Worldwide Summary*. New York: Price Waterhouse & Co.

Rubinstein, Mark. 1974. "An Aggregation Theorem for Securities Markets." *Journal of Financial Economics* 1:225–244.

Sah, Raaj, and Kenji Wada. 2001. "Can Government Collect Resources without Hurting Investors? Taxation of Returns from Assets." Working paper 01.27. Chicago: Harris School of Public Policy, University of Chicago.

Sandmo, Agnar. 1977. "Portfolio Theory, Asset Demand and Taxation: Comparative Statics with Many Assets." *Review of Economic Studies* 44:369–378.

Sandmo, Agnar. 1985. "The Effects of Taxation on Savings and Risk Taking," in *Handbook of Public Economics*, ed. Alan J. Auerbach and Martin Feldstein, 265–311. New York: North-Holland.

Sandmo, Agnar. 1989. "Differential Taxation and the Encouragement of Risk-Taking." *Economics Letters* 31:55–59.

Stiglitz, Joseph E. 1969. "The Effects of Income, Wealth, and Capital Gains Taxation on Risk-Taking." *Quarterly Journal of Economics* 83:263–283.

Stiglitz, Joseph E. 1972. "Taxation, Risk Taking, and the Allocation of Investment in a Competitive Economy," in *Studies in the Theory of Capital Markets*, ed. Michael C. Jensen, 294–374. New York: Praeger.

24

Reforming the Taxation of Human Capital: A Modest Proposal for Promoting Economic Growth

Paul A. David

This chapter presents a new proposal to modify existing income tax regimes in a way that would render them more supportive of human capital formation and hence more encouraging to long-term economic growth.

A bias against human capital formation expenditures exists in many national tax codes, which tend to favor investments in tangible capital formation and intangible business expenditures for R&D and in-house production of computer software. Differentials in the tax treatment of different classes of assets are "inefficient" in the static welfare-analytic sense, and these inefficiencies become magnified where the various assets are strong complements in production or in consumption. Due to the complementarities between human capital formation and the accumulation of other classes of productive assets, and the role of human capital in generating technological and organizational innovations,[1] this particular aspect of "nonneutrality" in the workings of the tax system may well have significant perverse consequences for economic growth.

The progressive taxation of personal income, moreover, tends to exacerbate the distortions in the allocation of investment that arise from the failure of most modern tax regimes to treat human and nonhuman capital formation in a neutral fashion. Because it proves more feasible under most tax regimes to shelter personal property income streams from the effects of rising marginal tax rates than is the case for wage and salary income, educational and training investments that yield incremental earned income are particularly punished.

To significantly reduce or eliminate progressive taxation of incomes, at best, will offer only partial amelioration of the tax-induced distortions of investment, and that approach to reform is an unattractive as a solution on other counts. Important noninstrumental, ethical reasons exist for redistributing income to poorer members of society in the high income countries, as well as reinforcing considerations that turn on the consequences of such redistributive policies for productivity improvement and growth in developing countries. Taken together, these constitute a cogent rationale against general proposals for tax regime reforms that would have the effect of eliminating progressive taxation.

What then can be done? Rather than continuing the debates over radical fiscal reforms—in which the elimination of income taxation and its replacement by taxes levied only on consumption expenditures, or various flat tax proposals, have figured prominently—a less ambitious, more pragmatic approach is advocated here. Economists are more likely to be effective in this area if their meliorative energies are directed to more modest, piecemeal proposals that do not entail a disruptive overhaul of the entire tax regime.

The reform proposed here would make the private costs of education and training fully deductible expenditures for purposes of calculating individuals' taxable income. Instead of allowing the tax deduction to be claimed immediately, or to be claimed by a third party, however, it would be credited to an account in the name of the person receiving the qualified form of education and/or training. Under the scheme envisaged, the value of this deduction account would then grow at a rate equal to the real yield on long-term government debt, up until the point at which it was exercised to reduce the personal income tax liabilities of the individual account holder. The period within which this could be done would be confined to a comparatively short time interval.

In effect, a novel financial instrument is proposed to achieve the objectives of a tax regime that was neutral in its treatment of intangible human capital and other productivity assets, without sacrificing the principle of progressive taxation. It is an individually held, nontransferable financial asset: an untaxed, interest-bearing educational (expense) deduction account. This novel device is conveniently described by its acronym, UIBEDA, which sounds like "we-bedda."

The strong rationale that can be found in the economics literature for reforming the tax treatment of human capital formation is reviewed briefly in section 1. This provides a background for the features of the proposal that are set out in section 2. A concrete (numerical) illustration of the operation of the scheme is supplied in section 3. The conditions under which the UIBEDA scheme could satisfy an intertemporal balanced budget constraint are examined in section 4, which broaches the important empirical question of how potent this form of subsidy would be in inducing incremental human capital investments that yielded larger earned income streams, and hence enlarged future tax revenues.

Section 5 calls attention to two further and distinctive virtues of the proposed scheme. One is that there is no reason to prevent the recipients of this form of educational subsidy from finding employment for their acquired skills outside their "home" labor markets. The second is that the governments of skill-deficient regions need not restrict the scope of the UIBEDA scheme to their respective native born populations or domestic residents. UIBEDA accounts thus lend themselves readily to use in implementing liberal policies of selective immigration and emigration.

The chapter concludes in section 6 with some remarks on the importance of setting in place provisions that establish credible commitment to this scheme on the part of the state, and related issues about the appropriate time horizon for such commitments.

1 The Fiscal Bias Against Human Capital Formation: Diagnosis and Previously Proposed Remedies

Although the process of developing human capabilities through education and other kinds of training may yield consumption satisfactions for the recipients, today the process is regarded widely as an investment activity from which will flow an incremental stream of future human productive services (and corresponding earnings). Systems of taxation that treat workers as agents of production (analogous to machines) distort the allocation of resources in a direction that militates against human capital formation. The personal income tax is the prime exemplar of such systems.

Contrary to common opinion, examination of modern tax codes in the United States, United Kingdom, and some other advanced economies reveals that some portion of human capital investments may be taxed more heavily than the financial investment and tangible physical investments made by households.[2] This state of affairs has emerged clearly where (for the ostensible purpose of raising the national conventional personal savings rate) special tax provisions have permitted the sheltering of income in pension funds, individual retirement accounts, and other savings vehicles. The use of the latter class of instruments for shifting income from the present into the future has thus been favored in comparison with others that can accomplish the same purpose—human capital investment being prominent among them.

On the other hand, it can be pointed out that under conventional systems of income taxation, based upon current earnings rather than the accrual accounting method that typically apply in the cases of physical capital goods, human capital investments are a favored vehicle for young households to use in transfering income (and consumption) into the future.[3] The thrust of this observation, however, is considerably blunted when one considers the structure of marginal income tax rates.

General formulations of optimal tax theory, such as the classic papers of Diamond and Mirrilees (1971), consequently have argued that there should be no taxes levied on intermediate goods. Plainly, human capital investments fall under the heading of intermediate goods, as they are an instrumentality for shifting resources from the present to the future. The practical implications for policy design that can be derived from optimal taxation principles, however, remain less than immediately clear. This is so because in practice human capital may be a mixture of labor supply, capital investment, and a final good, and because it may be necessary to consider general equilibrium effects, as well as the first-order impacts upon the behavior of individual agents.[4]

To move toward specific policy recommendations in this area, it is helpful to reduce the tension between the principle that human capital (being "an intermediate good") should not be taxed at all, and the practical difficulties of attempting to tax income from labor services in a way that would not distort human capital investments. Thus, Judd (1998) suggests continuing to tax workers' incomes but immediately expensing all human capital expenditures: proposing to extend the (automatic) deductibility of foregone earnings costs to all direct education and training outlays. Were a significant portion of educational (and/or training) expenditures to represent "consumption" goods (or bads) it would be appropriate to tax the portion of educational expenditures that generated these. The obvious problems of strictly implementing such a tax policy, however, suggest that reasonably generous caps, instead, might be imposed on the deductibility of direct education and training related expenditures.[5]

Nevertheless, the elimination of taxation of all investment in human capital has been recommended repeatedly by economists and tax analysts (e.g., Boskin 1977, and Kaplow 1996). This partial tax reform proposal, although quite sweeping, nevertheless falls rather short of a second-best policy, because it is not likely to result in a tax regime that is neutral to the formation of different types of capital.[6]

Those who view the persistence of differential tax treatment of different types of capital as a potential source of serious allocational inefficiencies cite this among the arguments favoring still more radical reforms, such as the adoption of taxes on consumption expenditures alone. But the consumption tax proposal—to which public finance economists widely subscribe—compounds two distinct departures from most existing tax regimes' treatment of human capital. First, it removes the tax disadvantage of human capital investments due to the difference between the nondeductibility of the direct cost component of human capital investment and the deductibility of depreciation charges on tangible nonhuman capital. Second, by eliminating the taxation of labor income, it does away with the effects of progressive marginal taxation on the amount of human capital invested privately by individuals (both foregone earnings and direct educational and training costs).[7]

Although the abandonment of progressive taxation is from some viewpoints the radical aspect of consumption tax (and related flat tax) schemes, that aspect of the reformers' proposal is not a logical requirement of shifting from labor incomes to consumption expenditures as the basis for taxation. Furthermore, eliminating the inefficiencies in resource allocation created by differential "tax wedges" (gaps between pretax and after-tax rates of return that vary according to the type of asset) is not an obviously compelling goal for tax policies to pursue. One should bear in mind here the trade-off between static efficiency and dynamic efficiency. Thus, a consistent growth-promoting logic may be read in the tax treatment of investment so as to favor both shorter-lived tangible assets (and intangible nonhuman assets such as patents and software), and comparatively long-lived, intangible human capital on the other hand.[8]

The implications for human capital formation of differences among tax regimes in the methods of income accounting are quite separable from those that derive from the structure of marginal personal income tax rates. The typical, progressive structure of the personal income tax schedules exerts an unambiguously discouraging influence upon the choice of investments in human capital as vehicles for income shifting. This effect is due entirely to the temporal positioning of this particular mode of saving within the household's life cycle. The expensing of foregone earnings costs, as well as any deductions that are allowed for direct education and training costs, comes during the early phase of workers' lives, when incomes and marginal tax rates are low in any case. These investments, especially when supplemented by taking advantage of on-the-job options, however, generate a rising stream of labor earnings that are exposed to higher marginal rates under progressive tax regimes.[9]

Is the adverse impact upon human capital investment a serious drawback of the progressive taxation of labor incomes? Good "natural" experimental data might permit the matter to be resolved empirically, but in its absence economists have turned to simulation models. The latter combine theoretical specifications and parameters estimated from microeconomic data to create quantitative models of household behavior that can be used to evaluate effects of hypothetical alternations in the regime of taxation.[10] According to the results obtained recently with such an approach by Dupor et al. (1996), the results of substituting a flat tax schedule for progressive rates such as exist in the U.S. 1990 tax code indicate that a 10 percent rise of the marginal tax rate over the increasing portion of the individual earnings profile has the effect of reducing investment in human capital by 15 percent.[11]

Quite obviously it is important to consider the general equilibrium repercussions of any significant tax policy changes. It is possible that the immediate positive impact upon the level of human capital investments of setting lower tax rates on labor income—vis-à-vis taxes levied on the returns to physical capital—may well be substantially mitigated over the long run. Indeed, it might be completely nullified by the induced change in the economy's asset portfolio.[12] In the absence of countervailing skill-deepening biases in technological change, the induced increase of the pace of accumulation of human capital (in relationship to the supply of raw labor-power through population growth) should operate to depress the marginal productivity of additional educational training.

Furthermore, to the extent that the contemplated tax reforms induce agents to substitute human capital for physical capital investments, the long-run effect on the level of physical capital per worker in the economy would depress the marginal productivity of labor and drag down before-tax rates of return to human capital.[13]

Dynamic general equilibrium considerations of this kind are particularly relevant when analyzing fiscal policy proposals for large, substantially closed economies. In the situation of small and highly open economies, however, the conclusions of the partial equilibrium analyses previously reviewed remain more applicable, because when international financial flows and labor migration are unobstructed they tend to operate in the long run to peg the before-tax rates of return on human capital and physical capital investments. A small open economy would thus be comparatively free of the counterforces that might otherwise work to curtail the rise in the rate of human capital formation among the indigenous population.

An economy that is open to the movements of workers from abroad, as well as to commodity trade and capital flows, also presents an environment in which reforms that positively affect the level of private after-tax returns on human capital may gain added potency, by inducing selective immigration. These are circumstances that characterize many smaller developed and developing economies, for which the modest tax reform proposal presented in the following sections may well be particularly relevant.

As long as the effect of the reform is to push a substantial portion of the distribution of after-tax private marginal yields on human capital above those elsewhere, it is likely to draw in people with greater potential earnings capacities. The pull would be stronger for individuals who also are more strongly disposed to utilize their inherent and acquired capabilities to gain further education and training, and ultimately to exploit that asset by entering the more highly remunerated occupations.[14] The possibilities of exploiting such effects will therefore be considered more closely in section 5 after the basic features of the UIBEDA scheme have been detailed.

2 A New Proposal: Principal Features of UIBEDAs

The main task here is to set out the features of the proposed reform instrument in detail sufficient to indicate the empirical information that would be required to establish its general feasibility. Although this is best tackled by offering concrete specifications of a hypothetical system, the particulars supplied here are those that lend

themselves well to purposes of exposition, rather than engaging with
the realities of existing administrative institutions and tax codes. The
goal here is to stimulate further discussion of the basic idea and to
engage the expertise of those most acquainted with the institutional
arrangements that would render its implementation practical.

Let us start by considering the simplest practical circumstances, in
which direct costs of educational investment are met out of current
income flows, as would be the case either where the young adult
student had independent means or was receiving inter vivos income
transfers for the purpose from family members. Under the proposed
scheme, neither the recipient nor the household that had borne these
current direct costs would be allowed immediately to enjoy such tax
savings as would be generated by taking them as deductions from
taxable income. Instead, the nominal value of the tax savings would
be recorded in the current year's tax return filed by the student, and
would be credited to an untaxed interest-bearing deduction account
(UIBEDA) established in the name of that individual and identified
by a taxpayer number.

Comprehensiveness is desirable in defining "direct costs" for these
purposes. Thus, this category should be taken to include expenditures for tuition and educational fees, for textbooks, equipment and
supplies purchased in connection with enrollment in formal training
programs, as well as additional expenses for living away from one's
place of residence while engaged in educational and training. It
should be understood that the phrase "formal training programs"
includes instruction at accredited educational and training institutions, and programs of on-the-job training whose reported costs to
the employer or other entity are accepted by the tax authority as an
appropriately deductible business expenditure.[15]

The maximum life of these UIBEDAs would be set uniformly, with
consideration given to the possibility that post-university professional education, and post-graduate training that occasioned direct
costs should likewise generate additional "credits" in the individual's account. The actual life of an account, however, would be a
matter for the account holder's discretion within specified limits.
Thus, after some stipulated initial waiting period from the date at
which it was established, the account either could be liquidated, or
that action could be further deferred until some specified maximum
age (of the account) was reached. The aggregate nominal value of an

UIBEDA—that is, of the portfolio consisting of a bundle variously dated "certified deposits" (direct cost expenditures), each of which would be growing exponentially at their respective government bond rates—could be cashed in for the sole purpose of claiming deductions from the account holder's domestic wage earnings.

Ideally, the UIBEDA should resemble a tax-free "retirement savings bond" in at least one respect: its value grows at a fixed rate of interest (set at, say, the Treasury's long-term borrowing rate in the year that the credit was established) through automatic reinvestment of yields, up to some maximum attainable surrender value. Unlike bonds, however, UIBEDAs would not be transferable, nor would they throw off any "coupon" yields prior to being cashed in. And they would have a variable surrender value even when held as long as was possible.

Once the UIBEDA had been broached, the stream of annual tax deductions would resemble a term annuity in that it would have to be taken in equal amounts (or according to some other pre-specified formula) in each consecutive year during a period of pre-defined length. But unlike annuities, their monetary value would be the resulting annual tax savings and therefore would depend upon the account holder's current income, given the prevailing tax rate schedule(s) that would apply to the UIBEDA account.

The benefits offered under this scheme in the form of future personal tax-savings are intended to induce the account holders to make use of such capabilities as they gain through human capital investment, by working at the higher income occupations that their education qualifies them to enter. The restrictions that have been imposed upon the way in which these benefits can be realized are meant to prevent taxpayers in high-income brackets from abusing the system to escape taxation. Otherwise, they might seek to benefit by claiming a deduction for education-related expenditures in the name of other individuals, especially those who do not intend or are unlikely ever to utilize that "investment" by working in their home country at subsequent dates.[16]

A further problematic issue that the foregoing provisions are designed to address is that an individual account holder might be myopically opportunistic, and so seek to cash in the deduction immediately upon completing her studies, after which she would permanently exit the domestic labor force. The imposed minimum waiting period should serve to diminish the attractiveness of the scheme to such individuals. In addition, because it seems desirable to provide the Treasury with greater predictability in the reduction of taxable incomes due to the liquidation of UIBEDAs, their conversion into an annuity-like stream of deductions should be restricted to take place within a prespecified number of consecutive tax-years.[17]

More generally, although it is desirable not to impose any limitations on individuals' freedom of action by virtue of their having opened an UIBEDA, that principle is not violated by setting the provisions and parameters in a way that would curtail abuse of the entitlement under the scheme.[18] For example, tighter restrictions could be introduced to curtail opportunistic behavior by requiring that to be eligible to exercise the liquidation option, the surrender date, T,[19] be preceded by a minimum number M years during which the account-holder had filed national income tax returns showing positive tax payments.

The effective after-tax yield on UIBEDAs would thus be determined by three sets of conditions: the intervening history of the Treasury's borrowing rate(s), the progressiveness of the prevailing income tax schedule at the time of the account's liquidation, and the steepness of the individual's earnings profile during the period following their education and training investments. The first two of these being under the government's control, it is important that the rates in effect at the time the particular individual's "credit" was deposited in the UIBEDA remained fixed throughout its life, whether or not the Treasury's borrowing rate actually changed. Keeping track of the implicit fiscal obligations of the Treasury to the credits in these accounts will not pose any real burden for modern financial information systems.

It will be apparent that the novel instruments—UIBEDAs—created under such a scheme not only would work to offset the taxation of the interest component in the returns on investment in human capital, but, because their value is increased by utilizing that asset in employment at higher earnings rates within the domestic economy, they add to agents' incentives to use their acquired skills in that manner. UIBEDAs, therefore, have the expected effect of raising future tax revenues derived from whatever public subsidies had been given to the individuals during their education in their country of origin.

3   A Numerical Illustration

To illustrate the magnitudes of the incentives that might be created under a scheme of this kind, we can assume the following investment cost, earnings profile, and tax parameters:

1. Total private costs of university education amount to 60K

2. 0.33 of total private costs are direct costs, the remainder being foregone earnings

3. The 15K of total private direct costs are prepaid by the individual's family and an UIBEDA in her name is established at the end of the tax year in which she matriculated, at age 17

4. 0.06 per annum is the government's nominal borrowing, set for the account at that date

5. The graduate's earnings profile starts at 15K and rises by 7 percent per annum from graduation at age 20 until age 30, and grows thereafter at 3.5 percent per annum until age 45 after which it remains flat (at 50.7K) until retirement at age 60

6. Noneducational deductions amounting to 5.0 percent are allowed on gross earnings above 10K

7. The marginal rate of tax on taxable wage earning is rising between broad earnings bands, as follows: 0.10 in 8K–14.99K, 0.15 in the 15K–24.99K, 0.25 in the 25K–44.99K, and 0.30 for 45K and above

8. The UIBEDA account value is liquidated in equal annual deduction claims over $(M =)$ 5 years

9. The maximum allowed life of an UIBEDA is $T_2 = 25$ years; and the minimum permissive age before an account can be realized is $T_1 = 3$ years, that is, given assumption (3), upon graduation at age 20.

An array of alternative outcomes can be generated, by varying the date at which the account holder exercises her option to begin taking the (five years' worth of) UIBEDA deductions (see table 24.1).

It should be noticed that under the schedules assumed in this table, the nominal value of the UIBEDA's yield of tax savings becomes substantial if these are deferred until after age 40, thereby creating an incentive to defer exercising the deduction and, instead, using it as a vehicle for (educational earnings contingent) savings. This may be seen by comparing the present value at age 20 of 4K

Table 24.1
Calculation of the UIBEDA's scheme's tax impact for individual beneficiaries

	Graduate's age at start of liquidation					
	20	25	30	35	40	45
Nominal value of UIBEDA (000s)	24.0	32.4	43.6	49.0	80.0	107.0
Gross wage income (000s)	15.0	21.3	30.0	35.7	42.6	50.7
Annual value of realized UIBEDA (000s)	4.8	6.5	8.7	9.8	16.0	21.4
Taxable income after UIBEDA (000s)	9.6	14.2	19.1	24.1	25.0	27.3
Annual tax savings from UIBEDA (000s)	0.5	0.8	1.3	1.5	4.0	5.3

Note: See text discussion for underlying assumptions.

worth of annual tax savings realized at ages 40–44, which is 1.2K, or well more than twice the value of exercising the deduction entitlement at age 20, immediately upon post-graduation employment.[20]

Looking at the scheme from a different angle and assuming constancy of these parameters, the 20K (or 25K) in nominal tax savings received between at ages 40–44 (or ages 45–49, respectively), would be sufficient to meet the direct educational investment costs of one of the graduate's children, assuming that child had been born when the graduate herself was age 25–26 (or age 30–31).

By the same token, had the new graduate's *mother* achieved the same earned income level by the time she was age 40–44, under this scheme she would be in a position to receive 20K–25K worth of tax savings. Conveniently, under the assumptions, this amount would be available to be applied toward meeting the current direct educational costs of a college-bound child of her own. From the standpoint of the overlapping generations envisaged in these examples, the UIBEDA thus would function as an individual tax-sheltered, government guaranteed educational endowment fund.

4   Can UIBEAs Pay for Themselves? Public Financial Intermediation under an Intertemporal Balanced-Budget Restriction

An important issue for consideration now is whether the proposed scheme can or cannot satisfy an intertemporal balanced budget constraint—a condition that a prudent treasurer might well be disposed to impose on any such fiscal innovation that involved the surrender of tax revenues.

It is easiest to see what is involved in answering this question by starting from the conditions most favorable to the UIBEDA proposal, namely, where the individual completing university has been induced to do so by the existence of the prospective income tax deductions. It is then straightforward to show—under plausible specifications about the effects on the typical individual's expected earnings profile of having undertaken the educational investment described in section 3, table 24.1—that the Treasury can do better than break even in present value terms. By engaging in this form of financial intermediation, the public sector can emerge with a tax revenue surplus.

To demonstrate this, the foregoing set of assumptions—(1) through (9) in section 3—can be augmented by another:

10. Instead of attending and completing university, the representative agent's alternative opportunity is to enter the labor market with a high school completion certificate and receive a stream of earnings that yield taxable wage income of 12K at age 17, rising to 14K at 20, 17K at 25, and 20K by age 30, but remaining constant thereafter.

Given that empirically plausible specification, the average "college differential" in earnings streams and the corresponding expected incremental income tax revenues recovered on those differences can be calculated, and they can be discounted to find their present value at the date at which the UIBEDA deduction credit was initially granted. For simplicity the latter will be taken to be the individual's twentieth birthday.

A rough approximation, using the tax rates and other parameters in the previous illustrative example, and therefore discounting at the 6 percent long-term government borrowing rate, puts the present value at age 20 of the incremental education-associated tax revenues generated up though age 44 in the neighborhood of 24K.

As all but 3K of the latter is generated during the ages between 29 and 44, it is plain that the Treasury can recover the (present value) of the educational cost deduction credits awarded at age 20 without worrying about the early labor market behavior of recent university graduates. In other words, complete recoupment will be achieved even were the young worker to take her training abroad after graduating, so long as she returned ten years later to recommence working in her home country—and was able to command at least the same, stipulated earnings profile for an university graduate with the equivalent of ten years post-graduation work experience.

Now consider what happens when the UIBEDA account is cashed in by a worker at age 45 who had been in continuous employment up to that point. A total of 26.5K in current tax savings enjoyed by her during that year and the following four years has an initial (age 20) present value of 5.1K. To find the present value (at that date) of the Treasury's net incremental revenue burden, however, one must consider that even with the UIBEDA deductions, the university graduate's taxable income is higher than that of the high school graduate. It therefore yields as much as an extra 6.8K worth of nominally valued tax revenue per year when she is in the age range from 45 through 49. The cumulated amount has a present value of 6.5K at age 20, which means that there would be a small net gain for the Treasury, amounting to $(6.5 - 5.1 =)$ 1.4K—even during the years when the UIBEDA deductions were being realized.

Quite obviously, there are further earnings differentials and corresponding incremental tax revenues to be enjoyed, if our representative worker does not withdraw from the domestic labor force after exercising her deduction credit entitlements. Suppose she continues in employment between age 50 and 60: in the scenario envisaged, the present value (at age 20) of the cumulated incremental income tax receipts flowing to the Treasury from this educated agent's earnings in the decade preceding retirement would approach 9K.

There are several ways in which to interpret the availability of the aggregated $(4K + 1.4K + 9K = 14.4K)$ worth of present value tax revenue surplus that emerges from the foregoing calculations.

1. Under the assumption that the representative worker in each case would be employed continuously up until age 60, the intertemporal balance budget constraint would be satisfied even if much smaller differentials existed between the expected earnings profiles of high school and university graduates.

2. The same would hold were an allowance to be made for less than full-time employment by the average college graduate: an expected rate of unemployment from all causes that averaged out at 9 percent per year (in every year from age 20 through age 60), combined with a proportionate one-third lowering of the graduate's full-time earnings profile would leave the intertemporal balanced budget constraint satisfied, that is, $(0.09 + 0.33)(24K + 1.4K + 9K) = 20K$.

3. Alternatively, the figures imply that the direct costs of university-training these additional college attendees could be publicly sub-sidized at a cost of 14.4K, so that a total (public and private) educational investment outlay amounting to 34.4K per student could be justified under this proposal as being consistent with main-tenance by the Treasury of its intertemporal balanced constraint.

4. One also may conclude from the foregoing that the growing risks of disability and death, or of retirement and emigration after age 50, would not pose a considerable threat to the Treasury's ability to sat-isfy the intertemporal balanced budget constraint.

It is now necessary to reconsider the premise for the preceding calculation, namely, that the gains and costs to the Treasury are solely those arising from the behavior of agents who the UIBEDA scheme induced to attend and complete a university education. Obviously, that is not realistic. The UIBEDA benefits (which produce losses of tax revenue for the Treasury) also would be enjoyed by some people who in any case would have completed their univer-sity education (and gained the associated differential earnings). The Treasury gains no incremental tax revenues by granting such per-sons a UIBEDA deduction.

So, the question of interest can be framed this way: In the context of our illustrative example, what fraction (p) of each cohort of col-lege graduates would have to be induced by the UIBEDA scheme to obtain their degree for the Treasury to cover the lost revenues on the other $(1 - p)$ portion, and thus break even?

The answer can be obtained almost immediately from the esti-mates produced in the foregoing calculations. Since the $1 - p$ of the cohort cost the Treasury a present value tax revenue loss of 5.1K per capita, and p generate a present value tax revenue surplus of 34.4K per capita, the magnitude that perfectly balances the one against the other in this case is $p = 0.12$. In other words, an increase in the pre-UIBEDA number of high school graduates who go on to graduate from college of only 13.6 percent ($[0.12/0.88] \times 100$) would suffice for the UIBEDA scheme to pay for itself in present value terms.

On its face, this seems a rather modest required impact on college participation (and completion) rates. Even allowing for a 10 percent average probability of yearly earnings losses (due to unemployment and disabilities) among the induced increment of college degree holders, the inducement effect required for the UIBEDA scheme to break even still remains quite low at only 16 percent. It must be said that for a country (such as the United States), where the faction of the high school graduates who go on to complete college is already as large as 0.7–0.8, moving up to the 0.81–0.93 range is not likely to be so readily accomplished simply by means of financial subsidies.[21] On the other hand, in a country where the faction of secondary school leavers that complete university is closer to 0.4 (as it is in contemporary Britain), the 16 percent gain entailed in reaching the 0.46 level does not appear unachievable by means of incentives such as those which the UIBEDA scheme would provide.

Unfortunately, there is not much quantitative evidence that allows one to carry this exploratory discussion much farther. A notable exception to the paucity of direct evidence is the body of econometric findings recently provided by Heckman and his collaborators. It has led them to conclude that in the United States the financing of post-secondary school education does not constitute a significant obstacle to university attendance by males, save for a quite small segment of the population.[22] The observation of a marked positive correlation between parental family income and college participation rates, however, is on this view attributable to structural factors of a more long-run nature: motivational and environmental factors that result in the disadvantages of poor educational preparation, and self-image that burden children in many low-income households environments, reducing their ability to meet university admission requirements and lowering confidence in being able complete a degree program leading to credentials that will prove valuable in the labor market.

If short-term financing constraints were indeed the serious obstacle to human capital formation in countries other than the United States, tax reforms of the sort considered here probably would not be the best policy instrument with which to tackle that problem. Yet, there is another source of difficulty relating to the private financing of higher education that may be successfully addressed by the introduction of the UIBEDA scheme. It appears that in some high-income societies, young adults and their parents in lower income households are reluctant to accumulate substantial personal indebtedness—especially without there being any corresponding tangible asset (such as a house, or a car) that could serve eventually to repay the debt.[23] Even in the United States it has been noticed that the take-up rate on subsidized college loans under government programs targeted toward students from low-income families remains low: more people are eligible to claim this form of support than do so.[24]

Such behavior is not so difficult to understand. Coming from family settings where as a rule there is no prior history of successful education-based economic advancement, these youngsters would be reasonable in attaching a high-risk discount to the economic returns that they are told can be anticipated on this form of investment. It is true that the loan default penalties as a rule are not exacting. But the tenets of financial responsibility that aspirant middle-class parents of modest means are likely to implant in their offspring prospect do not encourage a relaxed attitude toward the prospects of carrying an unpaid debt of significant size in relation to post-graduate earnings. They are thus wary of the risks of beginning adult life and having to seeking responsible positions of employment while burdened by a bad credit rating, should they become unable to maintain the scheduled educational loan repayments.

This latter line of explanation is at least consistent with the observation that rates of continuation to university among secondary school leavers vary positively with family context factors that are correlated with persistent parental income levels, with parental (especially mother's) educational attainments, and with indicators of the individual's academic ability.[25]

Thus, by giving individuals a deferred yield, work-contingent asset coupled to their educational debts, the UIBEDA scheme conceivably could contribute to counteracting such inhibitions about borrowing for one's university education and encourage planning for that of one's children.

It may be remarked, further, that the conceptually and empirically useful distinction that may be drawn between short-run credit constraints and long-run (family background) factors constraining participation in higher education should not obscure the point that expectations matter, so that it is only unanticipated short-run constraints that are clearly distinguishable.

The point frequently made is that human capital formation is an extended dynamic process in which each stage builds upon foundations created at a prior stage.[26] The logic of this justifies the view that providing higher education subsidies for youths whose families did not expect them to be able to attend university is not likely to be effective in fostering higher rates of college enrollment among those groups in the population. Hence, the very same considerations which argue that there will be only rather weak short-run effects of educational subsidies targeted to students from low-income families, suggests that that institutionalized credible expectations of the future availability of loans and tax subsidies for scholastically qualified young people would have much bigger positive effects in eliciting higher university enrollment rates. Their effects would work through the alteration of the family environment during childhood and adolescence, and hence they would exceed those identified simply with the removal of short-run credit constraints during the period of university attendance.

5   Extending UIBEDA Eligibility to International Migrants

An extensive economic literature has been devoted to the subject of international migration and its effects upon income in the sending countries. The portions of it that are generally thought to be most immediately germane to policies affecting a region's human capital endowments usually focus upon the effects of so-called brain drains.[27] Emigration of the more able, and more highly educated and skilled members of the population provides a form of windfall capital transfer to immigration regions. The prospect of an uncontrolled redistribution from developing economies where human capital is relatively scarce, toward the economically advanced, high income economies where complementary resources are available to employ such assets at much higher private marginal rates of return, is indeed a source for serious concern.[28]

This is so especially in development contexts where there are critical scarcities of educated personnel required to maintain the minimal functions of a modern government, to effect the transfer of superior technologies, and to facilitate economic and political interactions with other more economically advanced societies. On the other hand, in countries that enjoy substantial supply-side capabilities for expanding the numbers who can be trained, and where the problem is one of insufficient private demand for investment in human capital, efforts to curtail out-migration of the highly trained may well be counterproductive. Their effect may be to further weaken private incentives to invest in education.

Conversely, investment in human capital might be increased in some situations by allowing nationals (whose expected earnings potentials would thereby be raised) to choose to work abroad to realize those benefits gains. This effect could alter the investment behavior of a much larger portion of the population than that which actually would emigrate, and therefore might well increase the net positive impact of public subsidies upon the domestic rate of human capital formation.[29]

Where a liberal policy stance on the "brain drain" question is thus warranted, the implications for the implementation of the UIBEDA scheme are quite clear. All who had borne some of the direct and indirect costs of investing in their education and training should be eligible to accumulate and hold deduction credits in a UIBEDA, whether or not they subsequently take their human capital abroad. Transparently, the UIBEDA would be of value to those who emigrated only if they returned to take employment at home at a later point in their careers, hopefully with their productivity having been enhanced by the intervening foreign work experience.

Establishing automatic deductibility would result in emigrating nationals receiving claims to UIBEDA benefits whose rising future value would constitute an inducement for them to return to their country of origin after gaining further training and work experience abroad. This aspect of the proposal thus may be viewed as a means of encouraging voluntary repatriation among more highly educated nationals whose knowledge, skills and overseas connections are likely to be of considerable value in their country of origin.[30]

Although it is also likely that such individuals would have made further, indirect investments in human capital while working outside their country of origin, such expenditures need not eligible for further deduction credits in their UIBEDA accounts. Closing that option will eliminate a source of considerable administrative costs.

Turning now from the question of the eligibility of emigrating nationals for UIBEDA benefits, it should be observed that the application of the scheme in the case of immigrants is likely to be even more potent for a small open economy. Encouraging a substantial inflow of individual who have special, high-skill qualifications would tend to lower the costs and raise the profitability of the domestic industries that made intensive use of such workers. Under competitive conditions the benefits would be shared indirectly by others, as purchasers of their goods and services.

If the effects in the employing industries were to increase investment for additional plant and equipment capacity, the accompanying increases in labor input demands could be sufficient to counteract the downward relative price effect of immigration on the level of remuneration offered to new, domestically trained workers. Consequently, the moderating effects of an inflow of trained workers from abroad upon the incipiently rising local wage premia paid to workers with particular occupational skills need not result in a weakening of the long-run incentives for the domestic population to invest in such training.

The general point here is that programs promoting selective immigration on the one hand, and tax policies promoting human capital formation in the domestic population on the other, can be designed in ways that render them dynamic complements. When their effects are considered over a suitably extended but nonetheless finite time horizon, it appears quite natural to make short-run use of the features of the UIBEDA scheme as an instrument to promote selective immigration by nonnationals who have made education and training investments in other parts of the world.

The mechanism of selection available to the government in this case is the determination of the list of eligible overseas training institutions, and the date of receipt of specified degrees and competence certifications that would qualify immigrants to set up UIBEDA accounts when they first entered employment. Evidence would need to be submitted also to establish the direct expenditures incurred overseas in connection with obtaining those credentials. For administrative simplicity, however, no deduction credits would be allowed for indirect investments in the form of foregone earnings.

Where a foreign government has made provision for the extinguishing of such educational debts as a condition for permitting the trainees to emigrate or to remain abroad in employment, the government of a skill-deficit region might manage to recruit such workers by extending the UIBEDA scheme's benefits to them. Loan guarantees from the government in the region of immigration can facilitate refinancing of external student indebtedness, and the expenditures represented by the new, domestic loan can then be made eligible for treatment within the UIBEDA scheme on the same basis as newly contracted educational investments.[31]

Immigration offers the most direct and flexible means for a small economy to transform its domestic labor supply conditions to facilitate particular lines of economic expansion. The evident intention of the foregoing proposals is to place in the hands of the government another (fiscal) tool that could encourage a rapid inflow of migrants, thereby not only raising the average human capital endowment of the working age population, but doing so in a controlled and selectively targeted manner.

What of the drawbacks? It is likely that a country that extended its UIBEDA scheme to encourage selective immigration and repatriation would be accused of engaging in a "beggar thy neighbor" tax policy. If successful, it would be seen as inducing brain drains from other regions. Nevertheless, it is important to distinguish the present idea from the broad class of industrial policies and commercial policies that are more properly labeled "protectionist" and detrimental to global economic welfare. Tariffs and subsidies for domestic producers are instruments of national economic policy that give rise to both local and global inefficiencies. By contrast, however, the removal of differential taxation that is discouraging to individual investment in human capital would work to improve the allocation of resources in the economy that implements the reform.

As is the case with protective tariffs and strategic trade policies more generally, extension of the UIBEDA scheme's benefits to cover immigrants could provoke retaliation from other countries, especially those who perceived themselves to be losing the services of their highly trained and uncommonly productive workers.[32] Retaliation in kind would seek to neutralize the effects of the external reform by removing the disability that their own tax regime placed upon human capital investments, and possibly would introduce similar tax concessions for immigrants.

Unlike retaliatory protectionism, however, the result of generalized reactions of this sort would make capital markets function more inefficiently in the long run—both intra- and internationally. It is true that the benefits to the initiating reformer(s) eventually would be dissipated as a result of the global response. That, however, is not an argument against implementing the proposed reform in the first place. Indeed, if the threat of retaliation carries any implications for policy, it would seem to argue for moving quickly to introduce the UIBEDA and thereby realize the "first-mover" advantages that a small, open economy would obtain under the scheme.

6   Concluding Observations on Issues of Implementation

For such a program to be effective, it is essential that its statutory provisions should clearly prevent subsequent alterations (whether by executive or legislative action) in the obligations of the government as those are defined by the terms of established UIBEDA holdings.

Apart from the necessarily variable current government nominal borrowing rate that sets the yield on deduction credits, the terms of individual UIBEDAs ought to remain fixed throughout the life of these accounts. Establishing a reasonable measure of "credible commitment" on this issue, however, would not require binding future governments to leave tax rates unaltered, or rule out changes in expenditure eligibility provisions that applied in the cases of new entrants to the system.

Conceptually, what is appropriate is to render the assets formed within each UIBEDA as secure from the risk of default as are the government's debt instruments. Domestic inflation is a form of constructive default on the part of the state, the risk of which would (or should) be a concern for those being encouraged to acquire the new species of public obligation represented by the UIBEDA. In view of the fact that the great bulk of these obligations will held by tax-paying residents, this issue can readily be addressed by fixing the real yield on deductions credited to these accounts and linking the nominal value of the latter to the domestic consumer price index. There would be no need to provide separate protection against the risk of depreciation in the country's currency vis-à-vis other currencies.

The problem of establishing the credibility of the government's commitment to the proposed program of tax reform can be approached from another direction, noting a feature of the UIBEDA scheme that would have the effect of rendering its adoption less readily reversible. Once in place, it would complement policies of replacing direct subsidies for higher education expenditures with regime of financing based on a mixture of (publicly guaranteed) loans and (means tested) grants to needy students. That is a transition many high-income countries will find themselves having to undertake as they seek to raise the proportion of secondary school leavers who go on to university.[33]

Once "all but free tuition" and maintenance allowances for all but university students from low-income families had been withdrawn and replaced by government guaranteed education loans, the benefits promised under of the UIBEDA scheme would become quite difficult for a representative government to abrogate or significantly curtail without inciting middle-class outrage and retaliation at the polls.

Plainly, one intention underlying the proposal to introduce UIBEDA-like reforms in the context of developing economies is to create a future material opportunity that would not only transform popular attitudes about the value of undertaking investment in the further education of secondary school leavers and university graduates, but would tend to promote a more general attitudinal change. Governmental commitment to these modest fiscal reforms could go some way toward fostering a greater awareness of the palpable benefits that individuals and their families could anticipate by embracing the more general cultural and psychological orientation that is associated commonly with deferral of gratification and personal commitments to forward planning touching many aspects of human life.

Acknowledgments

My initial thinking about this subject was clarified in conversations about it with Kenneth Judd, Ronald McKinnon and James Poterba, at Stanford during Fall 2000. I am grateful to have had the benefit of Murray Shadbolt's penetrating comments on an earlier draft (circulated under the title "UIBEDA—A Modest Proposal for Reforming the Tax Treatment of Intangible Human Capital Investments.") Peter Temin also made very useful suggestions for improving the exposition, and James Heckman's comments drew my attention to important recent econometric evidence bearing upon human capital policy. The final draft has benefited from the editorial advice of Ravi Kanbur and comments by an anonymous reviewer. None of the people who I have the pleasure of thanking here necessarily subscribe to the tax reform proposal advanced in this essay, nor should they be held responsible for failing to correct such deficiencies as it may be found to contain.

Notes

1. David and Goddard (2001, sect. II 2) provides an extensive review of the theoretical and empirical economics literature about these propositions, including material from

historical studies. See Bassanini and Scarpetta (2001) for a recent study of the OECD countries that finds recent econometric support for the asserted impact of human capital formation on economic growth during the second half of the twentieth century. For a related discussion of the links between policy settings, institutions, and economic growth in twenty-one OECD countries during 1971–1998, based on a survey of recent economics journal publications, descriptive quantitative material and cross-country time-series regression analyses, see Bassanini, Scarpetta, and Hemmings (2001).

2. See, for example, Judd (1998) and Steuerle (1996).

3. See Kaplow (1996). Under accrual accounting, the returns from investment are included in current income; the costs of the asset are capitalized (not immediately expensed) and depreciated at a rate reflecting its "economic service life," that is, the temporal change in the present value of the remaining stream of returns; current depreciation charges are set against current income. Were accrual income taxes to be applied to human capital, the effect would be less favorable to investment in education and training than the conventional income tax regime. The reason is that such investments tilt the time-profile of earnings upward, and conventional income taxes do not impose additional taxes on the implicit interest component of higher later returns—whereas an accrual income system would do so.

4. See, for example, Boskin (1977), Davies and Whalley (1991), Trostel (1993), Dupor et al. (1996), Heckman, Lochner, and Taber (1998), and Judd (1998).

5. Furthermore, for the sake of consistency and completeness, the central tax authority should allow individuals to deduct from taxable income any mandatory community tax payments that were devoted to local public education and training activities. The latter step would preserve neutrality in the tax treatment of privately versus publicly provided educational services.

6. Physical capital goods purchased by businesses cannot be fully expensed, that is, set off against earnings by firms that pay corporate income taxes; instead, most national and local tax codes allow depreciation charges on these durables to be deducted from gross earnings.

7. Both features of the proposed reform are mimicked by the less sweeping proposal to shift to a "flat tax" on wage income, with full deductibility of human capital costs.

8. In the first case the tax bias tends to promote rapid turnover of elements of the tangible capital stock that embody recent technological innovations; in the second case the tax bias works to compensate for the greater systematic obsolescence risks to which owners of human capital are exposed by policies that promote more rapid rates of advance of fundamental knowledge and technological progress.

9. By comparison, the option of sheltering pension contributions (with equal pretaxes rates of return) is a more attractive vehicle for personal savings; pension proceeds—unlike the returns from educational investments—typically are realized (during retirement) when earned income levels and marginal rates of income taxation are expected to be lower.

10. The paradigmatic approach to the problem (following Heckman 1976) postulates that individuals make educational investment decisions within the framework of a model of intertemporal expected utility maximization, subject to the constraints of a human capital production function and private borrowing in perfect (financial) capital

markets. Dupor et al. (1996), for example, econometrically estimate the parameters of a life-cycle human capital investment model of U.S. white males (based upon synthetic cohort data for various educational attainment groups in the 1970 census), and use these to simulate the effects of various tax regimes.

11. In other words, the (arc-) elasticity of education and training investment with respect to the marginal tax rate is roughly −1.5.

12. This proposition is brought out in the work of Auerbach and Kotlikoff (1987), Davies and Whaley (1991), Heckman, Lochner, and Taber (1998), and Trostel (1993).

13. Consequently, as Trostel (1993) shows, the after-tax interest rate in the economy's steady-state equilibrium need not be raised by removing taxes on human capital investment.

14. Although this may achieve the purpose of augmenting the stock of human capital in the receiving country, it would do so without stimulating additional investment in education and training among the preexisting population—except indirectly, under some special conditions. Indeed, if immigrants who have been educated abroad bring capabilities that render them substitutes rather than complements for domestically trained members of the workforce, it is conceivable that an unrestricted inflow from overseas will so alter domestic labor supply conditions as to depress the demand for in-country training. See section 6 for further discussion.

15. It may be noted that where local tax authorities subsidize educational and vocational training programs and use local excise and property taxes for that purpose, and where all such taxes are not already treated as deductible under the national tax code, that fraction of local tax rates attributable to the subsidies (as announced by local authorities) could be used by households to calculate an allowable deduction.

16. If the tax benefits derived were to be significantly separated from the size of the incremental earnings power created by the "deductible expenses," a serious problem of moral hazard would arise: there would be little incentive for "educational investors" seeking to tax-shelter future (other) income to care about the efficacy of the educational/training services they purchased.

17. As described thus far, these deductions would start no sooner than year T_1, and end no later than T_2 after the account was first established; the entire value of the account would have to be liquidated by exercising deduction claims (in equal amounts) spread over the N consecutive years, where $N = T_2 - T_1$. Individuals would be free to privately insure against the risks of disability or other sources of taxable personal income losses during the N years when their UIBEDA was being liquidated.

18. Or enable it to satisfy an intertemporal balanced budget constraint, a requirement that is considered in section 4.

19. Following the notation in note 9, the surrender date must satisfy the restrictions: $T_1 \leq T \leq (T + M) \leq T_2$.

20. As will be seen in section 4, the viability of the scheme from the Treasury's standpoint will depend upon the gross pretax rate of incremental earnings growth from educational investments being expected to maintain a long-term yield rate that exceeds the yield on long-term government borrowing. Otherwise, the scheme becomes a (low) minimum yield guarantee for private investments in human capital formation.

21. More will be said on this matter in what follows.

22. This view has emerged from the findings reported by Cameron and Heckman (1998), Carneiro and Heckman (2002), Carneiro, Heckman and Manoli (2002). They report that short-run credit constraints are binding in the case of only 4 percent of the male population.

23. Or, in the case of appreciating assets, provide collateral for additional borrowing in future emergency circumstances. Systematic evidence on "the willingness to borrow" is lacking. In Britain, however, the fear among low-income students and their families of having accumulated substantial debt upon graduation is widely accepted as a constraint on the restructuring higher education finances. This reluctance to make use of existing student loan programs is cited in connection with the observation that the Labour government's withdrawal of student maintenance grants and the introduction of modest fees in 2000 was followed by a decline in the proportion of university enrollments comprised of students from low-income families. As a consequence, favorable consideration is being given by the Treasury to provide "higher education maintenance allowances" (HEMAs) on a means-tested basis to students in the 16–18 age range who remained in full-time (secondary) education, and to university student in the 18 plus age range. For many students whose parental family incomes fall in the range below £30,000, the contemplated MEMA would cover the present university fees. See, for example, "Grants may be restored for poorer students," *The Guardian*, 9 August 2002, 2.

24. Carneiro and Heckman (2002) cite Orfield's (1992) findings that students who are eligible for Pell Grants and Perkins Loans do not claim support from those sources. Various explanations have been suggested, ranging from the complexity of the applications process to the view that students from low-income families anticipate low (risk adjusted) rates of return that simply do not justify the investment of the opportunity costs of college atteendance. See Carneiro, Heckman, and Manoli (2002) for further discussion.

25. See Cameron and Heckman (1998) and Carniero, Heckman, and Manoli (2002).

26. See, for example, David and Goddard (2001) for a synthetic review of the literature on this theme; Carneiro, Heckman, and Manoli (2002, 69) sum up the same point succinctly: "Learning begets learning because of dynamic complementarities."

27. See, for example, Bhagwati and Wilson (1989) and World Bank (1995).

28. Thus, the *World Development Report* (World Bank, 1995, 64) asks: "Can something be done to stop the exodus of trained workers from poorer countries?"

29. See, for example, Stark, Helmenstein, and Prskawetz (1997) and Stark and Wang (2000).

30. Given the parameters of the calculations in sections 3 and 4, it can be seen that for individuals in the age range between 35 and 45, the relocation costs of repatriation otherwise would become a disincentive that firms in the home region would have to overcome in order to repatriate them.

31. In effect, immigrants with approved educational credentials could be made eligible (upon entering domestic employment) to receive educational loans in the amount of their preexisting indebtedness on the same terms as are available to residents, provided those funds are applied to extinguish their previously incurred debts. Upon doing so, the full amount of such outlays could be made the basis on which UIBEDA credits would be accumulated. A more cautious approach might be adopted to

increase the probability that the refinancing loans would be repaid: UIBEDA credits would be granted only upon production of evidence of actual domestic loan repayments. In principle, such a scheme could be implemented using private lenders for the refinancing activity, with some government guarantees to keep interest rates at the same level as those being offered to domestic students.

32. Other nations might chose an alternative strategic response to an externally induced brain drain: curtailing the freedom of its population to work abroad. This, however, is completely analogous to blocking the outward movement of financial capital, and, *as a* long-run policy it, too, would be injurious to the economic interests of the population.

33. This issue currently confronts the United Kingdom, where the university continuation rate among secondary school-leavers has risen to a bit over 42 percent and the Labour government has announced 50 percent as the target rate to be reached by 2010. The latter will still fall well below current U.S. levels. Indeed, the U.S. college participation rate fluctuated in the 40–52 percent range over the course during the 1970–1998 period even for male high school completers (ages 18–24) whose parental families occupied *the bottom quartile of the family income distribution*. The corresponding participation rates for the top half of the family income distribution ranged from 61–81 percent. (See Caniero and Heckman 2002, figure 1.) At present the Labour government in Britain finds itself trying to cope with the legacy of the fiscally reckless but politically adroit Conservative Party initiatives begun in the 1980s, which set in motion the rise in university enrollment rates without providing proportionate incremental funding for higher education from general tax revenues. As a consequence, public funding for higher education per student per university student declined by roughly 40 percent since the late 1970s. See, for example, "Higher education for all: The missing ingredient is a graduate tax," *The Guardian*, 9 August 2002, 19.

References

Auerbach, Alan-J., and Laurence J. Kotlikoff. 1987. *Dynamic Fiscal Policy*. Cambridge: Cambridge University Press.

Bassanini, Andrea, and Stefano Scarpetta. 2001. "Does Human Capital Matter for Growth in OECD Countries?: Evidence from Pooled Mean-group Estimates." OECD Economics Department working paper no. 282. ECO/WKP (2001) 8, 31 January.

Bassanini, Andrea, Stefano Scarpetta, and Phillip Hemmings. 2001. "Economic Growth: The Role of Policies and Institutions." OECD Economics Department working paper no. 283 ECO/WKP (2001) 9, 31 January.

Bhagwati, Jagdish, and John D. Wilson. 1989. *Income Taxation and International Mobility*. Cambridge, MA: MIT Press.

Boskin, Michael J. 1977. "Notes on the Tax Treatment of Human Capital," in U.S. Department of Treasury Office of Tax Analysis, *Conference on Tax Research, 1975*, 185–195. Washington, DC: U.S. GPO.

Cameron, Steven, and James J. Heckman. 1998. "Life Cycle Schooling and Dynamic Selection Bias: Models and Evidence for Five Cohorts of American Males." *Journal of Political Economy* 106 (2): 262–333.

Carneiro, Pedro, and James J. Heckman. 2002. "The Evidence on Credit Constraints in Post-Secondary Schooling." *The Economic Journal* 112 (October): 1–29.

Carniero, J., J. Heckman, and D. Manoli. 2002. "Human Capital Policy." Department of Economics working paper, University of Chicago, July.

David, Paul A., with John Gabriel Goddard [Lopez]. 2001. "Knowledge, Capabilities and Human Capital Formation in Economic Growth." *New Zealand Treasury working paper*, no. 13 (June), 143. Available in pdf format at: ⟨www.treasury.govt.nz/workingpapers/2001⟩.

Davies, James, and John Whalley. 1991. "Taxes and Capital Formation: How Important Is Human Capital?," in *National Saving and Economic Performance*, ed. B. Douglas Bernheim and John B. Shoven, 163–200. Chicago: University of Chicago Press (for NBER).

Diamond, Peter, and James A. Mirrlees. 1971. "Optimal Taxation and Public Production: I, and II." *American Economic Review* 61 (1 and 3, respectively): 8–27, 261–278.

Dupor, Bill, Lance Lochner, Christopher Taber, and Mary Beth Witteking. 1996. "Some Effects of Taxes on Schooling and Training." *American Economic Review* 86 (1): 340–346.

Eaton, Jonathan, and Harvey S. Rosen. 1980. "Taxation, Human Capital and Uncertainty." *American Economic Review* 70 (4): 705–715.

Goddard, J. Gabriel. 2000. "The Conditions of Entrepreneurship: Non-verifiable Human Capital, Endogenous Technological Opportunities, and Financial Institutions." University of Oxford, mimeo.

Heckman, James J. 1976. "Estimates of a Human Capital Production Function Embedded in a Life-Cycle Model of Labor Supply," in *Household Production and Consumption*, ed. Nestor E. Terleckyj, 227–264. New York: Columbia University Press (for NBER).

Heckman, James J., Lance Lochner, and Christopher Taber. 1998. "Explaining Rising Wage Inequality: Explorations with a Dynamic General Equilibrium Model of Labor Earnings with Heterogeneous Agents." *Review of Economic Dynamics* 1 (1): 1–58.

Heckman, James J., Jeffrey A. Smith, and Rebecca R. Roselius. 1994. "U.S. Education and Training Policy: A Re-evaluation of the Underlying Assumptions Behind the 'New Consensus,'" in *Labor Markets, Employment Policy, and Job Creation*, ed. Lewis C. Solomon and Alec R. Levenson, 83–121. Boulder, CO: Westview.

Judd, Kenneth L. 1998. "Taxes, Uncertainty and Human Capital." *American Economic Review* 88 (2): 289–292.

Kaplow, Louis. 1996. "On the Divergence between "Ideal" and Conventional Income-Tax Treatment of Human Capital." *American Economic Review* 86 (2): 347–352.

Orfield, G. 1992. "Money, Equity and College Access." *Harvard Educational Review* 2 (3): 337–372.

Steuerle, C. Eugene. 1996. "How Should Government Allocate Subsidies for Human Capital?" *American Economic Review* 86 (1): 353–357.

Stark, Oded, Christian Helmenstein, and Alexia Prskawetz. 1997. "A Brain Gain with a Brain Drain." *Economics Letters* 55 (2): 227–234.

Stark, Oded, and Yong Wang. 2000. "Inducing Human Capital Formation: Migration as a Substitute for Subsidies." University of Oslo, Economics Department working paper. November.

Trostel, Philip A. 1993. "The Effects of Taxation on Human Capital." *Journal of Political Economy* 101 (2): 327–350.

World Bank. 1995. *World Development Report 1995*. New York: Oxford University Press.

25

Births, Recoveries, Vaccinations, and Externalities

Mark Gersovitz

At the core of an economic definition of public health are the market failures and equity concerns that justify public interventions in the health sector. One important intervention is public promotion of vaccinations. A prominent rationale for these programs is a particular market failure, the externalities that arise when people who become infectious do not take account of the costs they impose on others.

Every economist knows that Stiglitz has made vast and varied contributions of importance to economics. As far as I know, however, he has never written any paper in the new field of economic epidemiology: the economic approach to infectious diseases and their control. Nonetheless, he has become a party, perhaps even an unknowing one, to a controversy over whether externalities associated with infections justify government promotion of vaccinations. The reason is that editions of his text, *Economics of the Public Sector* (1986, 1988, 2000), briefly discuss infectious diseases and vaccinations as examples of externalities:

Those who are vaccinated incur some cost (discomfort, time, money, risk of getting the disease from a bad batch of the vaccine). They receive some private benefit, in reduced likelihood of getting the disease, but a major part of the benefit is a public good, the reduced incidence of the disease in the community, from which all benefit. In many cases, the private costs exceed the private benefits, but the social benefits ... far exceed the costs. Because of the free rider problem, governments frequently require individuals to become vaccinated. (Stiglitz 1988, 120)

... while the main beneficiary of a vaccination may be the individual protected, and there is a significant marginal cost of vaccinating an additional individual, the public health benefits from universal vaccination—the reduced incidence of the disease, possibly its eradication—are benefits from which no one can be excluded. (Stiglitz 2000, 134)

These quotations stake out a clear position that vaccination against infectious diseases poses problems of externalities and that public policy can mitigate them. Consequently, the earliest quotation has provided a starting point for Francis (1997) who presents a model with the contrary conclusion, that infectious diseases do not generate externalities, at least not ones that should be offset by public policy. In turn, Francis's questioning of Stiglitz's position is shared by Philipson (2000, especially 1763–1764):

> Indeed, relying on standard arguments about the positive external effects of disease prevention, economists often [argue] for an active public role in the prevention of infectious diseases, such as AIDS. However, economists have rarely attempted to explain patterns of disease occurrence or to evaluate public interventions in the context of a society with individuals who do the best they can given their constraints. Such recent analysis ... has cast ... doubt on the old textbook arguments by economists. (Stiglitz 1997, 15).

Despite the attractive intuition of Stiglitz's discussion, one important aspect of vaccinations does militate against externalities: vaccinations are plausibly a discrete choice. Francis makes this natural assumption and adds to it the assumption that decision makers are homogenous in ways both explicit and implicit. There are, therefore, very limited internal margins of adjustment (either vaccinate or not) and no external margins of adjustment. These assumptions cast suspicion on Francis's conclusion and the questioning of Stiglitz's position by him and others. The issue of vaccinations in public health therefore badly needs some further modeling.

Although brief, Stiglitz's comments raise some additional important subsidiary issues. For one thing, he emphasizes the possibilities of eradication, one important consideration in modeling the dynamics of infectious diseases and the role for policy. For another, he introduces the issue of compulsory vaccination programs versus market-based subsidy schemes.

To further understand externalities in vaccinations, the following sections set out two models of infectious disease dynamics and optimal policy that subsume Francis's model and conclusions. Francis's conclusions only obtain as a special case. There is, in general, an externality connected to vaccinations and one that justifies government intervention.

1   The Social Planner's Problem

1.1   *The Dynamic Constraints*

The starting point for the study of optimal policy toward infectious diseases is mathematical epidemiology (Anderson and May 1991). It provides the dynamic constraints that condition decisions about infectious diseases. This chapter focuses on vaccination against diseases transmitted from person to person rather than ones transmitted by vectors.

The total number of people (N) comprises: (1) the susceptibles (S); (2) the infected and infectious (I); and (3) the vaccinated and thereby *u*ninfectible (U):

$$N = S + I + U. \tag{1}$$

The respective population proportions are s, i, and u, with $s + i + u = 1$. The birth rate of the population is $\varepsilon \geq 0$. Deaths occur as a proportion, $\delta \geq 0$, of all groups at the same rate; in this sense, the disease is not fatal. Net population change is

$$\dot{N} = (\varepsilon - \delta)N. \tag{2}$$

The number of susceptibles changes according to

$$\dot{S} = \varepsilon N - \delta S - Q - \alpha Si. \tag{3}$$

The first part of the right-hand side presupposes that all newborns are susceptible. The second part deducts those susceptibles who die. The third part deducts those susceptibles, Q, who are vaccinated at time t. The fourth part deducts those susceptibles who become infected. Under the assumption of random contacts, the probability per contact of a susceptible person's meeting an infected (and infectious) person is the proportion of infected people in the population, $i = I/N$ and Si is the number of susceptibles who do so. The factor α is an adjustment incorporating both the rate of contact and the inherent infectiousness of an infected (or susceptibility of a susceptible).

The number of infecteds evolves according to

$$\dot{I} = \alpha Si - \delta I. \tag{4}$$

The first term on the right-hand side has been discussed in conjunction with equation (3) and the second in conjunction with equation (2). Finally, the number vaccinated evolves according to

$$\dot{U} = Q - \delta U. \tag{5}$$

The infected never recover to become susceptible again or immune, nor do they cease being infectious.

These equations imply changes in the three proportions s, i, u:

$$\dot{s} = (1 - s)\varepsilon - q - \alpha s i, \tag{6}$$

in which $q = Q/N$,

$$\dot{i} = \alpha s i - \varepsilon i, \tag{7}$$

and

$$\dot{u} = q - \varepsilon u. \tag{8}$$

1.2   The Costs and Benefits of Interventions and the Social Planner's Optimization

The social planner maximizes social welfare as given by the present discounted value of total income net of the total costs of the disease and the total costs of vaccinations, the only intervention:

$$W = \int_0^\infty \{V_0 N - [p_I i N + p_q q N]\} e^{-rt} \, dt, \tag{9}$$

in which r is the discount rate, V_0 is income in the absence of the disease (received by everyone who is alive whether well or sick), p_I is the current money cost of being infected (and sick), such as foregone wages and the monetary equivalent of pain and suffering, and iN is the total number of the sick, and the last term is the price of a vaccination p_q times the number of vaccinations at any time, qN. Like Francis, I assume that utility is linear in income and that neither prevention (other than vaccination) nor therapies are options. The integrand of equation (9) is therefore the sum of the current incomes of the infected, the uninfected, and the vaccinated, less the total costs of illness and health interventions.

Equation (9) provides the objective function while equations (2) and (6)–(8) provide the dynamic equations that constrain the optimization problem. The current-value Hamiltonian, H, is

$$H = N\{V_0 - [p_I i + p_q q]\} + \lambda_N N[\varepsilon - \delta]$$
$$+ (\lambda_i N)[\alpha s i - \varepsilon i] + (\lambda_u N)[q - \varepsilon u] \tag{10}$$

in which λ_N, $(\lambda_i N)$ and $(\lambda_u N)$ are the current value multipliers.

At an internal solution for the optimal rate of vaccination $(s \geq q \geq 0)$, the first derivative of H with respect to the control, q, set equal to zero implies:

$$\lambda_u = p_q. \tag{11a}$$

The dynamic equations for the multipliers imply:

$$\dot{\lambda}_N = \lambda_N(r + \delta - \varepsilon) - [V_0 - (p_I i + p_q q)], \tag{11b}$$

$$\dot{\lambda}_i = (r + \delta)\lambda_i + p_I + \lambda_i \alpha i + \lambda_i \alpha(i + u - 1)$$

$$= (r + \delta)\lambda_i + p_I + \lambda_i \alpha i - \lambda_i \alpha s, \tag{11c}$$

and

$$\dot{\lambda}_u = (r + \delta)\lambda_u + \lambda_i \alpha i. \tag{11d}$$

The interpretation of these expressions is relatively straightforward, but I call attention to the last part of the center and right-hand side expressions of equation (11c).

These terms appear because the social planner recognizes that its decisions affect the path of the probability of becoming infected, that is, the path of the aggregate infection rate. These terms disappear if the proportion of susceptibles equals zero. To anticipate subsequent conclusions, therefore, it is not sufficient for there to be a difference between the social planner's decisions and private decisions for the social planner to consider its effect on the aggregate infection rate while private individuals do not. The proportion of susceptibles must also be strictly positive. Inspection of equations (6), (7), and (11a–d) also shows that the dynamic equations for i, u, and the λ_j, $j = i$, u do not involve N so that the dynamic system is independent of N although not of ε.

In the steady state of this system, equations (7), (8), and (11c–d) equal zero. That equation (7) equals zero implies that in the steady state:

$$s^* \equiv (1 - i^* - u^*) = \frac{\varepsilon}{\alpha}. \tag{12a}$$

Thus if $1 > s > 0$ so that there is a strictly internal solution to the model, $\alpha > \varepsilon > 0$, and conversely. In particular, s can only equal 0 if the birth rate is zero. This fact is important to the question of an externality, as will be clear once I specify the representative agent and the solution to its optimization problem in contrast to that of the social planner.

The conditions for the steady state together imply that the steady state value of i is

$$i^* = \frac{(r + \delta - \varepsilon)(r + \delta)p_q}{\alpha[p_I - (r + \delta)p_q]}. \tag{12b}$$

If $0 < i^* < (\alpha - \varepsilon)/\alpha$, the steady-state infection rate without vaccinations, then the steady-state optimal infection rate of i^* is maintained by vaccination, the case I consider. The condition $r + \delta - \varepsilon > 0$ is the standard requirement that the interest rate exceed the rate of population growth. The condition $p_I - (r + \delta)p_q > 0$ is the requirement that the cost of the infection per period exceeds the cost of capital (interest plus depreciation, i.e., probability of death) invested in the vaccination; otherwise the vaccination is worse than the disease. The steady-state value of i increases with the discount rate (r) and the death rate (δ), which both lessen the weight of the future in decisions, consistent with vaccination being an investment. It falls with increases in the cost of infection (p_I), in the ease of becoming infected (α), and the birth rate (ε), and rises with an increase in the cost of vaccination (p_q).

2   The Representative Agent's Problem

2.1   The General Problem of Decentralization

The simplest way to investigate externalities and associated policy is to assume that private decisions are made by a group of people that I call a household, a construct that is the representative decision-making agent. This construct provides a logically consistent and analytically tractable model to contrast with the model of the social planner: First, the household's objective function is fully congruent with the social planner's. Furthermore, the household understands and anticipates how the epidemic will evolve and is fully forward looking about its members' possible future statuses as well as their present situation. It is therefore the case that the rationale for government intervention depends neither on myopia nor on a discrepancy between the social planner's and the representative agent's valuation of outcomes over the path of the epidemic. The household members are Philipson's previously quoted "individuals who do the best they can given their constraints." The model therefore isolates the pure effect of externalities.

The only distinction between the social planner and the representative agent is that the household is small, relative to the whole population, so that the proportion of the household in any disease status does not affect the dynamics of the infection. In particular, this household takes as given the proportions of the population that is infected. The household, however, is sufficiently large that it can fulfill the role of a representative agent. The proportion of the household in each disease status is therefore identical to the population proportions.

2.2 The Specifics of Decentralization

The equations of the household's model are the same as the social planner's problem, equations (2), (7)–(9), except in two ways: First, all variables are interpreted to represent household variables rather than social ones except in equation (7) where the first term involving i is modified to substitute the society-wide value of the probability of infection, π, for i which now denotes the fraction of the household that is infected. It is this probability, π, that the household takes as exogenous. Consequently, equation (7') replaces equation (7):

$$\dot{i} = \alpha s\pi - \varepsilon i. \tag{7'}$$

Second, a further change has to be made to the objective function to reflect possible government interventions. If the government finds it optimal to affect the price of vaccinations, the representative household faces prices of $w_q = (1 + t_q)p_q$. So that interventions are revenue neutral and do not have incentive effects beyond the t_q, the household receives a lump sum payment (perhaps negative) of T per member that it takes as exogenous but that equals $t_q p_q q$. Without this lump sum, the household's welfare would be affected by a change in its income as the government intervenes with taxes or subsidies to offset the externality. The household's Hamiltonian is therefore

$$H = N\{V_0 - [p_I i + w_q q] + T\} + \lambda_N N[\varepsilon - \delta]$$
$$+ (\lambda_i N)[as\pi - \varepsilon i] + (\lambda_u N)[q - \varepsilon u]. \tag{10'}$$

At an internal solution for the optimal rate of vaccination ($s \geq q \geq 0$), the first derivative of H with respect to the control, q, set equal to zero implies

$$\lambda_u = w_q. \tag{11a'}$$

The dynamic equations for the multipliers imply

$$\dot{\lambda}_N = \lambda_N(r + \delta - \varepsilon) - [V_0 - (p_I i + w_q q)], \tag{11b'}$$

$$\dot{\lambda}_i = (r + \delta)\lambda_i + p_I + \lambda_i a\pi, \tag{11c'}$$

and

$$\dot{\lambda}_u = (r + \delta)\lambda_u + \lambda_i a\pi. \tag{11d'}$$

Absent government intervention, $w_q = p_q$, and equations (11a–d) and (11a'–d') only differ in the omission from equation (11c') of the last term in the center and right-hand sides of (11c). This omission occurs because the household takes the probability of infection (the aggregate infection rate), as exogenous. As in the social planner's problem, the dynamic equations for i, u, and λ_j, $j = i$, u do not involve N so the system is independent of N but not of ε.

Because this household is the representative agent, $\pi = i$, although the household took π as an exogenous function of time. The following calculations incorporate the substitution of $\pi = i$. In the steady state, equations (7'), (8), and (11c'–d') equal zero. As in the social planner's problem, equation (7') equal to zero implies

$$s^* \equiv (1 - i^* - u^*) = \frac{\varepsilon}{\alpha}. \tag{12a'}$$

The steady state value of i is

$$i^* = \frac{(r + \delta)(r + \delta)w_q}{\alpha[p_I - w_q(r + \delta)]}. \tag{12b'}$$

In contrast to equation (12b), equation (12b') does not involve the birth rate, ε, but does involve the tax-inclusive price of vaccination rather than the tax-exclusive one. Otherwise the expressions are identical and without these differences, the values of i in the steady state would be identical for the social planner and the household. Because public policy seeks to decentralize the social planner's problem, there would be nothing to do without these differences. In fact, when there are no new births ($\varepsilon = 0$) and no taxes/subsidies, there is no difference between the social planner's problem and the household's, no need for intervention, and in this sense, no externality.

This special case corresponds to Francis's assumptions and its conclusions to his. In the more general case $\varepsilon > 0$, and equality of the right-hand sides of equations (12b) and (12b′) implies that a subsidy is necessary to equate the social planner's and the household's steady-state values of i and thereby decentralize the planner's solution. The value of the subsidy is

$$t_q^* = \frac{-\varepsilon[p_I - p_q(r + \delta)]}{(r + \delta)(p_I - \varepsilon p_q)};$$

its absolute value depends positively on ε and p_I, negatively on p_q, r and δ, but not at all on α. Thus, the optimal subsidy in this model can be calculated based on parameters that are easily observed.

My intuition for Francis's case (although not necessarily his) is: when there are no births or deaths, and no one is vaccinated, the proportion of susceptibles is continuously falling and the proportion of infecteds is continuously rising. Eventually the proportion of infecteds (and therefore the probability of infection) reaches a threshold value, given by either equation (12b) or (12b′). At this threshold, the value of vaccination has just reached its cost (which is constant). If it is worth vaccinating anyone, it is worth vaccinating every susceptible because the proportion of infecteds (and the probability of infection of the remaining susceptibles) will otherwise continue to rise. The only way to maintain the steady state value of i is to vaccinate every susceptible once the threshold is reached. In the steady state, the proportion of the susceptibles is therefore equal to zero (from equation (7), in steady state $s^* = 0$ whenever $\varepsilon = 0$). And, because $s = 0$, the right-hand sides of equations (11c) and (11c′) are the same at the steady state. So the type of rule is a threshold rule for both the social planner and the household.

Furthermore, the value of the threshold is the same, and so there is no externality, at least not one that justifies intervention. It might be tempting to infer that the social planner would want a lower threshold which is reached earlier. But why? With a threshold, once it is reached, everyone gets vaccinated anyway, and if everyone is vaccinated when anyone is, there is no one left to benefit from earlier vaccination of others that would keep down the aggregate infection rate. Therefore, there is no point to the social planner's inducing an earlier time for vaccinating everyone, hence the thresholds are the same.

Now consider the case in which there are new births; $\varepsilon > 0$. There are now people who would benefit from a lower threshold that is reached earlier. They are born susceptible and would prefer that their elders are already vaccinated. The household neglects this factor because it takes the aggregate infection rate as given; the government takes this factor into account and chooses a lower threshold infection rate at which to begin vaccination. Furthermore, once this threshold is reached, not every susceptible is vaccinated. An assertion that it is optimal to vaccinate everyone when the threshold is reached would involve a contradiction: with a rule of universal vaccination, all new susceptibles would be vaccinated thereby diluting the infected pool as a proportion of the population and lowering the infection rate below the threshold. This result, however, is in contradiction to a threshold after which everyone is vaccinated. Therefore, the optimal strategy is to begin vaccinating a proportion of the susceptibles strictly less than one once a threshold has been reached and to keep vaccinating a proportion of the susceptible pool so that the proportions of susceptible, vaccinated, and infected people are constant.

Without government subsidization of vaccination to equalize the two thresholds, the household follows the same qualitative rule, but its threshold is higher because it neglects its impact on the aggregate probability of others' becoming infected. In effect, births introduce a heterogeneity into the population. Not everyone is alive at the same time, the unborn cannot take decisions simultaneously with those already born, and the household does not weigh its impact on the unborn who are not its members because the household takes the aggregate infection rate as exogenous. A positive subsidy obtains whether population growth is positive or not; all that is needed is that the *birth* rate is positive and it need not exceed the death rate. The next section shows that recovery, like a positive birth rate, generates an externality and a motive for government intervention.

3   A Model with Recovery

3.1   *The Dynamic Constraints*

In this model there are neither births nor deaths—everyone lives forever. Unless vaccinated, people cycle between being susceptible or infected (and infectious). That people do not become immune is not inconsistent with an effective vaccine, or at least the search for one; examples include HIV and parasitic diseases such as malaria.

Once again, the total number of people (N) comprises: (1) the susceptible (S); (2) the infected and infectious (I); and (3) the vaccinated (U):

$$N = S + I + U. \tag{13}$$

The corresponding proportions are: s, i, and u, with $s + i + u = 1$. There is no net population change:

$$\dot{N} = 0, \tag{14}$$

and the population is normalized at $N = 1$.

The number of susceptibles changes according to

$$\dot{S} = \beta I - Q - \alpha Si. \tag{15}$$

The first term on the right-hand side represents the infecteds who recover to be susceptible; β is the recovery rate. The other terms are the same as in equation (3). The number infected evolves according to

$$\dot{I} = \alpha Si - \beta I. \tag{16}$$

These terms are the reverse of the corresponding terms in equation (15). Finally, the number of people who have been vaccinated evolves according to

$$\dot{U} = Q. \tag{17}$$

These equations imply changes in the proportions i and u (and s):

$$\dot{i} = \alpha si - \beta i \tag{16a}$$

and

$$\dot{u} = q. \tag{17a}$$

3.2 The Costs and Benefits of Interventions and the Social Planner's Optimization

The social planner's objective function is the same as in section 1, namely, equation (9) with $N = 1$. The social planner's current-value Hamiltonian, H, is

$$H = \{V_0 - [p_I i + p_q q]\} + \lambda_i [\alpha s i - \beta i] + \lambda_u q \tag{18}$$

in which λ_i and λ_u are the current value multipliers.

At an internal solution for the optimal rate of vaccination ($s \geq q \geq 0$), the first derivative of H with respect to the control, q, set equal to zero implies

$$\lambda_u = p_q. \tag{19a}$$

The dynamic equations for the multipliers imply

$$\dot{\lambda}_i = r\lambda_i + p_I + \lambda_i(\alpha i + \beta) + \lambda_i \alpha(i + u - 1)$$

$$= r\lambda_i + p_I + \lambda_i(\alpha i + \beta) - \lambda_i \alpha s \tag{19b}$$

and

$$\dot{\lambda}_u = r\lambda_u + \lambda_i \alpha i. \tag{19c}$$

As in equation (11c), equation (19b) embodies the recognition by the social planner that its decisions affect the path of the probability of infection, that is, the path of the aggregate infection rate.

In steady state, equations (16a), (17a), and (19b–c) equal zero, and so

$$s^* \equiv (1 - i^* - u^*) = \frac{\beta}{\alpha}. \tag{20a}$$

Thus if $1 > s > 0$ so that there is a strictly internal solution to the model, $\alpha > \beta > 0$, and conversely. In particular, s only equals 0 if the recovery rate is zero. As in sections 1 and 2, this fact plays an important role in the question of the externality. The steady state value of i is

$$i^* = \frac{r^2 p_q}{\alpha[p_I - p_q r]}. \tag{20b}$$

If $0 < i^* < (\alpha - \beta)/\alpha$, the steady-state infection rate without vaccinations, then the steady-state optimal infection rate of i* is maintained by vaccination, and is the case I consider.

3.3 The Specifics of Decentralization

As in sections 1 and 2, the dynamic equations of the household's, model are the same as the corresponding social planner's problem except for the distinction between the household's, and the aggregate infection rates and the appearance of tax inclusive prices and lump-sum taxes in the objective function. The household's Hamiltonian is therefore

$$H = \{V_0 - [p_I i + w_q q] + T\} + \lambda_i [as\pi - \beta i] + \lambda_u q. \tag{18'}$$

At an internal solution for the optimal rate of vaccination $(s \geq q \geq 0)$, the first derivative of H with respect to the control, q, set equal to zero implies

$$\lambda_u = w_q. \tag{19a'}$$

The dynamic equations for the multipliers imply

$$\dot{\lambda}_i = r\lambda_i + p_I + \lambda_i(a\pi + \beta), \tag{19b'}$$

and

$$\dot{\lambda}_u = r\lambda_u + \lambda_i a\pi. \tag{19c'}$$

Without government intervention, $w_q = p_q$, and equations (19a–c) and (19a'–c') only differ in the omission from equation (19b') of the last term in the center and right-hand sides of (19b). As in sections 1 and 2, this difference arises because the household takes the aggregate infection rate as exogenous.

Because this household is the representative agent, the following calculations incorporate the substitution of $\pi = i$. In the steady state, equations (16a), (17a), and (19b'–c') equal zero, and so

$$s^* \equiv (1 - i^* - u^*) = \frac{\beta}{a}. \tag{20a'}$$

The steady-state value of i is

$$i^* = \frac{r w_q (r + \beta)}{a[p_I - w_q r]}. \tag{20b'}$$

In contrast to equation (20b), equation (20b′) involves the recovery rate, β. Otherwise the expressions would be identical if the government did not intervene. If $\beta = 0$, the values of i would be the same without government intervention, and there would be no need for government intervention. This case again corresponds to Francis's assumptions and its conclusions to his. When $\beta > 0$, however, the steady-state value of i would be lower when the social planner rather than the household optimizes, absent a government subsidy. To decentralize the social planner's problem, the government subsidizes vaccinations so that $w_q < p_q$ to offset $\beta > 0$.

The value of the subsidy is

$$t_q^* = \frac{-\beta[p_I - p_q r]}{[rp_I + \beta(p_I - p_q r)]};$$

its absolute value depends positively on β and p_I and negatively on p_q and r, but not at all on α. As in sections 1 and 2, the optimal subsidy depends on easily observable parameters.

This case shows that externalities can arise even without births; all the household's members are alive when it is making all its decisions, but the household, by its nature, ignores its impact on the aggregate infection rate. Although the household of section 2 in no way disregarded the interests of its own future members, this example perhaps makes clearer than sections 1 and 2 that the government is not correcting a disregard by the family of the interests of its own unborn. Instead, the government is correcting for the disregard by the household of its effects on the aggregate infection rate, a disregard that only matters when there are susceptibles in the steady state. Nor is the household in any sense myopic; it forms fully rational expectations.

4 Further Reflections on Vaccinations, Externalities, and Public Health

Both the models with births and with recovery argue for externalities in people's decisions to vaccinate against infectious diseases and for a government role in internalizing these externalities.

As is standard in mathematical epidemiology, the stock of infecteds declines at a fractional rate and therefore neither model allows for eradication in finite time. Eradication is at best asymptotic. But these models do allow for the possibility of zero incidence of the disease, in which all susceptibles are vaccinated. If the cost of infection is infinite or the cost of vaccination is zero, the government's optimal threshold for beginning vaccination equals zero so that the disease is eradicated asymptotically. In these special cases, however, the government threshold coincides with the private threshold in the absence of a subsidy and so there is no need for government intervention to bring about eradication.

To move away from the no-eradication property of the model would require a more cumbersome model of finite lives. An important question would be whether settling for an internal steady state with positive infection is dominated by a push for eradication in finite time. So when Stiglitz emphasizes eradication, he is pointing to the need for an important alteration in modeling strategy.

There are other factors that should be investigated, and all would seem relevant to externalities: vaccines need not be fully effective. The population may be inherently heterogeneous, with different costs of illness and vaccination inclusive of time, trouble, and the risks of side effects. People and governments may have additional options, such as prevention and therapies, that bring with them externalities.

References

Anderson, R. M., and R. M. May. 1991. *Infectious Diseases of Humans*. Oxford: The University Press.

Francis, P. J. 1997. "Dynamic Epidemiology and the Market for Vaccinations." *Journal of Public Economics*. 63: 383–406.

Philipson, T. 2000. "Economic epidemiology and infectious diseases," in *Handbook of Health Economics*, ed. A. J. Cuyler and J. P. Newhouse, 1761–1797. Amsterdam: North-Holland.

Stiglitz, J. E. 1986, 1988, 2000. *Economics of the Public Sector*. New York: Norton.

Stiglitz, J. E. 1997. "Introduction," in World Bank, *Confronting AIDS*, xv–xvi. Oxford: The University Press for the World Bank.

26

The Road Less Traveled: Oligopoly and Competition Policy in General Equilibrium

J. Peter Neary

It is a truth universally acknowledged that product markets are often far from competitive. Economists have taken two main routes in addressing this fact. At the microlevel, the field of industrial organization has developed a sophisticated array of models that focus on strategic interactions among firms in a single market. At the macrolevel, many fields, including international trade, macroeconomics, and growth, have used models of monopolistic competition to incorporate increasing returns to scale and product differentiation into general equilibrium. Each of these approaches has contributed enormously to our understanding of real-world economies; however, each ignores the insights of the other. Models of industrial organization typically take factor prices and aggregate income as given, and pay little attention to interactions between markets. General-equilibrium models of monopolistic competition typically ignore strategic behavior by incumbents; and they assume a perfectly elastic supply of identical new firms, ready and able to enter in response to the smallest profit opportunity.

Many important issues could be illuminated by combining these two approaches, in other words, by modeling oligopoly in general equilibrium. Progress in this direction, however, has been held back by a number of related problems. First, if firms are large in their own market, and if that market constitutes a significant segment of the economy, then the firms have direct influence on economy-wide variables. Assuming they behave rationally, they should exploit this influence, taking account of their effect on both aggregate income and economy-wide factor prices when choosing their output or price. Such behavior is both implausible (apart from relatively rare cases where firms have monopsony power in local factor markets) and difficult to model. Second, large firms influence the cost of living, and rational shareholders should take this into account in choosing the profit-maximizing level of output or price. This difficulty was first highlighted by Gabszewicz and Vial (1972), who interpreted it as implying that the predictions of general-equilibrium oligopoly models are sensitive to the choice of numeraire (see also Böhm 1994). Finally, Roberts and Sonnenschein (1977) showed that oligopolistic firms in general equilibrium typically have reaction functions so badly behaved that no equilibrium may exist.

These problems have held back the development of tractable models of oligopoly in general equilibrium. They have even found their way into textbooks (see, e.g., Bhagwati et al. 1998, 382, and Kreps 1990, 727). This chapter draws on recent work (Neary 2002a, b, c) where I argue that they can all be avoided in a simple way. This allows firms to be "large" in their own sector, but requires them to be "small" in the economy as a whole. Technically, the key to doing this is to assume a continuum of sectors, each with a small number of firms. (In fact, any reasonably large number of sectors would suffice, but it is much easier to work with the continuum case than with a large finite number of sectors.) Just as in models of perfect or monopolistic competition, firms cannot influence national income or factor prices and so take them as given. Since the output of any one sector is infinitesimal relative to national output, maximization of profits leads to the same real allocation irrespective of how they are deflated. Finally, with income effects absent for any one sector, reaction functions are more likely to be well-behaved, and existence of equilibrium is no more problematic than it is in partial equilibrium.

The purpose of this chapter is to put this modeling strategy in context and to consider its implications for competition policy in a closed economy. Section 1 reviews the literature on oligopoly in general equilibrium, a tiny one compared to the huge number of papers on either oligopoly in partial equilibrium or monopolistic competition in general equilibrium. Section 2 addresses a key element in implementing my approach, the specification of preferences. Section 3 presents a simple model of oligopoly in general equilibrium and derives some surprising implications for competition policy. Section 4 shows that analogous results also apply in a free-entry model of monopolistic competition that is dual to the oligopoly model of section 3.

1 Alternative Approaches

A variety of approaches has been taken to resolving the difficulties with embedding oligopoly in general equilibrium which I have highlighted. One strand of literature ignores them, assuming that the partial equilibrium oligopoly first-order condition, $p_i(1 - \alpha_i/\varepsilon) = c_i$, continues to apply in general equilibrium, even though firms are large relative to the economy as a whole. (Here α_i is the market share of firm i under Cournot competition, and ε is the price elasticity of demand.) For example, Batra (1972) explored the implications of monopoly for the two-sector growth model, while Melvin and Warne (1973) and Markusen (1981) introduced monopoly and oligopoly into the two-sector Heckscher-Ohlin trade model, respectively. This tradition is continued by Ruffin (2003), though he explicitly describes the typical agent in his model as behaving "schizophrenically, changing price as a producer and accepting prices as given as a consumer."

One aspect of firms' schizophrenia in these models is that they ignore their ability to influence factor prices. A small number of papers address this, explicitly assuming that firms exercise monopsony power (see Bishop 1966; Feenstra 1980; Markusen and Robson 1980; McCulloch and Yellen 1980). Even in simple models, such as when output prices are fixed by the small open economy assumption, this leads to considerable complications without yielding much additional insight.

A different tradition assumes that preferences are quasi-linear, so the utility function is $x_0 + u(x)$, where x_0 and x are the consumption levels of goods produced under perfect and oligopolistic competition respectively. The inverse demand curve for x is then independent of income. This approach has been widely used in industrial organization and related fields (see, for example, Dixit 1981; Vives 1985; Ottaviano, Tabuchi, and Thisse 2002). Models with quasi-linear preferences are sometimes defended as being general equilibrium (see, for example, Brander and Spencer 1984, 198; Konishi, Okuno-Fujiwara, and Suzumura 1990, 69). But most authors concede that, since all income effects fall on the good produced in the perfectly competitive sector, and factor prices are typically assumed to be determined in that sector, quasi-linear preferences provide a secure foundation for partial equilibrium analysis but nothing more.

Finally, a number of writers face up to the numeraire problem, warts and all. Gabszewicz and Vial (1972) and Cordella and Gabszewicz (1997) assume that firms are owned by worker-producers, who maximize utility rather than profits. In the same vein, Dierker and Grodal (1998) assume that firms maximize shareholders' real wealth, taking account of how their decisions affect the deflator for nominal wealth. These papers avoid the problem of sensitivity to the choice of numeraire. Their behavioral assumptions, however, are not very plausible, and the analysis required for even the simplest models of this kind is complex.

Given these difficulties of modeling oligopoly in general equilibrium, much more effort has been devoted to modeling monopolistic competition.[1] This is sometimes defended on the grounds that models with a fixed number of firms are short-run (see, for example, Ohyama 1999, 14), suggesting that free entry is the more general long-run case. But a casual glance at many real-world markets shows that they continue to be dominated by a small number of firms for long periods of time. A different rationale for monopolistic competition is that, with profits driven to zero by free entry and exit, the problems noted above seem to disappear. But as d'Aspremont, Dos Santos Ferreira, and Gérard-Varet (1996) pointed out, this is only strictly true if a continuum of monopolistically competitive firms is assumed.[2]

A number of authors have explored the implications of allowing firms to be large in their own market but small in the economy. Hart (1982) constructs an "island" economy in which firms on one island are owned by shareholders on other islands, so avoiding the problems of an endogenous deflator for profits. Shleifer (1986) and Murphy, Shleifer, and Vishny (1989) assume a large number of sectors, in each of which a monopolist faces a competitive fringe. Rotemberg and Woodford (1992) construct a dynamic model of implicit collusion among firms in a large (though finite) number of sectors. These papers, however, were not primarily focused on my goal of integrating the theory of industrial organization with general equilibrium analysis. In the remainder of this chapter I sketch how this can be done.

2 Preferences

The key technical step in operationalizing the approach I advocated in the introduction is to find a tractable specification of preferences.

An obvious starting point is to assume that utility is an additively separable function of a continuum of goods:

$$U[\{x(z)\}] = g\left[\int_0^1 u\{x(z)\}\,dz\right], \qquad g' > 0,\ u' > 0,\ u'' < 0. \tag{1}$$

This specification could be extended in a number of ways. The measure of integration could be endogenous rather than fixed, permitting a dynamic version of the model; the subutility functions could vary with z as well as $x(z)$; and they could allow for differentiated products produced by each firm in sector z. In the remainder of this chapter, however, it is convenient to concentrate on (1).

Assume therefore that a representative consumer maximizes (1) subject to the budget constraint:

$$\int_0^1 p(z)x(z)\,dz \leq I, \tag{2}$$

where I is aggregate income. The inverse demand functions are

$$p(z) = \frac{1}{\lambda}u'[x(z)], \tag{3}$$

where λ is the marginal utility of income, the Lagrange multiplier attached to the budget constraint, normalized by the derivative g'. The key feature of (3) is that, apart from λ, the demand price of good z depends only on variables pertaining to sector z itself. The marginal utility of income serves as a "sufficient statistic" for the rest of the economy in each sector. It is this property of what Browning, Deaton, and Irish (1985) call "Frisch demand functions," combined with the continuum assumption, which allows a consistent theory of oligopoly. In each sector z, firms take λ as given, but in general equilibrium it is determined endogenously. To solve for λ, multiply (3) by $p(z)$ and integrate, using (2), to obtain

$$\lambda = \frac{1}{\sigma_p^2}\int_0^1 p(z)u'[x(z)]\,dz, \quad \text{where} \quad \sigma_p^2 \equiv \int_0^1 p(z)^2\,dz. \tag{4}$$

So λ equals a price-weighted mean of the marginal utilities of individual goods, divided by the (uncentered) variance of prices.

While any additively separable utility function gives the sufficient statistic property, the general form $u[x(z)]$ is not tractable, since the endogenous consumption levels appear on the right-hand side of (4).

Hence, we need to consider some special forms for the subutility function. The simplest case is where preferences are Cobb-Douglas:

$$g(h) = \exp h, \qquad u[x(z)] = \beta(z) \ln x(z), \qquad \int_0^1 \beta(z)\, dz = 1. \tag{5}$$

Here λ is the reciprocal of income, $\lambda = 1/I$, and the inverse demand functions are unit-elastic, with $\beta(z)$ denoting the (infinitesimal) budget share of good z:

$$p(z) = \frac{1}{\lambda} \frac{\beta(z)}{x(z)} = \frac{\beta(z)I}{x(z)}. \tag{6}$$

These demand functions are attractively simple or extremely restrictive, depending on your point of view. In any case, they are inconsistent with profit maximization by a monopolist.

Alternatively, preferences may take the constant-elasticity-of-substitution form as in Dixit and Stiglitz (1977):

$$g(h) = h^{1/\theta}, \qquad u[x(z)] = x(z)^{\theta}, \qquad 0 < \theta < 1. \tag{7}$$

Now the inverse demand functions are isoelastic:

$$p(z) = \frac{\theta}{\lambda} x(z)^{-\eta}, \qquad \eta \equiv \frac{1}{1-\theta} > 1, \tag{8}$$

where the elasticity of demand η is also the elasticity of substitution between every pair of goods; while λ is an inverse Cobb-Douglas function of income and the true cost-of-living index P:

$$\lambda[\{p(z)\}, I] = \frac{\theta}{P^{\theta} I^{1-\theta}}, \qquad \text{where} \quad P \equiv \left[\int_0^1 p(z)^{1-\eta}\, dz \right]^{1/(1-\eta)}. \tag{9}$$

These demand functions allow convenient solutions in models of monopolistic competition, where they were first introduced. But in oligopoly they have unattractive implications; outputs are often strategic complements in Cournot competition, and reaction functions may be nonmonotonic.

Finally, as in Neary (2002c), consider the case where each subutility function is quadratic:

$$g(h) = h, \qquad u[x(z)] = ax(z) - 1/2bx(z)^2. \tag{10}$$

Now the inverse demand functions and the marginal utility of income are

$$p(z) = \frac{1}{\lambda}[a - bx(z)] \quad \text{and} \quad \lambda[\{p(z)\}, I] = \frac{a\mu_p - bI}{\sigma_p^2},\tag{11}$$

where μ_p is the mean of prices and we have already defined σ_p^2 as their (uncentred) variance. Hence, a rise in income, a rise in the (uncentred) variance of prices, or a fall in the mean of prices, all reduce λ and so shift the demand function for each good outward. From the perspective of firms, however, λ is an exogenous variable over which they have no control. While (11) is the true demand curve, the perceived demand curve is linear, as in Negishi (1961), since firms treat λ as constant. Oligopoly models with linear demand functions are easy to solve in partial equilibrium, which allows us to construct a tractable but consistent model of oligopoly in general equilibrium.

3 Competition Policy in General Oligopolistic Equilibrium

The specification of preferences discussed in the last section could be combined with any one of a huge variety of assumptions about the supply side of the economy. For simplicity I adopt here probably the simplest possible approach. It combines Cournot competition and a given number n of firms in each sector with a Ricardian specification of technology and factor markets. The first-order condition for a typical firm in sector z is: $p(z) - c(z) = by(z)/\lambda$. Solving for equilibrium output,

$$y(z) = \frac{a - \lambda c(z)}{b(n+1)}.\tag{12}$$

The unit cost of production in each sector, $c(z)$, equals the economy-wide wage rate, w, times the sector's labor requirement per unit output, denoted by $\alpha(z)$: $c(z) = w\alpha(z)$. The equilibrium condition in the labor market requires that the exogenous labor supply L equal the total demand for labor from all sectors:

$$L = \int_0^1 \alpha(z) n y(z)\, dz.\tag{13}$$

Inspecting equations (12) and (13) shows that they are homogeneous of degree zero in two nominal variables, the wage rate w and the inverse of the marginal utility of income, λ^{-1}. As is normal in real models, the absolute values of these variables are indeterminate and, indeed, uninteresting. Hence, we can choose an arbitrary numeraire. (This will be a true numeraire: unlike the cases discussed in section 1, the choice of numeraire has no implications for the model's behavior.) It is most convenient to choose utility itself as numeraire, so that λ is unity by choice of units.

To solve the model, evaluate the integral in (13), using (12):

$$w = \left[a\mu - \frac{n+1}{n} bL \right] \frac{1}{\sigma^2}. \tag{14}$$

μ and σ^2 denote the first and second moments of the technology distribution:

$$\mu \equiv \int_0^1 \alpha(z)\, dz \quad \text{and} \quad \sigma^2 \equiv \int_0^1 \alpha(z)^2\, dz. \tag{15}$$

For later use, note that the variance v^2 of the technology distribution is given by $v^2 = \sigma^2 - \mu^2$. A special case, which serves as a convenient benchmark, is the *featureless economy*, where all sectors have the same technology parameter α_0: the variance v^2 is zero, and so $\sigma = \mu = \alpha_0$.

The first issue to examine is the effect of competition policy (in the sense of an increase in the number of firms n in all sectors) on the functional distribution of income. National income I, measured in utility units, equals the sum of wages wL and total profits Π:

$$I = wL + \Pi, \qquad \Pi = \int_0^1 n\pi(z)\, dz. \tag{16}$$

To evaluate total profits, note that profits in each sector $\pi(z)$ equal $[p(z) - c(z)]y(z)$. Using the first-order condition and equation (12) gives:

$$\Pi = bn \int_0^1 y(z)^2\, dz = \frac{n}{b(n+1)^2} (a^2 - 2a\mu w + \sigma^2 w^2). \tag{17}$$

The appendix shows that this can be written in terms of parameters as follows:

$$\Pi = \frac{na^2}{b(n+1)^2} \frac{v^2}{\sigma^2} + \frac{bL^2}{n} \frac{1}{\sigma^2}. \tag{18}$$

From (14), the wage rate w is strictly increasing in n; while from (18) total profits are strictly decreasing in n. Hence it follows that

RESULT 1   A rise in n raises the share of wages in national income.

Thus competition policy has the expected effect on income distribution.

Next, we want to determine the effects of competition policy on welfare. Substituting the direct demand functions implied by (11) into the utility function (1) and (10), gives the indirect utility function (ignoring a constant):

$$\tilde{U} = a^2 - \sigma_p^2. \tag{19}$$

To calculate the variance of the distribution of prices, we can use the Cournot equilibrium price formula, $p(z) = [a + nc(z)]/(n + 1)$. Squaring and integrating yields

$$\sigma_p^2 = \frac{1}{(n + 1)^2} (a^2 + 2an\mu w + n^2\sigma^2 w^2). \tag{20}$$

Substituting from (14) for w, this becomes (as shown in the appendix)

$$\sigma_p^2 = \frac{a^2}{(n + 1)^2} \frac{v^2}{\sigma^2} + \frac{(a\mu - bL)^2}{\sigma^2}. \tag{21}$$

This is clearly decreasing, but not strictly so, in the number of firms. Hence,

RESULT 2   An increase in n raises welfare, strictly so if $v^2 > 0$.

Since there are no other distortions in the model, we would expect this to be so. The result is not strict, however, unlike result 1, which has a surprising implication:

COROLLARY   In the featureless economy, competition policy has no effect on welfare: $d\tilde{U}/dn = 0$.

Inducing entry by more firms in all sectors raises the demand for labor. But since the aggregate labor supply constraint is binding, this merely redistributes income from profits to wages without any gains in efficiency.

This result should not be seen as an argument against activism in competition policy. The model is far too stylized to provide a basis for policy making. In the realistic case where sectors are heterogeneous, the welfare costs of oligopoly implied by (21) may be greater than those implied by partial-equilibrium calculations in the tradition of Harberger (1954). Rather, the result should be seen as an extreme case that brings out the importance of a general-equilibrium perspective. It was clearly stated by Lerner (1933–1934), who also conjectured that a suitable measure of the economy-wide degree of monopoly is the standard deviation of the "degree of monopoly" (i.e., the price-cost margin) across all sectors. Equation (21) confirms Lerner's intuition and shows how it relates to the underlying structural parameters in the economy.

Finally, consider the effects of an increase in the technology variance, v^2, at constant μ. The appendix shows that equations (14), (18), and (21) imply

RESULT 3   A mean-preserving spread in the technology distribution raises aggregate welfare but lowers the share of wages in national income.

So aggregate welfare and the share of wages need not move together.

4   Competition Policy in Monopolistic Competition

Competition policy was modeled in the previous section as an exogenous increase in the number of firms in each sector of the economy. In this section I show that the same results follow, if instead the fixed costs of operating a firm are taken as parametric and entry of new firms is assumed to be free. The model therefore becomes one of monopolistic competition rather than of oligopoly.

It would be possible to assume that firms' fixed costs vary in some systematic way with z. There is no basis for doing this within the model, however, so assume instead that they take a constant value f in all sectors. Hence, the equilibrium condition for free entry in sector z is

$$f = \pi(z) = by(z)^2. \tag{22}$$

We can solve this for the equilibrium output of each firm and use (12) to solve for the equilibrium number of firms in sector z (ignoring the integer constraint):

$$y(z) = \sqrt{f/b} \quad \text{and} \quad n(z) = \frac{a - w\alpha(z)}{\sqrt{bf}} - 1. \tag{23}$$

As in models of monopolistic competition based on Dixit-Stiglitz preferences, the equilibrium size of each firm depends only on cost and taste parameters. Adjustment to shocks in other parameters comes about solely through changes in the number of firms.

We can now solve for the equilibrium wage. As in the previous section, we integrate the labor-market equilibrium condition (13). The difference is that now the number of firms in each sector and not the output of each varies with z. This yields

$$w = [(a - \sqrt{bf})\mu - bL]\frac{1}{\sigma^2}. \tag{24}$$

Comparing this with equation (14) in the last section, it is clear that a reduction in fixed costs in monopolistic competition has a similar effect on the equilibrium wage as an increase in the number of firms in oligopoly: both tend to raise w. Moreover, the competitive limits of the two models (as f approaches zero and n approaches infinity, respectively) are identical.

To solve for welfare, use the first-order condition and the free-entry condition (22) to solve for the equilibrium price in sector z:

$$p(z) = \sqrt{bf} + w\alpha(z). \tag{25}$$

Note that this implies a fixed absolute price-cost margin, whereas in monopolistic competition with Dixit-Stiglitz preferences, the relative price-cost margin is fixed. From (25), the appendix shows that the variance of prices equals

$$\sigma_p^2 = bf\frac{v^2}{\sigma^2} + \frac{(a\mu - bL)^2}{\sigma^2}. \tag{26}$$

This is clearly increasing (but not strictly so) in the fixed cost of production. Hence we can conclude the following:

RESULT 4   A fall in f raises welfare, strictly so provided $v^2 > 0$.

The interpretation of this result is identical to that of result 2 in the previous section. Competition policy has a similar effect on welfare under monopolistic competition as it has under oligopoly: welfare cannot fall and must increase, provided the variance of the technology distribution is strictly positive.

5   Conclusion

This chapter has reviewed previous approaches to modeling oligopoly in general equilibrium, and it has drawn on Neary (2002c) to propose a new view that in principle overcomes their deficiencies: modeling firms as large in their own market but small in the economy as a whole. On the one hand, firms face a small number of local competitors, so they have an incentive to compete strategically against them in the manner familiar from the theory of industrial organization. On the other hand, there is a continuum of sectors, so firms cannot influence economy-wide variables such as national income and factor prices. Furthermore, provided all profits are returned costlessly to the aggregate household, the implications of profit maximization are independent of tastes and of the normalization rule for prices. Hence, the approach avoids all the problems that have bedeviled previous studies of oligopoly in general equilibrium.

Implementing this approach requires a tractable specification of preferences. In principle, any form of additively separable preferences could be used, since they share the convenient property that the demand facing each sector depends only on variables pertaining to that sector and on the economy-wide marginal utility of income. For example, Dixit-Stiglitz preferences (which imply isoelastic perceived demand functions) could be used. I have chosen to work instead with continuum-quadratic preferences (which imply linear perceived demand functions), since they guarantee existence and uniqueness of equilibrium at the sectoral level and hence allow convenient aggregation across sectors.

To illustrate my proposed approach, I constructed a simple model of oligopoly in general equilibrium and used it to derive some surprising implications for competition policy. In particular, I showed that the desirability of increasing competition depends crucially on the distribution of what Lerner (1933–1934) called the "degree of monopoly" across sectors. While some authors, such as Francois and Horn (2000), have recognized that competition policy should take account of general equilibrium constraints, a satisfactory analytic framework in which to do so has not been available so far.

Of course, competition policy is modeled here in an extremely simple way: a parametric increase in the number of firms in section 3, or a parametric reduction in the fixed costs of operating a firm in section 4. In other respects, too, this chapter has clearly only scratched the surface of the new approach I have proposed. Even if continuum-quadratic preferences are retained, a wide range of alternative assumptions about market structure, firm behavior, and the workings of factor markets awaits exploration. For example, a richer theory of firm behavior should allow for strategic entry and entry-deterrence, since the assumption in section 3 that the number of firms in all sectors is exogenous is highly artificial. The standard assumption, however, of completely free entry in all sectors is just as unrealistic. I hope I have suggested the potential gains from exploring alternatives to the free-entry competitive paradigm, while still retaining a general-equilibrium perspective.

Appendix

Proof of Result 1   To evaluate total profits, substitute for w from (14) into the expression in brackets in (17) and rewrite as a difference in squares:

$$a^2 - 2a\mu w + \sigma^2 w^2 = a^2 - w(2a\mu - \sigma^2 w)$$

$$= a^2 - \left(a\mu - \frac{n+1}{n}bL\right)\left(a\mu + \frac{n+1}{n}bL\right)\frac{1}{\sigma^2}$$

$$= a^2\frac{v^2}{\sigma^2} + \left(\frac{n+1}{n}bL\right)^2\frac{1}{\sigma^2}. \tag{27}$$

Substituting back into (17) gives the expression for profits in (18).

Proof of Result 2   To evaluate the level of welfare, proceed as in the proof of result 1:

$$a^2 + 2an\mu w + n^2\sigma^2 w^2$$

$$= a^2 + nw(2a\mu + n\sigma^2 w)$$

$$= a^2 + [an\mu - (n+1)bL][a(n+2)\mu - (n+1)bL]\frac{1}{\sigma^2}$$

$$= a^2 + [(n+1)(a\mu - bL) - a\mu][(n+1)(a\mu - bL) + a\mu]\frac{1}{\sigma^2}$$

$$= a^2\frac{v^2}{\sigma^2} + (n+1)^2(a\mu - bL)^2\frac{1}{\sigma^2}. \tag{28}$$

Substituting back into (20) gives (21).

Proof of Result 3   To establish how v^2 affects welfare, differentiate (21):

$$\frac{d\sigma_p^2}{dv^2} \propto \frac{a^2}{(n+1)^2}\mu^2 - (a\mu - bL)^2$$

$$= -\frac{n(n+2)}{(n+1)^2}\left(a\mu - \frac{n+1}{n+2}bL\right)\left(a\mu - \frac{n+1}{n}bL\right) < 0. \tag{29}$$

This is negative, and so welfare in increasing in v^2, provided w in (14) is positive. The effect of v^2 on wages is negative, by inspection of (14). Finally, from (18), the effect on profits is

$$\frac{d\Pi}{dv^2} \propto \frac{na^2}{b(n+1)^2}\mu^2 - \frac{bL^2}{n}$$

$$= \frac{n}{b(n+1)^2}\left(a\mu + \frac{n+1}{n}bL\right)\left(a\mu - \frac{n+1}{n}bL\right) > 0. \tag{30}$$

Proof of Result 4 To evaluate the variance of prices, square and integrate (25) and then proceed as in the proofs of results 1 and 2:

$$\sigma_p^2 = bf + 2\sqrt{bf}\mu w + \sigma^2 w^2$$

$$= bf + w(2\sqrt{bf}\mu + \sigma^2 w)$$

$$= bf + [(a\mu - bL) - \sqrt{bf}\mu][(a\mu - bL) + \sqrt{bf}\mu]\frac{1}{\sigma^2}, \tag{31}$$

which leads to (26).

Acknowledgments

I am grateful to Joe Francois, Henrik Horn, Ravi Kanbur, Lars Persson, Johan Stennek, and Jacques Thisse for valuable discussions and comments. This research is part of the Globalisation Programme of the Centre for Economic Performance at LSE, funded by the UK ESRC, and of the International Trade and Investment Programme of the Institute for the Study of Social Change at University College Dublin.

Notes

1. I follow most of the literature in using imperfect competition to denote any type of market structure other than perfect competition, and monopolistic competition to refer to the Chamberlin large-group case, where entry and exit are free. Not all writers use the terms in this way. For example, monopolistic competition in Böhm (1994) and in Roberts and Sonnenschein (1977) refers to models with a fixed number of firms and perceived independence, which I prefer to describe as oligopoly models.

2. Ironically, Dixit and Stiglitz adopted this assumption in an early draft of their 1977 paper, but they dropped it from the published version at the request of a referee. See Brakman and Heijdra (2003).

References

Batra, Raveendra. 1972. "Monopoly theory in general equilibrium and the two-sector model of economic growth." *Journal of Economic Theory* 4: 355–371.

Bhagwati, Jagdish N., Arvind Panagariya, and T. N. Srinivasan. 1998. *Lectures on International Trade*, 2d ed. Cambridge, MA: MIT Press.

Bishop, Robert L. 1966. "Monopoly under general equilibrium: Comment." *Quarterly Journal of Economics* 80: 652–659.

Böhm, Volker. 1994. "The foundation of the theory of monopolistic competition revisited." *Journal of Economic Theory* 63: 208–218.

Brakman, Steven, and Ben J. Heijdra, eds. 2003. *The Monopolistic Competition Revolution after Twenty-Five Years*. Cambridge: Cambridge University Press.

Brander, James A., and Barbara Spencer. 1984. "Tariff protection and imperfect competition," in *Monopolistic Competition and International Trade*, ed. H. Kierzkowski, 194–206. Oxford: Clarendon Press.

Browning, Martin, Angus Deaton, and Margaret Irish. 1985. "A profitable approach to labor supply and commodity demands over the life-cycle." *Econometrica* 53: 503–543.

Cordella, Tito, and Jean Jaskold Gabszewicz. 1997. "Comparative advantage under oligopoly." *Journal of International Economics* 43: 333–346.

d'Aspremont, Claude, Rodolphe Dos Santos Ferreira, and Louis-André Gérard-Varet. 1996. "On the Dixit-Stiglitz model of monopolistic competition." *American Economic Review* 86: 623–629.

Dierker, Egbert, and Birgit Grodal. 1998. "Modelling policy issues in a world of imperfect competition." *Scandinavian Journal of Economics* 100: 153–179.

Dixit, Avinash K. 1981. "The role of investment in entry deterrence." *Economic Journal* 90: 95–106.

Dixit, Avinash K., and Joseph E. Stiglitz. 1977. "Monopolistic competition and optimum product diversity." *American Economic Review* 67: 297–308.

Feenstra, Robert C. 1980. "Monopsony distortions in an open economy: A theoretical analysis." *Journal of International Economics* 10: 213–235.

Francois, Joseph F., and Henrik Horn. 2000. "National and international competition policy." Mimeo., IIES, University of Stockholm.

Gabszewicz, Jean Jaskold, and Jean-Philippe Vial. 1972. "Oligopoly à la Cournot in a general equilibrium analysis." *Journal of Economic Theory* 4: 381–400.

Harberger, Arnold. 1954. "Monopoly and resource allocation." *American Economic Review (Papers and Proceedings)* 44: 77–87.

Hart, Oliver. 1982. "A model of imperfect competition with Keynesian features." *Quarterly Journal of Economics* 97: 109–138.

Konishi, Hideki, Masahiro Okuno-Fujiwara, and Kotaro Suzumura. 1990. "Oligopolistic competition and economic welfare: A general equilibrium analysis of entry regulation and tax-subsidy schemes." *Journal of Public Economics* 42: 67–88.

Kreps, David. 1990. *A Course in Microeconomic Theory*. Hemel Hempstead: Harvester Wheatsheaf.

Lerner, Abba P. 1933–1934. "The concept of monopoly and the measurement of monopoly power." *Review of Economic Studies* 1: 157–175.

Markusen, James R. 1981. "Trade and the gains from trade with imperfect competition." *Journal of International Economics* 11: 531–551.

Markusen, James R., and Arthur Robson. 1980. "Simple general equilibrium and trade with a monopsonized sector." *Canadian Journal of Economics* 3: 389–402.

McCulloch, Rachel, and Janet L. Yellen. 1980. "Factor market monopsony and the allocation of resources." *Journal of International Economics* 10: 237–248.

Melvin, James R., and Robert D. Warne. 1973. "Monopoly and the theory of international trade." *Journal of International Economics* 3: 117–134.

Murphy, Kevin M., Andrei Shleifer, and Robert V. Vishny. 1989. "The big push." *Journal of Political Economy* 97: 1003–1026.

Neary, J. Peter. 2002a. "Competition, trade and wages," in *Trade, Migration, Investment and Labour Market Adjustment*, ed. D. Greenaway, R. Upward, and K. Wakelin, 28–45. London: Macmillan.

Neary, J. Peter. 2002b. "Foreign competition and wage inequality." *Review of International Economics* 10: 680–693.

Neary, J. Peter. 2002c. "International trade in general oligopolistic equilibrium." University College Dublin, mimeo.

Negishi, Takashi. 1961. "Monopolistic competition and general equilibrium." *Review of Economic Studies* 28: 196–201.

Ohyama, Michihiro. 1999. "Market, trade and welfare in general equilibrium." *Japanese Economic Review* 50: 1–24.

Ottaviano, Gianmarco, Takatoshi Tabuchi, and Jacques-François Thisse. 2002. "Agglomeration and trade revisited." *International Economic Review* 43: 409–435.

Roberts, John, and Hugo Sonnenschein. 1977. "On the foundations of the theory of monopolistic competition." *Econometrica* 45: 101–113.

Rotemberg, Jerome, and Michael Woodford. 1992. "Oligopolistic pricing and the effects of aggregate demand on economic activity." *Journal of Political Economy* 100: 1153–1207.

Ruffin, Roy J. 2003. "Oligopoly and trade: What, how much and for whom?" *Journal of International Economics* 60: 313–335.

Shleifer, Andrei. 1986. "Implementation cycles." *Journal of Political Economy* 94: 1163–1190.

Vives, Xavier. 1985. "On the efficiency of Bertrand and Cournot equilibria with product differentiation." *Journal of Economic Theory* 36: 166–175.

27

Trade, Geography, and
Mmonopolistic
Competition: Theory and
an Application to Spatial
Inequalities in
Developing Countries

Anthony J. Venables

The Dixit-Stiglitz model of monopolistic competition transformed international trade theory, as it did other fields of economics, and provided one of the key building blocks for the new economic geography literature that developed in the 1990s. "Monopolistic competition and optimum product diversity" (Dixit and Stiglitz 1977), as its title suggests, was directed to analysis of the welfare economics of product selection. The central question posed was: in an industry with differentiated products and increasing returns to scale, how is the trade-off between the numbers of varieties and firm scale resolved? In particular, does the monopolistically competitive equilibrium produce too many or too few varieties, at too small or too large a scale? The authors showed that in a central case—a symmetric constant elasticity of substitution utility function—the equilibrium is identical to the allocation in which welfare is maximized subject to the constraint that firms make nonnegative profits.

The celebrity of the model stems, however, not from its analysis of product diversity, but from its development of a model of increasing returns and imperfect competition that lends itself to tractable inclusion in a general equilibrium framework. Putting increasing returns to scale in general equilibrium encounters two main difficulties. One is that the multiplicity of models of strategic behavior creates a danger of getting mired in taxonomy of cases. The other is that discontinuities can arise as entry or exit of firms is associated with nonmarginal changes in quantities and prices. The Dixit-Stiglitz approach (henceforth DS) sidesteps these problems by working with a large number (possibly a continuum) of firms, each producing its own variety of product. Market power comes only from each firm's monopoly in its own variety, avoiding issues of oligopolistic interaction. Industry aggregate variables are continuous functions of the number (or measure) of firms. Yet, at the same time, each individual firm has increasing returns to scale and makes integer choices. In the spatial context, increasing returns means that firms have to choose where to locate, since they would forego economies of scale by operating multiple plants. In short, "Dixit-Stiglitz lets us have our cake in discrete lumps, while doing calculus on it, too" (Fujita, Krugman, and Venables 1999).

This chapter has two objectives. One is to outline the DS model of monopolistic competition showing how, from the standpoint of trade and geography, it captures key ingredients that are essential to the modeling of the spatial economy. The other is to develop a simple application of a DS-based model of economic geography. The application asks the question: as an economy develops, what happens to spatial inequalities within the country?

1   The Dixit-Stiglitz Model of Monopolistic Competition

The original DS paper was completely aspatial, working with a single closed economy. It can be readily extended, however, to a multi-location framework, where locations can be interpreted as countries, regions, or cities within a country. The model generates trade flows among these locations and, more importantly, provides a theory of the location of industrial activity. The following section outlines this theory.

1.1   Bilateral Trade Flows

Trade data indicate that there is two-way trade between almost all pairs of countries. Even at quite a fine level of commodity disaggregation, at least for the larger countries, bilateral trade flows in both directions. Such flows constitute intraindustry trade, as compared to the interindustry trade studied by traditional trade theory. Furthermore, these trade flows attenuate rapidly with distance, pointing to the importance of trade costs of various types in choking off trade. None of these features are captured by what were, until the new trade theory revolution of the 1970s and 1980s, the standard models of trade theory based on perfect competition with homogeneous products. These models offer predictions about which commodities a country exports but, in a multicountry world, are silent on the question of where they are exported to and fail to predict the existence of intraindustry trade, except as a trivial consequence of how an industry is defined.

The DS formulation of product differentiation provides a tractable way of capturing all of these features. Its multicountry (or multiregion) variant is as follows. Suppose that the world consists of $i = 1, \ldots R$ locations. In a particular sector—here called manufacturing—each firm's product is differentiated from that of other firms, the degree of differentiation measured by a constant elasticity of substitution (CES) between pairs of products, denoted σ. Products are otherwise symmetric, entering utility in the same manner. Utility in location j is therefore represented by a CES aggregator taking the form

$$U_j = \left[\sum_i^R \int_{n_i} x_{ij}(z)^{(\sigma-1)/\sigma} dz \right]^{\sigma/(\sigma-1)}$$

$$= \left[\sum_i^R n_i x_{ij}^{(\sigma-1)/\sigma} \right]^{\sigma/(\sigma-1)}, \quad \sigma > 1, \tag{1}$$

where z denotes manufacturing varieties, n_i is the set of varieties produced in location i, and $x_{ij}(z)$ is the location j demand for the zth product from this set. It is typically assumed that all varieties produced in a particular location have the same costs and therefore, in equilibrium, are sold in the same quantity. The second equation in (1) makes use of this fact, so dispenses with the index z and rewrites the integral as a product. Dual to this quantity aggregator is a price index for manufactures in each country, G_j, defined over the prices of individual varieties produced in i and sold in j, p_{ij},

$$G_j = \left[\sum_i^R \int_{n_i} p_{ij}(z)^{1-\sigma} dz \right]^{1/(1-\sigma)} = \left[\sum_i^R n_i p_{ij}^{1-\sigma} \right]^{1-\sigma}, \tag{2}$$

where the second equation uses symmetry of equilibrium prices.

Bilateral trade flows follow directly from this structure. If country j's total expenditure on manufactures is denoted E_j, then its demand for each product produced in country i is (by Shephard's lemma on the price index)

$$x_{ij} = p_{ij}^{-\sigma} E_j G_j^{(\sigma-1)}. \tag{3}$$

Thus, the own price elasticity of demand is σ, and the term $E_j G_j^{\sigma-1}$ gives the position of the demand curve facing a single firm in market

j. The value of bilateral trade flows from i to j in the industry is therefore

$$n_i p_{ij} x_{ij} = n_i p_{ij}^{1-\sigma} E_j G_j^{(\sigma-1)}. \tag{4}$$

The model therefore predicts that values of bilateral trade flows depend on characteristics of demand in importer country j, the number and price of varieties produced in country i, together with any between country factors, such as transport costs, that enter the consumer (cif) price p_{ij}.

Relationships like equation (4) have launched countless gravity modeling exercises. Importer and exporter country characteristics are usually proxied by income, and between country trade costs proxied by distance and other variables such as sharing a common border. The observation that product differentiation creates intraindustry trade predates DS, however, and Armington (1969) had used product differentiation and a CES utility function to model such flows. But at that stage there was no theory to explain the number of varieties produced in each country. This was the next step made possible by the DS model.

1.2   Monopolistic Competition and the Location of Production

DS identified each variety with a single firm, assumed to operate with increasing returns to scale. The profits of a single representative country i firm π_i, can be expressed as

$$\pi_i = \sum_j^R p_{ij} x_{ij} - c_i \left[F + \sum_j^R x_{ij} T_{ij} \right]. \tag{5}$$

The first term is revenue earned from sales in all markets, and the second term is costs. The total output of the firm is $x_i \equiv \sum_j^R x_{ij} T_{ij}$, which is the sum of quantities sold in each market times the "iceberg" trade costs incurred in shipping the product. Thus, to meet consumer demand of x_{ij}, $T_{ij} x_{ij}$ units have to be produced and shipped. If $T_{ij} = 1$ trade is costless, then $T_{ij} - 1$ measures the proportion of output lost in shipping from i to j. Production incurs both a constant marginal cost c_i and, to capture increasing returns to scale, a fixed cost $c_i F$.

With demand functions (3), profit maximizing firms set a price according to

$$p_{ij}(1 - 1/\varepsilon_{ij}) = T_{ij}c_i. \tag{6}$$

where ε_{ij} is the perceived elasticity of demand. The form this elasticity takes depends on the nature of oligopolistic competition between firms in the industry. Under price and quantity competition, respectively B and C, they are

$$\varepsilon_{ij}^B = \sigma + (\eta - \sigma)s_{ij}, \qquad \frac{1}{\varepsilon_{ij}^C} = \frac{1}{\sigma} + \left(\frac{1}{\eta} - \frac{1}{\sigma}\right)s_{ij} \tag{7}$$

where s_{ij} is the share of a single firm from country i in market j and $1 - \eta$ is the elasticity of expenditure, E_j, with respect to the price index, G_j. While these forms capture strategic interaction they are unwieldy, so DS adopted the large-group assumption of Chamberlin (1950). With a continuum of firms the market share of any one is zero; setting $s_{ij} = 0$, the pricing rule is simply

$$p_i \equiv \frac{p_{ij}}{T_{ij}} = \frac{c_i \sigma}{\sigma - 1}. \tag{8}$$

This means that a firm in country i sets a single producer (fob) price, p_i, and the price in market j is $p_{ij} = p_i T_{ij}$. Furthermore, given this pricing behavior, profits of a country i firm are

$$\pi_i = c_i \left[\frac{x_i}{\sigma - 1} - F \right]. \tag{9}$$

Thus, the firm breaks even if the total volume of its sales equals a constant, denoted $\bar{x} = (\sigma - 1)F$.

In the closed economy, all that remains is to determine the number of firms. This number adjusts until the demand curve facing each is such that all make zero profits, that is, sell output $\bar{x}$. Formally, prices are set by equation (8), and the number of firms adjusts until the price index (2) takes the value at which demand for each firm's output (3) equals the break-even level.

The spatial extension of the model requires that one also finds the number of firms active in each country, region or city. There are two cases to consider. The first is when there are no trade frictions of any kind, so $T_{ij} = 1$ for all i, j. This case was explored by Helpman and Krugman (1985), who showed that DS can be added on top of traditional Heckscher-Ohlin trade theory. With no trade frictions there is a single integrated world product market; the price index is the same in all countries and all firms face identical demands, regardless of where they are located. To break even they must therefore have the same costs, so production is determined by technology and factor supply. In the absence of international technology differences, production and interindustry trade are determined just as in Heckscher-Ohlin trade theory. The location of production is determined by factor intensities and factor endowments, and net exports are identical to those predicted by Heckscher-Ohlin. There is also intraindustry trade, however, as each firm sells its output to all countries.

The more interesting case arises when there are trade costs, so $T_{ij} > 1$ for some i, j. Then it is not only the location of factors of production that determine the structure of production, but also the location of demand. This can be seen by writing the expression for the total sales of a firm that is producing in country i. Adding equation (3) across markets gives

$$x_i = \sum_j^R x_{ij} T_{ij} = p_i^{-\sigma} \sum_j^R E_j G_j^{\sigma-1} T_{ij}^{1-\sigma}. \tag{10}$$

The term $\sum_j^R E_j G_j^{\sigma-1} T_{ij}^{1-\sigma}$ is the market access of location i, and is the theoretically founded version of the old concept of market potential (Harris 1954). It says that, given the spatial distribution of demands (depending on expenditure and the price index in each market), firms located close to locations with large demands (i.e., locations i where $T_{ij}^{1-\sigma}$ is small) will, other things being equal, have higher sales.

In equilibrium all firms sell the same level of output, so other things are not equal. The effect must therefore show up in the equilibrium values of other variables, typically some combination of the number of firms and factor prices in each location. If factor prices are constrained to be the same in all locations (perhaps because of the presence of other tradeable sectors or factor mobility), then locations with good market access will tend to have many firms. Numbers of firms adjust to bring about a spatial distribution of price indices, G_j, such that $x_i = \bar{x}$ in all locations where $n_i > 0$. Achieving this involves an amplification effect, in the sense that if one location has twice the demand of others it will have more than twice as many firms.

If factor prices in a location are bid up by expansion of industry, then the corollary is that locations with good market access will have higher factor prices. Thus, if labor is the only input to production (so c_i equals the wage, w_i), then $x_i = \bar{x}$ implies (using (8) in (10)) that wages must satisfy the equation

$$\bar{x}\left(\frac{w_i \sigma}{\sigma - 1}\right)^\sigma = \sum_{j}^{R} E_j G_j^{\sigma-1} T_{ij}^{1-\sigma}. \tag{11}$$

This relationship is termed the wage equation (Fujita, Krugman, and Venables 1999) and gives the maximum level of wages consistent with zero profits for firms in location i. Since the right-hand side is decreasing in T_{ij}, it suggests there is a wage gradient from core regions (those with good market access) to peripheral ones. Furthermore, if labor is mobile, there is a positive feedback mechanism that can cause agglomeration of industrial activity. Regions with large markets pay high wages, thus attracting labor inflow which in turn causes the region to become large. Krugman (1991) shows how this may, depending on parameter values, lead to agglomeration of all manufacturing in a single location.

1.3 Cost and Demand Linkages

The DS apparatus can be applied to the production of intermediate goods as well as consumer goods. This was first picked up by Ethier (1982), who interpreted U_j as production of a composite intermediate, and G_j as its unit cost function. This interpretation was used in Romer (1987) and thereby entered the literature on endogenous growth.

The formulation was applied to the international location of production by Krugman and Venables (1995). The simplest case is where each manufacturing firm uses labor and manufacturing goods as inputs to production and produces output used both as a final consumption good and as an intermediate in manufacturing. If the technology is Cobb-Douglas, then manufacturing unit costs become $c_i = G_i^\alpha w_i^{1-\alpha}$, where α is the intermediate share. Demand for each firm's output now comes both from final consumer demand and derived demand from manufacturing firms, the location i value of which is $\alpha n_i p_i x_i$.

These two relationships create cost and demand linkages among firms. Locations where there are many manufacturing firms benefit from a good supply of intermediate goods, reducing the price index G_i and hence manufacturing costs. They also have high levels of demands for manufacturing, arising from the derived demands for manufacturing inputs. These linkages constitute pecuniary externalities, making it profitable for firms to locate close to other firms.

1.4   The Location of Industry

Putting these effects into general equilibrium gives a theory of industrial location combining factor supply, product market size, and competition effects, and linkages among firms. To see how these work, consider the thought experiment of relocating a firm from country j to country i. How does this affect the profitability of firms in country i?

The first effect is in the factor market. Additional factor demand in country i will tend to raise factor prices, depending on general equilibrium responses in other sectors of the economy, thus reducing profit levels in country i. The second effect arises through competition in the product market. The relocation changes price indices in each location, reducing the location i price index, G_i. If there are trade costs, then the net effect will be to shift down the demand curve faced by country i firms, reducing profit levels in country i.

The third effect is in the price of intermediates. The change in the price index described above means that manufactured intermediates become cheaper in country i (the cost linkage), tending to raise profits. Finally, relocation of a firm to country i increases derived demands. This shift in demand curves benefits local firms (the demand linkage), again raising the profitability of firms in country i.

Of the four forces, only the first—factor price effects—is captured in traditional trade theory. Both factor market and product market competition effects are forces for dispersion of activity, since adding a firm tends to reduce profits in the location. The two further effects, cost and demand linkages, however, are radically different; they suggest that adding a firm tends to raise profits of other firms in the location. The equilibrium location of the industry is therefore a balance between these dispersion and agglomeration forces.

The balance is studied in a number of contexts by Fujita, Krugman, and Venables (1999). For example, in a benchmark case in which countries are identical in underlying technology, demand, and endowments, falling trade barriers bring a pattern of divergence followed by convergence in the location of industry and hence in the world income distribution. When trade costs are very high, the location of industry must be dispersed; high trade barriers mean that local demands in every location must be met by local production. In contrast, when trade costs are very low, location is determined by factor supplies, implying dispersion and factor price equalization.

When trade costs are at intermediate levels and linkages are strong enough, however, industry concentrates in a subset of countries. Countries with industry have high wages, but it is not profitable for any single firm to relocate, as doing so would mean foregoing demand and cost linkages. The world therefore divides into a high-income region with manufacturing and a low-income region specializing in agriculture. The model yields the conclusion that, even if economies are ex ante identical, equilibrium involves international differences in production structure and inequality in incomes. Agglomeration forces captured by the DS framework break the symmetry of the model.

2   Spatial Inequalities in Development: An Application

These ideas are now pursued further in the context of spatial inequalities within a developing country. As a country industrializes, what happens to its internal geography? It has been suggested that as countries grow from low-income levels they go through a period of regional divergence with concentration of development and industrialization in just a restricted portion of the country. As development proceeds, industrial deconcentration occurs, with development of hinterland areas and a move toward regional convergence (see the discussion in Henderson, Shalizi, and Venables 2001).

The remainder of this chapter develops a simple variant of a new economic geography model to address these issues. Assume that the country under study has many locations, arranged linearly—the beach model. There are internal transport costs that depend on the distance between locations. The rest of the world is treated as an exogenous supplier and demander of goods, and several different geographies (or more simply, port locations) are considered through which the country interacts with the rest of the world.

The country under study has two sectors: manufacturing and agriculture. Manufacturing contains DS firms that each produce their own variety of output and are linked through the input-output structure discussed above. Since we seek to model the spatial implications of manufacturing development, rather than the causes of such development, we will deviate from the DS monopolistic competition model by simply assuming that the total number of manufacturing firms in the country is exogenous, and that each can produce a fixed level of output. With fixed production capacity, the price charged by each firm is that which clears the market for its variety. Firms' profits depend on where they produce, and profit maximizing locational choices are made. In addition to manufacturing, there is an agricultural sector modeled by supposing that every point in the country has an endowment of land that can be used with labor to produce a freely tradable agricultural product.

To complete the model, we must specify factor market clearing and income determination. Workers are completely mobile among locations and sectors, so at equilibrium real wages are the same in all locations and activities. As manufacturing expands, workers are drawn out of agriculture, bidding up wage levels in the economy. We will also assume that there is a diseconomy to agglomeration of manufacturing. Utility of manufacturing workers is decreasing in the number of manufacturing workers in the same location, so that (given perfect mobility of labor) wages must be higher in locations that have high levels of manufacturing employment. In this framework, what is the equilibrium location of firms in the economy? And as the number of manufacturing firms is exogenously increased, what happens to the equilibrium pattern of industrial location?

2.1 Industrialization under Autarky

Numerical methods to explore equilibria of this model are used, and results are presented in a series of contour plots.[1] In figure 27.1 and subsequent figures, the vertical axis represents locations in the economy; thus, the top and bottom of the vertical axis are the two ends of the linear economy. The horizontal axis is the share of the labor force in manufacturing, varying from 1 percent to 30 percent. The contour lines on the figures give manufacturing activity levels in each location.

Each point on the horizontal axis corresponds to an exogenously given number of manufacturing firms in the country as a whole, and the model computes the equilibrium location of these firms. Models of this type typically exhibit path dependence, so the process by which more firms are added to the economy needs to be specified. The results shown compute an initial equilibrium (at the left-hand end of each figure). A nearly uniform measure of firms is then added to all locations, on top of the equilibrium pattern at the previous equilibrium, and the new equilibrium computed. The process is repeated, moving to the right along the figure. The reason why a

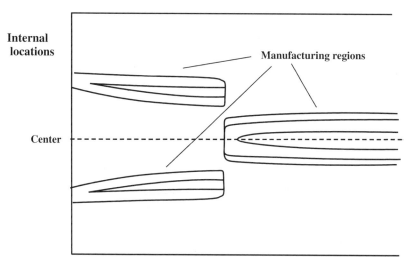

Figure 27.1
Location of industry under autarky

nearly uniform distribution is added is that to test for stability of the equilibrium, it is necessary to perturb the starting conditions slightly away from symmetry.

The closed economy is illustrated in figure 27.1. At low levels of manufacturing development, there are two manufacturing regions, located approximately one third and two-third of the way along the length of the economy. This locational pattern exhibits clustering because of the demand and cost linkages in the model. Working against clustering, however, is the presence of demand for manufactures in all locations. The distribution of land across locations means that income is generated everywhere, and complete agglomeration of manufacturing in a single central cluster would leave opportunities to profit from entry in peripheral regions. At low levels of overall manufacturing activity, the tension between the agglomeration and dispersion forces produces an outcome with two distinct manufacturing regions.

As the economy becomes more developed, one sees that the two manufacturing region structure breaks down and a single region forms, making the spatial distribution of activity more concentrated. Why does this happen? The two-region structure becomes unstable because as the economy becomes more industrialized, agglomeration forces become stronger. In particular, as manufacturing grows relative to agriculture, the proportion of demand for manufactures coming from the industrial regions becomes greater. This is a force for moving the industrial centers inward and away from the edges of the economy. Because of the lock-in effect created by agglomeration, however, this does not happen smoothly. Instead, the two-center structure remains an equilibrium up to some point at which there is a bifurcation in the system and a new structure develops, with a single central industrial region. Further growth of manufacturing increases the number of firms in this region and also (because of the diseconomies to city size that are present in the model) causes some spread of the region to either side of the central location. What we see then is the closed economy developing a monocentric structure, with a large central manufacturing region.

2.2 Industrialization with Two Ports

How do things differ in a more open economy? This is first addressed by looking at the case where the geography of the economy remains symmetric, with one port at each end of the country. Results are illustrated in figure 27.2.

At low levels of industrialization, there is now a single industrial region, located in the center of the economy. This is due to the presence of foreign competition, making peripheral locations unprofitable. Firms derive natural protection from locating in the center of the economy.

As the number of firms increases, two things happen. First, central regions of the economy become increasingly well supplied with manufactures, thus driving down their prices. And second, cost linkages strengthen, reducing costs and making manufacturing better able to compete with the rest of the world production. Both of these forces encourage a dispersion of activity from the central region toward the edges of the economy. Once again, there is a bifurcation point, but now the single cluster of activity divides into two clusters closer to the ports. Despite the lock-in forces due to agglomeration, these centers exhibit some movement toward the edge of the economy, becoming more dependent on export markets as a destination for the growing volume of output. At some point the clusters reach and concentrate at the port locations.

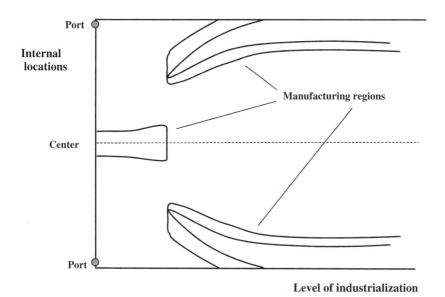

Figure 27.2
Location of industry with two ports

The broad picture is therefore one in which industrial development in the open economy is associated with transition from a small centrally located and inward-oriented manufacturing sector to its replacement by large export-oriented clusters at the ports. Two qualifications need to be made. First, if the domestic economy were made much larger, then the central cluster, devoted largely to supplying the domestic market, could also survive. And second, if returns to clustering were made stronger, then it is possible that manufacturing would agglomerate at a single port. The gains to agglomeration at just one of the ports would outweigh any diseconomies due to congestion or costs of supplying domestic consumers on the other side of the economy.

2.3 Industrialization with a Single Port

Finally, let us look at the case where geography is such that trade can occur through only one end of the economy, a port located at the bottom edge of figure 27.3.

Like the previous case, at low levels of industrialization there is a single industrial cluster. This is now located more than half the

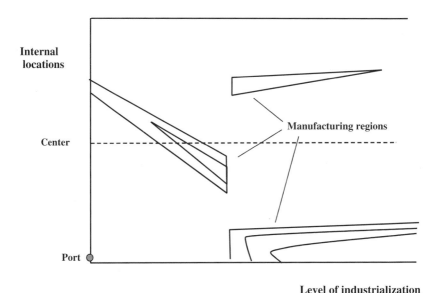

Figure. 27.3
Location of industry with one port

length of the economy away from the port to benefit from the natural protection of distance. Industrialization makes industry more outward oriented and causes movement of this cluster toward the port. This movement means that interior regions of the economy become progressively less well served by manufacturing industry, and the economy reaches a bifurcation point at which a new spatial structure emerges. A new industrial cluster forms in the interior of the economy, oriented toward meeting local demands, and the original cluster is replaced by a cluster of manufacturing in the port city. There is therefore a radical change in internal economic geography, with the original monocentric structure being replaced by two industrial clusters, one export oriented and the other predominantly supplying the domestic market.

Further growth in the number of firms is concentrated in the export-oriented cluster, as diminishing returns (in the product market) are encountered less rapidly in export sales than in domestic sales. But as this occurs, the coastal cluster gains an increasing cost advantage, due to the deepening of cost linkages. This undermines the competitiveness of the internal cluster which, in this example, starts to decline and eventually disappears.

2.4 Comparison

These cases are suggestive of the forces at work in determining the changing pattern of industrial location during development. They show how in open economies development can be associated with a deconcentration of activity. And in a cross-section of countries, they are consistent with the Ades and Glaeser (1995) finding that more open economies have less spatially concentrated economic activity.

The cases given here are examples rather than general findings, and the literature remains short of having findings that are robust enough to be the basis for policy advice. Results are sensitive to details of the geography of countries, including both external trade opportunities and internal infrastructure (the example here holds transport costs constant). Results also depend on the strengths of linkages within industries and, with many manufacturing sectors, the strength of linkages between industries. The model outlined here is static, and while agglomeration tends to lock-in an existing industrial structure, other forces for lock-in, such as sunk costs, are ignored. Thus, while some of the cases outlined above had the property that industrial structure only changed through the birth and death of industrial centers, others had the less satisfactory property of industrial centers moving continuously with parameters of the model. All of this points to the need for further work, both theoretical and empirical, to pin down these effects.

3 Conclusions

The question of where economic activity takes place is central to economics. The location of industry across countries is a major determinant of cross-country income distribution. Within countries there are important questions about regional inequalities and the design of urban structures. Yet, for many years, the spatial organization of activity was largely ignored by the economics mainstream. The likely reason for this is that convincing stories about regional and urban development hinge crucially on increasing returns to scale. In a world of constant or diminishing returns, the economy should be characterized by backyard capitalism, in which local markets are supplied by small plants. It is only increasing returns to scale that force firms to concentrate production in relatively few locations and thus confront them with the decision of where to operate. Yet increasing returns to scale pose difficulties for general equilibrium theorists. They cannot be satisfactorily reconciled with competitive market structures, and leave messy choices about what market structure should be assumed in its place.

The DS model of monopolistic competition offers a way out of this impasse, supplying the profession with a tractable and consistent model of firm level increasing returns and monopolistic competition. The range of its application across the fields of industrial organisation, technical change, growth theory, and trade theory is astonishing. Even more remarkable is the fact that with each application it has continued to open up new insights. In economic geography the combination of the DS model with spatial frictions (trade and transport costs) turns out to yield pecuniary externalities among firms, as we have seen here. As a consequence, not only are there increasing returns to scale within the firm, but there are also increasing returns to scale to groups of firms. This opens the door to rigorous analysis of clustering and of the cumulative causation processes that have loomed so large in informal discussions of regional and international development. It is now informing empirical work and will, perhaps, come to provide a basis for policy analysis.[2]

Notes

1. Details of the simulations are available from the author on request.

2. For a survey of empirical work, see Overman, Redding, and Venables (2001).

References

Ades, A. F., and E. L. Glaeser. 1995. "Trade and Circuses: Explaining Urban Giants," *Quarterly Journal of Economics* 110: 195–227.

Armington, P. S. 1969. "The Geographic Pattern of Trade and the Effects of Price Changes," IMF staff papers 17: 488–523.

Chamberlin, E. 1950. "Product Heterogeneity and Public Policy," *American Economic Review* 40: 85–92.

Dixit, A. K., and J. E. Stiglitz. 1977. "Monopolistic Competition and Optimum Product Diversity," *American Economic Review* 67: 297–308.

Ethier, W. J. 1982. "National and international returns to scale in the modern theory of international trade." *American Economic Review* 72: 389–405.

Fujita, M., P. Krugman, and A. J. Venables. 1999. *The Spatial Economy: Cities, Regions, and International Trade.* Cambridge, MA: MIT Press.

Harris, C. 1954. "The Market as a Factor in the Localization of Industry in the United States," *Annals of the Association of American Geographers* 64: 315–348.

Helpman, E., and P. Krugman. 1985. *Market Structure and Foreign Trade.* Cambridge, MA: MIT Press.

Henderson, J. V., Z. Shalizi, and A. J. Venables. 2001. "Geography and Development," *Journal of Economic Geography*, 1: 81–105.

Krugman, P. 1991. "Increasing Returns and Economic Geography," *Journal of Political Economy* 99(3): 483–499.

Krugman, P., and Venables, A. J. 1995. "Globalisation and the Inequality of Nations," *Quarterly Journal of Economics* 110(4): 857–880.

Overman, H. G., S. Redding, and A. J. Venables. 2001. "The Economic Geography of Trade, Production, and Income: A Survey of Empirics," CEP discussion paper, 508, forthcoming in J. Harrigan, ed. *Handbook of International Trade.* Basil Blackwell.

Romer, P. M. 1987. "Growth Based on Increasing Returns Due to Specialization," *American Economic Review* 77: 56–72.

28

Public Policy for Growth and Poverty Reduction

Nicholas Stern

The Nobel Committee and the economics profession as a whole have celebrated Joseph Stiglitz's work in the economics of information. I would like to focus attention on two other areas of economics where Joe has made—and is continuing to make—substantial contributions: public economics and development economics (including the economics of the transition).

One of the most outstanding of the many important contribution Joe has made is to bring those three areas closer together. During the nearly twenty years when I was an editor of the *Journal of Public Economics* (working with Tony Atkinson), I had many fruitful exchanges and collaborations with Joe, who was part of the editorial team, and the author of the now-classic *Economics of the Public Sector* as well as his book with Tony Atkinson, *Lectures on Public Economics*. My close friendship with Joe and our collaboration on the topics of development and transition has spanned an even longer period, starting when we were young researchers in the late 1960s walking in the Kenyan countryside. Later we explored the relatively uncharted terrain of transition from command to market economies when I was chief economist at the European Bank for Reconstruction and Development (EBRD) and Joe was chief economist of the World Bank.[1] Finally, Joe and I worked closely on the transition as I succeeded him in that job at the World Bank.[2] In all of these interactions I have learned enormously from him.

In this chapter I want to bring our discussions in public economics and development together, offering an approach to public policy that is focused on fighting poverty and based on an understanding of growth and development. Thus I begin by asking what are the key determinants of a development that benefits poor people? In answering I shall draw particularly on research at the World Bank at

the time of Joe's leadership, and I ask how public policy can influence these determinants. In answering these questions, I will try to
tell a story of what determines pro-poor growth and how to promote
it. In putting the questions this way, we are setting ourselves the
task of building a dynamic public economics: a public economics of
development.

1   Foundations in Public Economics and Key Elements of a Dynamic Approach

Brief Review

A major contribution of the theories of public economics over the last
thirty years has been in deepening an understanding of the complementarity between states and markets.

• The public economics of Boiteux (1949, 1956) and Diamond-
Mirrlees (1971) embodied the recognition that the state did not have
the capability or information necessary to direct production. Diamond and Mirrlees focused on production incentives for producers,
both private and public, together with prices and taxes facing consumers. They examined consistency and optimality.

• The analysis of market failures based on imperfect and asymmet-
rical information by Joseph Stiglitz, George Akerlof, and Michael
Spence lead to the modern field of information economics and
showed the ubiquity and seriousness of these market failures.

These are, of course, insights from theory but if we learned one
thing from the experience of the economies in Eastern Europe and
the former Soviet Union in transition to a market economy, it is that
markets need sound government if they are to function well. The
result of all this work was that neither the state nor market could be
seen as the solution; there is a basic complementarity between the
state and markets. But the question is not how much of each or the
balance between the two; the question is how they might combine
and be mutually supportive.

From Statics to Dynamics in Public Economics

The insights sketched above represent real achievements of lasting
value. This theory, however, does not have much to say about what I

will argue are the key drivers of pro-poor growth. These drivers are the main topic here: the investment climate and the empowerment of and investing in poor people. This approach goes beyond size and distribution of the cake and sees the issues of development and poverty reduction in terms of generating growth and participating in growth. Both elements are essentially processes with history, dynamic structure, and learning rather than one-shot events as in the static theory. Thus, the challenge of public policy becomes one of how to understand and influence these processes.

Within this perspective, entrepreneurship is central. How, analytically, can one bring entrepreneurship into the story? How can we usefully model and strengthen the insights of the Austrian School (e.g., von Mises, Schumpeter, Hayek, Kirzner) that, from the early twentieth century, recognized the centrality of entrepreneurship in the market process? The Austrians have emphasized that limitations on knowledge and information are key to understanding and appreciating the market process. In *Whither Socialism?* Stiglitz shows how these intuitive insights, and the accompanying critique of neoclassical theories assuming perfect information (including the Lerner/Lange model of the "price mechanism" under market socialism), can be deepened using the modern machinery of information economics. How can we now move toward theories, and related policies, about the conditions for entrepreneurship to flourish?

As Schumpeter (1934) emphasized so clearly and strongly, a competitive environment is fundamental to the flowering of entrepreneurship. It has to be possible to enter markets, to innovate, and to gain the rewards to innovation. Those working on development issues around the world surely see the potential for entrepreneurship in all societies. All too often, however, it is suppressed by obstacles and hurdles erected, operated, and maintained by those in privileged positions. It is undermined by weak governance and bureaucratic harassment—both organized and opportunistic. And it is frequently thwarted and discouraged by crime, both organized and otherwise.

These notions were central to our attempts at the EBRD to understand the process of transition in Eastern Europe and the former Soviet Union at the EBRD. They are also central to a broader examination of development that is the subject here. And they warn against imposing some standard blueprint for either transition or development. This has not been a mistake made by the Chinese as they embarked on and developed their own transition from 1979. They moved step-by-step; experimenting, building on what went before and finding their own way.

The analytical path ahead should not be a search for one grand unified theory. That would be fruitless, confusing, and misguided. We should be seeking a combination of strong empirics and a battery of theories. The issues concern the analysis of the twin and intertwined processes of the investment climate and empowering and investing in poor people. In focusing on these two processes as key drivers of pro-poor growth, note that we are not talking about steady states, about being on a production frontier, or about comparisons of two equilibria. We are talking about processes of change, adaptation, creativity, learning, and inclusion.

2   Building the Investment Climate

The central public policy question here is: how can a country develop governance and institutions to support entrepreneurship and well-functioning markets; or, in other words, how can it build an investment climate that will generate growth and development?

The Investment Climate and the Role of Public Economics

The policy challenge is thus the promotion of growth through improvements in the investment climate; it is about creating conditions so that the pie keeps expanding. It is not just a question of how to avoid or limit losing slices of the pie as measured by Dupuit-Harberger triangles or even rent-seeking quadrilaterals, which are, crudely speaking, the type of losses that lie behind standard trade-offs between size and distribution of the cake in basic static public economics.

The investment climate notion forces one to look at government through the eyes of the private sector—first and foremost, farmers and small entrepreneurs in both urban and rural areas. How will farmers learn about and be able to invest in new techniques or crops? Suppose one or more people from a village go to a town to work in a factory, workshop, or other establishment and learn about some basic activity, for example, how to produce some simple component or product. What sort of an investment environment would foster their applying what they have learned through the creation of a new enterprise in the village or elsewhere? As we have seen with the Chinese village enterprises, this sort of innovation (much more down-to-earth than innovation in the sense of new patents) has great developmental multiplier effects. For instance, in addition to jobs and income, parents will give greater support to girls' education when they see that their daughters with an education and literacy might get jobs in a local off-farm rural enterprise.

In focusing on SMEs we are not neglecting or forgetting entrepreneurship elsewhere. Policy and institutional reforms that improve the climate for small and medium-sized enterprises (SMEs) would usually also improve the climate for large and foreign enterprises. For growth to happen, entrepreneurs need to be able to recognize and create opportunities to increase productivity and make productive investments. And they need an environment where they can pursue those opportunities effectively.

Thus, we need to think of a dynamic model of their behavior involving (1) constraints on their entrepreneurship or, put another way, the strength of the supporting environment (including role models for being successful); (2) their ability to recognize and create opportunity; and (3) their learning processes. It is about risk and return, but what we are trying to do here is to understand not only the determinants of risk and return but also the determinants of perception and the ability to respond. The normative theory of the relevant public policy will have to be based on positive models of the investment climate and how it gets changed.

Ideally, a clear structural theory of the investment climate would lead directly to a definition of appropriate indicators for its measurement. I suspect that a careful examination of more modern growth theory in the Schumpeterian spirit has much to offer (see, e.g., Aghion and Howitt 1997). That is something which I hope theorists can help with.

At present, however, I offer a pragmatic definition and approach for the investment climate that is based on the underlying intuitive notion as described and on experience with surveys of firms concerning their perceptions of impediments to entrepreneurship.

The Investment Climate: Identifying the Obstacles

The identification of obstacles to investment and productivity growth must take place in a given country context. Different countries face different constraints and problems, and the institutional and governance responses to the challenge of improving the investment climate thus will also vary across countries. In this, as in other policy areas, while there are common principles, there should be no "one size fits all."

How can one gather information? There are a number of fruitful routes.

• Consultation with relevant groups. This will usually involve a strong element of the qualitative. This consultation should go beyond chambers of commerce or other representatives of large firms and multinationals and include diverse representatives of all firms including particularly farmers and microentrepreneurs. The World Bank has been associated with a number of approaches to these consultations, including those involved in the preparation of poverty reduction strategy papers for very poor countries.

• Learning through direct experience of the private investment activities of the multilateral development banks (International Finance Corporation, EBRD).

• Careful surveys of firms to identify constraints. These should include strong quantitative analysis.

Let me draw on results from India where the research department (DEC) of the World Bank is collaborating with the Confederation of Indian Industry (CII) on firm-level surveys of the investment climate. One example that illustrates what can be discovered came from a comparison of the investment climate in the state of Maharashtra in India, with a population of 100 million, and the state of Uttar Pradesh (UP), with a population of 170 million. One measurable dimension is the number of visits from local authorities that are twice as common in the survey in UP than Maharashtra. It is unlikely that these visitations are constructive and probable that they are predatory. And, indeed, one finds that those Indian states with better investment climates are both growing and reducing poverty more quickly.

3 Involving Poor People in Growth

The kind of research on the investment climate described here helps shape public policy in responding to the challenge of promoting investment, productivity, and growth. At the same time, the task of fighting poverty requires that public policy also work to ensure that poor people can participate in growth. This second process, fundamentally intertwined with the first, is a second crucial challenge for development-oriented public economics.

Participation, Poverty, and Public Policy

Growth is central to poverty reduction but it is a much more powerful force if poor people are empowered to participate.

Key to the participation of poor people in growth is making sure that they are equipped to participate and that institutional structures facilitate rather than prevent their participation. There are a number of crucial elements to public policy here, including working to involve poor people in decision making in the public sector, promoting participatory social organizations, and ensuring legal protection. Activities here, together with education, health, and social protection, can provide the circumstances for effective participation.

Just as firm-level surveys can help formulate policies to improve the investment climate, household and individual surveys that ask about empowerment and participation, as well as surveys of basic service providers (health units, schools, etc.) and government units, can help formulate public policy on empowering and investing in poor people. The World Bank has been investing strongly in such surveys; see, for example, the three volumes of *Voices of the Poor* by Narayan et al. (2000a, b) and Narayan and Petesch (2002), and the work on basic service providers that is under way for the forthcoming *World Development Report* on making services work for poor people. I would suggest that empirical public economics going forward will and should have a strong focus on these three types of surveys—firms/investment climate, households, and service providers/government units—just as the empirical work stimulated by the theory of the 1970s focused on household expenditure surveys and aggregate demand functions.

In assessing where we now stand in understanding the first pillar of the investment climate, I suggested that the empirics were ahead of theory. On the second pillar of empowering and investing in poor people I would suggest that the same ranking is true. In the second case, however, neither the empirics nor the theory has gone as far as the first. In both cases we are at the beginning of a long program of research and we have much further to go on the second pillar than the first. I suspect that modern theories of organization and incentives may have quite a lot to tell about why some modes of service provision work better than others.

The perspective here is not primarily about the static redistribution of income, but about ensuring both that the pie grows and poor people are part of the drivers and beneficiaries of the process. The lives and prospects of individuals and their families can be transformed by:

• Education and health care that increase their employability and ability to become successful entrepreneurs.

• Social protection that allows them to take the risks that participation in a dynamic market economy entails—the dynamic perspective on social protection is as a springboard, whereas the static perspective sees it as a social safety net.

• Social organization and empowerment through the administrative and legal system that improve the chances their voices will be heard, they can use their assets, and they will not be cheated or excluded.

Let me emphasize that these dynamic perspectives do not exclude, contradict, or reject the standard analyses of public policy for education, health, and redistribution. They build on them.

Promoting the Participation of Poor People: Start with Basic Services

From our analysis of how poor people can get involved in growth, we find some fairly direct public policy lessons or approaches. The challenge of empowering and investing in poor people is, in large measure, the challenge of ensuring effective and efficient creation and availability of basic services. This is the topic of the *World Development Report 2004* (to appear in September 2003). In responding to the challenge, both the level of resources and how they are used will be crucial. Just as with work on the investment climate, we are learning how to use both qualitative and quantitative information in understanding how to make services work for poor people.

• Quantitatively, it is important to gather information about whether services are actually reaching poor people and in what quality. For example, do people have access to clean water, are children being immunized, are teachers showing up at schools and doctors at clinics, do the schools have books and computers, and do the clinics have drugs and functioning equipment?

• Qualitatively, we must work to ensure that citizens', consumers', and parents' groups have a chance to make their voices heard.

One challenge, for example, is to encourage teachers to attend school; teachers show up for work more when parents are involved in the governance of schools. We have also seen the power of information, for example, in the Uganda expenditure tracking project that involved publishing the amounts of funds supposedly distributed from the government to the school districts (see Reinikka 2001). We should not assume that these examples operate solely through the greater monitoring and reward-oriented motivation that might come from greater participation by beneficiaries and their representatives. There is likely, for example, to be much greater job satisfaction and self-esteem if teachers see parents as constructively involved (see Uphoff 1994 or Tendler 1997 for examples of successful programs that emphasized the commitment and dedication of service workers).

4 Where Does this Perspective of Entrepreneurship and Learning Lead to in Public Economics?

As an illustration of where this approach to development can go, let us examine briefly five examples. They are all concerned with the endogeneity of innovations, behavior, and institutions.

Returns to Scale

Latifundia economies and soviet-style communism are two examples where seeking after productivity using returns to scale had the effect of killing the long-term developmental effects for most participants. Apparent short-term efficiency (often distorted by entrenched vested interests) was pursued in a way that damaged long-term development and the empowerment of people to create and innovate.

Stiglitz and I (separately) had the opportunity in Cambridge, England, in the 1960s to hear Joan Robinson and Nicholas Kaldor chastise neoclassical economics for its assumption of constant or diminishing returns. Karl Marx and Piero Sraffa were lauded in contrast for abandoning that assumption. Kaldor frequently quoted

Marx's "Accumulate, accumulate; that is Moses and the Prophets" (vol. I of *Kapital*, chapter 24, section 3 where he discusses increasing scale), which Kaldor took to be Marx's description of competition among capitalists for lower costs via scale. This embracing of increasing returns was taken by both the planners of the communist societies and many Marxist theorists as one of the distinguishing hallmarks of the command economy/Marxist approach to economic development.[3]

Adam Smith, on the other hand, clearly recognized the potentially deadening effect of the repetitive factory work directed by others which was involved in many large-scale activities. The effects on human development of types of work with no room for initiative, learning, and growth can be profoundly disempowering. Thomas Jefferson had a similar perspective with his vision of small farmers and businessmen as providing a constant revitalizing effect, which he contrasted with the static efficiency of big combines. A more recent and important example lies in the dynamism of Chinese township and village enterprises (TVEs). These were much more dynamic and creative than the monolithic and often gigantic state-owned enterprises (SOEs) which became a heavy burden on the economy.

Central to the approaches of Smith, Jefferson, and the TVEs are the dynamics of learning and creativity. Any policy directed toward development, industrial structure, and regulation risks being profoundly misleading if it does not take such forces into account.

Specialization with Gains from Trade

Some further aspects of the contrasts between China and the Soviet Union are instructive here. The Soviet Union went for gargantuan, highly specialized plants. This was partly due to misplaced confidence in static returns to scale but also as a means of economic and political control, thus highly specialized units and regions were all "held hostage" to each other and could be controlled by Stalin's central command. China, on the other hand, went for broad regional self-sufficiency. The result was that the rigidity and over-specialization of the Soviet system led to collapse of much of the industrial structure when it was exposed to market forces, whereas the Chinese transition showed great returns to enhanced internal trade. There is perhaps an analogy with education here; one common strategy is to do general education first—learn to do many things a little bit—and then specialize later—learn a lot about a little bit. This general-first approach expands the possibilities for specialization. It broadens the range of search and have a better opportunity to find out what one might be good at.

A policy lesson here is to seek flexibility and adaptability. Do not try to pick a single winner early on; do not force over-focus. Try to create conditions for learning where entrepreneurs can not only act and move, but are led to seek out potential areas of advantage and growth across a broad spectrum of economic activity.

Growth and Inequality

Growth with large inequality can suppress the potential for future growth. Initial winners can use their influence with the government to "remove the ladder," that is, to limit competition from other elements of society. The long-term effect can be the strangulation of continuing growth. A recent historical example will illustrate the point.

One interpretation of what happened in Russia in the 1990s is that the oligarchs first grabbed their positions and then tried to consolidate and protect their winnings (some would say "loot") by limiting the development of a broad economy of independent small and medium-sized firms.

Jane Jacobs has a wonderful way of making this point. If a spaceship landed from another solar system, we would surely be "agog" to learn about their marvelous technologies.

The important question, however, would be something quite different: What kinds of governments had they invented which had succeeded in keeping open the opportunities for economic and technological development instead of closing them off? Without helpful advice from outer space, this remains one of the most pressing and least regarded problems. (Jacobs 1969, 250)

Internalizing Externalities

One part of the static theory of externalities points to combining units that exhibit mutual externalities into a big unit where all the interactions are taken into account. But such overlayered and powerful entities are likely to stifle innovation. It is much more likely that an appropriate public sector response lies in trying to regulate and tax in a way that allows different entities to innovate and compete while paying the price for damages inflicted on others or being regulated to prevent them from inflicting damage.

Environment and Sustainability

Related issues arise when one looks at the environment and sustainability. There are those who appear to argue that the only way to live in harmony with the environment is to restrain growth. That is unlikely to be a route that will meet with success. It is probably also a mistake to see the issue as sustainability (and it is a mistake made by much of growth theory) in terms of long-run equilibrium or steady-state growth. It is better to see sustainability in terms of the challenge of creating new opportunities, anticipating and responding to problems, and innovating as circumstances change. In many structures, the incentives for adaptation are distorted in that they take inadequate account of the long-term and destructive effects of many actions on the environment. The right reaction is not to restrict growth and change but to restructure incentives through taxation, regulation, and the promotion of appropriate institutions. In this way we can try to foster the kind of learning and searching that finds ways of growing and changing without damage, or indeed ones that can overcome damage to the environment. This approach to sustainability lies at the heart of *World Development Report*, published in 2002.

5   Some Lessons and Conclusions

There are some lessons for the dynamic political economy of reform that run through the examples here. Let me present them in terms of two quotes from distinguished and thoughtful writers on these issues.

it is the nature of most innovations that its beneficiaries are anonymous, inarticulate, and unaware of the benefits-to-accrue (they include among others the consumers that are yet unborn), while those who stand to lose from the innovation are highly vocal vested interests.

That was Albert Hirschman over forty years ago (see Hirschman 1961, 61).

It must be considered that there is nothing more difficult to carry out, nor more doubtful of success, nor more dangerous to handle, than to initiate a new order of things. For the reformer has enemies in all those who profit by the old order, and only lukewarm defenders in all those who would profit by the new order.... Thus it arises that on every opportunity for attacking the reformer, his opponents do so with the zeal of partisans, the others only defend him half-heartedly, so that between them he runs great danger.

That was Machiavelli about 500 years ago (see Machiavelli 1940 (1513), chapter 6).

The dynamic notions of public economics sketched here not only provide a way forward economically, but the story told also has political advantages that take into account the difficulties highlighted by Hirschman and Machiavelli. Static redistribution, for example, is more difficult to sell politically and to implement in the face of entrenched interests than the notion that all children should have sufficient education to allow them to participate in the process of growth.

I have argued for an approach that asks what drives improving living standards, particularly of poor people, and then how to influence these drivers. The drivers identified as twin pillars of pro-poor growth were the creation of an investment climate for entrepreneurship, investment, and growth and the empowerment of and investment in poor people so that they can participate in the growth process.

What I am asking for is the introduction of the spirit of the public policy approach exemplified in the writings of Boiteux, Samuelson, Diamond, Mirrlees, Berglas, and Stiglitz into models that embody an approach to growth based on the insights of Hirschman and Schumpeter.

Acknowledgments

The paper has benefited from discussions when an earlier version was given at the Berglas School of Economics at Tel Aviv University at a lecture in honor of the memory of Eitan Berglas. Joe, Eitan, and I and several other contributors were all working on public economics, particularly in the 1970s and 1980s (see Pines, Sadka, and Zilcha 1998 for a tribute to Eitan's work). David Ellerman has contributed greatly to the preparation of this chapter and I am very grateful to him. For advice and guidance, I would like to thank Phillipe Aghion, Peter Diamond, Coralie Gevers, Karla Hoff, Joyce Msuya, Halsey Rogers, and Scott Wallsten.

Notes

1. See Stern and Stiglitz (1997) and Hussain, Stern, and Stiglitz (2000).

2. See Chang (2001) for nine of Stiglitz's better-known speeches made while chief economist at the World Bank.

3. Rereading that chapter of Kapital, however, suggests to me that Marx was talking at that part about increasing scale rather than increasing returns to scale. Actually, Kaldor himself took the dynamics of innovation and technical progress very seriously (see Kaldor and Mirrlees 1962 as well as Atkinson and Stiglitz 1969).

References

Aghion, Philippe, and Peter Howitt. 1997. *Endogenous Growth Theory*. Cambridge: MIT Press.

Atkinson, Anthony B., and Joseph Stiglitz. 1969. "A New View of Technological Change." *Economic Journal* 79, no. 315, September: 573–578.

Atkinson, Anthony B., and Joseph Stiglitz. 1980. *Lectures in Public Economics*. New York and London: McGraw-Hill.

Boiteux, Marcel. 1949. "La tarification des demandes en point: application de la théorie de la vente au coût marginal." *Revue Générale de l'électricité* 58 (August): 22–40.

Boiteux, Marcel. 1956. "Sur la gestion des monopoles public astreints à l'équilibre budgétaire." *Econometrica* 24 (January): 22–40; translated by W. J. Baumol as "On the Management of Public Monopolies Subject to Budgetary Constraints." *Journal of Economic Theory* 3 (September): 219–240.

Chang, Ha-Joon, ed. 2001. *Joseph Stiglitz and the World Bank: The Rebel Within*. London: Anthem.

Diamond, Peter A., and James A. Mirrlees. 1971. "Optimal Taxation and Public Production I: Production Efficiency" and "II: Tax Rules." *American Economic Review* 61: 8–27 and 261–278.

Hirschman, Albert O. 1961 (1958). *The Strategy of Economic Development*. Paperback ed. New Haven: Yale University Press.

Hussain, Athar, Nicholas Stern, and Joseph Stiglitz. 2000. "Chinese Reforms from a Comparative Perspective," in *Incentives, Organization, and Public Economics: Papers in Honour of Sir James Mirrlees*, ed. Peter Hammond and Gareth Myles, 243–277. New York: Oxford University Press.

Jacobs, Jane. 1969. *The Economy of Cities*. New York: Random House.

Kaldor, Nicholas, and James Mirrlees. 1962. "A New Model of Economic Growth." *Review of Economic Studies* 29, no. 3 (June): 174–192.

Machiavelli, Niccolò. [1513] 1940. *The Prince and the Discourses*. New York: Random House.

Narayan, Deepa, Raj Patel, Kai Schafft, Anne Rademacher, and Sarah Koch-Schulte. 2000a. *Voices of the Poor: Can Anyone Hear Us?* Published for the World Bank. New York: Oxford University Press.

Narayan, Deepa, Robert Chambers, Meera Kaul Shah, and Patti Petesch. 2000b. *Voices of the Poor: Crying Out for Change.* Published for the World Bank. New York: Oxford University Press.

Narayan, Deepa, and Patti Petesch. 2002. *Voices of the Poor: From Many Lands.* Published for the World Bank. New York: Oxford University Press.

Pines, David, Efraim Sadka, and Itzhak Zilcha, eds. 1998. *Topics in Public Economics.* Cambridge: Cambridge University Press.

Reinikka, Ritva. 2001. "Recovery in Service Delivery: Evidence from Schools and Clinics," in *Uganda's Recovery: The Role of Farms, Firms, and Government,* ed. Ritva Reinikka and Paul Collier. Washington, DC: World Bank.

Schumpeter, Joseph. 1934. *The Theory of Economic Development.* Redvers Opie trans. London: Oxford University Press.

Stern, Nicholas, and Joseph Stiglitz. 1997. A Framework for a Development Strategy in a Market Economy," in *Development Strategy and Management of the Market Economy,* vol. I, ed. E. Malinvaud et al., 253–296. Oxford: Clarendon Press (for the United Nations, New York).

Stiglitz, Joseph. 1986. *Economics of the Public Sector.* New York: W. W. Norton.

Stiglitz, Joseph. 1994. *Whither Socialism?* Cambridge, MA: MIT Press.

Tendler, Judith. 1997. *Good Government in the Tropics.* Baltimore: Johns Hopkins University Press.

Uphoff, Norman, ed. 1994. *Puzzles of Productivity in Public Organizations.* San Francisco: ICS Press.

29   Risk, Reform, and
       Privatization

David M. Newbery

By 1976 the consequences of the first oil shock on prices, output, and growth were becoming painfully apparent. Joe Stiglitz had attracted an exciting group of colleagues to visit Stanford, where we mostly worked on the economics of depletable resources and the economics of risk and uncertainty. In response to the boom and bust of most primary commodities during 1973–1975, UNCTAD proposed an Integrated Program for Commodities (IPC) to stabilize the prices of ten core commodities. Joe Stiglitz and I were asked by the World Bank and USAID to examine the desirability of the IPC. We expected to take existing theory on commodity price stabilization, build a simple model, and apply social cost-benefit analysis. Over the next three years, we realized the limitations of received wisdom and had to develop a more comprehensive approach, which appeared as *The Theory of Commodity Price Stabilization: A Study in the Economics of Risk* (Newbery and Stiglitz 1981).

The logical case for public intervention in commodity markets, which was the essence of the IPC, is that there is some market failure that needs correction. Primary commodities (almost uniquely) satisfy almost all the requirements of Arrow-Debreu standard commodities. Lots of 5,000 bushels of U.S. soft red winter wheat, fob Atlantic Ports for delivery in March 2002 can (like other primary commodities) be traded by phone with remarkably low transaction costs. Why, then, might markets fail for such homogenous goods produced by large numbers of individually small producers under near perfect competition? The standard answer was that the first theorem of welfare economics requires market completeness, or a market for each good not just at each place (Atlantic ports), and date (March 2002), but for each state of the world in which prices may differ. Commodity price risk was potentially a problem because of such market incompleteness, and hence there was no guarantee that a competitive equilibrium would be Pareto efficient.

Certainly since Coase (1960), economists have been wary of concluding that market incompleteness necessarily leads to inefficiency, for other forms of transaction (bilateral negotiation) and other institutions (the law of contracts and tort) may emerge in response to potential inefficiencies. The theory of the second best, particularly as interpreted by public finance theorists such as Diamond and Mirrlees (1971) and by Stiglitz himself, also warned against using an unreasonable benchmark in which any market could be costlessly created and agents fully and costlessly provided with all market-relevant information. There are usually good reasons why the market structure is incomplete. The cost of creating and running the market may be too high, information is costly to produce, and is likely to be asymmetrically held, with the attendant problems of moral hazard, adverse selection, and market implosion.

We therefore asked the more reasonable question whether the competitive equilibrium for agents selling homogenous goods on spot and futures markets but facing output and price risk would be constrained Pareto efficient, and, more fundamentally, whether individually rational agents would be lead to set up the right set of markets. In the first case, we proved that constrained efficiency required such stringent conditions that it was generically improbable, while in the second we showed that creating a new market could make all agents worse off. The case for commodity market failure in the presence of risk was thus theoretically plausible.

While this gave apparent comfort to those proposing to stabilize commodity prices, we cautioned that our theoretical investigations cast considerable doubt on the wisdom of the various proposals under discussion. Specifically, we argued that the benefits of intervention had to be measured against an institutional environment in which there were futures markets and private storage, and that most proposed buffer stock schemes were vulnerable to arbitrage and speculation. The efficiency gains of additional interventions appeared very small in cases where we could quantify them, while the likely financial cost of buffer stocks were appreciable. The distortionary costs of raising taxes to finance their losses would likely eliminate these small benefits, unless market compatible interventions were carefully designed and implemented. We also noted that the distributional impacts of market intervention might be considerably larger than the distortionary costs (as must be the case to justify redistributive taxation that is inevitably distortionary), though whether they would constitute an adequate defence of such intervention would depend sensitively on rather arcane characteristics of aggregate demand schedules and risk aversion.

If commodity price shocks and risk were the policy preoccupations of the 1970s, transition from state socialism to the market economy, and the attendant issues of privatization, were the big issues of the 1990s. Indeed, to quote Stiglitz (1999): "This century has been marked by two great economic experiments. The outcome of the first set, the socialist experiment that began, in its more extreme form, in the Soviet Union in 1917, is now clear. The second experiment is the movement back from a socialist economy to a market economy." This transition required far more than just allowing markets rather than the bureaucracy to allocate goods and incomes, for to function well these needed the supporting "institutions of capitalism," as well as a democratically responsive state. Stiglitz's policy pronouncements on these challenges reveal the value of the sophisticated economic analysis of the role of information for market functioning for which he was awarded the Nobel Prize. My task here is more modest: to draw out the link between the analysis of risk and risk-reducing institutions, and the design of reform, both for economic transition, but also for the reform of the electricity supply industry (ESI). Recent events in California, where Stiglitz and I worked on risk, suggest that such issues are still of considerable practical importance.

The Vertically Integrated Insurance Nexus and the Challenge for Reform

Kornai (2000) has forcefully reminded us that state socialism is a system to be sharply contrasted with the capitalist system, where the concept of a system is broad enough to embrace variants, but clear enough to distinguish sharply between these two alternatives. In his schema, the defining features of the systems are: "what characterizes political power, the distribution of property rights, and the constellation of coordination mechanisms. Once these are in place, they largely determine ... the type of behavior typical of the economic actors, and ... the typical economic phenomena.... (T)he socialist system does not originate spontaneously ... (but) is imposed on society by the communist party by brute force, when it gains power" (Kornai 2000, 29, 31). The party's vision of society is hostile to and eliminates private property and the free market, replacing them with state ownership and bureaucratic coordination or planning. Once this "genetic program" has been inserted into the economy, it sets in motion forces to transform economic relations and reject incompatible institutions. One key but largely unremarked aspect of this transformation is the way in which risk is handled under socialism compared to capitalism.

Economic activity involves risk, and all societies evolve institutions to reduce the costs of this risk. Agricultural societies face risks of drought, famine, flood, and pestilence. They store grain, diversify cropping patterns, divide their holdings into dispersed strips, hold livestock, accumulate gold, store and manage water, intermarry with distant villages, and evolve kinship and political structures to reallocate resources in hard times. As economies become more specialized, individual risks increase as the transaction price between successive stages in production introduce new variabilities into the determination of income. A farmer who grows subsistence crops need only worry about the quantity produced, but a farmer growing a cash crop worries both about the quantity and the price. When the sales price is low, the consumer enjoys the benefits of low prices so income is redistributed from producers to consumers, and conversely when prices are high. The more transactions take place in the chain from initial production to final consumption, the greater the potential for income redistributions caused by supply and demand shocks.

A large part of the emergence of a satisfactory market economy consists in the development of institutions to hedge or insure against these kinds of risks. Banks, credit agencies, futures markets, and securities markets all evolve in response to the need for these insurance activities. The absence of such institutions gives rise to a market failure—the failure to provide facilities for trading risk and insurance (Newbery 1989). As noted earlier, their presence may not completely eliminate (constrained) inefficiencies, but they dramatically alter and reduce them. The Soviet-type economy can be thought of as a comprehensive insurance institution in that it severs the link between economic shocks and income distribution. It is like the subsistence farm in which the income redistributive aspects of transactions have all been suppressed. Economists have criticized the socialist economy for the inefficiencies caused by the suppression of these markets and the absence of satisfactory price signals for resource allocation. There is a danger that such criticisms will overlook the other function that it served in providing insurance.

The transition to capitalism requires removing the barriers to exercising private property rights (which also requires the creation of institutions to ensure their defence). Kornai argues that this alone would be sufficient to set the economy on the transition path, though clearly the speed of transition and the nature of the end-state are likely to depend critically on the set of reforms implemented. The huge disparity of wealth and growth rates among the market economies is ample evidence that there is more to successful transition that just removing the barriers to private ownership. One of the critical issues facing Central European reformers in the early stage was how to sustain political support for the reforms while facing the implosion of their major trading partner, the former Soviet Union, and the consequent fall in demand for exports that were uncompetitive on other markets. The problem of sequencing reforms was not just to avoid unattractive irreversibilities, such as creating private monopolies (Newbery 1992), but also to create constituencies for maintaining the market economy, and reducing the extent of harmful shocks and the number of voters adversely affected. Risk management is thus central to the political sustainability of transition.

The preferred model of electricity reform for mature systems also involves creating new markets, by unbundling the former vertically integrated structure to separate out the natural monopoly transmission and distribution functions from the potentially competitive generation and supply (contracting and retailing) activities. Whereas before the final price was regulated and responded primarily to changes in fuel prices (often incompletely and with a lag, providing additional insurance), now only the transport cost (often less than 30 percent of the total cost) might be regulated. In Britain, where the ESI was unbundled and privatized in 1990, the wholesale price on occasion varied from 1.5 cents/kWh to 150 cents/kWh over a twenty-four hour period, not in response to varying fuel prices but to the tightness of demand relative to supply (Newbery 1995). The variation in average prices from year to year in Britain was relatively low, but average electricity prices in the California wholesale market during the off-peak winter season of January to April 2001 were ten times that in the same period in 1999, and the estimates of the additional profits that generators earned above the competitive level for the year 2000 amounted to over $8 billion (Wolak and Nordhaus 2001). Clearly, unbundling can create serious price risks where previously there were virtually none. While electricity reform in Britain has maintained popular support (even when under political attack, see Newbery 1998), the political backlash in California has not only threatened to reverse the whole reform process, but even at times threatened the industry with nationalization. Managing price risks during reform or transition is therefore potentially of the first importance.

The Chinese Reform Experience

China presents an interesting challenge to Kornai's schema, as it is apparently moving to a market economy without the removal of the communist party and ideology, and without obviously creating the institution of secure private property. China's reforms and dramatic increase in growth rate date from the open-door policy and liberalization introduced in 1978. From 1952–1978 the GDP growth rate was 2.5 percent per year, but from 1978 to 1997 the growth rate was 8.8 percent for the economy as a whole and 10.2 percent for the coastal provinces, excluding the city provinces of Shanghai and Tianjin. In contrast the output collapse in Central and Eastern Europe (CEE) after the start of transition (normally marked by the fall of the Berlin Wall in 1989) has been faster and more profound than almost any previous depression in history. The contrasts between the two market liberalization experiments are sharp and demand explanation (Newbery 1993). The comments here are more narrowly focused on the success with which China appears to have avoided adverse price and income shocks when introducing market-guided reforms.

The root cause of the inefficiency in Soviet-type economies was the monopoly power of state-owned enterprises (SOEs), and the solution is therefore to introduce competition. The size distribution of firms in market economies is generated and sustained by the entry and growth of new firms and the disappearance of inefficient firms, neither of which is allowed in Soviet-type economies. Competition can be introduced into a Soviet-type economy in three ways, ranked in order of difficulty: by opening the economy to international competition, by encouraging entry into the industry by domestic competitors, or by breaking up the existing SOEs. The first remedy may not be very effective if the exchange rate necessary for external equilibrium leads to an excessive real devaluation and underpricing of domestic factors, as was the case in Poland immediately after the big bang. Nor does it work for nontraded sectors, or those protected by high transport costs. The second approach was adopted by China and requires access to finance and resources. It is therefore likely to take longer, but it has the desirable consequence of mobilizing additional resources, introducing the forces of natural selection, and requiring little active regulation or state intervention, thus reducing the risks of mistaken policies.

The last solution may be simple in some cases (the road transport sector being an obvious example), and many service and distribution activities also have a small minimum economic scale, modest requirements in terms of skills and capital, and are thus natural candidates for small privatizations. Breaking up large conglomerates or vertically integrated industries is far more challenging and time consuming, as the experience of the Treuhandanstalt in the former GDR and the privatization of British utilities demonstrates. Nevertheless, the potential benefits from such restructuring are considerable, and the danger of privatization before restructuring is that it may be almost impossible to restructure after privatization, therefore foreclosing future desirable reforms (Newbery 1991).

China avoided the difficult problem of transforming large SOEs, but was able to find a positive solution to the problem of introducing competition and so revitalizing production. This was a remarkable, if accidental, by-product of the Chinese strategy. Two steps were necessary. The first was to liberalize a part of the market in the inputs and outputs of SOEs by the dual-track approach in which above-plan outputs could be freely marketed. This had the two-fold advantage of making inputs available outside the plan sector at market prices, while providing useful price signals to the state sector. It avoided the more fundamental changes that would have been required if prices had been liberalized for the entire output, for this would have led to large income redistributions and subjected the whole insurance system to unnecessary strains (see also Jin and Qian 1998).

The second and crucial element was to encourage entry by new competitive firms facing hard budget constraints but also access to finance. The solution was to facilitate the creation of township and village enterprises (TVEs) that had access to both credit and inputs from the state sector, and faced a buoyant demand for light manufacturing goods within their technological competence (Wang Xiaoquiang 1993). They were, however, the responsibility of the local authority, and as financial resources were limited, the local authority had every incentive to ensure that the enterprises were managed efficiently even though they were not privately owned. Shortage of local finance created the hard budget constraint lacking in the state sector, and encouraged authorities to close bankrupt enterprises and to adopt flexible labor market policies.

SOEs in both China and CEE were alike in that they were responsible for insuring lifetime employment, had egalitarian income distributions, and provided pensions and other social services to their former employees, thus providing extensive (and economically costly) insurance services to their workers. Any successful reform that exposes SOEs to competitive market forces will erode these internally provided insurance services, and a successful transition will almost certainly require either their replacement by alternative insurance institutions, or the confidence of the population that the risks to which they are exposed are relatively small. Health insurance should not be affected by the transition, but the risks of unemployment, poverty, and retirement may change dramatically. Ideally, reform should take place against a background of dynamic growth to minimize the risks of unemployment and poverty, and a demographic transition to a lower birth rate, which defers the moment at which the proportion of pensioners to workers rises. China scores well on these criteria, while the CEE countries score very poorly.

The less widespread and comprehensive the original insurance system born by the state, the easier it will be to make the transition to a more decentralized and market economy, and the smaller will be the proportion of state resources allocated to redistribution and not available for investment and growth. The main difference between China and the CEE countries lies in the relative size of the SOE sector, and the devolution of responsibilities for insurance down to the township and village or commune level, with much less importance attached to regional income redistribution. Wong (1992) documents the process by which this occurred, as the central government devolved increased responsibility to local levels without a compensating devolution of tax revenue. For example, the central government allocates funds to cover a fixed quota of price subsidies, with any expansion in the quantity to be financed at the local level, thus giving incentives for curtailing their expansion while preventing sudden redistributions of revenues and incomes. This devolution of expenditure, designed to assign responsibility for balancing budgets to the appropriate government level, was not accompanied by a transfer of formal tax instruments to the local level, as these continue to be set centrally. Consequently, local government has been forced to rely increasingly on extra-budgetary revenues from local enterprises, as revenues from enterprises are allocated by ownership (central or local).

The effect of China's liberalization policies was that the share of national industrial output produced by SOEs (in urban areas under state planning before liberalisation) fell from 78 percent in 1978 to 43 percent in 1993 (Jin and Qian 1997). The deadening effect of market suppression in the SOE sector and its related excess insurance was not dealt with directly, but its relative importance declined. The dual-track price system allowed market-determined price signals to work at the margin (where they are needed), without overly disturbing income distribution (which is primarily determined by the average prices, initially dominated by the centrally determined planned prices). Min Zhu (1993) argued that a shift from a profits tax on SOEs by central government to an increasing share of fixed and nominal tax contracts improved incentives facing enterprises, while gradually but inevitably eroding the central government's ability to make equalizing transfers to provinces. Over-insurance in China was therefore gradually eliminated or minimized, avoiding politically disruptive shocks.

Transitional and Risk-Reducing Contracts for Electricity Reform

U.K. electricity reform provides an excellent example of the benefits of restructuring and the importance of structural decisions. The United Kingdom tried all three possible reform models: in England and Wales the Central Electricity Generating Board (CEGB) was unbundled into three generating companies and the grid, the twelve distribution companies were privatized, and a wholesale market— the electricity pool—created. Scotland retained the two incumbent vertically integrated companies with minimal restructuring. Northern Ireland adopted the single buyer model with the combined transmission/distribution company NIE holding long-term power purchase agreements (PPAs) with the three independent generating companies.

Newbery and Pollitt (1997) and Pollitt (1997, 1998) have completed social cost benefit analyses of the three different models with striking and intuitively plausible results. The restructuring of the CEGB immediately introduced daily competitive price bidding for each power station. All generating companies dramatically increased productivity and drove down costs, including the state-owned Nuclear Electric. The audit of the first five years was that the social benefits amounted to a reduction of costs of 6 percent forever compared to the counterfactual, equivalent to a 100 percent return on the sales price. These benefits were almost entirely captured by companies, for profits rose as costs fell and prices remained stubbornly high until continued and aggressive regulatory intervention forced extensive divestment of capacity.

Scotland was a different story. In 1990 electricity prices were 10 percent lower than in England, but the lack of competitive pressure meant that by the end of the decade prices were some 5 percent higher. The very modest benefits of privatization were entirely absorbed by the costs of restructuring, delivering no net benefit. Northern Ireland gives a mixed picture. The long-term PPAs provided powerful incentives for increased plant availability and cost reductions, so that the improved generator performance outstripped that of the CEGB by three times. These PPAs, however, retained the benefits with the generating companies, and consumers were only able to benefit by aggressive price reductions on the nongenerating elements of cost, combined with government subsidies to reduce the embarrassing price gap between Northern Ireland and Britain.

The lessons from U.K. electricity restructuring are clear. Increased competitive pressure on generation is needed to reduce costs, and that requires separating generation from transmission and distribution. Whether these benefits will be passed on to consumers depends upon the intensity of competition, particularly the number of competitors and the existence of an open access wholesale market. Unrestructured industries, even if privatized, appear to deliver few benefits.

Unbundling creates new risks. To ensure both a smooth transition and to create predictable revenue streams on the back of which to privatize the generation and distribution companies, the government put in place "vesting contracts" for coal purchase and electricity sales. The contracts were financial, written before the companies were vested (i.e., created as limited liability companies) and mostly for three years, with some of shorter duration. They took the form of "contracts for differences," and were similar to futures contracts in that they had a strike price for a fixed quantity. As with futures markets (and dual-track prices), they confronted decision makers with the spot price for spot (quantity) decisions but provided income risk insurance for the bulk of sales or purchases at fixed prices. Similar contracts were used to make the generation market contestable, for independent power producers were then able to convince the distribution companies to sign fifteen-year contracts for the sale of base-load electricity. These contracts provided security for signing fifteen-year contracts for the purchase of gas, issuing debt to finance the purchase of the plant, creating a highly geared financial structure with low risk, and hence relatively low cost. Such a package made the generation market contestable, as the potential entrant could lock-in future prices and hence avoid the risk of retaliatory pricing behavior by the incumbents before entry. So attractive was this package that within a few months contracts had been signed for 10GW of CCGT plant, about one-fifth existing capacity, which was more than adequate to meet peak demand. Contracts thus both reduced the risk of price disruptions during the transition of a free market and helped make an initially rather uncompetitive market contestable, and ultimately one that is (with some enforced and negotiated divestment) relatively unconcentrated.

Contrast this with the experience of the California electricity reforms. California originally reformed and liberalized its electricity market because of dissatisfaction over high consumer prices. Average wholesale prices in 2000, however, were more than three times those of 1999, and 2001 started with rolling blackouts, and the major public utility, PG&E, filing for chapter 11 bankruptcy protection. California shows that poor market design coupled with inappropriate regulatory and political intervention, can rapidly produce extremely unsatisfactory outcomes when capacity is tight, particularly if the shortages are unexpected.

There were several compounding causes for the Californian crisis, notably a long history of underinvestment in generation, which was sustainable because California imported extensively from the Pacific Northwest, making use of the apparently abundant and cheap surplus hydroelectric power from the Columbia River. Second, and illustrative of the argument here, after generation was unbundled from transmission and distribution, distribution companies were strongly dissuaded from signing long-term contracts for electricity or hedging. This regulatory restraint was caused by the California Public Utilities Commission's poor experiences with earlier excessively priced PPAs from qualifying facilities, which earlier reforms had forced on the utilities. The commission recognized the spot market price as the principal measure of wholesale electricity costs, and utilities were required to trade all their power through the power exchange (PX). In addition, gas prices rose dramatically, and with them PPAs linked to gas prices, as did NOx emission prices, with permits trading at $80,000/ton at their peak, compared with $400/ton on the East Coast (Laurie 2001). Electricity prices rose, not just in California, but in the whole western interconnection in which wholesale power is traded. Thus the average price for the whole year of 2000 at the Mid-Columbia hub in the northwest (i.e., not in California) was $137/MWh compared with $27/MWh in 1999, higher than in California (where it averaged $115/MWh on the PX). California's largest distribution companies were unable to pass on the high wholesale prices, precipitating a financial shortfall as revenue fell far short of expenditure.

High plant utilization in the summer and autumn of 2000 induced by high spot prices necessitated greater scheduled maintenance downtime in the normally quieter winter period. Unfortunately, the combination of a dry winter in the Columbia River Basin lowering hydro output potential, with higher demand due to the colder weather, and plant outages in California, caused a severe shortage of capacity and energy, leading to higher prices, defaults, and bankruptcy. Inept price caps caused generators to export to neighboring states rather than sell in California, while the nonutility generators refused to supply for fear of not being paid. The repeated interventions of California's governor made a bad situation far worse, as threatened seizures, price caps, and regulatory hurdles initially prejudiced investment in generation. Poorly designed trading arrangements, with caps on some markets that encouraged participants to undercontract in the day-ahead market and diverted power to the real-time market at very high prices, amplified market power (Wolak and Nordhaus 2000).

There are numerous lessons that can be drawn from the Californian experience for electricity reform (Newbery 2002), but two are relevant here. Discouraging contracts exposed either consumers or companies to risk. As final prices were regulated, against the whole logic of unbundling, the companies were made bankrupt when prices rose. Other price caps had similar perverse effects. The regulatory/political response to high prices and capacity shortages has been one of panic-induced long-term contracting for new capacity at very high prices, that will eventually have to be paid either by consumers or tax-payers (essentially the same people in different ways). Wolak (2001) has argued that the required additional capacity could have been secured by a better combination of regulated price contracts and unregulated spot markets. If market design and regulation can ensure that generators contract all (or almost all) their output, then this will remove the incentive for exercising market power, facilitate investment and capacity availability, while eliminating price risks that might undermine the reforms and precipitate hasty and inappropriate policy responses.

The study of institutions to reduce risk, such as contracts, suggests their importance in the design of reforms for individual industries like electricity, or whole economies undergoing transition. It is no surprise that Stiglitz, who started his career with seminal work on risk, made his major policy pronouncements on the problems of privatization and transition.

References

Coase, Ronald H. 1960. "The Problem of Social Cost." *Journal of Law and Economics* 3: 1–44.

Diamond, Peter. A., and James A. Mirrlees. 1971. "Optimal Taxation and Public Production, I: Production Efficiency." *American Economic Review* 61 (1): 8–27.

Jin, Hehui, and Yingyi Qian. 1998. "Public vs Private Ownership of Firms: Evidence from Rural China." Mimeo., Department of Economics, Stanford University.

Kornai, János. 2000. "What the Change of System From Socialism to Capitalism Does and Does Not Mean." *Journal of Economic Perspectives* 14 (1): 27–42.

Laurie, R. A. 2001. "Distributed Generation: Reaching the Market Just in Time." *The Electricity Journal* 14: 87–94.

Newbery, David M. 1989. "Agricultural Institutions for Insurance and Stabilization," in *The Economic Theory of Agrarian Institutions*, ed. P. Bardhan, chap. 14, 267–296. Oxford: Clarendon Press.

Newbery, David M. 1991. "Reform in Hungary: Sequencing and Privatisation." *European Economic Review* 35 (May): 571–580.

Newbery, David M. 1992. "Sequencing the Transition," 181–199, in *The Transition of Socialist Economies Symposium 1991*, ed. H. Siebert. Tübingen: J. C. B. Mohr (Paul Siebeck).

Newbery, David M. 1993. "Transformation in Mature versus Emerging Economies: Why has Hungary been less successful than China?" *China Economic Review* 4 (2): 89–116.

Newbery, David M. 1995. "Power Markets and Market Power." *Energy Journal* 16 (3): 41–66.

Newbery, David M. 1998. "Pool Reform and Competition in Electricity," in M. Beesley, ed. *Regulating Utilities: Understanding the Issues*, 117–166. London: Institute of Economic Affairs.

Newbery, David M. 2002. "Regulating Unbundled Network Utilities." *Economic and Social Review*.

Newbery, David M., and Michael G. Pollitt. 1997. "The Restructuring and Privatisation of the CEGB- Was it Worth it?" *Journal of Industrial Economics* 45 (3): 269–303.

Newbery, David M., and Joseph E. Stiglitz. 1981. *The Theory of Commodity Price Stabilization: A Study in the Economics of Risk*. Oxford: Clarendon Press.

Pollitt, Michael G. 1997. "The Restructuring and Privatization of the Electricity Supply Industry in Northern Ireland—Will it be Worth it?" University of Cambridge Department of Applied Economics discussion paper no. 9701.

Pollitt, Michael G. 1998. "The Restructuring and Privatization of the Electricity Supply Industry in Scotland." Mimeo., Cambridge.

Stiglitz, Joseph E. 2001. "Whither Reform?—Ten Years after the Transition," in *Joseph Stiglitz and the World Bank: The Rebel Within*, ed. Ha-Joon Chang. London: Anthem Press. Annual Bank Conference on Development Economics, Washington, DC (1999).

Wang, Xiao-quiang. 1993. "Groping for stones to cross the river: Chinese price reform against the 'Big-Bang.' " Discussion paper on Economic Transition, DAE, Cambridge.

Wolak, F. A. 2001. "A comprehensive market power mitigation plan for the California electricity market." California ISO Market Surveillance Committee, April 24. Available online at ⟨www.stanford.edu/~wolak⟩.

Wolak, F. A., and R. Nordhaus. 2000. "An Analysis of the June 2000 Price Spikes in the California ISO's Energy and Ancillary Services Market." California ISO Market Surveillance Committee, September 6. Available from ⟨www.stanford.edu/~wolak⟩.

Wolak, F. A., and R. Nordhaus. 2001. "Comments on Staff Recommendations on Prospective Market Monitoring and Mitigation for the California Wholesale Electricity Market." California ISO Market Surveillance Committee, March 22.

Wong, Christine. 1992. "Central-Local Relations in an Era of Fiscal Decline: The paradox of Fiscal Decentralization in Post-Mao China." *The China Quarterly* 131: 691–715.

Zhu, Min. 1993. "The Mechanics and Consequences of Revenue Contract System in China." Mimeo., Public Division, PRD, World Bank, Washington, DC. Paper prepared for the Symposium on Economic Transition in China, July 1–3, Haikou, China.

30

Can Privatization Come Too Soon? Politics after the Big Bang in Post-Communist Societies

Karla Hoff

Economists have long recognized the importance of law for behavior, but they are just beginning to recognize that the law is endogenous. One of the most important instances of social change in recent years is the transition in Russia and Eastern Europe from public to private ownership of the means of production. These countries share a stated objective of establishing market economies: not only privatization of state enterprises but also systemic change, calling for the creation of an institutional environment, based on the "rule of law," where competitive market transactions can take place.[1]

In the early 1990s, the dominant paradigm in the West about this transition was that granting individuals the control of property would create a political constituency for the rule of law, where there is protection for private property rights.[2] All over the post-communist world, Western donors promoted "Big Bang" privatization—the mass transfer of state-owned assets to private agents (Przeworski 1995, viii, note 2). But there was no theory to explain how this process of institutional evolution would occur and, in fact, it has not yet occurred in Russia, in other former Soviet Union countries, in the Czech Republic, and elsewhere. A central reason for that, according to many scholars, is the weakness of the political demand for the rule of law. For example, Black, Kraakman, and Tarassova (2000) observe that in Russia, it was

hoped that broad private ownership would create a constituency for strengthening and enforcing [the new Civil and Commercial Codes]. That didn't happen. Instead, company managers and kleptocrats opposed efforts to strengthen or enforce the capital market laws. They didn't want a strong Securities Commission or tighter rules on self-dealing transactions. *And what they didn't want, they didn't get* (1753, emphasis added).

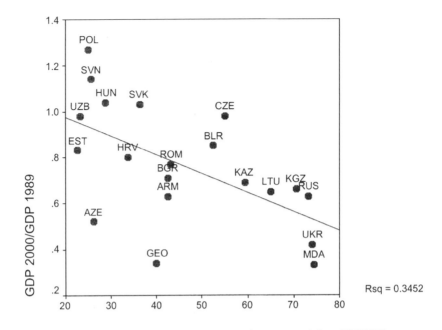

Index of insecurity of property and contract rights (BEEPS)

Figure. 30.1
Growth and property rights insecurity in twenty transition economies
Source: For the GDP data, EBRD (2001). For the survey data, ⟨http://www.worldbank.
org/wbi/governance/beepsinteractive.htm⟩. The survey is documented and analyzed in Hellman, Jones, and Kaufmann (2000).
Note: The index of insecurity is the percentage of respondents who disagree with the
statement: "I am confident that the legal system will uphold my contract and property
rights in business disputes." Response categories are "agree in most cases, tend to
agree, tend to disagree, disagree in most cases, strongly disagree." In constructing the
index, the response "tend to disagree" is counted as disagreement.

Figure 30.1 gives a snapshot of property rights insecurity and
growth for all transition countries for which such data are available.
The horizontal axis plots the fraction of firms in a 1999 EBRD/World
Bank survey reporting that they do not trust the legal system to
uphold their property and contract rights. In response to the question, "Do you agree with the statement, I am confident that the legal
system will uphold by contract and property rights in business
disputes?" a staggering 75 percent of firms in Russia, Kyrgystan,
Moldova, and the Ukraine disagreed. The vertical axis plots the ratio
of GDP in 2000 to GDP in 1989. In each of the six economies where
property rights are most insecure, GDP has contracted by more than

30 percent. (By comparison, the U.S. GDP contracted by 27 percent in the Great Depression.)

Those who forecast that Big Bang reforms would create a powerful lobby for the rule of law were wrong. Why were they wrong, or is it still too early to judge? The fact that political interactions do not play out in idealized competitive markets, but instead are often best modeled as interactions in markets with externalities or as bargaining games, suggests that one needs to be circumspect about allegations of the efficiency of the process.

This chapter is designed to provide an overview of my work, joint with Joe Stiglitz, that explores the political economy of property rights in the transition economies.[3] While it is of course true that some legal framework will follow mass privatization, we argue that the framework is not necessarily the rule of law. We focus on two "technologies" that can cripple the demand for the rule of law in equilibrium: (1) asset stripping, which can give individuals a stake in prolonging the no-rule-of-law state; and (2) bribery, which can lead to the protection of monopolies and so deter entry by political outsiders who may make up the natural constituency for the rule of law.[4]

The two main sections of this focus, respectively, on these two technologies. Section 1 considers a set of assumptions seemingly highly favorable to the creation of the rule of law: political power is widely dispersed; an individual can obtain contract enforcement only through the rule of law, not by buying rules just for himself; and all agents are better off building value under the rule of law than stripping. Yet I show in a simple example that a unique stable equilibrium may exist where the constituency for the rule of law is very small.

Section 2 considers oligarchic entrenchment. Taking into account the asymmetries in political power, some individuals may believe that they can extract for themselves more rents from the arbitrary exercise of their economic influence than they can obtain through any rule-bound system. Individuals for whom the rule of law is not desirable may "drive out" those for whom it is desirable, and who would otherwise have formed a powerful business constituency for the rule of law. Sequencing matters because it affects the ability of one group or another to engender a pernicious or broadly beneficial institutional consolidation.

I met Joe Stiglitz in the fall of 1984 when I arrived as a graduate student in Princeton, with a background as a French major in college. Much of literature is an exploration of the humanly created constraints facing individuals. In contrast, in the then central paradigm in economics, scarcity arises only from physical constraints: allocations under existing institutions replicate allocations under markets and are efficient; humanly created constraints do not matter. I knew something important was missing. In his lectures, Stiglitz applied the machinery of neoclassical economics to upturn the standard results. Like a magician drawing rabbits from a hat, he could make demand curves slope up, supply curves slope down, markets in competitive equilibrium fail to clear, cross-subsidies make everyone better off, students over-educate themselves, and farmers produce the wrong quantities of goods. And then he would show how the magic reflected some very human and rational response to imperfect information.[5] The theorem that individual rationality leads to social rationality applies to a special case, not the general case. Humanly created constraints did matter after all! The work described below is inscribed in that perspective.

1   "Ex Nihilo, the Jungle"

Yegor Gaidar, prime minister of Russia during 1991–1992, retrospectively characterized the leap from the collapse of socialist institutions to Big Bang privatization as "ex nihilo, the jungle" (Speech at the Annual World Bank Conference in Development Economics, Oslo, June 2002). Here I present a model in which an economy might fail to coordinate on the rule of law and instead coordinate on something more like the law of the jungle, which may be worse for everyone.

Consider an economy in which the possible legal structures vary only along the dimension of the security of property rights. There are two possible legal regimes that capture the ends of the spectrum: the rule of law and no rule of law, that is, a legal regime that does not enforce property and contract rights.

Agents with control rights over privatized property seek to maximize their wealth and choose between two strategies: building value, whose payoff depends on the legal regime in place, and stripping assets, which provides a sure return. The probability of the establishment of the rule of the law depends on the political constituency for it in equilibrium. I will set out a very simple example of this framework. The example points up a "chicken and egg" problem, where the legal environment leads individuals to adopt certain economic strategies and, given the economic choices that they have made, they in fact do not support the rule of law.

Agents

Time consists of two periods. Each agent exercises some control rights over enterprises in the first period and chooses between two actions:

- *Build value*: Make an irreversible investment to increase the enterprise's value.
- *Strip assets*: Strip the assets of the enterprise, whisk capital to a safe place, and tunnel value out.

The economy consists of a continuum of agents indexed by θ, where θ is uniformly distributed on $[0,1]$. Those with a higher value of θ strip better. (The payoff from stripping an enterprise is larger, the more liquid its assets and the greater the equity of minority shareholders.)

Political Environment

The initial state is one without the rule of law. Agents who build value demand reform—the rule of law—because it is the only legal regime that enforces contracts. Asset-strippers, who follow a strategy of take the money and run and may illegitimately profit from their control rights, do not. The economic strategy of an agent thus determines his political position.[6] Let x denote the fraction of agents who support the status quo, no rule of law. The probability $\pi(.)$ of the establishment of the rule of law depends on the size of the constituency that supports it, $1 - x$. This assumption is captured as $\pi(x) = (1 - x)^2$.

Payoffs

Technology is constant returns to scale. An agent of type θ who strips obtains a return θ per unit asset. An agent who builds values obtains a return of 1 if the rule of law is established, and $1/4$ if it is not.

Given x, the threshold below which agents build value and demand the rule of law, and above which they do not, is a type θ^* such that

$$\theta^*(x) = \pi(x) + [1 - \pi(x)]\frac{1}{4}, \qquad\qquad \text{switch line} \quad (1)$$

and so a population fraction $1 - \theta^*$ strips and supports the status quo (no rule of law).

Equilibrium
An equilibrium is a value of the constituency for the status quo, no rule of law, that solves

$$x = 1 - \theta^*(x). \tag{2}$$

Equation (2) states that for a fraction x of the agents, the expected return to stripping assets exceeds the return to building value. Substituting from (1), equation (2) implies $x = 3/4 - 3/4(1 - x)^2$. Equilibria are $x^* = 0$ and $x^{**} = 2/3$; see figure 30.2.

This simple example illustrates several points. Even if building value under the rule of law dominates stripping assets for every agent, a small constituency for the rule of law may be the unique stable equilibrium. At $x = 0$, the "switch line" in (1) is steeper than the "stripping ability curve" (defined by the uniform distribution of stripping abilities). Any slight increase in x above zero lowers the switch point by more than it lowers the return of the marginal asset-stripper, which induces movement away from the equilibrium. Thus the efficient equilibrium, where the transition to the rule of law occurs with certainty in the next period, is unstable. By similar reasoning, the inefficient equilibrium, where only $1/3$ of the agents support the rule of law, is stable. In this unique stable equilibrium, the probability of the establishment of the rule of law is just $1/9$.

But do the implications of that model extend to a dynamic framework? Shouldn't the forward-looking behavior of the agents affect their political actions of voting? If so, even an asset-stripper might vote for the rule of law.

To analyze this problem, we have extended the model to a dynamic framework (Hoff and Stiglitz 2002b). In our extension, two variables link an agent's current decisions to his future opportunities. First, a current decision to strip assets reduces the stake that

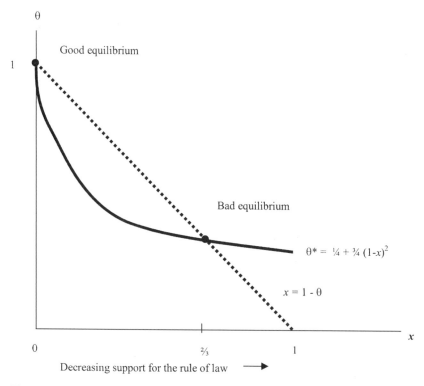

Figure. 30.2
The inefficient equilibrium is the unique stable equilibrium

an agent has in the future legal regime. Second, such a decision reduces his relative return from the rule of law (relative to no-rule-of-law) because the establishment of the rule of law at the end of a given period constrains his ability to strip.[7] Given these links between present and future, stripping can give agents an interest in prolonging the no-rule-of-law state. We are thus able to show that the qualitative results of the static model carry over to a dynamic framework with politically sophisticated agents.

In the model, how agents vote influences other agents' actions (a spillover effect), and how each agent acts influences his political position (an *intertemporal* incentive effect). Each individual, in attempting to influence the choice of the environment, focuses on the impact on himself, not on others. Externalities that affect political outcomes beget externalities that affect economic choices.

A deeper point is that if there were perfect capital markets (with nongovernmental enforcement), then the prospect of the establishment of the rule of law in the future would make it in the interests of each individual to take actions that maximize the social value of assets he controls because he could "capture" that value. In that case, all agents in the model would build value and all would support the rule of all. In this view, the imperfections in capital markets cause the inefficient behaviors that, in turn, cause the inefficient outcomes in the political equilibrium. As in the children's story "The House that Jack Built," one problem leads to another.

2 Oligarchic Entrenchment

In practice, the privatization in Russia was more adverse to the establishment of the rule of law than the preceding analysis would suggest, for it led to the creation of a small group of oligarchs, with vast fortunes and influence over the media and political processes.[8] Here, we analyze some aspects of what might be called an oligopolistic model. Three salient differences should be noted between that world and the one analyzed above. (1) In such a world, of course, it is not true that participants will believe that their actions will have no affect on the behavior of other participants. (2) The oligopolists/ oligarchs will typically obtain significant rents and will accordingly direct some of their political energies to the preservation of these rents. To the extent that they succeed, the legal framework that emerges will not be one that promotes economic efficiency.[9] (3) In some cases, the oligarchs may actually be against a rule-based system, believing that they can extract for themselves more rents from the arbitrary exercise of their economic influence than they can obtain through any rule-bound system. Such a result is predicated on the existence of plausible constraints on the kinds of rules that they can impose. Under the political process, for example, they may be restricted from writing down rules that are too patently discriminatory. Because bargaining goes on behind closed doors, the oligarchs may be able to achieve more under such behind-the-scenes bargaining than through any rule-based system. They may be willing to bear the risks associated with the nonrule based system, given the amount that the oligarchs as a whole would have to transfer to the nonoligarchs under the alternative.

This section first sets out an hypothesis about the logic of reform and then sketches a simple model to shed light on the equilibrium constituency for the rule of law.

2.1 An Hypothesis about the Logic of Political Constraints

At the outset of the collapse of socialist institutions in Russia and Eastern Europe, most observers agreed that, were it politically feasible to establish quickly the rule of law to underpin a market economy as or before state enterprises were privatized, it would be desirable to do so. It was argued, however, that it was politically infeasible to do so. This section explores the possible implications of that statement.

Assume two reforms a and b are under consideration. Let P_{ab} denote the power of the coalition in favor of a over b. The statement that a particular coalition is stronger in a certain circumstance than another coalition means that it is either larger, or that those within the coalition are willing or able to provide more resources to pushing for (or against) a certain set of proposals than another set of proposals.

It is alleged that a is not politically feasible, and b is observed to occur. Together this implies that

$$P_{bs} > P_{as}, \quad P_{bs} > P_s \quad \text{and} \quad P_{as} < P_s.$$

The coalition in favor of b over the status quo (P_{bs}) is stronger than the coalition in favor of a over the status quo (P_{as}), the coalition in favor of b over the status quo is stronger than the coalition in favor of remaining in the status quo (P_s), and the coalition in favor of a is weaker than the coalition in favor of remaining in the status quo.

Consider one such alternative reform and look at the reform process from the perspective of reformers within a government that is divided between reformers (R) and *nomenklatura* (N).[10] Reformers are considering two alternative reforms: (1) Reform r: Regulation and restructuring, followed by privatization; or (2) Reform p: privatization without prior regulation and restructuring.

Let $P_{ps}(R)$ denote the political power of the reformers in favor of p over the status quo, and let $P_{ps}(N)$ denote the political power of the *nomenklatura* in favor of p over the status quo. Suppose, for simplicity, that power is additive.

The usefulness of the logic of reform can be seen in evaluating the following often-heard assertions:

1. The reform p is politically feasible, but r is not. Formally,

$$P_{ps}(R) + P_{ps}(N) > P_s(R) + P_s(N) \tag{3}$$

$$P_{rs}(R) + P_{rs}(N) < P_s(R) + P_s(N) \tag{4}$$

2. The *nomenklatura* are currently using their control over the public sector to obtain rents for themselves, impeding its efficiency.

3. Privatization will result in owners who have the incentive to use those resources efficiently. That is, while p is feasible but r is not, p will result in increased efficiency. Those who get "control rights" under the privatization will use their new power to lobby for reforms in the legal structure (which by hypothesis were not feasible earlier) that will protect property and contracts and restrict anticompetitive practices. That is, reforms that could not be implemented initially can be implemented later.

Two implications follow. First, under the assumption that regulation is socially efficient, (3) and (4) imply that before privatization actually occurs, bargaining within government fails to yield the efficient outcome.[11] Second, (4) implies that if reformers have no power under the status quo,[12] and yet privatization is feasible, then for the *nomenklatura* privatization and the status quo are equivalent. That, in turn, implies that if privatization occurs, then government officials must prefer privatization to the rents that they receive under state ownership.

There is a clear and highly disturbing implication: there must be more corruption (in dollar value to those currently in power) associated with the privatization process than with the process in which enterprises remain under government control. Privatization may allow those currently in power to extract the present discounted value of future rents—in effect, to capitalize corruption. This was not difficult to do in the 1990s in Russia. A common method was to "convince" the local privatization committee to physically bar anyone outside one's own group from participating in the privatization auction. One oligarch, after explaining how he proceeded, commented,

We didn't shoot anyone and we didn't violate any laws. These are the normal business practices in Russia (Klebnikov 2000, 131).

The point is that the logic drives us at least to consider as a serious possibility that privatization provided an enormously powerful tool for redistribution toward those currently in political power.

To be sure, one may still decide that privatization enhances welfare, because the distortions associated with rent extraction in the one-time privatization process are less than those associated with rent extraction out of on-going government operation. That is, hypothesis C may be true even if the corruption under privatization is greater, in some sense, than under government ownership. The model I sketch below will question that implication in the context of societies with ill-defined property rights. The premise of the model is that incumbents have the ability to shape economic institutions in their favor after privatization, and political outsiders can reveal their preferences for more public protection of property rights only once they have entered a business activity.[13] In the model, the method of privatization may have implications for political evolution, that is, for the power of various coalitions in the future, and thus for the design of—or even the existence of—the rule of law.

2.2 A Model of Entrenchment

The economy has a continuum of goods. Each good is produced in its own sector. In a proportion γ of these sectors, there is a single, privatized firm. In addition, in each sector there is a competitive fringe of potential entrants. After the agents in the competitive fringe have moved, the legal framework is established and agents obtain payoffs conditional on the legal framework.

The probability of the establishment of the rule of law, π, depends on the size of the constituency that supports it. By assumption, only agents who are active in business have the information and the concentrated interests to lobby government and thereby reveal their preferences.

In each sector, individuals in the competitive fringe are of measure one and are indexed by f. A higher value f corresponds to a higher fixed cost of production. f is uniformly distributed on $[0, 1]$.

In a monopolized sector, the payoff to new entry is negative; hence, no individual enters such a sector. In a sector that is not monopolized, the payoff is $y - f$, if the rule of law is established, and otherwise it is $-f$. I assume that $y \in (0, 1)$. Then there is a critical value of f,

$$f^* = \pi y, \tag{5}$$

which is the type of the marginal entrant who is just indifferent between entering or not.

The fraction of potential entrants in the competitive fringe who choose to enter is $f^*[1 - \gamma]$: this is because a fraction $1 - \gamma$ of the sectors is not monopolized, and a fraction f^* of the competitive fringe of each of these sectors enters.

I write the probability of the establishment of the rule of law, π, as a function of the size of the constituency for it. The equilibrium value f^* solves

$$D \equiv y\pi(f^*[1 - \gamma]) - f^* = 0. \tag{6}$$

Equation (6) says that the difference between expected return and fixed costs for the marginal entrant is zero. There always exists at least one equilibrium, and it is stable if

$$\frac{\partial D}{\partial f}(f^*) = y\pi'[1 - \gamma] < 1. \tag{7}$$

Restructuring, which reduces γ, gives the constituency for the rule of law $(f^*[1 - \gamma])$ a double boost: evaluated in the neighborhood of a stable equilibrium, a fall in γ not only increases the set of sectors into which new entrants flow but also increases the number of new entrants in each sector by

$$\frac{df^*}{-d\gamma} = \frac{\partial D/\partial \gamma}{\partial D/\partial f} = \frac{y\pi'f^*}{1 - y\pi'[1 - \gamma]} > 0. \tag{8}$$

The outcome of a high value of γ and weak support for the rule of law may actually be worse than that captured in this simple model. In the absence of the rule of law, political insiders can monopolize new sectors—sectors that were not monopolies before privatization.

A notorious example of the capture of new markets is the takeover of the Lada car distribution in Russia. A police investigation in 1997 (following an earlier attempted investigation had ended with the assassination of the chief investigator), found that gangsters connected to the automaker had waged a kind of war to establish the monopoly. There was evidence of more than sixty-five murders of company managers and business rivals (Klebnikov 2000, 368).

Conclusion

The presumption of Big Bang reforms was that the faster state property was turned over to private hands, the faster a true market economy, including the legal regime to support it, would be established. This presumption was not based on a theoretical analysis of how the process would work. This chapter has described two technologies—stripping of assets and bribing—that may block the emergence of the natural constituency for the rule of law. Our analysis shows that, even if eventually a rule of law is established, the Big Bang, by increasing the profitability of these technologies, may put into play forces that *delay* its establishment.

Without privatization, control would have resided in the hands of government officials, who would also have stripped assets (the process occurred widely under *perestroika* and came to be known as "spontaneous privatization"). The point is that their ability to strip was enhanced by official privatization.[14] Privatization prior to restructuring also created the means and incentives to use one's wealth and influence to preserve monopoly rents and bar entry of new firms.

If, in particular, natural resource-rich sectors had not been privatized,[15] then both the ability to strip and the power to capture the state and block entry would not have been so great. The manner of privatization influences the constituency for a beneficial legal regime. If there had been more time—more time to ensure that privatization had more political legitimacy than the loans-for-shares privatization (they could hardly have had less legitimacy)—then it might have been easier to provide security for those insiders who invested inside the country rather than sending their assets abroad. In this case, there would have been more political support for the rule of law and thus a better political and economic equilibrium might have emerged.

Notes

1. By the rule of law I mean a legal regime where property rights are secure, since there are rules on which even the ruler cannot infringe; access to legal rights is broad; and rules for solving legal disputes are predictable. The rule of law is the institution that makes possible a competitive market economy as formulated in a neoclassical model. Empirical work confirms that the rule of law is critical to the success of actual market economies. Three strands of this literature are macrostudies on the security of

property rights (e.g., Barro 1997 and La Porta et al. 1998), firm-level studies (e.g., Johnson, McMillan, and Woodruff 2002), and case studies on the breadth of access to property rights (e.g., Kahn and Sokoloff 1998).

2. The phrase "dominant paradigm in the West" is due to Sachs, Zinnes, and Eilat (2000). A summary of that paradigm is provided by Murrell (1995). We use the term control in this context to distinguish it from ownership, which implies a clear legal framework defining rights and obligations. To be sure, in any society there is some legal framework, and control rights are circumscribed by that legal framework. For instance, in a highly primitive society one could imagine no enforcement of basic criminal codes, for example, against murder and theft. In such a world, actual practical control rights are highly circumscribed: a person can do as he pleases with an asset only so long as no one takes it away from him. Larger individuals (who can beat up on others) or those who can organize larger groups to fight in their defense have more effective control rights.

3. Hoff and Stiglitz (2002a, b, c, d). This work relates to two other literatures: work on the Nash equilibrium choice of the enforcement of property rights (e.g., de Meza and Gould 1992; Greif 1994); and work on the political economy of reform (e.g., Fernandez and Rodrik 1991; Dewatripont and Roland 1995; Hellman 1998). Like de Meza and Gould, the model of section 1 demonstrates the possibility of a coordination failure. But Hoff and Stiglitz (2000b) goes beyond existing literature on coordination failures in institutions by showing in a fully dynamic model how a bad equilibrium can persist.

4. The empirical importance of both technologies is well documented. The extent of capital outflow in Russia during the period 1995–2001 was $15–20 billion (Loungani and Mauro 2001; Reuters, February 20, 2002). Extensive data for the transition economies on bribery aimed at securing special treatment from the state is in Hellman et al. (2000).

5. References are respectively to: (1) Stiglitz (1987), where higher prices have selection and incentive effects; (2) Stiglitz (1974), where a fall in the unemployment rate brought about by the creation of government jobs increases turnover costs by more than it increases aggregate output; (3) Shapiro and Stiglitz (1984), where unemployment disciplines workers; and Stiglitz and Weiss (1981), where the interest rate influences the quality of the loan portfolio; (4) Rothschild and Stiglitz (1976), where a pooling equilibrium may Pareto dominate a separating equilibrium, (5) Stiglitz (1975), where a suboptional equilibrium is driven by the desire of high ability individuals to separate themselves from less able ones; and (6) Newbery and Stiglitz 1981, where farmers do not internalize the effect of their production decisions on aggregate risk. This work radically expanded ideas about the sources and pervasiveness of externalities, an idea emphasized by Greenwald and Stiglitz (1986) and, in the context of development, by Hoff (2001).
  Since many important externalities are local, some of the tools that Stiglitz and his coauthors developed to study externalities (such as single-crossing properties) have proved useful in modeling spatial sorting. An example from my own work is Hoff and Sen (2002), which develops a kind of a community sharecropping model, where each individual's return to civic effort depends on the distribution of civic actions in the population.

6. This is not the case in the dynamic extension of this model, but the results remain robust (Hoff and Stiglitz 2002b).

7. The basis for the rule of law cannot be only power; the rules must have some legitimacy. This limits the extent to which under any rule of law the returns from stripping can be grandfathered.

8. See note 15.

9. To be sure, one might argue that these problems would be eliminated if all the wealth were given to a single individual; a monopolist would have an incentive to promote economic efficiency. From this perspective, the problem with the privatization is not that it was too undemocratic, but that it was too democratic. But in few countries would political processes condone such an arbitrary exercise of power; and monopolies are efficient only under highly restrictive conditions, for example, that they can act in a perfectly discriminating way, which requires perfect information.

10. This formalizes the idea of a divided government in Boycko, Shleifer, and Vishny (1996).

11. Subtracting (3) from (4) gives $P_{rs}(R) - P_{ps}(R) < -[P_{rs}(N) + P_{ps}(N)]$, which can, equivalently, be written as $P_{rp}(R) < -P_{rp}(N)$. In words, the power of the reformers to impose regulation rather than privatization is less than the power of the *nomenklatura* to resist regulation rather than privatization.

12. That is the case where $P_{ps}(R) = P_s(R) = 0$.

13. Under that assumption, those who argued that quick privatization would create a constituency for free market institutions, including the rule of law, were looking for lobbyists in the wrong place.

14. Whether inefficient stripping by government is better or worse than inefficient stripping and monopolistic rent-seeking by the private sector is a question that is outside the scope of this chapter.

15. Many of the major enterprises in these sectors—the industrial jewels of Russia—were privatized under the loans-for-shares program in 1995–1997. This was a second wave of privatization. The first wave was a voucher privatization program through which 14,000 medium and large enterprises were privatized in 1992–1994. But the two programs are not viewed as independent events. In 1995–1996, President Yeltsin feared the loss of the election in part because the population didn't see the benefits of the mass privatization of 1992–1994. The loans-for-shares arrangement was a ploy in which a top business elite was persuaded to support Yeltsin's reelection in exchange for Yeltsin's agreement to transfer to them shares in some of Russia's most valuable enterprises.

References

Barro, R. 1997. *Determinants of Economic Growth: A Cross-Section Empirical Study*. Cambridge, MA: MIT Press.

Black, B., R. Kraakman, and A. Tarassova. 2000. "Russian Privatization and Corporate Governance: What Went Wrong?" *Stanford Law Review* 52: 1731–1801.

Boycko, M., A. Shleifer, and R. Vishny. 1996. "Second Best Economic Policy for a Divided Government." *European Economic Review* 40: 767–774.

de Meza, D., and J.R. Gould. 1992. "The Social Efficiency of Private Decisions to Enforce Property Rights." *Journal of Political Economy* 100 (3): 561–580.

Dewatripont, M., and G. Roland. 1995. "The Design of Reform Packages under Uncertainty." *American Economic Review* 85 (5): 1207–1223.

Fernandez, R., and D. Rodrik. 1991. "Resistance to Reform: Status Quo Bias in the Presence of Individual-Specific Uncertainty." *American Economic Review* 81 (5), December: 1146–1155.

Freeland, C. 2000. *Sale of the Century: Russia's Wild Ride from Communism to Capitalism.* Random House: New York.

Greenwald, B., and J. E. Stiglitz. 1986. "Externalities in Economics with Imperfect Information and Incomplete Markets." *Quarterly Journal of Economics* (May): 229–264.

Greif, A. 1994. "Cultural Beliefs and the Organization of Society: A Historical and Theoretical Reflection on Collectivist and Individualist Societies." *Journal of Political Economy* 102 (5): 912–950.

Hellman, J. 1998. "Winners Take All—The Politics of Partial Reform in Postcommunist Transitions." *World Politics* 50 (January): 203–234.

Hellman, J., G. Jones, and D. Kaufmann. 2000. "'Seize the State, Seize the Day': State Capture, Corruption, and Influence in Transition." World Bank Policy Research working paper no. 2444.

Hoff, K. 2001. "Beyond Rosenstein-Rodan: The Modern Theory of Coordination Problems," in Development. *Annual World Bank Conference on Development Economics 2000,* 145–188. Washington DC: World Bank.

Hoff, K., and A. Sen. 2002. "Home-ownership, Community Interactions, and Segregation." World Bank, manuscript.

Hoff, K., and J. E. Stiglitz. 2002a. "The Transition Process in Post-Communist Societies: Towards a Political Economy of Property Rights." *Proceedings of the Annual Bank Conference on Development Economics.* Oslo.

Hoff, K., and J. E. Stiglitz. 2002b. "A Dynamic Model of the Demand for the Rule of Law." World Bank, manuscript.

Hoff, K., and J. E. Stiglitz. 2002c. "The Political Economy of Property Rights in the Transition Economies: The Role of New Entry." Work in progress.

Hoff, K., and J. E. Stiglitz. 2002d. "After the Big Bang? Obstacles to the Emergence of the Rule of Law in Post-Communist Societies." NBER working paper no. 9282.

Johnson, S., J. McMillan, and C. Woodruff. 2002. "Property Rights and Finance." *American Economic Review* 92 (5): 1335–1356.

Khan, Z. B., and K. L. Sokoloff. 1998. "Patent Institutions, Industrial Organization and Early Technological Change: Britain and the United States, 1790–1850," in *Technological Revolutions in Europe,* ed. M. Berg and K. Bruland. Elgar: Cheltenham.

Klebnikov, P. 2000. *Godfather of the Kremlin: Boris Berezovsky and the Looting of Russia.* Harcourt: New York.

La Porta, R., F. Lopez-de-Silanes, A. Shleifer, and R. Vishny. 1998. "Law and Finance." *Journal of Political Economy* 106(6), December: 1133–1155.

Loungani, P., and P. Mauro. 2001. "Capital Flight from Russia." *The World Economy* 24 (5): 689–706.

Murrell, P. 1995. "Transition According to Cambridge, Mass." *Journal of Economic Literature* 33 (1), March: 164–178.

Newbery, D. G., and J. E. Stiglitz. 1981. *The Theory of Commodity Price Stabilization.* Oxford, UK: Oxford University Press.

Przeworski, A. 1995. *Sustainable Democracy.* Cambridge: Cambridge University Press.

Rothschild, M., and J. E. Stiglitz. 1976. "Equilibrium in Competitive Insurance Markets: An Essay on the Economics of Imperfect Information." *Quarterly Journal of Economics* 90 (4), November: 629–649.

Sachs, J., C. Zinnes, and Y. Eilat. 2000. "Systemic Transformation in Transition Economies." HIID, CAER II discussion paper no. 61.

Shapiro, C., and J. E. Stiglitz. 1984. "Equilibrium Unemployment as a Worker Discipline Device." *American Economic Review* 74 (3): 433–444.

Stiglitz, J. E. 1974. "Alternative Theories of Wage Determination and Unemployment in L.D.C.'s: The Labor Turnover Model." *Quarterly Journal of Economics* 88(2): 194–227.

Stiglitz, J. E. 1975. "The Theory of Screening, Education and the Distribution of Income." *American Economic Review* 65 (3), June: 283–300.

Stiglitz, J. E. 1987. "The Causes and Consequences of the Dependence of Quality on Price." *Journal of Economic Literature* 25 (March): 1–48.

Stiglitz, J. E., and A. Weiss. 1981. "Credit Rationing in Markets with Imperfect Information." *The American Economic Review* 71 (3), June: 393–410.

Appendix

31

Information and the Change in the Paradigm in Economics

Joseph E. Stiglitz

The research for which George Akerlof, Michael Spence, and I are being recognized is part of a larger research program which today embraces a great number of researchers around the world. In this article, I want to set the particular work which was cited within this broader agenda, and that agenda within the still broader perspective of the history of economic thought. I hope to show that information economics represents a fundamental change in the prevailing paradigm within economics.

Information economics has already had a profound effect on how we think about economic policy and is likely to have an even greater influence in the future. Many of the major policy debates over the past two decades have centered around the related issues of the efficiency of the market economy and the appropriate relationship between the market and the government. The argument of Adam Smith (1776) that free markets lead to efficient outcomes, "as if by an invisible hand," has played a central role in these debates: It suggested that we could, by and large, rely on markets *without government intervention* (or, at most, with a limited role for government). The set of ideas that I will present here undermined Smith's theory and the view of the role of government that rested on it. They have suggested that the reason that the hand may be invisible is that it is simply not there—or at least that if is there, it is palsied.

When I began the study of economics some forty-one years ago, I was struck by the incongruity between the models that I was taught and the world that I had seen growing up in Gary, Indiana. Founded in 1906 by U.S. Steel, and named after its chairman of the board, Gary has declined to but a shadow of its former self. But even in its heyday, it was marred by poverty, periods of high unemployment, and massive racial discrimination. Yet the economic theories we were taught paid little attention to poverty, said that all markets cleared—including the labor market, so that unemployment must be nothing more than a phantasm—and claimed that the profit motive ensured that there could not be economic discrimination (Becker 1971). As a graduate student, I was determined to try to create models with assumptions—and conclusions—closer to those that accorded with the world I saw, with all of its imperfections.

My first visits to the developing world in 1967, and a more extensive stay in Kenya in 1969, made an indelible impression on me. Models of perfect markets, as badly flawed as they might seem for Europe or America, seemed truly inappropriate for these countries. While many of the key assumptions that went into the competitive equilibrium model seemed not to fit these economies well, I was particularly struck by the imperfections of information, the absence of markets, and the pervasiveness and persistence of seemingly dysfunctional institutions, such as sharecropping. I had seen cyclical unemployment—sometimes quite large—and the hardship it brought as I grew up, but I had not seen the massive unemployment that characterized African cities, unemployment that could not be explained either by unions or minimum wage laws (which, even when they existed, were regularly circumvented). Again, there was a massive discrepancy between the models we had been taught and what I saw.

In contrast, the ideas and models I will discuss here have proved useful not only in addressing broad philosophical questions, such as the appropriate role of the state, but also in analyzing concrete policy issues. For example, I believe that some of the huge mistakes which have been made in policy in the last decade, in for instance the management of the East Asian crisis or the transition of the former communist countries to the market, might have been avoided had there been a better understanding of issues—such as financial structure, bankruptcy, and corporate governance—to which the new information economics has called attention. And the so-called "Washington consensus"[1] policies, which have predominated in the policy advice of the international financial institutions over the past quarter century, have been based on market fundamentalist policies which ignored the information-theoretic concerns; this explains, at least partly, their widespread failures. Information affects decision-making in every context—not just inside firms and households. More recently, as I discuss below, I have turned my attention to some aspects of what might be called the *political economy* of information: the role of information in political processes and collective decision-making. There are asymmetries of information between those governing and those governed, and just as participants in markets strive to overcome asymmetries of information, we need to look for ways by which the asymmetries of information in political processes can be limited and their consequences mitigated.

1   The Historical Setting

I do not want here to review in detail the models that were constructed exploring the role of information; in recent years, there has been a number of survey articles and interpretive essays, even several books in this area.[2] I do want to highlight some of the dramatic impacts that information economics has had on how economics is approached today, how it has provided explanations for phenomena that were previously unexplained, how it has altered our views about how the economy functions, and, perhaps most importantly, how it has led to a rethinking of the appropriate role for government in our society. In describing the ideas, I want to trace out some of their origins. To a large extent, these ideas evolved from attempts to answer specific policy questions or to explain specific phenomena to which the standard theory provided an inadequate explanation. But any discipline has a life of its own, a prevailing paradigm, with assumptions and conventions. Much of the work was motivated by an attempt to explore the limits of that paradigm—to see how the standard models could embrace problems of information imperfections (which turned out to be not very well).

For more than 100 years, formal modeling in economics had focused on models in which information was assumed to be perfect. Of course, everyone recognized that information was in fact imperfect, but the hope, following Marshall's dictum *"Natura non facit saltum,"* was that economies in which information was not too imperfect would look very much like economies in which information was perfect. One of the main results of our research was to show that this was not true; that even a small amount of information imperfection could have a profound effect on the nature of the equilibrium.

The creators of the neoclassical model, the reigning economic paradigm of the twentieth century, ignored the warnings of nineteenth-century and still earlier masters about how information concerns might alter their analyses—perhaps because they could not see how to embrace them in their seemingly precise models, perhaps because doing so would have led to uncomfortable conclusions about the efficiency of markets. For instance, Smith, in anticipating later discussions of adverse selection, wrote that as firms raise interest rates, the best borrowers drop out of the market.[3] If lenders knew perfectly the risks associated with each borrower, this would matter little; each borrower would be charged an appropriate risk premium. It is because lenders do not know the default probabilities of borrowers perfectly that this process of adverse selection has such important consequences.

I have already noted that *something* was wrong—indeed seriously wrong—with the competitive equilibrium models which represented the prevailing paradigm when we went to graduate school. The paradigm seemed to say that unemployment did not exist, and that issues of efficiency and equity could be neatly separated, so that economists could set aside problems of inequality and poverty as they went about their business of designing more efficient economic systems. But beyond these questionable conclusions there were also a host of empirical puzzles—facts that were hard to reconcile with the standard theory, institutional arrangements left unexplained. In microeconomics, there were public finance puzzles, such as why firms appear not to take actions which minimize their tax liabilities; security market paradoxes,[4] such as why asset prices are so volatile (Shiller 2000) and why equity plays such a limited role in the financing of new investment (Mayer 1990); and other important behavioral questions, such as why firms respond to risks in ways markedly different from those predicted by the theory. In macroeconomics, the cyclical movements of many of the key aggregate variables proved difficult to reconcile with the standard theory. For example, if labor-supply curves are highly inelastic, as most evidence suggests is the case (especially for primary workers), then falls in employment during cyclical downturns should be accompanied by large declines in the real consumption wage. This does not appear to happen. And if the perfect market assumptions were even approximately satisfied, the distress caused by cyclical movements in the economy would be much less than seems to be the case.[5]

There were, to be sure, some Ptolemaic attempts to defend and elaborate on the old model. Some authors, like George J. Stigler

(1961), Nobel laureate in 1982, while recognizing the importance of information, argued that once the real costs of information were taken into account, the standard results of economics would still hold. Information was just a transactions cost. In the approach of many Chicago School economists, information economics was like any other branch of applied economics; one simply analyzed the special factors determining the demand for and supply of information, just as one might analyze the factors affecting the market for wheat. For the more mathematically inclined, information could be incorporated into production functions by inserting an I for the input "information," where I itself could be produced by inputs, like labor. Our analysis showed that this approach was wrong, as were the conclusions derived from it.

Practical economists who could not ignore the bouts of unemployment which had plagued capitalism since its inception talked of the "neoclassical synthesis": If Keynesian interventions were used to ensure that the economy remained at full employment, the story went, the standard neoclassical propositions would once again be true. But while the neoclassical synthesis (Samuelson 1947, Nobel laureate in 1970) had enormous intellectual influence, by the 1970s and 1980s it had come under attack from two sides. One side attacked the underpinnings of Keynesian economics, its microfoundations. Why would rational actors fail to achieve equilibrium— with unemployment persisting—in the way that John Maynard Keynes (1936) had suggested? This form of the argument effectively denied the existence of the phenomena that Keynes was attempting to explain. Worse still, from this perspective some saw the unemployment that did exist as largely reflecting an interference (e.g., by government in setting minimum wages, or by trade unions using their monopoly power to set too-high wages) with the free workings of the market. The implication was that unemployment would be eliminated if markets were made more *flexible*, that is, if unions and government interventions were eliminated. Even if wages fell by a third in the Great Depression, they should have, in this view, fallen even more.

There was however an alternative perspective (articulated more fully in Greenwald and Stiglitz 1987a, 1988b) which asked why we shouldn't believe that massive unemployment was just the tip of an iceberg of more pervasive market efficiencies that are harder to detect. If markets seemed to function *so* badly some of the time, they must be underperforming in more subtle ways much of the time. The economics of information bolstered this view. Indeed, given the nature of the debt contracts, falling prices in the Depression led to bankruptcy and economic disruptions, actually exacerbating the economic downturn. Had there been more wage and price flexibility, matters might have been even worse.

In a later section, I shall explain how it was not just the discrepancies between the standard competitive model and its predictions which led to its being questioned, but the model's lack of robustness—even slight departures from the underlying assumption of perfect information had large consequences. But before turning to those issues, it may be useful to describe some of the specific questions which underlay the beginnings of my research program in this area.

2   Some Motivating Ideas

Education as a Screening Device

Key to my thinking on these issues was the time between 1969 and 1971 I spent at the Institute for Development Studies at the University of Nairobi with the support of the Rockefeller Foundation. The newly independent Kenyan government was asking questions that had not been raised by its former colonial masters, as it attempted to forge policies which would promote its growth and development. For example, how much should the government invest in education? It was clear that a better education got people better jobs—the credential put one at the head of the job queue. Gary S. Fields, a young scholar working at the Institute of Development Studies there, developed a simple model (published in 1972) suggesting, however, that the private returns to education—the enhanced probability of getting a good job—might differ from the social return. Indeed, it was possible that as more people got educated, the private returns got higher (it was even more necessary to get the credential) even though the social return to education might decline. From this perspective, education was performing a markedly different function than it did in the traditional economics literature, where it simply added to human capital and improved productivity.[6] This analysis had important implications for Kenya's decision about how much to invest in higher education. The problem with Fields' work was that it did not provide a full *equilibrium* analysis: wages were fixed, rather than competitively determined.

This omission led me to ask what the market equilibrium would look like if wages were set equal to mean marginal products *conditional on the information that was available* (Stiglitz 1975c). And this in turn forced me to ask: what were the *incentives* and *mechanisms* for employers and employees to acquire or transmit information? Within a group of otherwise similar job applicants (who therefore face the same wage), the employer has an incentive to identify who is the most able, to find some way of *sorting* or *screening* among them, *if he could keep that information private*. But often he cannot; and if others find out about a worker's true ability, the wage will be bid up, and the employer will be unable to appropriate the return to the information. At the very beginning of this research program we had thus identified one of the key issues in information economics: the difficulty of *appropriating* the returns to creating information.

On the other hand, if the employee knew his own ability (that is, if there were *asymmetries of information* between the employee and the employer), then a different set of incentives were at play. Someone who knows his abilities are above average has an incentive to convince his potential employer of that, but a worker at the bottom of the ability distribution has an equally strong incentive to keep the information private. Here was a second principle that was to be explored in subsequent years: there are incentives on the part of individuals for information not to be revealed, for secrecy, or, in modern parlance, for a lack of transparency. This raised questions: How did the forces for secrecy and for information disclosure get balanced? What was the equilibrium that emerged? I will postpone until the next section a description of that equilibrium.

Efficiency Wage Theory

That summer in Kenya I began three other research projects related to information imperfections. At the time I was working in Kenya, there was heavy urban unemployment. My colleagues at the Institute for Development Studies, Michael Todaro and John Harris, had formulated a simple model of labor migration from the rural to the urban sector which accounted for the unemployment.[7] High urban wages attracted workers, who were willing to risk unemployment for the chance at those higher wages. Here was a simple, general equilibrium model of unemployment, but again there was one missing piece: an explanation of high urban wages, well in excess of the legal minimum wage. It did not seem as if either government or unions were *forcing* employers to pay these high wages. One needed an equilibrium theory of wage determination. I recalled discussions I had once had in Cambridge with Harvey Leibenstein, who had postulated that in very poor countries, because of nutrition, higher wages led to higher productivity (Leibenstein 1957). The key insight was that imperfections in information and contracting might also rationalize a dependence of productivity on wages.[8] In that case, firms might find it profitable to pay a higher wage than the minimum necessary to hire labor; such wages I referred to as *efficiency wages*. With efficiency wages, unemployment could exist in equilibrium. I explored four explanations for why productivity might depend on wages (other than through nutrition). The simplest was that lower wages lead to higher turnover, and therefore higher turnover costs for the firm.[9] It was not until some years later than we were able to explain more fully—based on limitations of information—why it was that firms have to bear these turnover costs (Arnott and Stiglitz 1985; Arnott et al. 1988).

Another explanation for efficiency wages was related to the work I was beginning on asymmetric information. Any manager will tell you that paying higher wages attracts better workers—this is just an application of the general notion of adverse selection, which played a central role in earlier insurance literature (Arrow 1965). Firms in a market do not passively have to accept the "market wage." Even in competitive markets, firms could, if they wanted, offer higher wages than others; indeed, it might pay a firm to offer a higher wage, to attract more able workers. Again, the efficiency wage theory explained the existence of unemployment *in equilibrium*. It was thus clear that the notion that underlay much of traditional competitive equilibrium analysis—that markets *had* to clear—was simply not true if information were imperfect.

The formulation of the efficiency wage theory that has received the most attention over the years, however, has focused on problems of *incentives*. Many firms claim that paying high wages induces their workers to work harder. The problem that Carl Shapiro and I (1984) faced was to try to make sense of this claim. If all workers are identical, then if it benefited one firm to pay a high wage, it would likewise benefit all firms. But if a worker was fired for shirking, and there were full employment, he could immediately get another job at the same wage. The high wage would thus provide no incentive. Only if there were unemployment would the worker pay a price for shirking. We showed that *in equilibrium* there *had* to be unemployment: unemployment was the discipline device that forced workers to work hard (see Rey and Stiglitz 1996 for an alternative general-equilibrium formulation). The model had strong policy implications, some of which I shall describe below. Our work illustrated the use of highly simplified models to help clarify thinking about quite complicated matters. In practice, of course, workers are not identical, so problems of adverse selection become intertwined with those of incentives. For example, being fired usually does convey information—there is typically a stigma.

There was a fourth version of the efficiency wage, where productivity was related to *morale* effects, perceptions about how *fairly* they were being treated. While I briefly discussed this version in my earlier work (see in particular Stiglitz 1974d), it was not until almost twenty years later that the idea was fully developed in the important work of Akerlof and Yellen (1990).

Sharecropping and the General Theory of Incentives

This work on the economics of incentives in labor markets was closely related to the third research project that I began in Kenya. In traditional economic theory, while considerable lip service was paid to incentives, there was little serious attention to issues of incentives, motivation, and monitoring. With perfect information, individuals are paid to perform a particular service. If they perform the service they receive the contracted amount; and if not, they do not. With *imperfect* information, firms have to motivate and monitor, rewarding workers for observed good performance and punishing them for bad. My interest in these issues was first aroused by thinking about sharecropping, a common form of land tenancy in developing countries. Under sharecropping, the worker surrenders half (sometimes two-thirds) of the produce to the landlord in return for the use of his land. At first blush, this seemed a highly inefficient arrangement, equivalent to a 50 percent tax on workers' labor. But what were the alternatives? The worker could rent the land. He would have full incentives but then he would have to bear all the risk of fluctuations in output; and beside, he often did not have the requisite capital to pay the rent ahead of time and access to credit was limited (for reasons to be explained below). He could work as wage labor, but then the landlord would have to monitor him, to ensure that he worked. Sharecropping represented a compromise between balancing concerns about risk sharing and incentives. The underlying information problem was that the input of the worker could not be observed, but only his output, which was not perfectly correlated with his input. The sharecropping contract could be thought of as a combination of a rental contract *plus* an insurance contract, in which the landlord "rebates" part of the rent if crops turn out badly. There is not full insurance (which would be equivalent to a wage contract) because such insurance would attenuate all incentives. The adverse effect of insurance on incentives to avoid the insured-against contingency is referred to as *moral hazard*.[10]

In Stiglitz (1974b) I analyzed the equilibrium sharecropping contract. In that paper, I recognized the similarity of the incentive problems I explored to those facing modern corporations, for example, in providing incentives to their managers—a type of problem later to be called the *principal agent problem* (Ross 1973). There followed a large literature on optimal and equilibrium incentive schemes, in labor, capital, and insurance markets.[11] An important principle was that contracts had to be based on *observables*, whether they be inputs, processes, or outcomes. Many of the results obtained earlier in the work on adverse selection had their parallel in this area of "adverse incentives." For instance, Arnott and I (1988a, 1990) analyzed equilibria which entail partial insurance as a way of mitigating the adverse incentive effects (just as partial insurance characterized equilibrium with adverse selection).

Equilibrium Wage and Price Distributions

The fourth strand of my research looked at the issue of wage differentials from a different perspective. My earlier work had suggested that firms that faced higher turnover might pay higher wages to mitigate the problem. But one of the reasons that individuals quit is to obtain a higher-paying job, so the turnover rate in turn depends on the wage distribution. The challenge was to formulate an *equilibrium* model that incorporated both of these observations, that is, where the wage distribution *itself* which motivated the search was *explained* as part of the equilibrium.

More generally, efficiency wage theory said that firms might pay a higher wage than necessary to obtain workers; but the level of the efficiency wage might vary across firms. For example, firms with higher turnover costs, or for which worker inefficiency could lead to large losses of capital, or for which monitoring was more difficult, might find it desirable to pay higher wages. The implication was that similar labor might receive quite different compensation in different jobs. The distribution of wages might not, in general, be explicable solely in terms of differences in abilities.

I was to return to these four themes repeatedly in my research over the following three decades.

3   From the Competitive Paradigm to the Information Paradigm

In the previous section, I described how the disparities between the models economists used and the world that I saw, especially in Kenya, had motivated a search for an alternative paradigm. But there was another motivation, driven more by the internal logic and structure of the competitive model itself.

The competitive model virtually made economics a branch of engineering (no aspersions on that noble profession intended), and the participants in the economy better or worse engineers. Each was solving a maximization problem, with full information: households maximizing utility subject to budget constraints, firms maximizing profits (market value), and the two interacting in competitive product, labor, and capital markets. One of the peculiar implications was that there never were disagreements about what the firm should do. Alternative management teams would presumably come up with the same solution to the maximization problems. Another peculiar implication was for the meaning of risk: When a firm said that a project was risky, that (should have) meant that it was highly correlated with the business cycle, not that it had a high chance of failure (Stiglitz 1989g). I have already described some of the other peculiar implications of the model: the fact that there was no unemployment or credit rationing, that it focused on only a limited subset of the information problems facing society, that it seemed not to address issues such as incentives and motivation.

But much of the research in the profession was directed not at these big gaps, but at seemingly more technical issues—at the mathematical structures. The underlying *mathematics* required assumptions of convexity and continuity, and with these assumptions one could prove the existence of equilibrium and its (Pareto) efficiency (see Debreu 1959; Arrow 1964). The standard proofs of these fundamental theorems of welfare economics did not even list in their enumerated assumptions those concerning information: the perfect information assumption was so ingrained it did not have to be explicitly stated. The *economic* assumptions to which the proofs of efficiency called attention concerned the absence of externalities and public goods. The market failures approach to the economics of the public sector (Bator 1958) discussed alternative approaches by which these market failures could be corrected, but these market failures were highly circumscribed by assumption.

There was, moreover, a curious disjunction between the language economists used to explain markets and the models they constructed. They talked about the information efficiency of the market economy, though they focused on a single information problem, that of scarcity. But there are a myriad of other information problems faced by consumers and firms every day, concerning, for instance, the prices and qualities of the various objects that are for sale in the market, the quality and efforts of the workers they hire, or the potential returns to investment projects. In the standard paradigm, the competitive general-equilibrium model (for which Kenneth J. Arrow and Gerard Debreu received Nobel Prizes in 1972 and 1983, respectively), there were no shocks, no unanticipated events: At the beginning of time, the full equilibrium was solved, and everything from then on was an unfolding over time of what had been planned in each of the contingencies. In the real world, the critical question was: how, and how well, do markets handle fundamental problems of information?

There were other aspects of the standard paradigm that seemed hard to accept. It argued that institutions did not matter—markets could see through them, and equilibrium was simply determined by the laws of supply and demand. It said that the distribution of wealth did not matter, so long as there were well-defined property rights (Coase 1960, who won the Nobel Prize in 1991). And it said that (by and large) history did not matter—knowing preferences and technology and initial endowments, one could describe the time path of the economy.

Work on the economics of information began by questioning each of these underlying premises. Consider, to begin with, the convexity assumptions which corresponded to long-standing principles of diminishing returns. With imperfect information (and the costs of acquiring it) these assumptions were no longer plausible. It was not just that the cost of acquiring information could be viewed as fixed costs.[12] My work with Roy Radner (Radner and Stiglitz 1984) showed that there was a *fundamental nonconcavity in the value of information*, that is, under quite general conditions, it never paid to buy just a little bit of information. Arnott and Stiglitz (1988a) showed that such problems were pervasive in even the simplest of moral hazard problems (where individuals had a choice of alternative actions, e.g. the amount of risk to undertake). While we had not repealed the law of diminishing returns, we had shown its domain to be more limited than had previously been realized.

Michael Rothschild and I (1976) showed that under natural formulations of what might be meant by a competitive market with imperfect information, equilibrium often did not exist[13]—even when there was an arbitrarily small amount of information imperfection.[14] While subsequent research has looked for alternative definitions of equilibrium (e.g., Riley 1979), we remain unconvinced; most of these alternatives violate the natural meaning of "competition," that each participant in the market is so small that he believes that he will have no effect on the behavior of others (Rothschild and Stiglitz 1997).

The new information paradigm went further in undermining the foundations of competitive equilibrium analysis, the basic "laws" of economics. For example, we have shown how, when prices affect "quality"—either because of incentive or selection effects— equilibrium may be characterized by demand not equaling supply; firms will not pay lower wages to workers, even when they can obtain such workers, because doing so will raise their labor costs. Contrary to the law of one price, we have shown that the market will be characterized by wage and price distributions, even when there is no exogenous source of "noise" in the economy, and even when all firms and workers are (otherwise) identical. Contrary to standard competitive results, we have shown that in equilibrium, firms may charge a price in excess of the marginal costs, or workers may be paid a wage in excess of their reservation wage, so that the incentive to maintain a reputation is maintained (see also Klein and Leffler 1981; Shapiro 1983). Contrary to the efficient markets hypothesis

(Fama 1970), which holds that stock prices convey all the relevant information from the informed to the uninformed, Sanford J. Grossman and I (1976, 1980a) showed that, when information is costly to collect, stock prices necessarily aggregate information imperfectly (to induce people to gather information, there must be an "equilibrium amount of disequilibrium"). Each of these cornerstones of the competitive paradigm was rejected, or was shown to hold only under much more restrictive conditions.

The most fundamental reason that markets with imperfect information differ from those in which information is complete is that, with imperfect information, market actions or choices convey information. Market participants know this and respond accordingly. For example, firms provide guarantees not only because they are better able to absorb the risk of product failure but to convey information about their confidence in their products. A person takes an insurance policy with a large deductible to convey to the insurer his belief that the likelihood of his having an accident is low. Information may also be concealed: A firm may not assign an employee to a highly visible job, because it knows that the assignment will be interpreted as an indication that the employee is good, making it more likely that a rival will try to hire the person away.

One of the early insights (Akerlof 1970) was that, with imperfect information, markets may be thin or absent. The absence of particular markets, for example, for risk, has profound implications for how *other* markets function. The fact that workers and firms cannot buy insurance against many of the risks which they face affects labor and capital markets; it leads, for instance, to labor contracts in which the employer provides *some* insurance. But the design of these more complicated, but still imperfect and incomplete, contracts affects the efficiency, and overall performance, of the economy.

Perhaps most importantly, under the standard paradigm, markets are Pareto efficient, except when one of a limited number of market failures occurs. Under the imperfect information paradigm, markets are almost never Pareto efficient.

While information economics thus undermined these long-standing principles of economics, it also provided explanations for many phenomena that had long been unexplained. Before turning to these applications, I want to present a somewhat a more systematic account of the *principles* of the economics of information.

Some Problems in Constructing an Alternative Paradigm

The fact that information is imperfect was, of course, well recognized by all economists. The reason that models with imperfect information were not developed earlier was that it was not obvious how to do so: While there is a single way in which information is perfect, there are an infinite number of ways in which information can be imperfect. One of the keys to success was formulating simple models in which the set of relevant information could be fully specified—and so the precise ways in which information was imperfect could also be fully specified. But there was a danger in this methodology, as useful as it was: In these overly simplistic models, full revelation of information was sometimes possible. In the real world, of course, this never happens, which is why in some of the later work (e.g., Grossman and Stiglitz 1976, 1980a), we worked with models with an infinite number of states. Similarly there may well be ways of fully resolving incentive problems in simple models, which collapse when models are made more realistic, for example by combining selection and incentive problems (Stiglitz and Weiss 1986).

Perhaps the hardest problem in building the new paradigm was modeling equilibrium. It was important to think about both sides of the market—employers and employees, insurance company and the insured, lender and borrower. Each had to be modeled as "rational," in some sense, making inferences on the basis of available information and behaving accordingly. I wanted to model *competitive* behavior, where each actor in the economy was small, and believed he was small—and so his actions could not or would not affect the equilibrium (though others' inferences about himself might be affected). Finally, one had to think carefully about what was the feasible set of actions: what might each side do to extract or convey information to others.

As we shall see, the variety of results obtained (and much of the confusion in the early literature) arose partly from a failure to be as clear as one might have been about the assumptions. For instance, the standard adverse selection model had the quality of the good offered in the market (say of used cars, or riskiness of the insured) depending on price. The car buyer (the seller of insurance) knows the *statistical* relationship between price and quality, and this affects his demand. The market equilibrium is the price at which demand equals supply. But that is an equilibrium if and only if there is no way by which the seller of a good car can convey that information to the buyer—so that he can earn a quality premium—and if there is no way by which the buyer can sort out good cars from bad cars. Typically, there are such ways, and it is the attempt to elicit that information which has profound effects on how markets function. To develop a new paradigm, we had to break out from long-established premises, to ask what should be taken as assumptions and what should be derived from the analysis. Market clearing could not be taken as an assumption; neither could the premise that a firm sells a good at a particular price to all comers. One could not *begin* the analysis even by assuming that in competitive equilibrium there would be zero profits. In the standard theory, if there were positive profits, a firm might enter, bidding away existing customers. In the new theory, the attempt to bid away new customers by slightly lowering prices might lead to marked changes in their behavior or in the mix of customers, in such a way that the profits of the new entrant actually became negative. One had to rethink all the conclusions from first premises.

We made progress in our analyses because we began with highly simplified models of particular markets, that allowed us to think through carefully each of the assumptions and conclusions. From the analysis of particular markets (whether the insurance market, the education market, the labor market, or the land tenancy/sharecropping market), we attempted to identify general principles, to explore how these principles operated in each of the other markets. In doing so, we identified particular features, particular informational assumptions, which seemed to be more relevant in one market or another. The nature of competition in the labor market is different from that in the insurance market or the capital market, though these markets have much in common. This interplay, between looking at the ways in which such markets are similar and dissimilar, proved to be a fruitful research strategy.[15]

Sources of Information Asymmetries

Information imperfections are pervasive in the economy: indeed, it is hard to imagine what a world with perfect information would be like. Much of the research I describe here focuses on *asymmetries* of information, that fact that different people know different things.

Workers know more about their own abilities than the firm does; the person buying insurance knows more about his health, for example, whether he smokes and drinks immoderately, than the insurance firm. Similarly, the owner of a car knows more about the car than potential buyers; the owner of a firm knows more about the firm that a potential investor; the borrower knows more about the riskiness of his project than the lender does; and so on.

An essential feature of a decentralized market economy is that different people know different things, and in some sense, economists had long been thinking of markets with information asymmetries. But the earlier literature had neither thought about how these were created, or what their consequences might be. While such information asymmetries inevitably arise, the extent to which they do so and their consequences depend on how the market is structured, and the recognition that they will arise affects market behavior. For instance, even if an individual has no more information about his ability than potential employers, the moment he goes to work for a specific employer, an information asymmetry has been created—the employer may now know more about the individual's ability than others do. A consequence is that the "used labor" market may not work well. Other employers will be reserved in bidding for the worker's services, knowing that they will succeed in luring him away from his current employer only if they bid too much. This impediment to labor mobility gives market power to the first employer, which he will be tempted to exercise. But then, because a worker knows he will tend to be locked into a job, he will be more risk averse in accepting an offer. The terms of the initial contract thus have to be designed to reflect the diminution of the worker's bargaining power that occurs the moment he accepts a job.

To take another example, it is natural that in the process of oil exploration, a company may obtain information relevant to the likelihood that there will be oil in a neighboring tract—an informational externality (see Stiglitz 1975d; Leitzinger and Stiglitz 1984). The existence of this asymmetric information affects the nature of the bidding for oil rights on the neighboring tract. Bidding when there is known to be asymmetries of information will be markedly different from that where such asymmetries do not exist (Wilson 1977). Those who are uninformed will presume that they will win only if they bid too much—information asymmetries exacerbate the problem of the "winner's curse" (Wilson 1969; Capen et al. 1971). The government (or other owners of large tracts to be developed) should take this into account in its leasing strategy. And the bidders in the initial leases too will take this into account: part of the value of winning in the initial auction is the information rent that will accrue in later rounds.

While early work in the economics of information dealt with how markets overcame problems of information asymmetries, later work turned to how actors in markets *create* information problems, for example in an attempt to exploit market power. An example is managers of firms who attempt to entrench themselves, and reduce competition in the market for managers, by taking actions to increase information asymmetry (Shleifer and Vishny 1989; Edlin and Stiglitz 1995). This is an example of the general problem of corporate governance, to which I will return later. Similarly, the presence of information imperfections give rise to market power in product markets. Firms can exploit this market power through "sales" and other ways of differentiating among individuals who have different search costs (Salop 1977; Salop and Stiglitz 1977, 1982; Stiglitz 1979a). The price dispersions which exist in the market are *created* by the market—they are not just the failure of markets to arbitrage fully price differences caused by shocks that affect different markets differently.

Overcoming Information Asymmetries

I now want to discuss briefly the ways by which information asymmetries are dealt with, how they can be (partially) overcome.

1. Incentives for Gathering and Disclosing Information

There are two key issues: what are the *incentives* for obtaining information, and what are the *mechanisms*. My brief discussion of the analysis of education as a screening device suggested the fundamental incentive: More able individuals (lower risk individuals, firms with better products) will receive a higher wage (will have to pay a lower premium, will receive a higher price for their products) if they can establish that they are more productive (lower risk, higher quality).

We noted earlier that while some individuals have an incentive to disclose information, some have an incentive not to have the information disclosed. Was it possible that in market equilibrium, only *some* of the information would be revealed? One of the early important results was that, if the more able can costlessly establish that they are more able, then the market will be fully revealing, even though those who are below average would prefer that no information be revealed. In the simplest models, I described a process of unraveling: If the most able could establish his ability, he would; but then all but the most able would be grouped together, receiving the mean marginal product of that group; and the most able of that group would have an incentive to reveal his ability. And so on down the line, until there was full revelation. (I jokingly referred to this as "Walras' Law of Sorting"—if all but one group sorts itself out from the others, then the last group is also identified.)

What happens if those who are more able cannot credibly convince potential employers of their ability? The other side of the market has an incentive too to gather information. An employer that can find a worker that is better than is recognized by others will have found a bargain, because the worker's wage will be determined by what others think of him. The problem, as we noted, is that if what the employer knows becomes known to others, the worker's wage will be bid up, and the employer will be unable to appropriate the returns on his investment in information acquisition.

The fact that competition makes it difficult for the screener to appropriate the returns from screening has an important implication: In markets where, for one reason or another, the more able cannot fully convey their attributes, investment in screening requires *imperfect competition in screening*. The economy, in effect, has to choose between two different imperfections: imperfections of information or imperfections of competition. Of course, in the end, there will be both forms of imperfection, and no particular reason that these imperfections will be "balanced" optimally (Stiglitz 1975b; Jaffee and Stiglitz 1990). This is but one of many examples of the *interplay* between market imperfections. Earlier, for instance, we discussed the incentive problems associated with sharecropping, which arise when workers do not own the land that they till. This problem could be overcome if individuals could borrow to buy their land. But capital market imperfections—limitations on the ability to borrow, which themselves arise from information imperfections—explain why this "solution" does not work.

There is another important consequence: if markets were fully informationally efficient—that is, if information disseminated instantaneously and perfectly throughout the economy—then no one would have any incentive to gather information, so long as there was any cost of doing so. Hence markets cannot be fully informationally efficient (Grossman and Stiglitz 1976, 1980a).

2. Mechanisms for Elimination of/Reducing Information Asymmetries

In simple models where (for example) individuals know their own abilities there might seem an easy way to resolve the problem of information asymmetry: Let each person tell his true characteristic. Unfortunately, individuals do not necessarily have the incentive to tell the truth. Talk is cheap. Other methods must be used to convey information credibly.

The simplest way by which that could be done was an exam. Models of competitive equilibrium (Arrow 1973; Stiglitz 1974a) with exams make two general points. First, in equilibrium *the gains of the more able were largely at the expense of the less able.* Establishing that an individual is of higher ability provides that person with higher wages, but simultaneously establishes that others are of lower ability. Hence the private returns to expenditures on educational screening exceed the social returns. It was clear that there were important *externalities* associated with information, a theme which was to recur in later work. Second, and a more striking result, there could exist multiple equilibria—one in which information was fully revealed (the market identified the high and low ability people) and another in which it was not (called a pooling equilibrium). The pooling equilibrium Pareto-dominated the equilibrium with full revelation. This work, done some thirty years ago, established two results of great policy import, which remarkably have not been fully absorbed into policy discussions even today. First, markets do not provide appropriate incentives for information disclosure. There is, in principle, a role for government. And second, expenditures on information may be too great (see also Hirshleifer 1971).

3. Conveying Information Through Actions

But much of the information firms glean about their employees, banks about their borrowers, or insurance companies about their insured, comes not from examinations but from making inferences based on their *behavior*. This is a commonplace in life—but it was not in our economic models. As I have already noted, the early discussions of adverse selection in insurance markets recognized that as an insurance company raised its premiums, those who were least likely to have an accident might decide not to purchase the insurance; the willingness to purchase insurance at a particular price conveyed information to the insurance company. George Akerlof recognized that this phenomenon is far more general: the owner's willingness to sell a used car, for instance, conveyed information about the car's quality.

Bruce C. Greenwald (1979, 1986) took these ideas one important step further, showing how adverse selection applied to labor and capital markets (see also Greenwald et al. 1984; Myers and Majluf 1984). For example, the willingness of insiders in a firm to sell stock at a particular price conveys information about their view of what the stock is really worth. Akerlof's insight that the result of these information asymmetries was that markets would be thin or absent helped explain why labor and capital markets often did not function well. It provided part of the explanation for why firms raised so little of their funds through equity (Mayer 1990). Stigler was wrong: imperfect information was not just like a transactions cost.

There is a much richer set of actions which convey information beyond those on which traditional adverse selection models have focused. An insurance company wants to attract healthy applicants. It might realize that by locating itself on the fifth floor of a walk-up building, only those with a strong heart would apply. The willingness or ability to walk up five floors conveys information. More subtly, it might recognize that how far up it needs to locate itself, if it only wants to get healthy applicants, depends on other elements of its strategy, such as the premium charged. Or the company may decide to throw in a membership in a health club, but charge a higher premium. Those who value a health club—because they will use it—willingly pay the higher premium. But these individuals are likely to be healthier.

There are a host of other actions which convey information. The quality of the guarantee offered by a firm can convey information about the quality of the product; only firms that believe that their product is reliable will be willing to offer a good guarantee. The guarantee is desirable not just because it reduces risk, but because it conveys information. The number of years of schooling may convey information about the ability of an individual. More able individuals may go to school longer, in which case the increase in wages associated with an increase in schooling may not be a consequence of the human capital that has been added, but rather simply be a result of the sorting that occurs. The size of the deductible that an individual chooses in an insurance policy may convey information about his view about the likelihood of an accident or the size of the accidents he anticipates—*on average*, those who are less likely to have an accident may be more willing to accept high deductibles. The willingness of an entrepreneur to hold large fractions of his wealth in a firm (or to retain large fractions of the shares of the firm) conveys information about his beliefs in the firm's future performance. If a firm promotes an individual to a particular job, it may convey information about the firm's assessment of his ability.

The fact that these actions may convey information affects behavior. In some cases, the action will be designed to obfuscate, to limit information disclosure. The firm that knows that others are looking at who it promotes, and will compete more vigorously for those workers, may affect the willingness of the firm to promote some individuals or assign them to particular jobs (Michael Waldman 1984). In others, the action will be designed to convey information in a credible way to alter beliefs. The fact that customers will treat a firm that issues a better guarantee as if its product is better—and therefore be willing to pay a higher price—may affect the guarantee that the firm is willing to issue. Knowing that selling his shares will convey a negative signal concerning his views of the future prospects of his firm, an entrepreneur may retain more of the shares of the firm; he will be less diversified than he otherwise would have been (and accordingly, he may act in a more risk-averse manner).

A simple lesson emerges: Some individuals wish to convey information; some individuals wish not to have information conveyed (either because such information might lead others to think less well of them, or because conveying information may interfere with their ability to appropriate rents). In either case, the fact that actions convey information leads people to alter their behavior, and changes how markets function. This is why information imperfections have such profound effects.

Once one recognizes that actions convey information, two results follow. First, in making decisions about what to do, individuals will not only think about what they like (as in traditional economics) but how it will affect others' beliefs about them. If I choose to go to school longer, it may lead others to believe that I am more able. I may therefore decide to stay in school longer, not because I value what is being taught, but because I value how it changes others' beliefs concerning my ability. This means, of course, that we have to rethink completely firm and household decision-making.

Secondly, we noted earlier that individuals have an incentive to "lie"—the less able to say that they are more able. Similarly, if it becomes recognized that those who walk up to the fifth floor to apply for insurance are more healthy, then I might be willing to do so even if I am not so healthy, simply to fool the insurance company. Recognizing this, one needs to look for ways by which information is conveyed *in equilibrium*. The critical insight in how that could occur was provided in a paper I wrote with Michael Rothschild (1976). If those who were more able, less risk prone, or more creditworthy *acted* in some observable way (had different preferences) than those who were less able, less risk prone, or less creditworthy, then it might be possible to design a set of *choices*, which would result in those with different characteristics in effect *identifying* themselves through their *self-selection*. The particular mechanism which we explored in our insurance model illustrates how self-selection mechanisms work. People who know they are less likely to have an accident will be more willing to accept an insurance policy with a high deductible, so that an insurance company that offered two policies, one at a high premium and no deductible, one with a low premium and high deductible, would be able to sort out who were high risk and who low. It is an easy matter to construct choices which thus *separate* people into classes.

It was clear that information was conveyed because the actions were costly, and more costly for some than others. The attempt to convey information had to *distort* behavior. Our analysis also made it clear that it was not just information asymmetries, but information imperfections more generally, that were relevant. Even if those buying insurance did not know their accident probabilities (or know them with greater accuracy than the insurance company), so long as those with higher accident probabilities *on average* differed in some way reflected in their preferences and actions, self-selection mechanisms could and would be employed to sort.

Yet another set of issues arise from the fact that actions may not be costlessly observable. The employer would like to know how hard his worker is working; the lender would like to know the actions which borrower will undertake. These asymmetries of information about *actions* are as important as the earlier discussed asymmetries. Just as in the adverse selection model, the seller of insurance may try to overcome the problems posed by information asymmetries by *examination*, so too in the moral hazard or adverse incentive model, he may try to *monitor* the actions of the insured. But examinations and monitoring are costly, and while they yield some information, typically there remains a high level of residual information imperfection. One response to this problem is to try to induce desired behavior through the setting of contract terms. For example, borrowers' risk-taking behavior may be affected by the interest rate charged by the lender (Stiglitz and Weiss 1981).

Consequences for Market Equilibrium

The law of supply and demand had long been treated as a fundamental principle of economics. But there is in fact no law that requires the insurance firm to sell to all who apply at the announced premium, or the lender to lend to all who apply at the announced interest rate, or the employer to employ all those who apply at the posted wage. With perfect information and perfect competition, any firm that charged a price higher than the others would lose all of its customers; and at the going price, one faced a perfectly elastic supply of customers. In adverse selection and incentive models, what mattered was not just the supply of customers or employees or borrowers, but their "quality"—the riskiness of the insured or the borrower, the returns on the investment, the productivity of the worker.

Since "quality" may increase with price, it may be profitable (for example) to pay a higher wage than the "market-clearing" wage, whether the dependence on quality arises from adverse selection or adverse incentive effects (or, in the labor market, because of morale or nutritional effects). The consequence, as we have noted, is that market equilibrium may be characterized by demand not equaling supply in the traditional sense. In credit market equilibrium, the supply of loans may be rationed (Keeton 1979; Eaton and Gersovitz 1981; Stiglitz and Weiss 1981). Or, in the labor market, the wage rate may be higher than that at which the demand for labor equals the supply (an efficiency wage), leading to unemployment.[16]

Analyzing the choices which arise in *full* equilibrium, taking into account fully not only the knowledge that the firms have, say, about their customers but also the knowledge that customers have about how firms will make inferences about them from their behavior, and taking into account the fact that the inferences that a firm might make depends not only on what that firm does, but also on what other firms do, turned out, however, to be a difficult task. The easiest situation to analyze was that of a monopolist (Stiglitz 1977). The monopolist could construct a set of choices that would *differentiate* among different types of individuals, and analyze whether it was profit maximizing for him to do so fully, or to (partially) "pool"— that is, offer a set of contracts such that several types might choose the same one. This work laid the foundations of a *general theory of price discrimination*. Under standard theories of monopoly, with perfect information, firms would have an incentive to price discriminate perfectly (extracting the full consumer surplus from each). If they did this, then monopoly would in fact be nondistortionary. Yet most models assumed no price discrimination (that is, the monopolist offered the same price to all customers), without explaining why they did not do so. The new work showed how, given limited information, firms could price discriminate, but could do so only imperfectly. Subsequent work by a variety of authors (such as Adams and Yellen 1976; Salop 1977) explored ways by which a monopolist might find out relevant characteristics of his customers. Information economics thus provided the first coherent theory of monopoly.

The reason that analyzing monopoly was easy is that the monopolist could structure the entire choice set facing his customers. The hard question is to describe the full competitive equilibrium, for example, a set of insurance contracts such that no one can offer an alternative set that would be profitable. Each firm could control the choices that it offered, but not the choices offered by others; and the decisions made by customers depended on the entire set of choices available. In our 1976 paper, Rothschild and I succeeded in analyzing this case.

Three striking results emerged from this analysis. The first I have already mentioned: Under plausible conditions, given the natural definition of equilibrium, equilibrium might not exist. There were two possible forms of equilibria: *pooling equilibria*, in which the market is not able to distinguish among the types, and *separating equilibria*, in which it is. The different groups "separate out" by taking different actions. We showed in our context that there never could be a pooling equilibrium—if there were a single contract that everyone bought, there was another contract that another firm could offer which would "break" the pooling equilibrium. On the other hand, there might not exist a separating equilibrium either, if the cost of separation was too great. Any putative separating equilibrium could be broken by a profitable pooling contract, a contract which would be bought by both low risk and high risk types.[17]

Second, even small amounts of imperfections of information can change the standard results concerning the existence and characterization of equilibrium. Equilibrium, for instance, never exists when the two types are very near each other. As we have seen, the competitive equilibrium model is simply not robust.

Third, we now can see how the fact that actions convey information affects equilibrium. In perfect information models, individuals would fully divest themselves of the risks which they face, and accordingly would act in a risk neutral manner. We explained why insurance markets would not work well—why most risk-averse individuals would buy only partial insurance. The result was important not only for the insights it provided into the workings of insurance markets, but because there are important elements of insurance in many transactions and markets. The relationship between the landlord and his tenant, or the employer and his employee, contains an insurance component.

In short, the general principle that actions convey information applies in many contexts. Further, limitations on the ability to divest oneself of risk are important in explaining a host of contractual relationships.

Sorting, Screening, and Signaling

In equilibrium, both buyers and sellers, employers and employees, insurance company and insured, and lender and creditor are aware of the informational consequences of their actions. In the case where, say, the insurance company or employer takes the initiative in sorting out applicants, self-selection is an alternative to examinations as a sorting device. In the case where the insured, or the employee, takes the initiative to identify himself as a more attractive contractual partner, then it is conventional to say he is *signaling* (Spence 1973). But of course, in equilibrium both sides are aware of the consequences of alternative actions, and the differences between signaling and self-selection screening models lie in the technicalities of game theory, and in particular whether the informed or uninformed player moves first.[18]

Still, some of the seeming differences between signaling and screening models arise because of a failure to specify a *full* equilibrium. We noted earlier that there might be many separating contracts, but a unique separating equilibrium. We argued that if one considered any other separating set of contracts, then (say, in the insurance market) a firm could come in and offer an alternative set of contracts and make a profit. Then the original set of separating contracts could not have been an equilibrium. The same is true in, say, the education signaling model. There are many educational systems which "separate"—that is, the more able choose to go to school longer, and the wages at each level of education correspond to the productivity of those who go to school for that length of time. But all except one are not *full equilibria*. Assume, for instance, there were two types of individuals, of low ability and of high ability. Then if the low-ability person has twelve years of schooling, then any education system in which the high-ability person went to school sufficiently long—say, more than fourteen years—might separate. But the low-ability types would recognize that if they went to school for eleven years, they would still be treated as having low ability. The unique equilibrium level of education for the low-ability person is that which maximizes his net income (taking into account the productivity gains and costs of education). The unique equilibrium level of education for the high-ability type is the lowest level of education such that the low-ability type does not have the incentive to mimic the high-ability person's educational attainment.

The education system, of course, was particularly infelicitous for studying *market* equilibrium. The structure of the education system is largely a matter of public choice, not of market processes. Different countries have chosen markedly different systems. The minimum level of education is typically not a matter of choice, but set by the government. Within educational systems, examinations play as important a role as self-selection or signaling, though *given* a certain standard of testing, there is a process of self-selection involved in deciding whether to stay in school, or to try to pass the examination. For the same reason, the problems of existence which arise in the insurance market are not relevant in the education market—the "competitive" supply side of the market is simply absent. But when the signaling concepts are translated into contexts in which there is a robust competitive market, the problems of existence cannot be so easily ignored. In particular, when there is a continuum of types, as in the Spence (1973) model, there never exists a screening equilibrium.

Equilibrium Contracts

The work with Rothschild was related to earlier work that I had done on incentives (such as the work on sharecropping) in that both lines of work entailed an "equilibrium in contracts." The contracts that had characterized economic relations in the standard competitive model were extraordinarily simple: I will pay you a certain amount if you do such and such. If you did not perform as promised, the pay was not given. But with perfect information, individuals simply would not sign contracts that they did not intend to fulfill. Insurance contracts were similarly simple: A payment occurred if and only if particular specified events occurred.

The work on sharecropping and on equilibrium with competitive insurance markets showed that with imperfect information, a far richer set of contracts would be employed and thus began a large literature on the theory of contracting. In the simple sharecropping contracts of Stiglitz (1974b), the contracts involved shares, fixed payments, and plot sizes. More generally, optimal payment structures related payments to *observables*, such as inputs, processes, or outputs.[19] Further, because what goes on in one market affects other parts of the economy, the credit, labor, and land markets are *interlinked*; one could not decentralize in the way hypothesized by the standard perfect information model (Braverman and Stiglitz 1982, 1986a, b, 1989).

These basic principles were subsequently applied in a variety of other market contexts. The most obvious was the design of labor contracts (Stiglitz 1975a). Payments to workers can depend not only on output, but on *relative* performance, which may convey more relevant information than absolute performance. For example, the fact that a particular company's stock goes up when all other companies' stock goes up may say very little about the performance of the manager. Nalebuff and Stiglitz (1983a, b) analyzed the design of these relative performance compensation schemes (contests).

Credit markets too are characterized by complicated equilibrium contracts. Lenders may specify not only an interest rate, but also impose other conditions (collateral requirements, equity requirements) which would have both incentive and selection effects.[20] Indeed, the simultaneous presence of both selection and incentive effects is important in credit markets. In the absence of the former, it might be possible to increase the collateral requirement *and* raise interest rates, still ensuring that the borrower undertook the safe project.

As another application, "contracting"—including provisions that help information be conveyed and risks be shared—have been shown to play an important role in explaining macroeconomic rigidities. See, for instance, Costas Azariadis and Stiglitz (1983), the papers of the symposium in the 1983 *Quarterly Journal of Economics*, the survey article by Sherwin Rosen (1985), Arnott et al. (1988), and Werin and Wijkander (1992). Moreover, problems of asymmetries of information can help explain the perpetuation of seemingly inefficient contracts (Stiglitz 1992b).

Equilibrium Wage and Price Distributions

One of the most obvious differences between the predictions of the model with perfect information and what we see in everyday life is the conclusion that the same good sells for the same price everywhere. In reality, we all spend a considerable amount of time shopping for good buys. The differences in prices represent more than just differences in quality or service. There are *real* price differences. Since Stigler's classic paper (1961), there has been a large literature exploring optimal search behavior. However Stigler, and most of the search literature, took the price or wage distribution as given. They did not ask how the distribution might arise and whether, given the search costs, it could be sustained.

As I began to analyze these models, I found that there could be a nondegenerate equilibrium wage or price distribution even if all agents were identical, for example, faced the same search costs. Early on, it had become clear that even small search costs could make a large difference to the behavior of product and labor markets. Peter

A. Diamond (1971) had independently made this point in a highly influential paper, which serves to illustrate powerfully the lack of robustness of the competitive equilibrium theory. Assume for example, as in the standard theory, that all firms were charging the competitive price, but there is an epsilon cost of searching, of going to another store. Then any firm which charged half an epsilon more would lose no customers and thus would choose to increase its price. Similarly, it would pay all other firms to increase their prices. But at the higher price, it would again pay each to increase price, and so on until the price charged at every firm is the monopoly price, even though search costs are small. This showed convincingly that the competitive price was not the equilibrium. But in some cases, not even the monopoly price was an equilibrium. In general, Salop and Stiglitz (1977, 1982, 1987) and Stiglitz (1979b, 1985c, 1987b, 1989c) showed that in situations where there were even small search costs, markets might be characterized by a price distribution. The standard wisdom that said that not everyone had to be informed to ensure that the market acted perfectly competitive was simply not, in general, true (see Stiglitz 1989c, for a survey).

4   Efficiency of the Market Equilibrium and the Role of the State

The fundamental theorems of neoclassical welfare economics state that competitive economies will lead, as if by an invisible hand, to a (Pareto-) efficient allocation of resources, and that every Pareto-efficient resource allocation can be achieved through a competitive mechanism, provided only that the appropriate lump-sum redistributions are undertaken. These theorems provide both the rationale for the reliance on free markets, and for the belief that issues of distribution can be separated from issues of efficiency, allowing the economist the freedom to push for reforms which increase efficiency, regardless of their seeming impact on distribution. (If society does not like the distributional consequences of a policy, it should simply redistribute income.)

The economics of information showed that neither of these theorems was particularly relevant to real economies. To be sure, economists over the preceding three decades had identified important market failures—such as the externalities associated with pollution—which required government intervention. But the scope for market failures was limited, and thus the arenas in which government intervention was required were correspondingly limited.

Early work, already referred to, had laid the foundations for the idea that economies with information imperfections would not be Pareto efficient, *even taking into account the costs of obtaining information*. There were interventions in the market that could make all parties better off. We had shown, for instance, that incentives for the disclosure and acquisition of information were far from perfect. On the one hand, imperfect appropriability meant that there might be insufficient incentives to gather information; but on the other, the fact that much of the gains were "rents," gains by some at the expense of others, suggested that there might be excessive expenditures on information. A traditional argument for unfettered capital markets was that there are strong incentives to gather information; discovering that some stock was more valuable than others thought would be rewarded by a capital gain. This price discovery function of capital markets was often advertised as one of its strengths. But while the individual who discovered the information a nanosecond before anyone else might be better off, was society as a whole better off? If having the information a nanosecond earlier did not lead to a change in real decisions (e.g., concerning investment), then it was largely redistributive, with the gains of those obtaining the information occurring at the expense of others (Stiglitz 1989c).

There are potentially other inefficiencies associated with information acquisition. Information can have adverse effects on volatility (Stiglitz 1989i). And information can lead to the destruction of markets, in ways which lead to adverse effects on welfare. For example, individuals may sometimes have incentives to create information asymmetries in insurance markets, which leads to the destruction of those markets and a lowering of overall welfare. Welfare might be increased if the acquisition of this kind of information could be proscribed. Recently, such issues have become sources of real policy concern in the arena of genetic testing. Even when information is available, there are issues concerning its use, with the use of certain kinds of information having either a discriminatory intent or effect, in circumstances in which such direct discrimination itself would be prohibited.[21]

While it was perhaps not surprising that markets might not provide appropriate incentives for the acquisition and dissemination of information, the market failures associated with imperfect information may be far more profound. The intuition can be seen most simply in the case of models with moral hazard. There, the premium charged is associated with the *average* risk and, therefore, the average care, taken by seemingly similar individuals. The moral hazard problem arises because the level of care cannot be observed. Each individual ignores the effect of his actions on the premium; but when they all take less care, the premium increases. The lack of care by each exerts a negative externality on others. The essential insight of Greenwald and Stiglitz (1986)[22] was to recognize that such externality-like effects are pervasive whenever information is imperfect or markets incomplete—that is always—and as a result, markets are essentially never constrained Pareto efficient. In short, market failures are pervasive. Arnott et al. (1994) provide a simple exposition of this point using the standard self-selection and incentive compatibility constraints.

An important implication is that efficient allocations cannot in general be decentralized via competitive markets. The notion that one could decentralize decision-making to obtain (Pareto-) efficient resource allocation is one of the fundamental ideas in economics. Greenwald and Stiglitz (1986) showed that that was not possible in general. A simple example illustrates what is at issue. An insurance company cannot monitor the extent of smoking, which has an adverse effect on health. The government cannot monitor smoking any better than the insurance company, but it can impose taxes, not only on cigarettes, but also on other commodities which are complements to smoking (and subsidies on substitutes which have less adverse effects). See Arnott and Stiglitz (1991a) and Stiglitz (1989a, 1998b).

A related result from the new information economics is that issues of efficiency and equity cannot easily be delinked. For example, with imperfect information, a key source of market failure is *agency problems*, such as those which arise when the owner of land is different from the person working the land. The extent of agency problems depends on the distribution of wealth, as we noted earlier in our discussion of sharecropping. Moreover, the notion that one could separate out issues of equity and efficiency also rested on the ability to engage in lump sum redistributions. But as Mirrlees (1971) had pointed out, with imperfect information, this was not possible; all redistributive taxation must be distortionary. But this fact implies that interventions in the market which change the before-tax distribution of income could be desirable, because they lessened the burden on redistributive taxation (Stiglitz 1998a). Again, the conclusion: The second welfare theorem, effectively asserting the ability to separate issues of distribution and efficiency, was not true.

In effect, the Arrow-Debreu model had identified the *single set* of assumptions under which markets were efficient. There had to be perfect information; more accurately, information could not be *endogenous*, it could not change either as a result of the actions of any individual or firm or through investments in information. But in the world we live in, a model which assumes that information is *fixed* seems irrelevant.

As the theoretical case that markets in which information is imperfect were not efficient became increasingly clear, several new arguments were put forward against government intervention. One we have already dealt with: that the government too faces informational imperfections. Our analysis had shown that the incentives and constraints facing government differed from those facing the private sector, so that even when government faced exactly the same *informational* constraints, welfare could be improved (Stiglitz 1989a).

There was another rear-guard argument, which ultimately holds up no better. It is that market failures—absent or imperfect markets—give rise to nonmarket institutions. For example, the absence of death insurance gave rise to burial societies. Families provide insurance to their members against a host of risks for which they either cannot buy insurance, or for which the insurance premium is viewed as too high. But in what I call the *functionalist fallacy*, it is easy to go from the observation that an institution arises to fulfill a function to the conclusion that actually, *in equilibrium*, it serves that function. Those who succumbed to this fallacy seemed to argue that there was no need for government intervention because these nonmarket institutions would "solve" the market failure, or at least do as well as any government. Richard Arnott and I (1991a) showed that, to the contrary, nonmarket institutions could actually make matters worse. Insurance provided by the family could crowd out market insurance, for example. Insurance companies would recognize that the insured would take less risk because they had obtained insurance from others, and accordingly cut back on the amount of insurance that they offered. But since the nonmarket (family) institutions did a poor job of divesting risk, welfare could be decreased.

The Arnott-Stiglitz analysis reemphasized the basic point made at the end of the last subsection: it was only under very special circumstances that markets could be shown to be efficient. Why then should we expect an equilibrium involving nonmarket institutions and markets to be efficient?

5 Further Applications of the New Paradigm

Of all the market failures, the extended periods of underutilization of resources—especially human resources—is of the greatest moment. The consequences of unemployment are exacerbated in turn by capital market imperfections, which imply that even if the future prospects of an unemployed individual are good, he cannot borrow enough to sustain his standard of living.

We referred earlier to the dissatisfaction with traditional Keynesian explanations, in particular, the lack of microfoundations. This dissatisfaction gave rise to two schools of thought. One sought to use the old perfect market paradigm, relying heavily on representative agent models. While information was not perfect, expectations were rational. But the representative agent model, by construction, ruled out the information asymmetries which are at the heart of macroeconomic problems. If one begins with a model that *assumes* that markets clear, it is hard to see how one can get much insight into unemployment (the failure of the labor market to clear).

The construction of a macroeconomic model which embraces the consequences of imperfections of information in labor, product, and capital markets has become one of my major preoccupations over the past fifteen years. Given the complexity of *each* of these markets, creating a general-equilibrium model—simple enough to be taught to graduate students or used by policy makers—has not proven to be an easy task. At the heart of that model lies a new theory of the firm, for which the theory of asymmetric information provides the foundations. The modern theory of the firm in turn rests on three pillars, the theory of corporate finance, the theory of corporate governance, and the theory of organizational design.

Theory of the Firm

Under the older, perfect information theory (Modigliani and Miller 1958, 1961; see also Stiglitz 1969a, 1974c, 1988d), it made no difference whether firms raised capital by debt or equity, in the absence of tax distortions. But information is at the core of finance. The information required to implement equity contracts is greater than for debt contracts (Townsend 1979; Greenwald and Stiglitz 1992). Most importantly, the willingness to hold (or to sell) shares conveys information (Leland and Pyle 1977; Ross 1977; Stiglitz 1982c; Greenwald et al. 1984; Myers and Majluf 1984; Hellman and Stiglitz 2000; for empirical verification see, e.g., Paul Asquith and David W. Mullins, Jr. 1986), so that how firms raise capital does make a difference. In practice, firms rely heavily on debt (as opposed to equity) finance (Mayer 1990), and bankruptcy, resulting from the failure to meet debt obligations, matters. Both because of the cost of bankruptcies and limitations in the design of managerial incentive schemes, firms act in a risk-averse manner—with risk being more than just correlation with the business cycle (Greenwald and Stiglitz 1990a; Stiglitz 1989g). Moreover, because of the potential for credit rationing, not only does the firm's net worth matter, but so does its asset structure, including its liquidity.[23]

While there are many implications of the theory of the risk-averse firm facing credit rationing, some of which are elaborated upon in the next section, one example should suffice to highlight the importance of these ideas. In traditional neoclassical investment theory, investment depends on the real interest rate and the firm's perception of expected returns. The firm's cash flow or its net worth should make no difference. The earliest econometric studies of investment, by Edwin Kuh and John R. Meyer (1957), suggested however that this was not the case. Nevertheless these variables were excluded from econometric analyses of investment for two decades following the work of Robert E. Hall and Dale W. Jorgenson (1967). It was not until work on asymmetric information had restored theoretical respectability that it became acceptable to introduce financial variables into investment regressions. When that was done, it was shown that—especially for small- and medium-sized enterprises—these variables are crucial. (For a survey of the vast empirical literature see Hubbard 1998.)

In the traditional theory, firms simply maximized the expected present discounted value of profits (which equaled market value); with perfect information, how that was to be done was simply an engineering problem. Disagreements about what the firm should do were of little moment. In that context, *corporate governance*—how firm decisions were made—mattered little as well. But again, in reality, corporate governance matters a great deal. There *are* disagreements about what the firm should do—partly motivated by differences in judgments, partly motivated by differences in objectives (Stiglitz 1972b; Grossman and Stiglitz 1977, 1980b). Managers can take actions which advance their interests at the expense of that of shareholders, and majority shareholders can advance their interests at the expense of minority shareholders. The owners not only could not monitor their workers and managers, because of asymmetries of information, they typically did not even know what these people who were supposed to be acting on their behalf *should* do. That there were important consequences for the theory of the firm of the separation of ownership and control had earlier been noted by Adolph A. Berle and Gardiner C. Means (1932), but it was not until information economics that we had a coherent way of thinking about the implications (Jensen and Meckling 1976; Stiglitz 1985a).

Some who still held to the view that firms would maximize their market value argued that (the threat of) takeovers would ensure competition in the market for managers and hence promote stock market value maximization. If the firm were not maximizing its stock market value, then it would pay someone to buy the firm, and change its actions so that its value would increase. Early on in this debate, I raised questions on theoretical grounds about the efficacy of the takeover mechanism (Stiglitz 1972b). The most forceful set of arguments were subsequently put forward by Grossman and Hart (1980), who observed that any small shareholder who believed that the takeover would subsequently increase market value would not be willing to sell his shares. The subsequent work by Shleifer and Vishny (1989) and Edlin and Stiglitz (1995), referred to earlier, showed how existing managers could take actions to reduce the effectiveness of competition for management, i.e., the threat of takeovers, by increasing asymmetries of information.

So far, we have discussed two of the three pillars of the modern theory of the firm: corporate finance and corporate governance. The third is *organizational design*. In a world with perfect information, organizational design too is of little moment. In practice, it is of central concern to businesses. For example, as we have already discussed, an organizational design that has alternative units performing comparable tasks can enable a firm to glean information on the basis of which better incentive systems can be based. (Nalebuff and Stiglitz 1983a, b). But there is another important aspect of organization design. Even if individuals are well intentioned, with limited information, mistakes get made. To err is human. Raaj K. Sah and I, in a series of papers (1985, 1986, 1988a, b, 1991) explored the consequences of alternative organizational design and decision-making structures for organizational mistakes: for instance, whether good projects get rejected or bad projects get accepted. We suggested that, in a variety of circumstances, decentralized polyarchical organizational structures have distinct advantages (see also Sah 1991; Stiglitz 1989d). These papers are just beginning to spawn a body of research; see, for example, Bauke Visser (1998), Amar Bhidé (2001), and Michael Christensen and Thorbjorn Knudsen (2002).

Macroeconomics

With these points made, we can return to the important area of *macroeconomics*. The central macroeconomic issue is unemployment. The models I described earlier explained why unemployment could exist *in equilibrium*. But much of macroeconomics is concerned with *dynamics*, with explaining why sometimes the economy seems to amplify rather than absorb shocks, and why the effects of shocks may long persist. In joint work with Bruce Greenwald and Andy Weiss, I have shown how theories of asymmetric information can help provide explanations of these phenomena. (For an early survey, see Greenwald and Stiglitz 1987a, 1988b, 1993b and Stiglitz 1988b, 1992a.) The imperfections of capital markets—the phenomena of credit and equity rationing which arise because of information asymmetries—are key. They lead to risk-averse behavior of firms and to households and firms being affected by cash flow constraints.

Standard interpretations of Keynesian economics emphasized the importance of wage and price rigidities, but without a convincing explanation of how those rigidities arise. For instance, some theories had shown the importance of costs of adjustment of prices (Akerlof and Yellen 1985; Mankiw 1985). Still at issue, though, is why firms tend to adjust quantities rather than prices, even though the costs of adjusting quantities seem greater than those of prices. The Greenwald-Stiglitz theory of adjustment (1989) provided an explanation based on capital market imperfections arising from information imperfections. In brief, it argued that the risks created by informational imperfections are generally greater for price and wage adjustments than from quantity adjustments. Risk-averse firms would make smaller adjustments to those variables for which the consequences of adjustment were more uncertain.

But even though wages and prices were not perfectly flexible, neither were they perfectly rigid, and indeed in the Great Depression, they fell by a considerable amount. There had been large fluctuations in earlier periods, and in other countries, in which there had been a high degree of wage and price flexibility. Greenwald and I (1987a, b, 1988b, c, d, 1989, 1990b, 1993a, b, 1995) argued that other market failures, in particular, the imperfections of capital markets and incompleteness in contracting, were needed to explain key observed macroeconomic phenomena. In debt contracts, which are typically not indexed for changes in prices, whenever prices fell below the level expected (or in variable interest rate contracts, whenever real interest rates rose above the level expected) there were transfers from debtors to creditors. In these circumstances, excessive downward price flexibility (not just price rigidities) could give rise to problems; Irving Fisher (1933) and Stiglitz (1999d) emphasize the consequences of differences in the speed of adjustment of different prices. These (and other) redistributive changes had large real effects, and could not be insured against because of imperfections in capital markets. Large shocks could lead to bankruptcy, and with bankruptcy (especially when it results in firm liquidation) there was a loss of organizational and informational capital.[24] Even if such large changes could be forestalled, until there was a resolution, the firm's access to credit would be impaired, and for good reason. Moreover, without "clear owners" those in control would in general not have incentives to maximize the firm's value.

Even when the shocks were not large enough to lead to bankruptcy, they had impacts on firms' ability and willingness to take risks. Since all production is risky, shocks affect aggregate supply, as well as the demand for investment. Because firm net worth would only be restored over time, the effects of a shock persisted. By the same token, there were hysteresis effects associated with policy: An increase in interest rates which depleted firm net worth had impacts even after the interest rates were reduced. Firms that were bankrupted with high interest rates remain so. If firms were credit rationed, then reductions in liquidity could have particularly marked effects (Stiglitz and Weiss 1992). Every aspect of macroeconomic behavior is affected: The theories helped explain, for instance, the seemingly anomalous cyclical behavior of inventories (the procyclical movements in inventories, counter to the idea of production smoothing, result from cash constraints and the resulting high shadow price of money in recessions); or of pricing (in recessions, when the "shadow price" of capital is high, firms do not find it profitable to invest in acquiring new customers by cutting prices). In short, our analysis emphasized the supply-side effects of shocks, the interrelationships between supply and demand side effects, and the importance of *finance* in propagating fluctuations.

Earlier, I described how the information paradigm explained credit rationing. A second important strand in our macroeconomic research explored the link between credit rationing and macroeconomic activity (Blinder and Stiglitz 1983), explained the role of banks as risk-averse firms, as information institutions involved in screening and monitoring, in determining the supply of credit (Greenwald and Stiglitz 1990b, 1991, 2002; Stiglitz and Weiss 1990), described the macroeconomic impacts of changes in financial regulations, and analyzed the implications for monetary policy under a variety of regimes, including dollarization (Stiglitz 2001d). These differed in many respects from the traditional theories, such as those based on the transactions demand for money, the microfoundations of which were increasingly being discredited as money became increasingly interest bearing (the interest rate was not the opportunity cost of holding money) and as credit, not money, was increasingly being used for transactions. We also explained the importance of credit linkages (e.g., not only between banks and firms but among firms themselves) and their role in transmitting shocks throughout the economy. A large body of empirical work has subsequently verified the importance of credit constraints for macroeconomic activity, especially investment (see Kuh and Meyer 1957; Calomiris and Hubbard 1990; and Hubbard 1990).

Growth and Development[25]

While most of the macroeconomic analysis focused on exploring the implications of imperfections of credit markets for cyclical fluctuations, another strand of our research program focused on growth. The importance of capital markets for growth had long been recognized; without capital markets firms have to rely on retained earnings. But how firms raise capital is important for their growth. In particular, "equity rationing"—especially important in developing countries, where informational problems are even greater—impedes firms' willingness to invest and undertake risks, and thus slows growth. Changes in economic policy which enable firms to bear more risk (e.g., by reducing the size of macroeconomic fluctuations, or which enhance firms' equity base, by suppressing interest rates, which result in firm's having larger profits) enhance economic growth. Conversely, policies, such as those associated with IMF interventions, in which interest rates are raised to very high levels, discourage the use of debt, forcing firms to rely more heavily on retained earnings.

The most challenging problems for growth lie in economic development. Typically, market failures are more prevalent in less developed countries, and these market failures are often associated with information problems—the very problems that inspired much of the research described in this paper (see Stiglitz 1985b, 1986a, 1988a, 1989e, h, 1991a, 1997a; Braverman et al. 1993). While these perspectives help explain the failures of policies based on *assuming* perfect or well-functioning markets, they also direct attention to policies which might remedy or reduce the consequences of informational imperfections (World Bank 1999).

One of the most important determinants of the pace of growth is the acquisition of knowledge. For developed countries, this requires investment in research; for less developed countries, efforts at closing the knowledge gap between themselves and more developed countries. Knowledge is, of course, a particular *form* of information, and many of the issues that are central to the economics of information are also key to understanding research—such as the problems of appropriability, the fixed costs associated with investments in research (which give rise to imperfections in competition), and the public good nature of information. It was thus natural that I turned to explore the implications in a series of papers that looked at both equilibrium in the research industry and the consequences for economic growth.[26] While it is not possible to summarize briefly the results, one conclusion does stand out: Market economies in which research and innovation play an important role are not well described by the standard competitive model, and that the market equilibrium, without government intervention, is not in general efficient.

Theory of Taxation[27]

One of the functions of government is to redistribute income. Even if it did not actively wish to redistribute, the government has to raise revenues to finance public goods, and there is a concern that the revenue be raised in an equitable manner, e.g., that those who are more able to contribute do so. But government has a problem of identifying these individuals, just as (for example) a monopolist may find it difficult to identify those who are willing to pay more for its product. Importantly, the self-selection mechanisms for information revelation that Rothschild and I had explored in our competitive insurance model or that I had explored in my paper on discriminating monopoly can be applied here. (The problem of the government, maximizing social "profit," i.e., welfare, subject to the information constraints, is closely analogous to that of the monopolist, maximizing private profit subject to information constraints. For this reason, Mirrlees' (1971) paper on optimal taxation, though not couched in information-theoretic terms, was an important precursor to the work described here.)

The critical question for the design of a tax system thus becomes *what is observable.* In older theories, in which information was perfect, lump-sum taxes and redistributions made sense. If ability is not directly observable, the government had to rely on other observables—like income—to make inferences; but, as in all such models, market participants, as they recognize that inferences are being made, alter their behavior. In Mirrlees (1971) only income was assumed observable. But in different circumstances, either more or less information might be available. It might be possible to observe hours worked, in which case wages would be observable. It might be possible to observe the quantity of each good purchased by any particular individual or it might be possible to observe only the aggregate quantity of goods produced.

For each information structure, there is a *Pareto-efficient tax structure*, that is, a tax structure such that no group can be made better off without making some other group worse off. The choice among such tax structures depends on the social welfare function, including attitudes towards inequality.[28] While this is not the occasion to provide a complete description of the results, two are worth noting: What had been thought of as optimal commodity tax structures (Ramsey 1927) were shown to be part of a Pareto-efficient tax system only under highly restricted conditions, e.g., that there was no income tax (see Atkinson and Stiglitz 1976; Sah and Stiglitz 1992; Stiglitz 1998a). On the other hand, it was shown that in a central benchmark case, it was not optimal to tax interest income.

Theory of Regulation and Privatization

The government faces the problems posed by information asymmetries in regulation as well as in taxation. Over the past quarter century, a huge literature has developed making use of self-selection mechanisms (see, e.g., Sappington and Stiglitz 1987a; Laffont and Tirole 1993), allowing far better and more effective systems of regulation than had existed in the past. An example of a sector in which government regulation is of particular importance is banking; we noted earlier that information problems are at the heart of credit markets, and it is thus not surprising that market failures be more pervasive, and the role of the government more important in those markets (Stiglitz 1994d). Regulatory design needs to take into account explicitly the limitations in information (see, e.g., Hellman et al. 2000; Patrick Honahan and Stiglitz 2001; Stiglitz 2001c; Greenwald and Stiglitz 2002).

The 1980s saw a strong movement towards privatizing state enterprises, even in areas in which there was a natural monopoly, in which case government ownership would be replaced with government regulation. While it was apparent that there were frequently problems with government ownership, the theories of imperfect information also made it clear that even the best designed regulatory systems would work imperfectly. This naturally raised the question of under what circumstances we could be sure that privatization would enhance economic welfare. As Herbert A. Simon (1991), winner of the 1978 Nobel Prize, had emphasized, both public and private sectors face information and incentive problems; there was no compelling theoretical argument for why large private organizations would solve these incentive problems better than public organizations. In work with Sappington (1987b), I showed that the conditions under which privatization would necessarily be welfare enhancing were extremely restrictive, closely akin to those under which competitive markets would yield Pareto-efficient outcomes (see Stiglitz 1991b, 1994c for an elaboration and applications).

6   Some Policy Debates

The perspectives provided by the new information paradigm not only shaped theoretical approaches to policy, but in innumerable concrete issues also led to markedly different policy stances from those wedded to the old paradigm.

Perhaps most noted were the controversies concerning development strategies, where the *Washington consensus* policies, based on market fundamentalism—the simplistic view of competitive markets with perfect information, inappropriate even for developed countries, but particularly inappropriate for developing countries—had prevailed since the early 1980s within the international economic institutions. Elsewhere, I have documented the failures of these policies in development (Stiglitz 1999c), as well as in managing the transition from communism to a market economy (see, e.g., Hussein et al. 2000; Stiglitz 2000a, 2001e) and in crisis management and prevention (Stiglitz 2000b). Ideas matter, and it is not surprising that policies based on models that depart as far from reality as those underlying the Washington consensus so often led to failure.

This point was brought home perhaps most forcefully by the management of the East Asia crisis which began in Thailand on July 2, 1997. While I have written extensively on the many dimensions of the failed responses (Furman and Stiglitz 1998; Stiglitz 1999e), here I want to note the close link between these failures and the theories put forward here. Our work had emphasized the importance of maintaining the credit supply and the risks of (especially poorly managed) bankruptcy. Poorly designed policies could lead to an unnecessarily large reduction in credit availability and unnecessary large increases in bankruptcy, both leading to large adverse effects on aggregate supply, exacerbating the economic downturn. But this is precisely what the IMF did: by raising interest rates to extremely high levels in countries where firms were already highly leveraged, it forced massive bankruptcy, and the economies were thus plunged into deep recession. Capital was not attracted to the country, but rather fled. Thus, the policies even failed in their stated purpose, which was to stabilize the exchange rate. There were strong hysteresis effects associated with these policies: when the interest rates were subsequently lowered, firms that had been forced into bankruptcy did not become "unbankrupt," and the firms that had seen their net worth depleted did not see an immediate restoration. There were alternative policies available, debt standstills followed by corporate financial restructurings, for example; while these might not have avoided a downturn, they would have made it shorter and more shallow. Malaysia, whose economic policies conformed much more closely to those that our theories would have suggested, not only recovered more quickly, but was left with less of a legacy of debt to impair its future growth, than did neighboring Thailand, which conformed more closely to the IMF's recommendation. (For discussions of bankruptcy reform motivated by these experiences see Miller and Stiglitz 1999; Stiglitz 2000e.)

On another front, the *transition from communism to a market economy* represents one of the most important economic experiments of all time, and the failure (so far) in Russia, and the successes in China, shed considerable light on many of the issues which I have been discussing. The full dimension of Russia's failure is hard to fathom. Communism, with its central planning (requiring more information gathering, processing, and dissemination capacity than could be managed with *any* technology), its lack of incentives, and its system rife with distortions, was viewed as highly inefficient. The movement to a market, it was assumed, would bring enormous increases in incomes. Instead, incomes plummeted, a decline confirmed not only by GDP statistics and household surveys, but also by social indicators. The numbers in poverty soared, from 2 percent to upwards of 40 percent, depending on the measure used. While there were many dimensions to these failures, one stands out: the privatization strategy, which paid little attention to the issues of corporate governance which we stressed earlier. Empirical work (Stiglitz 2001e) confirms that countries that privatized rapidly but lacked "good" corporate governance did not grow more rapidly. Rather than providing a basis for wealth creation, privatization led to asset stripping and wealth destruction (Hussein et al. 2000; Stiglitz 2000a).

7   Beyond Information Economics

We have seen how the competitive paradigm that dominated economic thinking for two centuries was not robust, did not explain key economic phenomena, and led to misguided policy prescriptions.

The research over the past thirty years on information economics that I have just described has focused, however, on only one aspect of my dissatisfaction with that paradigm. It is not easy to change views of the world, and it seemed to me the most effective way of attacking the paradigm was to keep within the standard framework as much as possible. I only varied one assumption—the assumption concerning perfect information—and in ways which seemed to me highly plausible.

There were other deficiencies in the theory, some of which were closely connected. The standard theory assumed that technology and preferences were fixed. But changes in technology, R&D, are at the heart of capitalism. The new information economics—extended to incorporate changes in knowledge—at last began to address systematically these foundations of a market economy.

As I thought about the problems of development, I similarly became increasingly convinced of the inappropriateness of the assumption of fixed preferences, and of the importance of embedding economic analysis in a broader social and political context. I have criticized the Washington consensus development strategies partly on the grounds that they perceived of development as nothing more than increasing the stock of capital and reducing economic distortions. But development represents a far more fundamental transformation of society, including a change in "preferences" and attitudes, an acceptance of change, and an abandonment of many traditional ways of thinking (Stiglitz 1995, 1999c). This perspective has strong policy implications. For instance, some policies are more conducive to effecting a development transformation. Many of the policies of the IMF—including the manner in which it interacted with governments, basing loans on conditionality—were counterproductive. A fundamental change in development strategy occurred at the World Bank in the years I was there, one which embraced this more comprehensive approach to development. By contrast, policies which have ignored social consequences have frequently been disastrous. The IMF policies in Indonesia, including the elimination of food and fuel subsidies for the very poor as the country was plunging into depression, predictably led to riots. The economic consequences are still being felt.

In some ways, as I developed these perspectives, I was returning to a theme I had raised thirty years ago, during my work on the efficiency wage theory in Kenya. In that work I had suggested psychological factors—morale, reflecting a sense that one is receiving a fair wage—could affect efforts, an alternative, and in some cases more persuasive reason for the efficiency wage theory. It is curious how economists have almost studiously ignored factors, which are not only the center of day-to-day life, but even of business school education. Surely, if markets were efficient, such attention would not be given to such matters, to issues of corporate culture and intrinsic rewards, unless they were of some considerable importance. And if such issues are of importance within a firm, they are equally important within a society.

Finally, I have become convinced that the dynamics of change may not be well described by equilibrium models that have long been at the center of economic analysis. Information economics has alerted us to the fact that history matters; there are important hysteresis effects. Random events—the Black Plague, to take an extreme example—have consequences that are irreversible. Dynamics may be better described by evolutionary processes and models, than by equilibrium processes. And while it may be difficult to describe fully these evolutionary processes, this much is already clear: there is no reason to believe that they are, in any general sense, "optimal." (I discussed these issues briefly in Stiglitz 1975b, 1992e, 1994c, and Sah and Stiglitz 1991; some of the problems are associated with capital market imperfections.)

Many of the same themes that emerged from our simpler work in information economics applied here. For instance, in the information-theoretic models discussed above we showed that multiple equilibria (some of which Pareto-dominated others) could easily arise. So, too, here (Stiglitz 1995). This in turn has several important consequences, beyond the observation already made that history matters. First, it means that one cannot simply predict where the economy will be by knowing preferences, technology, and initial endowments. There can a high level of indeterminacy (see, e.g., Stiglitz 1973c). Second, as in Darwinian ecological models, the major determinant of one's environment is the behavior of others, and their behavior may in turn depend on their beliefs about others' behavior (Hoff and Stiglitz 2001). Third, government intervention can sometimes move the economy from one equilibrium to another; and having done that, continued intervention might not be required.

8   The Political Economy of Information

Information affects political processes as well as economic ones. First, we have already noted the distributive consequences of information disclosures. Not surprisingly, then, the "information rules of the game," both for the economy and for political processes, can become a subject of intense political debate. The United States and the IMF argued strongly that lack of transparency was at the root of the 1997 financial crisis, and said that the East Asian countries had to become more transparent. The attention to quantitative data on capital flows and loans by the IMF and the U.S. Treasury could be taken as conceding the inappropriateness of the competitive paradigm (in which *prices* convey all the relevant information); but the more appropriate way of viewing the debate was *political*, a point which became clear when it was noted that partial disclosures could be of only limited value. Indeed, they could possibly be counterproductive, as capital would be induced to move through channels involving less disclosure, channels like off-shore banking centers, which were also less well regulated. When demands for transparency went beyond East Asia to Western hedge funds and offshore banking centers, suddenly the advocates of more transparency became less enthralled, and began praising the advantages of partial secrecy in enhancing incentives to gather information. The United States and the Treasury then opposed the OECD initiative to combat money laundering through greater transparency of offshore banking centers—these institutions served particular *political and economic interests*—until it became clear that terrorists might be using them to help finance their operations. At that point, the balance of American interests changed, and the Treasury changed its position.

Political processes inevitably entail asymmetries of information (for a more extensive discussion, see Patrick D. Moynihan 1998; Stiglitz 2002b): our political leaders are *supposed* to know more about threats to defense, about our economic situation, etc., than ordinary citizens. There has been a delegation of responsibility for day-to-day decision-making, just as there is within a firm. The problem is to provide incentives for those so entrusted to act on behalf of those who they are supposed to be serving—the standard principal-agent problem. Democracy—contestability in political processes—provides a check on abuses of the powers that come from delegation just as it does in economic processes; but just as we recognize that the takeover mechanism provides an imperfect check on management, so too we should recognize that the electoral process provides an imperfect check on politicians. As in the theory of the firm where the current management has an incentive to *increase* asymmetries of information in order to enhance market power, so too in public life. And as disclosure requirements—greater transparency—can affect the effectiveness of the takeover mechanism and the overall quality of corporate governance, so too these factors can affect political contestability and the quality of public governance.

In the context of political processes, where "exit" options are limited, one needs to be particularly concerned about abuses. If a firm is mismanaged—if the managers attempt to enrich themselves at the expense of shareholders and customers and entrench themselves against competition, the damage is limited—customers, at least, can switch. But in political processes, switching is not so easy. If all individuals were as selfish as economists have traditionally modeled them, matters would indeed be bleak, for—as I have put it elsewhere—ensuring the public good is itself a public good. But there is a wealth of evidence that the economists' traditional model of the individual is too narrow—and that indeed intrinsic rewards, e.g., of public service, can be even more effective than extrinsic rewards, e.g., monetary compensation (which is not to say that compensation is not of some importance). This public spiritedness (even if blended with a modicum of self-interest) is manifested in a variety of civil society organizations, through which individuals voluntarily work together to advance their perception of the collective interests.

There are strong incentives on the part of those in government to reduce transparency. More transparency reduces their scope for action—it not only exposes mistakes, but also corruption (as the expression goes, "sunshine is the strongest antiseptic"). Government officials may try to enhance their power by trying to advance specious arguments for secrecy, and then saying, in effect, to justify their otherwise inexplicable or self-serving behavior, "trust me ... if you only knew what I knew."

There is a further rationale for secrecy, from the point of view of politicians: Secrecy is an artificially created scarcity of information, and like most artificially created scarcities, it gives rise to rents, rents which in some countries are appropriated through outright corruption (selling information). In other contexts these rents become part of a "gift exchange," as when reporters trade "puff pieces" and distorted coverage in exchange for privileged access to information. I was in the unfortunate position of watching this process work, and work quite effectively. Without unbiased information, the effectiveness of the check that can be provided by the citizenry is limited; without good information, the contestability of the political processes can be undermined.

One of the lessons of the economics of information is that these problems cannot be fully resolved, but that laws and institutions can decidedly improve matters. Right-to-know laws, for example, which require increased transparency, have been part of governance in Sweden for 200 years; they have become an important if imperfect check on government abuses in the United States over the past quarter century. In the past five years, there has become a growing international acceptance of such laws; Thailand has gone so far as to include such laws in its new constitution. Regrettably, these principles of transparency have yet to be endorsed by the international economic institutions.

9 Concluding Remarks

In this article I have traced the replacement of one paradigm with another. The deficiencies of the neoclassical paradigm—the failed predictions, the phenomena that were left unexplained—made it inevitable that it would be challenged. One might ask, though, how can we explain the persistence of this paradigm for so long? Despite its deficiencies, the competitive paradigm did provide insights into many economic phenomena. There are some markets in which the issues which we have discussed are not important—the market for wheat or corn—though even there, pervasive government interventions make the reigning competitive paradigm of limited relevance. The underlying forces of demand and supply are still important, though in the new paradigm, they become only part of the analysis; they are not the whole analysis. But one cannot ignore the possibility that the survival of the paradigm was partly because the belief in that paradigm, and the policy prescriptions that were derived from it, has served certain interests.

As a social scientist, I have tried to follow the analysis, wherever it might lead. My colleagues and I know that our ideas can be used or abused—or ignored. Understanding the complex forces that shape our economy is of value in its own right; there is an innate curiosity about how this system works. But, as Shakespeare said, "All the world's a stage, and all the men and women merely players." Each of us in our own way, if only as a voter, is an actor in this grand drama. And what we do is affected by our perceptions of how this complex system works.

I entered economics with the hope that it might enable me to do something about unemployment, poverty, and discrimination. As an economic researcher, I have been lucky enough to hit upon some ideas that I think do enhance our understanding of these phenomena. As an educator, I have had the opportunity to reduce some of the asymmetries of information, especially concerning what the new information paradigm and other developments in modern economic science have to say about these phenomena, and to have had some first-rate students who, themselves, have pushed the research agenda forward.

As an individual, I have however not been content just to let others translate these ideas into practice. I have had the good fortune to be able to do so myself, as a public servant both in the American government and at the World Bank. We have the good fortune to live in democracies, in which individuals can fight for their perception of what a better world might be like. We as academics have the good fortune to be further protected by our academic freedom. With freedom comes responsibility: the responsibility to use that freedom to do what we can to ensure that the world of the future be one in which there is not only greater economic prosperity, but also more social justice.

Acknowledgments

This article is a revised version of the lecture Joseph E. Stiglitz delivered in Stockholm, Sweden, on December 8, 2001, when he received the Bank of Sweden Prize in Economic Sciences in Memory of Alfred Nobel. The article is copyright © The Nobel Foundation 2001 and is published here with the permission of the Nobel Foundation.

Notes

1. See John Williamson (1990) for a description and Stiglitz (1999c) for a critique.

2. Review articles include Stiglitz (1975b, 1985d, 1987a, 1988b, 1992a, 2000d) and John G. Riley (2001). Booklength references include, among others, Drew Fudenberg and Jean Tirole (1991), Jack Hirshleifer and Riley (1992), and Oliver D. Hart (1995).

3. "If the legal rate ... was fixed so high ... the greater part of the money which was to be lent, would be lent to prodigals and profectors, who alone would be willing to give this higher interest. Sober people, who will give for the use of money no more than a part of what they are likely to make by the use of it, would not venture into the competition" (Smith 1776). See also Jean-Charles-Leonard Simonde de Sismondi (1815), John S. Mill (1848), and Alfred Marshall (1890), as cited in Stiglitz (1987a).

4. There was so many of these that the *Journal of Economic Perspectives* ran a regular column with each issue highlighting these paradoxes. For a discussion of other paradoxes, see Stiglitz (1973b, 1982d, 1989g).

5. Robert E. Lucas, Jr. (1987), who won the Nobel Prize in 1995, uses the perfect markets model with a representative agent to try to argue that these cyclical fluctuations in fact have a relatively small welfare costs.

6. See, e.g., Theodore W. Schultz (1960), who won the Nobel Prize in 1979, and Jacob Mincer (1974). At the time, there was other ongoing work criticizing the human-capital formulation, which focused on the role of education in socialization and providing credentials; see, for example, Samuel Bowles and Herbert Gintis (1976).

7. See Michael P. Todaro (1969) and John R. Harris and Todaro (1970). I developed these ideas further in Stiglitz (1969b).

8. Others were independently coming to the same insight, in particular, Edmund S. Phelps (1968). Phelps and Sidney G. Winter (1970) also realized that the same issues applied to product markets, in their theory of customer markets.

9. In Nairobi, in 1969, I wrote a long, comprehensive analysis of efficiency wages, entitled "Alternative Theories of Wage Determination and Unemployment in LDC's." Given the custom of writing relatively short papers, focusing on one issue at a time, rather than publishing the paper as a whole, I had to break the paper down into several parts. Each of these had a long gestation period. The labor turnover paper was published as Stiglitz (1974a); the adverse selection model as Stiglitz (1982a, 1992d, a revision of a 1976 unpublished paper). I elaborated on the nutritional efficiency wage theory in Stiglitz (1976). Various versions of these ideas have subsequently been elaborated on in a large number of papers, including Andrew W. Weiss (1980), Stiglitz (1982f, 1986b, 1987a, 1987g), Akerlof and Yellen (1986), Andrés Rodríguez and Stiglitz (1991a, b), Raaj K. Sah and Stiglitz (1992), Barry J. Nalebuff et al. (1993), and Patrick Rey and Stiglitz (1996).

10. This term, like adverse selection, originates in the insurance literature. Insurance firms recognized that the greater the insurance coverage, the less incentive there was for the insured to take care; if a property was insured for more than 100 percent of its value, there was even an incentive to have an accident (a fire). Not taking appropriate care was thought to be "immoral"; hence the name. Arrow's work in moral hazard (Arrow 1963, 1965) was among the most important precursors, as it was in the economics of adverse selection.

11. For a classic reference see Hart and Bengt Holmström (1987). In addition, see Stiglitz (1975a, 1982c), Kevin J. Murphy (1985), Michael C. Jensen and Murphy (1990), Joseph G. Haubrich (1994), and Brian J. Hall and Jeffrey B. Liebman (1998).

12. In the natural "spaces," indifference curves and isoprofit curves were ill behaved. The nonconvexities which naturally arose implied, in turn, that equilibrium might be characterized by randomization (Stiglitz 1975b), or that Pareto-efficient tax and optimal tax policies might be characterized by randomization (see Stiglitz 1982g, Arnott

and Stiglitz 1988a, and Dagobert L. Brito et al. 1995). Even small fixed costs (of search, of finding out about characteristics of different investments, of obtaining information about relevant technology) imply that markets will not be *perfectly* competitive; they will be better described by models of *monopolistic competition* (see Avinash K. Dixit and Stiglitz 1977, Steven Salop 1977, and Stiglitz 1979a, b, 1989f), though the basis of imperfect competition was markedly different from that originally envisioned by Edward H. Chamberlin (1933).

13. Nonconvexities naturally give rise to discontinuities, and discontinuities to problems of existence, but the nonexistence problem that Rothschild and I had uncovered was of a different, and more fundamental nature. The problem was in part that a single action of an individual—a choice of one insurance policy over another—discretely changed beliefs, e.g., about his type; and that a slight change in the actions of, say an insurance firm—making available a new insurance policy—could lead to discrete changes in actions, and thereby beliefs. Partha Dasgupta and Eric Maskin (1986) have explored mixed strategy equilibria in game-theoretic formulations, but these seem less convincing than the imperfect competition resolutions of the existence problems described below. I explored other problems of nonexistence in the context of moral hazard problems in work with Richard Arnott (1987, 1991b).

14. This had a particularly inconvenient implication: when there was a continuum of types, such as in the A. Michael Spence (1973, 1974) models, a full equilibrium never existed.

15. Some earlier work, especially in general-equilibrium theory, by Leonid Hurwicz (1960, 1972), Jacob Marschak and Radner (1972), and Radner (1972), among others, had recognized the importance of problems of information, and had even identified some of the ways that limited information affected the nature of the market equilibrium (e.g., one could only have contracts that were contingent on states of nature that were observable by both sides to the contract). But the attempt to modify the abstract theory of general equilibrium to incorporate problems of information imperfects proved, in the end, less fruitful than the alternative approach of beginning with highly simplified, quite concrete models. Arrow (1963, 1965, 1973, 1974, 1978), while a key figure within the general-equilibrium approach, was one of the first to identify the importance of adverse selection and moral hazard effects.

16. Constructing *equilibrium models* with these effects is more difficult than might seem to be the case at first, since each agent's behavior depends on opportunities elsewhere, i.e., the behavior of others. For example, the workers that a firm attracts at a particular wage depend on the wage offers of other firms. Shapiro and Stiglitz (1984), Rodríguez and Stiglitz (1991a, b), and Rey and Stiglitz (1996), represent attempts to come to terms with these general-equilibrium problems.

17. Of course, insurance markets do exist in the real world. I suspect that a major limitation of the applicability of Rothschild-Stiglitz (1976) is the assumption of perfect competition. Factors such as search costs and uncertainty about how easy it is to get a company to pay a claim make the assumption of perfect competition less plausible. Self-selection is still relevant, but some version of monopolistic competition, may be more relevant than the model of perfect competition.

18. See, in particular, Stiglitz and Weiss (1983a, 1994) and Shiro Yabushita (1983). As we point out, in the real world, who moves first ought to be viewed as an endogenous variable. In such a context, it appears that the screening equilibria are more robust than the signaling equilibrium. Assume, for instance, that there were some signaling

equilibrium that differed from the screening equilibrium, e.g., there were a pooling equilibrium, sustained because of the out-of-equilibrium beliefs of firms. Then such an equilibrium could be broken by a prior or later move of firms.

19. In Stiglitz (1974b) the contracts were highly linear. In principle, generalizing payment structures to nonlinear functions was simple. Though even here, there were subtleties, e.g., whether individuals exerted their efforts before they knew the realization of the state of nature, and whether there were bounds on the penalties that could be imposed, in the event of bad outcomes (James A. Mirrlees 1975b; Stiglitz 1975a; Mirrlees 1976). The literature has not fully resolved the reason that contracts are often much simpler than the theory would have predicted (e.g., payments are linear functions of output), and do not adjust to changes in circumstances (see, e.g., Franklin Allen 1985; Douglas Gale 1991).

20. See, for instance, Stiglitz and Weiss (1983b, 1986, 1987). Even with these additional instruments there could still be nonmarket-clearing equilibria.

21. See, for example, Rothschild and Stiglitz (1982, 1997). For models of statistical discrimination and some of their implications, see Arrow (1972), Phelps (1972), and Stiglitz (1973a, 1974d). See also Stiglitz (1984a).

22. Greenwald and Stiglitz (1986) focus on models with adverse selection and incentive problems. Greenwald and Stiglitz (1988a) showed that similar results hold in the context of search and other models with imperfect information. Earlier work, with Shapiro (1983) had shown, in the context of a specific model, that equilibria in an economy with an agency or principal-agent problem were not (constrained) Pareto efficient. Later work, with Arnott (1990), explored in more detail the market failures that arise with moral hazard. Earlier work had shown that with imperfect risk markets, themselves explicable by imperfections of information, market equilibrium was Pareto inefficient. See David M. G. Newbery and Stiglitz (1982, 1984) and Stiglitz (1972a, 1981, 1982b).

23. The very concept of liquidity—and the distinction between lack of liquidity and insolvency—rests on information asymmetries. If there were perfect information, any firm that was liquid would be able to obtain finance, and thus would not face a liquidity problem.

24. In traditional economic theories bankruptcy played little role, partly because control (who made decisions) did not matter, and so the change in control that was consequent to bankruptcy was of little moment, partly because with perfect information, there would be little reason for lenders to lend to someone, rather than extending funds through equity (especially if there were significant probabilities of, and costs to, bankruptcy). For an insightful discussion about control rights see Hart (1995).

25. For discussions of growth, see Greenwald et al. (1990) and Stiglitz (1990, 1992c, 1994a, b). The somewhat separate topic of development is analyzed in Stiglitz (1985b, 1986a, 1988a, 1989b, e, h, 1991a, 1993, 1995, 1996, 1997a, b, 1998b, 1999b, c, 2000c, 2001a, b), Sah and Stiglitz (1989a, b), Karla Hoff and Stiglitz (1990, 1998, 2001), Nicholas Stern and Stiglitz (1997), and Stiglitz and Shahid Yusuf (2000).

26. There were, of course, several precursors to what has come to be called endogenous growth theory. See in particular, the collection of essays in Karl Shell (1967) and Anthony B. Atkinson and Stiglitz (1969). For later work, see, in particular, Dasgupta and Stiglitz (1980a, b, 1981, 1988), Dasgupta et al. (1982), and Stiglitz (1987c, d, 1990).

27. The discussion of this section draws upon Mirrlees (1971, 1975a), Atkinson and Stiglitz (1976), Stiglitz (1982e, 1987f), Arnott and Stiglitz (1986), and Brito et al. (1990, 1991, 1995).

28. In that sense, Mirrlees' work confounded the two stages of the analysis. He described the point along the Pareto frontier that would be chosen by a government with a utilitarian social welfare function. Some of the critical properties, for example, the zero marginal tax rate at the top, were, however, characteristics of *any* Pareto-efficient tax structure, though that particular property was not *robust*—that is, it depended strongly on his assumption that relative wages between individuals of different abilities were fixed (see Stiglitz 2002a).

References

Adams, William J. and Yellen, Janet L. "Commodity Bundling and the Burden of Monopoly." *Quarterly Journal of Economics*, August 1976, *90*(3), 475–498.

Akerlof, George A. "The Market for 'Lemons': Quality Uncertainty and the Market Mechanism." *Quarterly Journal of Economics*, August 1970, *84*(3), 488–500.

Akerlof, George A. and Yellen, Janet L. "A Near-Rational Model of the Business Cycle with Wage and Price Inertia." *Quarterly Journal of Economics*, 1985, Supp., *100*(5), 823–838.

Akerlof, George A. and Yellen, Janet L., eds. *Efficiency wages model of the labor market.* New York: Cambridge University Press, 1986.

Akerlof, George A. and Yellen, Janet L. "The Fair Wage-Effort Hypothesis and Unemployment." *Quarterly Journal of Economics*, May 1990, *105*(2), 255–283.

Allen, Franklin. "On the Fixed Nature of Sharecropping Contracts." *Economic Journal*, March 1985, *95*(377), 30–48.

Arnott, Richard J.; Greenwald, Bruce C. and Stiglitz, Joseph E. "Information and Economic Efficiency." *Information Economics and Policy*, March 1994, *6*(1), 77–88.

Arnott, Richard J.; Hosios, Arthur J. and Stiglitz, Joseph E. "Implicit Contracts, Labor Mobility, and Unemployment." *American Economic Review*, December 1988, *78*(5), 1046–1066.

Arnott, Richard J. and Stiglitz, Joseph E. "Labor Turnover, Wage Structures, and Moral Hazard: The Inefficiency of Competitive Markets." *Journal of Labor Economics*, October 1985, *3*(4), 434–462.

Arnott, Richard J. and Stiglitz, Joseph E. "Moral Hazard and Optimal Commodity Taxation." *Journal of Public Economics*, February 1986, *29*(1), 1–24.

Arnott, Richard J. and Stiglitz, Joseph E. "Equilibrium in Competitive Insurance Markets with Moral Hazard." Princeton University Discussion Paper No. 4, October 1987.

Arnott, Richard J. and Stiglitz, Joseph E. "Randomization with Asymmetric Information." *RAND Journal of Economics*, Autumn 1988a, *19*(3), 344–362.

Arnott, Richard J. and Stiglitz, Joseph E. "The Basic Analytics of Moral Hazard." *Scandinavian Journal of Economics*, September 1988b, *90*(3), 383–413.

Arnott, Richard J. and Stiglitz, Joseph E. "The Welfare Economics of Moral Hazard," in H. Louberge, ed., *Risk information and insurance: Essays in the memory of Karl H. Borch*. Norwell, MA: Kluwer, 1990, 91–122.

Arnott, Richard J. and Stiglitz, Joseph E. "Moral Hazard and Nonmarket Institutions: Dysfunctional Crowding Out or Peer Monitoring?" *American Economic Review*, March 1991a, *81*(1), 179–190.

Arnott, Richard J. and Stiglitz, Joseph E. "Price Equilibrium, Efficiency, and Decentralizability in Insurance Markets." National Bureau of Economic Research (Cambridge, MA) Working Paper No. 3642, March 1991b.

Arrow, Kenneth J. "Uncertainty and the Welfare Economics of Medical Care." *American Economic Review*, December 1963, *53*(5), 941–973.

Arrow, Kenneth J. "The Role of Securities in the Optimal Allocation of Risk-bearing." *Review of Economic Studies*, April 1964, *31*(2), 91–96.

Arrow, Kenneth J. *Aspects of the theory of risk-bearing (Yrjo Jahnsson lectures)*. Helsinki, Finland: Yrjo Jahnssonin Saatio, 1965.

Arrow, Kenneth J. "Some Mathematical Models of Race in the Labor Market," in A. H. Pascal, ed., *Racial discrimination in economic life*. Lanham, MD: Lexington Books, 1972, 187–204.

Arrow, Kenneth J. "Higher Education as a Filter." *Journal of Public Economics*, July 1973, *3*(2), 193–216.

Arrow, Kenneth J. "Limited Knowledge and Economic Analysis." *American Economic Review*, March 1974, *64*(1), 1–10.

Arrow, Kenneth J. "Risk Allocation and Information: Some Theoretical Development." *Geneva Papers on Risk and Insurance*, June 1978, *8*.

Asquith, Paul and Mullins, David W., Jr. "Equity Issues and Offering Dilution." *Journal of Financial Economics*, January–February 1986, *15*(1–2), 61–89.

Atkinson, Anthony B. and Stiglitz, Joseph E. "A New View of Technological Change." *Economic Journal*, September 1969, *79*(315), 573–578.

Atkinson, Anthony B. and Stiglitz, Joseph E. "The Design of Tax Structure: Direct Versus Indirect Taxation." *Journal of Public Economics*, July–August 1976, *6*(1–2), 55–75.

Azariadis, Costas and Stiglitz, Joseph E. "Implicit Contracts and Fixed Price Equilibria." *Quarterly Journal of Economics*, 1983, Supp., *98*(3), 1–22.

Bator, Francis M. "The Anatomy of Market Failure." *Quarterly Journal of Economics*, August 1958, *72*(3), 351–379.

Becker, Gary. *The economics of discrimination*, 2nd Ed. Chicago: University of Chicago Press, 1971.

Berle, Adolph A. and Means, Gardiner C. *The modern corporation and private property*. New York: Harcourt Brace and World, 1932.

Bhidé, Amar. "Taking Care: Ambiguity, Pooling and Error Control." Working paper, Columbia Business School, November 2001.

Blinder, Alan S. and Stiglitz, Joseph E. "Money, Credit Constraints, and Economic Activity." *American Economic Review*, May 1983 (*Papers and Proceedings*), 73(2), 297–302.

Bowles, Samuel and Gintis, Herbert. *Schooling in capitalist America*. New York: Basic Books, 1976.

Braverman, Avishay; Hoff, Karla and Stiglitz, Joseph E., eds. *The economics of rural organization: Theory, practice, and policy*. New York: Oxford University Press, 1993.

Braverman, Avishay and Stiglitz, Joseph E. "Sharecropping and the Interlinking of Agrarian Markets." *American Economic Review*, September 1982, 72(4), 695–715.

Braverman, Avishay and Stiglitz, Joseph E. "Cost-Sharing Arrangements under Sharecropping: Moral Hazard, Incentive Flexibility, and Risk." *Journal of Agricultural Economics*, August 1986a, 68(3), 642–652.

Braverman, Avishay and Stiglitz, Joseph E. "Landlords, Tenants and Technological Innovations." *Journal of Development Economics*, October 1986b, 23(2), 313–332.

Braverman, Avishay and Stiglitz, Joseph E. "Credit Rationing, Tenancy, Productivity, and the Dynamics of Inequality," in P. Bardhan, ed., *The economic theory of agrarian institutions*. Oxford University Press, 1989, 185–202.

Brito, Dagobert L.; Hamilton, Jonathan H.; Slutsky, Steven M. and Stiglitz, Joseph E. "Pareto Efficient Tax Structures." *Oxford Economic Papers*, January 1990, 42(1), 61–77.

Brito, Dagobert L.; Hamilton, Jonathan H.; Slutsky, Steven M. and Stiglitz, Joseph E. "Dynamic Optimal Income Taxation with Government Commitment." *Journal of Public Economics*, February 1991, 44(1), 15–35.

Brito, Dagobert L.; Hamilton, Jonathan H.; Slutsky, Steven M. and Stiglitz, Joseph E. "Randomization in Optimal Income Tax Schedules." *Journal of Public Economics*, February 1995, 56(2), 189–223.

Calomiris, Charles W. and Hubbard, R. Glenn. "Firm Heterogeneity, Internal Finance, and Credit Rationing." *Economic Journal*, March 1990, 100(399), 90–104.

Capen, Edward; Clapp, Robert and Campbell, William. "Competitive Bidding in High Risk Situations." *Journal of Petroleum Technology*, June 1971, 23(1), 641–653.

Chamberlin, Edward H. *The theory of monopolistic competition*. Cambridge, MA: Harvard University Press, 1933.

Christensen, Michael and Knudsen, Thorbjorn. "The Architecture of Economic Organization: Toward a General Framework." University of Southern Denmark Working Paper No. 02-7, January 2002.

Coase, Ronald H. "The Problem of Social Cost." *Journal of Law and Economics*, October 1960, 3, 1–44.

Dasgupta, Partha; Gilbert, Richard J. and Stiglitz, Joseph E. "Invention and Innovation under Alternative Market Structures: The Case of Natural Resources." *Review of Economic Studies*, October 1982, 49(4), 567–582.

Dasgupta, Partha and Maskin, Eric. "The Existence of Equilibrium in Discontinuous Economic Games, I: Theory." *Review of Economic Studies*, January 1986, 53(1), 1–26.

Dasgupta, Partha and Stiglitz, Joseph E. "Industrial Structure and the Nature of Innovative Activity." *Economic Journal*, June 1980a, *90*(358), 266–293.

Dasgupta, Partha and Stiglitz, Joseph E. "Uncertainty, Market Structure and the Speed of R&D." *Bell Journal of Economics*, Spring 1980b, *11*(1), 1–28.

Dasgupta, Partha and Stiglitz, Joseph E. "Entry, Innovation, Exit: Toward a Dynamic Theory of Oligopolistic Industrial Structure." *European Economic Review*, February 1981, *15*(2), 137–158.

Dasgupta, Partha and Stiglitz, Joseph E. "Learning by Doing, Market Structure, and Industrial and Trade Policies." *Oxford Economic Papers*, 1988, *40*(2), 246–268.

Debreu, Gerard. *The theory of value.* New Haven, CT: Yale University Press, 1959.

Diamond, Peter A. "A Model of Price Adjustment." *Journal of Economic Theory*, June 1971, *3*(2), 156–168.

Dixit, Avinash K. and Stiglitz, Joseph E. "Monopolistic Competition and Optimal Product Diversity." *American Economic Review*, June 1977, *67*(3), 297–308.

Eaton, Jonathan and Gersovitz, Mark. "Debt with Potential Repudiation: Theoretical and Empirical Analysis." *Review of Economic Studies*, April 1981, *48*(2), 289–309.

Edlin, Aaron S. and Stiglitz, Joseph E. "Discouraging Rivals: Managerial Rent-Seeking and Economic Inefficiencies." *American Economic Review*, December 1995, *85*(5), 1301–1312.

Fama, Eugene F. "Efficient Capital Markets: a Review and Empirical Work." *Journal of Finance*, May 1970, *25*(2), 383–417.

Fields, Gary S. "Private and Social Returns to Education to Labor Surplus Economies." *Eastern Africa Economic Review*, June 1972, *4*(1), 41–62.

Fisher, Irving. "The Debt Deflation Theory of Great Depressions." *Econometrica*, October 1933, *1*(4), 337–357.

Fudenberg, Drew and Tirole, Jean. *Game theory.* Cambridge, MA: MIT Press, 1991.

Furman, Jason and Stiglitz, Joseph E. "Economic Crises: Evidence and Insights from East Asia." *Brookings Papers on Economic Activity*, 1998, (2), 1–114.

Gale, Douglas. "Optimal Risk Sharing through Renegotiation of Simple Contracts." *Journal of Financial Intermediation*, December 1991, *1*(4), 283–306.

Greenwald, Bruce C. *Adverse selection in the labor market.* New York: Garland Press, 1979.

Greenwald, Bruce C. "Adverse Selection in the Labor Market." *Review of Economic Studies*, July 1986, *53*(3), 325–347.

Greenwald, Bruce C.; Kohn, Meir and Stiglitz, Joseph E. "Financial Market Imperfections and Productivity Growth." *Journal of Economic Behavior and Organization*, June 1990, *13*(3), 321–345.

Greenwald, Bruce C. and Stiglitz, Joseph E. "Externalities in Economies with Imperfect Information and Incomplete Markets." *Quarterly Journal of Economics*, May 1986, *101*(2), 229–264.

Greenwald, Bruce C. and Stiglitz, Joseph E. "Keynesian, New Keynesian and New Classical Economics." *Oxford Economic Papers*, March 1987a, *39*(1), 119–133.

Greenwald, Bruce C. and Stiglitz, Joseph E. "Imperfect Information, Credit Markets and Unemployment." *European Economic Review*, 1987b, *31*(1–2), 444–456.

Greenwald, Bruce C. and Stiglitz, Joseph E. "Pareto Inefficiency of Market Economies: Search and Efficiency Wage Models." *American Economic Review*, May 1988a (*Papers and Proceedings*), *78*(2), 351–355.

Greenwald, Bruce C. and Stiglitz, Joseph E. "Examining Alternative Macroeconomic Theories." *Brookings Papers on Economic Activity*, 1988b, (1), 207–260.

Greenwald, Bruce C. and Stiglitz, Joseph E. "Imperfect Information, Finance Constraints and Business Fluctuations," in M. Kohn and S. C. Tsiang, eds., *Finance constraints, expectations, and macroeconomics*. Oxford: Oxford University Press, 1988c, 103–140.

Greenwald, Bruce C. and Stiglitz, Joseph E. "Money, Imperfect Information and Economic Fluctuations," in M. Kohn and S. C. Tsiang, eds., *Finance constraints, expectations and macroeconomics*. Oxford: Oxford University Press, 1988d, 141–165.

Greenwald, Bruce C. and Stiglitz, Joseph E. "Toward a Theory of Rigidities." *American Economic Review*, May 1989 (*Papers and Proceedings*), *79*(2), 364–369.

Greenwald, Bruce C. and Stiglitz, Joseph E. "Asymmetric Information and the New Theory of the Firm: Financial Constraints and Risk Behavior." *American Economic Review*, May 1990a (*Papers and Proceedings*), *80*(2), 160–165.

Greenwald, Bruce C. and Stiglitz, Joseph E. "Macroeconomic Models with Equity and Credit Rationing," in R. Glenn Hubbard, ed., *Asymmetric information, corporate finance, and investment*. Chicago: University of Chicago Press, 1990b, 15–42.

Greenwald, Bruce C. and Stiglitz, Joseph E. "Toward a Reformulation of Monetary Theory: Competitive Banking." *Economic and Social Review*, October 1991, *23*(1), 1–34.

Greenwald, Bruce C. and Stiglitz, Joseph E. "Information, Finance and Markets: The Architecture of Allocative Mechanisms." *Industrial and Corporate Change*, 1992, *1*(1), 37–68.

Greenwald, Bruce C. and Stiglitz, Joseph E. "Financial Market Imperfections and Business Cycles." *Quarterly Journal of Economics*, February 1993a, *108*(1), 77–114.

Greenwald, Bruce C. and Stiglitz, Joseph E. "New and Old Keynesians." *Journal of Economic Perspectives*, Winter 1993b, *7*(1), 23–44.

Greenwald, Bruce C. and Stiglitz, Joseph E. "Labor Market Adjustments and the Persistence of Unemployment." *American Economic Review*, May 1995 (*Papers and Proceedings*), *85*(2), 219–225.

Greenwald, Bruce C. and Stiglitz, Joseph E. *Towards a new paradigm for monetary economics*. London: Cambridge University Press, 2002 (forthcoming).

Greenwald, Bruce C.; Stiglitz, Joseph E. and Weiss, Andrew W. "Informational Imperfections in the Capital Markets and Macroeconomic Fluctuations." *American Economic Review*, May 1984 (*Papers and Proceedings*), *74*(2), 194–199.

Grossman, Sanford J. and Hart, Oliver D. "Take-over Bids, the Free-Rider Problem, and the Theory of the Corporation." *Bell Journal of Economics*, Spring 1980, *11*(1), 42–64.

Grossman, Sanford J. and Stiglitz, Joseph E. "Information and Competitive Price Systems." *American Economic Review*, May 1976 (*Papers and Proceedings*), *66*(2), 246–253.

Grossman, Sanford J. and Stiglitz, Joseph E. "On Value Maximization and Alternative Objectives of the Firm." *Journal of Finance*, May 1977, *32*(2), 389–402.

Grossman, Sanford J. and Stiglitz, Joseph E. "On the Impossibility of Informationally Efficient Markets." *American Economic Review*, June 1980a, *70*(3), 393–408.

Grossman, Sanford J. and Stiglitz, Joseph E. "Stockholder Unanimity in the Making of Production and Financial Decisions." *Quarterly Journal of Economics*, May 1980b, *94*(3), 543–566.

Hall, Brian J. and Liebman, Jeffrey B. "Are CEO's Really Paid Like Bureaucrats?" *Quarterly Journal of Economics*, August 1998, *113*(3), 653–691.

Hall, Robert E. and Jorgenson, Dale W. "Tax Policy and Investment Behavior." *American Economic Review*, June 1967, *57*(3), 391–414.

Harris, John R. and Todaro, Michael P. "Migration, Unemployment and Development: A Two-Sector Analysis." *American Economic Review*, March 1970, *60*(1), 126–142.

Hart, Oliver D. *Firms, contracts, and financial structure*. Oxford: Oxford University Press, 1995.

Hart, Oliver D. and Holmström, Bengt. "The Theory of Contracts," in T. Bewley, ed., *Advances of economic theory: Fifth World Congress*. Cambridge: Cambridge University Press, 1987, 71–155.

Haubrich, Joseph G. "Risk Aversion, Performance Pay, and the Principal-Agent Problem." *Journal of Political Economy*, April 1994, *102*(2), 258–276.

Hellman, Thomas F. and Stiglitz, Joseph E. "Credit and Equity Rationing in Markets with Adverse Selection." *European Economic Review*, February 2000, *44*(2), 281–304.

Hellman, Thomas F.; Murdock, Kevin C. and Stiglitz, Joseph E. "Liberalization, Moral Hazard in Banking and Prudential Regulation: Are Capital Requirements Enough?" *American Economic Review*, March 2000, *90*(1), 147–165.

Hirshleifer, Jack. "The Private and Social Value of Information and the Reward to Inventive Activity." *American Economic Review*, September 1971, *61*(4), 561–574.

Hirshleifer, Jack and Riley, John G. *The analytics of uncertainty and information*. Cambridge: Cambridge University Press, 1992.

Hoff, Karla and Stiglitz, Joseph E. "Imperfect Information and Rural Credit Markets—Puzzles and Policy Perspectives." *World Bank Economic Review*, September 1990, *4*(3), 235–250.

Hoff, Karla and Stiglitz, Joseph E. "Moneylenders and Bankers: Price-Increasing Subsidies in a Monopolistically Competitive Market." *Journal of Development Economics*, April 1998, *55*(2), 485–518.

Hoff, Karla and Stiglitz, Joseph E. "Modern Economic Theory and Development," in G. Meier and J. E. Stiglitz, eds., *Frontiers of development economics: The future in perspective*. New York: Oxford University Press, March 2001, 389–485.

Honahan, Patrick and Stiglitz, Joseph E. "Robust Financial Restraint," in G. Caprio, P. Honohan, and J. E. Stiglitz, eds., *Financial liberalization: How far, how fast?* New York: Cambridge University Press, October 2001, 31–62.

Hubbard, R. Glenn, ed. *Asymmetric information, corporate finance, and investment*. Chicago: University of Chicago Press, 1990.

Hubbard, R. Glenn. "Capital-Market Imperfections and Investment." *Journal of Economic Literature*, March 1998, *36*(1), 193–225.

Hurwicz, Leonid. "Optimality and Informational Efficiency in Resource Allocation Processes," in K. J. Arrow; S. Karlin, and P. Suppes, eds., *Mathematical methods in the social sciences*. Stanford, CA: Stanford University Press, 1960, 27–46.

Hurwicz, Leonid. "On Informationally Decentralized Systems," in C. B. McGuire and R. Radner, eds., *Decision and organization*. Amsterdam: North-Holland, 1972, 297–336.

Hussein, Athar; Stern, Nicholas and Stiglitz, Joseph E. "Chinese Reforms from a Comparative Perspective," in P. J. Hammond and G. D. Myles, eds., *Incentives, organization, and public economics: Papers in honour of Sir James Mirrlees*. Oxford: Oxford University Press, 2000, 243–277.

Jaffee, Dwight and Stiglitz, Joseph E. "Credit Rationing," in B. Friedman and F. Hahn, eds., *Handbook of monetary economics*, Vol. 2. Amsterdam: North-Holland, 1990, 837–888.

Jensen, Michael C. and Meckling, William H. "Theory of the Firm: Managerial Behavior, Agency Costs and Ownership Structure." *Journal of Financial Economics*, October 1976, *3*(4), 305–360.

Jensen, Michael C. and Murphy, Kevin J. "Performance Pay and Top-Management Incentives." *Journal of Political Economy*, April 1990, *98*(2), 225–264.

Keeton, William R. *Equilibrium credit rationing*. New York: Garland Press, 1979.

Keynes, John Maynard. *The general theory of employment, interest and money*. New York: Harcourt Brace, 1936.

Klein, Benjamin and Leffler, Keith B. "The Role of Market Forces in Assuring Contractual Performance." *Journal of Political Economy*, August 1981, *89*(4), 615–641.

Kuh, Edwin and Meyer, John R. *The investment decision: An empirical study*. Cambridge, MA: Harvard University Press, 1957.

Laffont, Jean-Jacques and Tirole, Jean. *A theory of incentives in procurement and regulation*. Cambridge, MA: MIT Press, 1993.

Leibenstein, Harvey. "The Theory of Underemployment in Backward Economies." *Journal of Political Economy*, April 1957, *65*(2), 91–103.

Leitzinger, Jeffrey J. and Stiglitz, Joseph E. "Information Externalities in Oil and Gas Leasing." *Contemporary Policy Issues*, March 1984, (5), 44–57.

Leland, Hayne E. and Pyle, David H. "Informational Asymmetries, Financial Structure, and Financial Intermediation." *Journal of Finance*, May 1977, 32(2), 371–387.

Lucas, Robert E., Jr. *Models of business cycles*. New York: Blackwell, 1987.

Mankiw, N. Gregory. "Small Menu Costs and Large Business Cycles: A Macroeconomic Model of Monopoly." *Quarterly Journal of Economics*, May 1985, 10(2), 529–537.

Marschak, Jacob and Radner, Roy. *Economic theory of teams*. New Haven, CT: Yale University Press, 1972.

Marshall, Alfred. *Principles of economics*. London: Macmillan, 1890.

Mayer, Colin. "Financial Systems, Corporate Finance, and Economic Development," in R. G. Hubbard, ed., *Asymmetric information, corporate finance and investment*. Chicago: University of Chicago Press, 1990, 307–332.

Mill, John S. *Principles of political economy with some of their applications to social philosophy*. London: John W. Parker, 1848.

Miller, Marcus and Stiglitz, Joseph E. "Bankruptcy Protection Against Macroeconomic Shocks: The Case for a 'Super Chapter 11.'" Unpublished manuscript presented at the World Bank Conference on Capital Flows, Financial Crises, and Policies, April 1999.

Mincer, Jacob. *Schooling, experience and earnings*. New York: Columbia University Press, 1974.

Mirrlees, James A. "An Exploration in the Theory of Optimum Income Taxation." *Review of Economic Studies*, April 1971, 38(2), 175–208.

Mirrlees, James A. "Optimal Commodity Taxation in a Two-Class Economy." *Journal of Public Economics*, February 1975a, 4(1), 27–33.

Mirrlees, James A. "The Theory of Moral Hazard and Unobservable Behaviour I." Mimeo, Nuffield College, 1975b.

Mirrlees, James A. "The Optimal Structure of Incentives and Authority within an Organization." *Bell Journal of Economics*, Spring 1976, 7(1), 105–131.

Modigliani, Franco and Miller, Merton H. "The Cost of Capital, Corporation Finance, and the Theory of Investment." *American Economic Review*, June 1958, 48(3), 261–297.

Modigliani, Franco and Miller, Merton H. "Dividend Policy, Growth, and the Valuation of Shares." *Journal of Business*, October 1961, 34(4), 411–433.

Moynihan, Patrick D. *Secrecy: The American experience*. New Haven, CT: Yale University Press, 1998.

Murphy, Kevin J. "Corporate Performance and Managerial Remuneration: An Empirical Analysis." *Journal of Accounting and Economics*, 1985, 7(1–3), 11–42.

Myers, Stewart C. and Majluf, Nicholas S. "Corporate Financing and Investment Decisions When Firms Have Information That Investors Do Not Have." *Journal of Financial Economics*, June 1984, 13(2), 187–221.

Nalebuff, Barry J.; Rodriguez, Andres and Stiglitz, Joseph E. "Equilibrium Unemployment as a Worker Screening Device." National Bureau of Economic Research (Cambridge, MA) Working Paper No. 4357, May 1993.

Nalebuff, Barry J. and Stiglitz, Joseph E. "Information, Competition and Markets." *American Economic Review*, May 1983a (*Papers and Proceedings*), *73*(2), 278–283.

Nalebuff, Barry J. and Stiglitz, Joseph E. "Prizes and Incentives: Toward a General Theory of Compensation and Competition." *Bell Journal of Economics*, Spring 1983b, *14*(1), 21–43.

Newbery, David M. G. and Stiglitz, Joseph E. "The Choice of Techniques and the Optimality of Market Equilibrium with Rational Expectations." *Journal of Political Economy*, April 1982, *90*(2), 223–246.

Newbery, David M. G. and Stiglitz, Joseph E. "Pareto Inferior Trade." *Review of Economic Studies*, January 1984, *51*(1), 1–12.

Phelps, Edmund S. "Money-Wage Dynamics and Labor-Market Equilibrium." *Journal of Political Economy*, July–August 1968, Pt. 2, *76*(4), 678–711.

Phelps, Edmund S. "The Statistical Theory of Racism and Sexism." *American Economic Review*, September 1972, *62*(4), 659–661.

Phelps, Edmund S. and Winter, Sidney G. "Optimal Price Policy under Atomistic Competition," in E. Phelps, et al., eds., *Microeconomic foundations of employment and inflation theory*. New York: Norton, 1970, 309–337.

Radner, Roy. "Existence of Equilibrium of Plans, Prices, and Price Expectations in a Sequence of Markets." *Econometrica*, March 1972, *40*(2), 289–303.

Radner, Roy and Stiglitz, Joseph E. "A Nonconcavity in the Value of Information," in M. Boyer and R. Khilstrom, eds., *Bayesian models in economic theory*. New York: Elsevier, 1984, 33–52.

Ramsey, Frank P. "A Contribution to the Theory of Taxation." *Economic Journal*, March 1927, *37*(145), 47–61.

Rey, Patrick and Stiglitz, Joseph E. "Moral Hazard and Unemployment in Competitive Equilibrium." Unpublished manuscript, University of Toulouse, July 1996.

Riley, John G. "Informational Equilibrium." *Econometrica*, March 1979, *47*(2), 331–360.

Riley, John G. "Silver Signals: Twenty-Five Years of Screening and Signaling." *Journal of Economic Literature*, June 2001, *39*(2), 432–478.

Rodríguez, Andrés and Stiglitz, Joseph E. "Equilibrium Unemployment, Testing, and the Pure Theory of Selection." Unpublished manuscript presented at the NBER/CEPR Conference on Unemployment and Wage Determination, Boston, October 1991a.

Rodríguez, Andrés and Stiglitz, Joseph E. "Unemployment and Efficiency Wages: The Adverse Selection Model." Unpublished manuscript presented at NBER/CEPR Conference on Unemployment and Wage Determination, Boston, October 1991b.

Rosen, Sherwin. "Implicit Contracts: A Survey." *Journal of Economic Literature*, September 1985, *23*(3), 1144–1175.

Ross, Stephen A. "The Economic Theory of Agency: The Principals Problem." *American Economic Review*, May 1973 (*Papers and Proceedings*), *63*(2), 134–139.

Ross, Stephen A. "The Determination of Financial Structure: The Incentive-Signalling Approach." *Bell Journal of Economics*, Spring 1977, *8*(1), 23–40.

Rothschild, Michael and Stiglitz, Joseph E. "Equilibrium in Competitive Insurance Markets: An Essay on the Economics of Imperfect Information." *Quarterly Journal of Economics*, November 1976, *90*(4), 629–649.

Rothschild, Michael and Stiglitz, Joseph E. "A Model of Employment Outcomes Illustrating the Effect of the Structure of Information on the Level and Distribution of Income." *Economic Letters*, 1982, *10*(3–4), 231–236.

Rothschild, Michael and Stiglitz, Joseph E. "Competition and Insurance Twenty Years Later." *Geneva Papers on Risk and Insurance Theory*, December 1997, *22*(2), 73–79.

Sah, Raaj K. "Fallibility in Human Organizations and Political Systems." *Journal of Economic Perspectives*, Spring 1991, *5*(2), 67–88.

Sah, Raaj K. and Stiglitz, Joseph E. "Human Fallibility and Economic Organization." *American Economic Review*, May 1985 (*Papers and Proceedings*), *75*(2), 292–296.

Sah, Raaj K. and Stiglitz, Joseph E. "The Architecture of Economic Systems: Hierarchies and Polyarchies." *American Economic Review*, September 1986, *76*(4), 716–727.

Sah, Raaj K. and Stiglitz, Joseph E. "Committees, Hierarchies and Polyarchies." *Economic Journal*, June 1988a, *98*(391), 451–470.

Sah, Raaj K. and Stiglitz, Joseph E. "Qualitative Properties of Profit-Maximizing K-out-of-N Systems Subject to Two Kinds of Failure." *IEEE Transactions on Reliability*, December 1988b, *37*(5), 515–520.

Sah, Raaj K. and Stiglitz, Joseph E. "Sources of Technological Divergence between Developed and Less Developed Economies," in G. Calvo, R. Findlay, P. Kouri, and J. Braga de Macedo, eds., *Debt, stabilizations and development: Essays in memory of Carlos Diaz-Alejandro*. Cambridge, MA: Blackwell (for WIDER of the United Nations University), 1989a, 423–446.

Sah, Raaj K. and Stiglitz, Joseph E. "Technological Learning, Social Learning and Technological Change," in S. Chakravarty, ed., *The balance between industry and agriculture in economic development: Proceedings of the Eighth World Congress of the International Economic Association, Delhi, India, volume 3, Manpower and transfers*. New York: St. Martin's, 1989b, 285–298.

Sah, Raaj K. and Stiglitz, Joseph E. "The Quality of Managers in Centralized Versus Decentralized Organizations." *Quarterly Journal of Economics*, February 1991, *106*(1), 289–295.

Sah, Raaj K. and Stiglitz, Joseph E. *Peasants versus city-dwellers: Taxation and the burden of economic development*. Oxford: Clarendon Press, 1992.

Salop, Steven. "The Noisy Monopolist: Information, Price Dispersion and Price Discrimination." *Review of Economic Studies*, October 1977, *44*(3), 393–406.

Salop, Steven. "Monopolistic Competition with Outside Goods." *Bell Journal of Economics*, Spring 1979, *10*(1), 141–156.

Salop, Steven and Stiglitz, Joseph E. "Bargains and Ripoffs: A Model of Monopolistically Competitive Price Dispersions," *Review of Economic Studies*, October 1977, *44*(3), 493–510; reprinted in S. A. Lippman and D. K. Levine, eds., *The economics of information*. Aldershot, U.K.: Elgar, 1995, 198–215.

Salop, Steven and Stiglitz, Joseph E. "The Theory of Sales: A Simple Model of Equilibrium Price Dispersion with Identical Agents." *American Economic Review*, December 1982, *72*(5), 1121–1130.

Salop, Steven and Stiglitz, Joseph E. "Information, Welfare and Product Diversity," in G. Feiwel, ed., *Arrow and the foundations of the theory of economic policy*. New York: New York University Press, 1987, 328–340.

Samuelson, Paul A. *Foundations of economic analysis*. Cambridge, MA: Harvard University Press, 1947.

Sappington, David E. M. and Stiglitz, Joseph E. "Information and Regulation," in E. Bailey, ed., *Public regulation*. London: MIT Press, 1987a, 3–43.

Sappington, David E. M. and Stiglitz, Joseph E. "Privatization, Information and Incentives." *Journal of Policy Analysis and Management*, 1987b, *6*(4), 567–582.

Schultz, Theodore W. "Capital Formation by Education." *Journal of Political Economy*, December 1960, *68*(6), 571–583.

Shapiro, Carl. "Premiums for High Quality Products as Returns to Reputations." *Quarterly Journal of Economics*, November 1983, *98*(4), 659–680.

Shapiro, Carl and Stiglitz, Joseph E. "Equilibrium Unemployment as a Worker Discipline Device." *American Economic Review*, June 1984, *74*(3), 433–444.

Shell, Karl, ed. *Essays on the theory of optimal economic growth*. Cambridge, MA: MIT Press, 1967.

Shiller, Robert J. *Irrational exuberance*. Princeton, NJ: Princeton University Press, 2000.

Shleifer, Andrei and Vishny, Robert W. "Management Entrenchment: The Case of Manager-Specific Assets." *Journal of Financial Economics*, November 1989, *25*(1), 123–139.

Simon, Herbert A. "Organizations and Markets." *Journal of Economic Perspectives*, Spring 1991, *5*(2), 25–44.

Simonde de Sismondi, Jean-Charles-Leonard. *Political economy*. New York: Kelley, 1966 (first published in 1815).

Smith, Adam. *An inquiry into the nature and causes of the wealth of nations*. Chicago: University of Chicago Press, 1977 (first published in 1776).

Spence, A. Michael. "Job Market Signaling." *Quarterly Journal of Economics*, August 1973, *87*(3), 355–374.

Spence, A. Michael. *Market signaling: Information transfer in hiring and related processes*. Cambridge, MA: Harvard University Press, 1974.

Stern, Nicholas and Stiglitz, Joseph E. "A Framework for a Development Strategy in a Market Economy," in E. Malinvaud and A. K. Sen, eds., *Development strategy and the management of the market economy*. Oxford: Clarendon Press, 1997, 253–295.

Stigler, George J. "The Economics of Information." *Journal of Political Economy*, June 1961, *69*(3), 213–225.

Stigler, George J. "Imperfections in the Capital Market." *Journal of Political Economy*, May/June 1967, *75*(3), 287–292.

Stiglitz, Joseph E. "A Re-Examination of the Modigliani-Miller Theorem." *American Economic Review*, December 1969a, *59*(5), 784–793.

Stiglitz, Joseph E. "Rural-Urban Migration, Surplus Labour, and the Relationship between Urban and Rural Wages." *East African Economic Review*, December 1969b, *1*(2), 1–27.

Stiglitz, Joseph E. "On the Optimality of the Stock Market Allocation of Investment." *Quarterly Journal of Economics*, February 1972a, *86*(1), 25–60.

Stiglitz, Joseph E. "Some Aspects of the Pure Theory of Corporate Finance: Bankruptcies and Take-Overs." *Bell Journal of Economics*, Autumn 1972b, *3*(2), 458–482.

Stiglitz, Joseph E. "Approaches to the Economics of Discrimination." *American Economic Review*, May 1973a (*Papers and Proceedings*), *62*(2), 287–295; reprinted in W. Darity and C. Boshamer, eds., *Economics and discrimination*. Aldershot, U.K.: Elgar, 1993, 325–333.

Stiglitz, Joseph E. "Taxation, Corporate Financial Policy and the Cost of Capital." *Journal of Public Economics*, February 1973b, *2*(1), 1–34.

Stiglitz, Joseph E. "The Badly Behaved Economy with the Well Behaved Production Function," in J. A. Mirrlees and N. H. Stern, eds., *Models of economic growth*. London: MacMillan, 1973c, 118–137.

Stiglitz, Joseph E. "Alternative Theories of Wage Determination and Unemployment in L.D.C.'s: The Labor Turnover Model." *Quarterly Journal of Economics*, May 1974a, *88*(2), 194–227.

Stiglitz, Joseph E. "Incentives and Risk Sharing in Sharecropping." *Review of Economic Studies*, April 1974b, *41*(2), 219–255.

Stiglitz, Joseph E. "On the Irrelevance of Corporate Financial Policy." *American Economic Review*, December 1974c, *64*(6), 851–866.

Stiglitz, Joseph E. "Theories of Discrimination and Economic Policy," In G. von Furstenberg, B. Harrison, and A. R. Horowitz, eds., *Patterns of racial discrimination*. Lanham, MD: Lexington Books, 1974d, 5–26.

Stiglitz, Joseph E. "Incentives, Risk and Information: Notes Toward a Theory of Hierarchy." *Bell Journal of Economics*, Autumn 1975a, *6*(2), 552–579.

Stiglitz, Joseph E. "Information and Economic Analysis," in J. M. Parkin and A. R. Nobay, eds., *Current economic problems*. Cambridge: Cambridge University Press, 1975b, 27–52.

Stiglitz, Joseph E. "The Theory of Screening, Education and the Distribution of Income." *American Economic Review*, June 1975c, *65*(3), 283–300.

Stiglitz, Joseph E. "The Efficiency of Market Prices in Long Run Allocations in the Oil Industry," in G. M. Brannon, ed., *Studies in energy tax policy*. Cambridge, MA: Ballinger, 1975d, 55–99.

Stiglitz, Joseph E. "The Efficiency Wage Hypothesis, Surplus Labour, and the Distribution of Income in L.D.C.s." *Oxford Economic Papers*, July 1976, *28*(2), 185–207.

Stiglitz, Joseph E. "Monopoly, Non-linear Pricing and Imperfect Information: The Insurance Market." *Review of Economic Studies*, October 1977, *44*(3), 407–430.

Stiglitz, Joseph E. "Equilibrium in Product Markets with Imperfect Information." *American Economic Review*, May 1979a (*Papers and Proceedings*), 69(2), 339–345.

Stiglitz, Joseph E. "On Search and Equilibrium Price Distributions," in M. Boskin, ed., *Economics and human welfare: Essays in honor of Tibor Scitovsky*. New York: Academic Press, 1979b, 203–236.

Stiglitz, Joseph E. "Pareto Optimality and Competition." *Journal of Finance*, May 1981, 36(2), 235–251.

Stiglitz, Joseph E. "Alternative Theories of Wage Determination and Unemployment: The Efficiency Wage Model," in M. Gersovitz, C. F. Diaz-Alejandro, G. Ranis, and M. R. Rosenzweig, eds., *The theory and experience of economic development: Essays in honor of Sir Arthur W. Lewis*. London: Allen and Unwin, 1982a, 78–106.

Stiglitz, Joseph E. "The Inefficiency of the Stock Market Equilibrium." *Review of Economic Studies*, April 1982b, 49(2), 241–261.

Stiglitz, Joseph E. "Information and Capital Markets," in W. F. Sharpe and C. Cootner, eds., *Financial economics: Essays in honor of Paul Cootner*. Upper Saddle River, NJ: Prentice Hall, 1982c, 118–158.

Stiglitz, Joseph E. "Ownership, Control and Efficient Markets: Some Paradoxes in the Theory of Capital Markets," in K. D. Boyer and W. G. Shepherd, eds., *Economic regulation: essays in honor of James R. Nelson*. East Lansing, MI: Michigan State University Press, 1982d, 311–341.

Stiglitz, Joseph E. "Self-Selection and Pareto Efficient Taxation." *Journal of Public Economics*, March 1982e, 17(2), 213–240.

Stiglitz, Joseph E. "The Structure of Labor Markets and Shadow Prices in L.D.C.'s," in R. Sabot, ed., *Migration and the labor market in developing countries*. Boulder, CO: Westview, 1982f, 13–64.

Stiglitz, Joseph E. "Utilitarianism and Horizontal Equity: The Case for Random Taxation." *Journal of Public Economics*, June 1982g, 18(1), 1–33.

Stiglitz, Joseph E. "Information, Screening and Welfare," in M. Boyer and R. Khilstrom, eds., *Bayesian models in economic theory*. New York: Elsevier, 1984a, 209–239.

Stiglitz, Joseph E. "Price Rigidities and Market Structure." *American Economic Review*, May 1984b (*Papers and Proceedings*), 74(2), 350–356.

Stiglitz, Joseph E. "Credit Markets and the Control of Capital." *Journal of Money, Credit, and Banking*, May 1985a, 17(2), 133–152.

Stiglitz, Joseph E. "Economics of Information and the Theory of Economic Development." *Revista de Econometria*, April 1985b, 5(1), 5–32.

Stiglitz, Joseph E. "Equilibrium Wage Distribution." *Economic Journal*, September 1985c, 95(379), 595–618.

Stiglitz, Joseph E. "Information and Economic Analysis: A Perspective." *Economic Journal*, 1985d, Supp., 95, 21–41.

Stiglitz, Joseph E. "The New Development Economics." *World Development*, 1986a, 14(2), 257–265.

Stiglitz, Joseph E. "Theories of Wage Rigidities," in J. L. Butkiewicz, K. J. Koford, and J. B. Miller, eds., *Keynes' economic legacy: Contemporary economic theories.* New York: Praeger, 1986b, 153–206.

Stiglitz, Joseph E. "The Causes and Consequences of the Dependence of Quality on Prices." *Journal of Economic Literature*, March 1987a, *25*(1), 1–48.

Stiglitz, Joseph E. "Competition and the Number of Firms in a Market: Are Duopolies More Competitive Than Atomistic Markets?" *Journal of Political Economy*, 1987b, *95*(5), 1041–1061.

Stiglitz, Joseph E. "Design of Labor Contracts: Economics of Incentives and Risk-Sharing," in H. Nalbantian, ed., *Incentives, cooperation and risk sharing.* Totowa, NJ: Rowman and Littlefield, 1987c, 47–68.

Stiglitz, Joseph E. "Learning to Learn, Localized Learning and Technological Progress," in P. Dasgupta and P. Stoneman, eds., *Economic policy and technological performance.* Cambridge: Cambridge University Press, 1987d, 125–153.

Stiglitz, Joseph E. "On the Microeconomics of Technical Progress," in J. M. Katz, ed., *Technology generation in Latin American manufacturing industries.* New York: St. Martin's Press, 1987e, 56–77.

Stiglitz, Joseph E. "Efficient and Optimal Taxation and the New New Welfare Economics," in A. Auerbach and M. Feldstein, eds., *Handbook of public economics.* New York: Elsevier, 1987f, 991–1042.

Stiglitz, Joseph E. "The Wage-Productivity Hypothesis: Its Economic Consequences and Policy Implications," in M. J. Boskin, ed., *Modern developments in public finance.* Oxford: Blackwell, 1987g, 130–165.

Stiglitz, Joseph E. "Economic Organization, Information, and Development," in H. Chenery and T. N. Srinivasan, eds., *Handbook of development economics.* New York: Elsevier, 1988a, 185–201.

Stiglitz, Joseph E. "Money, Credit, and Business Fluctuations." *Economic Record*, December 1988b, *64*(187), 62–72.

Stiglitz, Joseph E. "On the Relevance or Irrelevance of Public Financial Policy," in K. J. Arrow and M. J. Boskin, ed., *The economics of public debt: Proceedings of a conference held by the International Economic Association.* New York: St. Martin's, 1988c, 41–76.

Stiglitz, Joseph E. "Why Financial Structure Matters." *Journal of Economic Perspectives*, Autumn 1988d, *2*(4), 121–126.

Stiglitz, Joseph E. "On the Economic Role of the State," in A. Heertje, ed., *The economic role of the state.* Oxford, U.K.: Blackwell, 1989a, 9–85.

Stiglitz, Joseph E. "Financial Markets and Development." *Oxford Review of Economic Policy*, Winter 1989b, *5*(4), 55–68.

Stiglitz, Joseph E. "Imperfect Information in the Product Market," in R. Schmalensee and R. D. Willig, eds., *Handbook of industrial organization*, Vol. 1. New York: Elsevier, 1989c, 769–847.

Stiglitz, Joseph E. "Incentives, Information and Organizational Design." *Empirica*, January 1989d, *16*(1), 3–29.

Stiglitz, Joseph E. "Markets, Market Failures and Development." *American Economic Review*, May 1989e (*Papers and Proceedings*), 79(2), 197–203.

Stiglitz, Joseph E. "Monopolistic Competition and the Capital Market," in G. Feiwel, ed., *The economics of imperfect competition and employment—Joan Robinson and beyond.* New York: New York University Press, 1989f, 485–507.

Stiglitz, Joseph E. "Mutual Funds, Capital Structure, and Economic Efficiency," in S. Bhattacharya and G. Constantinides, eds., *Theory of valuation—frontiers of modern financial theory*, Vol. 1. Totowa, NJ: Rowman and Littlefield, 1989g, 342–356.

Stiglitz, Joseph E. "Rational Peasants, Efficient Institutions and the Theory of Rural Organization," in P. Bardhan, ed., *The economic theory of agrarian institutions.* Oxford: Clarendon Press, 1989h, 18–29.

Stiglitz, Joseph E. "Using Tax Policy to Curb Speculative Short-Term Trading." *Journal of Financial Services Research*, December 1989i, 3(2–3), 101–115.

Stiglitz, Joseph E. "Growth Theory: Comments: Some Retrospective Views on Growth Theory," in P. Diamond, ed., *Growth/productivity/unemployment: Essays to celebrate Bob Solow's birthday.* Cambridge, MA: MIT Press, 1990, 50–68.

Stiglitz, Joseph E. "Development Strategies: The Roles of the State and Private Sector," in S. Fischer, D. de Tray, and S. Shekhar, eds., *Proceedings of the World Bank annual conference on development economics 1990.* Washington, DC: World Bank, 1991a, 430–433.

Stiglitz, Joseph E. "Some Theoretical Aspects of the Privatization: Applications to Eastern Europe," in *Rivista di Politica Economica*, December 1991b, 81(158), 199–224; reprinted in M. Baldassarri, L. Paganetto, and E. S. Phelps, eds., *Privatization processes in Eastern Europe.* Rome: St. Martin's, 1993, 179–204.

Stiglitz, Joseph E. "Capital Markets and Economic Fluctuations in Capitalist Economies." *European Economic Review*, April 1992a, 36(2–3), 269–306.

Stiglitz, Joseph E. "Contract Theory and Macroeconomic Fluctuations," in L. Werin and H. Wijkander, eds., *Contract economics.* Cambridge, MA: Blackwell, 1992b, 292–322.

Stiglitz, Joseph E. "Explaining Growth: Competition and Finance." *Rivista di Politica Economica*, November 1992c, 82(169), 277–243.

Stiglitz, Joseph E. "Prices and Queues as Screening Devices in Competitive Markets," in D. Gale and O. Hart, eds., *Economic analysis of markets and games: Essays in honor of Frank Hahn.* Cambridge, MA: MIT Press, 1992d, 128–166.

Stiglitz, Joseph E. "Notes on Evolutionary Economics: Imperfect Capital Markets, Organizational Design, Long-run Efficiency." Unpublished manuscript presented at a Conference at Osaka University, 1992e.

Stiglitz, Joseph E. "Consequences of Limited Risk Markets and Imperfect Information for the Design of Taxes and Transfers: An Overview," in K. Hoff, A. Braverman, and J. Stiglitz, eds., *The economics of rural organization: Theory, practice, and policy.* New York: Oxford University Press, 1993.

Stiglitz, Joseph E. "Economic Growth Revisited." *Industrial and Corporate Change*, 1994a, 3(1), 65–110.

Stiglitz, Joseph E. "Endogenous Growth and Cycles," in Y. Shionoya and M. Perlman, eds., *Innovation in technology, industries, and institutions: Studies in Schumpeterian perspectives*. Ann Arbor, MI: University of Michigan Press, 1994b, 121–156.

Stiglitz, Joseph E. *Whither socialism?* Cambridge, MA: MIT Press, 1994c.

Stiglitz, Joseph E. "The Role of the State in Financial Markets," in M. Bruno and B. Pleskovic, eds., *Proceeding of the World Bank conference on development economics, 1993*. Washington, DC: World Bank, 1994d, 41–46.

Stiglitz, Joseph E. "Social Absorption Capability and Innovation," in Bon Ho Koo and D. H. Perkins, eds., *Social capability and long-term economic growth*. New York: St. Martin's, 1995, 48–81.

Stiglitz, Joseph E. "Some Lessons from the East Asian Miracle." *World Bank Research Observer*, August 1996, *11*(2), 151–177.

Stiglitz, Joseph E. "The Role of Government in Economic Development," in M. Bruno and B. Pleskovic, eds., *Annual World Bank conference on development economics, 1996*. Washington, DC: World Bank, 1997a, 11–23.

Stiglitz, Joseph E. "The Role of Government in the Economies of Developing Countries," in E. Malinvaud and A. K. Sen, eds., *Development strategy and the management of the market economy*. Oxford: Clarendon, 1997b, 61–109.

Stiglitz, Joseph E. "Pareto Efficient Taxation and Expenditure Policies, With Applications to the Taxation of Capital, Public Investment, and Externalities." Unpublished manuscript, presented at conference in honor of Agnar Sandmo, January 1998a.

Stiglitz, Joseph E. "Towards a New Paradigm for Development: Strategies, Policies and Processes." Unpublished manuscript, 9th Raul Prebisch Lecture delivered at the Palais des Nations, Geneva, UNCTAD, October 1998b.

Stiglitz, Joseph E. "Interest Rates, Risk, and Imperfect Markets: Puzzles and Policies." *Oxford Review of Economic Policy*, 1999a, *15*(2), 59–76.

Stiglitz, Joseph E. "Knowledge for Development: Economic Science, Economic Policy, and Economic Advice," in B. Pleskovic and J. E. Stiglitz, eds., *Proceedings from the annual bank conference on development economics, 1998*. Washington DC: World Bank, 1999b, 9–58.

Stiglitz, Joseph E. "More Instruments and Broader Goals: Moving Toward the Post-Washington Consensus." *Revista de Economia Politica*, January–March 1999c, *19*(1), 94–120; reprinted in Ha-Joon Chang, ed., *The rebel within: Joseph Stiglitz at the World Bank*. London: Anthem, 2001, 19–56.

Stiglitz, Joseph E. "Toward a General Theory of Wage and Price Rigidities and Economic Fluctuations." *American Economic Review*, May 1999d (*Papers and Proceedings*), *89*(2), 75–80.

Stiglitz, Joseph E. "Responding to Economic Crises: Policy Alternatives for Equitable Recovery and Development." *Manchester School*, 1999e, Spec. Iss., *67*(5), 409–427.

Stiglitz, Joseph E. "Whither Reform? Ten Years of the Transition," in B. Pleskovic and J. E. Stiglitz, eds., *Proceedings of the annual bank conference on development economics, 1999*. Washington, DC: World Bank, 2000a, 27–56.

Stiglitz, Joseph E. "Capital Market Liberalization, Economic Growth, and Instability." *World Development*, June 2000b, *28*(6), 1075–1086.

Stiglitz, Joseph E. "Formal and Informal Institutions," in P. Dasgupta and I. Serageldin, eds., *Social capital: A multifaceted perspective*. Washington, DC: World Bank, 2000c, 59–68.

Stiglitz, Joseph E. "The Contributions of the Economics of Information to Twentieth Century Economics." *Quarterly Journal of Economics*, November 2000d, *115*(4), 1441–1478.

Stiglitz, Joseph E. "Some Elementary Principles of Bankruptcy," in *Governance, equity and global markets (proceedings of annual bank conference for development economics in Europe, June 1999)*. Paris: La Documentation Francaise, 2000e.

Stiglitz, Joseph E. "Challenges in the Analysis of the Role of Institutions in Economic Development," in G. Kochendorfer-Lucius and B. Pleskovic, eds., *The institutional foundations of a market economy*, Villa Borsig Workshop Series 2000. Berlin: German Foundation for International Development (DSE), 2001a, 15–28.

Stiglitz, Joseph E. "From Miracle to Recovery: Lessons from Four Decades of East Asian Experience," in Shahid Yusuf, ed., *Rethinking the East Asian miracle*. Washington, DC: World Bank, 2001b.

Stiglitz, Joseph E. "Principles of Financial Regulation: A Dynamic Approach." *World Bank Observer*, Spring 2001c, *16*(1), 1–18.

Stiglitz, Joseph E. "Crisis y Restructuración Financiera: el Papel de la Banca Central." *Cuestiones Económicas*, 2001d, *17*(2), 3–24.

Stiglitz, Joseph E. "Quis Custodiet Ipsos Custodes? Corporate Governance Failures in the Transition," in J. E. Stiglitz and P.-A. Muet, eds., *Governance, equity, and global markets: the annual bank conference on development economics in Europe*. New York: Oxford University Press, 2001e, 22–54.

Stiglitz, Joseph E. "New Perspectives on Public Finance: Recent Achievements and Future Challenges." *Journal of Public Economics*, 2002a (forthcoming).

Stiglitz, Joseph E. "On Liberty, the Right to Know and Public Discourse: The Role of Transparency in Public Life," in M. Gibney, ed., *Globalizing rights*. Oxford, U.K.: Oxford University Press, 2002b (forthcoming).

Stiglitz, Joseph E. and Weiss, Andrew W. "Credit Rationing in Markets with Imperfect Information." *American Economic Review*, June 1981, *71*(3), 393–410.

Stiglitz, Joseph E. and Weiss, Andrew W. "Alternative Approaches to the Analysis of Markets with Asymmetric Information." *American Economic Review*, March 1983a, *73*(1), 246–249.

Stiglitz, Joseph E. and Weiss, Andrew W. "Incentive Effects of Termination: Applications to the Credit and Labor Markets." *American Economic Review*, December 1983b, *73*(5), 912–927.

Stiglitz, Joseph E. and Weiss, Andrew W. "Credit Rationing and Collateral," in J. Edwards, J. Franks, C. Mayer, and S. Schaefer, eds., *Recent developments in corporate finance*. New York: Cambridge University Press, 1986, 101–135.

Stiglitz, Joseph E. and Weiss, Andrew W. "Credit Rationing: Reply." *American Economic Review*, March 1987, 77(1), 228–231.

Stiglitz, Joseph E. and Weiss, Andrew W. "Banks as Social Accountants and Screening Devices for the Allocation of Credit." *Greek Economic Review*, Autumn 1990, Supp., 12, 85–118.

Stiglitz, Joseph E. and Weiss, Andrew W. "Asymmetric Information in Credit Markets and Its Implications for Macroeconomics." *Oxford Economic Papers*, October 1992, 44(4), 694–724.

Stiglitz, Joseph E. and Weiss, Andrew W. "Sorting Out the Differences Between Screening and Signaling Models," in M. O. L. Bacharach, M. A. H. Dempster, and J. L. Enos, eds., *Mathematical models in economics*. Oxford: Oxford University Press, 1994.

Stiglitz, Joseph E. and Yusuf, Shahid. "Development Issues: Settled and Open," in G. M. Meier and J. E. Stiglitz, eds., *Frontiers of development economic: The future in perspective*. Oxford: Oxford University Press, May 2000, 227–268.

Todaro, Michael P. "A Model of Labor Migration and Urban Unemployment in Less Developed Countries." *American Economic Review*, March 1969, 59(1), 138–148.

Townsend, Robert J. "Optimal Contracts and Competitive Markets with Costly State Verifications." *Journal of Economic Theory*, October 1979, 21(2), 265–293.

Visser, Bauke. "Binary Decision Structures and the Required Detail of Information." European University Institute Working Paper No. 89/1, February 1998.

Waldman, Michael. "Job Assignments, Signaling and Efficiency." *RAND Journal of Economics*, Summer 1984, 15(2), 255–267.

Weiss, Andrew W. "Job Queues and Layoffs in Labor Markets with Flexible Wages." *Journal of Political Economy*, June 1980, 88(3), 526–538.

Werin, Lars and Wijkander, Hans, eds. *Contract economics*. Cambridge, MA and Oxford, U.K.: Blackwell, 1992. [Proceedings of *Contract: Determinants, Properties and Implications*, 1990 Nobel Symposium 77, Saltsjöbaden, Sweden.]

Williamson, John. "What Washington Means by Policy Reform," in J. Williamson, ed., *Latin American adjustment: How much has happened*? Washington, DC: Institute of International Economics, April 1990, 5–20.

Wilson, Robert B. "Competitive Bidding with Disparate Information." *Management Science*, March 1969, 15(7), 446–448.

Wilson, Robert B. "A Bidding Model of Perfect Competition." *Review of Economic Studies*, 1977, 44(3), 511–518.

World Bank, ed. *Knowledge for development: 1998/99 world development report*. Washington, DC: World Bank, 1999.

Yabushita, Shiro. "Theory of Screening and the Behavior of the Firm." *American Economic Review*, March 1983, 73(1), 242–245.

Articles

1966

"Investment, Income, and Wages," (abstract), with G. A. Akerlof. *Econometrica*, 34 (5), supplementary issue, 1966, 118. (Presented at December meetings of the Econometric Society, New York.)

1967

"Allocation of Investment in a Dynamic Economy," with K. Shell. *Quarterly Journal of Economics*, 81, November 1967, 592–609.

"A Two-Sector, Two-Class Model of Economic Growth." *Review of Economic Studies*, 34, April 1967, 227–238.

1968

"A Note on Technical Choice Under Full Employment in a Socialist Economy." *Economic Journal*, 78 (311), September 1968, 603–609.

"Output, Employment and Wages in the Short Run," with R. Solow. *Quarterly Journal of Economics*, 82, November 1968, 537–560.

1969

"Allocation of Heterogeneous Capital Goods in a Two-Sector Economy." *International Economic Review*, 10, October 1969, 373–390. (Presented at the 1965 Chicago Symposium on the Theory of Economic Growth.)

"Behavior Toward Risk with Many Commodities." *Econometrica*, 37 (4), October 1969, 660–667.

"Capital Gains, Income and Savings," with K. Shell and M. Sidrauski. *Review of Economic Studies*, 36, January 1969, 15–26.

"Capital, Wages and Structural Unemployment," with George A. Akerlof. *Economic Journal*, 79 (314), June 1969, 269–281.

"Distribution of Income and Wealth Among Individuals." *Econometrica*, 37 (3), July 1969, 382–397. (Presented at the December 1966 meetings of the Econometric Society, San Francisco.)

"The Effects of Income, Wealth and Capital Gains Taxation on Risk-Taking." *Quarterly Journal of Economics*, 83 (2), May 1969, 263–283.

"The Implications of Alternative Saving and Expectations Hypotheses for Choices of Technique and Patterns of Growth," with D. Cass. *Journal of Political Economy*, 77, July–August 1969, 586–627. (Presented at the 1967 Chicago Symposium on the Theory of Economic Growth.)

"A New View of Technological Change," with A. Atkinson. *Economic Journal*, 79 (315), September 1969, 573–578.

"A Re-Examination of the Modigliani-Miller Theorem." *American Economic Review*, 59 (5), December 1969, 784–793. (Presented at the 1967 meetings of the Econometric Society, Washington, D.C.)

"Rural-Urban Migration, Surplus Labor and the Relationship Between Urban and Rural Wages." *East African Economic Review*, 1–2, December 1969, 1–27.

"Theory of Innovation: Discussion," with Evsey Domar. *American Economic Review*, AEA Papers and Proceedings, 59 (2), May 1969, 44–49.

1970

"A Consumption Oriented Theory of the Demand for Financial Assets and the Term Structure of Interest Rates." *Review of Economic Studies*, 37 (3), July 1970, 321–351. (Presented at the August 1968 meetings of the Econometric Society, Boulder, Colorado.)

"Factor Price Equalization in a Dynamic Economy." *Journal of Political Economy*, 78 (3), May–June 1970, 456–489.

"Increasing Risk: I. A Definition," with M. Rothschild. *Journal of Economic Theory*, 2 (3), September 1970, 225–243. Subsequently published in *Foundations of Insurance Economics*, G. Dionne and S. Harrington, eds. Kluwer Academic Publishers, 1992.

"Non-Substitution Theorems with Durable Capital Goods." *Review of Economic Studies*, 37 (4), October 1970, 543–553.

"Reply to Mrs. Robinson on the Choice of Technique." *Economic Journal*, 80 (318), June 1970, 420–422.

"The Structure of Investor Preferences and Asset Returns, and Separability in Portfolio Allocation: A Contribution to the Pure Theory of Mutual Funds," with D. Cass. *Journal of Economic Theory*, 1, June 1970, 122–160.

1971

"Differential Taxation, Public Goods, and Economic Efficiency," with P. Dasgupta. *Review of Economic Studies*, 38 (2), April 1971, 151–174.

"Increasing Risk: II. Its Economic Consequences," with M. Rothschild. *Journal of Economic Theory*, 5 (1), March 1971, 66–84.

1972

"Addendum to Increasing Risk: I. A Definition," with M. Rothschild. *Journal of Economic Theory*, 5 (2), October 1972, 306.

"Four Lectures on Portfolio Allocation with Many Risky Assets," in *Mathematical Methods in Investment and Finance*, Szege-Shell, eds. Amsterdam: North-Holland Publishing, 1972, 76–108.

"On Optimal Taxation and Public Production," with P. Dasgupta. *Review of Economic Studies*, 39 (1), January 1972, 87–103.

"On the Optimality of the Stock Market Allocation of Investment." *Quarterly Journal of Economics*, 86 (1), February 1972, 25–60. (Presented to the Far Eastern Meetings of the Econometric Society, June 1970, Tokyo, Japan.)

"Risk Aversion and Wealth Effects on Portfolios with Many Assets," with D. Cass. *Review of Economic Studies*, 39 (3), July 1972, 331–354.

"Some Aspects of the Pure Theory of Corporate Finance: Bankruptcies and Take-Overs." *Bell Journal of Economist*, 3 (2), Autumn 1972, 458–482.

"The Structure of Indirect Taxation and Economic Efficiency," with A. Atkinson. *Journal of Public Economics*, 1, March 1972, 97–119.

"Taxation, Risk Taking, and the Allocation of Investment in a Competitive Economy," in *Studies in the Theory of Capital Markets*, M. Jensen, ed. New York: Praeger, 1972, 294–361. (Proceedings of a conference at the University of Rochester, August 1969.)

1973

"Approaches to the Economics of Discrimination." *American Economic Review*, 62 (2), May 1973, 287–295. Reprinted in *Economics and Discrimination*, W. Darity and C. Boshamer, eds. Edward Elgar Publishing, 1993.

"The Badly Behaved Economy with the Well Behaved Production Function," in *Models of Economic Growth*, J. Mirrlees, ed. MacMillan Publishing Company, 1973, 118–137. (Presented at the International Economic Association Conference on Growth Theory, Jerusalem, 1970.)

"Education and Inequality." *Annals of the American Academy of Political and Social Sciences*, 409, September 1973, 135–145.

"Recurrence of Techniques in a Dynamic Economy," in *Models of Economic Growth*, J. Mirrlees, ed. MacMillan, 1973, 138–161.

"Some Further Results on the Measurement of Inequality," with M. Rothschild. *Journal of Economic Theory*, 6 (2), April 1973, 188–204.

"Taxation, Corporate Financial Policy and the Cost of Capital." *Journal of Public Economics*, 2, February 1973, 1–34. (Subsequently published in *Modern Public Finance*, 1,

International Library of Critical Writings in Economics, no. 15, A. Atkinson, ed. Elgar, 1991, 96–129.)

1974

"Alternative Theories of Wage Determination and Unemployment in L.D.C.'s: The Labor Turnover Model." *Quarterly Journal of Economics*, 88 (2), May 1974, 194–227. Subsequently published in *Development Economics*, 1, D. Lal, ed. Elgar, 1992, 288–321.

"Benefit-Cost Analysis and Trade Policies," with P. Dasgupta. *Journal of Political Economy*, 82 (1), January–February 1974, 1–33. (Presented to Conference on Project Evaluation, Nairobi, July, 1971.)

"The Cambridge-Cambridge Controversy in the Theory of Capital; A View From New Haven: A Review Article." *Journal of Political Economy*, 82 (4), July–August 1974, 893–904.

"Demand for Education in Public and Private School Systems." *Journal of Public Economics*, 2, November 1974, 349–386.

"Growth With Exhaustible Natural Resources: Efficient and Optimal Growth Paths." *Review of Economic Studies*, 41, Symposium on the Economics of Exhaustible Resources, March 1974, 123–137.

"Growth With Exhaustible Resources: The Competitive Economy." *Review of Economic Studies*, 41, Symposium on the Economics of Exhaustible Resources, March 1974, 139–152.

"Incentives and Risk Sharing in Sharecropping." *Review of Economic Studies*, 41 (2), April 1974, 219–255.

"Increases in Risk and in Risk Aversion," with P. Diamond. *Journal of Economic Theory*, 8 (3), July 1974, 337–360. (Presented at a Conference on Decision Rules and Uncertainty, Iowa City, May 1972.)

"On the Irrelevance of Corporate Financial Policy." *American Economic Review*, 64 (6), December 1974, 851–866. (Presented at a conference in Hakone, Japan, 1970.)

"Theories of Discrimination and Economic Policy," in *Patterns of Racial Discrimination*, G. von Furstenberg et al., eds. D. C. Heath and Company (Lexington Books), 1974, 5–26.

1975

"The Efficiency of Market Prices in Long Run Allocations in the Oil Industry," in *Studies in Energy Tax Policy*, G. Brannon, ed. Cambridge: Ballinger Publishing, 1975, 55–99. (Report written for the Ford Foundation Energy Policy Project, August 1973.)

"Incentives, Risk and Information: Notes Toward a Theory of Hierarchy." *Bell Journal of Economics*, 6 (2), Autumn 1975, 552–579. (Presented at Berlin Symposium on Planning, August 1973.)

"Information and Economic Analysis," in *Current Economic Problems*, J. M. Parkin and A. R. Nobay, eds. Cambridge: Cambridge University Press, 27–52. (Proceedings of the Association of University Teachers of Economics, Manchester, England, April 1974.)

"Reply to Mr. Stapleton on 'Some Aspects of the Pure Theory of Corporate Finance: Bankruptcies and Take-Overs.'" *Bell Journal of Economics*, 6 (2), Autumn 1975, 711–714.

"The Theory of Screening, Education and the Distribution of Income." *American Economic Review*, 65 (3), June 1975, 283–300.

1976

"The Corporation Tax." *Journal of Public Economics*, 5, April–May 1976, 303–311.

"The Design of Tax Structure: Direct Versus Indirect Taxation," with A. Atkinson. *Journal of Public Economics*, 6, July-August 1976, 55–75. Subsequently published in *Modern Public Finance*, 2, International Library of Critical Writings in Economics, no. 15, A. Atkinson, ed. Elgar, 1991, 82–102.

"The Efficiency Wage Hypothesis, Surplus Labor and the Distribution of Income in L.D.C.'s." *Oxford Economic Papers*, 28 (2), July 1976, 185–207.

"Equilibrium in Competitive Insurance Markets: An Essay on the Economics of Imperfect Information," with M. Rothschild. *Quarterly Journal of Economics*, 90 (4), November 1976, 629–649. Subsequently reprinted in *Industrial Economics*, O. E. Williamson, ed. Edward Elgar, 1990, 141–61; in *Foundations of Insurance Economics*, G. Dionne and S. Harrington, eds. Kluwer Academic Publishers, 1992; and in *Economic Theory and the Welfare State*, Nicholas Barr, ed. Cheltenham, U.K.: Edward Elgar, 2000.

"Estate Taxes, Growth and Redistribution," in *Essays in Honor of W. Vickrey*, R. Grieson, ed. Lexington: Lexington Publishing Company, 1976, 225–232.

"Information and Competitive Price Systems," with S. Grossman. *American Economic Review*, 66 (2), May 1976, 246–253.

"Monopoly and the Rate of Extraction of Exhaustible Resources." *American Economic Review*, 66 (4), September 1976, 655–661. Reprinted in *The Economics of Exhaustible Resources*, G. Heal, ed. Brookfield, VT: Edward Elgar, 1993, 184–190.

"Notes on Estate Taxes, Redistribution, and the Concept of Balanced Growth Path Incidence." *Journal of Political Economy*, 86 (2), part 2, 137–150. (Paper presented at NBER Conference on Taxation, Stanford University, January 1976.)

"Sharecropping: Risk Sharing and the Importance of Imperfect Information," with D. Newbery, in *Risk, Uncertainty and Development*, J. A. Roumasset et al., eds. Southeast Asia Research Center for Agriculture, Agricultural Development Council, 1976, 311–341. (Originally presented at a conference in Mexico City, March 1976.)

1977

"Bargains and Ripoffs: A Model of Monopolistically Competitive Price Dispersions," with S. Salop. *Review of Economic Studies*, 44 (3), October 1977, 493–510. Reprinted in *The Economics of Information*, S. A. Lippman and D. K. Levine, eds. Edward Elgar, 1995, 198–215.

"Monopolistic Competition and Optimum Product Diversity," with A. Dixit. *American Economic Review*, 67 (3), June 1977, 297–308. Republished in *Microeconomics: Theoretical and Applied*, 2, R. Kuenne, ed. Aldershot, U.K.: Elgar, 1991, 183–194.

"Monopoly, Non-Linear Pricing and Imperfect Information: The Insurance Market." *Review of Economic Studies*, 44 (3), October 1977, 407–430.

"On Value Maximization and Alternative Objectives of the Firm," with S. Grossman. *Journal of Finance*, 32 (2), May 1977, 389–402.

"Some Further Remarks on Cost-Benefit Analysis," in *Social and Economic Dimensions of Project Evaluation*, H. Schwartz and R. Berney, eds. Inter-American Development Bank, 1977, 253–282. (Proceedings of the Symposium on Cost-Benefit Analysis, IDB, Washington, March 1973.)

"Some Lessons from the New Public Finance," with M. Boskin. *American Economic Review*, 67 (1), February 1977, 295–301.

"Symposium on the Economics of Information: Introduction." *Review of Economic Studies*, 44 (3), October 1977, 389–391.

"Tariffs Versus Quotas As Revenue Raising Devices Under Uncertainty," with P. Dasgupta. *American Economic Review*, 67 (5), December 1977, 975–981.

"Theory of Local Public Goods," in *The Economics of Public Services*, M. S. Feldstein and R. P. Inman, eds. MacMillan Publishing Company, 1977, 274–333. (Paper presented to IEA Conference, Turin, 1974.)

1978

"Efficiency in the Optimum Supply of Public Goods," with L. J. Lau and E. Sheshinski. *Econometrica*, 46 (2), March 1978, 269–284.

"Equity, Taxation and Inheritance," in *Personal Income Distribution*, W. Krelle and A. F. Shorrocks, eds. North-Holland Publishing Company, 1978, 271–303. (Proceedings of IEA Conference, Noordwijk aan Zee, Netherlands, April 1977.)

1979

"Aggregate Land Rents, Expenditure on Public Goods and Optimal City Size," with R. Arnott. *Quarterly Journal of Economics*, 93 (4), November 1979, 471–500.

"Energy Resources and Research and Development," with P. Dasgupta and R. Gilbert, in *Erschopfbare Ressourcen*. Berlin: Duncker & Humbolt, 85–108. (Presented at a conference in Mannheim, 1979.)

"Equilibrium in Product Markets with Imperfect Information." *American Economic Review*, 69 (2), May 1979, 339–345.

"Intergenerational Transfers and Inequality," with D. Bevan. *The Greek Economic Review*, 1 (1), August 1979, 8–26.

"Monopolistic Competition and Optimum Product Diversity: Reply," with A. Dixit. *American Economic Review*, 69 (5), December 1979, 961–963.

"A Neoclassical Analysis of the Economics of Natural Resources," in *Scarcity and Growth Reconsidered*, V. K. Smith, ed. Baltimore: Johns Hopkins Press, 1979, 36–66. Subsequently reprinted in *The Economics of Exhaustible Resources*, G. Heal, ed. Brookfield, VT: Edward Elgar, 1993, 131–161; and in *Natural Resource Economics: A Book of Readings*, C. Gopalakrishnan, ed. University of California Press, 1992. (Originally presented at Conference of Resources for the Future, October 1976.)

"On Search and Equilibrium Price Distributions," in *Economics and Human Welfare: Essays in Honor of Tibor Scitovsky*, M. Boskin, ed. York: Academic Press Inc., 1979, 203–236.

"The Theory of Commodity Price Stabilization Rules: Welfare Impacts and Supply Responses," with D. Newbery. *The Economic Journal*, 89 (356), December 1979, 799–817. Subsequently published in *Development Economics*, 4, D. Lal, ed. Elgar, 1992, 200–218.

1980

"Industrial Structure and the Nature of Innovative Activity," with P. Dasgupta. *Economic Journal*, 90 (358), June 1980, 266–293. Reprinted in *The Economics of Technical Change*. Elgar Reference Collection, International Library of Critical Writings in Economics, 31, Edwin Mansfield and Elizabeth Mansfield, eds. Aldershot, U.K.: Elgar. 133–160.

"On the Impossibility of Informationally Efficient Markets," with S. Grossman. *American Economic Review*, 70 (3), June 1980, 393–408. Subsequently reprinted in *Financial Markets and Incomplete Information—Frontiers of Modern Financial Theory*, 2, S. Bhattacharya and G. Constantinides, eds. Rowman and Littlefield, 1989, 123–136.

"Risk, Futures Markets and the Stabilization of Commodity Prices," in *The Proceedings of the First Annual Sponsor's Conference Frontiers in Futures*. Columbia University Center for the Study of Futures Markets, September 1980.

"Stockholder Unanimity in the Making of Production and Financial Decisions," with S. Grossman. *Quarterly Journal of Economics*, 94 (3), May 1980, 543–566.

"The Taxation of Exhaustible Resources," with P. Dasgupta and G. Heal, in *Public Policy and the Tax System*, G. A. Hughes and G. M. Heal, eds. London: George Allen and Unwin, 1980, 150–172.

"Uncertainty, Market Structure and the Speed of R&D," with P. Dasgupta. *Bell Journal of Economics*, 11 (1), Spring 1980, 1–28. Also Princeton University Econometric Research Program Research Memorandum 255.

1981

"Aggregate Land Rents and Aggregate Transport Costs," with R. Arnott. *Economic Journal*, 91 (362), June 1981, 331–347. Also NBER working paper 523.

"Credit Rationing in Markets with Imperfect Information," with A. Weiss. *American Economic Review*, 71 (3), June 1981, 393–410. Subsequently reprinted in *New Keynesian Economics*, 2, G. Mankiw and D. Romer, eds. Cambridge, Mass.: MIT Press, 1991 247–276. Also Princeton University Econometric Research Program Research Memoranda 267 and 268. (Presented at a meeting of the Western Economic Association, June 1978.)

"Entry, Innovation, Exit: Toward a Dynamic Theory of Oligopolistic Industrial Structure," with P. Dasgupta. *European Economic Review*, 15 (2), Feb. 1981, 137–158.

"Market Structure and Resource Extraction Under Uncertainty," with P. Dasgupta. *Scandinavian Economic Journal*, 83, 1981, 318–333. Reprinted in *The Impact of Rising Oil Prices on the World Economy*, L. Mattiessen, ed. MacMillan, 1982, 178–193. Princeton University Econometric Research Program Research Memorandum 262.

"On the Almost Neutrality of Inflation: Notes on Taxation and the Welfare Costs of Inflation," in *Development in an Inflationary World*, M. June Flanders and Assaf Razin, eds. New York: Academic Press, 1981, 419–457. Also NBER working paper 499.

"Pareto Optimality and Competition." *Journal of Finance*, 36 (2), May 1981, 235–251.

"Potential Competition May Reduce Welfare." *American Economic Review*, 71 (2), May 1981, 184–189. (Papers and proceedings of the AEA meetings in Denver, CO, September 1980.)

"Project Appraisal and Foreign Exchange Constraints," with C. Blitzer and P. Dasgupta. *Economic Journal*, 91 (361), March 1981, 58–74. (Presented at the Econometric Society Meeting, August 1976, Helsinki.)

"Resource Depletion Under Technological Uncertainty," with P. Dasgupta. *Econometrica*, 49 (1), January 1981, 85–104.

1982

"Alternative Theories of Wage Determination and Unemployment: The Efficiency Wage Model," in *The Theory and Experience of Economic Development: Essays in Honor of Sir Arthur W. Lewis*, M. Gersovitz et al., eds. London: George Allen & Unwin, 1982, 78–106.

"The Choice of Techniques and the Optimality of Market Equilibrium with Rational Expectations," with D. Newbery. *Journal of Political Economy*, 90 (2), April 1982, 223–246. (Also Princeton University Econometric Research Program Research Memorandum 277.)

"The Inefficiency of the Stock Market Equilibrium." *Review of Economic Studies*, 49 (2), April 1982, 241–261. Also Princeton University Econometric Research Program research memorandum 256, November 1980. (Paper presented at a Conference on Uncertainty and Insurance in Economic Theory in Honor of Karl Borch, Bergen, April 1979.)

"Information and Capital Markets," in *Financial Economics: Essays in Honor of Paul Cootner*, William F. Sharpe and Cathryn Cootner, eds. Prentice Hall, New Jersey, 1982, 118–158. Also NBER working paper 678.

"Invention and Innovation Under Alternative Market Structures: The Case of Natural Resources," with R. Gilbert and P. Dasgupta. *Review of Economic Studies*, 49 (4), 1982, 567–582. Also Princeton University Econometric Research Program Research Memorandum 263.

"Market Structure and Resource Depletion: A Contribution of the Theory of Intertemporal Monopolistic Competition," with P. Dasgupta. *Journal of Economic Theory*, 28 (1), October 1982, 128–164. Previously Princeton University Econometric Research Program research memorandum 261, March 1980.

"A Model of Employment Outcomes Illustrating the Effect of the Structure of Information on the Level and Distribution of Income," with M. Rothschild. *Economic Letters*, 10, 1982, 231–236.

"On the Impossibility of Informationally Efficient Markets: Reply," with S. Grossman. *American Economic Review*, 72 (4), September 1982, 875.

"Optimal Commodity Stock-Piling Rules," with D. Newbery. *Oxford Economic Papers*, November 1982, 403–427.

"Ownership, Control and Efficient Markets: Some Paradoxes in the Theory of Capital Markets," in *Economic Regulation: Essays in Honor of James R. Nelson*, Kenneth D. Boyer and William G. Shepherd, eds. Michigan State University Press, 1982, 311–341.

"The Rate of Discount for Cost-Benefit Analysis and the Theory of the Second Best," in *Discounting for Time and Risk in Energy Policy*, R. Lind, ed. Resources for the Future, 1982, 151–204.

"Risk Aversion, Supply Response, and the Optimality of Random Prices: A Diagrammatic Analysis," with D. Newbery. *Quarterly Journal of Economics*, 97 (1), February 1982, 1–26. Also Princeton University Econometric Research Program Research Memorandum 276.

"Self-Selection and Pareto Efficient Taxation." *Journal of Public Economics*, 17, 1982, 213–240. Also NBER working paper 632.

"Sharecropping and the Interlinking of Agrarian Markets," with A. Braverman. *American Economic Review*, 72 (4), September 1982, 695–715. Also Princeton University Econometric Research Program research memorandum 299.

"The Structure of Labor Markets and Shadow Prices in L.D.C.'s," in *Migration and the Labor Market in Developing Countries*, R. Sabot, ed. Boulder, CO: Westview, 1982, 13–64. (Presented at World Bank Conference, February 1976.)

"The Theory of Sales: A Simple Model of Equilibrium Price Dispersion with Identical Agents," with S. Salop. *American Economic Review*, 72 (5), December 1982, 1121–1130. Also Princeton University Econometric Research Program research memorandum 283.

"Utilitarianism and Horizontal Equity: The Case for Random Taxation." *Journal of Public Economics*, 18, 1982, 1–33. Also NBER working paper 694.

1983

"Alternate Approaches to the Analysis of Markets with Asymmetric Information," with A. Weiss. *American Economic Review*, 73 (1), March 1983, 246–249.

"Futures Markets and Risk: A General Equilibrium Approach," in *Futures Markets, Modeling, Managing and Monitoring Futures Trading*, Manfred Streit, ed. Basil Blackwell Publishers, October 1983, 75–106. (Paper presented at a conference at the European Institute, Florence, March 1982.) Subsequently revised as "Futures Markets and Risk: A General Equilibrium Approach," Princeton University Financial Research Center Memorandum 47, April 1984.

"Implicit Contracts and Fixed Price Equilibria," with C. Azariadis. *Quarterly Journal of Economics* Supplement, 98, 1983, 1–22. Subsequently reprinted in *New Keynesian Economics*, 2, N. G. Mankiw and D. Romer, eds. MIT Press, 1991, 187–210.

"Incentive Effects of Termination: Applications to the Credit and Labor Markets," with A. Weiss. *American Economic Review*, 73 (5), December 1983, 912–927.

"Information, Competition and Markets," with B. Nalebuff. *American Economic Review*, 73 (2), May 1983, 278–284.

"Money, Credit Constraints and Economic Activity," with A. Blinder. *American Economic Review*, 73 (2), May 1983, 297–302.

"On the Relevance or Irrelevance of Public Financial Policy: Indexation, Price Rigidities and Optimal Monetary Policy," in *Inflation, Debt and Indexation*, R. Dornbusch and M. Simonsen, eds. MIT Press, 1983, 183–222. (Presented at a Conference at Rio de Janeiro, December 1981.)

"On the Theory of Social Insurance: Comments on 'The State and the Demand for Security in Contemporary Societies' by Raymond Barre." *The Geneva Papers*, 8 (27), Sixth Annual Lecture of the Geneva Association, April 1983, 105–110.

"Preemption, Leapfrogging and Competition in Patent Races," with D. Fudenberg, R. Gilbert, and J. Tirole. *European Economic Review*, 22, June 1983, 3–32.

"Prizes and Incentives: Toward a General Theory of Compensation and Competition," with B. Nalebuff. *Bell Journal*, 14 (1), Spring 1983, 21–43. Also Princeton University Econometric Research Program Research Memorandum 293.

"Public Goods in Open Economies with Heterogeneous Individuals," in *Locational Analysis of Public Facilities*, J. F. Thisse and H. G. Zoller, eds. Amsterdam: North-Holland, 1983, 55–78.

"Review of 'Samuelson and Neoclassical Economics' by G. R. Feiwel." *Journal of Economic Literature*, 21 (3), September 1983, 997–999.

"Risk, Incentives and Insurance: The Pure Theory of Moral Hazard." *Geneva Papers*, 8 (26), January 1983, 4–32. Also Princeton University Financial Research Center memorandum 42. (Fifth Annual Geneva Lecture delivered at Zurich, March 1981.)

"Some Aspects of the Taxation of Capital Gains." *Journal of Public Economics*, 21, July 1983, 257–294.

"Strategic Considerations in Invention and Innovation: The Case of Natural Resources," with P. Dasgupta and R. Gilbert. *Econometrica*, 51 (5), September 1983, 1430–1448. Subsequently reprinted in *Economic Organizations as Games*, K. Binmore and P. Dasgupta, eds. New York: Basil Blackwell, 1986, 165–175.

"The Theory of Local Public Goods Twenty-Five Years After Tiebout: A Perspective," in *Local Provision of Public Services: The Tiebout Model After Twenty-Five Years*, G. R. Zodrow, ed. New York: Academic Press, 1983, 17–53.

"Toward a Reconstruction of Keynesian Economics: Expectations and Constrained Equilibria," with P. Neary. *Quarterly Journal of Economics*, 98, supplement, 1983, 199–228. Reprinted in *The Keynesian Heritage Volumes I*, G. K. Shaw, ed., in a series: *Schools of Thought in Economics*, Mark Blaug, ed. Edward Elgar Publishing Ltd. Also NBER working paper 376. (Presented at the Athens meeting of the Econometric Society, September 1979.)

1984

"Budget Policy and Processes: Where Do We Go From Here?," with M. Boskin, W. Niskanen, and R. Penner. *Contemporary Policy Issues*, Fall 1984–1985, 53–78. (Panel discussion at the meetings of the Western Economic Association, July 1984.)

"The Economics of Price Scissors," with R. Sah. *American Economic Review*, 74 (1), March 1984, 125–138.

"Equilibrium Unemployment as a Worker Discipline Device," with Carl Shapiro. *American Economic Review*, 74 (3), June 1984, 433–444. Subsequently reprinted in *New Keynesian Economics*, 2, N. G. Mankiw and D. Romer, eds. MIT Press, 1991, 123–142. Also in *Macroeconomics and Imperfect Competition*, Jean-Pascal Bénassy, ed. Edward Elgar Publishing, 1995, 453–464.

"Information Externalities in Oil and Gas Leasing," with J. Leitzinger. *Contemporary Economic Policy Issues*, 5, March 1984, 44–57. (Paper presented at the Western Economic Association Meetings, July 1983.)

"Information, Screening and Welfare," in *Bayesian Models in Economic Theory*, Marcel Boyer and Richard Khilstrom, eds. Elsevier Science Publications, 1984, 209–239.

"Informational Imperfections in the Capital Markets and Macroeconomic Fluctuations," with A. Weiss and B. Greenwald. *American Economic Review*, 74 (2), May 1984, 194–199.

"The New Public Finance: A Perspective" (in Spanish). *Hacienda Publica Espanola*, 91, 1984, 341–348.

"A Nonconcavity in the Value of Information," with R. Radner, in *Bayesian Models in Economic Theory*, Marcel Boyer and Richard Khilstrom, eds. Elsevier Science Publications, 1984, 33–52.

"Pareto Inferior Trade," with D. Newbery. *Review of Economic Studies*, 51 (1), January 1984, 1–12.

"Price Rigidities and Market Structure." *American Economic Review*, 74 (2), May 1984, 350–356. Subsequently reprinted in *New Keynesian Economics*, 2, N. G. Mankiw and D. Romer, eds. MIT Press, 1991, 377–388. Also in *Macroeconomics and Imperfect Competition*, Jean-Pascal Bénassy, ed. Edward Elgar Publishing, 1995, 221–226.

1985

"Can Unemployment be Involuntary? Reply," with C. Shapiro. *American Economic Review*, 75 (5), December 1985, 1215–1217.

"The Consumption Expenditure Tax," in *The Promise of Tax Reform*, J. Pechman, ed. Englewood Cliffs: Prentice-Hall, 1985, 107–127.

"Credit Markets and the Control of Capital." *Journal of Money, Banking, and Credit*, 17 (2), May 1985, 133–152. Subsequently reprinted in *La Theoria del Mercata Finanziari*, G. Viciago and G.Verga, eds. Bologna: Societa Editrice il Mulino, 1992.

"Economics of Information and the Theory of Economic Development." *Revista De Econometria*, 5 (1), April 1985, 5–32.

"Equilibrium Unemployment as a Worker Discipline Device: Reply," with C. Shapiro. *American Economic Review*, 75 (4), September 1985, 892–893.

"Equilibrium Wage Distributions." *Economic Journal*, 95 (379), September 1985, 595–618.

"The General Theory of Tax Avoidance." *National Tax Journal*, 38 (3), September 1985, 325–338. Also NBER reprint no. 987.

"Human Fallibility and Economic Organization," with R. Sah. *American Economic Review*, 75 (2), May 1985, 292–296.

"Information and Economic Analysis: A Perspective." *Economic Journal*, 95, supplement: conference papers, 1985, 21–41.

"Labor Turnover, Wage Structure & Moral Hazard: The Inefficiency of Competitive Markets," with R. Arnott. *Journal of Labor Economics*, 3 (4), October 1985, 434–462.

"The Social Cost of Labor, and Project Evaluation: A General Approach," with R. Sah. *Journal of Public Economics*, 28, 1985, 135–163. Economic Growth Center discussion paper no. 470, Yale University, March 1985.

1986

"The Architecture of Economic Systems: Hierarchies and Polyarchies," with R. Sah. *American Economic Review*, 76 (4), September 1986, 716–727. Also a shortened version in AEA papers and proceedings.

"Comments on 'Tax Asymmetries and Corporate Tax Reform' by Saman Majd and Stewart C. Myers," in *The Effects of Taxation on Capital Formation*, M. Feldstein, ed. NBER, 1986, 374–376.

"Cost Sharing Arrangement Under Sharecropping: Moral Hazard, Incentive Flexibility and Risk," with A. Braverman. *Journal of Agricultural Economics*, 68 (3), August 1986, 642–652. (Revised version of "Moral Hazard, Incentive Flexibility & Risk: Cost Sharing Arrangements under Sharecropping," with A. Braverman, Economic Research Program, research memorandum 298, Princeton, 1988.)

"Credit Rationing and Collateral," with A. Weiss, in *Recent Developments in Corporate Finance*, Jeremy Edwards et al., eds. New York: Cambridge University Press, 1986, 101–135. Also a Bell Communications research discussion paper.

"The Economics of Price Scissors: Reply," with R. Sah. *American Economic Review*, 76 (5), December 1986, 1195–1199. Published version of "The Economics of Town-versus-Country Problems," Yale Economic Growth Center paper 508.

"Externalities in Economies with Imperfect Information and Incomplete Markets," with B. Greenwald. *Quarterly Journal of Economics*, May 1986, 229–264. Reprinted in *Economic Theory and the Welfare State*, Nicholas Barr, ed. Cheltenham, U.K.: Edward Elgar, 2000. Originally entitled "Pecuniary and Market Mediated Externalities: Toward a General Theory of the Welfare Economics of Economies with Imperfect Information and Incomplete Markets," NBER working paper 1304.

"Hemmis Hohe Lohne." *Wirtschafts Woche*, 43 (17), October 1986, 98–105.

"Introduction to Proceedings of the International Economic Association Roundtable Conference on New Developments in the Theory of Market Structure," in *New Developments in the Theory of Market Structure*, J. E. Stiglitz and F. Mathewson, eds. MacMillan, 1986. (Conference held in Ottawa, Canada, May 10, 1982.)

"Landlords, Tenants and Technological Innovations," with A. Braverman. *Journal of Development Economics*, 23 (2), October 1986, 313–332.

"Moral Hazard and Optimal Commodity Taxation," with R. Arnott. *Journal of Public Economics*, 29, 1986, 1–24.

"The New Development Economics." *World Development*, 14 (2), 1986, 257–265. Subsequently reprinted in *The Political Economy of Development and Underdevelopment*, C. K. Wilber, ed. New York: Random House, 1988, 393–407.

"Pure Theory of Country Risk," with J. Eaton and M. Gersovitz. *European Economic Review*, 30 (3), June 1986, 481–513. Reprinted in *Development Economics*, 4, D. Lal, ed. Elgar, 1992, 241–273. Also NBER working paper no. 1864, April 1986, and NBER reprint 793.

"Theories of Wage Rigidities," in *Keynes' Economic Legacy: Contemporary Economic Theories*, J. L. Butkiewicz, et al., eds. New York: Praeger Publishers, 1986, 153–206. (Presented at a conference on Keynes' Economic Legacy, University of Delaware, December 1983.)

"Theory of Competition, Incentives and Risk," in *New Developments in the Theory of Market Structure*, J. E. Stiglitz and F. Mathewson, eds. MacMillan/MIT Press, 1986, 399–449. Also Princeton University Econometric Research Program research memorandum 311.

"Toward a More General Theory of Monopolistic Competition," in *Prices, Competition, & Equilibrium*, M. Peston and R. Quandt, eds. Oxford: Philip Allan/Barnes & Noble Books, 1986, 22–69. Also Princeton University Econometric Research Program research memorandum 316.

1987

"The Causes and Consequences of the Dependence of Quality on Prices." *Journal of Economic Literature*, 25, March 1987, 1–48. Subsequently reprinted in *Impresa, Instituzione e Informazione*, M. Franzini and M. Messori, eds. Bologna: Cooperative Libraria Universitaria, 1991.

"Competition and the Number of Firms in a Market: Are Duopolies More Competitive Than Atomistic Markets?" *Journal of Political Economy*, 95 (5), 1987, 1041–1061. (Revised version of "Duopolies are More Competitive than Atomistic Markets," Princeton University Econometric Research Program research memorandum 310, February 1984.)

"Credit Rationing: Reply," with A. Weiss. *American Economic Review*, 77 (1), March 1987, 228–231.

"Design of Labor Contracts: Economics of Incentives and Risk-Sharing," in *Incentives. Cooperation and Risk Sharing*, H. Nalbantian, ed. Totowa, N.J.: Rowman & Allanheld, 1987, 47–68.

"Pareto Efficient and Optimal Taxation and the New New Welfare Economics," in *Handbook of Public Economics*, 2, A. Auerbach and M. Feldstein, eds. Amsterdam: North-Holland, 1987, 991–1042.

"Human Nature and Economic Organization." Jacob Marashak Lecture, presented at Far Eastern Meetings of the Econometric Society, October 1987.

"Imperfect Information, Credit Markets and Unemployment," with B. Greenwald. *European Economic Review*, 31, 1987, 444–456.

"Information and Regulation," with D. Sappington, in *Public Regulation*, E. Bailey, ed. London: MIT Press, 1987, 3–43.

"Information, Welfare and Product Diversity," with S. Salop, in *Arrow and the Foundations of the Theory of Economic Policy*, G. Feiwel, ed. London: MacMillan, 1987, 328–340. (Revised version of a paper presented to a conference on imperfect information at Bell Labs, February 1978.)

"The Invariance of Market Innovation to the Number of Firms," with R. Sah. *Rand Journal of Economics*, 18 (1), Spring 1987, 98–108.

"Keynesian, New Keynesian and New Classical Economics," with B. Greenwald. *Oxford Economic Papers*, 39, March 1987, 119–133. Subsequently reprinted in *Price, Quantities, and Expectations*, P. J. N. Sinclair, ed. Oxford University Press, 1987, 119–133; in the French translation of *Collected Papers on the Current State of Keynesian Theory*, R. Arena and D. Torre, eds. Les Presses Universitaires de France; in the French translation of *Origins and Prospects of Keynesianism: Some New Developments*, R. Arena and D. Torre, eds.; and in *Keynes et les nouveaux Keynesiens*, R. Arena and D. Torre, eds. Paris: Les Presses Universitaires de France, 1992, 169–191.

"Learning to Learn, Localized Learning and Technological Progress," in *Economic Policy and Technological Performance*, P. Dasgupta and Stoneman, eds. Cambridge University Press, 1987, 125–153.

"On the Microeconomics of Technical Progress," in *Technology Generation in Latin American Manufacturing Industries*, Jorge M. Katz, ed. Macmillan Press Ltd. 1987, 56–77. (Presented to IDB-Cepal Meetings, Buenos Aires, November 1978.)

"Pareto Efficient and Optimal Taxation and the New New Welfare Economics," in *Handbook on Public Economics*, A. Auerbach and M. Feldstein, eds. North Holland: Elsevier Science Publishers, 1987, 991–1042. Also NBER working paper 2189.

"Price Scissors and the Structure of the Economy," with R. Sah. *Quarterly Journal of Economics*, 102, 1987, 109–134.

"Privatization, Information and Incentives," with D. Sappington. *Journal of Policy Analysis and Management*, 6 (4), 1987, 567–582. Reprinted in *The Political Economy of Privatization and Deregulation*, E. Baily and J. Hower, eds. Edward Elgar, 1993. NBER working paper no. 2196 and reprint no. 1021.

"Safety, User Fees, and Public Infrastructure," with R. Arnott, in *Transportation Deregulation and Safety*. conference proceedings, The Transportation Center, Northwestern University, June 1987, 411–445.

"Sharecropping," in *The New Palgrave: A Dictionary of Economics*, MacMillan Press, 1987. Subsequently reprinted in *The New Palgrave: Economic Development*, J. Eatwell et al., eds. Macmillan, 1989, 308–315.

"Some Theoretical Aspects of Agriculture Policies." *World Bank Research Observer*, 2 (1), January 1987, 43–60. Reprinted as "Algunos Aspectos Teoricos de la Polutica Agraria." *Revista de Analisis del Norte Alternativa*, June 1989, 7–34.

"Tax Reform: Theory and Practice," in *The Economics of Tax Reform*, Kalamazoo, MI: Upjohn Institute, 1987.

"Taxation and Pricing of Agricultural and Industrial Goods in Developing Economies," with R. Sah, in *The Tax Theory for Developing Countries*, D. Newbery and N. Stern, eds. Oxford: Oxford University Press, 1987, 430–458.

"Technological Change, Sunk Costs, and Competition." *Brookings Papers on Economic Activity*, 3, 1987. Also in special issue of *Microeconomics*, M. N. Baily and C. Winston, eds. 1988, 883–947.

"Wage Rigidity, Implicit Contracts, Unemployment and Economic Efficiency," with D. Newbery. *Economic Journal*, 97 (386), June 1987, 416–430.

1988

"The Basic Analytics of Moral Hazard," with R. Arnott. *Scandinavian Journal of Economics*, 90 (3), 1988, 383–413. Also NBER working paper 2484.

"Comments on Symposium on Monetary Theory," with A. Stockman and M. Woodford, in *Symposium on Monetary Theory* (Proceedings of Taipei), Institute of Economics, Acadamia Sinica, 1988, 299–336.

"Committees, Hierarchies and Polyarchies," with R. Sah. *The Economic Journal*, 98 (391), June 1988, 451–470.

"Computerized Tax Collecting," Chapter 20 in *Tax Policy in the Twenty-First Century*, Herbert Stein, ed. John Wiley and Sons, 1988, 278–288. (Originally presented at the Conference on Tax Policy in the Twenty First Century, Washington DC, 1987, as "Technical Change and Taxation.")

"Economic Organization, Information, and Development," in *Handbook of Development Economics*, H. Chenery and T. N. Srinivasan, eds. Elsevier Science Publishers, 1988, 185–201.

"Examining Alternative Macroeconomic Theories," with B. Greenwald. *Brookings Papers on Economic Activity*, 1, 1988, 207–270. Subsequently reprinted in *Recent Developments in Macroeconomics*, Edmund Phelps, ed. Edward Elgar, 1991, 335–388.

"Financial Intermediaries and the Allocation of Capital," published as "Ruolo dei Fondi de Capitallizzazione Nello Szilluppo dell'Economia di un Paese Industrializzato." *Assicurazioni*, Luglio-Agosto 1988, 1–16. (Originally delivered to Academia de Lincei, May 29, 1988, Rome.)

"Imperfect Information, Finance Constraints and Business Fluctuations," with B. Greenwald, in *Finance Constraints, Expectations, and Macroeconomics*, M. Kohn and S. C. Tsiang, eds. Oxford: Oxford University Press, 1988, 103–140.

"Implicit Contracts, Labor Mobility and Unemployment," with R. Arnott and A. Hosios. *American Economic Review*, 78 (5), December 1988, 1046–1066. Also NBER working paper no. 2316.

"Information, Finance Constraints and Business Fluctuations," with B. Greenwald. *Symposium on Monetary Theory* (Proceedings of Taipei), Institute of Economics, Academia Sinica, 1988, 299–336.

"Learning by Doing, Market Structure, and Industrial and Trade Policies," with P. Dasgupta. *Oxford Economic Papers*, 40 (2), 1988, 246–268.

"Money, Credit, and Business Fluctuations." *Economic Record*, 64 (187), December 1988, 62–72. Reprinted as "Dinero, Crédito y Fluctuaciones Economicas." *Revista de Economia*, Banco Central del Uruguay, 3 (3), April 1989. Also NBER working paper no. 2823 and reprint no. 1390.

"Money, Imperfect Information and Economic Fluctuations," with B. Greenwald, in *Finance Constraints, Expectations and Macroeconomics*, M. Kohn and S. C. Tsiang, eds. Oxford: Oxford University Press, 1988, 141–165. Also NBER working paper no. 2188.

"On the Market for Principles of Economics Textbooks: Innovation and Product Differentiation." *Journal of Economic Education*, 19 (2), Spring 1988, 171–177.

"On the Relevance or Irrelevance of Public Financial Policy," in *The Economics of Public Debt*, proceedings of the 1986 International Economics Association Meeting, London: Macmillan Press, 1988, 4–76.

"Pareto Inefficiency of Market Economies: Search and Efficiency Wage Models," with B. Greenwald. *American Economic Review*, 78 (2), May 1988, 351–355.

"Potential Competition, Actual Competition and Economic Welfare," with P. Dasgupta. *European Economic Review*, 32, May 1988, 569–577. Also Princeton University discussion paper 8, August 1987.

"Qualitative Properties of Profit-Maximizing K-out-of-N Systems Subject to Two Kinds of Failure," with R. Sah. *IEEE Transactions on Reliability*, 37 (5), December 1988, 515–520.

"Randomization with Asymmetric Information," with R. Arnott. *Rand Journal of Economics*, 19 (3), Autumn 1988, 344–362. Also NBER working paper no. 2507.

"Taxation, Information, and Economic Organization," with M. Wolfson. *Journal of the American Taxation Association*, 9 (2), spring 1988, 7–18. Paper presented for delivery to the American Accounting Association, August 1987.

"The Wage-Productivity Hypothesis: Its Economic Consequences and Policy Implications," in *Modern Developments in Public Finance*, M. J. Boskin, ed. Basil Blackwell, 1988, 130–165. (Paper presented to the American Economic Association, December 1982.)

"Vertical Restraints and Producers' Competition," with P. Rey. *European Economic Review*, 32, March 1988, 561–568. Also NBER working paper no. 2601 and Princeton University discussion paper 13.

"Why Financial Structure Matters." *Journal of Economic Perspectives*, 2 (4), 1988, 121–126.

1989

"Congestion Pricing to Improve Air Travel Safety," with R. Arnott, in *Transportation Safety in an Age of Deregulation*, L. N. Moses and I. Savage, eds. Oxford University Press, 1989, 167–185. Also in Princeton University discussion paper 27, "Two Essays on Travel Safety," with "The Economics of Transportation Safety and Deregulation."

"Credit Rationing, Tenancy, Productivity and the Dynamics of Inequality," with A. Braverman, in P. Bardhan, ed. *The Economic Theory of Agrarian Institutions,* Oxford: Clarendon Press, 1989, 185–201. Previously World Bank policy research working paper 176, May 1989; also Princeton University discussion paper 23, 1988.

"Financial Markets and Development." *Oxford Review of Economic Policy,* 5 (4), 1989, 55–68.

"Impact of the Changing Tax Environment on Investments and Productivity," with B. Greenwald. *The Journal of Accounting, Auditing and Finance,* 4 (3), Summer 1989, 281–301. (Revised version of paper prepared for a conference on "Tax Policy in a Complex and Dynamic Economic Environment: Challenges and Opportunities," New York University, December 1988.)

"Imperfect Information in the Product Market," in *Handbook of Industrial Organization,* 1, Elsevier Science Publishers, 1989, 769–847.

"Incentives, Information and Organizational Design." *Empirica,* 16 (1), January 1989, 3–29. Also NBER working paper no. 2979. (NOG Lecture, Austrian Economic Association, September 1988.)

"The Informational Content of Initial Public Offerings," with I. Gale. *Journal of Finance,* 44 (2), June 1989, 469–478. Also NBER working paper no. 3259.

"Markets, Market Failures and Development." *American Economic Review,* 79 (2), May 1989, 197–203. Subsequently published in *Boletin de Informacion Comercial Espanola,* Madrid.

"Monopolistic Competition and the Capital Market," in *The Economics of Imperfect Competition and Employment—Joan Robinson and Beyond,* G. Feiwel, ed. New York: New York University Press, 1989, 485–507.

"Mutual Funds, Capital Structure, and Economic Efficiency," in *Theory of Valuation—Frontiers of Modern Financial Theory,* 1, S. Bhattacharya and G. Constantinides, eds. Totowa, NJ: Rowman and Littlefield, 1989, 342–356.

"Notes on Stochastic Capital Theory," with W. Brock and M. Rothschild, in *Joan Robinson and Modern Economic Theory (vol. 1),* G. Feiwel, ed. Macmillan Press, 1989, 591–622. Also NBER technical working paper no. 23, May 1982, and Social Systems Research Institute reprint series 373. (Revised version presented at Conference in Honor of Karl Borch, Bergen, Norway, April 1989.)

"Principal and Agent," in *The New Palgrave: Allocation, Information and Markets,* J. Eatwell, et al., eds. London: MacMillan Press, 1989, 241–253. Also Princeton University discussion paper 18.

"Rational Peasants, Efficient Institutions and the Theory of Rural Organization," in *The Economic Theory of Agrarian Institutions,* P. Bardhan, ed. Oxford: Clarendon Press, 1989, 18–29.

"Reflections on the State of Economics: 1988." *Economic Record,* March 1989, 66–72. (Presented at Australian Economic Meetings, Canberra, August 1988.)

"Sources of Technological Divergence between Developed and Less Developed Countries," with R. Sah, in *Debt, Stabilizations and Development: Essays in Memory of Carlos Diaz-Alejandro*, G. Calvo, et al., eds. Basil Blackwell, 1989, 423–446. Also Princeton University discussion paper 22.

"Technological Learning, Social Learning and Technological Change," with R. Sah, in *The Balance between Industry and Agriculture in Economic Development*, S. Chakravarty, ed. MacMillan Press/IEA, 1989, 285–298. Also Yale University Economic Growth Center paper 433.

"Toward a Theory of Rigidities," with B. Greenwald. *American Economic Review*, 79 (2), May 1989, 364–69. Also NBER working paper no. 2938.

"Using Tax Policy to Curb Speculative Short-Term Trading." *Journal of Financial Services Research*, 3 (2/3), December 1989, 101–115.

1990

"Asymmetric Information and the New Theory of the Firm: Financial Constraints and Risk Behavior," with B. Greenwald. *American Economic Review*, 80 (2), May 1990, 160–165. Also NBER working paper no. 3359.

"Banks as Social Accountants and Screening Devices for the Allocation of Credit," with A. Weiss. *Greek Economic Review*, 12, supplement, autumn 1990, 85–118. Reprinted in *Financial Intermediaries*, Mervin K. Lewis, ed. Aldershot, U.K.: Elgar, 1995, 297–330. Also NBER working paper no. 2710, September 1988.

"Credit Rationing," with D. Jaffee, in *Handbook of Monetary Economics*, B. Friedman and F. Hahn, eds. Amsterdam: Elsevier Science Publishers, 1990, 837–888.

"Financial Market Imperfections and Productivity Growth," with B. Greenwald and M. Kohn. *Journal of Economic Behavior and Organization*, 13 (3), June 1990, 321–345. Also NBER working paper no. 2945.

"Imperfect Information and Rural Credit Markets: Puzzles and Policy Perspectives," with K. Hoff. *World Bank Economic Review*, 4 (3), September 1990, 235–250. Subsequently revised and reprinted in *The Economics of Rural Organization: Theory, Practice, and Policy*, K. Hoff, A. Braverman, and J. Stiglitz, eds. New York: Oxford University Press for the World Bank, 1993, 33–52.

"Macroeconomic Models with Equity and Credit Rationing," with B. Greenwald, in *Asymmetric Information, Corporate Finance, and Investment*, R. B. Hubbard, ed. University of Chicago Press, 1990, 15–42.

"Pareto Efficient Tax Structures," with D. L. Brito, J. H. Hamilton and S. M. Slutsky. *Oxford Economic Papers*, 42, 1990, 61–77. Subsequently reprinted in *Taxation, Private Information and Capital*, P. J. N. Sinclair and M. D. E. Slater, eds. Oxford: Clarendon Press, 1991, 61–77.

"Peer Monitoring and Credit Markets." *World Bank Economic Review*, 4 (3), September 1990, 351–366. Also in *The Economics of Rural Organization: Theory, Practice, and Policy*, World Bank, 1993, 70–86.

"Remarks on the Occasion of the Presentation of the UAP Prize," in *Journées Scientifiques & Prix UAP, 1988, 1989, 1990*, 2, Conseil Scientifique de l'UAP, ed. December 1990, 23–32.

"Some Retrospective Views on Growth Theory presented on the occasion of the Celebration of Robert Solow's 65th Birthday," in *Growth/Productivity/Unemployment*, P. Diamond, ed. Cambridge, MA: MIT Press, 1990, 50–68.

"Symposium on Bubbles." *Journal of Economic Perspectives*, 4 (2), Spring 1990, 13–18.

"The Welfare Economics of Moral Hazard," with R. Arnott, in *Risk Information and Insurance: Essays in the Memory of Karl H. Borch*, H. Louberge, ed. Norwell: Kluwer Academic Publishers, 1990, 91–122. Also NBER working paper no. 3316.

1991

"Another Century of Economic Science." *Economic Journal* anniversary issue, 101 (404), January 1991, 134–141. Also published in *The Future of Economics*, J. D. Hey, ed. Blackwell Publishers, 1992.

"Comments on David Bradford, 'Market Value vs. Accounting Measures of National Saving'," in *National Saving and Economic Performance*, B. D. Bernheim and J. B. Shoven, eds. University of Chicago Press, 1991, 15–48. (Presented at NBER Conference on Savings, Maui, Hawaii, January 1989.)

"Development Strategies: The Roles of the State and the Private Sector," in *Proceedings of the World Bank's Annual Conference on Development Economics 1990*, 1991, 430–435.

"Dynamic Optimal Income Taxation With Government Commitment," with D. L. Brito, J. H. Hamilton and S. M. Slutsky. *Journal of Public Economics*, 44, 1991, 15–35. Also NBER working paper no. 3965.

"The Economic Role of the State: Efficiency and Effectiveness," in *Efficiency and Effectiveness in the Public Domain. The Economic Role of the State*, T. P. Hardiman and M. Mulreany, eds. Dublin: Institute of Public Administration, 1991, 37–59.

"Foreword," in *Informal Credit Markets and the Institution of Economics*, S. Claro and P. Yotopoulos, eds. Westview Press, 1991.

"Introduction to Symposium on Organizations and Economics." *Journal of Economic Perspectives*, 5 (2), spring 1991, 15–24.

"The Invisible Hand and Modern Welfare Economics," in *Information Strategy and Public Policy*, D. Vines and A. Stevenson, eds. Oxford: Basil Blackwell, 1991, 12–50. Also NBER working paper no. 3641. (Stevenson Lecture given at Glasgow University, December 1988.)

"Moral Hazard and Non-Market Institutions: Dysfunctional Crowding Out or Peer Monitoring," with R. Arnott. *American Economic Review*, 81 (1), March 1991, 179–190.

"The Quality of Managers in Centralized Versus Decentralized Organizations," with R. Sah. *Quarterly Journal of Economics*, 106 (1), February 1991, 289–325. Also Yale University Economic Growth Center discussion paper 624, April 1990.

"Some Theoretical Aspects of the Privatization: Applications to Eastern Europe." *Revista di Politica Economica*, December 1991, 179–204. IPR-USAID working paper, September 1991. Also in *Privatization Processes in Eastern Europe*. M. Baldassarri, L. Paganetto, and E. S. Phelps, eds. New York: St. Martin's Press, 1993.

"Symposium on Organizations and Economics." *Journal of Economic Perspective*, 5 (2), Spring 1991, 15–24.

"Toward a Reformulation of Monetary Theory: Competitive Banking," with B. Greenwald. *Economic and Social Review* 23 (1), October 1991, 1–34. Also NBER working paper no. 4117. (Paper prepared for the Irish Economic Association Annual Conference, Dublin, May 1991, and Caffee Lectures presented to the University of Rome and the Bank of Italy, Rome, April 1991.)

1992

"Alternative Tactics and Strategies for Economic Development," in *New Directions in Development Economics*, K. Jameson, and A. Dutt, eds. Edward Elgar, 1992, 57–80. (AT&T Lecture presented at Notre Dame, April 1990.)

"Asymmetric Information in Credit Markets and Its Implications for Macroeconomics," with A. Weiss. *Oxford Economic Papers*, 44 (4), October 1992, 694–724.

"Banks versus Markets as Mechanisms for Allocating and Coordinating Investment," in *The Economics of Cooperation: East Asian Development and the Case for Pro-Market Intervention*, J. A. Roumasset and S. Barr, eds. Boulder: Westview Press, 1992, 15–38. (Presented at Investment Coordination in the Pacific Century: Lessons from Theory and Practice Conference, given at the University of Hawaii, January 1990.)

"Capital Markets and Economic Fluctuations in Capitalist Economies." *European Economic Review*, 36, North-Holland, 1992, 269–306. (Marshall Lecture prepared for the European Economic Association Annual Meeting, Cambridge, U.K., August 1991.)

"Contract Theory and Macroeconomic Fluctuations," in *Contract Economics*, L. Werin and H. Wijkander, eds. Basil Blackwell, 1992, 292–322.

"The Design of Financial Systems for the Newly Emerging Democracies of Eastern Europe," in *The Emergence of Market Economies in Eastern Europe*, C. Clague and G. C. Rausser, eds. Cambridge: Basil Blackwell, 1992, 161–184. Also Institute for Policy Reform working paper IPR21, 1991.

"Explaining Growth: Competition and Finance." *Rivista di Politica Economica (Italy)*, 82 (169), November 1992, 225. (Paper prepared for the Villa Mondragone International Economic Seminar, Rome, June 1992.)

"Futures Markets and Risk Reduction," with D.M.G. Newbery, in *The Theory of Futures Markets*, P. Weller, ed. Oxford: Basil Blackwell, 1992, 36–55.

"Information, Finance and Markets: The Architecture of Allocative Mechanisms," with B. Greenwald. *Industrial and Corporate Change*, 1 (1), 1992, 37–63. Also in *Finance and the Enterprise*, V. Zamagni, ed. Academic Press, 1992, 11–36.

"Introduction: S&L Bailout," in *The Reform of Federal Deposit Insurance: Disciplining the Government and Protecting Taxpayers*, J. Barth and R. Brumbaugh, Jr., eds. Harper Collins Publishers, 1992, 1–12.

"The Meanings of Competition in Economic Analysis." *Rivista internazionale de scienze sociali*, 2, April–June 1992, 191–212.

"Methodological Issues and the New Keynesian Economics." *Alternative Approaches to Macroeconomics*, A. Vercelli and N. Dimitri, eds. Oxford University Press, 1992, 38–86. Also NBER working paper no. 3580 and reprint no. 1801.

"Prices and Queues as Screening Devices in Competitive Markets," in *Economic Analysis of Markets and Games: Essays in Honor of Frank Hahn*, D. Gale and O. Hart, eds. Cambridge: MIT Press, 1992, 128–166. Also IMSSS technical report 212, Stanford University, August 1976.

"Stochastic and Deterministic Fluctuations in a Non-Linear Model with Equity Rationing," with M. Gallegati. *Giornale Degli Economisti e Annali di Economia (Italy)*, 60, January–April 1992, 97–108.

1993

"Comments on 'Toward a Counter-Counter-Revolution in Development Theory'," in *Proceedings of the World Bank's Annual Conference on Development Economics 1992*, Washington, D.C.: World Bank, 1993, 39–49.

"Consequences of Limited Risk Markets and Imperfect Information for the Design of Taxes and Transfers: An Overview," in *The Economics of Rural Organization: Theory, Practice, and Policy*, K. Hoff, A. Braverman, and J. Stiglitz, eds. New York: Oxford University Press for the World Bank, 1993, 33–49.

"Financial Market Imperfections and Business Cycles," with B. Greenwald. *Quarterly Journal of Economics*, 108 (1), February 1993, 77–114. Also NBER working paper no. 2494. (Paper prepared for the Far-Eastern Meeting of the Econometric Society, Seoul, June 1991.)

"Incentives, Organizational Structures, and Contractual Choice in the Reform of Socialist Agriculture," in *The Agricultural Transition in Central and Eastern Europe and the Former U.S.S.R.*, A. Braverman, K. Brooks, and C. Csaki, eds. World Bank, 1993, 27–46. (Presented at the World Bank conference "Agricultural Reform in Eastern Europe and the USSR," Budapest, August 1990.)

"International Perspectives in Undergraduate Education." *American Economic Review*, 83 (2), May 1993, 27–33.

"Market Socialism and Neoclassical Economics," in *Market Socialism: The Current Debate*, P. Bardhan and J. Roemer, eds. New York: Oxford University Press, 1993, 21–41.

"Measures for Enhancing the Flow of Private Capital to the Less Developed Countries." *Development Issues*, Development Committee, World Bank, 1993, 201–211.

"Monopolistic Competition and Optimum Product Diversity: Reply," with A. Dixit. *American Economic Review*, 83 (1), March 1993, 301–304.

"New and Old Keynesians," with B. Greenwald. *Journal of Economic Perspectives*, 7 (1), Winter 1993, 23–44.

"Perspectives on the Role of Government Risk-Bearing within the Financial Sector," in *Government Risk-bearing*, M. Sniderman, ed. Norwell, MA: Kluwer Academic Publishers, 1993, 109–130. (Paper prepared for Conference on Government Risk Bearing, Federal Reserve Bank of Cleveland, May 1991.)

"Post Walrasian and Post Marxian Economics." *Journal of Economic Perspectives*, 7 (1), Winter 1993, 109–114.

"The Role of the State in Financial Markets." *Proceeding of the World Bank Conference on Development Economics 1993*, Washington, D.C.: World Bank, 41–46. Also Institute for Policy Reform working paper IPR 56, 1992.

1994

"Economic Growth Revisited." *Industrial and Corporate Change*, 3 (1), 65–110, 1994.

"Endogenous Growth and Cycles," in *Innovation in Technology, Industries, and Institutions*, Y. Shionoya and M. Perlman, eds. The University of Michigan Press, 1994, 121–156. Also NBER working paper no. 4286.

"Information and Economic Efficiency," with R. Arnott and B. Greenwald. *Information Economics and Policy*, 6 (1), March 1994, 77–88. Also NBER working paper no. 4533. (Paper prepared for the New Orleans Meeting of the American Economic Association, 1992.)

"Reflections on Economics and on Being and Becoming an Economist," in *The Makers of Modern Economics*, vol. II, Arnold Heertje, ed. Harvester Wheatsheaf (Simon & Schuster International Group), May 1994, 140–183.

"Rethinking the Economic Role of the State: Publicly Provided Private Goods/ Replanteamiento del papel económico del estado: bienes privados suministrados públicamente." *Celección els Llibres Dels Fulls Econòmics*, 10, Generalitat de Catalunya Departament de Sanitat I Seguretat Social, 19–47. (Paper originally delivered at Universitat Pompeu Fabra, Barcelona, November 15, 1992.)

"Sorting Out the Differences Between Screening and Signaling Models," with A. Weiss, in *Mathematical Models in Economics*, M. O. L. Bacharach, M. A. H. Dempster, and J. L. Enos, eds. Oxford: Oxford University Press, 1994. Previously NBER technical working paper 93, November 1990.

1995

"Discouraging Rivals: Managerial Rent-Seeking and Economic Inefficiencies," with A. Edlin. *American Economic Review*, 85 (5), December 1995, 1301–1312. Also NBER working paper no. 4145, 1992.

"Interest Rate Puzzles, Competitive Theory and Capital Constraints," in *Economics in a Changing World*, IEA Conference Volume, Economic Growth and Capital and Labour markets, 111 (5), Jean-Paul Fitoussi, ed. New York: St. Martin's Press, 1995, 145–175. (Prepared for the International Economics Association Meetings, Moscow, August 1992.)

"Labor Market Adjustments and the Persistence of Unemployment," with B. Greenwald. *American Economic Review*, 85 (2), May 1995, 219–225.

"Randomization in Optimal Income Tax Schedules," with D. Brito, J. Hamilton, and S. Slutsky. *Journal of Public Economics*, 56 (189), February 1995, 189–223.

"The Role of Exclusive Territories in Producers' Competition," with P. Rey. *Rand Journal of Economics*, 26 (3), Autumn 1995, 431–451. Previously NBER working paper no. 4618, January 1994.

"Setting Budget Priorities." *Vital Speeches of the Day*, 6 (4), December 1, 1995, 121–124.

"Social Absorption Capability and Innovation," in *Social Capability and Long-Term Economic Growth*, Bon Ho Koo and D. H. Perkins, eds. New York: St. Martin's Press, 1995, 48–81.

1996

"Deposit Mobilisation Through Financial Restraint," with T. Hellmann and K. Murdock, in *Financial Development and Economic Growth*, N. Hermes and R. Lensink, eds. Routledge, 1996, 219–246. Also in *Banking and Financial Institutions*, 3 (5B), February 7, 1996; and Stanford Graduate School of Business research paper 1354, July 1995.

"Financial Markets, Public Policy, and the East Asian Miracle," with M. Uy. *World Bank Research Observer*, 11 (2), August 1996, 249–276.

"Institutional Innovations and the Role of Local Government in Transition Economies: The Case of Guangdong Province of China," with Yingyi Qian, in *Reforming Asian Socialism: The Growth of Market Institutions*, John McMillan and Barry Naughton, eds. Ann Arbor, MI: The University of Michigan Press, 1996, 175–193.

"International Economic Justice and National Responsibility: Strategies for Economic Development in the Post Cold War World." *Oxford Development Studies*, 24 (2), June 1996, 101–109.

"Introduction: Scope of the Assessment," with J. Goldemberg, et al. as chapter 1, and "Intertemporal Equity, Discounting, and Economic Efficiency," with K. Arrow, et al. as chapter 4 in *Climate Change 1995: Economic and Social Dimensions of Climate Change*, J. Bruce, H. Lee, and E. Haites, eds. Cambridge: Cambridge University Press, 1996, 21–51 and 125–144. The latter also chapter 1 in *Global Climate Change: Economic and Policy Issues*, M. Munasinghe, ed. World Bank environment paper 12, Washington, D.C., 1995, 1–32.

"Some Lessons from the East Asian Miracle." *World Bank Research Observer*, 11 (2), August 1996, 151–177. Reprinted as "Algunas ensenanzas del milagro del Este Asiatico (with English summary)," *Desarrollo Economico*, 37 (147), Oct.–Dec. 1997, 323–349.

1997

"Competition and Insurance Twenty Years Later," with Michael Rothschild. *Geneva Papers on Risk and Insurance Theory*, 22 (2), December 1997, 73–79.

"Dumping on Free Trade: The U. S. Import Trade Laws." *Southern Economic Journal*, 64 (2), 1997, 402–424. Also London School of Economics Centre for Economic Performance discussion paper 210, with P. Orszag, 1994.

"A Framework for a Development Strategy in a Market Economy," with Nicholas Stern, in *Development Strategy and the Management of the Market Economy*, E. Malinvaud and A. K. Sen, eds. Oxford: Clarendon Press, 1997, 253–295. Also European Bank for Reconstruction and Development working paper 20, April 1997.

"Financial Restraint: Toward a New Paradigm," with T. Hellmann and K. Murdock, in *The Role of Government in East Asian Economic Development*, M. Aoki, H. Kim, and M. Okuna-Fujiwara, eds. Oxford: Clarendon Press, 1997, 163–207.

"Looking Out for the National Interest: the Principles of the Council of Economic Advisers." *American Economic Review*, 87 (2), May 1997, 109–113. (Speech to American Economic Association. New Orleans. January 5, 1996.)

"Moneylenders and Bankers: Price-increasing Subsidies in a Monopolistically Competitive Market," with Karla Hoff. *Journal of Development Economics* 52, 1997, 429–462. Corrected for printing errors in "Moneylenders and Bankers: Price-Increasing Subsidies with Monopolistic Competition." *Journal of Development Economics*, 55, 1998, 485–518. Previously "Theory of Imperfect Competition in Rural Credit Markets," Institute for Policy Reform working paper IPR 49, 1992; and "Moneylenders and Bankers: Fragmented Credit Markets with Monopolistic Competition," working paper 93–10, University of Maryland, Department of Economics, 1993.

"Reflections on the Natural Rate Hypothesis." *Journal of Economic Perspectives*, 11 (1), Winter 1997, 3–10.

"Reply: Georgescu-Roegen versus Solow/Stiglitz." *Ecological Economics*, Elsevier Science, 1997, 269–270.

"The Role of Government in Economic Development," in *Annual World Bank Conference on Development Economics 1996*, M. Bruno and B. Pleskovic, eds. World Bank, 1997, 11–23.

"The Role of Government in the Economies of Developing Countries," in *Development Strategy and the Management of the Market Economy*, E. Malinvaud and A. K. Sen, eds. Oxford: Clarendon Press, 1997, 61–109.

"The State and Development: Some New Thinking," in *Report: International Roundtable: "The Capable State,"* World Bank and German Foundation for International Development. Berlin, October 8. Transcript available at ⟨http://www.worldbank.org/html/extdr/extme/jssp100897.htm⟩.

1998

"An Agenda for Development in the Twenty-First Century," in *Annual World Bank Conference on Development Economics 1997*, J. E. Stiglitz and B. Pleskovic, eds. Washington, D.C.: World Bank, 1998, 17–31.

"Building Robust Financial Systems." *Central Bank of Barbados Economic Review*, 25 (1), June 1998, 49–56.

"Central Banking in a Democratic Society." *De Economist* (Netherlands), 146 (2), 1998, 199–226.

"Development Based on Participation—A Strategy for Transforming Societies." *Transition*, 9 (6), World Bank and Davidson Institute, December 1998, 1–3.

"Economic Crises: Evidence and Insights from East Asia," with Jason Furman. *Brookings Papers on Economic Activity*, 1998 (2), 1–114. (Presented at Brookings Panel on Economic Activity, Washington, September 3, 1998.)

"Financial Restraint and the Market Enhancing View," with T. Hellmann and K. Murdock, in *The Institutional Foundations of East Asian Economic Development*, Y. Hayami and M. Aoki, eds. London: MacMillan, 1998, 255–284.

"IFIs and the Provision of International Public Goods," in *Cahiers Papers*, 3 (2), European Investment Bank, 1998, 116–134.

"Inequality and Growth: Implications for Public Finance and Lessons from Experience in the U.S.," in *Beyond Tradeoffs: Market Reform and Equitable Growth in Latin America*," N. Birdsall, C. Graham, R. H. Sabot, ed. Inter-American Development Bank, 1998, 305–319.

"International Development: Is it Possible?," with Lyn Squire. *Foreign Policy*, 110, spring 1998, 138–151.

"Introduction," with Boris Pleskovic, in *Annual World Bank Conference on Development Economics 1997*, Pleskovic and Stiglitz, eds. Washington, D.C.: World Bank, 1998, 1–7.

"The Private Uses of Public Interests: Incentives and Institutions." *Journal of Economic Perspectives*, 12 (2), spring 1998, 3–22. (Originally presented at a Society of Government Economists conference in Chicago, Distinguished Lecture on Economics in Government, January 4, 1998.)

"The Role of Government in the Contemporary World," in *Income Distribution and High-Quality Growth*, Vito Tanzi and Ke-young Chu, eds. Cambridge, MA: MIT Press, 21–53. Also background paper no. 5 of the third meeting High Level Group on Development Strategy and Management of the Market Economy, UNU/WIDER, Helsinki, Finland, July 8–10.

"Road to Recovery: Restoring Growth in the Region Could Be a Long and Difficult Process." *Asiaweek* 24 (8), July 17, 1998, 66–67.

"Towards a New Paradigm for Development: Strategies, Policies and Processes." Ninth Raul Prebisch Lecture delivered at the Palais des Nations, Geneva, October 19, 1998, UNCTAD. Chapter 2 in *The Rebel Within*, Ha-Joon Chang, ed. London: Wimbledon Publishing Company, 2001, 57–93.

1999

"Aid Effectiveness and Development Partnership," in *Donor Coordination and the Effectiveness of Development Assistance*, UNU Public Lectures, November 1999, 17–30.

"Beggar-Thyself vs. Beggar-Thy-Neighbor Policies: The Dangers of Intellectual Incoherence in Addressing the Global Financial Crisis." *Southern Economic Journal*, 66 (1), July 1999, 1–38. (Paper presented to the Annual Meetings of the Southern Economics Association, Baltimore, November 8, 1998.)

"Economic Consequences of Income Inequality," with Jason Furman. *Symposium Proceedings—Income Inequality: Issues and Policy Options*. Jackson Hole, WY: Federal Reserve Bank of Kansas City, 1998, 221–263.

"The Future of the International Financial Architecture." *World Economic Affairs*, 2 (3), Winter 1999, 35–38.

"Interest Rates, Risk, and Imperfect Markets: Puzzles and Policies." *Oxford Review of Economic Policy* 15 (2), 1999, 59–76.

"Introduction." *Economic Notes*, 28 (3), November 1999, 249–254.

"Introduction," with Boris Pleskovic, in *Annual World Bank Conference on Development Economics 1998*. Boris Pleskovic and Joseph E. Stiglitz, eds. Washington, D.C.: World Bank, 1999, 1–8.

"Knowledge as a Global Public Good," in *Global Public Goods: International Cooperation in the 21st Century*, Inge Kaul, Isabelle Grunberg, Marc A. Stern, eds. United Nations Development Program. New York: Oxford University Press, 1999, 308–325.

"Knowledge for Development: Economic Science, Economic Policy, and Economic Advice," in *Annual World Bank Conference on Development Economics*, B. Pleskovic and J. Stiglitz, eds. Washington, D.C.: World Bank, 1998, 9–58.

"Lessons from East Asia." *Journal of Policy Modeling*, 21 (3), May 1999, 311–330. (Paper presented at the American Economic Association Annual Meetings, New York, January 4, 1999.)

"More Instruments and Broader Goals: Moving Toward the Post-Washington Consensus," in *Development Issues in the 21st Century*, G. Kochendorfer-Lucius and B. Pleskovic, eds. Berlin: German Foundation for International Development, 1999, 11–39. Also chapter 1 in *The Rebel Within*, Ha-Joon Chang, ed. London: Wimbledon Publishing Company, 2001, 17–56. (Originally presented as the 1998 WIDER Annual Lecture, Helsinki, January 1998; also keynote address at Villa Borsig winter workshop, February 1998.)

"Must Financial Crises Be This Frequent and This Painful?" *Policy Options* (Canada), 20 (5), June, 23–32. (Paper originally given on September 23, 1998, as University of Pittsburgh McKay Lecture).

"New Perspectives on the Role of the State," in *Akademische Reden und Kolloquien* (Academic Lectures and Colloquia), 18, University of Erlangen-Nuernberg, 1999. (Paper initially presented as Recktenwald Prize acceptance speech, February 3, 1998.)

"The Procyclical Role of Rating Agencies: Evidence from the East Asian Crisis," with G. Ferri and L.-G. Liu. *Economic Notes*, 28 (3), 1999, 335–355.

"Public-Private Technology Partnerships: Promises and Pitfalls," with Scott J. Wallsten. *American Behavioral Scientist*, 43 (1), September 1999, 52–74. Also published in *Public-Private Policy Partnerships*, P. Rosenau, ed. Cambridge, MA: MIT Press, 2000, 37–59.

"The Reasons Behind the Crash." *Etruria Oggi*, 17 (50), June 1999, 28–31.

"Reforming the Global Economic Architecture: Lessons from Recent Crises." *The Journal of Finance* 54 (4), August 1999, 1508–1521.

"Responding to Economic Crises: Policy Alternatives for Equitable Recovery and Development." *The Manchester School*, 67 (5), special issue 1999, 409–427. (Paper presented to North-South Institute, Ottawa, Canada, September 29, 1998.)

"The Role of Participation in Development." *Development Outreach*, 1 (1), summer 1999, 10–13. (Excerpted from presentation delivered at the Conference on Democracy, Market Economy and Development in Seoul, South Korea, February 1999.)

"State versus Market: Have Asian Currency Crises Affected the Reform Debate?" The University Press Limited for Bangladesh Economic Association: Dhaka, Bangladesh, 1999. (Presented at the 1999 Bangladesh Economic Association lecture.)

"Taxation, Public Policy and The Dynamics of Unemployment." *International Tax and Public Finance*, 6, 239–262. (Paper presented to the Institute of International Finance, Cordoba, Argentina, August 24, 1998.)

"Toward a General Theory of Wage and Price Rigidities and Economic Fluctuations." *American Economic Review*, 89 (2), May 1999, 75–80. (Paper prepared for the American Economic Association Annual Meetings, New York, January 4, 1999.)

"Trade and the Developing World: A New Agenda." *Current History*, 98 (631), November 1999, 387–393.

"The World Bank and the Overseas Economic Cooperation Fund in the New Millennium." *Journal of Development Assistance*, 5 (1), 11–17.

"The World Bank at the Millennium." *Economic Journal*, 109 (454), F577–F597.

"The WTO Millennium Round." *Social Development Review*, 3 (4), December 1999, 6–9.

2000

"Capital Market Liberalization, Economic Growth, and Instability." in *World Development*, 28 (6), 2000, 1075–1086.

"Chinese Reforms from a Comparative Perspective," with Athar Hussain and Nicholas Stern, in *Incentives, Organization, and Public Economics: Papers in Honour of Sir James Mirrlees*, Peter J. Hammond and Gareth D. Myles, eds. Oxford University Press, 2000, 243–277.

"Conclusions." *Economic Notes*, 29 (1), special issue, The East Asian Crisis: Lessons for Today and for Tomorrow, February 2000, 145–151.

"The Contributions of the Economics of Information to Twentieth Century Economics." *Quarterly Journal of Economics*, 115 (4), November 2000, 1441–1478.

"Credit and Equity Rationing in Markets with Adverse Selection," with T. Hellmann. *European Economic Review*, 44 (2), February 2000, 281–304. Earlier, longer version in "A Unifying Theory of Credit and Equity Rationing in Markets with Adverse Selection," Stanford Graduate School of Business research paper 1356, October 1995.

"Democratic Development as the Fruits of Labor." *Perspectives on Work*, 4 (1), 2000, 31–38. Also chapter 9 in *The Rebel Within*, Ha-Joon Chang, ed. London: Wimbledon Publishing Company, 2001, 279–315. (Originally keynote address at the Industrial Relations Research Association, Boston, January 2000.)

"Development Issues: Settled and Open,"in *Frontiers of Development Economics: The Future in Perspective*, G. Meiter and J. Stiglitz, eds. Oxford: Oxford University Press, 2000, 227–268.

"Formal and Informal Institutions," in *Social Capital: A Multifaceted Perspective*, P. Dasgupta and I. Serageldin, eds. Washington, D.C.: World Bank, 2000, 59–68.

"Introduction" and "Conclusions," with H. de Largentaye, P. Muet, and J. Rischard, in *Governance, Equity and Global Markets: Proceedings from the Annual Bank Conference on Development Economics in Europe, June 1999*. Paris: Conseil d'Analyse Economique, 2000, 9–18 and 237–238. Printed in French in *Revue d'Economie du Developpement*, 0 (1–2), June 2000.

"Introduction," with Boris Pleskovic, in *Annual World Bank Conference on Development Economics 1999*, Boris Pleskovic and Joseph E. Stiglitz, eds. Washington, D.C.: World Bank, 2000, 1–13.

"Introduction." *The World Bank: Structure and Policies*, Christopher L. Gilbert and David Vines, eds. Cambridge: Cambridge University Press, 2000, 1–9.

"Lessons from the Global Financial Crisis," in *Global Financial Crises: Lessons from Recent Events*, Joseph R. Bisignano, William C. Hunter, George G. Kaufman, eds. Boston: Kluwer Academic Publishers, 2000, 89–109. (Originally presented at the Conference on Global Financial Crises, Bank for International Settlements and Federal Reserve Bank of Chicago, May 6, 1999.)

"Liberalization, Moral Hazard in Banking and Prudential Regulation: Are Capital Requirements Enough?" *American Economic Review*, 90 (1), March 2000, 147–165. Also published in *Industrial Organization and Regulation*, 3 (17), August 2000; and in *Banking and Financial Institutions*, 5 (8), June 2000.

"New Bridges Across the Chasm: Macro- and Micro-Strategies for Russia and other Transitional Economies," with David Ellerman. *Zagreb International Review of Economics and Business*, 3 (1), 2000, 41–72.

"O Que Eu Aprendi com a Crise Mundial." *Revista de Economia Politica/Brazilian Journal of Political Economy*, 20 (3), July–September 2000, 169–174.

"Quis custodiet ipsos custodes? Corporate Governance Failures in the Transition," in *Governance, Equity and Global Markets, Proceedings from the Annual Bank Conference on Development Economics in Europe, June 1999*, Pierre-Alain Muet and J. E. Stiglitz, eds. Conseil d'Analyse economique, Paris, 2000, 51–84. Also published in *Challenge*, 42 (6), November/December 1999, 26–67. (Originally presented as keynote address at the Annual Bank Conference on Development Economics in Europe, Paris, June 23, 1999.) French version "Quis custodiet ipsos custodes? Les defaillances du gouvernement d'entreprise dans la transition," *Revue d'Economie du Developpement*, 0 (1–2), June 2000, 33–70.

"Reflections on Mobility and Social Justice, Economic Efficiency, and Individual Responsibility," in *New Markets, New Opportunities? Economic and Social Mobility in a Changing World*, Nancy Birdsall and Carol Graham, eds. Washington, D.C.: Brookings Institution Press, 2000, 36–65. (Paper prepared for presentation at MacArthur Research Network meeting, Bellagio, Italy, May 6, 1998.)

"Reflections on the Theory and Practice of Reform," in *Economic Policy Reform: The Second Stage*, Anne Krueger, ed. University of Chicago Press, 2000, 551–584.

"Scan Globally, Reinvent Locally: Knowledge Infrastructure and the Localization of Knowledge," in *Banking on Knowledge: the Genesis of the Global Development Network*, Diane Stone, ed. Routledge, 2000, 24–43. Also chapter 6 in *The Rebel Within*, Ha-Joon Chang, ed. London: Wimbledon Publishing Company, 2001, 194–219. (Originally keynote address to the First Global Development Network Conference, Bonn, December 1999.)

"Some Elementary Principles of Bankruptcy," in *Governance, Equity and Global Markets: Proceedings from the Annual Bank Conference on Development Economics in Europe, June 1999*. Paris: Conseil d'Analyse Economique, 2000, 605–620.

"Two Principles for the Next Round or, How to Bring Developing Countries in from the Cold." *World Economy*, 23 (4), 437–454.

"The Underpinnings of a Stable and Equitable Global Financial System: From Old Debates to New Paradigm," with Amar Bhattacharya, in *Annual World Bank Conference on Development Economics 1999*, B. Pleskovic and J. E. Stiglitz, eds. Washington, D.C.: World Bank, 2000, 91–130. (Paper presented to the annual World Bank Conference on Development Economics, April 28–30, 1999.)

"Whither Reform? Ten Years of Transition," in *Annual World Bank Conference on Economic Development*, B. Pleskovic and J. E. Stiglitz, eds. Washington: World Bank, 2000, 27–56. Also chapter 4 in *The Rebel Within*, Ha-Joon Chang, ed. London: Wimbledon Publishing Company, 2001, 127–171. Summary in *Transition Economics*, 3 (12), June 1999. (Originally presented on April 30, 1999.)

2001

"A Comparison of Economic Transition among China and Other Countries." *Economics Information*, 5, May, 2001, 43–46 (in Chinese).

"Challenges in the Analysis of the Role of Institutions in Economic Development," in *Villa Borsig Workshop Series 2000: The Institutional Foundations of a Market Economy*, Gudrun Kochendorfer-Lucius and Boris Pleskovic, eds. German Foundation for International Development (DSE), 2001, 15–28.

"Crisis y Restructuración Financiera: el Papel de la Banca Central." *Cuestiones Económicas*, 17 (2), 2001, 3–24.

"Development Issues: Settled and Open," in *Frontiers of Development Economics*, G. Meier and J. Stiglitz. New York: Oxford University Press, 2001, 227–268.

"Development Theory at a Crossroads," in *Proceedings from the Annual Bank Conference on Development Economics in Europe, June 2000*, Jean-Francois Rischard et al., eds. Paris: Conseil d'Analyse Economique, 2001, 65–74.

"Development Thinking at the Millennium," in *Proceedings from the Annual Bank Conference on Development Economics 2000*, Washington: World Bank, 2001, 13–38. (Paper presented to the annual World Bank Conference on Development Economics, Paris, June 26, 2000.)

"Failure of the Fund: Rethinking the IMF Response." *Harvard International Review*, 23 (2), Summer 2001, 14–18.

"Foreword," in *The Great Transformation: The Political and Economic Origins of Our Time*," Karl Polanyi, ed. Boston: Beacon Press, 2001, vii–xvii.

"From Miracle to Crisis to Recovery: Lessons from Four Decades of East Asian Experience," in *Rethinking the East Asian Miracle*, J. Stiglitz and S. Yusuf, eds. Oxford: Oxford University Press, 2001, 509–526.

"Mexico—Five Years After the Crisis," with D. Lederman, A. Menendez, and G. Perry. *Annual Bank Conference on Development Economics 2000*, Washington, D.C.: World Bank, 2001, 263–282.

"Modern Economic Theory and Development," with Karla Hoff, in G. Meier and J. Stiglitz. *The Future of Development Economics in Perspective*, New York: Oxford University Press, 2001, 389–459.

"Not Poles Apart: 'Whither Reform?' and 'Whence Reform?'," with David Ellerman. *The Journal of Policy Reform*, 4 (4), 2001, 325–338.

"On Liberty, the Right to Know and Public Discourse: The Role of Transparency in Public Life," chapter 8 in *The Rebel Within*, Ha-Joon Chang, ed. London: Wimbledon Publishing Company, 2001, 250–278. (Originally presented as 1999 Oxford Amnesty Lecture, Oxford, January 1999.)

"Participation and Development: Perspectives from the Comprehensive Development Paradigm," in *Democracy, Market Economics & Development: An Asian Perspective*, Farrukh Iqbal and Jong-Il You, eds. World Bank, 2001, 49–72. Also chapter 7 in *The Rebel Within*, Ha-Joon Chang ed. London: Wimbledon Publishing Company, 2001, 220–249.

"Preface," in *The New Russia: Transition Gone Awry*, L. Klein and M. Pomer, eds. Stanford, CA: Stanford University Press, 2001, xvii–xxiii.

"Principles of Financial Regulation: A Dynamic Approach." *The World Bank Observer*, 16 (1), spring 2001, 1–18.

"Redefining the Role of the State," chapter 2 in *The Rebel Within*, Ha-Joon Chang, ed. London: Wimbledon Publishing Company, 2001, 94–126. (Originally presented on the tenth anniversary of MITI Research Institute Tokyo, Japan, March 17, 1998.)

"Rethinking Pension Reform: Ten Myths About Social Security Systems" and "Introduction," with Peter Orszag, in *New Ideas About Old Age Security*, R. Holman and J. Stiglitz, eds. Washington, D.C.: World Bank, 2001, 17–56. (Presented at the conference on "New Ideas About Old Age Security," World Bank, Washington, D.C., September 14–15, 1999.)

"Robust Financial Restraint," in *Financial Liberalization: How Far, How Fast?* G. Caprio, P. Honohan, and J. Stiglitz, eds. Cambridge, U.K.: Cambridge University Press, 2001, 31–63.

"The Role of International Financial Institutions in the Current Global Economy," chapter 5 in *The Rebel Within*, Ha-Joon Chang, ed. London: Wimbledon Publishing Company, 2001, 172–193. (Originally an address to the Chicago Council on Foreign Relations, Chicago, February 27, 1998.)

"Shaken and Stirred: Volatility and Macroeconomic Paradigms for Rich and Poor Countries," with William Easterly and Roumeen Islam, in *Annual Bank Conference on Development Economics 2000*, Washington, D.C.: World Bank, 2001, 191–212. Also in *Advances in Macroeconomic Theory*, Jacques Drèze, ed. IEA Conference vol. 133, Houndsmill: Palgrave, 2001, 352–372. (Speech given for Michael Bruno Memorial Lecture, twelfth World Congress of IEA, Buenos Aires, August 27, 1999.)

2002

"Capital Market Liberalization and Exchange Rate Regimes: Risk without Reward." *The Annals of the American Academy of Political and Social Science* 579, January 2002, 219–248.

"Financial Market Stability and Monetary Policy." *Pacific Economic Review*, 7 (1), February 2002, 13–30. (Speech given at the HKEA first biennial conference, Hong Kong, December 15, 2000.)

"New Perspectives on Public Finance: Recent Achievements and Future Challenges." *Journal of Public Economics*, 86, 2002, 341–360.

"The Roaring Nineties." *The Atlantic Monthly* 290 (3), October 2002, 75–89.

2003

"Democratizing IMF and World Bank: Governance and Accountability." forthcoming in a special issue of *Governance* on *Deliberately Democratizing Multilateral Organization*, 16 (1), January 2003.

Books

An Economic Analysis of the Conservation of Depletable Natural Resources, with P. Dasgupta, G. Heal, R. Gilbert, and D. Newbery, prepared for the Federal Energy Administration, May 1977.

Effects of Risk on Prices and Quantities of Energy Supplies, with R. Gilbert, prepared for Electric Power Research Institute, EPRI EA–700, project 869–1, final report, 1–4, May 1978.

Lectures in Public Economics, with A. B. Atkinson. New York and London: McGraw-Hill Book Company, 1980. (Spanish translation 1988, Instituto de Estudios Fiscales; Chinese translation 1991, Shanghai San-Lian Publishing.)

The Theory of Commodity Price Stabilization, with D. Newbery. Oxford: Oxford University Press, 1981.

Economics of the Public Sector. New York: W. W. Norton, 1986. (Translations in Spanish in 1988, Turkish, and Japanese.)

Economics of the Public Sector, 2nd ed. New York: W. W. Norton, 2000.

The Economic Role of the State. Oxford, U.K.; Cambridge, MA: B. Blackwell, 1989.

The Economic Role of the State. A. Heertje, ed. Basil Blackwell and Bank Insinger de Beaufort NV, 1989, 9–85. (Italian edition *Il Ruolo Economico dello Stato*, Società editrice il Mulino, Bologna, 1992, translated by Marco Da Rin.)

Peasants versus City-Dwellers: Taxation and the Burden of Economic Development, with R. Sah, Oxford: Clarendon Press, 1992.

Economics, 1st ed. New York: W. W. Norton, 1993. (Translations in Spanish, Latvian, and Japanese.)

The Economics of Rural Organization: Theory, Practice, and Policy, ed. with K. Hoff and A. Braverman. New York: Oxford University Press, 1993.

Principles of Macroeconomics. New York: W. W. Norton, 1993. (Translations in Spanish, Bollati Boringhieri, Torino, 2001; and in Italian.)

Principles of Microeconomics. New York: W. W. Norton, 1993. (Translations in Spanish, Barcelona, 2001; and in Italian.)

Principles of Macroeconomics and the Canadian Economy. New York: W. W. Norton, 1993.

Principles of Microeconomics and the Canadian Economy. New York: W. W. Norton, 1993.

Economics and the Canadian Economy, with R. Boadway, Canadian edition. New York: W. W. Norton, 1994.

Whither Socialism? Cambridge, MA: MIT Press, 1994. (Expanded from a paper presented at the Wicksell Lectures, May 1990.)

Economics, 2nd ed. New York: W. W. Norton, 1997.

Economics and the Canadian Economy, 2nd ed., with R. Boadway, Canadian edition. New York: W. W. Norton, 1997.

Economics of the Public Sector, 3rd ed. New York: W. W. Norton, 2000.

Frontiers of Development Economics: the Future in Perspective, with Gerald M. Meier, eds. New York: Oxford University Press, 2001.

New Ideas about Old Age Security, with Robert Holzmann, ed. Washington, D.C.: World Bank, 2001.

Rethinking the East Asian Miracle, with S. Yusuf, ed. World Bank and Oxford University Press, 2001.

Financial Liberalization: How Far, How Fast? with Gerard Caprio and Patrick Honohan, eds. Cambridge, U.K.: Cambridge University Press, 2001.

The Rebel Within: Joseph Stiglitz and the World Bank, ed. with a commentary by Ha-Joon Chang. Anthem World Economics. London: Wimbledon Publishing Company, 2001.

Globalization and Its Discontents. Washington, D.C.: W. W. Norton Company, 2002. Also published in the U.K. by Penguin Books as paperback; in German by Siedler; in French by Fayard; in Spanish by Taurus; in Italian by Einaudi; in Catalan by Empuries; in Dutch by Het Spectrum; in Japanese by Tokuma Shoten; in Taiwanese by Locus; in Korean by Sejong; in Brazil by Siciliano; in Portugese by Terramar; in Serbian by Marvel; in Czech by Prostor; in Greek by Livani; in Turkish by PlanB and in Romanian by Economica.

Towards a New Paradigm for Monetary Economics, with Bruce Greenwald. London: Cambridge University Press, 2003.

Online Publications, Testimonies, and So Forth

"I Dissent: Unconventional Economic Wisdom," monthly column for Project Syndiacte, an association of over 150 newspapers around the world. ⟨http://www.project-syndicate.org/series/series_list.php4?id=11⟩

"The Role of Government in a Digital Age," with Peter Orszag and Jonathan Orszag, study commissioned by the Computer & Communications Industry Association, October 2000.

"The Impact of Paying for College on Family Finances," with Laura Tyson, Peter Orszag, and Jonathan Orszag, commissioned by UPromise, Inc., November 2000. ⟨http://www.upromise.com/pdfs/tysonStiglitzResearch.pdf⟩

"Statement of Joseph Stiglitz at Center on Budget and Policy Priorities Press Conference," Center on Budget and Policy Priorities Report, Oct. 26, 2001. ⟨http://www.cbpp.org/10–26–01bud.htm⟩

"Budget Cuts vs. Tax Increases at the State Level: Is One More Counter-Productive than the Other During a Recession?" with Peter Orszag, Center on Budget and Policy Priorities Report, November 6, 2001. ⟨http://www.cbpp.org/10–30–01sfp.htm⟩

"Tax Cuts are not Automatically the Best Stimulus: A Response to Glenn Hubbard," with Peter Orszag, Center on Budget and Policy Priorities Report, November 27, 2001. ⟨http://www.cbpp.org/11–27–01tax.pdf⟩

"Optimal Fire Departments: Evaluating Public Policy in the Face of Externalities," with Peter R. Orszag and Joseph E. Stiglitz, The Brookings Institution, January 4, 2002. ⟨http://www.brookings.edu/views/papers/orszag/20020104.htm⟩

"U.S. versus Microsoft, Declaration as Part of The Tunney Act Proceeding," with Jason Furman, commissioned by the Computer & Communications Industry Association, January 28, 2002. ⟨http://www.sbgo.com/Papers/tunney_jesjf.pdf⟩

"Implications of the New Fannie Mae and Freddie Mac Risk-based Capital Standard," with Jonathan M. Orszag and Peter R. Orszag. *Fannie Mae Papers*, I (2), March 2002. ⟨http://www.sbgo.com/Papers/fmp-v1i2.pdf⟩

Working Papers and Unpublished Papers

Economics of Information

"Contests and Cooperation: Toward a General Theory of Compensation and Competition," presented at a Conference on the Internal Organization of Firms, International Institute of the Internal Organization of Firms, International Institute of Management, Berlin, July 1980; and at a Conference on the Economics of Information, University of Pennsylvania, May 1981.

"Cutting off Credit: An Application of Constraints on Incentive Devices," with A. Weiss, April 1982.

"Equilibrium in Competitive Insurance Markets with Moral Hazard," with R. Arnott,. Princeton University Discussion Paper 4, 1987. Also NBER working paper 3588, 1991.

"Equilibrium Unemployment as a Worker Screening Device," with B. Nalebuff and A. Rodriguez, NBER working paper 4357, May 1993. (Paper presented as "Equilibrium Unemployment, Testing, and the Pure Theory of Selection" at the NBER/CEPR Conference on Unemployment and Wage Determination, Boston, October 1991.)

"Equilibrium Unemployment, Testing, and the Pure Theory of Selection," with A. Rodriguez, presented at NBER/CEPR Conference on Unemployment and Wage Determination, Boston, October 1991.

"The Existence and Characteristics of Competitive Equilibrium," with R. Arnott, revised 1985.

"Existence and Equilibrium in Markets with Imperfect Information," with M. Rothschild, presented to World Congress of Econometric Society, Toronto, 1975.

"Incentives Schemes Under Differential Information Structures: An Application to Trade Policy," with P. Dasgupta, IMSSS technical report no. 172, Stanford University, July 1972.

"Information and Competition," Inaugural lecture presented at All Souls College, Oxford, June 1978.

"Information and Exploration Externalities," SEER technical report, Stanford University, 1976.

"Information in a Decentralized (Market) Economy," presented at Spoleto Conference on Post Industrial Society, July 1986.

"Information, Planning and Incentives," presented at the CSCCRP Sino-American Conference on Alternative Development Strategies in Wingspread, Racine, WI, November 1980. (Chinese edition published 1982.)

"Knowledge of Technology and the Technology of Knowledge: New Strategies for Development," Background paper for *UNDP Human Report 2001*.

"Moral Hazard and Unemployment in Competitive Equilibrium," with P. Rey. October 1993. (Revised July 1996.)

"Price Equilibrium, Efficiency, and Decentralizability in Insurance Markets," with R. Arnott, NBER working paper 3642, 1991.

"Prices and Queues in Screening Services in Competitive Markets," IMSSS technical report 212, Stanford University, August 1976.

"Remarks on Inequality, Agency Costs, and Economic Efficiency," prepared for a workshop in "Economic Theories of Inequality," Stanford Institute for Theoretical Economics, Stanford University, March 11–13, 1993.

"Short-term Contracts as a Monitoring Device," with P. Rey, NBER working paper 4514, 1993.

"A Simple Proof that Futures Markets are Almost Always Informationally Imperfect," with I. Gale, April 1989. (Revised version of "Futures Markets Are Almost Always Informationally Inefficient," Princeton University Financial Research Center Memorandum No. 57, February 1985.)

"Unemployment and Efficiency Wages: The Adverse Selection Model," with A. Rodriguez, presented at NBER/CEPR Conference on Unemployment and Wage Determination, Boston, October 17–19 1991.

"Unemployment As a Worker Selection Device," with B. Nalebuff, Princeton University, 1985, (Revision of "Quality and Prices," Princeton University Econometric research memorandum no. 297, May 1982.)

Economics of Uncertainty

"Risk and Trade Policy," with D. Newbery, World Bank working paper no. 53, January 1983. (Revised 1985.)

Risk and Agriculture

"Alternate Stabilization Schemes for Supply Uncertainty," with D. Newbery, Economic theory discussion paper no. 4, University of Cambridge, January 1978.

"Determinants of the Distributional Impact of Commodity Price," with D. Newbery, Economic theory discussion paper no. 17, University of Cambridge, July 1979.

Financial Markets

"Economics of Small Business Lending," at "Bank Lending to Small Businesses: A Conference," Office of the Comptroller, November 15, 1991.

"The Effect of Financial Repression in an Economy with Positive Real Interest Rates: Theory and Evidence," with K. Murdock, August 1993.

"Equity Financing for New Firms," with I. Gale, May 1986.

"Financial Restraint: Toward a New Paradigm," with Thomas Hellmann and Kevin Murdock, Stanford Graduate School of Business research paper: 1355, April 1995. (Prepared for World Bank's EDI Workshop on "Role of Government in Economic Development: Analysis of East Asian Experiences," Kyoto, Japan, September 16–17, 1994.)

"Futures Markets and Risk: A General Equilibrium Approach," Princeton University Financial Research Center memorandum 47, April 1984.

"Futures Markets Are Almost Always Informationally Inefficient," with I. Gale, Princeton University Financial Research Center memorandum No. 57, February 1985. (Revised as "A Simple Proof that Futures Markets Are Almost Always Informationally Inefficient," working paper, 1989.)

"Multiple Stock Offering and the Financing of New Firms," with I. Gale, Princeton University Financial Research Center memorandum 73, November 1986.

"Perfect and Imperfect Capital Markets," presented to the Econometric Society Meetings, New Orleans, 1971.

Growth and Capital Theory

"Capital Constraints and Economic Growth," revised version of a paper prepared for a conference at Buffalo, May 1990.

"Imperfect Capital Markets and Productivity Growth," with B. Greenwald and M. Salinger. Paper presented at NBER Conference in Vail, CO, April 1990, revised March 1991 and April 1992.

"Notes on Learning, Capital Constraints, Growth and Efficiency," presented at Conference held by Institute for the Study of Free Enterprise Systems, Buffalo, NY, May 1990.

Natural Resources

"Stepping Toward Balance: Addressing Global Climate Change," presented at the Conference on Environmentally and Socially Sustainable Development. Washington, D.C., October 6, 1997.

"Climate Change: An Agenda for Global Collective Action," with Joseph E. Aldy and Peter R. Orszag, prepared for the conference on "The Timing of Climate Change Policies," Pew Center on Global Climate Change, October 2001.

Theory of Market Structure, R&D

"Analysis of Factors Affecting the R&D Choices of Firms," with P. David, Center for Research in Economic Growth memorandum 232, Stanford University, 1979.

"Creating Competition in Telecommunications," presented at the Conference on Managing the Telecommunications Sector Post-Privatization, George Washington University, Washington, D.C., April 27, 1998.

"Entry, Equilibrium, and Welfare," with R. Gilbert.

"Exercises in the Economics of Learning-By-Doing," with P. Dasgupta, Cambridge University, May 1985. (Presented at GTE Conference on Industrial Organization, Cambridge, August 1985.)

"Some Rough Notes on Diversity of Tastes and Diversity of Commodities," Oxford University, paper presented at Bell Labs Conference on Monopolistic Competition, February 1977.

"Sunk Costs, Competition, and Welfare," with P. Dasgupta, August 1985.

"Welfare and Competition with Sunk Costs," with P. Dasgupta, November 1985.

Macroeconomics

"Bankruptcy protection against macroeconomic shocks: the case for a 'super chapter 11'," with M. Miller, World Bank Conference on Capital Flows, Financial Crises, and Policies, April 15, 1999.

"Capital Market Imperfections and Labor Market Adjustments," with B. Greenwald, presented to NBER/CEPR Conference on Labor Market Dynamics, Cambridge, October 1991.

"An Economic Analysis of Labor Turnover," Institute for Mathematical Studies in the Social Sciences (ISMMM) working paper no. 53, Stanford University, February 1976.

"Expectations, Asset Accumulation and the Real-Balance Effect," with P. Neary, presented at Dublin Meetings of the Econometric Society, September 1982, working paper no. 1990.

"Household Labor Supply, Unemployment, and Minimum Wage Legislation," with Kaushik Basu and Garance Genicot, Policy research working paper no. 2049, Washington, D.C.: World Bank, 1999.

"Imperfect Information and Macroeconomic Analyses," with B. Greenwald.

"The Long Boom? Business Cycles in the 1980s and 1990s," given to CEPR conference "The Long Boom," Stanford University, September 5, 1997.

"Macroeconomic Equilibrium and Credit Rationing," with A. Weiss, NBER working paper no. 2164, 1987.

"The New Keynesian Economics: Money and Credit," Fisher-Schultz Lecture presented at the Meetings of Econometric Society, Copenhagen, August 1987.

"A Theorist's View of Policymaking and a Policymaker's View of Theory Perspectives on Modern Macroeconomics," Marshall Lectures presented at Cambridge University. April 29–30, 1996.

Monetary Economics

"Adverse Selection, Credit Rationing and Central Bank Policy," working paper, 1989.

"Capital Market Imperfections and Regional Economic Development," with B. Greenwald and A. Levinson, prepared for CEPR conference on Finance and Development in Europe, Santiago, Spain, December 1991.

"Money Neutrality in a Model of Firm Adjustment," with B. Greenwald and K. Clay, working paper, Stanford University, 1990.

"Monetary and Exchange Rate Policy in Small Open Economies: The Case of Iceland," Central Bank of Iceland working paper n. 15. at ⟨http://www.sedlabanki.is/uploads/files/WP-15.pdf⟩

"Monetary Policy and the Institutional Structure of Banking," with B. Greenwald, June 1991.

"Monetary Policy and the Theory of the Risk-Averse Bank," with B. Greenwald, prepared for the conference "Macroeconomic Stabilization Policy: Lessons for the Future," CEPR, Stanford University and the Federal Reserve Bank of San Francisco, March 5, 1993.

International Economics

"The Global Financial Crisis: Perspectives and Policies," presented to Stanford Institute for Economic Policy Research, Stanford, March 24, 1999. Also given as talk to Pacific Affairs Council and Pomona College.

"Two Principles for the Next Round or, How to Bring Developing Countries in from the Cold," Stockholm, Sweden, April 12, 1999. Revised and presented to WTO, Geneva, Switzerland, September 21, 1999.

"Back to Basics: Policies and Strategies for Enhanced Growth and Equity in Post-Crisis East Asia," Bangkok, Thailand, July 29, 1999.

"Responding to Economic Crises: Policy Alternatives for Equitable Recovery and Development," presented to North-South Institute, Ottawa, Canada, September 29, 1998.

"Towards a New International Architecture: Principles and Policies," presented to European Investment Bank in Fiesole, Italy, October 15, 1995.

Development

"Allocation of Capital in East Asia," with M. Uy, prepared for *The East Asian Miracle*, World Bank, 1993.

"Can Aid Facilitate Development? A New Vision for Development Cooperation in the 21st Century," paper presented in Tokyo, Japan, September 17, 1997.

"Confronting AIDS in Developing Countries," address to Members of the European Parliament, Brussels, November 25, 1997.

"Development Under Adversity? The Palestinian Economy in Transition," address to the Conference on Development Under Adversity, Gaza, November 22, 1997.

"The East Asian Crisis and Its Implications for India," Commemorative lecture for the Golden Jubilee Year Celebration of Industrial Finance Corporation of India, New Delhi, India, May 19, 1998.

"The Role of the Financial System in Development," presentation at the Fourth Annual World Bank Conference on Development in Latin America and the Caribbean (LAC ABCDE), San Salvador, El Salvador, June 29, 1998.

"Distribution, Efficiency and Voice: Designing the Second Generation of Reform," presented at Conference on Asset Distribution, Poverty, and Economic Growth. Ministry of Land Reform, Brazil and the World Bank, Brasília, Brazil, July 14, 1998.

"Second Generation Strategies for Reform for China," presented to Beijing University, Beijing, China, July20, 1998

"The Future of China," presented in "China: Challenges and Prospects," at the World Bank Group—International Monetary Fund Annual Meetings Program of Seminars, Hong Kong SAR, China, September 22, 1997.

"Government, Financial Markets, and Economic Development," NBER working paper no. 3669, 1991. (Presented at a conference by the Vargas Foundation, "The Economic Reconstruction of Latin America," in Rio de Janeiro, August 1989.)

"The Impact of Individual Accounts: Piecemeal vs. Comprehensive Approaches," with Mike Orszag, Peter Orszag, and Dennis Snower, presented at the World Bank Annual Development Conference, April 1999.

"An Issues Paper on Financial Markets and Policies in East Asian Economies," June 1992.

"Markets and Development," prepared for the American Economic Association Meetings, December 1980.

More Instruments and Broader Goals: Moving Toward the Post-Washington Consensus, World Institute for Development Economics Research (WIDER) annual lectures 2, Helsinki, Finland, January 1998.

"Participation and Development: Perspectives from the Comprehensive Development Paradigm," presented at the International Conference on Democracy, Market Economy, and Development. Seoul, Korea, February 27, 1999.

"A Report on the China Trip for the World Bank Project 'Public Policy and the Asian Miracle,'" with Y. Qian, January 1993.

"Sound Finance and Sustainable Development in Asia," Keynote Address to the Asia Development Forum Manila, the Philippines, March 12, 1998.

"Statement to the Meeting of Finance Ministers of ASEAN plus 6 with the IMF and the World Bank," Kuala Lumpur, Malaysia, December 1, 1997.

"Statement to the Meeting of the Heads of Multilateral Development Banks," Inter-American Development Bank, Washington, D.C., January 15, 1998.

"Survey of the Economics of International Debt," with J. Eaton and M. Gersovitz, 1985.

"Taxes, Prices, and the Balance Between Industry and Agriculture," with R. Sah, presented at eighth International Economic Congress in New Dehli, December 1986.

"Technology, Taxes, Prices, and the Balance between Industry and Agriculture," with R. Sah, prepared in EMBRAPA-Yale workshop, Brasilia, May 18–22, 1987.

"Theory of Imperfect Competition in Rural Credit Markets," with K. Hoff, Institute for Policy Reform working paper IPR 49, October 1992.

"A Theory of Rural Credit Markets with Costly Enforcement," with K. Hoff, October 1992.

"Toward a New Paradigm for Development: Strategies, Policies, and Processes," given as the 1998 Prebisch Lecture at UNCTAD, Geneva, October 19, 1998.

Distribution of Income and Wealth

"Simple Formulae for the Measurement of Inequality and the Optimal Linear Income Tax," IMSSS technical report no. 215, Stanford University, August 1976.

"Mobility and Inequality: A Utilitarian Analysis," with R. Kanbur, Economic theory discussion paper 57, University of Cambridge, May 1982.

"Intergenerational Mobility and Dynastic Inequality," with R. Kanbur, Princeton University Economic Research Program Research memorandum no. 324, April 1986.

"Remarks on Inequality, Agency Costs, and Economic Efficiency," prepared for a workshop in "Economic Theories of Inequality," Stanford Institute for Theoretical Economics, Stanford University, March 11–13, 1993.

Welfare Economics

"The Inefficiency of the Competitive Stock Market and Its Implications for the Depletion of Natural Resources," Studies in the Economics of Energy Resources, technical report no. 21, Stanford University, 1977.

"Pareto Inferior Trade and Optimal Trade Policy," with D. Newbery, Princeton University Econometric Research Program Research memorandum 281, May 1981.

Comparative Economic Systems/Organization Theory

"Economics of Committees," with R. Sah, center discussion paper 486, Economic Growth Center, Yale University, June 1985.

"Human Nature and Economic Organization," Jacob Marashak Lecture, presented at Far Eastern Meetings of the Econometric Society, October 1987.

"Lessons for Transition Economies from the Experience of the East Asian Tigers," Videorecording of a lecture given in an IMF Institute seminar series, November 7, 1996.

"Managerial Quality in Centralized versus Decentralized Economic Systems," with R. Sah, July 1986.

"Notes on Evolutionary Economics: Imperfect Capital Markets, Organizational Design, Long-run Efficiency." 1995.

"Perpetuation and Self-Reproduction of Organizations: The Selection and Performance of Managers," with R. Sah, presented at World Congress of Econometric Society, Cambridge, August 1985.

"Some Aspects of a General Theory of Economic Organization," lecture presented at the Ninth Latin American Meeting of the Econometric Society, Santiago, Chile, August 1989.

Political Economy

"Gender and Development: The Role of the State," World Bank Gender and Development Workshop, Washington, D.C., April 2, 1998.

"Public Policy for a Knowledge Economy," remarks at the Department for Trade and Industry and Center for Economic Policy Research, London, U.K., January 27, 1999.

"Reflections on the Theory and Practice of Reform," presented to Stanford University, September 17, 1998.

"Rethinking the Economic Role of the State: Publicly Provided Private Goods," lecture delivered at Universitat Pompeu Fabra, Barcelona, November 15, 1992.

Theory of Taxation/Public Finance

"Financial Structure and the Incidence of the Corporate Income Tax," with B. Greenwald, March 1987.

"Information and Multi-Period Optimal Income Taxation with Government Commitment," with D. Brito, J. Hamilton, and S. Slutsky, NBER working paper no. 2458, December 1987.

"Information and Multi-Period Optimal Taxation With Self-Selection," with D. Brito, J. Hamilton and S. Slutsky, Princeton University, October 1983.

"Local Financing Alternative to the International Incidence of Corporate Income Taxes," with B. Greenwald, presented to NBER Conference on International Aspects of Taxation, September 1991.

"Modelling the Effects of Capital Gains Taxes on the Accrual and Realization of Capital Gains," report prepared for the Department of the Treasury, October 1981.

"Pareto Efficient Taxation and Expenditure Policies, With Applications to the Taxation of Capital, Public Investment, and Externalities," presented at conference in honor of Agnar Sandmo, January 1998.

"Technological Change and Taxation," prepared for Conference on Tax Policy in the Twenty-First Century, Washington, D.C.

"Taxation and Agricultural Pricing Policies, Cost Benefit Analysis, and the Foreign Exchange Constraint," paper prepared for the World Bank, September 1982.

"The Town-Versus-Country Problem: Optimal Pricing in an Agrarian Economy," with A. Braverman and R. Sah, presented to a conference at the World Bank, June 1982.

Theory of Public Expenditures

"Project Appraisal and Foreign Exchange Constraints: A Simple Exposition," with C. R. Blitzer and P. Dasgupta, NBER working paper no. 2165, 1987.

"The Theory of International Public Goods and the Architecture of International Organizations," background paper no. 7, Third Meeting, High Level Group on Development Strategy and Management of the Market Economy, UNU/WIDER, Helsinki, Finland, July 8–10, 1995.

Miscellaneous

"Inequality and Capital Taxation," IMSSS technical report 457, Stanford University, July 1985.

"Incentives and Institutions in the Provision of Health Care in Developing Countries: Toward an Efficient and Equitable Health Care Strategy," keynote address, International Conference in Health and Economic Development, National Institutes of Health, November 15, 1999.

"China: Forging a Third Generation of Reforms," speech given on July 23, 1999.

Index